COMPUTER-AIDED DESIGN AND OTHER COMPUTING RESEARCH DEVELOPMENTS

COMPUTER-AIDED DESIGN AND OTHER COMPUTING RESEARCH DEVELOPMENTS

CLARA M. DE SMET
AND
JULIE A. PEETERS
EDITORS

Nova Science Publishers, Inc.
New York

LIBRARY OF CONGRESS CATALOGING-IN-PUBLICATION DATA

De Smet, Clara M.
Computer-aided design and other computing research developments / Clara M. De Smet and Julie A. Peeters.
p. cm.
Includes bibliographical references and index.
ISBN 978-1-60456-860-8 (hardcover : alk. paper)
1. Computer science--Research. 2. Computer-aided design. I. Peeters, Julie A. II. Title.
QA76.27.D48 2009
620'.00420285--dc22
2009015088

Published by Nova Science Publishers, Inc. ✦ New York

CONTENTS

PREFACE

Computer Aided Design has been the motivation for major breakthroughs in various fields of computer science such as computer graphics, visualization, and computer architecture. On the other hand, advancements in graph theory, geometric constraint solving, algorithms and data structures have enabled the use of computers in various fields such as manufacturing, VLSI design, reverse engineering, and restoration of artifacts. This new setting has established Computer Aided Design as a major framework for designing and editing machine parts, jewelry, archaeological findings, buildings, electronics and computers.This book provides leading-edge research on this field and other fields of computer research from around the globe.

Chapter 1 develops an ontology of computer-aided design, based on the function-behaviour-structure (FBS) ontology. It proposes two complementary views of the process of design. The object-centred view applies the FBS ontology to the artefact being designed. Integrating an ontology of three "design worlds", this view establishes a framework of designing as a set of transformations between the function, behaviour and structure of the design object, driven by interactions between the three design worlds. Building on this framework, the process-centred view applies the FBS ontology to the activities defined by the object-centred view. This increases the level of detail and provides a more well-defined set of representations of these activities. Our ontological framework can be used to provide a better understanding of the functionalities required of existing and future computer-aided design support.

Recently solid modelers have been popularized in mechanical CAD systems. However, 2D CAD systems are still used in medium-sized and/or small companies because generally solid modelers are more expensive and difficult in their operations than 2D CAD systems in the aspect of cost-effectiveness. As a result, the conversions of 2D drawings into solid models have been still operated manually in companies using 2D CAD systems. Although a great many methods have been proposed to automatically convert 2D drawings into solid models, they could not apply to most of actual 2D drawings because they handled only correct 2D drawings in geometry. Actually various kinds of simplified expressions such as partial omissions are usually used in 2D drawings. Also, in 2D assembly drawings, if assemblies consist of many parts, it becomes very difficult to recognize each part and to convert them into 3D assembly models by using only outlines of 2D assembly drawings. In Chapter 2, firstly previously proposed methods are referred. Then the author's methods are presented. The author's methods can convert simplified 2D drawings described above into solid models.

In the methods, dimensions, part numbers and parts lists of 2D assembly drawings are used to understand detailed structures of assemblies. As a result, a single solution can be usually obtained as a 3D assembly model from a 2D assembly drawing regardless of the number of parts. In omitted 2D drawings, it is difficult to convert the drawings into solid models because they are quite incorrect in geometry. In the methods, 2D drawings including partial omissions can be automatically restored to correct 2D drawings by learning and generalizing patterns of line segments. When the generalized patterns of line segments are applied to actual partial omissions of 2D drawings, they would be automatically restored in the methods.

The purpose of Chapter 3 is to examine cross-national data in order to identify possible factors related to the observable patterns of MVNO (Mobile Virtual Network Operator) penetration. For this purpose, a mobile market structure is analyzed considering important economic factors related to the penetration of MVNOs. MVNOs have gained popularity in the Western markets, but have a dismal track record in non-Western regions. In comparing the different regions, this study analyzes how the MVNO market has changed and what opportunities and/or threats network operators and potential MVNO entrants are likely to face. This study conducts an economic assessment of market structure and environment for different countries' MVNO penetration. The data on market structure is analyzed by means of cluster/factor analysis techniques, in order to group countries according to their market environments. Then, structural equation modeling is used to investigate the relations of MVNO penetration and independent variables. The results show that MVNO penetration significantly relates to market structure and performance. These results also imply an appropriate policy to promote MVNO diffusion.

A new generation of Computer Aided Design systems has become available in which geometric constraints can be defined to determine properties of large designs. The new design concept, often called constraint-based design or design by features offers users the capability of easily defining and modifying a design, but introduces the problem of solving complicated, not always well defined, constraint problems. Traditional parametric models can also be enhanced to partially support declarative constraint-based descriptions. Chapter 4 provides an overview of representation schemes for CAD applications. Then the authors present a survey of methods for geometric constraint solving appropriate for Computer Aided Design. The authors demonstrate how these representations and constraint solving methods can be combined or adapted to support a broad range of CAD applications by presenting two example cases of successfully using a feature-based constraint-based representation scheme to support two different CAD applications.

With the proliferation of portable computing platforms and small wireless devices, wireless networks have received more and more attention as a means for providing data communications among devices regardless of their physical locations. However, due to the slow advancement in battery technology, battery power continues to be a constrained resource in wireless networks and thus energy conservation remains to be an important issue. In Chapter 5, the authors provide a taxonomy of power management and power control algorithms and protocols for wireless networks.

The authors start with a description of energy consumption characteristics of wireless devices, and identify the power consumed in the wireless transmitters essentially consists of two parts: power consumed by the radio electronic and power consumed in the RF output. To save power, one can either turn off the radio electronic and put wireless devices into the power saving mode at appropriate times, or adjust the RF output power (and hence the wireless transmission range) subject to maintaining network connectivity and bi-directionality. The former techniques are termed as power management, while the latter power control. For each category, the authors then state the performance objectives, present representative, state-of-the-art algorithms and protocols in both wireless infrastructure and infrastructureless (a.k.a. ad hoc) networks, and discuss their advantages and drawbacks.

The combination of cellular wireless technology and wireless LAN technology offers great possibility of achieving anywhere, anytime Internet access. Wireless LAN technology can provide high bandwidth data transmission within a small coverage while cellular wireless network including 3G cellular wireless networks can serve relative low bandwidth data transmission in a wider area. The integration of these two wireless technologies will enhance the Internet access ability of mobile users to achieve "Always Best Connected". Loosely coupled architecture seems to be prospective to implement. One of the important issues in loosely coupled approach is the handoff between wireless LAN and 3G cellular networks. Chapter 6 presents an overall view on various techniques to perform the vertical handoff. The authors describe several state-of-the-art schemes to implement the vertical handoff and seamless connection processes in quite detail. The objective of this review is to present a general picture on the topic and the relevant techniques for further research.

Network emulation is an important research approach. It allows real-world traffic to interact with simulated traffic and experience various user-specified packet delaying, dropping, reordering, and duplication treatments. With emulation, one can test the function and performance of a real-world network device under various simulated network conditions without the need to get, know, or modify its internal protocol stack. Due to these capabilities, emulation is widely used to test network protocols and network devices. In Chapter 7, the authors introduce NCTUns, an innovative network simulator and emulator. They explain the novel simulation methodology used by it, present its new kernel-module-based design and implementation, and show its emulation capabilities and performance. Several examples are presented to illustrate its uses in wired and wireless network emulations. More information about this tool is available at its web site at http://NSL.csie.nctu.edu.tw/nctuns.html.

Many products are designed with aesthetic sculptured surfaces to enhance their aesthetic appear, an important factor in customer satisfaction, especially for automotive and consumer-electronics products. In other cases, products have sculptured surfaces to meet functional requirements. Examples of functional surfaces can be easily found out in aero-, gas- and hydrodynamic applications (turbine blades), optical (lamp reflector) and medical (parts of anatomical reproduction) applications, manufacturing surfaces (molding die, die face), *etc.* Functional surfaces interact with environment or with other surface. Due to this, functional surfaces also can be called *dynamic surface.*

Functional surfaces don't possess the property to slide over itself. This causes significant complexity in machining of sculptured surfaces. Application of multi-axis *NC* machine is the only way for efficient machining of sculptured surfaces.

Reduction of the machining time is a critical issue when machining sculptured surfaces on multi-axis *NC* machines. In order to decrease the machining cost of a sculptured surface the machining time must be as short as possible. Definitely, this is the case where the sentence "Time is money!" works. Generally speaking, the optimization of surface generation on multi-axis *NC* machine results in time savings. It is the right point to recall the words[1] "*gaining time is gaining everything*!"

Expert Commentary A is the author's attempt to cover briefly the modern theory of surface generation with focus on optimal machining of sculptured surfaces on multi-axis *NC* machine.

The advance of multi-sensor imaging systems enables the capability of producing multiple image modalities across the electromagnetic spectrum bands. These multimodality images should be combined together to generate a composite image, which is able to display plenty of information captured by the system. The technique named image fusion is developed for this purpose. Varies of image fusion approaches have been presented in the literature, a popular category of which is the multiresolution image fusion (MRIF). Expert Commentary B reviews the state of the art of the MRIF algorithms and the performance assessment issue in image fusion. The mechanism and applications of the MRIF are described. However, there is not a universal solution for all applications. The image fusion algorithm must be carefully selected or tailored based on the specific requirements of an application. This chapter discusses these relevant issues as well.

Powell-Sabin splines are bivariate C_1-continuous quadratic splines defined on an arbitrary triangulation. Their construction is based on a particular split of each triangle in the triangulation into six smaller triangles. Expert Commentary C gives an overview of the properties of Powell-Sabin splines in the context of computer aided geometric design. These splines can be represented in a compact normalized B-spline basis with an intuitive geometric interpretation involving control triangles. Using these triangles one can interactively change the shape of the splines in a predictable way. The authors describe the simple subdivision rules for Powell-Sabin splines, and discuss some applications. They consider a new efficient spline visualization technique based on subdivision. The authors also look at two useful generalizations of the Powell-Sabin splines, i.e., QHPS splines and NURPS surfaces. The QHPS splines are a hierarchical variant of Powell-Sabin splines. They have very similar properties as the Powell-Sabin splines, and their hierarchical nature allows a local refinement of the spline in a very straightforward way. The NURPS surface is the rational extension of the Powell-Sabin spline. By means of weights they give extra degrees of freedom to the designer for the modelling of surfaces.

Expert Commentary D addresses the issue of survivable Voice over IP (VoIP) network design. In the applied model the whole VoIP network is divided into two logical components: the access network and the transport network. The access network consists of VoIP end-points each representing a number of users, which connect to the transport network through edge routers serving as gateways. Since multiple edge routers may be available for any given VoIP node, one task of the design process is to assign gateways to the VoIP end-points. The edge routers have to be connected in a way that security and availability can be assured for the VoIP traffic. One obvious approach to fulfilling these requirements, which is assumed throughout the investigations, is to define a Virtual Private Network (VPN). Supposing a large volume of VoIP traffic, the cost of the VPN can be significant; thus, the other task of VoIP network design is to specify the transport VPN in the most economical way, while also taking the possible failures of transport network elements (i.e., routers and links) into consideration. Assuming a single network element failure at a time, the survivability of the

[1]John Shebbeare, 1709-1788.

VoIP network can be assured by assigning two gateways, namely a primary and a backup one, to each VoIP end-point, and calculating two disjoint paths between each pair of edge routers. To decrease the amount of backup reservations, a shared backup path protection scheme can be applied. The two tasks of survivable VoIP network design can be solved separately; however, in this chapter a novel solution is proposed in which the edge router assignment process takes both the objective function of VPN specification and the issues of survivability into consideration. Multiple methods realizing the novel approach are presented, which are based on the paradigms of evolutionary algorithms and simulated annealing. Moreover, a VPN specification algorithm is presented which utilizes the stepwise nature of the cost functions. The performance of the presented methods is evaluated with the help of simulations, using a well-known greedy algorithm as reference. It is shown that the proposed methods outperform the reference algorithm significantly in the simulation scenarios investigated.

Superconducting circuits of Josephson junctions can be used for quantum information processing. A superconducting loop of three Josephson junctions has been proposed and demonstrated as a quantum bit or qubit [1]-[4]. A coherent superposition of two persistent-current states can be obtained when the two classical states are coupled via quantum tunneling through an energy barrier. The classical states of persistent currents can also be used as two binary bits [5]. Logic functions can be realized by coupling two or more bits, i.e. the circuit loops [6]. The interaction between loops is via magnetic interference of the superconductors.

In Expert Commentary E, superconducting circuits of Josephson junctions are investigated with as aim to possibly use them in locally-connected processor structures [7]. Both a classical SIMD computer architecture and an array-based quantum computer structure are presented that use the same basic circuit, the Josephson junctions. Our ideal is that the classical computer can serve as a pre-, post- and intermediate processor for the quantum computation that is performed in the heart of the Josephson circuit array. As such, it then establishes a heterogeneous quantum/classical computer for implementations of algorithms such as Shor's factoring algorithm which mixes classical computation steps with quantum computation steps in a single algorithm.

A quantum CNN (cellular nonlinear networks) architecture using the Josephson circuits is also proposed, presenting a novel computing paradigm for Josephson circuits [8]. Since classical computing architectures (SIMD arrays), quantum computing architectures and semi-quantum computing architectures (quantum CNNs) can be simultaneously studied on the same device, the Josephson circuit is a good vehicle for investigating the architectural issues of quantum and nanoelectronic computer systems, independently from the question of which device will be the ultimate implementation vehicle.

In Computer Aided Geometric Design, several methods for approximating a data point set with a parametric curve or a parametric surface have been considered: approximation by least squares, approximation using radial basis functions and approximation using the progressive iteration approximation property. Short Communication A presents with a unified notation a concise survey on the approximation method derived from the progressive iteration approximation property.

The weird quantum mechanical effects governing the behavior of sub-atomic particles are about to revolutionize the way we perform computation and manipulate information. Genuine quantum mechanical features, like superposition of states, entanglement and interference, can be harnessed in order to speed up computation or enhance the security of data communications. But the fundamental ability of a quantum computer to process information at a deeper physical level than a conventional computer is able to, allows the former to tackle a much broader palette of information processing tasks, thus establishing its superiority in terms of computational power. Specifically, Short Communication B uncovers a class of information processing tasks (based on the problem of distinguishing among entangled quantum states) whose members are readily carried out by a quantum computer, yet are impossible to perform on any classical machine (whether deterministic or probabilistic).

The authors also demonstrate the importance of parallelism for the emerging field of quantum computation and quantum information by providing two examples of tasks for which a parallel approach can make the difference between success and failure. In the first case, the authors analyze the quantum distinguishability problem restricted to direct quantum measurements and show that the failure of a sequential approach accounts for the impossibility of constructing a Universal Computer. The second example deals with a practical instance of the rank-varying computational complexity paradigm, identified in the procedure for computing the quantum Fourier transform. The authors show that under the constraints imposed by quantum decoherence, only a parallel approach can guarantee a reliable solution or, alternatively, improve scalability.

The quantum Fourier transform is a very powerful tool, allowing for the design of fast quantum algorithms. The authors show herein that the quantum Fourier transform and its inverse can also be successfully used to build quantum key distribution protocols that offer improved eavesdropping detection rates due to an innovative disruption amplification process.

In: Computer-Aided Design...
Editors: C.M. De Smet et al, pp. 1-25
ISBN: 978-1-60456-860-8

Chapter 1

An Ontology of Computer-Aided Design

Udo Kannengiesser
NICTA, Australia, and School of Computer Science and Engineering, University of New South Wales, Sydney, Australia
John S. Gero
Krasnow Institute for Advanced Study and Volgenau School of Information Technology and Engineering, George Mason University, USA, and University of Technology, Sydney, Australia

Abstract

This chapter develops an ontology of computer-aided design, based on the function-behaviour-structure (FBS) ontology. It proposes two complementary views of the process of design. The object-centred view applies the FBS ontology to the artefact being designed. Integrating an ontology of three "design worlds", this view establishes a framework of designing as a set of transformations between the function, behaviour and structure of the design object, driven by interactions between the three design worlds. Building on this framework, the process-centred view applies the FBS ontology to the activities defined by the object-centred view. This increases the level of detail and provides a more well-defined set of representations of these activities. Our ontological framework can be used to provide a better understanding of the functionalities required of existing and future computer-aided design support.

1. Introduction

The notion of computer-aided design can be understood as an umbrella term for approaches to using computational tools to support human design activities. Its principal innovations to date include tools for computer-aided drafting (CAD), engineering (CAE) and manufacturing (CAM), which have been recognised as significant technological achievements of the past century (Weisberg 2000). These tools are now indispensable for practitioners in many design domains.

Some research has focused on expanding computer support to activities carried out in the early, conceptual stages of design. However, its impact on design practices and tool development in industry has generally been rather low. We believe that one of the reasons is that many of these approaches are based on an insufficient understanding of design. This concerns activities that are carried out by human designers, which include producing and re-interpreting drawings or sketches, and reflecting on current and previous design tasks. It has been shown that these activities are important drivers of designing (Schön and Wiggins 1992; Suwa et al. 1999; Suwa and Tversky 2002). Most traditional models of design are inadequate because they do not explicitly account for these findings.

Progress on a more comprehensive understanding of designing has been made only recently. Our situated function-behaviour-structure (FBS) framework (Gero and Kannengiesser 2004) represents designing as a situated act that is driven by the interactions between the designer and their environment. It uses a perspective that is oriented to the object being designed, so that designing can be shown as a set of transformations between the function, behaviour and structure of the artefact. The situated FBS framework has shown its potential to enhance human understanding of designing. This chapter develops extensions to this framework that provide a more detailed ontological basis on which computer-aided design support can be built.

Section 2 presents the situated FBS framework and shows how it derives from an object-centred view of designing driven by the interactions between three "design worlds". Section 3, adopting a process-centred view of designing, applies the FBS ontology to the design activities defined in Section 2. This adds a significant amount of detail and rigour to the representation of each activity. Section 4 uses this view to derive a framework that specifies the functions required of computational tools to support designing. Section 5 concludes the chapter.

2. An Object-Centred Ontology of Design

2.1. An Ontology of Design Objects

Most design models and design ontologies focus on the artefact or object of design. The FBS ontology distinguishes between three aspects of a design object (Gero 1990; Gero and Kannengiesser 2004): function (F), behaviour (B) and structure (S).

2.1.1. Object Function

Function (F) of an object is defined as its teleology ("what the object is for"). For example, some of the functions of a window include "to provide view", "to provide daylight" and "to provide rain protection". Function represents the usefulness of the object for another system.

2.1.2. Object Behaviour

Behaviour (B) of an object is defined as the attributes that can be derived from its structure ("what the object does"). Using the window example, behaviours include "thermal conduction", "light transmission" and "direct solar gain". Behaviour provides operational, measurable performance criteria for comparing different objects.

2.1.3. Object Structure

Structure (S) of an object is defined as its components and their relationships ("what the object consists of"). The structure of physical objects includes their form (i.e., geometry and topology) and material. More generally, form can be viewed as a description of an object's macro-structure, and material can be viewed as a shorthand description of the micro-structure. In the window example, macro-structure (form) includes "glazing length" and "glazing height", and micro-structure (material) includes "type of glass".

2.1.4. Relationships between Object Function, Behaviour and Structure

Humans construct relationships between function, behaviour and structure through experience and through the development of causal models based on interactions with the object. Specifically, function is ascribed to behaviour by establishing a teleological connection between the human's goals and observable or measurable effects of the object. There is no direct relationship between function and structure. Behaviour is causally related to structure, i.e. it can be derived from structure using physical laws or heuristics. This may require knowledge about external effects (exogenous variables) and their interaction with the artefact's structure. In the window example, deriving the behaviour "light transmission" requires considering external light sources.

2.2. An Ontology of Design Worlds

An aspect that has been ignored in most models of design relates to the interactions of the designer and their environment. Designers perform actions in order to change their environment. By observing and interpreting the results of their actions, they then decide on new actions to be executed on the environment. The designers' concepts may change according to what they are "seeing", which itself is a function of what they have done. One may speak of an "interaction of making and seeing" (Schön and Wiggins 1992). This interaction between the designer and the environment strongly determines the course of designing.

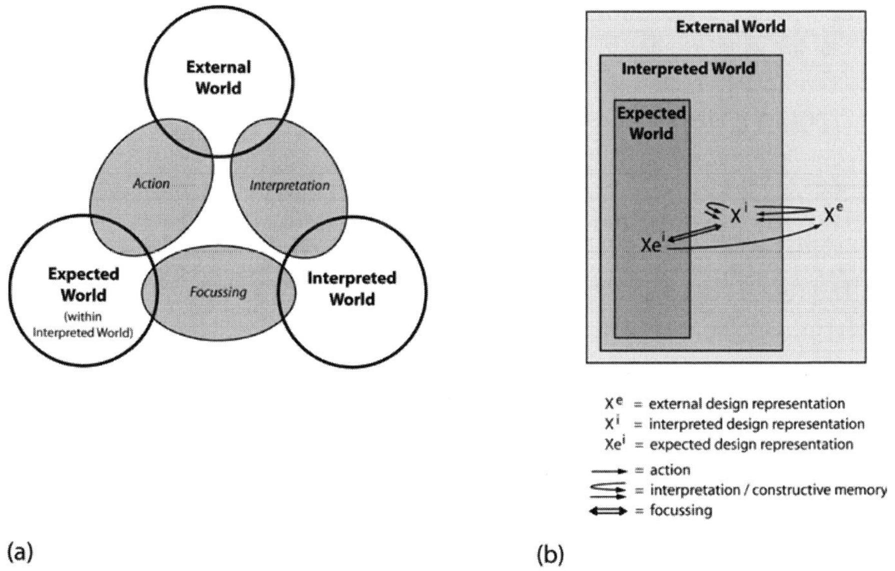

Figure 1. Situatedness as the interaction of three worlds: (a) general model, (b) specialised model for design representations.

This idea is called situatedness, whose foundational concepts go back to the work of Dewey (1896) and Bartlett (1932).

Gero and Kannengiesser (2004) have modelled situatedness by specifying three interacting worlds: the external world, interpreted world and expected world, Figure 1(a).

2.2.1. The External World

The external world is the world that is composed of representations outside the designer or design agent. The notion of "external" is meant in a conceptual sense rather than a physical one. It denotes an environment that contains design artefacts made available for interpretation.

2.2.2. The Interpreted World

The interpreted world is the world that is built up inside the design agent in terms of sensory experiences, percepts and concepts. It is the internal representation of that part of the external world that the design agent interacts with. The interpreted world provides an environment for analytic activities and discovery during designing.

2.2.3. The Expected World

The expected world is the world imagined actions of the design agent will produce. It is the environment in which the effects of actions are predicted according to current goals and interpretations of the state of the world.

2.2.4. Relationships between the Three Worlds

These three worlds are related through three classes of interaction. *Interpretation* transforms variables that are sensed in the external world into sensory experiences, percepts and concepts that compose the interpreted world. *Focussing* takes some aspects of the interpreted world and uses them as goals for the expected world. *Action* is an effect which brings about a change in the external world according to the goals in the expected world.

2.2.5. A More Detailed Framework of Design Interactions

Figure 1(b) presents a specialised view of the ontology of design worlds, with the design agent (described by the interpreted and expected world) located within the external world, and with general classes of design representations placed into this nested model. The set of expected design representations (Xe^i) corresponds to the notion of a design state space, i.e. the state space of all possible designs that satisfy the set of requirements. This state space can be modified during the process of designing by transferring new interpreted design representations (X^i) into the expected world and/or transferring some of the expected design representations (Xe^i) out of the expected world. This leads to changes in external design representations (X^e), which may then be used as a basis for re-interpretation changing the interpreted world. Novel interpreted design representations (X^i) may also be the result of memory (here called *constructive memory*), which can be viewed as a process of interaction among design representations within the interpreted world rather than across the interpreted and the external world.

Both interpretation and constructive memory are viewed as "push-pull" processes, i.e. the results of these processes are driven both by the original experience ("push") and by some of the agent's current interpretations and expectations ("pull") (Gero and Fujii 2000). This notion captures two ideas. First, interpretation and constructive memory have a subjective nature, using first-person knowledge grounded in the designer's interactions with their environment (Bickhard and Campbell 1996; Clancey 1997; Ziemke 1999; Smith and Gero 2005). This is in contrast to static approaches that attempt to encode all relevant design knowledge prior to its use. Anecdotal evidence in support of first-person knowledge is provided by the common observation that different designers perceive the same set of requirements differently (and thus produce different designs). And the same designer is likely to produce different designs at later times for the same requirements. This is a result of the designer acquiring new knowledge while interacting with their environment between the two times.

Second, the interplay between "push" and "pull" has the potential to produce emergent effects, leading to novel and often surprising interpretations of the same internal or external representation. This idea extends the notion of biases that simply reproduce the agent's current expectations. Examples have been provided from experimental studies of designers interacting with their sketches of the design object. Schön and Wiggins (1992) found that designers use their sketches not only as an external memory, but also as a means to reinterpret what they have drawn, thus leading the design in a surprising, new direction. Suwa et al. (1999) noted, in studying designers, a correlation of unexpected discoveries in sketches with the invention of new issues or requirements during the design process. They concluded that "sketches serve as a physical setting in which design thoughts are constructed on the fly in a situated way". Guindon's (1990) protocol analyses of software engineers, designing control software for a lift, revealed that designing is characterised by frequent discoveries of new requirements interleaved with the development of new partial design solutions. As Guindon puts it, "designers try to make the most effective use of newly inferred requirements, or the sudden discovery of partial solutions, and modify their goals and plans accordingly".

2.3. The Situated Function-Behaviour-Structure Framework

Gero and Kannengiesser (2004) have combined the ontology of design artefacts (Section 2.1) with the ontology of design worlds (Section 2.2), by specialising the model of situatedness shown in Figure 1(b). In particular, the variable X, which stands for design representations in general, is replaced with the more specific representations F, B and S. This provides the basis of the situated FBS framework, Figure 2 (Gero and Kannengiesser 2004). In addition to using external, interpreted and expected F, B and S, this framework uses explicit representations of external requirements given to the designer by another agent (usually the customer). Specifically, there may be external requirements on function (FR^e), external requirements on behaviour (BR^e), and external requirements on structure (SR^e). The situated FBS framework also introduces the process of comparison between interpreted behaviour (B^i) and expected behaviour (Be^i), and a number of processes that transform interpreted structure (S^i) into interpreted behaviour (B^i), interpreted behaviour (B^i) into interpreted function (F^i), expected function (Fe^i) into expected behaviour (Be^i), and expected behaviour (Be^i) into expected structure (Se^i). Figure 2 uses the numerals 1 to 20 to label the resultant set of processes; however, it should be noted that they do not represent any order of execution.

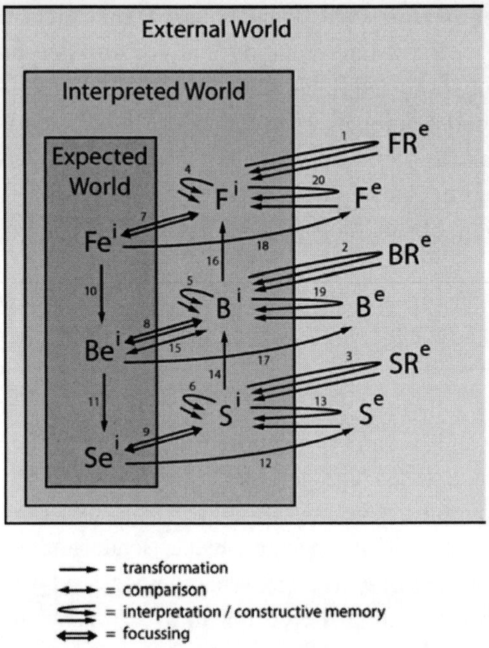

Figure 2. The situated FBS framework.

The 20 processes can be mapped onto eight fundamental design steps (Gero 1990; Gero and Kannengiesser 2004).

1. *Formulation*: consists of processes 1 – 10. It includes interpretation of external requirements, given to the designer by a customer, as function, behaviour and structure, via processes 1, 2 and 3. Requirements are also constructed as implicit requirements generated from within the designer, using constructive memory (processes 4, 5 and 6). Focussing transfers a subset of the (explicitly and implicitly) required function, behaviour and structure into the expected world (processes 7, 8 and 9). In summary, processes 1 – 9 represent activities that populate the interpreted and expected worlds with design concepts, providing the basis for subsequent transformations of these concepts. Process 10 transforms expected function into additional expected behaviour. The set of expected function, behaviour and structure, resulting from the formulation step, represents the design state space. It includes all the variables and their ranges of values that are relevant for the design task.
2. *Synthesis*: consists of process 11 to generate an instance of structure that is expected to meet the required behaviour, and the externalisation of that structure via process 12. This design step can be viewed as part of a search process through the (previously formulated) state space of all possible instances of structure.
3. *Analysis*: consists of interpretation of externalised structure (process 13) and the derivation of behaviour from that structure (process 14).

4. *Evaluation*: consists of a comparison of expected behaviour and behaviour derived through analysis (process 15).
5. *Documentation*: produces an external representation of a design solution for purposes of communicating that solution in terms of structure (process 12), and, optionally, behaviour (process 17) and function (process 18).
6. *Reformulation type 1*: consists of focussing on different structures than previously expected (process 9). Precursors of this process are the interpretation of external structure (process 13), constructive memory of structure (process 6) or the interpretation of new requirements on structure (process 3).
7. *Reformulation type 2*: consists of focussing on different behaviours than previously expected (process 8). Precursors of this process are the derivation of behaviour from structure (process 14), the interpretation of external behaviour (process 19), constructive memory of behaviour (process 5) or the interpretation of new requirements on behaviour (process 2).
8. *Reformulation type 3*: consists of focussing on different functions than previously expected (process 7). Precursors of this process are the ascription of function to behaviour (process 16), the interpretation of external function (process 20), constructive memory of function (process 4) or the interpretation of new requirements on function (process 1).

The numbering of the eight design steps, similar to the 20 processes, does not prescribe any order of execution. While it may be expected for some routine design tasks to follow a sequential execution of only the first five steps, it has been found that all three types of reformulation frequently occur throughout the process of designing (McNeill et al. 1998).

The situated FBS framework represents designing independently of the domain of the design and the specific methods used, and of the subject carrying out the process of designing. What we have referred to as the "design agent" in the definition of the three design worlds can be embodied by a human designer (or team of human designers), a computational tool, or a combination of both.

3. A Process-Centred Ontology of Design

The object-centred ontology of design presented in Section 2 has been helpful in establishing a basic understanding of design. Its emphasis on artefacts provides an intuitive, tangible perspective, representing the process of designing as a gradual evolution of the design object across three levels. The three-world model of design interactions, in which this representation is embedded, is sufficiently rich to account for the phenomena of situatedness.

However, the object-centred ontology lacks sufficient detail and rigour to be useful for comparing or developing different methods and computer support for designers. The key ideas and semantics conveyed by the situated FBS framework are only informally expressed using textual, natural-language descriptions such as in Sections 2.2 and 2.3. The graphical model in Figure 2 does not fully capture these semantics. The mapping of the 20 processes onto Gero's (1990) eight fundamental design steps has added some more meaning by locating these processes within typical phases of a design project. However, this mapping does not completely capture all the semantics and is too informal to be used as an ontological framework for computer-aided design. What is needed is an ontology that is process-centred, treating design processes as first-class entities rather than derivatives of object-centred constructs. This Section will present such an ontology, extending our recent work on an FBS ontology of processes (Gero and Kannengiesser 2007).

3.1. An Ontology of Processes

Processes are usually understood as entities that are less tangible than (physical) objects. Nonetheless, they can be represented using the same set of ontological constructs as used for describing objects: function, behaviour and structure. To clearly distinguish between the notations of the process-centred and the object-centred FBS ontology, we will use the indices "p" for "process" and "o" for "object".

3.1.1. Process Function

Function (F^p) of a process is ontologically no different to object function, as it is based on the observer's goals rather than on embodiment as an object or as a process. Instances of process functions are largely domain-dependent. However, most processes that we design and execute through actions have the general function of replacing an existing state of the world with a desired one.

3.1.2. Process Behaviour

Behaviour (B^p) of a process relates to attributes that allow comparison on a performance level as a basis for process evaluation. Typical process behaviours are speed, cost, amount of space required and accuracy. These behaviours can be specialised and/or quantified for instances of processes in particular domains.

3.1.3. Process Structure

Through an analogy with the structure of physical objects, we can distinguish between a macro- and a micro-structure (S^p) of processes.

The macro-structure of a process includes three components and two relationships, Figure 3.

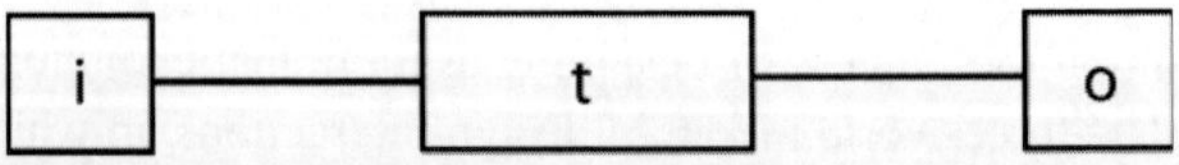

Figure 3. The macro-structure of a process (i = input; t = transformation; o = output).

The components are

- input (i),
- transformation (t) and
- output (o).

The relationships connect

- input and transformation (i – t) and
- transformation and output (t – o).

Input (i) and output (o) represent properties of entities being transformed in terms of their variables and/or their values. For example, the process of transportation changes the values for the location of a (physical) object (e.g. the values of its x-, y- and z-coordinates). The process of electricity generation takes mechanical motion as input and produces electrical energy as output.

A common way to describe the transformation (t) of a process is in terms of a plan, a set of rules or other procedural descriptions. A typical example is a software procedure that is expressed in source code or as an activity diagram in the Unified Modeling Language (UML). Such descriptions are often used to specify sub-components of the transformation.

The relationships between the three components of a process are usually uni-directional from the input to the transformation and from the transformation to the output. For iterative processes the t – o relationship is bi-directional to represent the feedback loop between the output and the transformation.

The micro-structure or "material" of a process differs from the macro-structure because its components and relationships cannot be distinguished (or are not relevant) at the same level of abstraction. For example, it is not common to specify the (business process) transformation "pay the supplier" in terms of more fine-grained activities (sub-components) such as "log in to online banking system", "fill out funds transfer form" and "click the submit button". This set of activities is best viewed as a micro-structure specified only through a shorthand qualifier such as "using internet banking". Micro-structure can also be associated with the input and output components of a process. For example, a set of measuring data that is the input of a statistical analysis process may be "materialised" through either digital or paper-based media.

While micro-structure is clearly needed to carry out ("materialise") a process, the components and relationships of that micro-structure are not explicitly represented. This fits with one of *Merriam-Webster*'s definitions of material as "the formless substratum of all things which exists only potentially and upon which form acts to produce realities".

The "formless substratum" of a transformation may reference not only processes but also objects. It then denotes the entity or agent executing the transformation. In the "pay the supplier" example, it is possible to specify "finance officer" or "purchasing department" as a general descriptor for the executing agent. Including such references to agents (as "actors" or "roles") has become well-established in process modelling (Curtis et al. 1992).

Since micro-structure does not specify components and relationships, it can be embodied by either (micro-) objects or (micro-) processes. In some instances, the micro-structure of objects can refer to (micro-) processes rather than (micro-) objects. For example, the chemical bonds (macro-relationships) between the atoms (macro-components) of a molecule are realised by physical processes, according to the laws of quantum electrodynamics. A view of the world as being based on processes rather than objects has generally been suggested in process philosophy (Rescher 2006).

3.1.4. Relationships between Process Function, Behaviour and Structure

Relationships among F^p, B^p and S^p are constructed according to the same principles as described for F^o, B^o and S^o (see Section 2.1.4). Function is ascribed to behaviour based on associations of process performance with human goals. Behaviour can be derived from structure either directly or indirectly based on external effects. An example of directly derived behaviour is the speed of a process, as this depends exclusively on the macro-structure ("what kind of transformation is used on what input to produce what output?") and the micro-structure ("how and by whom is the transformation carried out using what input/output media?"). An example of indirectly derived behaviour is accuracy, which needs an external benchmark against which the output of the process is compared.

3.2. An Ontology of Design Processes

The FBS ontology of processes can be used to re-represent the object-centred description of the 20 design processes (presented in Section 2.3) as a process-centred one. Most parts of the object-centred model depicted in Figure 2 directly map onto the input and output components of process macro-structure (S^p). For example, S^p of process 14 in Figure 2 includes (interpreted) object structure (S^o) as input (i) and (interpreted) object behaviour (B^o) as output (o).[1] No specific information is given about transformation components, as this is available only at an instance level.

Most of the semantics of the situated FBS framework can be captured by process function (F^p). Table 1 gives an overview of the structure and functions of each of the 20 design processes.

Interpretation processes (1, 2, 3, 13, 19 and 20) can have two different functions. One function is to transfer existing design concepts from one agent to another or the same agent without a change of the initial meaning of these concepts. This involves bringing external representations into a form that allows processing of these representations by the individual design agent. The other function of interpretation is to re-interpret design concepts based on existing ones. This generates design concepts and issues that are novel with respect to the ones initially intended.

Constructive memory processes (4, 5 and 6) have a similar set of functions. One function is to retrieve design concepts from some storage space in the same way as they were experienced at the time of storage. While this may include some computation or transformation, such as refinement or decomposition of design concepts, the results of this process will all have a pre-defined relationship with the initial concepts. The other function of the constructive memory processes is to re-construct and thereby modify existing design concepts, which corresponds to the notion of reflection (Schön 1983).

Focussing processes (7, 8 and 9) have the function to construct the design state space. This includes the construction of the initial design state space (maps onto the formulation step) and subsequent modifications of that space (maps onto the reformulation steps).

Action processes (12, 17 and 18) can have two different functions. One function is to communicate aspects of the design to other stakeholders (agents). Here, the notion of communication is used in its traditional sense of sharing information, based on unambiguous

[1] Indices for "interpreted" have been omitted here to improve notational clarity.

transfer of design concepts. The other function is to initiate reflective conversation, either with other stakeholders (agents) or the initiator of the action process itself. In other words, external representations are produced to be re-interpreted in new ways.

Table 1. Function (F^p) and macro-structure (S^p) of the 20 design processes

ID	Process class	(Macro-) S^p	F^p
1	Interpretation	$FR^e \rightarrow F^i$	1. transfer design concepts as intended 2. re-interpret design concepts
2		$BR^e \rightarrow B^i$	
3		$SR^e \rightarrow S^i$	
4	Constructive memory	$F^i \rightarrow F^i$	1. retrieve design concepts as stored 2. re-construct design concepts
5		$B^i \rightarrow B^i$	
6		$S^i \rightarrow S^i$	
7	Focussing	$F^i \rightarrow Fe^i$	construct function state space
8		$B^i \rightarrow Be^i$	construct behaviour state space
9		$S^i \rightarrow Se^i$	construct structure state space
10	Transformation	$Fe^i \rightarrow Be^i$	construct behaviour state space
11		$Be^i \rightarrow Se^i$	generate values for design structure
12	Action	$Se^i \rightarrow S^e$	1. communicate the design to others 2. initiate reflective conversation
13	Interpretation	$S^e \rightarrow S^i$	1. transfer design concepts as intended 2. re-interpret design concepts
14	Transformation	$S^i \rightarrow B^i$	1. analyse for current behaviours 2. determine additional behaviours
15	Comparison	$\{Be^i, B^i\} \rightarrow$ decision	evaluate the design
16	Transformation	$B^i \rightarrow F^i$	generate new design issues
17	Action	$Be^i \rightarrow B^e$	1. communicate the design to others 2. initiate reflective conversation
18		$Fe^i \rightarrow F^e$	
19	Interpretation	$B^e \rightarrow B^i$	1. transfer design concepts as intended 2. re- interpret design concepts
20		$F^e \rightarrow F^i$	

Processes 10, 11, 14 and 16 may be called "FBS^o transformations" based on their role as transformers between F^o, B^o and S^o. Process 10 has the function to construct the behaviour state space, and process 11 has the function to generate values within the (previously constructed) structure state space. Process 14 has two functions. One function is to analyse the design with respect to current behaviours. The other function is to determine additional behaviours that can be included as issues in the current design task. This is also the function of process 16. The comparison process (15) has the function to evaluate the design, based on decision making informed by comparison of expected and interpreted design performance.

It can be seen that some of the functions (F^p) – loosely speaking – relate to non-situated and others to situated aspects of designing. Non-situated aspects are captured by those functions that do not address the potential for change during designing. These are the functions that involve "transfer" (in interpretation processes), "retrieval" (in constructive memory processes) and "communication" (in action processes). Situated aspects of designing describing the potential for change are captured by functions that involve "re-interpretation" (in interpretation processes), "re-construction" (in constructive memory processes) and "reflective conversation" (in action processes).

Table 1 does not include the behaviours (B^p) of the 20 processes. This is because, at the current level of abstraction, they are no different from the general process behaviours described in Section 3.1.2. This is based on the independence of our ontology of specific methods or design domains. No detailed information about structure (S^p) and exogenous effects is available to be able to specialise or quantify general process behaviours (B^p) such as speed, accuracy and cost. An example for such detailed information would be when process structures (S^p) were considered that contain iterations (e.g., when using genetic algorithms (GAs) in design synthesis). In this case, the behaviour (B^p) "rate of convergence" could be derived that is a specialisation of the behaviour (B^p) "speed". However, as our aim here is to provide a general rather than an instance-specific ontology, different classes of design processes are distinguished only at the level of function (F^p) and structure (S^p).

4. An Ontological Framework for Computer-Aided Design Support

The ontological view presented in Sections 2 and 3 has provided a detailed description of 20 distinct processes in designing. This is useful for enhancing our understanding of designing as a human activity. However, the ultimate aim of most research in design is to enhance the performance of this activity, both in terms of higher effectiveness and efficiency. The key to improving performance or behaviour (B^p) of designing is in the structure (S^p) it is derived from. This requires more detailed representations of structure (S^p) than presented in Table 1, and mainly concerns micro-structure. Exploring the micro-level of process structure is a general research theme that has been recognised in a number of other disciplines (Osterweil 2005).

Research in the micro-structure (S^p) of designing can be characterised loosely as either method- or tool-oriented. Method-oriented approaches focus on process-centred representations of micro-structure. These representations can be viewed as composing a new macro-structure to be "materialised" by humans or tools. Tool-oriented design research focuses on object-centred representations of micro-structure in terms of new design tools. Computer-aided design research and development is clearly located in this field. Both method- and tool-oriented research streams are complementary, as each of them often uses results from the other.

Computer-aided design tools can themselves be regarded as design objects. Applying the FBS ontology to these tools provides a schema for the characteristics that the tools must exhibit to be useful in the process of designing. We will use the index "t" for "tool" to distinguish the FBS view of tools from the FBS view of design objects and design processes. The most essential characteristics of a tool relate to function (F^t) as they orient the specification of a tool's behaviour (B^t) and structure (S^t) towards the required goals and context of use. Many of the functions of computer-aided design tools do not differ from any other software product. They include such general characteristics as usability, reliability, maintainability and others (ISO 2001). However, there are a number of functions that are specific to computer-aided design tools. These functions relate to the tools' role as the "material" of design processes, and can generally be described as "to support design processes of class X". For example, a general function (F^t) of a commercial CAD tool is "to support design processes of class X = documentation" (one of the fundamental design steps presented in Section 2.3). These functions can be further specialised using particular combinations of the FBS^p properties of the 20 design processes presented in Table 1. An example of a more specific function (F^t) of a CAD tool is "to support the process structure (S^p) $Se^i \rightarrow S^e$ in a way to achieve the process function (F^p) of communicating the design to others".

The set of functions (F^t) derivable in this way can serve as high-level requirements for the development of new design tools. This approach makes research and development in computer-aided design look like a design process, generating computational models and architectures as the structure (S^t) of tools exhibiting certain behaviours (B^t) to achieve the required functions (F^t). The remainder of this Section will cast existing work on computer-aided design systems in this ontology, classifying that work based on tool functions (F^t) derived from combinations of F^p and S^p shown in Table 1. This aims to provide an overview of the current range of both commercial software and academic proof-of-concept demonstrators. For this purpose, detailed descriptions of their behaviour (B^t) and structure (S^t) are not required. Readers may consult our references to the literature for more specific information.

4.1. Computer-Aided Design Support for Action

The notion of a "tool" has traditionally been viewed as a mechanism for humans to perform actions. Computer-aided design tools can serve two possible functions (F^t) in their support of action (see Table 1):

- support communicating the design
- support initiating reflective conversation

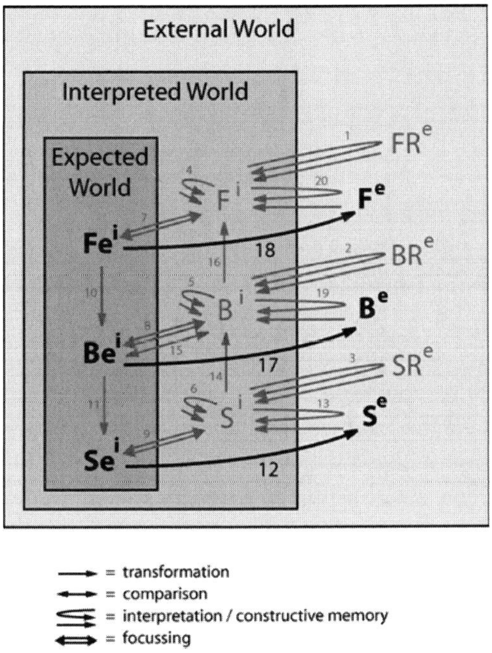

Figure 4. Action in the situated FBS framework.

Figure 4 highlights processes 12, 17 and 18 in the situated FBS framework to represent actions related to these two functions.

4.1.1. Support for Communicating the Design

- **$Se^i \rightarrow S^e$ (process 12)**: The ability to generate representations of external object structure (S^o) is provided by commercial CAD systems. These tools produce 2-D, 3-D or 4-D models and offer functionalities such as scaling, rotating and rendering to communicate different aspects of the object. The models generated by CAD systems are primarily used for data exchange with other designers, manufacturers or other stakeholders, or for providing input for tools that perform analyses of the designed objects. Communication across different tools has been recognised as an area of growing concern, as the tools generally use different languages (data formats) for representing object structure. A number of approaches address this problem by defining standardised product models, the best known of which are STEP and IFCs (Eastman 1999). Many CAD tools now have translators (called pre-processors) that map object structure onto a neutral format based on these standards. Some of our previous work was concerned with developing an agent-based approach to communicating product data in situations where no standard formats are available (Kannengiesser and Gero 2006; Kannengiesser and Gero 2007).
- **$Be^i \rightarrow B^e$ (process 17)**: Virtual reality (VR) systems are increasingly used to generate 3-D objects in a place-like context that usually include avatars representing potential users or stakeholders of the design. These tools support modelling not only the structure (S^o) but also the behaviour (B^o) of the designed object based on simulated interactions with avatars or other objects. Digital mock-ups (DMUs) are based on a similar concept, and are commonly used for the simulation of assembly operations or kinematics. Other tools that focus mainly on the communication of object behaviour (B^o) are those specialised in performing particular engineering analyses. Typical examples here include the representation of stresses and temperatures.
- **$Fe^i \rightarrow F^e$ (process 18)**: There are currently no commercial tools specialised in generating formal representations of object function (F^o). This is mainly due to the lack of a commonly agreed representation language. In most cases, function is described informally using natural language expressions, usually based on verb-noun pairs (Jacobsen et al. 1991) that are also used in this chapter. These descriptions can be produced by general-purpose word processors and annotation mechanisms provided by CAD systems. Future tool support may result from recent work on more formal representations of function (Chandrasekaran and Josephson 2000; Stone and Wood 2000; Szykman et al. 2001; Deng 2002).

4.1.2. Support for Initiating Reflective Conversation

- **$Se^i \rightarrow S^e$ (process 12)**: There are no commercial design tools that explicitly aim at supporting reflective conversation. However, there are some method-oriented approaches that may inform the development of such tools. For example, Jun and

Gero (1997) have demonstrated how shapes can emerge by representing the same geometrical structure in different ways. Current CAD systems do not have this ability, as their representations are fixed through the way they store a design's geometry in their database. An approach by Reymen et al. (2006) uses checklists and forms for designers to stimulate the creation of textual descriptions of designs from multiple perspectives, at regular intervals during the process of design.

- **$Be^i \rightarrow B^e$ (process 17)**: Reflective conversation at the behaviour level has not been well understood. However, the models of generating multiple representations described for the structure level can be applied when behaviour is represented using shapes. The notion of space, for example, can be viewed as a behaviour (derived from a walls-and-floor structure) that can be described geometrically.
- **$Fe^i \rightarrow F^e$ (process 18)**: Apart from cases in which functions represent references to shapes, reflective conversation at the function level has not been well understood. Tool support for generating multiple, textual representations of function may be developed based on research in natural language semantics. For example, de Vries et al. (2005) explore the use of the WordNet lexicon (Miller 1995) to generate a graph of synonyms and other semantic relations from a given set of words.

4.2. Computer-Aided Design Support for FBS^o Transformations and Evaluation

A number of research efforts have concentrated on tool support for performing those transformations and evaluations that have been viewed as fundamental in most traditional models of designing (e.g., Asimov (1962)). These include the transformations between the function, behaviour and structure of the design object, and evaluation based on comparing expected with "actual" behaviour. Figure 5 highlights processes 10, 11, 14, 15 and 16 to represent these activities.

- **$S^i \rightarrow B^i$ (process 14)**: There is a wide range of commercial tools that support the derivation of object behaviour from design structure. These are commonly referred to as analysis tools or simulation tools. Most of them are based on the physical laws and principles established in the engineering sciences. Examples of design analyses for which there is automated support include finite element analysis, thermal analysis, energy analysis and kinematic analysis. Some tools, such as design optimisation tools and parametric CAD systems, provide automated support for the $S^i \rightarrow B^i$ transformation as part of a collection of transformations that also include evaluation (process 15) and the generation of object structure (process 11). These tools will be presented in more detail under the bullet points for processes 11 and 15 (below). The function of determining additional behaviours (see Table 1) is addressed by some CAD systems performing runtime analyses of the design, such Design for X (DFX) analyses. Gero and Kazakov (1998) have developed a computational model of behaviour analogy where new behaviour variables are introduced into the target design based on structure similarity with the source design.

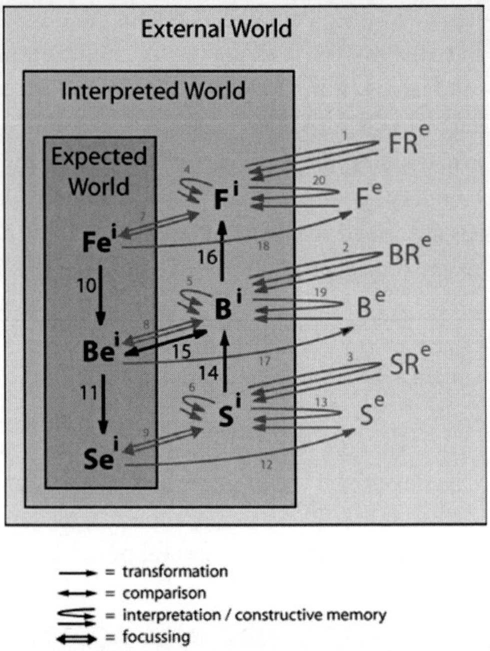

Figure 5. FBS° transformations and evaluation in the situated FBS framework

- **$Be^i \rightarrow Se^i$ (process 11)**: Parametric CAD systems have shown to significantly facilitate the creation of solid models (Shah and Mäntylä 1995), and many CAD vendors now offer parametric modelling features. These systems can be viewed as automating the process of computing an object structure once a set of parameters have been formulated for both structure and behaviour. Parametric CAD systems also allow for automated maintenance of parametric constraints (Sacks et al. 2004). This requires additional automation for analysing and evaluating the design for constraint violations, which can be mapped onto the transformation process $S^i \rightarrow B^i$ (process 14) and the evaluation process $\{Be^i, B^i\} \rightarrow$ decision (process 15). Design optimisation tools provide similar integrated functionalities supporting the same set of processes. They provide an extensive range of mechanisms to evolve object structure, including various deterministic and stochastic search methods (Papalambros and Wilde 2000).
- **$\{Be^i, B^i\} \rightarrow$ decision (process 15)**: Automated support for this process is provided in a number of computer-aided design systems, as indicated above. Optimisation tools, in particular, incorporate sophisticated strategies for controlling the execution of alternative search paths, based on the performance of the current design candidate. Research on agent-based design systems addresses evaluation using conflict resolution mechanisms, which have been applied to instances of multi-objective design optimisation (Grecu and Brown 1996; Campbell et al. 1999).
- **$Fe^i \rightarrow Be^i$ (process 10)**: Few systems have been developed that support the generation of object behaviours based on object function (Maiden and Sutcliffe 1992;

Bhatta et al. 1994; Umeda et al. 1996). This is mainly due to the lack of a formal language to represent function.

- **$B^i \rightarrow F^i$ (process 16)**: There has been no work to date on tool support for this process.

4.3. Computer-Aided Design Support for Focussing

There has been some work on tools to support focussing, the processes involved in the formulation of a design state space. These tools are mainly based on decision-making mechanisms that use various kinds of information. Figure 6 highlights processes 7, 8 and 9 to represent focussing.

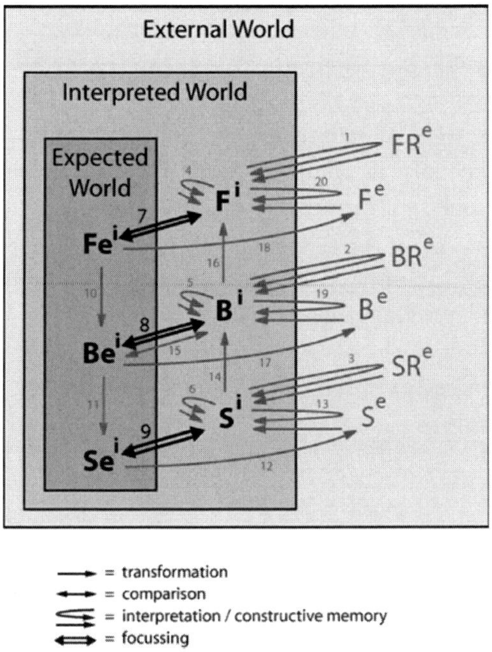

Figure 6. Focussing in the situated FBS framework.

- **$S^i \rightarrow Se^i$ (process 9)**: A number of computational approaches to focussing on object structure have been developed in the area of design optimisation. Some of this work uses information extracted from the current design. For example, Parmee's (1996) cluster-oriented genetic algorithms (COGAs) identify high-performance regions within the current structure state space. These features are then used for focussing on different structure variables and constraints, to concentrate the search for an optimum design on particular areas within the original structure state space. Other work uses information learnt from previous design tasks. A tool developed by Schwabacher et al. (1998) extracts characteristics of previous optimisation results and uses them to formulate new optimization problems. These characteristics include information such as optimal structure, mappings between structure and behaviour, infeasible behaviour and active constraints. This information is used to improve the problem formulation by reducing the structure state space.

- **$B^i \rightarrow Be^i$ (process 8)**: Some work has been done on focussing at the level of object behaviour, again mostly in the context of optimisation. Mackenzie and Gero (1987) have induced rules to detect certain features of Pareto optimal sets relating to curvature, sensitivity and other information. The rules use this information to reformulate the problem by carrying out focussing in a way that reduces the behaviour state space. Jozwiak's (1987) approach uses learning to acquire knowledge of inactive constraints, which is then used to predict whether or not the constraints of the current optimisation task may be neglected.
- **$F^i \rightarrow Fe^i$ (process 7)**: There has been no work to date on tool support for this process.

4.4. Computer-Aided Design Support for Interpretation

Tools usually have some form of interface to receive and utilise input provided externally either by humans or other tools. In computer-aided design, there are two possible functions (F^t) for interpretation by tools:

- support transferring design concepts as intended
- support re-interpreting design concepts

Figure 7 highlights processes 1, 2, 3, 13, 19 and 20 to represent interpretation.

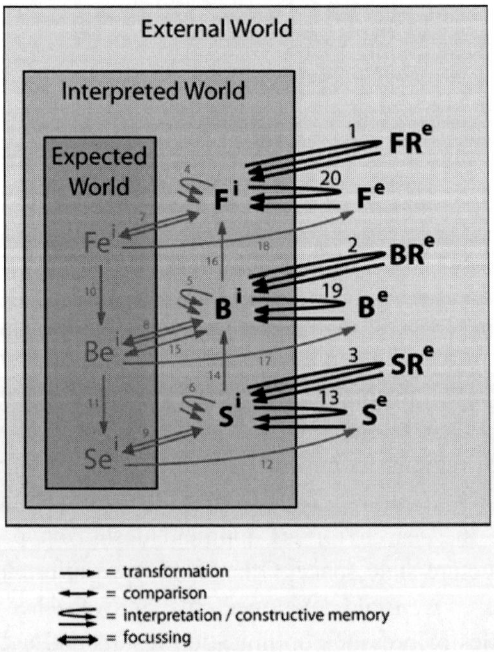

Figure 7. Interpretation in the situated FBS framework.

4.4.1. Support for Transfer of Design Concepts as Intended

- **$SR^e \rightarrow S^i$ (process 3) and $S^e \rightarrow S^i$ (process 13)**: There has been considerable research in the computational interpretation of external object structure. The standardisation approaches to product modelling, mentioned in Section 4.1.1, provide the basis for the development of import mechanisms (called post-processors) that translate the standard models into the tool's native format. Post-processors for STEP and IFC models are available in a number of commercial CAD/CAE/CAM systems. Another area of research is concerned with the interpretation of human sketches and freehand drawings by tools converting them into more exact graphical models or performing early design analyses (Taggart 1975; Gross 1996; Leclercq 2001).
- **$BR^e \rightarrow B^i$ (process 2) and $B^e \rightarrow B^i$ (process 19)**: Most design tools dealing with object behaviour directly derive that behaviour from structure (process 14) rather than interpreting it externally (e.g., from other tools). As a result, not much work exists on tool support for the interpretation of object behaviour. However, recent approaches to interoperability aiming to standardise the representation of function and behaviour besides structure (Szykman et al. 2001) may lead to the development of tool translators that automate this process.
- **$FR^e \rightarrow F^i$ (process 1) and $F^e \rightarrow F^i$ (process 20)**: Most tool support for the interpretation of object function is based on mechanisms of word recognition, given that many representations of function are described using natural language annotations. While there is a large number of general-purpose tools that provide interfaces for textual input (such as Word processors or electronic whiteboards), only few of them (e.g., the word generation system developed by de Vries et al. (2005)) offer more word-processing features than just editing. Future work on the interpretation of function can be expected to be driven by advances in both representing and reasoning about function, particularly in the area of design interoperability (Szykman et al. 2001).

4.4.2. Support for Re-Interpretation of Design Concepts

- **$SR^e \rightarrow S^i$ (process 3) and $S^e \rightarrow S^i$ (process 13)**: Most research in re-interpretation has been done at the level of object structure. A system presented by Saund and Moran (1994) supports the creation of multiple interpretations of line drawings, by first decomposing and then reassembling elements of freehand drawings. The emerging shapes are then presented to the user for selection. A design agent capable of re-interpretation has been developed by Smith and Gero (2001) on the basis of Gero and Fujii's (2000) "push-pull" model of situated cognition. This system has been able to learn new shapes over sequences of action and (re-)interpretation that are themselves the result of the agent's modified experience.
- **$BR^e \rightarrow B^i$ (process 2) and $B^e \rightarrow B^i$ (process 19)**: There has been no work to date on tool support for this process.
- **$FR^e \rightarrow F^i$ (process 1) and $F^e \rightarrow F^i$ (process 20)**: There has been no work to date on tool support for this process.

4.5. Computer-Aided Design Support for Constructive Memory

Most work on computer-aided design tools includes support for memory in some way. There are two possible functions (F^t) related to this notion:

- support retrieval of design concepts as stored
- support re-construction of design concepts

Figure 8 highlights processes 4, 5 and 6 to represent constructive memory.

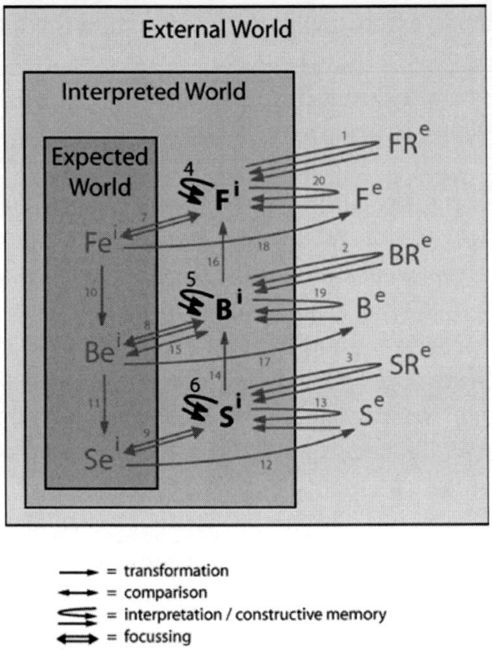

Figure 8. Constructive memory in the situated FBS framework.

4.5.1. Support for Retrieval of Design Concepts as Stored

- **$S^i \rightarrow S^i$ (process 6)**: Research in using memory of object structure includes work on feature-based modelling. A number of CAD systems provide design databases, repositories or libraries to store design features, such as pockets, holes and slots. Their reuse can lead to significant gains of productivity in designing. Techniques of feature extraction from geometrical CAD models can be viewed as another example of retrieving design concepts, although they require some additional computation. Here, features are implicitly stored in the pre-defined mappings underpinning common extraction techniques such as graph matching, syntactic pattern recognition and shape grammars (Shah 1991).
- **$B^i \rightarrow B^i$ (process 5)**: Some recent work on design repositories has concentrated on including properties related to behaviour (B^o) and function (F^o) of the design object (Szykman et al. 2001; Mocko et al. 2004). In addition, approaches to capturing and reusing design rationale have focused on appropriate representations of previous

object behaviour to be accessible for guiding the generation of new object structure (Chandrasekaran et al. 1993).

- **$F^i \rightarrow F^i$ (process 4)**: Simple retrieval of object function is best exemplified by work on storing and reusing function (F^o) hierarchies in design repositories (Szykman et al. 2001) or case bases (Navinchandra et al. 1991). Approaches to retrieving implicitly stored functions include work, mentioned earlier, on inferring word relations based on WordNet (de Vries et al. 2005). Other work focuses on the construction of sub-functions using decomposition knowledge encoded in grammars (Sridharan and Campbell 2005).

4.5.2. Support for Re-Construction of Design Concepts

- **$S^i \rightarrow S^i$ (process 6), $B^i \rightarrow B^i$ (process 5) and $F^i \rightarrow F^i$ (process 4)**: The idea of generating design concepts by situated re-construction rather than static retrieval from previous experience is quite new in design research. As a result, very little work has been done towards the development of computational models and tools that support this process. However, a number of research demonstrators have shown both the feasibility and the potential benefits of future constructive memory tools. Examples include neural network implementations used for the design of mechanical assemblies (Liew and Gero 2004), design optimisation (Peng and Gero 2006) and the exchange of product data between design tools (Kannengiesser and Gero 2007). The majority of this work provides support for re-construction of design concepts at all three levels, comprising function (F^o), behaviour (B^o) and structure (S^o).

5. Conclusion

Designing comprises a rich set of activities that is only beginning to be completely understood. Capturing these activities and defining them in a detailed framework is necessary to advance our understanding of design. The ontological framework presented in this chapter is a contribution to this aim. It extends our previous, object-centred work on representing the process of designing by adding a process-centred view. This view is based on the direct application of the FBS ontology to design activities, treating them as first-class entities with their own function, behaviour and structure, and no longer as mere derivatives of object-centred constructs. This provides a more structured description at a higher level of detail, which has the potential to make our framework of situated designing more amenable to other researchers.

We have shown that the process-centred ontology of designing also allows specifying a set of requirements for tool support. This is based on the connection we established between the FBS view of design processes and the FBS view of design tools. Specifically, tools are viewed as artefacts whose functions (F^t) are specialised to supporting particular aspects of design processes, which themselves consist of combinations of function (F^p), behaviour (B^p) and structure (S^p). We have demonstrated how some of the outcomes of existing computer-aided design research and development can be mapped onto 20 classes of design processes represented in this way. One result of our mappings is that a lack of tool support can be identified for a number of design activities. At the level of granularity presented in this chapter, this concerns activities of re-interpretation and re-construction of design concepts, and reasoning and focussing on object function (F^o).

Our ontology allows understanding the research field of computer-aided design as the "materials science" of designing, concerned with creating and analysing tools to form appropriate "materials" of design processes at different levels of granularity. This is possible because the FBS ontology represents all design objects, tools and processes uniformly. Future research may use this ontology to create more fine-grained specifications of design tools. For example, different classes of feature extraction processes can be defined based on different classes of inputs (e.g., cubic, cylindrical or free-form shapes) and on different classes of transformations (e.g., graph matching, shape grammars, neural networks, etc.), and consequently different functions (F^t) of feature extraction tools can be derived. Information about specific process behaviour (B^p) and process function (F^p), on an instance level, can be added to derive more refined tool functions (F^t). Researchers and developers in computer-aided design can then identify specific gaps in the functions (F^t) of existing tools and generate the behaviour (B^t) and ultimately the structure (S^t) of new tools to close these gaps.

Acknowledgements

NICTA is funded by the Australian Government as represented by the Department of Broadband, Communications and the Digital Economy and the Australian Research Council through the ICT Centre of Excellence program. This work is partly a result of research funded by the Australian Research Council, Project DP0559885.

References

[1] Asimov, M: 1962, *Introduction to Design*, Prentice-Hall, Englewood Cliffs.

[2] Bartlett, FC: 1932 reprinted in 1977, *Remembering: A Study in Experimental and Social Psychology*, Cambridge University Press, Cambridge.

[3] Bhatta, S, Goel, A and Prabhakar, S: 1994, Innovation in analogical design: A model-based approach, *in* JS Gero and F Sudweeks (eds) *Artificial Intelligence in Design '94*, Kluwer, Dordrecht, pp. 57-74.

[4] Bickhard, MH and Campbell, RL: 1996, Topologies of learning, *New Ideas in Psychology* **14**(2): 111-156.

[5] Campbell, MI, Cagan, J and Kotovsky, K: 1999, A-Design: An agent-based approach to conceptual design in a dynamic environment, *Research in Engineering Design* **11**(3): 172-192.

[6] Chandrasekaran, B, Goel, AK and Iwasaki, Y: 1993, Functional representation as design rationale, *IEEE Computer* **26**(1): 48-56.

[7] Chandrasekaran, B and Josephson, JR: 2000, Function in device representation, *Engineering with Computers* **16**(3-4): 162-177.

[8] Clancey, WJ: 1997, *Situated Cognition: On Human Knowledge and Computer Representations*, Cambridge University Press, Cambridge.

[9] Curtis, B, Kellner, MI and Over, J: 1992, Process modeling, *Communications of the ACM* **35**(9): 75-90.

[10] Deng, YM: 2002, Function and behavior representation in conceptual mechanical design, *Artificial Intelligence for Engineering Design, Analysis and Manufacturing* **16**(5): 343-362.
[11] Dewey, J: 1896 reprinted in 1981, The reflex arc concept in psychology, *Psychological Review* **3**: 357-370.
[12] Eastman, CM: 1999, *Building Product Models: Computer Environments Supporting Design and Construction*, CRC Press, Boca Raton.
[13] Gero, JS: 1990, Design prototypes: A knowledge representation schema for design, *AI Magazine* **11**(4): 26-36.
[14] Gero, JS and Fujii, H: 2000, A computational framework for concept formation for a situated design agent, *Knowledge-Based Systems* **13**(6): 361-368.
[15] Gero, JS and Kannengiesser, U: 2004, The situated function-behaviour-structure framework, *Design Studies* **25**(4): 373-391.
[16] Gero, JS and Kannengiesser, U: 2007, A function-behavior-structure ontology of processes, *Artificial Intelligence for Engineering Design, Analysis and Manufacturing* **21**(4): 379-391.
[17] Gero, JS and Kazakov, V: 1998, Using analogy to extend the behaviour state space in creative design, *in* JS Gero and ML Maher (eds) *Computational Models of Creative Design IV*, Key Centre of Design Computing and Cognition, University of Sydney, Australia, pp. 113-143.
[18] Grecu, DL and Brown, DC: 1996, Learning by single function agents during spring design, *in* JS Gero and F Sudweeks (eds) *Artificial Intelligence in Design '96*, Kluwer, Dordrecht, pp. 409-428.
[19] Gross, MD: 1996, The electronic cocktail napkin – a computational environment for working with design diagrams, *Design Studies* **17**(1): 53-69.
[20] Guindon, R: 1990, Designing the design process: Exploiting opportunistic thoughts, *Human-Computer Interaction* **5**: 305-344.
[21] ISO: 2001, *Software Engineering – Product Quality – Part 1: Quality Model*, ISO/IEC 9126-1, International Organization for Standardization, Geneva, www.iso.ch
[22] Jacobsen, K, Sigurjonsson, J and Jacobsen, O: 1991, Formalized specification of functional requirements, *Design Studies* **12**(4): 221-224.
[23] Jozwiak, SF: 1987, Improving structural optimization programs using artificial intelligence concepts, *Engineering Optimization* **12**: 155-162.
[24] Jun, HJ and Gero, JS: 1997, Representation, re-representation and emergence in collaborative computer-aided design, *in* ML Maher, JS Gero and F Sudweeks (eds) *Preprints Formal Aspects of Collaborative Computer-Aided Design*, Key Centre of Design Computing and Cognition, University of Sydney, Australia, pp. 303-320.
[25] Kannengiesser, U and Gero, JS: 2006, Towards mass customized interoperability, *Computer-Aided Design* **38**(8): 920-936.
[26] Kannengiesser, U and Gero, JS: 2007, Agent-based interoperability without product model standards, *Computer-Aided Civil and Infrastructure Engineering* **22**(2): 80-97.
[27] Leclercq, P: 2001, Programming and assisted sketching, *in* B de Vries, JP van Leeuwen and HH Achten (eds) *CAAD Futures 2001*, Kluwer Academic Publishers, Dordrecht, pp. 15-32.
[28] Liew, P and Gero, JS: 2004, Constructive memory for situated design agents, *Artificial Intelligence for Engineering Design, Analysis and Manufacturing* **18**(2): 163-198.

[29] Mackenzie, CA and Gero, JS: 1987, Learning design rules from decisions and performances, *Artificial Intelligence in Engineering* **2**(1): 2-10.

[30] Maiden, NA and Sutcliffe, AG: 1992, Exploiting reusable specifications through analogy, *Communications of the ACM* **35**(4): 55-63.

[31] McNeill, T, Gero, JS and Warren, J: 1998, Understanding conceptual electronic design using protocol analysis, *Research in Engineering Design* **10**(3): 129-140.

[32] Miller, GA: 1995, WordNet: A lexical database for English, *Communications of the ACM* **38**(11): 39-41.

[33] Mocko, G, Malak, R, Paredis, C and Peak, R: 2004, A knowledge repository for behavioral models in engineering design, *Computers and Information Science in Engineering Conference '04*, Salt Lake City, UT.

[34] Navinchandra, D, Sycara, KP and Narasimhan, S: 1991, Behavioral synthesis in CADET, a case-based design tool, *IEEE Conference on Artificial Intelligence Applications*, Miami Beach, FL, pp. 217-221.

[35] Osterweil, LJ: 2005, Unifying microprocess and macroprocess research, *in* M Li, B Boehm and LJ Osterweil (eds) *Unifying the Software Process Spectrum*, Springer-Verlag, Berlin, pp. 68-74.

[36] Papalambros, P and Wilde, DJ: 2000, *Principles of Optimal Design: Modeling and Computation*, Cambridge University Press, Cambridge.

[37] Parmee I.C. (1996) Towards an optimal engineering design process using appropriate adaptive search strategies, *Journal of Engineering Design* **7**(4): 341-362.

[38] Peng, W and Gero, JS: 2006, Concept formation in a design optimization tool, *in* J van Leeuwen and H Timmermans (eds) *Innovations in Design Decision Support Systems in Architecture and Urban Planning*, Springer-Verlag, Berlin, pp. 293-308.

[39] Rescher, N: 2006, *Process Philosophical Deliberations*, Ontos-Verlag, Frankfurt.

[40] Reymen, IMMJ, Hammer, DK, Kroes, PA, van Aken, JE, Dorst, CH, Bax, MFT and Basten, T: 2006, A domain-independent descriptive design model and its application to structured reflection on design processes, *Research in Engineering Design* **16**(4): 147-173.

[41] Sacks, R, Eastman, CM and Lee, G: 2004, Parametric 3D modeling in building construction with examples from precast concrete, *Automation in Construction* **13**(3): 291-312.

[42] Saund, E and Moran, TP: 1994, A perceptually-supported sketch editor, *ACM Symposium on User Interface Software and Technology*, ACM Press, New York.

[43] Schön, DA: 1983, *The Reflective Practitioner: How Professionals Think in Action*, Harper Collins, New York.

[44] Schön, DA and Wiggins, G: 1992, Kinds of seeing and their functions in designing, *Design Studies* **13**(2): 135-156.

[45] Schwabacher, M, Ellman, T and Hirsh, H: 1998, Learning to set up numerical optimizations of engineering designs, *Artificial Intelligence for Engineering Design, Analysis and Manufacturing* **12**(2): 173-192.

[46] Shah, JJ: 1991, Assessment of features technology, *Computer-Aided Design* **23**(5): 331-343.

[47] Shah, JJ and Mäntylä, M: 1995, *Parametric and Feature-Based CAD/CAM: Concepts, Techniques, and Applications*, John Wiley & Sons, New York.

[48] Smith, GJ and Gero, JS: 2001, Interaction and experience: Situated agents and sketching, *in* JS Gero and FMT Brazier (eds) *Agents in Design 2002*, Key Centre of Design Computing and Cognition, University of Sydney, pp. 115-132.

[49] Smith, GJ and Gero, JS: 2005, What does an artificial design agent mean by being 'situated'?, *Design Studies* **26**(5): 535-561.

[50] Sridharan, P and Campbell, MI: 2005, A study on the grammatical construction of function structures, *Artificial Intelligence for Engineering Design, Analysis and Manufacturing* **19**(3): 139-160.

[51] Stone, RB and Wood, KL: 2000, Development of a functional basis for design, *Journal of Mechanical Design* **122**(4): 359-370.

[52] Suwa, M, Gero, JS and Purcell, T: 1999, Unexpected discoveries and s-inventions of design requirements: A key to creative designs, *in* JS Gero and ML Maher (eds) *Computational Models of Creative Design IV,* Key Centre of Design Computing and Cognition, University of Sydney, Sydney, Australia, pp. 297-320.

[53] Suwa, M and Tversky, B: 2002, External representations contribute to the dynamic construction of ideas, *in* M Hegarty, B Meyer and NH Narayanan (eds) *Diagrams 2002*, Springer-Verlag, Berlin, pp. 341-343.

[54] Szykman, S, Fenves, SJ, Keirouz, W and Shooter, SB: 2001, A foundation for interoperability in next-generation product development systems, *Computer-Aided Design* **33**(7): 545-559.

[55] Taggart, J: 1975, Sketching: An informal dialogue between designer and computer, *in* N Negroponte (ed.) *Reflections on Computer Aids to Design and Architecture*, Petrocelli Charter, New York, pp. 147-162.

[56] Umeda, Y, Ishii, M, Yoshioka, M, Shimomura, Y and Tomiyama, T: 1996, Supporting conceptual design based on the function-behavior-state modeler, *Artificial Intelligence for Engineering Design, Analysis and Manufacturing* **10**(4): 275-288.

[57] de Vries, B, Jessurun, J, Segers, N and Achten, H: 2005, Word graphs in architectural design, *Artificial Intelligence for Engineering Design, Analysis and Manufacturing* **19**(4): 277-288.

[58] Weisberg, DE: 2000, The electronic push, *Mechanical Engineering* **122**(4): 52-59.

[59] Ziemke, T: 1999, Rethinking grounding, *in* A Riegler, M Peschl and A von Stein (eds) *Understanding Representation in the Cognitive Sciences: Does Representation Need Reality?*, Plenum Press, New York, pp. 177-190.

In: Computer-Aided Design...
Editors: C.M. De Smet et al, pp. 27-63
ISBN: 978-1-60456-860-8

Chapter 2

VARIOUS APPROACHES TO THE AUTOMATIC CONVERSION OF SIMPLIFIED 2D DRAWINGS INTO SOLID MODELS

Masaji Tanaka
Okayama Univ. of Science, Dept. of Mechanical Systems Engineering, Okayama, Japan

Abstract

Recently solid modelers have been popularized in mechanical CAD systems. However, 2D CAD systems are still used in medium-sized and/or small companies because generally solid modelers are more expensive and difficult in their operations than 2D CAD systems in the aspect of cost-effectiveness. As a result, the conversions of 2D drawings into solid models have been still operated manually in companies using 2D CAD systems. Although a great many methods have been proposed to automatically convert 2D drawings into solid models, they could not apply to most of actual 2D drawings because they handled only correct 2D drawings in geometry. Actually various kinds of simplified expressions such as partial omissions are usually used in 2D drawings. Also, in 2D assembly drawings, if assemblies consist of many parts, it becomes very difficult to recognize each part and to convert them into 3D assembly models by using only outlines of 2D assembly drawings. In this chapter, firstly previously proposed methods are referred. Then the author's methods are presented. The author's methods can convert simplified 2D drawings described above into solid models. In the methods, dimensions, part numbers and parts lists of 2D assembly drawings are used to understand detailed structures of assemblies. As a result, a single solution can be usually obtained as a 3D assembly model from a 2D assembly drawing regardless of the number of parts. In omitted 2D drawings, it is difficult to convert the drawings into solid models because they are quite incorrect in geometry. In the methods, 2D drawings including partial omissions can be automatically restored to correct 2D drawings by learning and generalizing patterns of line segments. When the generalized patterns of line segments are applied to actual partial omissions of 2D drawings, they would be automatically restored in the methods.

1. Introduction

In recent years, solid modelers have been popularized in mechanical CAD systems. Solid models are useful for present systems of CAM, CAE, CAPP, etc. However, 2D CAD systems are still used in medium-sized and/or small companies because generally solid modelers are more expensive and difficult in their operations than 2D CAD systems. Presently the necessity of 3D models has been increased step by step in the companies using 2D drawings. For example, automakers require solid models of each part to parts makers because they want to apply more precise 3D models of cars to CAE, etc. Also, the presentation of 3D models of various mechanical products would be effective for sales in many companies.

Actually the conversions of 2D drawings into solid models have been still operated manually in most of companies using 2D CAD systems. Although a great many methods have been proposed to automatically convert 2D drawings into solid models, they could not apply to most of actual 2D drawings. The most important reason is that previously proposed methods had handled only one mechanical part and only correct orthographic views in geometry. However, there are fatal issues in those methods for actual 2D drawings as follows.

(1) Simplified expressions such as sectional views and partial omissions are usually applied to actual 2D drawings. By using them, 2D drawings become clear and easy for designers and manufacturers. For example, symmetric parts such as bearings are always drawn only sectional views.
(2) Standardized mechanical parts such as bolts, nuts, bearings and gears are often expressed as symbolic figures in 2D drawings. Therefore, these figures are not correct in geometry.
(3) When most of parts are simple such as bars and plates in mechanical products, they are usually drawn only as 2D assembly drawings.
(4) Basically, mechanical drawings are messages to manufacturers to make actual mechanical products. Therefore, it is not necessary that mechanical drawings are correct orthographic views in geometry. Preferably, correct dimensions are often more important than correct outlines of products in the drawings for manufacturers. Additionally, various kinds of design information such as parts numbers and parts lists can aid to explain precise models of actual products in 2D drawings.

In general, complex curved surfaces are difficult to express in 2D drawings. For example, they are often used in the bodies of cars, planes, etc. Solid modelers are suitable for the design of products consisting of many complex curved surfaces. On the other hand, since mechanical structures such as cranes and garages consist of a great many simple parts such as bars and plates, the solid modeling of them usually wastes much time and is very troublesome for CAD operators. Therefore, in the aspect of cost-effectiveness, it becomes more suitable to make 2D drawings than to make solid models for designing mechanical structures. As a result, it is thought that 2D CAD systems and solid modelers would coexist for a long time in the future.

Figure 1.1 illustrates the overview of solid model of a crane in Mitsui Engineering and Shipbuilding (MES) Co., Ltd in Japan. Figure 1.2 illustrates the part of telescopic spreader and Figure 1.3 illustrates the parts of wheels in the crane. Since the crane consists of huge numbers of parts, immense time was required to make its correct solid model from 2D drawings. Figure 1.4 illustrates the 2D drawing of the overview of telescope spreader in Figure 1.2. In the author's research of this chapter, many 2D drawings were supplied from MES Co., Ltd, and the author's methods shown in this chapter have been developed by using these drawings.

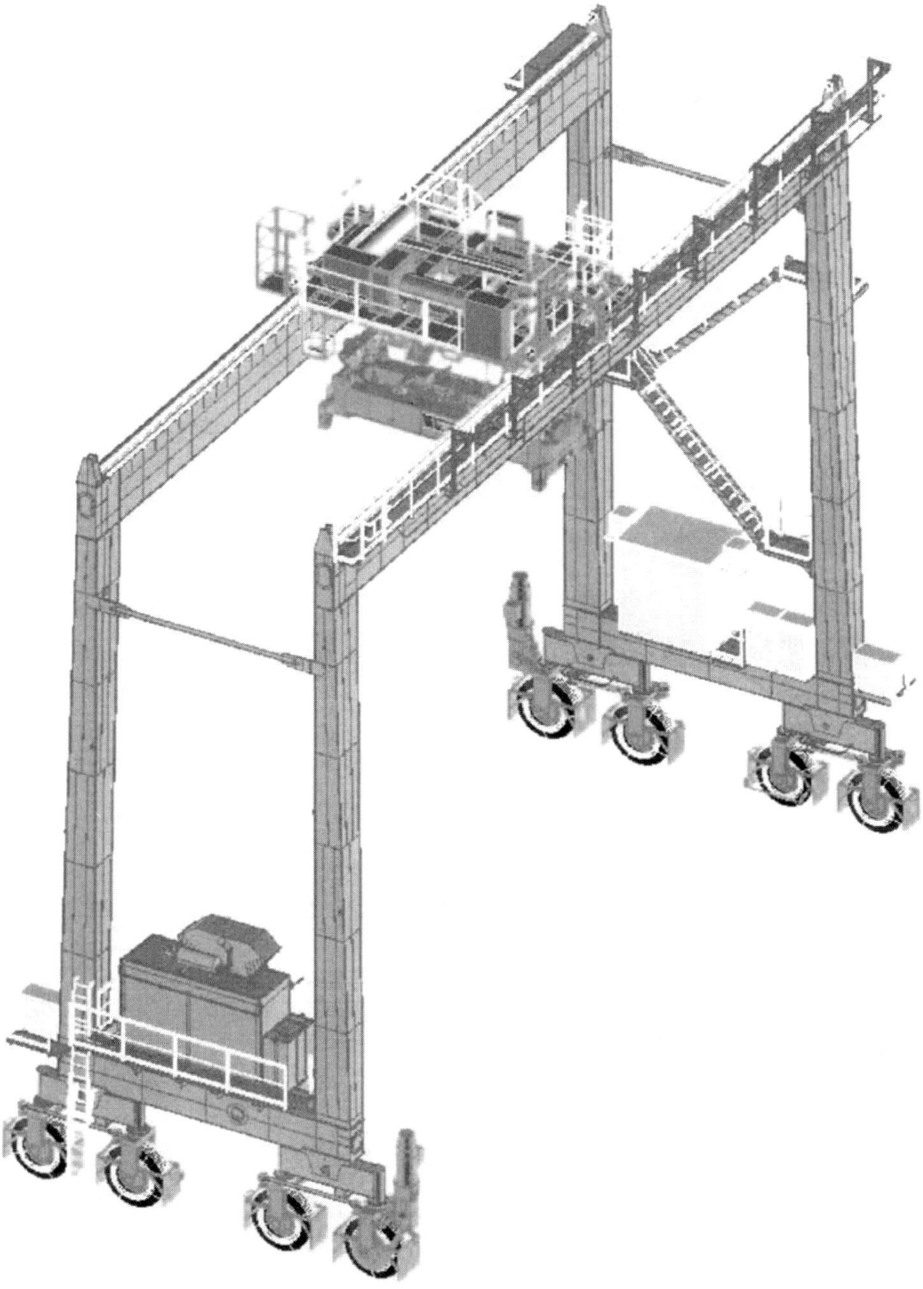

Figure 1.1. The solid model of a crane.

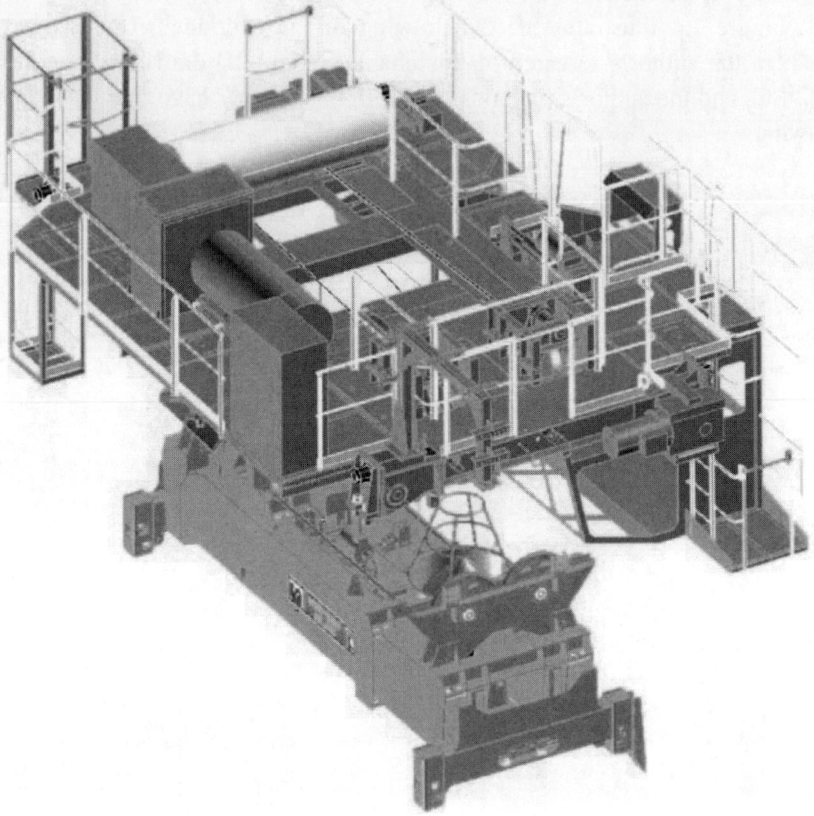

Figure 1.2. The telescopic spreader in Figure 1.1.

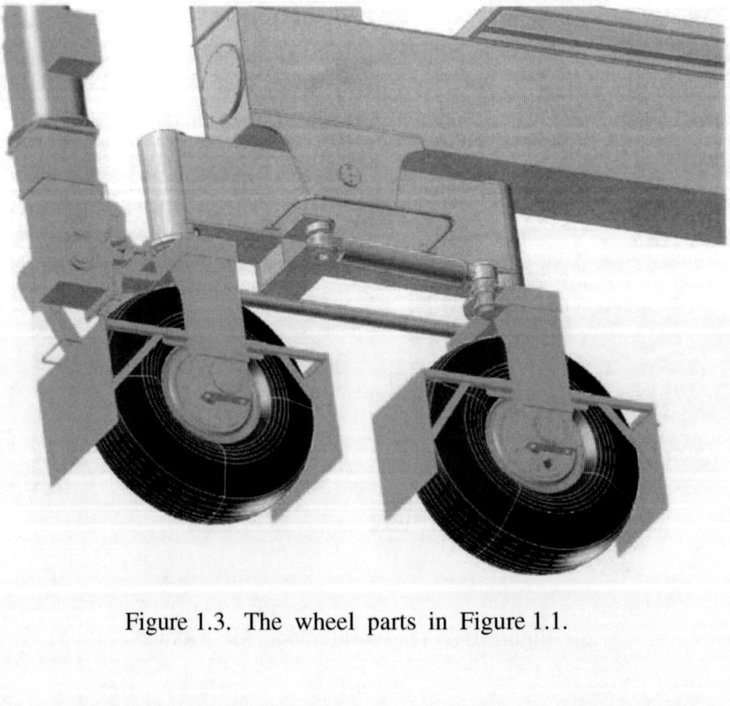

Figure 1.3. The wheel parts in Figure 1.1.

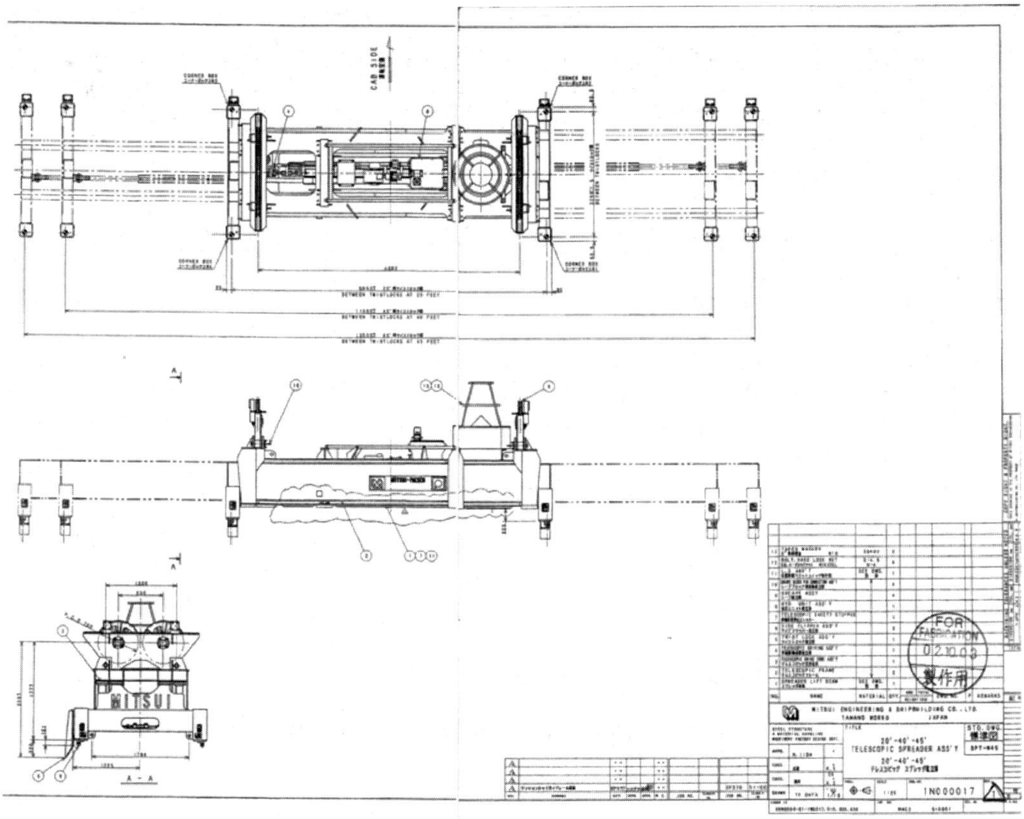

Figure 1.4. The overview of telescopic spreader in Figure 1.2.

Generally when 2D assembly drawings of mechanical structures are automatically converted to solid models by using only outlines, a great many solutions would be generated because each of parts cannot be recognized by only outlines in 2D assembly drawings. When the author firstly got 2D drawings of mechanical structures from the company, the most important issue was the explosion of the numbers of solutions. Example 1.1 as in Figure 1.5 that is a 2D drawing of mechanical structure was my first target to the conversion of 2D drawings to 3D models.

Since it is difficult to understand Figure 1.5, the author redraws simplified Example 1.1 as in Figure 1.6. In this figure, Example 1.1 consists of nine parts. By looking at the parts list of Example 1.1, it is found that from Part 1 to Part 7 are steel plates, Part 8 is a set of sixteen bolts and Part 9 is a kaowool cloth. Also, the size of each plate is indicated in the parts list. For example, the size of Part 1 is 14mmx145mmx560mm. These dimensions are also indicated in the outlines of Example1.1 and the area of Part 1 is pointed by the part number of that. The information of parts lists and part numbers enable manufacturers to understand easily the structures of assemblies in 2D assembly drawings. Therefore, manufacturers can usually obtain a single solution as a 3D model from a 2D assembly drawing.

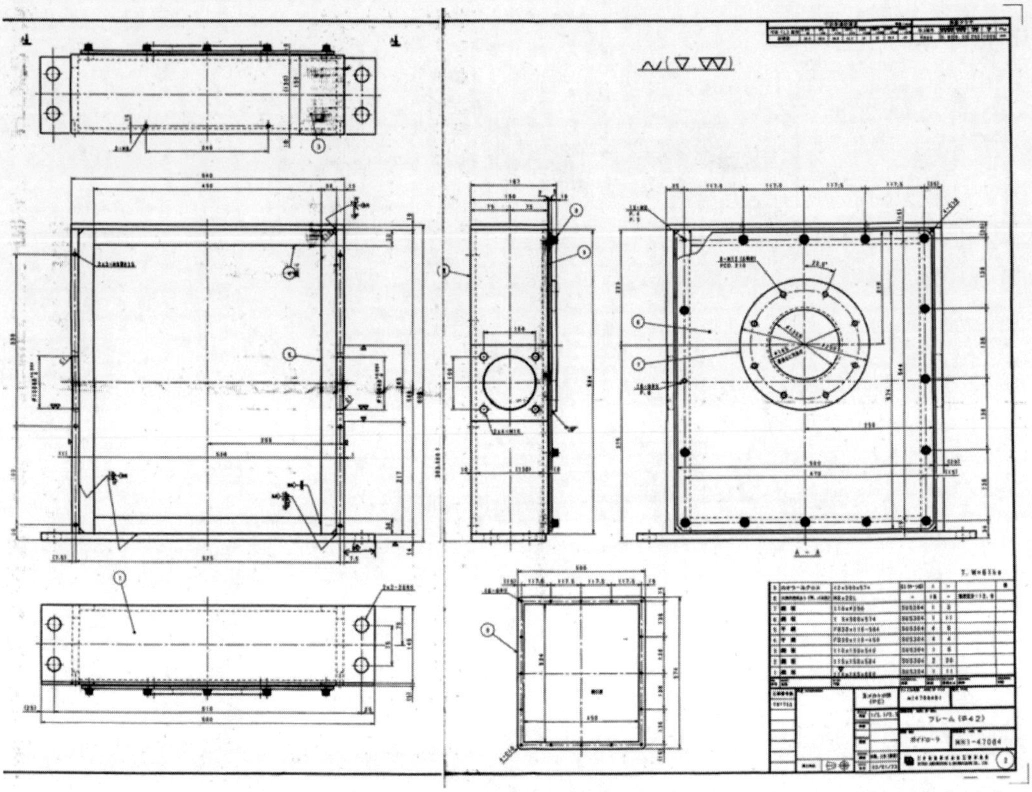

Figure 1.5. Example 1.1.

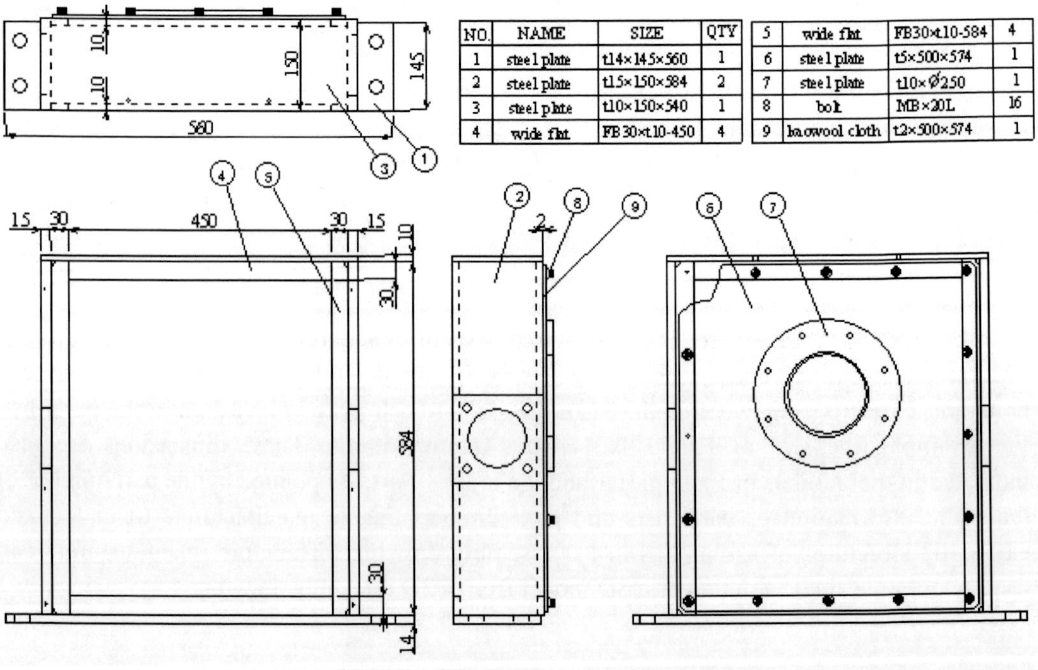

NO.	NAME	SIZE	QTY
1	steel plate	t14×145×560	1
2	steel plate	t15×150×584	2
3	steel plate	t10×150×540	1
4	wide flat	FB30×t10-450	4
5	wide flat	FB30×t10-584	4
6	steel plate	t5×500×574	1
7	steel plate	t10×Ø250	1
8	bolt	M8×20L	16
9	kaowool cloth	t2×500×574	1

Figure 1.6. Simplified Example 1.1.

The dimensions, part numbers and parts lists of 2D assembly drawings are applied in the author's method as follows. First of all, CAD files are formed as DXF (Drawing Interchange Formats) files in the author's method. DXF format is the most popularized format in 2D CAD systems. Each of DXF files is a text file and outlines, dimensions and texts can be distinguished as sections. So parts lists and part numbers can be recognized from DXF files of 2D assembly drawings. In Example 1.1, firstly Part 1 and its size can be recognized as steel plate and 14mm×145mm×560mm respectively. Next, the combinations of dimensions {14, 145, 560} are searched in the outlines of assembly drawing. So one combination consisting of 145mm and 560mm in the bottom view, and 14mm in the front view can be recognized in the drawing. Moreover, the part number of Part 1 is pointed in the bottom view. This combination can make a general solid model of a plate. In the same way, thirteen solid models of plates can be generated from Part 2 to Part 7. Since these solid models express plates that are not machined, detailed solid models of actual plates in the assembly are needed to make the correct 3D assembly model of Example 1.1. To make them, virtual 2D part drawings that are cut from assembly drawings in accordance with dimensions of parts are made in the author's method. The wireframe model, surface model and virtual blocks are made from each of virtual 2D part drawings. Each of virtual blocks consists of a closed region of faces in a surface model. The solid model of each part can be made by combining virtual blocks, and the 3D assembly model can be obtained by combining the solid models of parts.

In the author's method described above, a single solution would be usually obtained from a 2D assembly drawing. However, many issues remain. An important issue is the existence of simplified expressions in 2D drawings. Sectional views, partial omissions and partial detail drawings are often used in 2D drawings. For example, in Figure 1.6, there is a partial omission in Part 6 in the back view of Example 1.1. Though simplified expressions are difficult to handle them in a computer, they are useful for designers and manufacturers because they can express mechanical products more briefly. The last author's research result in this chapter is a method to automatically restore partial omissions in 2D drawings into correct 2D drawings in geometry. Correct wireframe models that can make 3D models will be made from the correct drawings. In general, partial omissions are often applied to draw long bars in 2D drawings. Since the partial omissions are not geometric but based on human understanding, learning algorithms are applied to handle them in the author's method. Firstly various kinds of properties such as type, length, center point, etc. are given to each line segment in the author's method. Then the relationships of line segments are learned and generalized such as repetitive features, vertical lines and straight lines. Finally, generalized patterns of line segments are applied to restore partial omissions of 2D drawings into correct drawings.

In the following sections, author's four methods are explained in detail. Firstly the author's method to automatically convert orthographic views into solid models is explained [1]. In this method, each orthographic view corresponds to one 3D object, and the equations of virtual blocks are explained to obtain the solutions of solid models. Secondly this method is applied to 2D assembly drawings to make 3D assembly models [2]. These conversion methods of 2D drawings into solid models are called the author's original method. Thirdly the author's method to automatically convert 2D assembly drawings of mechanical structures into 3D assembly models is explained [3]. This method is called the author's assembly method. Finally the author's method to automatically restore partial omissions in 2D drawings into correct 2D drawings in geometry is explained [4, 5]. This method is called the author's restoration method.

2. Related Works

There are a great many researches to automatically convert 2D drawings into solid models. The typical researches of them are presented in this section. The problem of the conversion was originally indicated by Idesawa's paper in 1973 [6]. In his paper, the method to make wireframe models and surface models from orthographic views was described. He discovered that imaginary wires and faces that do not construct solid models as the solutions were generated when wireframe models and surface models are made from orthographic views. Also, he discovered that the imaginary wires and faces are apt to generate many solutions. He proposed a method to delete the imaginary wires and faces by geometric constraints such as a condition that each 3D edge must be connected to two faces.

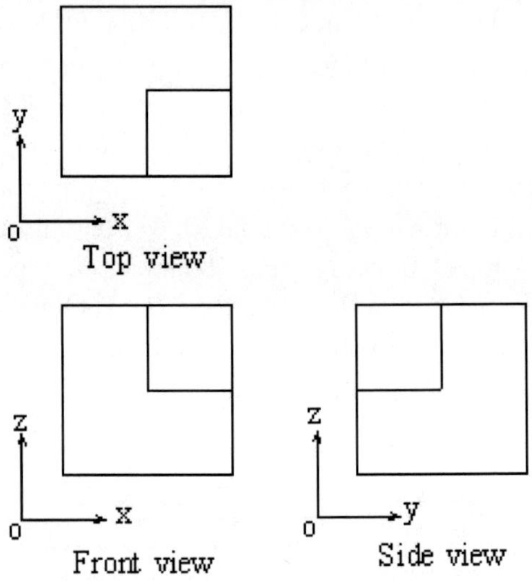

Figure 2.1. Example 2.1.

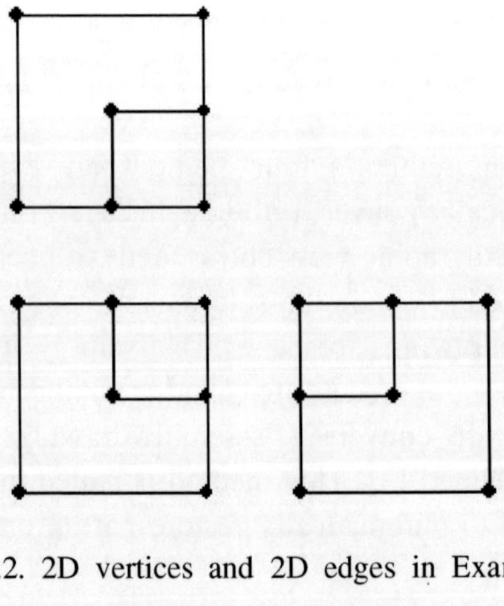

Figure 2.2. 2D vertices and 2D edges in Example 2.1.

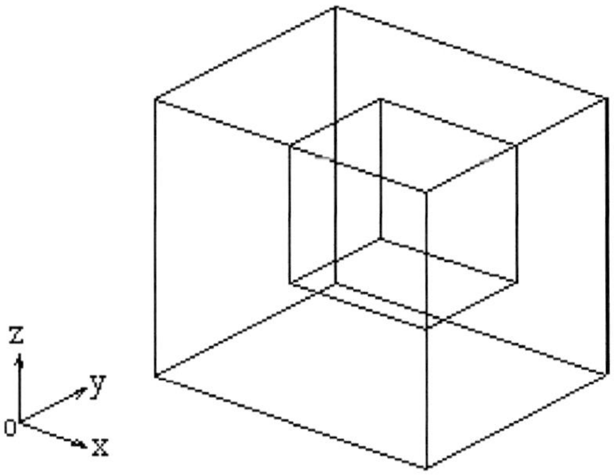

Figure 2.3. The wireframe model of Example 2.1.

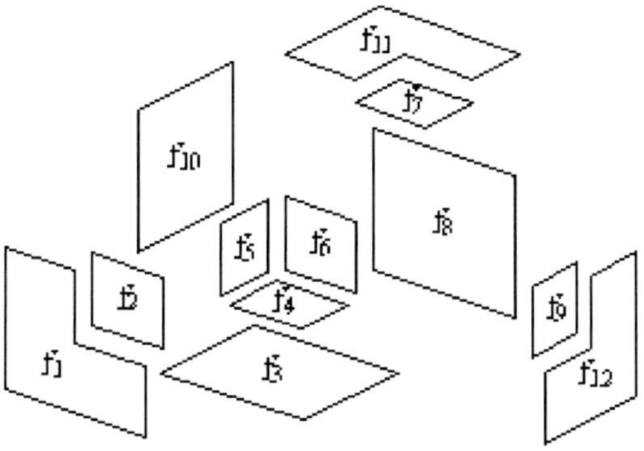

Figure 2.4. Each of faces in Example 2.1.

These problems are concretely explained as follows by using Example 2.1 as in Figure 2.1. An orthographic view consists of front view, top view and side view. In Example 2.1, *x-z*, *z-y*, *y-z* coordinate systems are set in each of views, and the origins of them are the same in 3D space. A 2D vertex is defined as an intersection of lines and a 2D edge is defined as a line segment whose endpoints are 2D vertices in orthographic views. 2D vertices of Example 2.1 are emphasized in Figure 2.2. In the same way, 3D vertices and 3D edges are defined in 3D space. In an orthographic view, the combinations of 2D vertices can make 3D vertices and the combinations of 2D, 3D vertices and 2D edges can make a wireframe model. Figure 2.3 illustrates the wireframe model of Example 2.1. It is found that there are three imaginary 3D edges that do not construct the solid model of Example 2.1. Surface models are made from wireframe models. Each of faces is a closed loop of 3D edges. Figure 2.4 illustrates each of numbered faces in Example 2.1. It is found that f_2, f_7 and f_9 are imaginary faces that are made from imaginary 3D edges. When Idesawa's condition described above is applied, the solid model of Example 2.1 can be obtained as in Figure 2.5. In the author's methods, imaginary geometric elements are called false elements and actual elements that construct solid models are called true elements.

The combinations of the truth of faces are equal to 2^n when the number of faces is n in a surface model. Therefore, to obtain solid models as the solutions, the computational complexity will exponentially increase when the numbers of faces increase in surface models. Afterward, Wesley and Markowsky invented virtual blocks each of which is a closed region of faces in their paper in 1981 [7]. In Example 2.1, two virtual blocks (B_1, B_2) are made as in Figure 2.6. It is obvious that B_1 is true and B_2 is false. The number of virtual blocks is very less than the number of faces when they are generated from an orthographic view. However, it is difficult to apply geometrical constraints to distinguish the truth of virtual blocks. In their paper, though several examples and the processes to obtain the solutions of solid models from orthographic views were indicated, there were no formed algorithms of the processes.

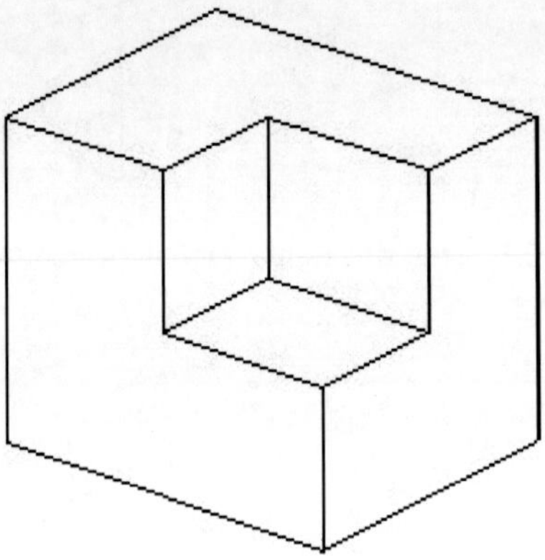

Figure 2.5. The solid model of Example 2.1.

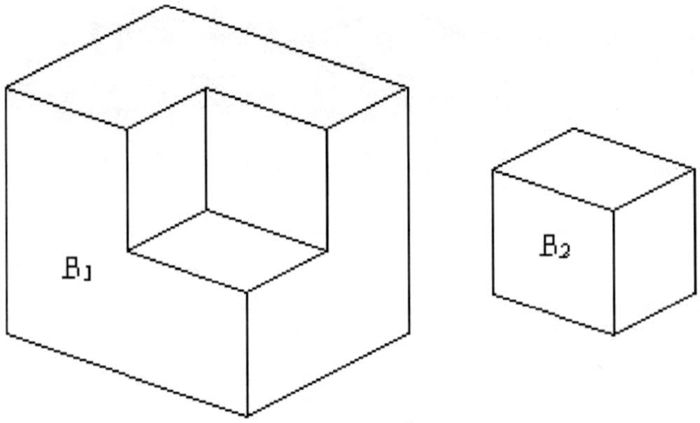

Figure 2.6. The virtual blocks of Example 2.1.

Since they handled only polyhedrons, virtual blocks consisted of only planar faces. Sakurai and Gossard [8] extended the kind of faces to curved faces. In their method, arcs and circles can be drawn in orthographic views and cylindrical, conical, spherical and toroidal faces can be applied to virtual blocks. Additionally, Dutta and Srinivas [9] handled two polygonal orthographic views. Though many solutions would be more generated from two polygonal orthographic views than from three views, two views are more useful than three views in actual 2D drawings. Gujar and Nagendra surveyed many researches of the conversion [10] and a method using virtual blocks is proposed [11].

Presently various kinds of methods have been still researched for the conversion of 2D drawings into 3D models. For example, Masuda and Numao [12] applied non-manifold topology and the assumption-based truth maintenance system (ATMS) to formulate the truth of virtual blocks. Kin et al. [13] introduced heuristics to distinguish the truth of faces. Lee et al. [14] proposed a CSG based method for symmetrical parts. Lu et al. [15] handled architectural 2D drawings. Dimri and Gurumoorthy [16] handled 2D sectional views. Gong et al. [17] generated hybrid wireframe models to process quadric surfaces in 2D drawings. Cao et al. [18] handled 2D drawings without hidden lines. Bhushan et al. [19] also handled 2D assembly drawings without part numbers. Also, many researches have been tried to automatically convert single freehand sketches to solid models (e.g. [20-21]). Moreover, several software packages had been marketed that automatically convert 2D drawings into solid models. However, these products could not be applied to most of actual 2D drawings because various kinds of simplified expressions are usually applied to 2D drawings.

3. Original Method to Convert 2D Drawings into Solid Models

3.1. The Method Using Lattice Faces and Cubic Models

Firstly the author considered simpler method than proposed methods to automatically reconstruct solid models from orthographic views because the generation of wireframe models and surface models from orthographic views seemed to be very difficult. So the author replaced the conversion problems with cubic models. When vertical and/or horizontal lines are added to make lattice faces in Example 2.1 as shown in Figure 3.1(a), a solid model consisting of eight cubes can be imaged. Here, let Figure 3.1(a) be Example 3.1. Figure 3.1(b) illustrates each of cubes (C_1, C_2, ... , C_8). Especially C_8 is hidden in this figure. Here, added lines to Figure 2.1 are called virtual 2D edges. So generally outlines of lattice faces consist of solid 2D edges, dotted 2D edges and virtual 2D edges. Figure 3.2 illustrates the relationships between the lattice faces and cubes in Figure 3.1. From this figure, the following five conditions can be defined.

(1) *Solid_2D edge_condition*
When two cubes are connected at a face in a cubic model and the boundaries of them appear as a solid 2D edge in one of the lattice faces, the two cubes are not both true.

(2) *Virtual_2D edge_condition*
When two cubes are connected at a face in a cubic model and the boundaries of them appear as a virtual 2D edge in one of the lattice faces, the truths of two cubes are the same.

(3) *Dotted_2D edge_condition*
When two cubes are connected at a face in a cubic model and the boundaries of them appear as a dotted 2D edge in one of the lattice faces, the truth of two cubes are the same and at least two cubes that can make the dotted 2D edge must exist.

(4) *Existence_condition*
When C_x is false, if some 2D edge of outlines in a orthographic view is deleted and/or added, C_x must be true.

(5) *Mass_condition*
When C_x is false, if all of true cubes do not form one solid model, C_x must be true.

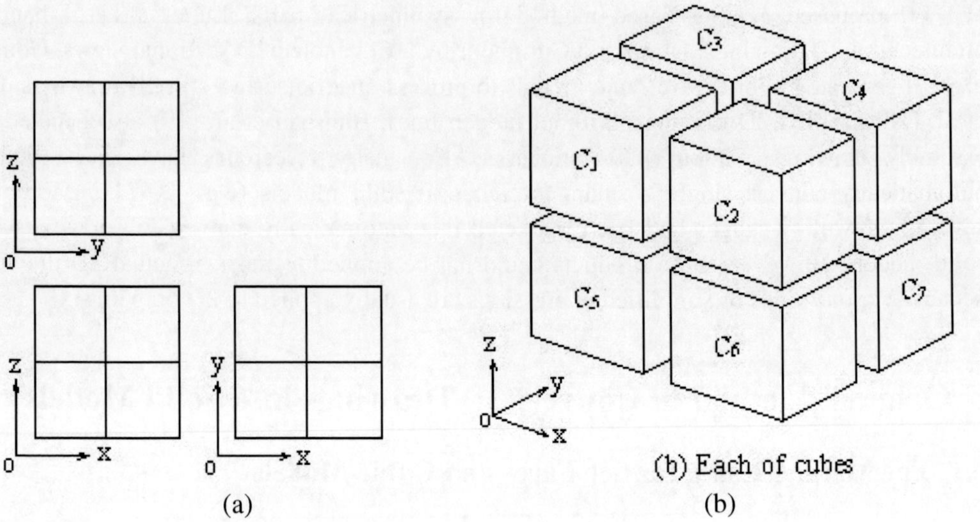

Figure 3.1. The cubic model of Example 3.1.

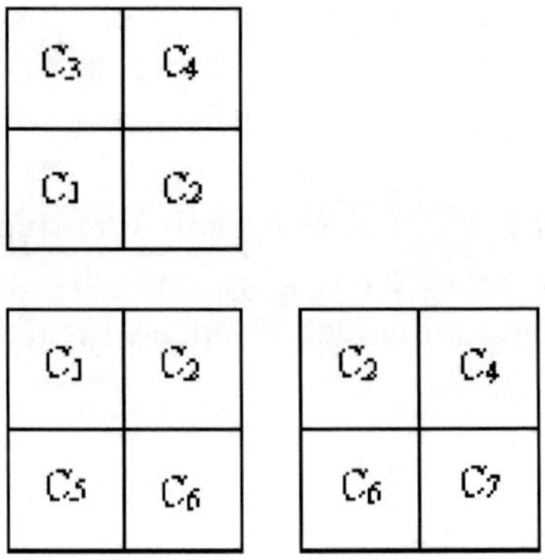

Figure 3.2. The relationships between lattice faces and cubes in Figure 3.1.

Here, two cubes whose truths are the same are formalized as C_x-C_y. Also, two cubes whose truth are not both true are formalized as $C_x \times C_y$. Figure 3.3 illustrates the equations of cubes in each view of Example 3.1. In this figure, since C_1, C_2, C_4 and C_6 are overlapped in the three views, the three equations can be connected as in Figure 3.4. In this figure, when *Existence_condition* is applied, C_1, C_3, C_4, C_5, C_6 and C_7 become true. Then C_2 becomes false by *Solid_2D edge_condition*. Though the truth of C_8 cannot be distinguished, if C_8 is false, several dotted 2D edges are added to Example 2.1. Therefore, C_8 must be true. As a result, the solution of Example 3.1 is formed by all of cubes except C_2. This solution is the same as B_1 in Figure 2.6.

Figure 3.5 illustrates Example 3.2 and Figure 3.6 illustrates the lattice faces of Example 3.2. From this figure, eighteen cubes can be made as shown in Figure 3.7. Figure 3.8 illustrates the relationships between the lattice faces and cubes in Example 3.2. Figure 3.9 illustrates the equations of cubes in each view of Example 3.2. These equations can be connected as in Figure 3.10. In this figure, when *Existence_condition* is applied, it is found that C_1, C_3, C_6, C_7, C_8, C_9, C_{10}, C_{11}, C_{12}, C_{13} and C_{16} are true. Therefore, C_2, C_4 and C_5 become false. Then C_{14}, C_{15}, C_{17} and C_{18} become true by *Existence_condition*. Therefore, the solution of Example 3.2 can be obtained as in Figure 3.11. Though lattice faces and cubic models can be made easily and the truth of each cube can be found easily by the equations of cubes, slanting 2D edges cannot be applied by the cubic method. So the author applied the cubic method to virtual blocks as follows.

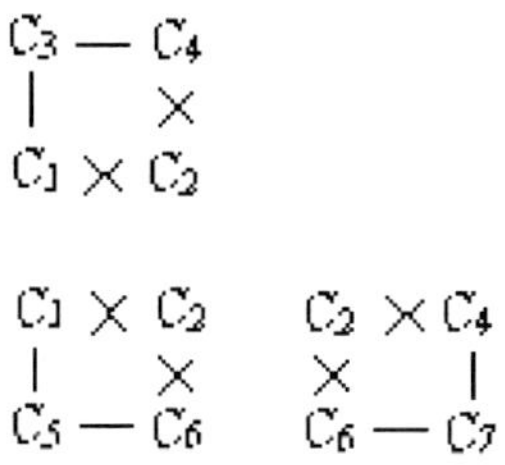

Figure 3.3. The equations of cubes in each view of Example 3.1.

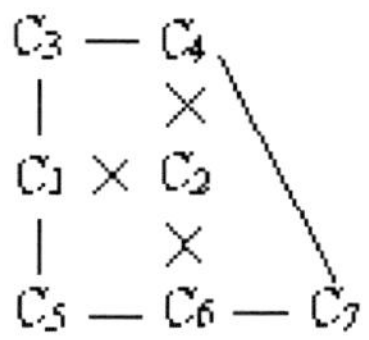

Figure 3.4. The equations of cubes in Example 3.1.

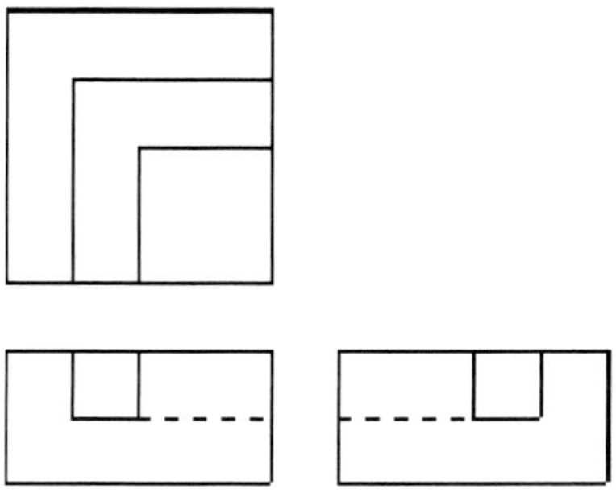

Figure 3.5. Example 3.2.

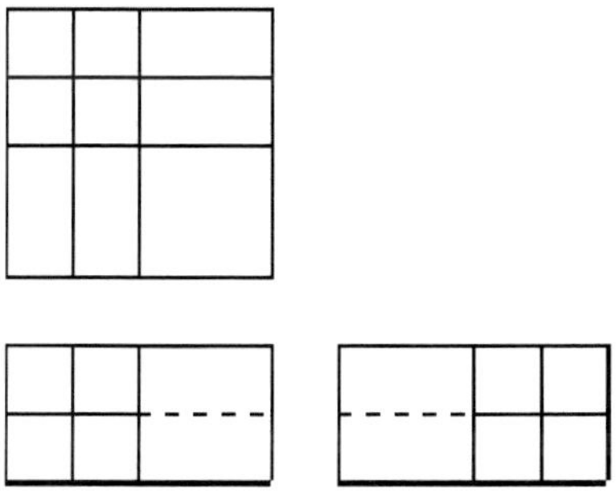

Figure 3.6. The lattice faces of Example 3.2.

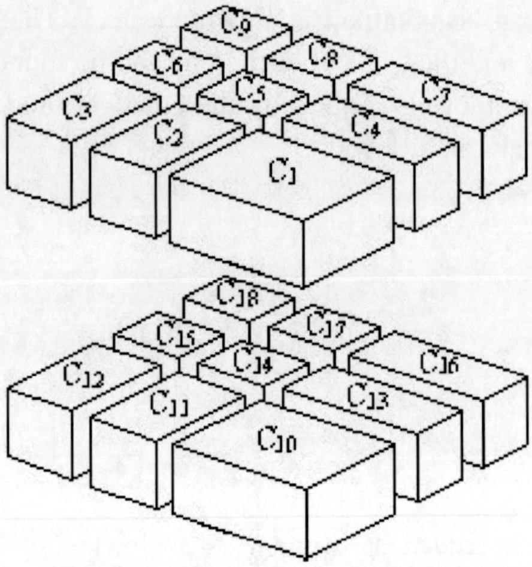

Figure 3.7. The cubic model of Example 3.2.

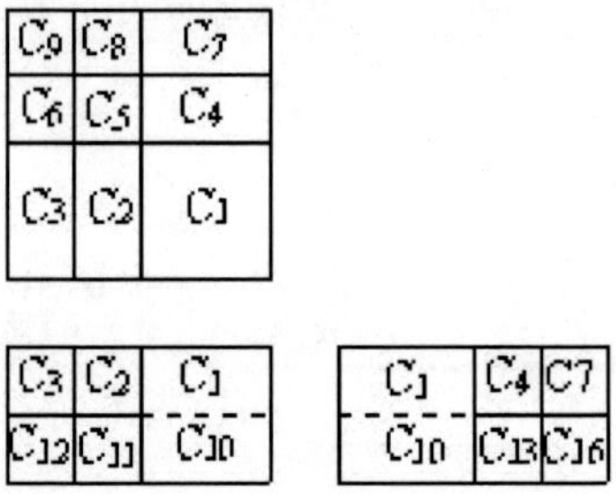

Figure 3.8. The relationships between lattice faces and cubes in Example 3.2.

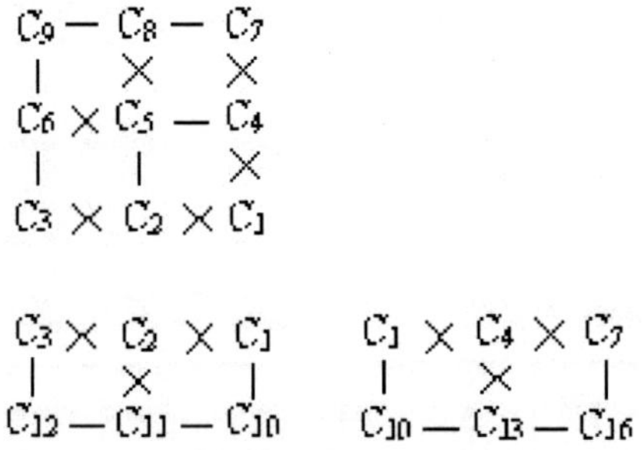

Figure 3.9. The equations of cubes in each view of Example 3.2.

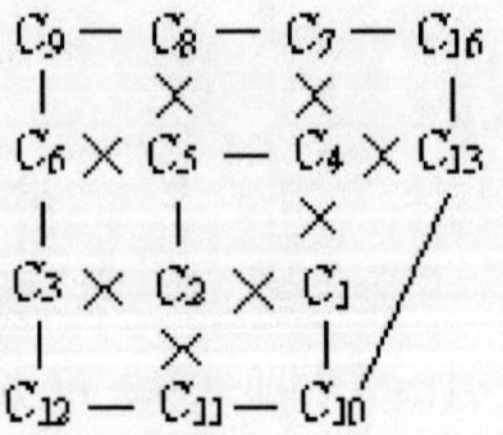

Figure 3.10. The equations of cubes in Example 3.2.

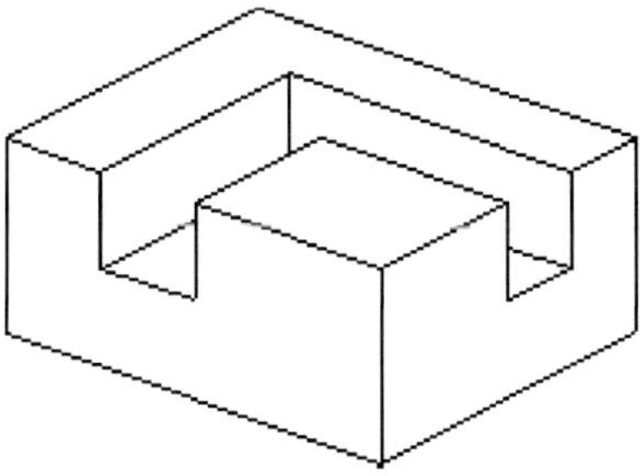

Figure 3.11. The solid model of Example 3.2.

3.2. The Method Using 2D Faces and Virtual Blocks

Figure 3.12 illustrates Example 3.3. There are many slanting 2D edges in Example 3.3. When Wesleys' method [2] is applied to Example 3.3, the wireframe model and virtual blocks (B_1, B_2, … , B_{12}) can be generated as in Figure 3.13 and Figure 3.14 respectively.

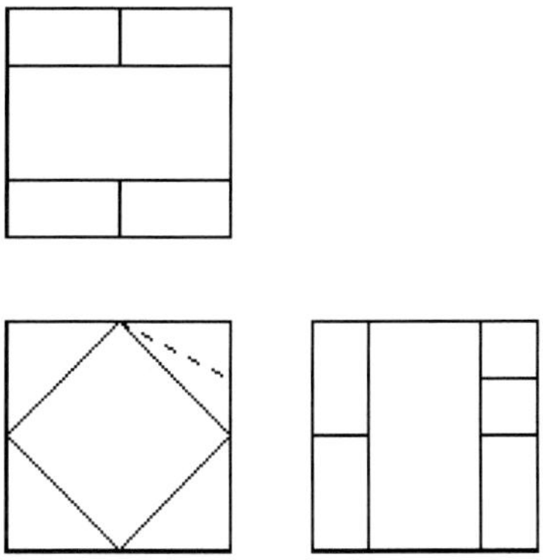

Figure 3.12. Example 3.3.

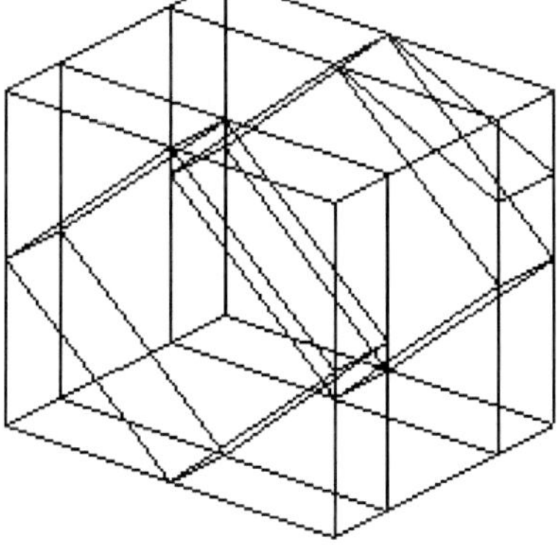

Figure 3.13. The wireframe model of Example 3.3.

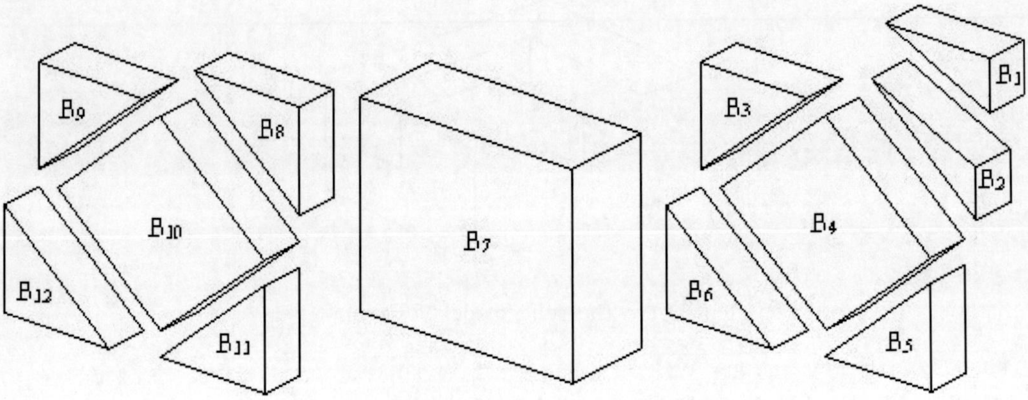

Figure 3.14. The virtual blocks of Example 3.3.

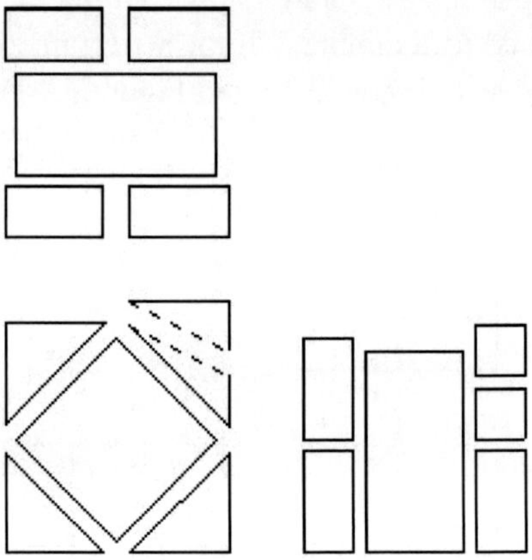

Figure 3.15. Each of 2D faces in Example 3.3.

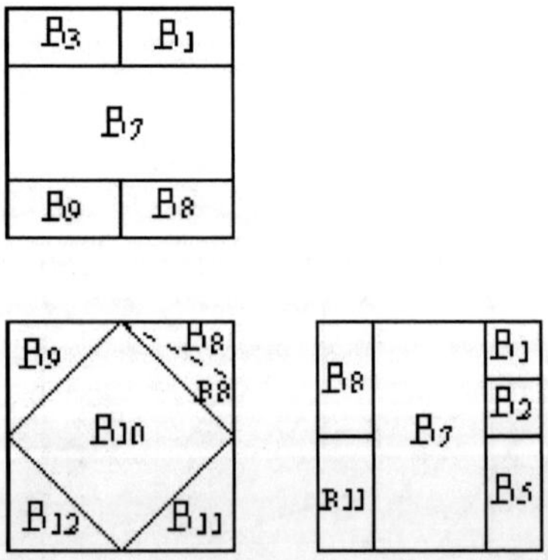

Figure 3.16. The relationships between 2D faces and virtual blocks in Example 3.3.

In the author's cubic method, lattice faces can correspond to cubic models. In the same way, since each of 3D faces corresponds to a closed loop of 2D edges between orthographic views and their surface models, each of closed loops of 2D edges can correspond to each of virtual blocks. Here, let a closed loop of 2D edges be a 2D face. Figure 3.15 illustrates each of 2D faces in Example 3.3. Figure 3.16 illustrates the relationships between 2D faces and virtual blocks in Example 3.3. Figure 3.17 illustrates the overview of virtual block model in Example 3.3. By comparing Figure 3.16 with Figure 3.17, the conditions of cubes described above can apply to virtual blocks except for *Virtual_2D edge_condition* as follows.

(1) *Solid_2D edge_condition*
When two virtual blocks are smoothly connected in their faces and the boundaries of them appear as a solid 2D edge in the boundaries of 2D faces, the two virtual blocks are not both true.

(2) *Dotted_2D edge_condition*
When two virtual blocks are smoothly connected in their faces and the boundaries of them appear as a dotted 2D edge in the boundaries of 2D faces, the truth of two virtual blocks are the same and at least two virtual blocks that can make the dotted 2D edge must exist.

(3) *Existence_condition*
When B_x is false, if some 2D edge of outlines in a orthographic view is deleted and/or added, B_x must be true.

(4) *Mass_condition*
When B_x is false, if all of true blocks do not form one solid model, B_x must be true.

For example, B_9 and B_{10} are separated by a solid 2D edge in the front view in Figure 3.16. However, in Figure 3.17, the faces of B_9 and B_{10} are connected smoothly. Therefore, if B_9 and B_{10} are both true, the solid 2D edge is deleted. As a result, B_9 and B_{10} are not both true by *Solid_2D edge_condition*. In the same way, the equations of virtual blocks in each view can be made as in Figure 3.18. When these three equations are connected, the equations of virtual blocks in Example 3.3 are formed as in Figure 3.19. The equations can be solved as follows. Firstly B_7 becomes true by *Existence_condition*. So B_1, B_2, B_3, B_5, B_8, B_9 and B_{11} become false. Then B_4 and B_{10} become true by *Existence_condition*. So B_{12} becomes false. As a result, only the truth of B_6 cannot be distinguished by the equations. B_6 becomes an undecided block. Generally undecided blocks can generate many solutions. Finally two solutions can be obtained from Example 3.3 by the equations as follows. B_6 is true in Figure 3.20(a) and false in Figure 3.20(b).

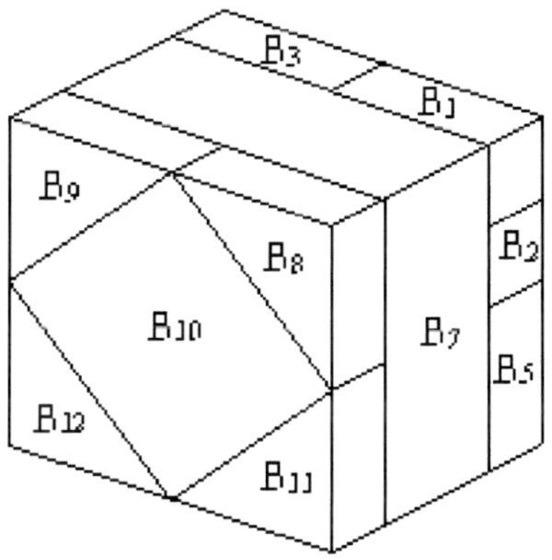

Figure 3.17. The overview of virtual block model in Example 3.3.

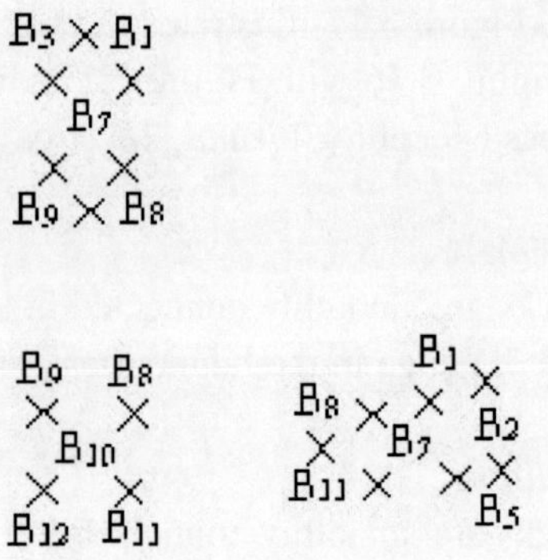

Figure 3.18. The equations in each view of Example 3.3.

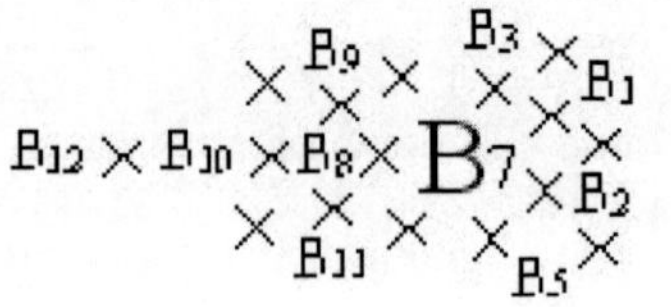

Figure 3.19. The equations of virtual blocks in Example 3.3.

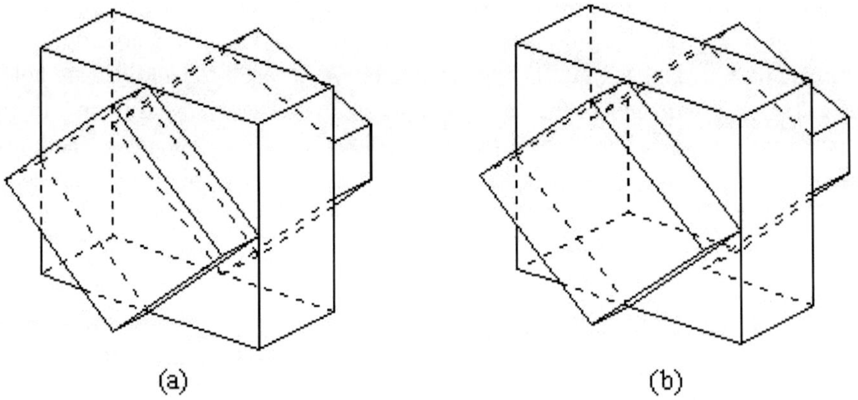

(a) (b)

Figure 3.20. Two solutions in Example 3.3.

The advantages of the author's original method in this section are summarized as follows.

(1) Since solid models as the solutions are made from not surface models but virtual blocks, the computational complexity is basically very less than surface models.
(2) Since the relationships of the truth of virtual blocks are formalized as the equations of virtual blocks, solid models as the solutions can be obtained by solving the equations.
(3) Since the equations of virtual blocks could only distinguish the truth of blocks appearing in the equations, the other blocks become undecided blocks that can generate many solutions. Therefore, if input orthographic views are not almost ambiguous, very few solid models as the solutions could be quickly obtained regardless of the numbers of virtual blocks.

4. Automatic Conversion of 2D Assembly Drawings into 3D Assembly Models

4.1. Application of the Equations of Virtual Blocks to 2D Assembly Drawings

The equations of virtual blocks in the author's original method can apply to 2D assembly drawings because all outlines of assemblies are usually drawn in 2D assembly drawings.

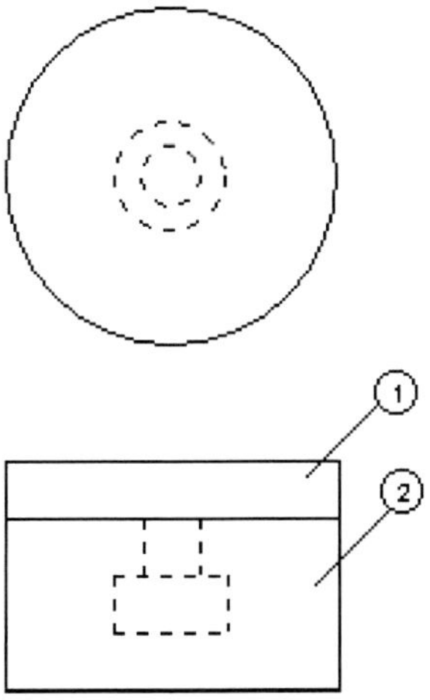

Figure 4.1. Example 4.1.

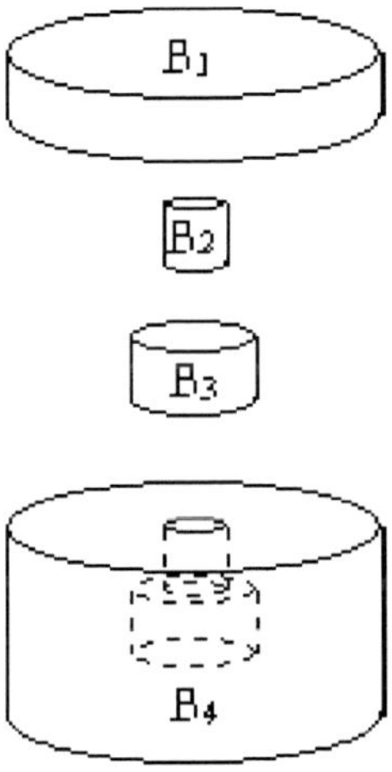

Figure 4.2. Each of virtual blocks in Example 4.1.

Therefore, necessary blocks to construct each of parts in assemblies can be generated from 2D assembly drawings. However, it is difficult to automatically recognize the shape of each part in 2D assembly drawings by using only their outlines. In general, the shapes of mechanical parts are not almost uniform though many prototypes such as bolts, gears, etc. exist. Since part numbers are usually indicated in 2D drawings, they can be hints to recognize each of parts. Figure 4.1 illustrates Example 4.1 that is a simple 2D assembly drawing consisting of two parts. When the wireframe model and surface model of Example 4.1 are made, four virtual blocks (B_1, B_2, B_3, B_4) are generated as shown in Figure 4.2. Figure 4.3 illustrates 2D faces and their corresponding virtual blocks in Example 4.1. In 2D assembly drawings, the solid model of each part can be obtained by distinguishing the truth of virtual blocks, and also the belonging of virtual blocks to each part must be distinguished. Therefore, the conditions of virtual blocks in section 3 are changed a little in 2D assembly drawings as follows.

(1) *Solid_2D edge_condition*
When two virtual blocks are smoothly connected in their faces and the boundaries of them appear as a solid 2D edge in the boundaries of 2D faces, the two virtual blocks do not belong to the same part or they are not both true.

(2) *Dotted_2D edge_condition*
When two virtual blocks are smoothly connected in their faces and the boundaries of them appear as a dotted 2D edge in the boundaries of 2D faces, the truth of two virtual blocks are the same and at least two virtual blocks that can make the dotted 2D edge must exist. If the two virtual blocks are both true, they belong to the same part.

(3) *Existence_condition*
When B_x is false, if some 2D edge of outlines in a orthographic view is deleted and/or added, B_x must be true. Additionally, if a part number points a 2D face, some virtual block that corresponds to the 2D face must exist.

(4) *Mass_condition*

When B_x is false, if all of true blocks do not form one solid model of a part, B_x must be true.

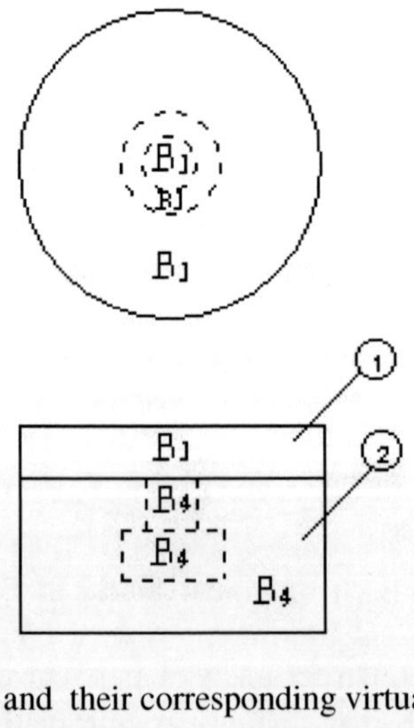

Figure 4.3. The 2D faces and their corresponding virtual blocks in Example 4.1.

In Figure 4.3, only "Part 1-$B_1 \times B_4$–Part 4" is obtained as the equations of virtual blocks. When Existence_condition is applied, it is found that B_1 belongs to Part 1 and B_2 belongs to Part 2. As a result, B_2 and B_3 become undecided blocks and they generate three solutions as in Figure 4.4. It is difficult to select a correct solution from the three solutions. In this case, some physical conditions could find a correct solution. For example, since the connection of two parts is unstable in solution (a), it is not correct. Also, since two parts cannot be assembled in solution (c), it is not correct. As a result, solution (b) can be found the correct solution of Example 4.1. However, it is difficult to formalize physical conditions of virtual block models to calculate correct solutions. Though Example 4.1 is a simple 2D assembly drawing, if assemblies consist of many parts, the numbers of solutions would exponentially increase and it would be impossible to find correct solutions.

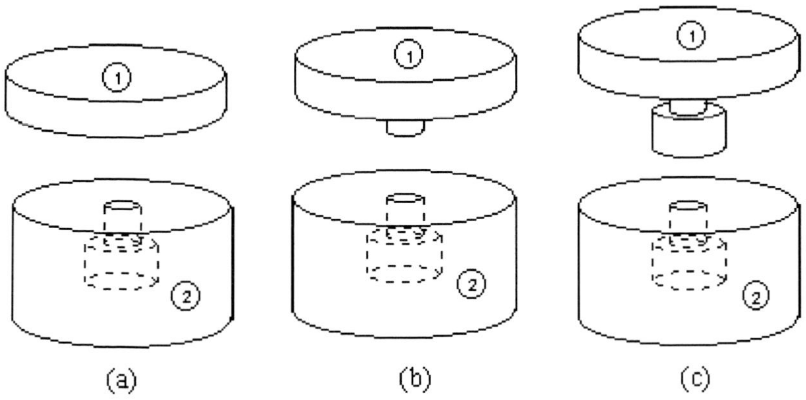

Figure 4.4. Three solutions in Example 4.1.

4.2. The Conversion of 2D Assembly Drawings into 3D Models to Obtain a Single Solution

If assemblies consist of simple and obvious parts, the identification of correct solutions becomes easy. For example, mechanical structures such as cranes are usually drawn as only 2D assembly drawings because most of their parts are simple such as bars and plates. In this case, drawn bars and plates are indicated in detail by their outward dimensions, parts numbers and parts lists in 2D assembly drawings. When these data of parts is automatically recognized in 2D assembly drawings, undecided blocks could be minimized to obtain correct solutions.

Figure 4.5 illustrates Example 4.2 that is a table consisting of six parts. The data of six parts are indicated as dimensions, parts numbers and a parts list in this figure. For example, it is found that the outward dimensions of Part 1 are 25×300×300 and the quantity of Part 1 is one in the parts list of Example 4.2. Also, the dimensions of each part are drawn in the outlines of assembly drawing in Example 4.2. In this example, if all of parts form cuboids like its parts list, it is not difficult to make its 3D assembly model because each of 3D part can be made by searching a correct combination of dimensions. However, generally the parts of assemblies are usually machined such as Part 2 in Example 4.2. To obtain detailed shapes of parts in 2D assembly drawings, the author invents virtual 2D part drawings as follows.

In Example 4.2, the outward size of Part 1 is 25×300×300. When the three dimensions are searched in its assembly drawing, two cubic combinations can be recognized. In the two combinations, when part number (1) is searched, a single combination can be found. When the areas where Part 1 exists are separated from the original drawing in accordance with its dimensions (25×300×300), the separated drawing is called the virtual 2D part drawing of Part

1. In the same way, each of virtual 2D part drawings in Example 4.2 is made as in Figure 4.6. Since virtual 2D part drawings could include all of outlines that express the shapes of parts, virtual blocks made from virtual 2D part drawings could make the solid models of parts in detail. Figure 4.7 illustrates virtual blocks made from virtual 2D part drawings in Figure 4.6. The following conditions of virtual blocks made from virtual 2D part drawings to make the solid models of parts are largely changed from the conditions of 2D assembly drawings described above.

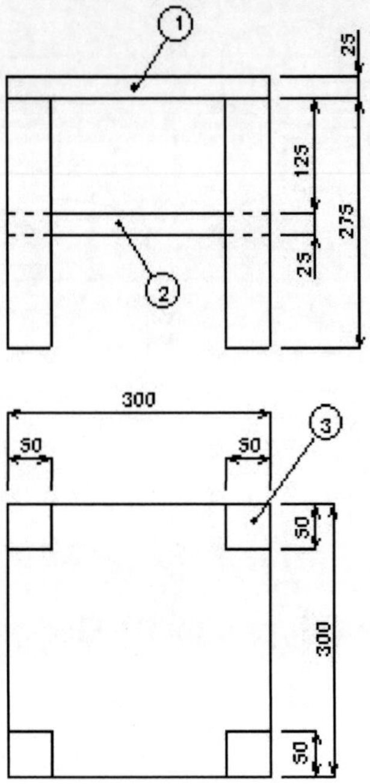

NO.	SIZE	QTY
1	25 × 300 × 300	1
2	25 × 300 × 300	1
3	50 × 50 × 275	4

Figure 4.5. Example 4.2.

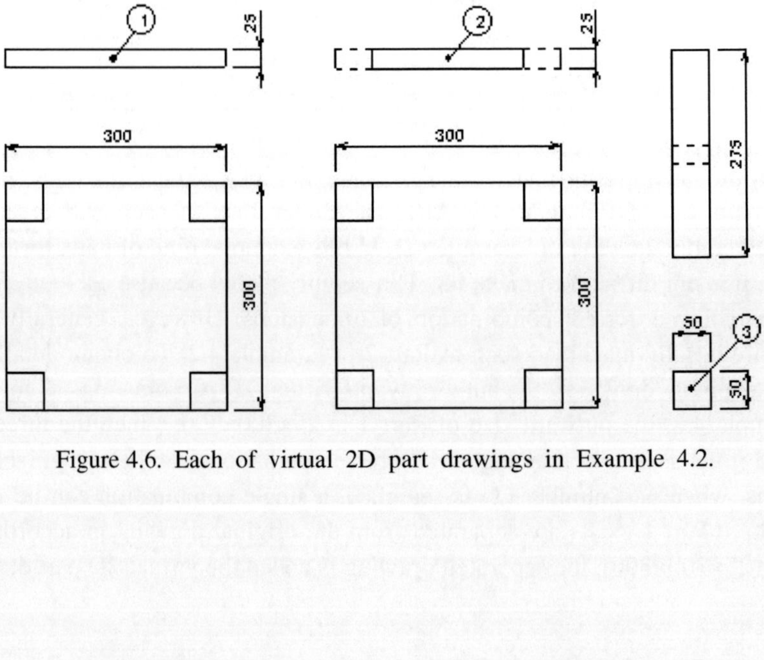

Figure 4.6. Each of virtual 2D part drawings in Example 4.2.

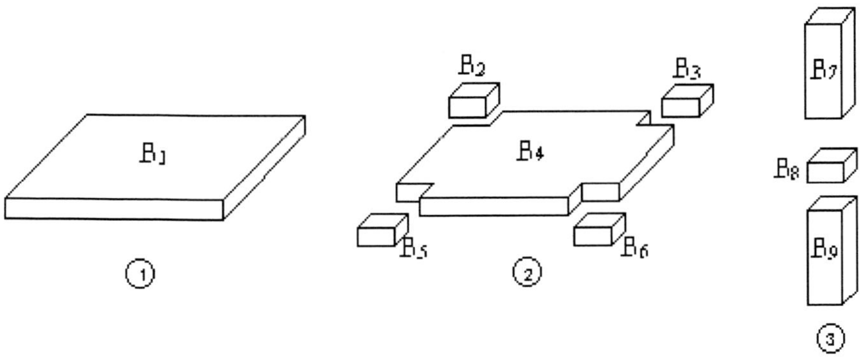

Figure 4.7. The virtual blocks of each part in Example 4.2.

(1) Existence_condition
Let a part be A in a 2D assembly drawing, and let a block be B that is recognized from the virtual 2D drawing of Part A. Suppose that B is false in Part A. If the dimensions or the part number of Part A are not correct or Part A does not form a solid, B must be true in Part A.

(2) Overlap_condition
Suppose that there are some overlapping blocks between plural parts. If there is a true block in the blocks, the other blocks are false in any parts.

(3) 2D edge_condition
When block B is true in Part A, if some 2D edges projected from B are changed, B is false in Part A.

(4) Identity_condition
Suppose that the quantity of Part A is two and they are called Part A and Part A'. When all of blocks in Part A is decided and undecided blocks exist in Part A', the undecided blocks must be decided as the shape of Part A' is the same as Part A.

When these conditions are applied to Example 4.2, the solution can be obtained as follows. Firstly B_1, B_4, B_7, B_8 and B_9 become true by applying Existence_condition. Then B_2, B_3, B_5 and B_6 become false by applying Overlap_condition. As a result, a single solution can be obtained in Example 4.2 as follows. Part 1 is B_1, Part 2 is B_4 and Part 3 consists of B_7, B_8 and B_9 as in Figure 4.8. Figure 4.9 illustrates the solution of 3D assembly model of Example 4.2.

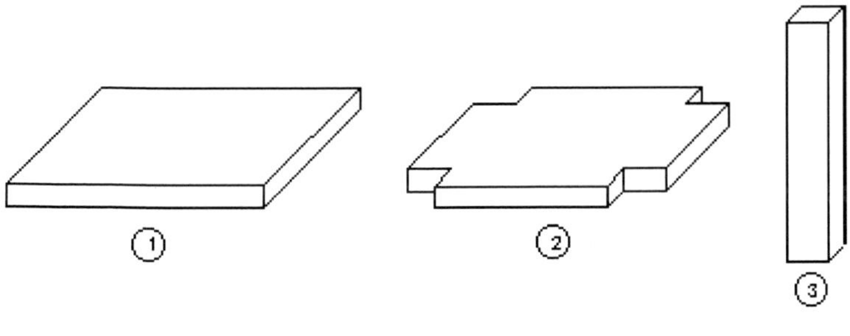

Figure 4.8. The solution of each part in Example 4.2.

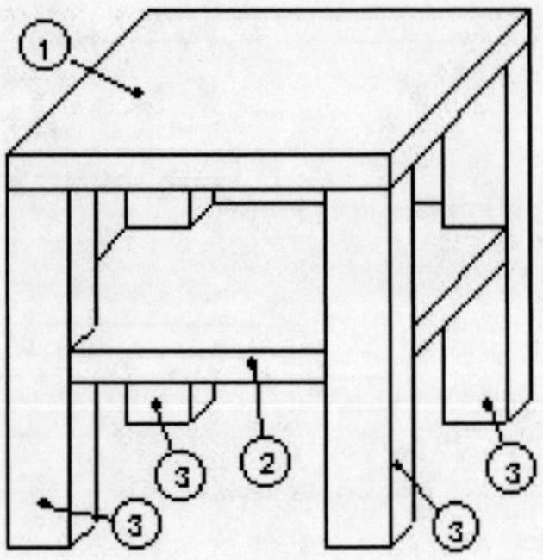

Figure 4.9. The 3D assembly model of Example 4.2.

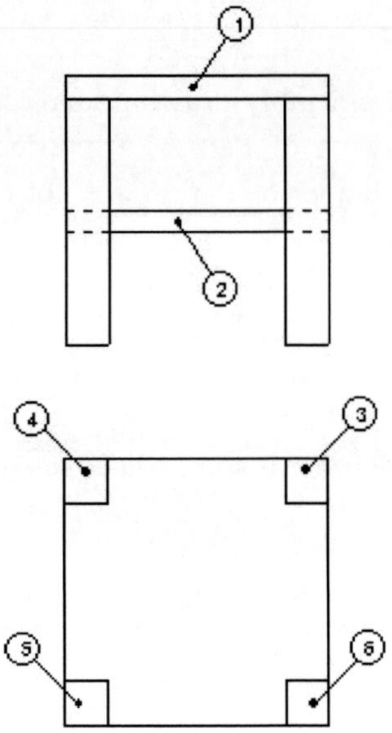

Figure 4.10. Example 4.2'.

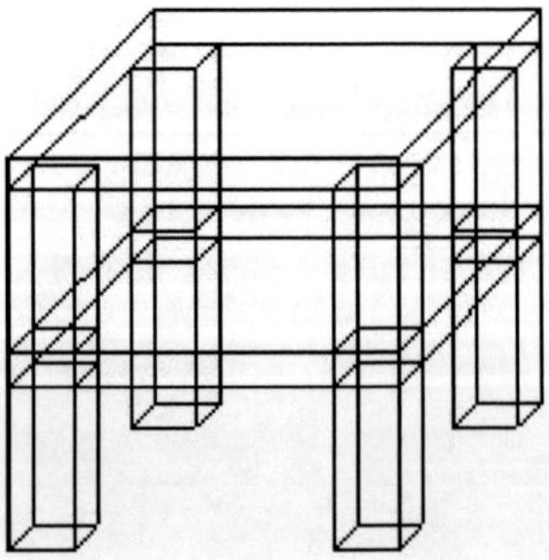

Figure 4.11. The wireframe model in Example 4.2'.

If the parts list of Example 4.2 does not exist, a single solution cannot be obtained. When dimensions and parts list are deleted and all of part numbers are added to Example 4.2, the assembly drawing of that is changed into Figure 4.10 (Example 4.2'). Figure 4.11 illustrates the wireframe model of Example 4.2' and fifteen virtual blocks are generated as shown in

Figure 4.12. Figure 4.13 illustrates the relationships between 2D faces and virtual blocks and the equations of these blocks are formed as shown in Figure 4.14. In the equations, the following relationships are obtained. B_1 belongs to Part 1. B7 belongs to Part 2. B_3, B_{10} and B_{12} belong to Part 4. B_5, B_{11} and B_{14} belong to Part 3. Therefore, basically the other seven virtual blocks become undecided blocks. As a result, 107 solutions are generated because of the seven undecided blocks. There are many strange cases in the solutions. Figure 4.15 illustrates two strange examples in the solutions. In the cases that the solid models of parts cannot be specified, the numbers of solutions would exponentially increase from 2D assembly drawings such as this example. In the author's assembly method, since the solid models of parts can be specified by using dimensions, part numbers and parts lists, a single solution would be usually obtained regardless of the number of parts in a 2D assembly drawing.

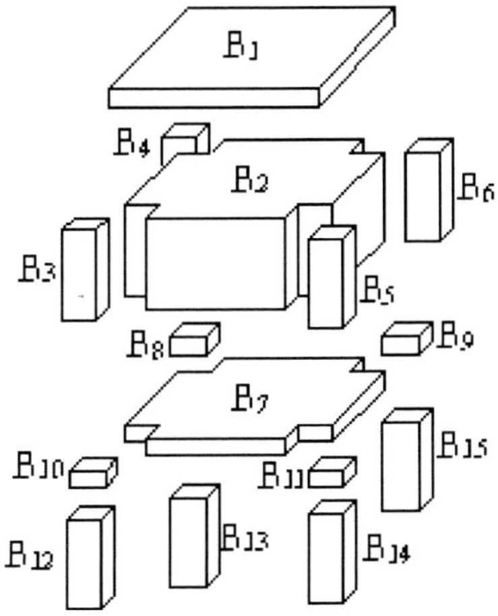

Figure 4.12. The virtual blocks in Example 4.2'.

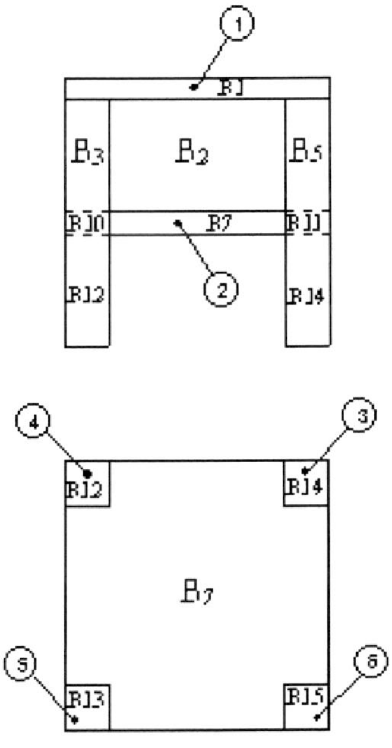

Figure 4.13. The relationships between 2D faces and virtual blocks in Example 4.2'.

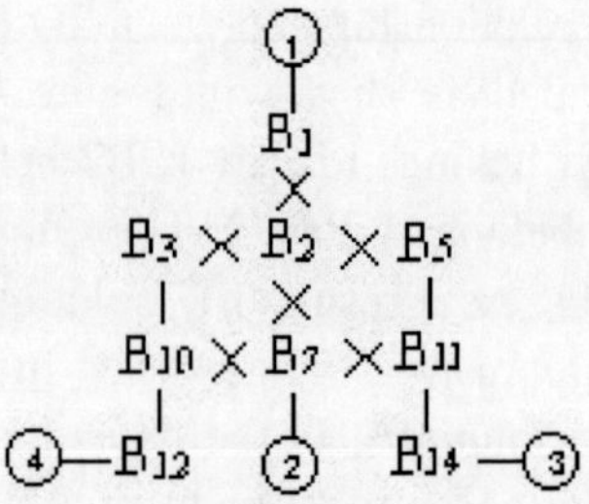

Figure 4.14. The equation of virtual blocks in Example 4.2'.

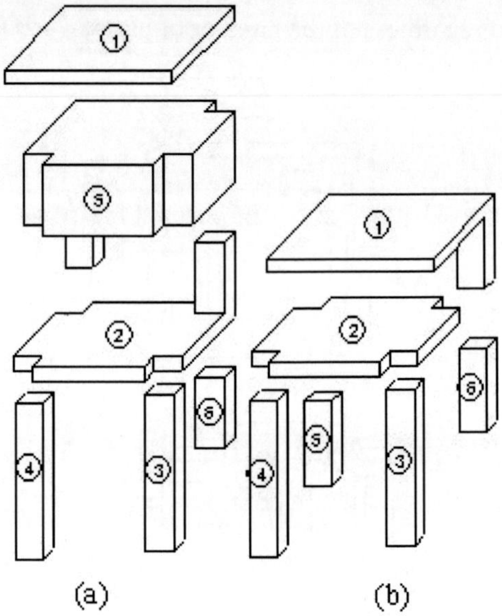

Figure 4.15. Two examples of the solutions in Example 4.2'.

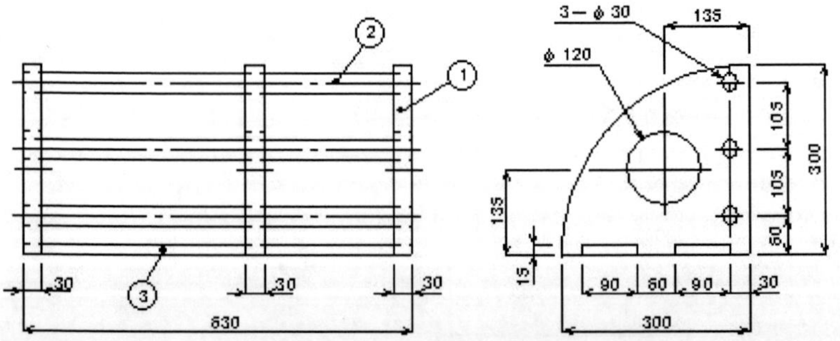

NO.	SIZE	QTY
1	30 × 300 × 300	3
2	φ 30 × 630	3
3	15 × 90 × 630	2

Figure 4.16. Example 4.3.

Figure 4.16 illustrates Example 4.3 that is a book shelf. Figure 4.17 illustrates each of virtual 2D drawings in Example 4.3. Figure 4.18 illustrates each of virtual blocks made from Figure 4.17. Firstly B_1, B_8, B_9, B_{10}, B_{11}, B_{12}, B_{13}, B_{14}, B_{15} and B_{16} become true by applying *Existence_condition*. Then B_2, B_3, B_4, B_6 and B_7 become false by applying *Overlap_condition*. Lastly B_5 become false by applying *2D edge_condition*.

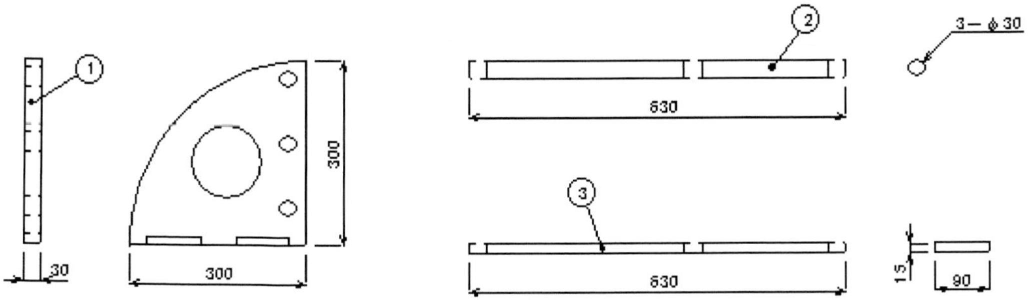

Figure 4.17. Each of the virtual 2D part drawings in Example 4.3.

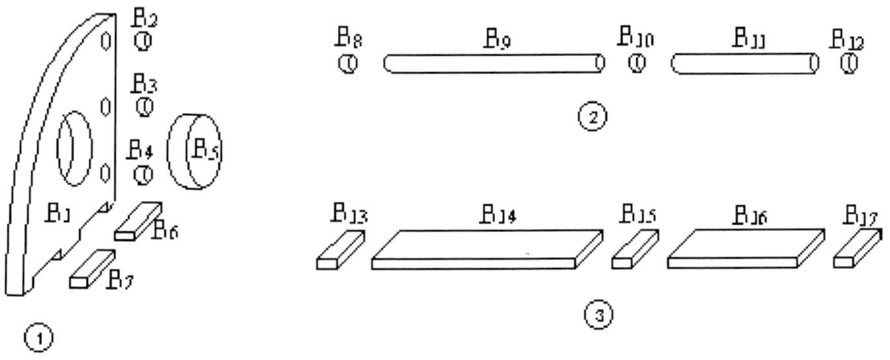

Figure 4.18. The virtual blocks of each part in Example 4.3.

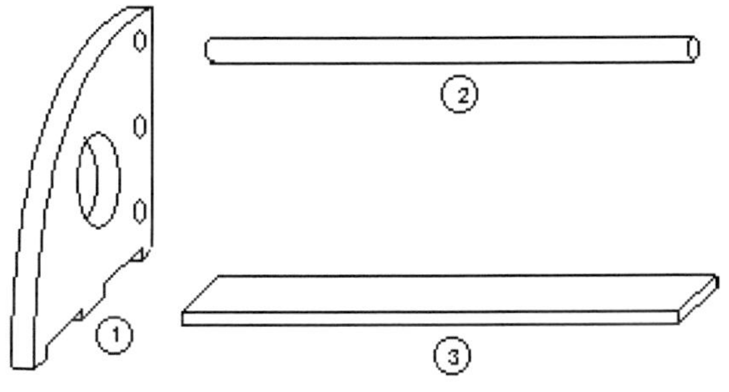

Figure 4.19. The solid model of each part in Example 4.3.

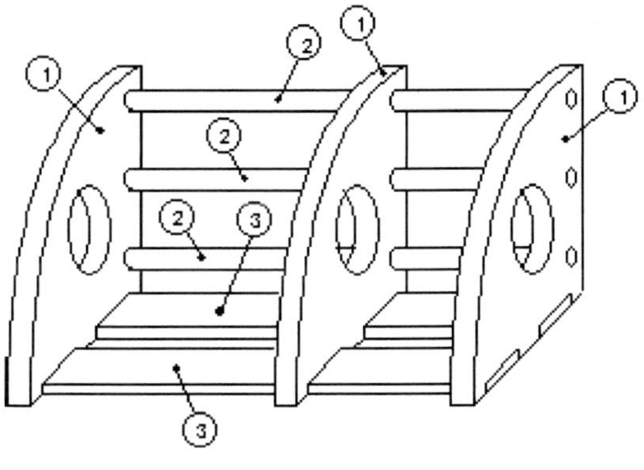

Figure 4.20. The 3D assembly model of Example 4.3.

As a result, a single solution can be obtained in Example 4.3 as follows. Part 1 is B_1. Part 2 consists of B_8, B_9, B_{10}, B_{11} and B_{12}. Part 3 consists of B_{13}, B_{14}, B_{15} and B_{16}. These solutions of each part are illustrated in Figure 4.19. Figure 4.20 illustrates the 3D assembly model of Example 4.3. If the parts list of Example 4.3 does not exist, 31 virtual blocks are generated and approximately 70,000 solutions are generated by applying the equations of virtual blocks.

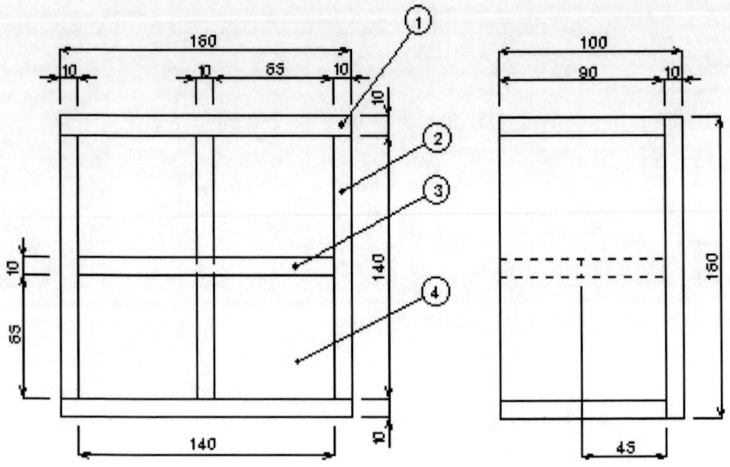

NO	SIZE	QTY
1	10×90×160	2
2	10×90×140	2
3	10×90×140	2
4	10×160×160	1

Figure 4.21. Example 4.4.

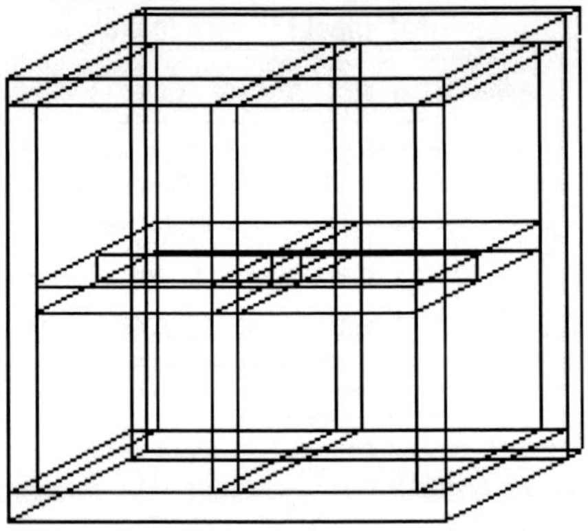

Figure 4.22. The wireframe model in Example 4.4.

Figure 4.21 illustrates Example 4.4 that is a small container. Figure 4.22 illustrates the wireframe model of Example 4.4. From this figure, 17 virtual blocks are generated as shown in Figure 4.23 and approximately 6,000,000 solutions are generated by applying the equations of virtual blocks. Figure 4.24 illustrates the virtual 2D part drawings of Part 1 and 4 in Example 3.4. In this figure, since each part generates only one block, the two generated blocks become Part 1 and 4. For Part 2 and 3, four possible virtual 2D part drawings are recognized as in Figure 4.25. In this figure, it is obvious that (a) and (b) correspond to Parts 2 and 3 because of their part numbers. Figure 4.26 illustrates virtual blocks made from Figure 4.25. Since B_3 and B_6 overlap with B_9 and B_{10}, all of them cannot be true. It is obvious that B_1 is Part 2. Suppose that (c) corresponds to Part 2 and (d) corresponds to Part 3. Then, B_{12} becomes Part 3. However, all of the overlapping blocks must become true by

Identity_condition. Therefore, it is found that (c) corresponds to Part 3 and (d) corresponds to Part 2. When 2D edge_condition is applied to the blocks of (b) and (c), it is found that B_5, B_6, B_7, B_8 and B_{11} are true and B_{10} is false. Then, B_9 becomes true and B_3 becomes false by the *Existence_condition* and *Overlap_condition*. When the *Identity_condition* is applied to B_2 and B_4, it is found that they are true. As a result, a single solution is obtained for Example 4.4 as in Figure 4.27. Figure 4.28 illustrates the 3D assembly model of Example 4.4.

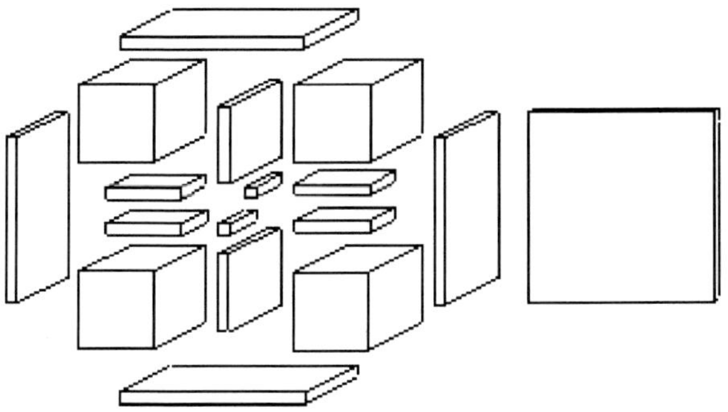

Figure 4.23. The virtual blocks in Example 4.4.

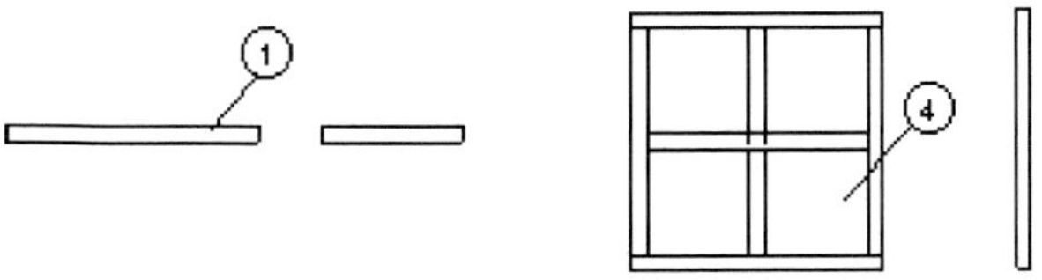

Figure 4.24. Virtual 2D part drawings of Part 1 and Part 4 in Example 4.4.

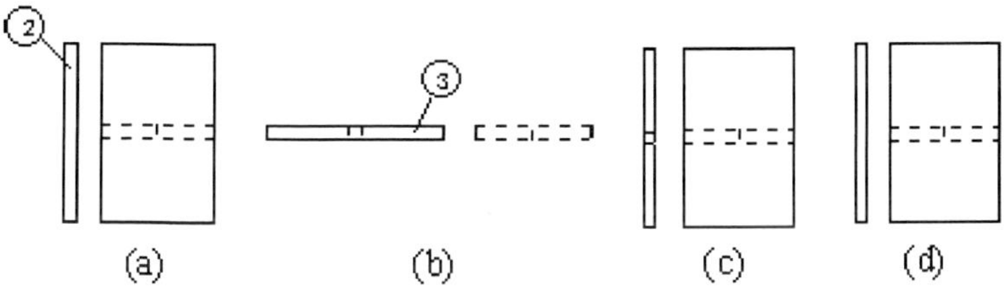

Figure 4.25. Four patterns of virtual 2D part drawings of Part 2 and 3 in Example 4.4.

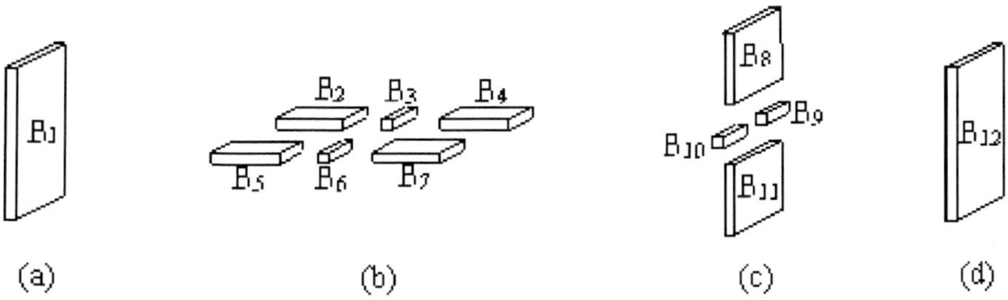

Figure 4.26. Virtual blocks made from Figure 4.17.

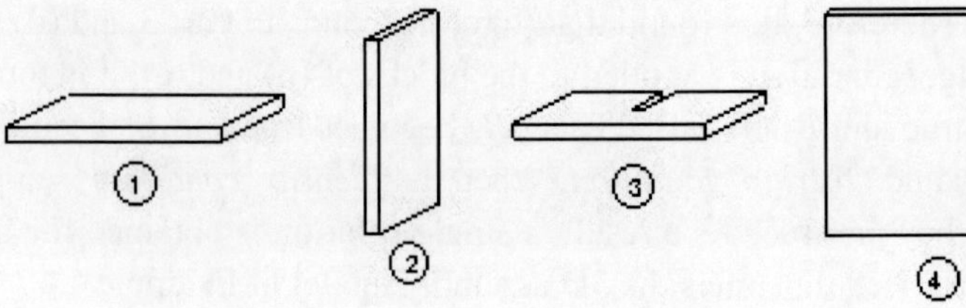

Figure 4.27. The solution of each part in Example 4.4.

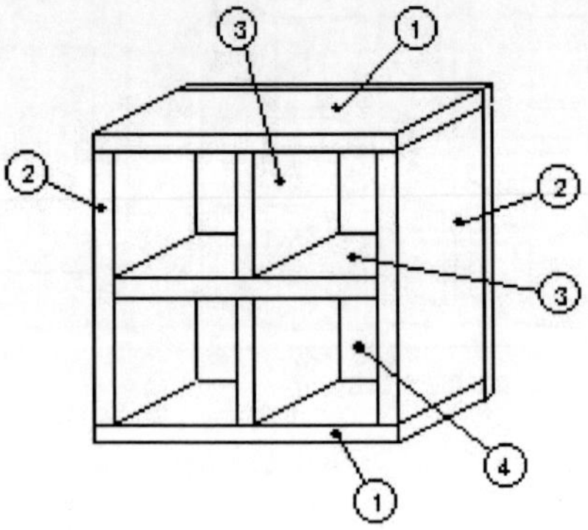

Figure 4.28. The 3D assembly model of Example 4.4.

5. Automatic Restoration of Omitted 2D Drawings into Correct Drawings

5.1. Basic Algorithm

Various kinds of simplified expressions such as sectional views and partial omissions are usually applied to 2D drawings. For example, when a long bar is drawn in a 2D drawing such as Example 5.1 illustrated in Figure 5.1, the middle part of bar is usually omitted. In this section, the author's restoration method is explained that 2D drawings including partial omissions are automatically restored to correct drawings in geometry. Partial omissions are often used in 2D assembly drawings. For example, in Figure 1.6, the part on the left of Part 6 is omitted to clarify the relationship of the connection of Part 4 and 5. In general, it is difficult to automatically restore the partial omissions because they are not geometric but based on human understanding. In the restoration method, the automatic restoration of partial omissions is realized by applying learning algorithms of patterns of the partial omissions. The basic algorithm of learning systems to restore the partial omissions is as follows.

(1) Various kinds of properties are defined to line segments.
(2) The relationships of two or three arranged line segments are defined as properties.
(3) Many patterns of arranged line segments are learned and generalized by extracting common properties.
(4) Generalized patterns are applied to restore partial omissions of 2D drawings into correct 2D drawings.

5.2. Properties of Line Segments and Generalized Patterns of Repetitive Line Segments

Properties are defined from one, two and three line segments in order as follows.

[The properties of one line segment]
(1) type (2) kind (3) start point (4) end point (5) radius (6) length (7) center point (8) slope.

Here, the type is straight, arc or circle. In the restoration method, break lines are drawn as free-form curves in 2D drawings. So they can be recognized from the other line segments. The kind is solid or dotted. The slope is expressed as a degree from x axis. The slope of an arc is a degree of a straight line drawn between its two end points. In the front view of Example 5.1, each of line segments is numbered (L1, L2, ... , L12) as in Figure 5.2. For example, the properties of L3 are as follows. (1) straight (2) solid (3) (50, 50) (4) (50, 250) (5) d (6) 200 (7) (50, 150) (8) 90° Here, "d" of (5) expresses "default". In the same way, the properties of L4 are as follows. (1) circle (2) solid (3) d (4) d (5) 25 (6) 157 (7) (100, 125) (8) d. Next, the relationships of two line segments that do not be intersected are defined as properties as follows.

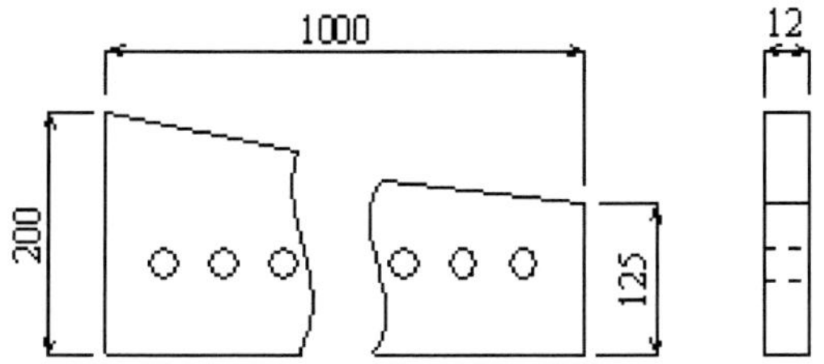

Figure 5.1. Example 5.1.

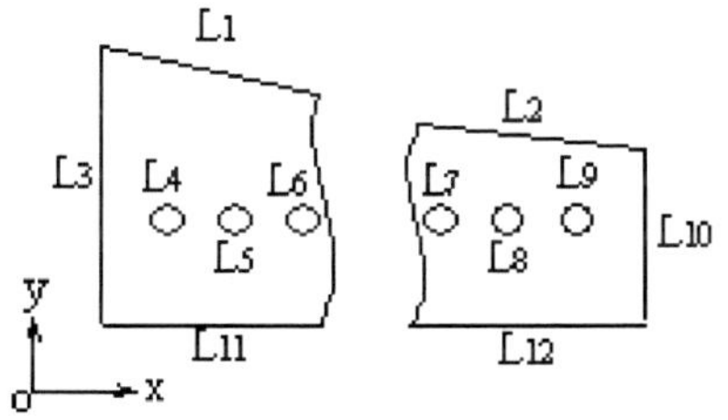

Figure 5.2. Numbered line segments in the front view of Example 5.1.

[The properties of two line segments]
(1) identity of two types (2) identity of two radiuses and lengths (3) identity of two kinds (4) identity of two slopes (5) vector between two center points (6) degree of two line segments (7) real intersection (8) imaginary intersection (9) arrangement of two line segments (10) minimum length of endpoints of two line segments (11) maximum length of endpoints of two line segments.

The values of (1) to (4) are "true" or "false". The vector of (5) is expressed as (*a*, *b*). Here, (*a*, *b*) is equal to (-*a*, -*b*). The value of (9) is "straight line" or "vertical". For example, the properties of L4 and L5 in Figure 5.2 are as follows. (1) true (2) true (3) true (4) d (5) (50, 0) (6) d (7) d (8) d (9) d (10) d (11) d. The relationships of three line segments can be defined as properties as follows by synthesizing the properties of two line segments described above.

[The properties of three line segments]

(1) identity of three types (2) identity of three radiuses and lengths (3) identity of three kinds (4) identity of two vectors (5) center of curvature (6) radius of curvature (7) identify of three slopes based on (5).

For example, the properties of L4, L5 and L6 in Figure 5.2 are as follows. (1) true (2) true (3) true (4) true (5) d (6) d (7) d.

Figure 5.3 illustrates three patterns of arranged line segments (Pattern 1, 2, 3). In Pattern 1, three line segments are arranged continuously. The properties of them are as follows.

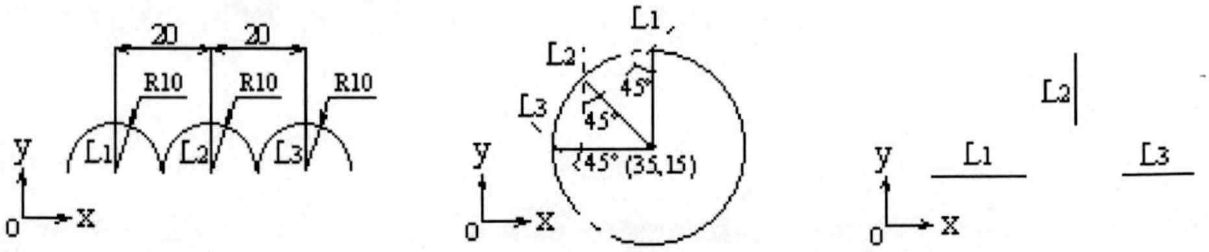

(a) Pattern 1 (b) Pattern 2 (c) Pattern 3

Figure 5.3. Three patterns of arranged line segments.

L1: (1) circle (2) solid (3) (10, 10) (4) (30, 10) (5) 10 (6) 63 (7) (20, 10) (8) 0°.
L2: (1) circle (2) solid (3) (30, 10) (4) (50, 10) (5) 10 (6) 63 (7) (40, 10) (8) 0°.
L3: (1) circle (2) solid (3) (50, 10) (4) (70, 10) (5) 10 (6) 63 (7) (60, 10) (8) 0°.

When these properties are synthesized, the properties of two line segments can be calculated as follows.

L1-L2: (1) true (2) true (3) true (4) true (5) (20, 0) (6) d (7) (30, 0) (8) d (9) d (10) 0 (11) 40.
L2-L3: (1) true (2) true (3) true (4) true (5) (20, 0) (6) d (7) (50, 0) (8) d (9) d (10) 0 (11) 40.

Moreover, when these properties are synthesized, the properties of three line segments can be calculated as follows.

L1-L2-L3: (1) true (2) true (3) true (4) true (5) d (6) d (7) d.

In the same way, when several similar patterns like Patten 1 are input, they can be generalized as follows.

[*Generalized_straight_pattern*] (1) true (2) true (3) true (4) true (5) d (6) d (7) d.

This pattern can apply to restore omitted repetitive line segments such as circles of Example 5.1. In Pattern 2, three line segments are arranged circularly as in Figure 5.3. In this pattern, the properties of line segments can be calculated as follows.

L1: (1) straight (2) dotted (3) (41, 41) (4) (29, 29) (5) d (6) 14 (7) (35, 35) (8) 45°.
L2: (1) straight (2) dotted (3) (21, 36) (4) (21, 22) (5) d (6) 14 (7) (21, 29) (8) 45°.
L3: (1) straight (2) dotted (3) (9, 21) (4) (21, 9) (5) d (6) 14 (7) (15, 15) (8) 45°.
L1-L2: (1) true (2) true (3) true (4) true (5) (-14, -6) (6) d (7) d (8) (21, 21) (9) d (10) 10 (11) 28.
L2-L3: (1) true (2) true (3) true (4) true (5) (-6, -14) (6) d (7) d (8) (21, 9) (9) d (10) 12 (11) 27.
L1-L2-L3: (1) true (2) true (3) true (4) false (5) (35, 15) (6) 20 (7) true.

In the same way, when several similar patterns like Patten 2 are input, they can be generalized as follows.

[*Generalized_circular_pattern*] (1) true (2) true (3) true (4) false (5) token (6) token (7) true.

Here, "token" expresses a variable.

5.3. Generalized Patterns of Two Isolated Line Segments

In Example 5.1, when two break lines are deleted, four line segments become isolated line segments that do not form any loops of line segments. To restore them, the following two generalized patterns are made in the restoration method by using Pattern 3 in Figure 5.3. Firstly, the properties of L1 and L3 are calculated as follows.

L1: (1) straight (2) solid (3) (10, 10) (4) (30, 10) (5) d (6) 20 (7) (20, 10) (8) 0°.
L3: (1) straight (2) solid (3) (50, 10) (4) (66, 10) (5) d (6) 20 (7) (58, 10) (8) 0°.
L1-L3: (1) true (2) false (3) true (4) true (5) (38, 0) (6) 0° (7) d (8) d (9) straight line (10) 20 (11) 56.

When several similar patterns whose arrangement is "straight line" are input, they can be generalized as follows.

[*Generalized_straight_line_pattern*]

(1) true (2) token (3) true (4) true (5) token (6) 0° (7) d (8) d (9) straight line (10) token (11) token.

Next, the properties of L1 and L2 are calculated as follows.

L2: (1) straight (2) solid (3) (40, 20) (4) (40, 35) (5) d (6) 15 (7) (40, 28) (8) 90°.
L1-L2: (1) true (2) false (3) true (4) false (5) (20, 18) (6) 90° (7) d (8) (40, 10) (9) vertical (10) 14 (11) 39.

When several similar patterns whose arrangement is "vertical" are input, they can be generalized as follows.

[*Generalized_vertical_line_pattern*]

(1) true (2) token (3) true (4) false (5) token (6) 90° (7) d (8) d (9) vertical (10) token (11) token.

5.4. The Automatic Restoration of Omitted Line Segments in 2D Drawings

When repetitive line segments exist and they are adjacent to break lines in a 2D drawing, they become the targets of restoring omitted repetitive line segments. Also, if isolated line segments exist after break lines are deleted in 2D drawings, they become the targets for the restoration. Firstly generalized patterns are applied to the line segments of targets and all properties of them can be calculated. Next, break lines are deleted in the 2D drawing and extend the repetitive and/or isolated line segments until they intersect to the other line segments. In Example 5.1, the following preprocessing is required. Firstly a contradiction can be searched by comparing a dimension (1000mm) and a scale (1:1) in Figure 5.1. Then identical surface is recognized that forms a closed loop of outlines. In Example 5.1, two surfaces can be recognized. Then they are rearranged in accordance with correct 1000mm and two break lines are deleted as in Figure 5.4.

In general, the restoration processes are firstly applied to isolated line segments, and secondly applied to repetitive line segments. In Figure 5.4, when *Generalized_straight_line_pattern* is applied to L1, L2 and L11, L12 respectively, their actual properties can be calculated, and when they extend until intersecting to the other line segments, they can be connected as in Figure 5.5. Then when *Generalized_straight_pattern* is applied to L4, L5, L6 or L7, L8, L9, their actual properties can be calculated. When they extend until intersecting to the other line segments, they can form correct repetitive circles as in Figure 5.6. This figure shows restored Example 5.1 as the solutions. Figure 5.7(a) illustrates Example 5.2 that is a circular saw and the bottom part of that is omitted. Each of the blades of Example 5.7(a) consists of two line segments. When *Generalized_circular_pattern* is applied to the blades, correct repetitive blades can be made as in Figure 5.7(b) after a break line deleted.

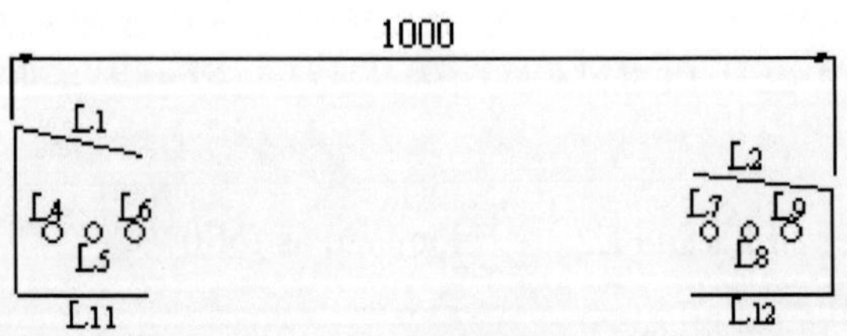

Figure 5.4. Rearranged two surfaces in accordance with 1000mm in Example 5.1.

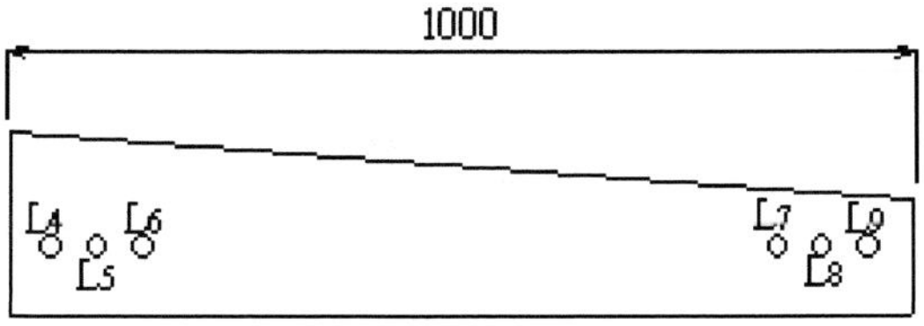

Figure 5.5. The restorations of isolated line segments in Example 5.1.

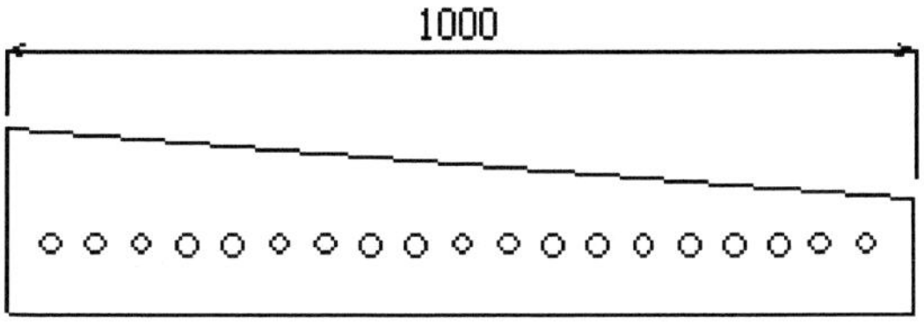

Figure 5.6. Restored Example 5.1.

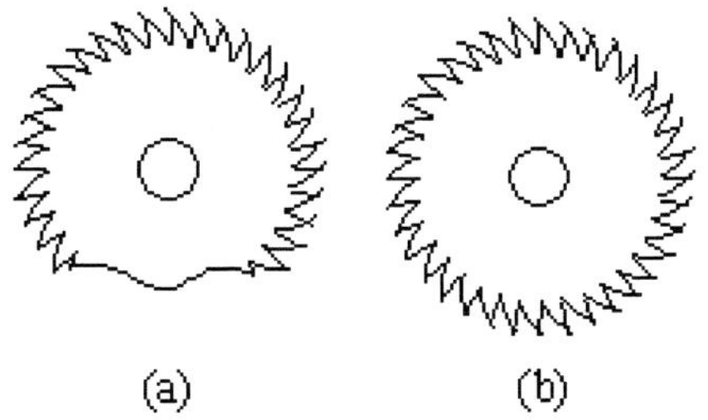

Figure 5.7. Example 5.2.

Figure 5.8(a) illustrates Example 5.3 that is a simplified Part 6 in Figure 1.6. If the break line of this figure is deleted, L1, L2, L3 and L4 become isolated line segments. L5, L6, L7 and L8, L9, L10 form repetitive circles respectively. When *Generalized_virtical_line_pattern* is applied to L2 and L4, L1 and L3 cannot be connected because they intersect to extended L2. Therefore, L1 and L4 must be connected firstly, and then L2 and L3 can be connected. As a result, all of isolated line segments are restored as in Figure 5.8(c). In the cases that many isolated line segments are related to each other such as this example, some combinations of restorations must be made to find the solutions. When *Generalized_straight_line_pattern* is applied to L5, L6, L7 or L8, L9, L10, the solution of Example 5.3 can be obtained as shown in Figure 5.3(d).

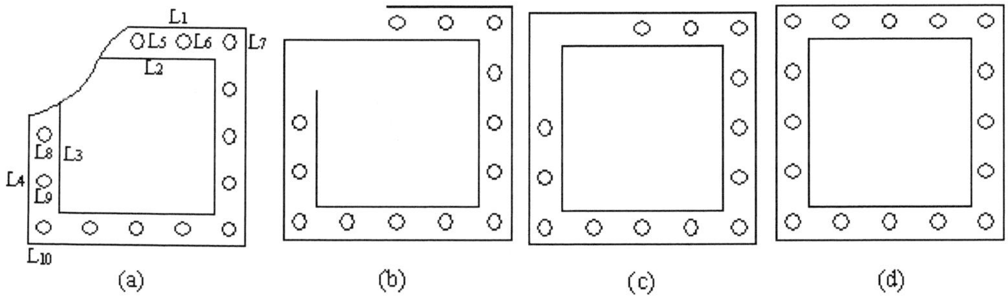

Figure 5.8. Example 5.3.

5. Conclusion

In this chapter, mainly the author's four methods are explained for the automatic conversion of various kinds of simplified 2D drawings into solid models as follows. (1) A method to automatically convert an orthographic view that expresses one object into solid models as the solutions by using the equations of virtual blocks (2) A method to automatically convert 2D assembly drawings into 3D assembly models consisting of the solid models of parts (3) A method to automatically convert a 2D assembly drawing of a mechanical structure consisting of bars and plates into a single 3D assembly model (4) A method to automatically restore 2D drawings including partial omissions into correct 2D drawings in geometry.

There are a great many simplified expressions in mechanical 2D drawings. In the author's method, though only correct 2D assembly drawings of mechanical structures consisting of bars and plates are handled, there are many ambiguous dimensions and parts lists in actual 2D assembly drawings. Also, though the restoration of partial omissions is handled in the method, there are various kinds of omissions that cannot be handled by the method. For example, if sectional views are added to the omissions, the restoration becomes very difficult. Therefore, it would be very difficult to automatically convert actual 2D drawings into correct solid models because actual 2D drawings are often incorrect and some comments that are important to understand the drawings are often inserted randomly to them.

In general, simplified expressions in 2D drawings are different in each domain of products. In this chapter, since mechanical structures are handled, mainly the parts of assemblies consist of bars and plates. In the other domains, for example, pillars and walls are usually drawn as double lines and rectangles, and parts numbers and parts lists are not usually included in architectural drawings. If 3D models are required only for presentations, precise 3D models are not necessary. So the author's method would be applied to make 3D models for presentations in various kinds of 2D drawings.

Also, in the restorations of omitted 2D drawings of the method, learning systems of line segments are applied. Repetitive, vertical and parallel line segments can be learned by the learning systems. It is thought that these algorithms would be applied to the conversion of ambiguous 2D drawings into 3D models for presentations, and applied to the automatic learning systems of elementary theorems of geometry in the domain of artificial intelligence.

References

[1] Tanaka, M., Iwama, K, & Watanabe, T. (1994). A Method of Constructing Solid Models from Orthographic Views by Using Solid Elements, *1st Symposium on ISICIMS*, pp. 219-224.

[2] Tanaka, M., Iwama, K., Hosada, A. & Watanabe, T. (1998). Decomposition of a 2D Assembly Drawing into 3D Part Drawings, *Computer-Aided Design*,Vol.30, No.1, pp.37-46.

[3] Tanaka, M., Anthony, L., Kaneeda, T. & Hirooka, J. (2004). A Single Solution Method for Converting 2D Assembly Drawings to 3D Part Drawings, *Computer-Aided Design*,Vol.36, No.8, pp.723-734.

[4] Tanaka, M., Kaneeda, T., Yamahira, T. & Iwama, K. (2006). A Method to Restore Partial Omissions in 2D Drawings, *Computer-Aided Design & Applications,* Vol.3, Nos.1-4, pp.341-347.
[5] Tanaka, M., Kaneeda, T., Yamahira, T., Sasae, D., Fukagawa, J. & Iwama, K. (2006). A Method to Restore Partial Omissions in 2D drawings by Learning Regularities of Features, *WSEAS Transactions on Information Science and Applications*, Issue 5, Volume 3, pp.878-884.
[6] Idesawa, M. (1973). A system to generate a solid figure from a three view, *Bull. JSME* Vol.16, pp.216-225.
[7] Wesley, M. A. & Markowsky, G. (1981). Fleshing Out Projections, *IBM J. Res. & Develop.*, Vol.25, No.6, pp.934-954.
[8] Sakurai, H. & Gossard, D. C. (1983). Solid Model Input Through Orthographic Views, *Computer Graphics,* Vol.17, No.3, pp.243-252.
[9] Dutta D & Srinivas YL. (1992). Reconstruction of curved solids from two polygonal orthographic views, *Computer-Aided Design* Vol.24, No.3, pp.149–159.
[10] Nagendra, I. V. & Gujar, U. G. (1988). 3-D Objects from 2-D Orthographic View—A Survey, *Comput. & Graphics*, Vol.12, No.1, pp.111-114.
[11] Gujar, U. G. & Nagendra, I. V. (1989). Construction of 3D Solid Objects from Orthographic Views, *Comput. & Graphics*, Vol.13, No.4, pp.505-521.
[12] Masuda, H. & Numao, M. (1997). A Cell-based Approach for Generating Solid Objects from Orthographic Projections, *Compter-Aided Design*, Vol.29, No.3, pp.177-187.
[13] Kim, C., Inoue, M. & Nishihara, S. (1992). Heuristic Understanding of Three Orthographic Views, *J. of Information Processing*, Vol.15, No.4, pp.510-518.
[14] Lee, H. & Han, S. (2005). Reconstruction of 3D interacting solids of revolution from 2D orthographic views, *Computer-Aided Design*, Vol.37, No.13, pp.1388-1398.
[15] Lu, T., Tai, C., Bao, L., Su, F., & Cai, S. (2005). 3D Reconstruction of Detailed Buildings from Architectual Drawings, *Computer-Aided Design and Applications*, Vol.2, Nos.1-4, pp.527-536.
[16] Dimri, J. & Gurumoorthy, B. (2005). Handling sectional views in volume-based approach to automatically construct 3D solid from 2D views, *Computer-Aided Design*, Vol.37, No.5, pp.485-495.
[17] Gong, J.-H., Zhang, H., Zhang, G.-F. & Sun, J.-G. (2006). Solid Reconstruction Using Recognition of Quadric Surfaces from Orthographic Views, *Computer-Aided Design*, Vol.38, No.8, pp.821-835.
[18] Cao, L., Liu, J. & Tang, X. (2005). 3D Object Reconstruction from a Single 2D Line Drawing without Hidden Lines, *ICCV'05,* pp.272-277.
[19] Bhushan, B. & Gurumoorthy, B. (2006). Volume Based Approach to Extract 3-D Parts from 2D Assembly Drawing, *Computer-Aided Design & Applications*, Vol.3, Nos.1-4, pp.119-128.
[20] Sugihara, K., (1986). *Machine Interpretation of Line Drawings*, The MIT Press.
[21] Lipson, H. & Shpitalni, M. (1996) Optimization-based reconstruction of a 3D object from a single freehand line drawing, *Computer-Aided Design*, Vol. 28, No. 8, pp. 651-663.

In: Computer-Aided Design...
Editors: C.M. De Smet et al, pp. 65-87
ISBN: 978-1-60456-860-8

Chapter 3

MOBILE VIRTUAL NETWORK OPERATORS IN THE WEST AND THE EAST: A TECHNO-ECONOMIC ANALYSIS

Dong Hee Shin
Pennsylvania State Berks, Pennsylvania State University, PA, USA

Abstract

The purpose of this study is to examine cross-national data in order to identify possible factors related to the observable patterns of MVNO (Mobile Virtual Network Operator) penetration. For this purpose, a mobile market structure is analyzed considering important economic factors related to the penetration of MVNOs. MVNOs have gained popularity in the Western markets, but have a dismal track record in non-Western regions. In comparing the different regions, this study analyzes how the MVNO market has changed and what opportunities and/or threats network operators and potential MVNO entrants are likely to face. This study conducts an economic assessment of market structure and environment for different countries' MVNO penetration. The data on market structure is analyzed by means of cluster/factor analysis techniques, in order to group countries according to their market environments. Then, structural equation modeling is used to investigate the relations of MVNO penetration and independent variables. The results show that MVNO penetration significantly relates to market structure and performance. These results also imply an appropriate policy to promote MVNO diffusion.

Keywords: mobile virtual network operator, vertical integration, market structure

1. Introduction

When Virgin Mobile withdrew its operation from Singapore in early 2003, the company cited "weak economic and market conditions" in the country as the reason behind the failure of the business (Wireless Asia, 2002). Its decision to exit the Asian market was followed by the recent failures of Mobile Virtual Network Operators (MVNOs) in Asian countries, such as Taiwan, Hong Kong, and Malaysia. As the Asian MVNO market development is not as visible as in Europe, the failures left some questions as to what market conditions would be required for MVNOs to succeed. Although there were other factors such as marketing strategy, prices, and culture that might contribute to the failure, this study focuses on market structure in a cross-national study to shed light on the question as to whether the observable differences between Eastern and Western market conditions are the outcome of a specific set of factors. This study investigates the set of factors influencing MVNO penetration in order to answer following questions:

RQ1: What are the market factors affecting the penetration of MVNOs?
RQ2: Is the penetration of MVNOs are related to market structure?

When looking at the emerging MVNO phenomenon, there may be two approaches: (1) from the perspective of the MVNO itself, in which the features for its sustainable business development are researched; (2) from the perspective of the overall mobile market and industry, in which the relation of MVNOs to the market should be analyzed. The present study takes the second approach in order to analyze MVNOs from a broader perspective by relating MVNO penetration and market structure: (1) 28 countries of the EU and the 2 countries of the Americas representing the West, (2) 17 Asian countries representing the East, and (3) 21 countries of Latin and South America are collected. After collecting data on market and industry from these groups, cluster and factor analysis are used to summarize patterns of market structure in the telecommunications industry. Each factor is characterized by a set of coefficients expressing its correlations with the observed variables. The variables are assigned to the factor with which they are most loaded. As a result, the market structure indicators are split into disjoint sets, with each indicator associated with a single factor. The estimated factor loadings applied to the country-specific market structure indicators make it possible to score countries according to each of the factors, so that rankings of countries can be obtained in terms of factor-specific scores. It is standard practice to retain a number of the factors which cumulatively explain a substantial part of the overall covariance. A multivariate regression model is developed to evaluate the effects of market variables on MVNO penetration.

This study finds that MVNO penetration significantly relates to market structure and industry performance. In Asia whose markets tend to be vertical structure, successful mobile operators have predominantly maintained high vertical market integration strategies, where they control or own the spectrum, base stations, connecting networks, systems infrastructure, customer service operations, pricing, packaging, billing, branding and points of sale. In contrast, European and North American mobile markets have become relatively horizontal structure over time (Weiss, 2006)—for example, networks, terminals, operating systems, application software and wireless channels are provided by different companies. In this horizontal structure of the industry, collaborations with other companies are quite necessary and companies in each horizontal layer are experts in what they do: network operators are more open to outsourcing parts of the value chain. Operators in these regions increasingly view MVNOs along with Mobile Virtual Network Enablers (MVNE) as efficient indirect sales channels that can decrease the focus on price because of strong brand loyalty, lower subscriber acquisition costs by tapping existing customer bases, and increase average revenue per user via differentiated content and services. From a theoretical point of view, this paper proves that vertically integrated oligopoly is not favorable to effective competition (Vickers, 1995). This study further implies that the impact of MVNOs will be significant and their penetration will depend on the roles of MVNEs, which together will change the structure and the dynamics of telecom markets.

2. Definition and Evolution of MVNOs

Since their origination in Europe in 2000, there are currently approximately 200 operational MVNOs world-wide, with various models and concepts. The number of MVNOs has been drastically increased since 2000. According to Ovum (2006), there were 59 MVNOs in Western Europe in 2002 and there are 190 MVNOs in 2006 in Western Europe. Countries like The Netherlands, France, Denmark, the U.K., Finland, Belgium, Australia and United States have the most MVNOs, whereas non-Western countries are just beginning to launch active MVNO business models. The MVNOs contained within their MVNO market study vary from consumer driven MVNOs to enterprise, non-consumer MNVOs, and data focused operations. The majority of MVNOs have been consumer focused and the future development of MVNOs will be within enterprise market developments.

There is no specific definition of an MVNO, but generally it can be defined as an organization that is more or less independent from its host network in terms of technology and service. Regulatory bodies around the world have adopted various definitions and different forms of regulatory intervention, depending on the extent to which an MVNO relies on the facilities of a mobile network operator. The ITU (2001) defines an MVNO as a carrier providing users with mobile services without its own government-issued license for bandwidth. Ulset (2002) defines it as an organization providing customers with mobile phone services without owning any airtime. Similarly, Ovum (2006) defines an MVNO as a carrier with the following characteristics: it provides customers with a mobile service, has an independent mobile network code, issues independent SIM cards, directly operates a mobile communications switch including a home location register, and does not own its own bandwidth. The present study defines an MVNO in a broad, functional sense: wireless companies that have their own brand, marketing, retail outlets, and phone offerings, but use another operator's infrastructure instead of building and operating their own. This definition is similar to that of Weiss (2006) and Dippon and Banerjee (2006). This broad definition allows this study to grasp the dynamics of MVNO markets which provide flexibility to potential MVNOs to establish business models according to their financial capability. This in turn increases the level of competition, which results in lower prices and innovative service offerings that benefit mobile users. Mobile network operators also have benefits from MVNO by increasing network utilization and by using of excess capacity (Capuano, 2005). As these benefits of MVNOs are similar to the consequences of liberalization, privatizations, and deregulation, MVNOs can be located in this wider literature of telecom market and policy. This aspect is what previous MVNOS studies have been neglected.

Although there have been many studies on MVNOs, few have attempted to look comparatively at MVNO effects and market structure. Most empirical studies on MVNOs are limited to single countries. This approach was partly related to the lack of internationally comparable data on market structures. A study by Boylaud and Nicoletti (2001) provides an example of how different market structures can be compared across countries. In addition, further studies (Noam, 2003a; Kiiski, 2003; Jang, 2003; Lehr, 2002; Dolye & Smith, 1998) helped to conceptualize the notion of market structure and link it to MVNOs.

The present study extends the Shin and Bartolacci's (2007) study, which investigate MVNOs in four countries. By including virtually all cases of MVNOs in the world, the present study can locate MVNOs in a wider context, which would help demonstrate its unique contribution to the ongoing policy debates.

3. The Relation of MVNOs to Market Structure

The MVNO is a new player in the telecom value chain, which used to be comprised of operators, service providers, application providers, and content providers. In a climate of competition and deregulation, virtual network operators have squeezed between operators and customers. In the past, telecommunications network operators used to oversee many functions themselves, maintaining strict control over physical networks and a good deal of control over services, content, marketing and billing (Frieden, 2003). However, this vertical integration began to crumble because of a downturn in the telecommunication market and because of the burden of high infrastructure costs (Shin & Bartolacci, 2006). The telecommunications market has changed considerably recently, with less vertical integration, a greater degree of outsourcing, and the abolition of monopolies, with easier entry of new players into the field (Chowdary, 1998). Such vertical disintegration has encompassed not only new telecommunications operators, but also content, service and application providers, as well as new equipment providers from the information technology field (Lehr, 2001).

The MVNO model has catalyzed vertical disintegration in the telecommunications industry and has created a situation where many major players separate from the mobile network operators, seeking to access the value chain at all levels (Shin & Bartolacci, 2006). In this light, Capuano (2005) likened MVNO to "liberalization frontier." Unlike other simple resellers of telecommunications services, MVNOs add value such as brand appeal, distribution channels, and other affinities to the resale of mobile services. In addition, unlike simple resellers, MVNOs have close and tight relationships with other players in the value chain. Effective MVNOs have sufficient agreements with existing operators to provide a good service coverage area, and some well-diversified MVNOs can offer a product mix that incumbent mobile operators cannot match.

Many studies have shown that the level of vertical integration is negatively related to competition and positively related to concentration (Hodendorn, 2005). The introduction of competition in the telecom market was followed by a decrease in market concentration, with new players entering into markets and a sharp drop in prices. Along with competition, liberalization has brought new players in both fixed and mobile markets. Market liberalization promotes competition by opening the market to new entrants backed by private capital. Liberalization is the opening of a monopolistic market to competitive provision of facilities and services (Melody, 1999). Therefore, liberalization and vertical integration are often negative correlation (Shin & Bartolacci, 2006). As the new players develop new and niche services, the market becomes more and more segmentized. For most telecom players who are concerned with decreasing ARPU due to segmented markets and customers, the MVNO business is another way to increase ARPU from a stagnant customer base, with potentials and perils similar to broadband. MVNOs can increase ARPU by providing content-based ARPU and keeping their subscribers satisfied. As many studies show (Doyle & Smith, 1998; Noam,

2002), all these variables are closely related. With the emergence of MVNOs, it is worthwhile to examine each variable of market components in relation to MVNO penetration.

4. Summarizing Market Structure for Empirical Analysis

Data of a set of variables are drawn time period from 2000 to 2006. This period is the time when MVNO emerged and is rising to the present.

4.1. The Choice of Indicators

For the purpose of evaluating the correlations of market structure and MVNO penetration, it is useful to focus on a limited set of indicators that capture the main relationship between MVNOs and market structure. In general, this study adopts the indicators of market structure identified by the OECD study (2004; 2001), which are also used in scholarly research: the degree of vertical integration (Krafft, 2003), the degree of liberalization (Sappington & Weisman, 1996), the degree of concentration (Noam, 2003a), and the degree of competition. The OECD investigated the linkages between regulation and telecom market structure/performance for 23 OECD countries. In the study, market structure was measured with the indicators of vertical integration, concentration, and segmentation: and market performance was measured with competition and liberalization. This study adds ARPU as a market performance measure, since the FCC commonly uses the ARPU measure when assessing mobile market performance.

In addition to these indicators, the pricing scheme, governance mechanisms, and regulatory institutions can have important effects on performance. However, these indicators are all qualitative in nature and are difficult to convert to into quantitative values. In addition, such data are not sufficiently available over long enough time periods and across countries to be useful. The current regulatory environment associated with mobile telecommunications could be included, but it is characterized by a relatively low cross-country similarity regarding both price regulation and regulatory institutions. These dimensions of regulation and governance were therefore omitted. The focus thus was reduced to two main issues: market structure and industry performance. These variables were also used by the FCC (2005) when assessing mobile telecommunication markets; (1) market structure; (2) carrier conduct; (3) consumer behavior; and (4) market performance. Because of difficulty in collecting and turning the qualitative data on carrier conduct and consumer behavior into useful quantitative data, these variables are excluded. The following variables of the market structure were chosen:

- *Degree of liberalization.* The degree of liberalization is calculated as a percentage of the number of regulations, where no restrictions have been attached to both market access and national treatment for a specific services sub-sector and mode of supply out of total possible commitments. Calculations have been done by the GATT Trade Unit based on the methodology developed by Hoekman (1995). This methodology is in line with the method used in the telecom sector by Gual and Trillas (2004) who measure liberalization policies through the degree to which market opening or deregulation policies are asymmetric or biased in favor of entrants.

H1: The degree of liberalization of telecom market is related to the MVNOs' penetration.

- *Degree of vertical integration in the telecommunications industry*, as measured by the percentage of significant market players in mobile industries' revenue of total telecom industry revenue. This measurement is used by Noam's (2004) study to investigate the Internet's vertical integration (percentage of top 10 companies in specific industries' revenue of total industry revenue). Ideally, degree of vertical integration should be measured by widely used to be the most suitable indicator (Haller, 1997, p. 319). According to Choi and Shin (1992), vertical integration illustrates how much an entity has created value on its own through its operating activities. Haller (1997) measures the degree of vertical integration by looking at the ratio of value added to total output. Data on the degree of vertical integration were either (1) collected from various sources of ITU, OECD, and WTO, or (2) calculated from the Noam's (2004) method.

H2: The degree of vertical integration is related to the MVNOs' penetration

- *The degree of market segmentation,* as measured by the Market Segmentation Index (Informa Research, 2005). The market segmentation method involves identifying and describing subgroups of the market. First, factor and cluster analysis profile customers. Based on survey responses, customers are grouped or segmented according to similar preferences or needs. Then, the Market Segmentation Index is computed by dividing the incidence of each market segment in a particular market by the incidence of each market segment in the total market. A score of 1.0 means that a market segment is the same as the total market in a market sample. Index values above 1.0 indicate that the market segment is over-represented in a given sample of the overall market, while index values below 1.0 indicate that the market segment is under-represented relative to the overall market in that sample. An index value of 1.2 means that market segment is 20 percent more likely to be found within the particular sample than in the general population.

H3: The degree of market segmentation is related to the MVNOs' penetration

- *The degree of mobile market performance*, as measured by average ARPU. Although there are other indicators of performance, such as CPGA (cost per gross acquisition), CCPU (cash cost per user), and churn, these data are hard to collect. Despite much criticism of its flaws, ARPU is widely used to measure market performance. Since the 1980s, the ITU has defined telecommunication performance indicators and ARPU has been a major indicator of performance (ITU, 2000). ARPU is calculated by dividing billable services-derived revenues for a given period by the average number of billable subscribers for that period.

H4: The degree of mobile market performance is related with the MVNOs' penetration

- *The degree of competition in the mobile telecommunications industry*, as compiled from data collected by the International Telecom Union and the World Bank (Standard Data) to construct a competition index variable. This variable is assigned a value of zero if the telecommunication sector is served by a national monopoly operator, a value of one if the sector has more than one operator in either the fixed-line or the mobile market segment, and a value of two if the sector has more than one operator in both fixed-line and mobile market segments. This method is used by Li and Xu (2004) for measuring competition in the telecom sector around the world.

H5: The degree of competition is related to the MVNOs' penetration.

- The degree of concentration in the wireless telecommunications industry, as measured by the HHI (Herfindahl-Hirschman Index),

$$HHI = 10{,}000\ [\Sigma(S_i)^2\ ] = 10{,}000\ [(S_1)^2 + (S_2)^2 + (S_3)^2 + \ldots + (S_n)^2\ ]$$

Where n equals the number of firms participating in an industry; S_i equals each firm's market share, and i equals the firm in a given industry.

H6: The degree of concentration is related to the MVNOs' penetration.

4.2. Parametric Regression Analysis: Multivariate Regression Analysis

Multivariate regression analysis is used to determine the relative importance of each MVNO market share within a group. The structural equation can be derived from the above variables in a reduced form to explain MVNO penetration, as follows:

MVNO penetration = f (concentration, competition, vertical integration, liberalization, performance, and segmentation)

In this study, a multivariate regression method was used to estimate model parameters. Factor analysis and cluster analysis methods were used in mapping the structure of the observations and relations between possible measures for the independent variables. Based on the theoretical model above, the following empirical model was formulated:

$$MVNOP = CONS + \beta 1{*}COMP + \beta 2{*}\ LIB + \beta 3{*}\ ARPU + \beta 4{*}\ SEG + \beta 5{*}COMP + \beta 6 VER + \varepsilon$$

with

MVNOD - MVNO penetration ; CONS - intercept (constant) ; CONP - concentration (HHI); LIB – liberalization ; ARPU - Average revenue per unit; SEG – segmentation; COMP - competition; VER - vertical integration; ε *- random error term.*

The dependent variable was defined as the total MVNO market share in a country as a percentage of the total wireless market (the number of MVNO subscribers as percentages of the total mobile subscribers; Table 1e). Data were collected over a period between 2003 and 2005 (Table 1).

4.3. Non-parametric Regression Analysis: Local Polynomial Regression

Since the relation between the MVNO penetration and independent variables cannot be guaranteed linearity, non-parametric regression analysis is complemented. In non-parametric regression, the MVNO penetration does not take a predetermined form (such as normal distribution), but is constructed according to information derived from the data (the data supply the model structure as well as the model estimates). As the relation may be natural log (non-linearity), the analysis can be smoother and produce theoretical robustness to the model selection using natural log of non-linearity. The equation can be established with (*ti*, *Yi*), where *ti* is time series (2003-2005) and *Yi i*s the dependent variable, which defined as the total MVNO market share in a country as a percentage of the total wireless market (the number of MVNO subscribers as percentages of the total mobile subscribers; Table 1e).

$$Yi = m(ti) + \varepsilon i,$$

The regression function *m* can be *f* (concentration, competition, vertical integration, liberalization, performance, and segmentation). Data were collected over a period between 2003 and 2005 (Table 1).

Table 1.a. Data collected

	HHI	VI	Lib	Segm	ARPU	COM
EU average	3,948	0.23	0.86	0.93	49.91%	0.73
Asian average	2,186	0.32	0.54	0.56	42.54%	0.53
North America average	1,337	0.59	0.34	0.84	28.4%	0.81

- Europe (28): Austria, Belgium, Denmark, Estonia, Finland, France, Germany, Greece, Hungary Ireland, Italy, Latvia, Liechtenstein, Lithuania, Luxembourg, Netherlands, Netherlands Antilles, Norway, Poland, Portugal, Russia, Slovenia, Spain, Sweden, Switzerland, Turkey, Ukraine, and United Kingdom.
- America (23): USA, Canada, Mexico, Caribbean countries, and Latin American countries.
- Asia (16): Hong Kong, Singapore, China, India, Japan, Indonesia, Korea, Malaysia, Myanmar, Mongo, Philippines, Taiwan, Australia, New Zealand, Thailand, and Vietnam.

Table 1.b. Mobile market

	Number of license holders	Share of largest operator	Share of second largest operator
Demark	8	39	19
Finland	4	67	30
Sweden	5	43	25
UK	5	32	20
USA	8	27	24
Singapore	3	54	19
Hong Kong	3	34	18

* EU's weighted average (i.e., HHI is weighted by the countries share of telecom revenue)

Sources: OECD Communications Outlook, ITU Database, World Mobile Market 1996-2010," OMSYC

Table 1.c. MVNO subscribers as percentage of total mobile subscribers in 2004.

Countries	EU	US	Asia
%	5.9%	1.3%	0.01%

Note: Data compiled from Market Research (2005).

Table 1.d. MVNO in Europe, America, and Asia

MVNO in Europe

Austria	3 MVNO relationships – A1 (0), H3G (0), ONE (2), tele.ring (1), T-Mobile (0)
Belgium	29 MVNO relationships - BASE (25, 3 via MVNE Transatel), Mobistar (1), Proximus (1)
Denmark	14 MVNO / SP relationships - H3G (0), Sonofon (3), TDC Mobil (11), Telia Mobil (0)
Estonia	2 MVNO relationships - AS EMT (0), Elisa (1), Tele2 Eesti (0)
Finland	10 MVNO / SP relationships – Elisa (1), Finnet (3), TeliaSonera (3)
France	13 MVNO / SP relationships - Bouygues (3, 2 via MVNEs), Orange (4), SFR (5)
Germany	32 MVNO / SP relationships
Greece	1 MVNO
Hungary	2 MVNO relationships
Ireland	3-4 MVNO relationships
Italy	1 MVNO
Latvia	1 MVNO / SP relationship – LMT (1), Tele2 (0)
Liechtenstein	1 MVNO
Lithuania	2 MVNO / SP relationships - BitSM (2), Omnitel (0), UAB Tele2 (0)
Luxembourg	1 MVNO relationship - LUXGSM (1), Tango AS (0), VOX Mobile (0)
Netherlands, The	24 MVNO / SP relationships - KPN Mobile (5), Orange (2), Telfort (14), T-mobile (0), Vodafone (3), unknown (1) planned / speculations (3)
Netherlands Antilles	1 MVNO relationship
Norway	11 MVNO relationships
Poland	2 MVNO relationships (?)
Portugal	0 MVNO relationships
Russia	2 MVNO relationships
Slovenia	1 MVNO / SP relationship
Spain	2-3 MVNO / SP relationships
Sweden	23 MVNO relationships
Switzerland	3 MVNO / SP relationships
Turkey	0 MVNO
Ukraine	1 MVNO relationship
U.K.	24 MVNO relationships

*SP: Service provider

Table 1.d. Continued.

MVNO in America

North America	Canada	7 MVNO relationships - Bell Mobility (1), E-Mobile (1), Microcell (2)
	U.S.	53 MVNO relationships
	Mexico	3 MVNO
Latin & South America	Argentina	3 MVNO
	Brazil	1 MVNO
	Bolivia	2 MVNO (COTAS)
	Puerto Rico	1 MVNO
	Venezuela	2 MVNO

*Rest of Latin and South America countries do not have MVNO.

MVNO in Asia

Australia	30 MVNO relationships - H3G (0), Optus (12), Telstra (6), Vodafone (8, 7 via MVNEs)
China	1 MVNO
Hong Kong	6 MVNO
India	2 MVNO
Indonesia	0 MVNO
Japan	8 MVNO
Korea	1 MVNO (operate in U.S.)
Malaysia	2 MVNO
Myanmar	0 MVNO
Mongo	0 MVNO
New Zealand	1 MVNO
Philippines	1 MVNO
Singapore	2 MVNO
Taiwan	2 MVNO
Thailand	0 MVNO
Vietnam	0 MVNO

Table 1.e. MVNO market share

	Mobile subscribers (million)			**MVNO subscribers (million)**			**MVNO market share (%)**		
	2003	**2004**	**2005**	**2003**	**2004**	**2005**	**2003**	**2004**	**2005**
Asia Pacific	621	733	912	0.9	1.02	1.04	0.1	0.01	0.01
Europe	610	721	878	10.4	11.9	17.1	1.7	1.7	1.9
North America	211	232	245	6.3	9.2	11.3	3	4.4	4.9
Latin America	198	237	247	0.4	0.42	0.44	0.02	0.01	0.01

4.3. Cluster Analysis and Factor Analysis

Based on the data above, a cluster analysis was used to categorize and group mobile markets according to market structure and performance. Cluster analysis is used to investigate the similarity of the countries based on scores on each of the estimated factors. Starting from the values taken by the scores in each country, this technique progressively groups countries in clusters of increasing size, based on (multi-dimensional) pair-wise comparisons. At each step in the clustering process, an index of inter-group similarity measuring the distance between the clusters being joined is calculated. It is standard practice to stop the clustering procedure (i.e., select the relevant number of clusters) when the distance between clusters becomes sizable.

Using cluster analysis, several groups of markets were identified based on their experience with MVNOs over the period analyzed, the most vertical being Hong Kong and Singapore, and the most horizontal, layered or open (horizontally diversified or consolidated) being the UK, Denmark, Netherlands, Norway, Sweden, and U.S. Country clusters based on market conditions were found to be as follows:

- Vertical structure (23 countries): Most Asian countries, Latin countries, etc.
- Horizontal structure (24 countries): Most of the EU, North America.
- Mixture (20 countries): Australia, New Zealand, etc.

After the groupings of countries were created through cluster analysis, a factor analysis was carried out to evaluate the underlying commitment factors and to reduce number of variables in order to avoid multi-colinearity (Table 2). The factors, which are linear combinations of the observed variables, can be interpreted using economic measures such as *market structure*, *openness*, and *dependency*. Each factor is characterized by a set of coefficients expressing its correlation with the observed variables, and the variables are assigned to the factor with which they are most loaded (Table 3). As a result, the market structure indicators are split into disjoint sets, each of which is associated with one factor. The estimated factor loadings applied to the country-specific market structure indicators make it possible to "score" countries according to each of the factors, so that rankings of countries can be obtained in terms of factor-specific scores. It is standard practice to retain a number of factors which cumulatively explain a substantial part of the overall covariance.

Table 2. Results of factor analysis: Rotated factor loadings

Variables/factors	Performance	Structure	Ancillary Regulation
Competition	0.628	0.052	-.0083
ARPU	0.721	-0.188	0.114
Segmentation	0.023	0.930	0.149
Concentration	-0.129	0.900	-0.033
Vertical integration	-0.093	-0.838	0.199
Liberalization	0.003	-0.254	0.349

*Factor loadings measure the correlation between the individual indicators and the latent factors. Indicators are assigned to the factor to which they are most correlated. The rotation of factor loadings is a transformation aimed at minimizing the number of indicators that are highly correlated with more than one factor.

Table 3. Correlation matrix (full model)

	Concentration	Competition	Segmentation	Liberalization	ARPU	Vertical integration
Concentration	1					
Competition	-0.3923	1				
Segmentation	-0.2328	0.7992	1			
Liberalization	-0.2134	0.5923	0.4283	1		
ARPU	-0.3769	0.5912	0.6913	0.5131	1	
Vertical integration	0.5460	-0.4942	-0.4093	-0.7022	-0.4623	1

5. Empirical Model and Analysis Results

5.1. Result from Parametric Analysis

Overall, the empirical results allow the identification of important factors that influence the observable pattern of MVNO penetration. Four hypotheses were confirmed, while two hypotheses were rejected (H4 & H6). Four main factors are found to best describe the trans-national variance in the set of indicators of MVNO and market structure.

Table 4.a. Estimation results

Variables/factors	Model1	Model2	Model3	Model4	Model5
Concentration	0.0078 *0,029*	0.00688 *0.305*		-0.01003 *-2.566*	**0.0382 *2.903*
Competition	0.0883 *-1.349*		-0.0232 *-2.301*	*-0.1372 *-1.212*	-0.0034 *-2.393*
Segmentation	**0.27442 *3.492*	***0.2432 *4.203*	***0.235 *3.999*	**0.1578 *2.942*	
Liberalization	0.0302 *0.624*	-0.214 *-0.992*	0.034 *1.932*	*0.134 *2.321*	
ARPU	*0.0899 *-3.392*	0.0603 *1.9323*	**0.00907 *-3.2093*		**0.0197 *-2.9332*
Vertical integration		*-0.183 *-2.032*	*0.192 *0.123*	-0.031 *3.234*	
Constant	-5.934 *-1.170*	-3.423 *-1.153*	-7.392 *-1.923*	-4.923 *-0.132*	0.323 *3.293*
Prob>F	***0.0071	**0.0162	***0.0012	***0.0052	**0.0129
R^2	0.5517	0.5711	0.5417	0.5291	0.323
Adj. R^2	0.4136	0.4053	0.4793	0.4293	0.203

Note: *significant at 90% level; ** significant at 95% level; *** significant at 99% level.
(Dependent variable MVNO market share in 2002-2003, t-statistic is italic)

Table 4.b. Summary measures (multiple regression)

R	R Square	Adjusted R Square	Std. Error of the Estimated
.8061	.8323	.8434	.0054

Table 4.b. Continued

	Sum of Square	df	Mean Square	F	Sig. (p-value)
Regression	52.613	10	5.261	67.676	.000
Residual	28.454	366	7.774		
Total	81.067	376			

Table 4.c. Regression coefficients

	Unstandardized coefficient (B)	Standard Error	t-value	Sig. (p-value)
Concentration	-.101	.003	-1.321	.000
Competition	.022	.007	3.103	.002
Segmentation	.116	.011	4.507	.010
Liberalization	.180	.078	6.401	.002
ARPU	.103	.007	1.297	.000
Vert. Integration	-.046	.021	-10.874	.022
Constant	.873	.082	10.625	.000

Table estimation results summarize the estimated effects of market structure on MVNO penetration for the selected model specifications (i.e., those that were not rejected by the tests). Overall, the market structure indicators performed quite well, significantly improving the fit of the regressions. By looking at the indicators most closely associated with each of the factors, a straightforward economic interpretation can be made. The first factor (associated with vertical integration of the mobile market) shows that the degree of vertical integration is significantly associated with MVNO penetration; the presence of more vertically integrated incumbents reduces the MVNO market share. The second (associated with segmentation in telecom services) factor expresses the positive significant relationship with the MVNO penetration. The third factor (associated with mobile market competition) shows a positive relation, in that higher competition is related to higher MVNO penetration; and the fourth factor (associated with liberalization) accounts for the positive relation the process of the MVNO penetration. The concentration factor has a negative correlation with MVNO penetration, but the relation is not statistically significant. While ARPU does not show a statistically significant result either, ARPU yields an interesting insight. The ARPU of MVNO (breakdown by region) shows that North American has increased ARPU since 2000, indicating higher-end segments are coming online through an emphasis on post-paid MVNOs such as ESPN and Disney. The ARPU of EU MVNO has declined, implying growth in the low-end segments and intense competition. The ARPU of Asia is relatively stable, indicating a slight offset by data revenues from data-only operators.

A principal components method with a varimax rotation of the 6 variables reveals 5 underlying factors with eigenvalues of greater than one. These 5 factors explain 75.9% of the variability in the eleven variables. Model 1 does not account for the vertical integration variable and Model 2 does not include the competition variable. Model 3 has a better overall explanatory capacity, but the variables of competition and liberalization are not significant. Model 4 does not include the dependency variable, but is generally acceptable. Model 5 drops four variables and shows the least explanatory power. There are some recurrent observations from these models. Vertical integration and segmentation are the most statistically significant factors. The effect of these two variables is also relatively robust.

Dividing the sample into the two groups (vertical and horizontal) identified by the cluster analysis yielded more insights (Table 5). The cluster analysis between the groups reveals that MVNO penetration among the groups correlates strongly with market structural factors (e.g., concentration, segmentation, liberalization, and vertical integration) and to a lesser extent with performance indicators (e.g., competition, ARPU).

The statistical analysis shows that the liberalization factor present in the horizontal group had a positive and significant impact on MVNO penetration. This can be explained by the EU's Access Directive, which helped to correct vertical integration in communications services and facilitated MVNO launches. In 2003, the European Commission issued a recommendation to national telecom regulators to examine the competitiveness of the market for wholesale access and call origination on public mobile telephone networks. The study resulted in new legislation in countries like Ireland and France that forces operators to open up their network to MVNOs. The EU's Access Directive contains requirements that vertically integrated network operators must impose accounting separation and initiate transfer pricing arrangements where they control access to essential input facilities that are used by their competitors in a retail market. In contrast, the liberalization factor for the vertical group was detrimental to MVNO penetration, although the effect also was not statistically significant. This can be inferred that the liberalized climate in Asian countries has provided established mobile operators with even more favorable markets. In other words, significant market players have been the biggest beneficiary of liberalization policy, while effective competition in the overall market has not been improved.

Table 5. Estimation results, country groups

Variables/factors	EU	North America	Asia
Concentration	-0.08752 *-1.979*	*-0.01003 *0.9302*	*0.2101 *0.210*
Competition	*0.19832 *2.392*	0.1238 *1.341*	0.09333 *1.101*
Segmentation	*0.07832 *3.232*	**0.0932 *2.942*	*-0.0920
Liberalization	**0.2983 *4.344*	**0.3903 *3.9434*	**0.3683 *4.233*
ARPU	0.0738 *5.1323*	*0.0423 *2.381*	0.0128 *0.4923*
Vertical integration	**-0.1374 *4.999*	**-0.0393 *3.2832*	**-2.034 *4.213*
Constant	**12.3049 *4.923*	0.3943 *2.123*	0.984 *1.032*
Prob>F R^2 Adj. R^2	***0.0071 0.5517 0.4136	**0.0162 0.5711 0.4053	***0.0052 0.5291 0.4293

Note: *significant at 90% level; ** significant at 95% level; *** significant at 99% level.
(dependent variable MVNO penetration from 2004 to 2005, t-static in italics)

Model runs at the level of country sub-groups show that the overall pattern is particularly visible in the horizontal group of countries. In this group, competition is correlated positively with MVNO penetration (with no significance), and concentration does not exhibit a significant effect. Within the countries in the vertical group, competition has the opposite effect and is negatively related to MVNO penetration.

Concentration (measured by HHI) shows a positive effect, but is not statistically significant on MVNO penetration. This finding contradicts a widely held belief exhibited in several previous studies (e.g., Noam, 2003b) that HHI is a standard indicator of concentration. The HHI of the U.S. is more effective than Europe. The U.S.'s HHI is 1,377 compared to that of Europe. Market concentration is low by international standards in the U.S., and the MVNO penetration, therefore, has been largely unaffected by market concentration. Concentration also is not a significant factor in Asia. For example, Hong Kong's HHI is low (1,936), but is an effective HHI figure. The HHI figures of the Asian countries contribute to the insignificant result of competition and concentration. As the competition variable shows, Hong Kong and Singapore are two of the world's most competitive mobile markets. The implication is that the Asian markets in general are small-scale markets, and therefore the incentive to innovate may be lower than in large markets. As shown in the EU and U.S. mobile markets, larger firms innovate more. The largest operators in Hong Kong and Singapore have relatively small market shares. These cities host two of the most fragmented world markets, and less fragmented markets, such as the EU and the U.S., have much higher MVNO penetration. An explanation may be that fragmentized or segmented submarkets in smaller overall markets obviate inter-operator collaboration on application development (Godfrey & Kam, 2004). As the ITU report (2004) shows, Hong Kong has a more fragmented market sector than any other country, and no mobile operator there accounts for more than 30% of the market. This segmented market produces a low HHI in Hong Kong. As to the HHI variable itself, it may not be a good measure in such a small market (Farrell & Shapiro, 1990; Demsetz, 1974). A more appropriate measure may be Gans' new measurement of HHI when it involves vertical structure, namely "vertical HHI" (Gans, 2005).

The market segmentation variable shows different results across groups. The segmentations in EU and North America show a significant correlation with the MVNO market share. This result reflects the current U.S.'s MVNE proliferation: there are more than 25 MVNE in the U.S. (Pyramid Research, 2006). An MVNE does not have a relationship with end-user customers. Instead, MVNEs provide infrastructure and services to enable MVNOs to offer services and have a relationship with end-user customers. MVNEs enable infrastructure and related services, ranging from network element provisioning, administration, operation support systems, and business support systems, by providing intermediation between MVNOs that do not want to have any control over network elements and those that want complete control. As of 2006, there are more than 39 MVNE's in the world; eighty percent of them are located in Western countries, and there is no MVNE in Asian countries (Pyramid Research, 2006). MVNEs accelerate market segmentation by allowing MVNOs to provide various segments such as prepaid, high-end, data-focused players, etc.

Interestingly, this segmentation variable shows a significant correlation with the vertical integration variable. This can be explained by the fact that the European MVNE's provide the telecom operators with a relationship to manage the ability to manage relationships through a single, trusted interface for different MVNOs (Kristensson, 2001). In other words, MVNE's provide a bundled platform for MVNOs. These equate to turnkey type solutions that typically include automated interfaces to a carrier's provisioning system, real-time or near-real-time usage, and gateways for Short Message Service and content, as well as the usual Telco back-office systems and services. MVNE's take such forms as Application Service Providers, billing companies, content providers, hardware manufacturers, and Internet or media companies. It can be said that MVNOs and MVNEs are motivated by the same factors but the latter influences the MVNO penetration (Shin & Bartolacci, 2006).

The highly vertically integrated markets in Asia have generally not been favorable to the MVNO model. The fact that the MVNO model has had difficulty establishing itself in such segmented market environments suggests that the intensity of the facilities-based competition creates limited opportunities for them to be economically viable, even with differentiated strategies in the face of aggressive price competition. Hong Kong's MVNOs, for example, lease network services from facilities-based providers and compete on the basis of retail service differentiation. However, because of the already fragmented sector in these markets, MVNOs have not been effective in focusing on niche markets that can be served at lower cost with a focused marketing strategy. MVNOs in Hong Kong have therefore become vertically integrated service providers who contribute to and enhance the vertical market structure.

In regard to market performance, the ARPU variable shows no significant correlation, although it does show a positive correlation. The insignificance of ARPU implies that the main challenge prospective MVNOs will face is not necessarily a low ARPU, but other challenges such as a niche market. In other words, regardless of whether mobile operators are making or losing profit, they are seeking new markets. As Jost (2004) predicts, MVNOs can potentially survive on $5 ARPU, but the MVNO model in general must find a way to survive on the cost side of the business. The positive relation implies that MVNOs are active in markets where they deal with low margin subscribers. The undesirable role of MVNOs in this scenario protects the host carrier from undesirable financial costs such as those related to volatile prepaid churn, high capital investment, and consumer fraud. All of these can accompany an MVNO that targets low-value subscribers. The positive correlation further suggests that MVNOs must find a niche among incumbent carriers who are willing to lease capacity, since most operators are unlikely to open their networks.

The estimation results of liberalization show that liberalization is a somewhat significant factor (Table 4a). It is interesting to note that the Asian markets' liberalization also significantly contributes to MVNO penetration (Table 5), despite the low penetration in general. Since market liberalization in EU, a huge number of competing MVNOs are operating, while in Asian markets, under pressure of regulations and entrepreneurs, the process of MVNO development has just started. This can be interpreted that several Asian countries like Japan, Malaysia, and India are making positive efforts to facilitate MVNOs by establishing guidelines requiring network operators to lease or remain open to MVNOs.

The contradiction between liberalization and low MVNO penetration in Asian countries also can be explained from the different nature of liberalization. Asian countries in general achieved liberalization in policy and regulation, but actual markets seem not to fully feel such liberalized environment (Chowdary, 1998). While the liberalizations in Western countries have been achieved in an autonomous interaction between government and market, Asian countries seem to achieve it solely by policy-driven liberalization (Shin, 2007). The liberalization indicators in Asian countries may be policy-based, which is different from the market-based liberalization of Western countries. Under the policy-based liberalization, the markets are artificially changing toward liberal markets, but liberalized markets are most effective in climates of effective competition (Wu, 2003). Although overall Asian markets are apparently liberalized by government intervention, Asian markets still seem to be not liberal enough to embrace the MVNO, and the MVNO does not appear to stabilize in markets without effective competition.

It is ironic that SK Telecom, Korea's biggest mobile operator, is running an MVNO business in U.S. by the name of Helio, which has been successful in targeting niche tech-savvy young adults seeking multiplayer gaming. SK Telecom obviously does not want to open their walled-garden vertical market, but takes advantage of the liberalized and segmented U.S. market. In this light, it can be said that even though liberalization shows contributing factors to MVNOs in Asia, the actual MVNO show low penetrations in general.

Overall, the empirical analysis does show key drivers of MVNO penetration, but it also implies that several constellations of factors can be conducive to MVNO penetration. The active operation of MVNEs supports the analyses of segmentization, vertical integration, concentration, and liberalization. This point needs to be further examined by using panel regression.

5.2. Result from Non-parametric Analysis

A non-parametric regression of MVNO market share is conducted using the Nadaraya-Watson (N-W), local linear (LP1) and quadratic (LP2) estimators, with a cross-validation bandwidth. Just like the parametric analysis above, single repressor of non-parametric analysis shows that vertical integration has a positive effect on MVNO. Positive effects are also shown in liberalization, segmentation, and competition. Vertical integration and concentration have negative effects on MVNO. The relationship between MVNO market share and segmentation seems close to linear, whereas that between MVNO and competition appears logarithmic. A logarithmic relation also found in between MVNO and concentration.

Using more than two repressors shows more insights. MVNO penetration rises with liberalization and competition. The relationships are noticeably affected by changes in other variables. The relationship of MVNO to liberalization becomes quite steep with an increase in the value of segmentation. Conversely, the relationship of MVNO to liberalization becomes logarithmic with an increase in the value of concentration. This is likely because liberalization and segmentation are positive relations with MVNO, whereas concentration is negative relation with MVNO.

The effect of performance (ARPU) is rather small, particularly when compared to that of liberalization. It seems that ARPU is not a predictor in MVNO penetration.

6. Tripartite Description of MVNO: America, EU, and Asia

The comparative analyses imply that the MVNO models may be effective in Western countries but have a limitation when applied to global markets. Based on the findings here, the EU market can be characterized as one of the most competitive, liberal, and least vertically integrated markets, and is therefore highly segmented among the markets. The liberalized market of the EU allows MVNOs to negotiate more freely with HNOs (Host

Network Operators, i.e., Sprint). A large number of MVNEs in the EU and the U.S. implies highly segmented markets, which facilitate the negotiation between MVNOs and HNOs. MVNEs such as Visage Mobile provide back-office services and facilitate the interface between the brand and the carrier. Essentially, MVNEs handle operations, so that the brand partner can focus on customer acquisition and content. The emergence and proliferation of MVNEs relates to the fact that mobile businesses in Western countries have based themselves on content and branding, while Asian mobile markets are still driven mainly by handsets and price.

In addition, the liberalized markets of the EU seem to expedite MVNO penetration in consolidated and integrated applications instead of segmented services. One example of such liberalization is that European policy on competition has been directed to promote MVNO (e.g., Open Network Provision, Interconnection Directives). While in most European member states the MVNO entry remains subject to commercial negotiation alone, there are a number of member states which have incorporated provisions into their national telecommunications law to govern such access. Spain, Ireland and Sweden have extended the mandatory access to all HNOs. Such mandatory access can be seen as a kind of affirmative liberalization policy.

While not as evolved as the European MVNO market, the North American market has matured to the point where success is determined by traditional business competency, including factors such as brand strength, marketing, sales, distribution, and perceived value by the consumers. In particular, MVNOs have been making significant headway in North America. MVNOs in the U.S. and Canada are primarily targeting niche markets, and many such markets remain untapped or underserved. As shown by the regression, the U.S. market seems to be more segmented than that of the EU; thus, MVNOs are focusing on niche segments. For example, Virgin Mobile U.S. caters to the youth market, while Movida focuses on the Hispanic population in the U.S.

It appears that the growth of MNVOs in the U.S. is related to the growing trend toward specialization in market segmentation by operators. As operators better define the segments that they serve most profitably, they will be better able to transfer their less profitable and more difficult segments to groups that are more efficient at serving these segments. These fundamental shifts in market structure are opening up the U.S. market to MVNO entry by the region's key service players: banks, distributors, and retailers. Each of these groups has created unique relationships with specific consumers and corporate segments that may well set the stage for an expansion into mobile services. Reflecting the highly segmented market, a large number of MVNO in the U.S. started as data-centric MVNOs as opposed to voice or reseller MVNOs. In the U.S., MNVOs are focusing on mobile data solutions such as real-time data offerings at a more affordable rate.

While the EU started ahead of the U.S., the MVNOs in North America have many similarities to the EU MVNOs. Both the EU and the U.S. have an overall Prepaid Focus, both have cased overall price deflation, both have used data to boost revenues, both are looking to take advantage of 3G (Third Generation Wireless) to differentiate and increase revenues, and both have used MVNOs to develop underserved market segments with a targeted MVNO offer.

Latin America, however, presents a situation quite different from that of North America. Although the Latin American mobile landscape presents many of the same types of obstacles that affect the U.S. mobile market, such as low ARPU and increasingly saturated markets, the

Latin American region has its own set of problems, such as regulatory constraints and lack of spectrum capacity. In addition, key factors of MVNOs, such as competition, performance, a liberal market, and niche markets, do not exist with enough momentum to make MVNOs a reality. These factors will limit the number of viable brand-based MVNOs, as the potential addressable market may not justify the investments. However, since 2003, many of these obstacles have been largely removed or substantially lowered by the growing implementation of 2.5G technologies and the resulting increase in network capacity. Furthermore, recent plans to auction W-CDMA spectra for 3G services are creating a shift in regulatory initiatives that will force new license owners to open up their networks to MVNOs.

Similarly, the MVNO market development in Asia is not as visible as in Western markets (Table 1b and 1c). As shown in this study, market and industry performance create challenges for MVNOs. It is difficult for new MVNOs to enter Asian markets as the overall marketplace is highly saturated by existing network operators. In addition, maybe more importantly, Asian regulators are reluctant to force operators to open up to MVNOs, and operators even more so. The regulators have promoted facilities-based competition, and the operators who fear customer base cannibalization seem to influence regulation and market viability for MVNOs. The regulators' intervention may be in line with the discrepancy between Asia's high liberalization and low MVNO penetration (Table 5). The liberalization indicators in Asian countries may be policy-based, which is different from the market-based liberalization of Western countries. Under the policy-based liberalization, the markets are artificially changing toward liberal markets, but liberalized markets are most effective in climates of effective competition (Wu, 2003). Although overall Asian markets are apparently liberalized by government intervention, Asian markets still seem to be not liberal enough to embrace the MVNO, and the MVNO does not appear to stabilize in markets without effective competition. It is ironic that SK Telecom, Korea's biggest mobile operator, is running an MVNO business in U.S. by the name of Helio, which has been successful in targeting niche tech-savvy young adults seeking multiplayer gaming. SK Telecom obviously does not want to open their walled-garden vertical market, but takes advantage of the liberalized and segmented U.S. market. All of these peculiar features of Asian operators regarding market structure and industry culture imply that the Asian factors and indicators should be interpreted with special care. In this light, the Asian markets will likely force the "Asianization" of the current MVNO models being implemented in other regions of the world. The emerging MVNO market model cannot be similar to the MVNO model used in mature markets. MVNO diffusion in Asia will come at a much slower pace and through diverse processes because governments are more cautious in their approach due to political costs.

These tripartite comparisons imply that MVNOs tend to be more prosperous in developed, mature, and consequently dynamic markets like those in the West, rather than in young markets like those in Asia and Latin America. In fact, MVNOs tend to follow an economy of scale according to a number game; the rich get richer, the poor get poorer. The findings of this study imply that a certain level of penetration must be attained before the MVNO model becomes feasible. The emergence of MVNOs poses opportunities for established markets but threats for new markets. While the Asian markets see MVNO posing a threat of price deflation and loss of customer control, the Western markets turn such possible threats to opportunities by reselling excess network capacity and by creating new market segments. To increase MVNO penetration, Asian governments are now making efforts to liberalize, disintegrate, deregulate, and privatize their markets to foster an environment with a rich diversity of MVNOs, which Western countries have built over the long term. Asian regulators seem to realize the benefits of MVNO's as a means of encouraging competition, which would ultimately lead to greater choice and lower prices. The regulators should evaluate the market and make policy recommendations for MVNOs based on competitive pricing and keeping the market viable and profitable.

7. Conclusion

The emergence and proliferation of MVNO is not simply matter of infrastructure sharing between HNO and MVNO. It may involve a more fundamental question of market condition as the emergence of MVNOs has revealed two main industry structures in the mobile telecommunications industry: a horizontally layered (either diversified or consolidated), market-driven structure with a modular product architecture, and a vertically integrated, walled-garden oligopoly with an integrated product architecture. As shown previously, MVNO services are much more successful in Western than in Asian countries. One major reason for this difference in success is the differences in the industry structures between the markets in both areas. Because of the complexity of MVNO services, a horizontally layered structure seems to be more inviting. This finding provides future carriers and potential MVNOs with a framework to determine whether or not the MVNO model is right for their respective business.

The Asian industrial framework is optimized for traditional mobile voice services. It does not allow MVNOs to develop their business models in ways that have turned to be popular in Western Europe. In other words, MVNO services are more successful in markets where virtual operators take intermediary and aggregating roles in order to offer a true end-to-end mobile service. The incumbent Asian operators are not eager to change the market structure. It seems that MVNOs would reap nothing but negative consequences from the consumer's point of view if the market structure changed. In his study on market structure, Economides (1996) leaves open the question of whether the horizontal or a vertical industry structure is better for MVNOs. That is, the open questions would be: Is it more valuable to have a transparent, market-driven industry structure or a vertically integrated oligapoliy enabling the provision of easy-to-use services? Would this more integrated structure provide a mobile telecommunications market with only one, monopolistic player. This study partly answers such questions by showing that a horizontally-layered market is better at facilitating MVNO penetration. It appears that the vertically integrated telecom business models are less effective in an environment where the demand for a whole range of value-added services is strong. Under such a horizontal value chain, vertical integration seems to minimized. Predicting which MVNO trends will prevail can be a hard question. In the long run, MVNOs, along with MVNEs, are likely to rise and decline in popularity as uncertain markets and industries and change. One thing is clear: regardless of whether MVNOs, prevail or fail, their impact will be significant throughout the wireless industry.

8. Limitations and Future Studies

Given its complexity, defining telecom market structure is always elusive and difficult. This study is an exploratory attempt to define mobile market structure to analyze the emerging phenomena of the MVNO. This study used an aggregation model, and data were collected for the limited time of 2003-2005. Therefore, it would be helpful in the future to conduct comparative studies at a less aggregated level, such as using cross-sectional time-series analysis methods. In addition, multivariate regression, as Cava-Ferreruela et al. (2006) indicate, has weak numeric and estimation features. Other sophisticated measures may be accompanied with multivariate regression, such as bootstrap re-sampling or stepwise selection techniques. A strong methodological framework will better predict the prospect for MVNOs. One question that remains uncertain for MVNOs in East and West alike is the long-term viability of the MVNO itself. This question relates to how the value chain will develop and where bottlenecks will remain.

The current study intentionally simplifies and limits the variables in order to grasp an overall understanding of MVNO penetration factors. The limited variables allowed this study to set aside regulations, and policy, and carrier conduct and behavior as dummy variables. As Economides (1996) contends, the structural differences are caused by dissimilarities in the national regulations. As the present study excludes national policy from variables, it neglects to note many important aspects: EU regulators are opening up network access in favor of MVNO models and the FCC has been generally favorable to MVNO, which is not the case in non-Western regions. In addition, the significant results of the dummy variable imply that there is something more behind MVNO penetration and market structure. For example, despite the overall similarities between the U.S. and the EU, the lower MVNO in the U.S. can be explained by the fact that the U.S. operators are carefully watching MVNO development because they believe that the transition period between 2.5G and 3G will be the most fruitful period for MVNOs. This kind of carrier behavior will have to be investigated with respect to regulation and policy.

References

Boylaud O, & Nicoletti G. (2001). Regulation, market structure and performance in telecommunications. *OECD Economic Studies*, **32**, 99-142.

Capuano, C. (2005). Access regulation in vertically integrated oligopolies. *Proceedings of 32th the European Association for Research in Industrial Economics (EARIE) Conference*.

Cava-Ferreruela, I. & Alabau-Munoz, A. (2006). Broadband policy assessment: A cross-national empirical analysis. *Telecommunications Policy*, article In Press.

Choi, C. & Shin, H. (1992). A comment on a model of vertical product differentiation. *The Journal of Industrial Economics*, **40** (2), 229-231.

Chowdary T.H. (1998). Telecom liberalization and competition in developing countries. *Telecommunications Policy,* **22** (4), 259-265.

Dippon, C., & Banerjee, A. (2006). *Mobile Virtual Network Operators: Blessing or curse?* NERA Economic Consulting, White Plains, NY.

Doyle C. & Smith J.C. (1998). Market structure in mobile telecoms: qualified indirect access and the receiver pays principle. *Information Economics Policy*, **10**(4), 471-488.

Economides, N. (1996). The economics of networks. *International Journal of Industrial Organization*, **14**(2), 675-699.

Farrell, J. & Shapiro, C. (1990). Horizontal Mergers: An Equilibrium Analysis. *American Economic Review*, **80** (1), 107-123.

Frieden, R. (2003). Adjusting the Horizontal and Vertical in Telecommunications Regulation: A Comparison of the Traditional and a New Layered Approach. *Federal Communications Law Journal,* **55**(2), 207-250.

Gans, J. S. (2005). Concentration-based merger tests and vertical market structure. *Journal of Economic Literature*, **43**(2), 238-256.

Godfrey, J. & Kam, J. (2004). *What it takes to kick start mobile data: the lessons from Japan and South Korea*. ITU Asia 2004, Online News Service.

Gual, J. & Trillas, J.F. (2004). Telecommunications policies: determinants and impact. (August 2004). *CEPR Discussion Paper* No. **4578**. Available at Social Science Research Network: http://ssrn.com/abstract=604468

Haller, A. (1997). *Die Wertschöpfungsrechnung - Ein Instrument zur Steigerung der Aussagefähigkeit von Unternehmensabschlüssen im internationale Jontext*, Poeschel Verlag, Stuttgart.

Hodendorn, C. (2005). Regulating vertical integration in broadband: Open access versus common carriage. *Review of Network Economics,* **4**(1), 19-32.

Hoekman, B. (1995). Trade laws and institutions: Good practices and the World Trade Organization, Supplementary paper presented at The Uruguay Round and Developing Economies, *a World Bank Conference*, 26-27 January 1995.

Informa Research (2005). Informa research services' telecom market segmentation and customer profiling program, 2005. Accessed in March 2006 http://www.markettrends.com/industry/telecom/telecomproj.htm#5

International Telecom Union (2001). *Mobile Virtual Network Operators*, Geneva. Geneva: ITU.

International Telecom Union (2004). *Trends in telecommunication reform*: Effective regulation. Geneva: ITU.

International Telecom Union (2002). *Asia-Pacific Telecommunications Indicators*. Geneva: ITU.

Jang, B. (2003). Vertical structure and network competition in telecommunications services market. *Information Society Research,* Fall: 81-101.

Jost, J. (2004). *Can MVNOs succeed in emerging markets?* Pyramid Research.

Krafft, J. (2003). Vertical structure of the industry and competition: an analysis of the evolution of the info-communications industry. *Telecommunications Policy,* **27**(8/9), 625-649.

Kristensson, S. (2001). *Mobile Virtual Network Operators. Assessing MVNO business opportunities.* School of Business, University of Stockholm, Master of Science Thesis, June 2001.

Lehr, W. (2002). Vertical integration, Industry Structure, and Internet Telephony. *Internet Telephony* (ed. McKnight, Lehr, and Clark), the MIT Press, 2001.

Levinstein, M.C. (2002). Vertical integration. In: Mokyr, J. editor. *Oxford Encyclopedia of Economic History*, New York.

Li, W. & Xu, C. (2000). The impact of privatization and competition in the telecommunications sector around the world. *Journal of Law and Economics,* **48** (October).

Market Research (2005). *Future of mobile virtual network operator series: Europe, America, Asia Africa 2006.* Market Research Publication Report (Rcport ID: RFB1188821).

Melody, W. (1999). Telecom reform. *Telecommunications Policy,* **25**, 7 – 34.

Noam, E. (2004). *The Internet: Still Wide Open and Competitive?* Oxford Internet Institute, Internet Issue Brief No. 1, August 2003.

Noam, E. (2003). The effect of deregulation on market concentration: an analysis of the Telecom Act of 1996 and the industry meltdown. *The Columbia Science and Technology Law Review*, **4**, 1-12.

Noam, E. (2003b). Deregulation and market concentration: An analysis of post-1996 consolidations. *Federal Communications Law Journal*, **58**, 539-550.

Noam, E. (2002). *How telecom is becoming a cyclical industry, and what to do about it.* Presentation at Columbia Institute for Tele-Information, Conference on Telecommunications Volatility, April 2002, Columbia University, New York.

OECD Economics Department Working Papers (2001). OECD Economics Department in its series by Olivier Boylaud and Giuseppe Nicoletti. Regulation, market structure and performance in telecommunications, 2001.

OECD (2000). Performance Indicators for Public Telecommunication Operators. Paris. Original OECD report available online at: http://www.oecd.org/dsti/sti/it/cm/prod/ICCP22.htm

Ovum (2005). *Virtual mobile services: Strategies for fixed and mobile operators*, June 30, 2005. Ovum Research & Consultancy, Market Research Report.

Ovum (2006). Virtual Mobile Services: Strategies for Fixed and Mobile Operators. Ovum Ltd. 2006, by John Matthews, Susan Sweet. http://www.ovum.com.

Perry, M. (1989). Vertical Integration: Determinants and Effects. (Eds) R. Schmalensee and R. Willig, *Handbook of Industrial Organization*, Volume I, Chapter 4.

Pyramid Research (2006). *MVNOs and MVNEs: Analyzing the Viability of Virtual Mobile Players.* February 2006 (ID: PYR1224156) Accessed in August 2006. http://www.marketresearch.com/product/display.asp?productid=1224156

Sappington, D. & Weisman, D. (1996). *Designing incentive regulation for the telecommunications industry.* MIT Press, Cambridge, MA.

Shin, D.H. & Bartolacci, M. (2007). A study of MVNO diffusion and market structure in the EU, US, Hong Kong, and Singapore. *Telematics & Informatics,* **24**, 86-100.

Shin, D. (2007). A critique of Korean national information strategy: case of national information infrastructures. *Government Information Quarterly.*

Ulset, S. (2002). Mobile virtual network operators: a strategic transaction cost analysis of preliminary experiences. *Telecommunications Policy,* **26**(9-10), 537-549.

Wireless Asia (2002). Virgin Mobile and SingTel jointly call off their Virgin-branded MVNO mobile service a mere eight months after its launch. August 21 2002.

Weiss, T. (2006). *Mobile Strategies.* Futuretext, London.

Wu, F. (2003). From monopoly to competition: a comparative study of telecommunications policy reform in four Asia countries. *Proceeding of Pacific Telecommunications Council,* January 2003, Manoa, Hawaii.

Vickers J. (1995). Competition and regulation in vertically related markets. *The Review of Economic Studies,* **62**(1), 1-17.

In: Computer-Aided Design...
Editors: C.M. De Smet et al, pp. 89-107
ISBN: 978-1-60456-860-8

Chapter 4

CONSTRAINT-BASED AND FEATURE-BASED CAD SYSTEMS AND APPLICATIONS

***Ioannis Fudos*[1] *and Vasiliki Stamati*[2]**
Department of Computer Science, University of Ioannina, Greece

Abstract

A new generation of Computer Aided Design systems has become available in which geometric constraints can be defined to determine properties of large designs. The new design concept, often called constraint-based design or design by features offers users the capability of easily defining and modifying a design, but introduces the problem of solving complicated, not always well defined, constraint problems. Traditional parametric models can also be enhanced to partially support declarative constraint-based descriptions. We provide an overview of representation schemes for CAD applications. Then we present a survey of methods for geometric constraint solving appropriate for Computer Aided Design. We demonstrate how these representations and constraint solving methods can be combined or adapted to support a broad range of CAD applications by presenting two example cases of successfully using a feature-based constraint-based representation scheme to support two different CAD applications.

1. Introduction

Computer Aided Design has been the motivation for major breakthroughs in various fields of computer science such as computer graphics, visualization, and computer architecture. On the other hand, advancements in graph theory, geometric constraint solving, algorithms and data structures have enabled the use of computers in various fields such as manufacturing, VLSI design, reverse engineering, and restoration of artifacts. This new setting has established Computer Aided Design as a major framework for designing and editing machine parts, jewelry, archaeological findings, buildings, electronics and computers. We present a

[1] E-mail addresses: fudos@cs.uoi.gr
[2] E-mail addresses: vicky@cs.uoi.gr

framework for representing and editing CAD models for various applications based on two main concepts:

Local characteristics which are commonly called features. These characteristics may determine structural properties such as connectivity and hierarchy of objects, geometric properties such as dimensions, distances, angles, smoothness, inclusion, and other topological relations and finally functionality properties that usually are application dependent and determine the behavior of the system when performing its required tasks.

Local or global constraints imposed on the model to enforce complex geometric structures and advanced functionality. Such constraints may be part of a feature or span a number of different features. Constraints are clearly declarative, meaning that there is no suggested enforcement procedure. The systems determine based of the application and the user interaction how to enforce the system of geometric constraints.

The rest of this survey is structured as follows: Section 2 presents a comparative survey of representation models for CAD applications. The hybrid feature-based and constraint-based scheme is argued to be the most appropriate for a diverse collection of CAD applications. Section 3 presents methods to tackle the bottleneck problem of geometric constraint solving. Traditional methods are described and modern approaches that are not domain sensitive are presented. Section 4 presents two example cases of applying the framework to two different CAD applications. Section 5 offers conclusions.

2. Computer Aided Design Representation Schemes

There is a variety of geometric representations that can be used at different levels of CAD applications. The suitable representation scheme for each application depends on the scope of the application and its peculiarities. Some modeling types are simple and aim at providing only an external representation of the object, whereas others aim at encapsulating and providing additional knowledge and data, such as design intent, functionality, and editability.

In the following we study common modeling schemes used in CAD applications. An object can be represented in the simple form of raw data, such as a point cloud corresponding to points on the surface of the object. A widespread scheme in solid modeling is the Boundary Representation (B-rep) model where the facets and edges that describe the boundary of a solid are modeled using a connectivity graph and a collection of surface and edge patches. On the other hand, Constructive Solid Geometry (CSG) and volume models handle objects as 3D solids. There are also higher-level representation schemes that capture not only the shape of the object but also provide information pertaining to design intent and functionality, which can be used later on for re-parameterization and modification. We briefly describe each scheme and evaluate its suitability for various CAD applications.

2.1. Raw Data

The most basic and simple way to represent a 3D object is as raw data. By raw data we mean an unstructured collection of geometric primitives such as a point cloud or a range image. Such data are usually produced directly from a 3D object scanning or 3D reconstruction setting. The density of the data sets produced by these methods depends on the sampling rate used to acquire information from the object's surface. Also, very often the point clouds obtained contain noisy data due to physical characteristics of the object or limitations and regulations of the acquisition method used. However, this problem has been dealt with and processing methods have been suggested that overcome this problem. The characteristic of this representation model is that it describes the object as discrete data, i.e. points, without providing any information about the connectivity, the topological relation among geometric primitives or the design intent. This type of representation is mainly used in point-based modeling, i.e. [1], [2] and reverse engineering applications [3].

2.2. Boundary Representation (Brep)

A more common representation model in CAD applications is the boundary representation model (Brep), which describes the edges and facets of the boundary of the object. This type of model consists of a collection of surface patches. Surfaces can capture objects of complex and freeform design. Thanks to advancements in computer graphics hardware we are able to handle efficiently the CPU-intensive processing required by Brep. These factors have resulted in the increased usage of this representation in a wide spectrum of applications. A Brep model is often realized as a mesh of triangular or quadrilateral (and in general polygonal) planar or higher degree surface facets.

Planar polygonal meshes (called polyhedral representations) are mostly suited for rendering and virtual reality and not for CAD applications since they do not provide sufficient detail. Often, other representation schemes are converted to polygonal representations for the purpose of rendering. Polyhedral representations such as triangulations are also used in reverse engineering applications, usually as intermediate representations during the re-engineering process. A drawback of representing a 3D object with a polygonal mesh is that it cannot capture design semantics, such as design intent, inter part relations and overall behavior. Also model editing is only feasible in a local corrective sense. Smooth object surfaces cannot efficiently and accurately be represented by a polygonal mesh, even when a large number of polygons are used, since the polyhedral representation by definition cannot accommodate for G^1 continuity. For example, to render areas of high curvature quite accurately we need to increase the number of polygons and decrease significantly the facet size.

Overall, polyhedral representation is not suitable for describing objects with specific design characteristics and functionality, such as mechanical and industrial parts. Also it is not appropriate for describing complex and detailed objects since the large number of polygons needed to sufficiently approximate the initial object makes the method unaffordable both time-wise and space-wise.

Applications such as aesthetic and industrial engineering, reverse engineering and jewellery design use commonly non-planar surfaces to capture the boundaries of complex objects [4]. A Brep model may be constructed using NURBS (Non-Uniform Rational B-Splines) or other parametric surface patches. This type of representation is useful in applications where free-form surfaces are part of the repertoire of primitive geometric entities. Brep can capture almost any type of object, such as mechanical parts and objects of aesthetic design. Surfaces can be described using appropriate parametric representations. Brep models make editing of local features feasible by interactively placing control points, therefore modifying the shape or curvature of the object's feature. However, Brep models on their own do not capture higher design characteristics of the object such as functionality and part relationships. The information provided through this type of model is limited and does not provide tools for modifying parts of the model that affect the whole design. Therefore, Brep models are used in combination with other techniques (e.g. features, constraints) to obtain higher-level descriptions that correspond to more flexible and useful models that are suitable for CAD applications. For instance, in [5], the authors present a beautification process based on constraints which is performed on B-rep models constructed from reverse engineering range data. B-rep models acquired by re-engineering can present various inaccuracies and errors, therefore the authors suggest the beautification of the models by describing topological regularities in terms of geometric constraints.

2.3. Volume Modeling

While surface raw data and Brep modeling schemes provide data concerning the boundary of a model, constructive solid geometry (CSG) and volumetric models represent the objects as a volume. This type of representation can be used for objects that B-rep cannot sufficiently describe. For example, a Brep model cannot represent unambiguously a sphere containing a hollow, whereas a volume model can easily capture such solids.

Constructive solid geometry (CSG) models are created by performing Boolean operations on solid primitives e.g. spheres, cones, cylinders and cubes. We perceive that CSG models represent objects that can be created from solid primitives. Unless we use a very large number of primitives we cannot use CSG to model higher degree free-form objects. In general, the CSG representation scheme is well suited for mechanical part design and for all applications where the design history can be expressed as a tree of Boolean operations on geometric primitives. Also editing and local shape modification is performed by intervening in the appropriate operation (internal tree node). Converting CSG models to render-able ones is extremely difficult and therefore CSG is commonly used in conjunction to Brep. In this case a Brep model is always maintained and every modification is transformed to an incremental Brep editing operation. Constraints may also be used in conjunction to CSG for performing multiple internal node modifications at a single step.

Volume pixels (voxels) are used in a volumetric approach to 3D object representation. A voxel is a geometric primitive and represents the smallest discrete volume used in this representation scheme. Voxel-based representations are commonly used for visualizing unstructured 3D volume date such as data from scientific computing, medical imaging etc. Although used in early CAD/CAM settings, volumetric representations have been proven to be very inefficient for computer aided editing, rendering and manufacturing. This representation scheme may be used as redundant auxiliary information in CAD applications [6] such as solid modeling, reverse engineering and feature-based and constraint-based modeling for the purposes of physical modeling and simulation.

2.4. Higher-level Representations for CAD

A current promising trend in computer-aided design is to use higher-level structures for model representation. These structures are based on one of the former representation types in combination with additional structural, topological or other information. A feature-based representation scheme describes the object as a combination of features, which are surfaces or solid parts with specific characteristics. A constraint-based representation scheme uses geometric constraints enforced on the model and its features to obtain a more accurate representation that captures designer requirements. The skeleton of a model can also be considered as a higher-level CAD representation that can be used for specific operations such as feature detection and extraction.

More specifically, the feature-based model is a representation scheme that is growing more and more popular. The model is described by defining collections of feature elements and relationships among them. The features are collections of points, surfaces or other features. For example a commonly used feature type is a cross-section of a solid. Constraints are applied to the features to create more accurate and robust models, but also for enforcing global criteria such as tolerance and beautification. This type of model representation has been established initially for manufacturing mechanical parts, where a library of features is created and then relationships among feature elements are enforced. The feature-based scheme is well suited to industrial design in general since it provides for advanced editability. This is due to the knowledge encapsulated by the model concerning tolerances, constraints, relationships and connectivity. For this reason, feature-based methods are often characterized as knowledge-based. Their main objective is to exploit any knowledge and information pertaining to design intent, functionality and construction process. Besides, this representation scheme supports collaborative CAD, reverse engineering and VLSI applications. This type of model also provides the user-designer with the capability of editing, redesigning and reconstructing the original design, depending on her preferences and needs by tailoring the model features [7].

A powerful higher-level structure for representing objects is the constraint-based scheme, which is often used in combination with features [8]. This representation scheme is particularly preferred in CAD applications where the objects being modeled, modified and manufactured are of geometric or freeform design and must conform to constraints determined locally on specific components or globally on the whole model [9]. Constraints defined on a model or its individual components can refer to almost any characteristic, i.e. geometric attributes, such as size and shape, topological characteristics, such as placement and connectivity, functionality and behavior. Constraint-based models are widely used in architecture, mechanical engineering, electronic design, aesthetic and industrial design, for design, modeling or re-engineering. The types of constraints defined depend on the nature of the CAD application. For example, in VLSI CAD a geometric constraint scheme may be used in conjunction to feature-based or other graph-based connectivity modeling. Constraints are imposed on each design feature used in the VLSI circuit referring to the feature's intra-connectivity and its local characteristics (i.e. area, size, geometry). Contraints may also be imposed to express inter-feature connectivity requirements. Finally, constraints are also enforced globally on the circuit, and are targeted to optimize the overall placement and routing of the features on the chip.

An object can also be represented by its skeleton. By skeleton we mean the closure of all points that have more than one closest point on the shape boundary (for example the medial axis transform). This representation provides the topology and shapes that exist in the object and also reflects the symmetries of an object. Depending on the type of application the skeleton is used for, it may be a 2D or 3D representation. For instance, in 3D the medial axis transform produces a medial surface. The exact computation of the 3D skeleton is a computationally intensive problem that returns a skeleton as complex as the object itself. Therefore we usually seek for an approximation. A skeleton representation scheme is used in various CAD applications for object recognition and retrieval [10], animation [11] and other solid modeling operations ([12], [13]). It is widely used in feature-based modeling, where it can be employed to describe the shape of features, in feature detection and extraction applications and shape deformation, for instance refer to [14] and [15].

3. Geometric Constraint Solving

Higher level representations are powerful, accurate and user friendly. However they have a major bottleneck; all complicated functionality has been shifted to the solution of a large non-linear system of geometric constraints with multiple valid solutions. In this section we present an overview of approaches to geometric constraint solving. We outline the most representative methods and evaluate their behavior in terms of the major concerns faced in CAD/CAM systems: solution selection, interactive speed, editability, handling of over and underconstrained configurations and scope [16].

3.1. Numerical Constraint Solvers

In numerical constraint solvers, the constraints are translated into a system of algebraic equations and are solved using iterative methods. To handle the exponential number of solutions and the large number of parameters, iterative methods require sharp initial guesses. Also, most iterative methods have difficulties handling overconstrained or underconstrained instances. The advantage of these methods is that they have the potential to solve large nonlinear system that may not be solvable using any of the other methods. All existing solvers more or less switch to iterative methods when the given configuration is not solvable by the native method. This fact emphasizes the need for further research in the area of numerical constraint solving.

Sketchpad [17] was the first system to use the method of relaxation as an alternative to propagation. Relaxation is a slow but quite general method. The Newton-Raphson method has been used in various systems [18] [19], and it proved to be faster than relaxation but it has the problem that it may not converge or it may converge to an unwanted solution after a chaotic behavior. For that reason, Juno [18] uses as initial state the sketch interactively drafted by the user. However, Newton-Raphson is so sensitive to the initial guess [20], that the sketch drafted must almost satisfy all constraints prior to constraint solving. A sophisticated use of the Newton-Raphson method was developed in [21], where an improved way for finding the inverse Jacobian matrix is presented. Furthermore, the idea of dividing the matrix of constraints into submatrices as presented in the same work has the potential of providing the user with useful information regarding the constraint structure of the sketch. Though this information is usually quantitative and nonspecific, it may help the user in basic modifications. To check whether a constraint problem is well-constrained, Chyz [22] proposes a preprocessing phase where the graph of constraints is analyzed to check whether a necessary condition is satisfied. The method is however quite expensive in time and it cannot detect all the cases of singularity. An alternative method to Newton-Raphson for geometric constraint solving is homotopy or continuation [23], that is argued in [24] to be more satisfactory in typical situations where Newton-Raphson fails. Homotopy, is global, exhaustive and thus slow when compared to the local and fast Newton's method [25], however it may be more appropriate for CAD/CAM systems when constructive methods fail, since it may return all solutions if designed carefully.

3.2. Constructive Constraint Solvers

This class of constraint solvers is based on the fact that most configurations in an engineering drawing are solvable by ruler, compass and protractor or using other less classical repertoires of construction steps. In these methods the constraints are satisfied in a constructive fashion, which makes the constraint solving process natural for the user and suitable for interactive debugging. There are two main approaches in this direction.

Rule-Constructive Solvers

Rule-constructive solvers use rewrite rules for the discovery and execution of the construction steps. In this approach, complex constraints can be easily handled, and extensions to the scope of the method are straightforward to incorporate [26]. Although it is a good approach for prototyping and experimentation, the extensive computations involved in the exhaustive searching and matching make it inappropriate for real world applications.

A method that guarantees termination, ruler and compass completeness and uniqueness using the Knuth-Bendix critical pair algorithm is presented in ([27], [28]). This method can be proved to confirm theorems that are provable under a given system of axioms [29]. A system based on this method was implemented in Prolog. Aldefeld in [30] uses a forward chaining inference mechanism, where the notion of direction of lines is imposed by introducing additional rules, and thus restricting the solution space. A similar method is presented in [31], where handling of overconstrained and underconstrained problems is given special consideration. Sunde in [32] uses a rule-constructive method but adopts different rules for representing directed and nondirected distances, giving flexibility for dealing with the solution selection problem. In [33], the problem of nonunique solutions is handled by imposing a topological order on three geometric objects. An elaborate description of a complete set of rules for 2D geometric constraint solving can be found in [34]. In their work, the scope of the particular set of rules is characterized. [35] presents an extension of the set of rules of [34], and provides a correctness proof based on the techniques of [36].

Graph-Constructive Solvers

The graph-constructive approach has two phases. During the first phase the graph of constraints is analyzed and a sequence of construction steps is derived. During the second phase these construction steps are followed to place the geometric elements. These approaches are fast and more methodical. In addition, conclusions characterizing the scope of the method can be easily derived. A major drawback is that as the repertoire of constraints increases the graph-analysis algorithm needs to be modified.

Fitzgerald [37] follows the method of dimensioned trees introduced by Requicha [38]. This method allows only horizontal and vertical distances and it is useful for simple engineering drawings. Todd in [39] first generalized the dimension trees of Requicha. Owen in [40] presents an extension of this principle that includes circularly dimensioned sketches. DCM [41] is a system that uses some extension of Owen's method. [42] presents an elaborative graph-constructive method, with fast analysis and construction algorithms, and extensions for handling classes of nonsolvable, underconstrained and consistently overconstrained configuration

3.3. Propagation Methods

Propagation methods follow the approach met in traditional constraint solving systems. In this approach, the constraints are first translated into a system of equations involving variables and constants. The equations are then represented by an undirected graph which has as nodes the equations, the variables and the constants, and whose edges represent whether a variable or a constant appears in an equation. Subsequently, we try to direct the graph so as to satisfy all the equations starting from the constants. To accomplish this, various propagation techniques have been used but none of them guarantees to derive a solution and at the same time have a reasonable worst case running time. For a review of these methods see [28]. In a sense, the constructive constraint solvers can be thought of as a sub case of the propagation method (fixed geometric elements for constants and variable geometric elements for variables). However, constructive constraint solvers utilize domain specific information to derive more powerful and efficient algorithms.

3.4. Symbolic Constraint Solvers

In symbolic solvers, the constraints are transformed to a system of algebraic equations which is solved using methods from algebraic manipulation, such as Grobner basis calculation [43] or Wu's method [44]. Although, these methods are interesting from a theoretical viewpoint, their practical significance is limited, since their time and space complexity is typically exponential or even hyperexponential.

3.5. Hierarchical and Hybrid Approaches

A major result in analysis of constraint graphs by [45] in which an efficient method for detecting dense constraint subgraphs is described has enabled the solution of large systems of geometric constraints in 2, 3 or more dimensions. By using this result we can build efficient algorithm for solving arbitrary systems of geometric constraints. We first find a set of minimal disjoint dense constraint subgraphs. Each subgraph is then reduced in a supernode of high dimension and the method is applied recursively to the resulting graph. In this way we build a hierarchy of constraint graphs that is treated bottom up or top down based on the application. Interfeature 3D constraints result in systems of 3D constraints. Such systems are very hard to solve with graph constructive methods since there is not even a necessary and sufficient condition for well-constrainedness in 3D. By using the decomposition suggested by this approach we may breakdown the large geometric constraint system in a multitude of small systems with few variables. Such systems are usually easy to solve using global optimization with topological constraints to narrow down the root selection process.

In this direction [46] has developed a novel method for placement and routing in VLSI by constructing a circuit hierarchy by detecting dense connectivity graphs and then employing global optimization algorithms for each sub-problem.

4. CAD Applications from a Feature-Based/Constraint-Based Point of View

Since the models constructed by CAD applications are most often meant for manufacturing or production in general, it is necessary that they are robust and accurate. Also, most applications require that the model can be modified and re-engineered. The use of constraints and features in such CAD applications is essential and is the only representation scheme that sufficiently supports these requirements. In this section we will present two example approaches that adopt this modeling scheme.

4.1. Parametric Feature Based Design in Manufacturing Systems

An example of a CAD application where the feature- and constraint-based representation model is most appropriate is parametric feature-based manufacturing [47].

Parametric modeling was commonly used for the construction of complex models on which parameters were used to provide for subsequent customization. The parameters defined during the design and modeling process are relative to the individual geometric characteristics of the model or to the model as a whole. For example, the parameters can control characteristics such as length, height, width and hole radius.

On the other hand, feature-based modeling is a representation scheme based on the combination of individual feature components. In this context a feature is a unit that can be defined as a connected set of geometric elements (i.e. a subpart) associated with attributes that describe its shape and behavior, such as geometry, topology, functionality and connectivity with other features. In traditional approaches each feature is linked to a set of local parameters that control its attribute values. Here, the feature-based model is complemented through the use of local and global constraints. The constraints are applied locally, in reference to the parameter values or the geometric characteristics of the primitives of the features to impose design or user-defined specifics such as hole size, pocket depth, and globally, in reference to the connectivity and the inter-feature relations of the model.

Much work has been performed on the definition of features in relation to various CAD applications. Features are often perceived as 3D solid components that can be classified into feature libraries depending on their shape or geometry. This point of view is described for instance in [48], where the authors present a library of features fit for manufacturing applications, and in [49], where design features for machining are examined. In [50] features are defined as pierced voxels that are used to create traditional pierced jewellery. However, features can also be defined from surfaces, which is especially common in freeform design applications. For instance, [51] examines freeform surface features, whereas [52] presents a taxonomy of freeform features. Other work uses the notion of feature points and feature lines ([53], [54]) for applications usually related to data segmentation for reverse engineering, or shape deformation and manipulation. Since the definition of a feature is not strict, Hoffmann and Joan-Arinyo in [55] suggest the use of user-defined features in feature based modeling.

Parametric and feature based modeling is an essential component of current CAD design systems. In traditional CAD systems, CSG and Brep models are created by adding and subtracting parts in the model and by applying transformations and various design operations. Design intent was not a concern in these systems and therefore precise editing that involved structural and arbitrary topological modifications of parts of the model was almost impossible without rebuilding the model from scratch. Editing a part of the model is feasible if the design steps are undone until the model returns to the previous state, when the part was created. This of course is possible if the design history of the model is recorded and it is obvious that even though editing theoretically concerns a part of the model, ultimately the whole design process is affected. Feature based CAD systems overcome this limitation by capturing design intent. Since the models are constructed using parameters and features, local editing is possible without necessarily affecting the whole model. Changes are propagated through the model based on the parameters and constraints defined in the system and based on the attributes and connectivity of the features. Feature-based constraint-based modeling systems provide libraries of feature components to be used in the design process and some support user-defined features. Applications such as custom design are feasible since components of models can be combined or re-designed to satisfy user defined preferences or requirements.

Many commercial CAD modeling systems support parametric and/or feature-based modeling. Systems such as PRO/Engineer [56], AUTOCAD [57], IRONCAD [58], CATIA [59], Solidworks [60], SolidEdge [61] and Alibre design [62], which have been developed mainly for mechanical engineering, manufacturing and industrial design applications, have been integrated with parametric and/or feature based modeling capabilities. Architectural Desktop and AUTOCAD are CAD systems used in architectural applications that support parametric modeling. 3D Studio Max [63] and Maya [64] are parametric feature-based modeling systems used for artwork and animation. There are also systems that have been developed for specific CAD applications, such as jewelry, clothing and textile design, marine applications and furniture.

The above modeling systems are very efficient for manufacturing and production applications. However more freeform applications, such as aesthetic and custom design, are still challenging even with these systems. An interesting case is jewellery design. A large number of CAD systems for jewellery design are parametric feature-based. They provide graphical interfaces with excellent rendering capabilities. The majority of these systems provide built-in libraries of settings and cut gems and stones and advanced feature-based design tools. Some systems provide advanced functionality that provides the use of builders for recording design steps and for defining parameter values for parts to be used in the process. Also, the majority of these systems have the capability of exporting models to rapid prototyping machines. However, in most CAD systems for jewellery, designing is performed manually using various tools and usually the design steps cannot be programmed to be executed automatically and accurately. This means that each different piece of jewellery has to be created basically from the beginning by hand, making custom design applications difficult and time-consuming. Also these systems require that the user has designing skills or knowledge of using CAD systems. In the following we will present an interesting example of jewellery application that is difficult to carry out with existing CAD systems: the construction of traditional pierced jewellery, .

In [50] ByzantineCAD, a feature-based CAD system suitable for the design of pierced Byzantine jewellery is presented. The system is automated and parametric meaning that the user-designer sets some parameter values and ByzantineCAD creates the jewellery model that corresponds to the specified values. This provides the designer with the ability to rapidly create custom-designed jewellery, based on the preferences of the customers such as including their initials on a ring. ByzantineCAD introduces a feature-based and voxel-based approach to designing jewellery, through the definition of elementary structural elements with specific attributes and properties that are used as building blocks to construct complex pierced designs.

More specifically, pierced Byzantine jewellery are gold jewels with pierced designs that were made along the coastlines of the eastern Mediterranean Sea during the period 3rd –7th century A.D. Their originality is due to the particular processing technique that is used for their creation resulting in a special aesthetic effect. Pierced jewellery was created from thin sheets of gold. The designs were engraved on these sheets of gold with a thin sharp tool. After the outlining of the designs, holes following their shape were created and these were decorated with triangular carvings, using an iron chisel.

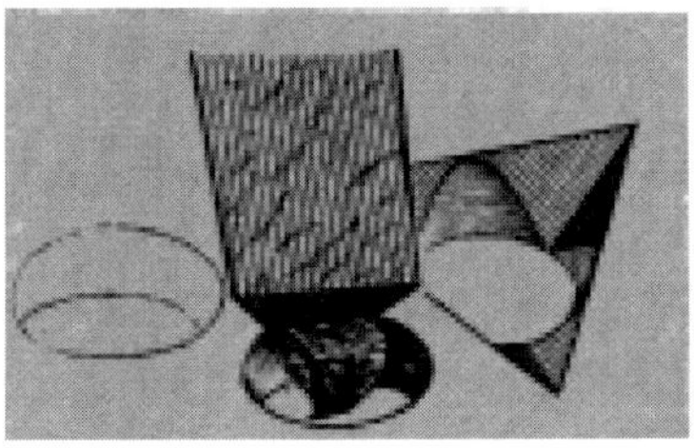

Figure 1. Using a chisel to create carvings around a hole.

In ByzantineCAD a feature library of carved, pierced voxel elements is defined in accordance to the craftsmanship used in traditional Byzantine jewellery. The design of pierced jewellery is made up of cylindrical holes that have carvings around them. Each hole with the corresponding carvings around it is considered for the purposes of reconstruction as a structural element (feature). Each feature is a solid made of a rectangular parallelepiped with a cylindrical hole and the corresponding carvings around the hole (Figures 1,2) . According to the aesthetic rules that characterize traditional pierced jewellery, all structural elements have the same size but differ in the position of the hole and the carvings around it. The hole can be located either in the center of the parallelepiped or in the center of any of the four quarters. Note that, in terms of computer aided design and manufacturing, the cylindrical hole can be positioned anywhere in the rectangular parallelepiped; the above restriction follows from careful interpretation of the traditional artistic patterns used. Attributes of these feature elements are characteristics such as the number of carvings around the cylindrical hole, the position of the hole in the parallelepiped, the directions of the carvings and more. A large number of different structural elements can be created by a hole and various carvings and, since not all of these feasible feature elements are valid for use in creating pierced designs, restrictions concerning the carving directions are defined based on aesthetic and artistic rules.

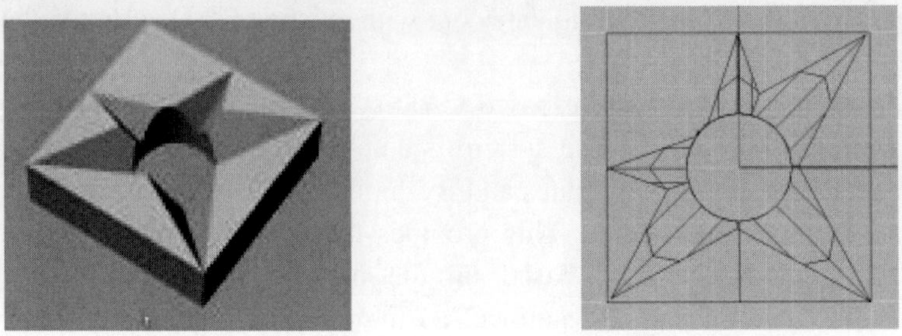

Figure 2. A structural element (feature).

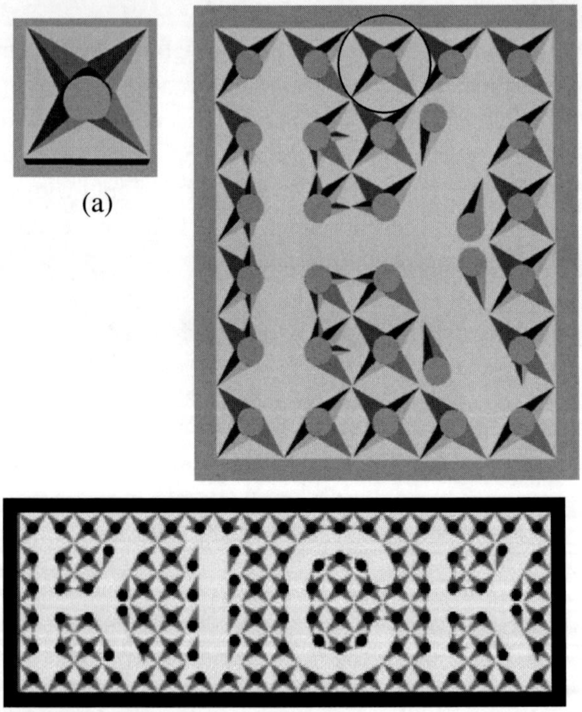

(a)

Figure 3. Pierced voxel elements such as (a) are used as features to create complex solid plaques representing designs, i.e. letters or words, that are sized and modified appropriately to construct custom-designed jewellery (i.e. ring).

These feature elements are combined like 3D building blocks to create complex carved plaques representing pierced designs (Figure 3). The structural elements are placed side by side, either on top, bottom, right or left of each other, and unioned into a new object. The rules determining how the different features can be combined are defined by the designs to be recreated. The construction of these plaques is constrained by the parameter values defined by the user-designer in reference to characteristics of the plaque such as length and width. The plaques are then used to create jewellery such as rings and necklace pendants. By parameterizing the process of creating pierced jewellery, it is very easy to modify characteristics of the jewellery such as the size and the designs represented.

4.2. Feature-Based Modeling for Reverse Engineering

Reverse engineering aims to analyze a real object and to determine its characteristics and mechanisms, with further aim to reconstruct and remanufacture it. The data concerning the physical object can be obtained by various methods. A common method is using a 3D laser scanner to obtain a point cloud corresponding to points on the surface of the scanned object. Given this, a more specific definition of reverse engineering would be to define it as the process of obtaining a geometric CAD model from measurements acquired by scanning an existing physical model [65].

Reverse engineering is vital for various industries because the computer models acquired help improve the quality and efficiency of designs and also speed up the manufacturing and analysis process. In mechanical part engineering and manufacturing, reverse engineering aims to replicate existing parts for which no CAD models exist. Also, it is possible to manufacture objects for which the original CAD model no longer corresponds to the physical part that was manufactured due to subsequent undocumented modifications made after the initial design stage. Reverse engineering is applied in industrial design, such as automobile exterior parts design. Stylists and artists very often create physical models of their concepts by using clay, plaster or wood. These real-scale models are then used to create CAD models for manufacturing the objects on an industrial scale. Also the CAD models provide the artists and stylists with the ability to re-evaluate their designs, especially when they can easily re-design or modify them as needed. Reverse engineering encourages conceptual design because the designer creates an initial prototype, scans it and manipulates it as desired.

Re-engineering objects of freeform design is relatively more difficult and complex than reconstructing mechanical parts. Mechanical parts usually have specific geometric characteristics, such as symmetries and swept profiles that are fairly easy to detect and parameterize. However, in the case of freeform objects, there are often features that are difficult to extract. In the case of restricted mechanical parts, features libraries can be defined and used for detecting features in the point cloud, whereas for freeform objects this is not feasible.

Since reverse engineering applications aim at reproduction and manufacturing, the re-engineering process must create highly accurate and robust CAD models. A characteristic of the objects re-engineered is that they are usually parts of larger objects and therefore have to fit and connect exactly with other parts, like pieces in a puzzle. For this reason, the models created through the reverse engineering process must be well defined and constrained [66]. Also, in some cases, the model created is to be edited in i.e. custom designing, therefore a simple B-rep model is not appropriate. Given this, it is natural that feature-based and constrained based models are used more and more in re-engineering applications.

A feature-based reverse engineering method was also used in [67] for reverse engineering a mannequin for garment design. The basic concept in this method is to create a generic mannequin model of a human torso, which is appropriately aligned with the 3D point cloud of the desired human torso model, and the generic model is "fitted" to the point cloud by matching up characteristic points of the models e.g. peaks. This method creates parameterized models by exploiting the features of the object and by using them to constrain the fitting process. It is an automated approach to reverse engineering human torsos that creates parameterized models with good accuracy.

Constraint definition and application has been used in building reconstruction and reverse engineering objects of aesthetic design. Specifically, [68] examines how a priori knowledge can be used to derive constraints to create more accurate models in architectural applications. Relevant work is also found in [69]. In [70] the authors suggest a constraint-based approach in reverse engineering for model beautification.

A paradigm of feature-based/constraint-based re-engineering is the REFAB ([71], [48]) project, which uses a feature-based and constraint-based method to reverse engineer mechanical parts. REFAB is a human interactive system where the 3D point cloud is presented to the user, and the user selects from a list a feature that exists in the cloud, specifies with the mouse the approximate location of the feature in the point cloud, and the system then fits the specified feature to the actual point cloud data using a least square means method iteratively. The authors give emphasis on the fitting of pockets, where the user draws a profile of the pocket on the point cloud and the system then fits the profile to the data and the profile is then extruded to create the pocket. This feature-fitting process is made more accurate by using constraints that are detected by the system, verified by the user and then exploited to achieve a better fitting of the features according to the data. The system supports constraints [72] such as parallelism, concentricity, perpendicularity and symmetry. The constraints defined and used in REFAB seek to reduce the degrees of freedom associated with the object as much as possible, so as to achieve high precision models in less time.

An interesting feature-based approach to re-engineering objects of freeform design is presented in [73]. Re-engineering objects of freeform design is essential for supporting custom design in a CAD model reconstruction system. It provides user-designers with the capability to modify re-engineered CAD models according to their preferences and to incorporate in novel designs. For instance, in the case of jewellery re-engineering, the user-designer might like to be able to modify the dimensions of a ring to produce one of larger size, or be able to choose certain parts of the object to use them to create other pieces of jewellery. To this end, one needs to exploit the features of the original model and the relationships and constraints that hold among them. In [73] a generic and global feature detection approach to reverse engineering point clouds of objects of freeform design is presented. A method is presented for detecting and segmenting a point cloud into individual subsets that correspond to features. This is achieved by using a point characteristic defined as "concavity intensity" to decompose the point cloud into subsets (components) that correspond to features of the physical object. The concavity intensity of a point corresponds to the smallest distance from the point to its convex hull that does not pass through the point cloud. This feature basically detects concave features in the object being reengineered. A concavity intensity map is shown in Figure 4. In the concavity intensity map the values are rendered using greyscale, where black corresponds to points belonging to the convex hull, whereas white corresponds to points that are farthest away from the convex hull. We can observe that edges (rapid variations in concavity intensity), saddle points and extrema can be used to partition the point cloud into components that can later be refined as the features of the object.

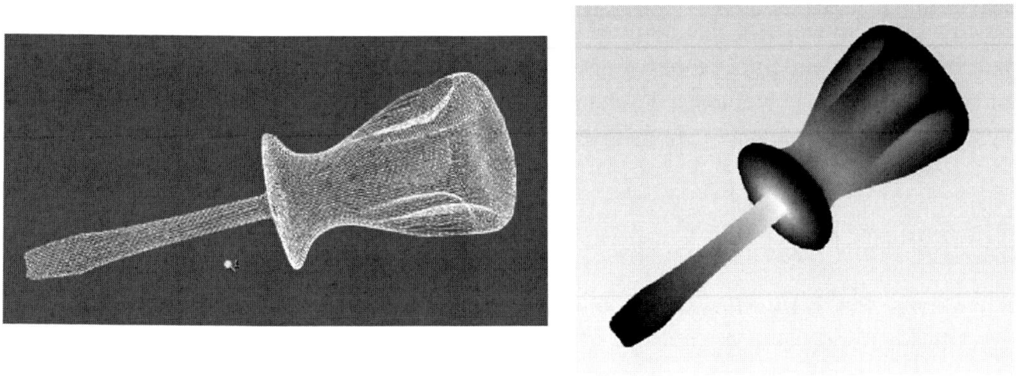

Figure 4. A point cloud of a screwdriver [75] (left) and its concavity intensity map (right).

The point concavity intensity values calculated are used to segment the point cloud into feature components. Alternative methods for segmentation used in CAD applications are presented in [74]. A feature component is bounded by areas where abrupt changes in the direction of the normal and/or rapid concavity intensity variations are observed. After calculating the concavity intensities of the all the points that form the point cloud, a region growing method to divide the point cloud into its components is applied (Figure 5). The region growing method is based on two criteria:

i) the normal vectors of neighboring points belonging to the same region should form an angle smaller than a threshold t and
ii) the approximate gradients of the concavity intensity function in directions x, y and z for neighboring points of the same region should maintain the same sign value, meaning that there are no zero crossings observed between them.

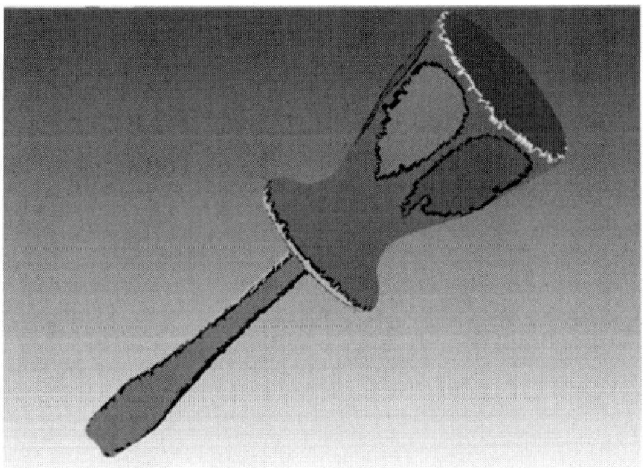

Figure 5. Feature extraction is performed by region growing.

5. Conclusions

We have presented a survey of representation schemes for CAD applications. Then we have introduced a framework for representing and performing complex design operations in CAD systems. This framework has evolved from the feature-based design paradigm augmented with intra-feature and inter-feature constraints and a hierarchical constraint analysis technique for placing geometric elements. To demonstrate the employment of this framework we have presented two example applications that we have developed using this new design concept.

References

[1] Cripps R.J., *Algorithms to support point-based cadcam,* International Journal of Machine Tools and Manufacture 2003, 43(4), 425-432.

[2] Kobbelt L. and Botsch M., *A survey of point-based techniques in computer graphic,* Computers and Graphics 2004, 28(6), 801-814.

[3] Hoppe H., Derose T., Duchamp T., McDonald J. and Stuetzle W., *Surface reconstruction from unorganized points,* Computer Graphics 1992, 26(2), 71--78.

[4] Benko P., Martin R.R. and Varady T., *Algorithms for reverse engineering boundary representation models,* Computer-Aided Design 2001, 33(11), 839-851.

[5] Langbein F.C., Marshall A.D. and Martin R.R., *Choosing consistent constraints for beautification of reverse engineered geometric models,* Computer-aided Design 2004, 36(3), 261-278.

[6] Jense G.J., *Voxel-based methods for CAD,* Computer Aided Design 1989, 21(10), 528-533.

[7] Hoffmann C.M. and Joan-Arinyo R., *Erep An editable high-level representation for geometric design,* Geometric Modeling for Product Realization, P. Wilson, M. Wozny , M. Pratt, eds., North Holland, 1993, 129-164.

[8] Benko P., Kos G., Varady T., Andor L. and Martin R.R., *Constrained fitting in reverse engineering,* Computer-Aided Design 2002, 19(3), 173-205.

[9] Anderl R. and Mendgen R., *Modelling with constraints: theoretical foundation and application,* Artificial Intelligence in Computer-Aided Design 1996, 28(3), 155-168.

[10] Cornea N.D., Demirci M.F., Silver D., Shokoufandeh A., Dickinson S.J. and Kantor P.B., *3D Object Retrieval using Many-to-many Matching of Curve Skeletons*, IEEE International Conference on Shape Modeling and Applications (SMI) 2005, Boston USA, 368-373.

[11] Bloomenthal J., *Medial-based Vertex Deformation*, Proceedings of the 2002 ACM SIGGRAPH/Eurographics Symposium on Computer Animation 2002, San Antonio, TX, USA, .

[12] Sheehy D., Armstrong C. and Robinson D., *Shape description by medial axis construction,* IEEE Transactions on Visualization and Computer Graphics 1996, 2(1), 62-72.

[13] Storti D.W., Turkiyyah G.M., Ganter M.A., Lim C.T. and Stal D.M., *Skeleton-based modeling operations on solids, Solid Modeling '97* 1997, Atlanta GA USA.

[14] Lien J., Keyser J. and Amato N.M., *Simultaneous Shape Decomposition and Skeletonization*, Proceedings of the ACM Syposium on Solid and Physical Modeling 2006. Cardiff, Wales, United Kingdom, 219-228

[15] Yoshizawa S., Belyaev A.G. and Seidel H-P., *Free-form skeleton-driven mesh deformation*, Proceedings of the eighth ACM Symposium on Solid Modeling and applications 2003, Seattle, Washington U.S.A., 247-253

[16] Fudos I., *Constraint Solving for Computer Aided Design*, Dept of Computer Sciences, Purdue University, 1995, PhD Thesis.

[17] Sutherland I., *Sketchpad, a man-machine graphical communication system.* Proceedings of the spring Joint Compo Conference, 1963,329-345.

[18] Nelson, G., *Juno, a constraint-based graphics system*, SIGGRAPH 1985, San Francisco USA.,235-243.

[19] Serrano D. and Gossard D., *Combining mathematical models and geometric models in CAE systems*, Proc. ASME Computers in Eng. Conf 1986, Chicago USA.,277-284.

[20] Beaty P.L., Fitzhorn P.A. and Herron G.J., *Extensions in variational geometry that generate and modify object edges composed of rational Bezier curves,* Computer-Aided Design 1994, 26(2), 98-108.

[21] Light R. and Gossard D., *Modification of geometric models through variational geometry,* Computer Aided Design 1982, 14(4), 209-214.

[22] Chyz W., *Constraint management for CSG*, MIT, 1985, Master's Thesis.

[23] Allgower E.L. and Georg K., *Continuation and path following,* Acta Numerica 1993, 1-64.

[24] Lamure H. and Michelucci D., *Solving geometric constraints by homotopy*, Proc. Third Symposium on Solid Modeling and Applications 1995, Salt Lake City, USA.,263-269.

[25] Morgan A., *Solving polynomial systems using continuation for engineering and scientific problems* 1987, Prentice Hall Inc.

[26] Bruderlin B. and Roller D., *Geometric constraint solving and applications* 1998, Springer Verlag.

[27] Bruderlin B., *Constructing three-dimensional geometric objects defined by constraints*, In Workshop on Interactive 3D Graphics 1986,111-129.

[28] Sohrt W., *Interaction with constraints in three-dimensional modeling*, Dept of Computer Science. The University of Utah, 1991, Master's Thesis.

[29] Bruderlin B., *Using geometric rewrite rules for solving geometric problems symbolically,* Theoretical Computer Science 1993, 116, 291-303.

[30] Aldefeld, B., *Variation of geometries based on a geometric-reasoning method,* Computer-Aided Design 1988, 20(3), 117-126.

[31] Suzuki H., Ando H. and Kimura F., *Variation of geometries based on a geometric-reasoning method,* Computers & Graphics 1990, 14(2), 211-224.

[32] Sunde G., *Specification of shape by dimensions' and other geometric constraints*, in Geometric modeling for CAD applications 1988, M. J. Wozny, H. W. McLaughlin, and J. L. Encarnacao, eds., North Holland, IFIP, 199-213.

[33] Yamaguchi Y. and Kimura F., *A constraint modeling system for variational geometry*, in Geometric Modeling for Product Engineering, M. J. Wozny, J.U. Turner and K. Preiss, eds., 1990, Elsevier Science Publishers B.V. (North Holland), 221-233.

[34] Verroust A., Schonek F. and Roller D., *Rule-oriented method for parameterized computer-aided design,* Computer Aided Design 1992, 24(10), 531-540.

[35] Joan-Arinyo R. and Soto A., *A rule-constructive geometric constraint solver*, Technical Report LSI-95-25-R, 1995, Universitat Politecnica de Catalunya.

[36] Fudos I. and Hoffmann C.M., *Correctness proof of a geometric constraint solver,* International Journal of Computational Geometry & Applications, 1996, 405-420

[37] Fitzgerald W.J., *Using axial dimensions to determine the proportions of line drawings in computer graphics,* Computer Aided Design 1981, 13(6), 377-382.

[38] Requicha, A., *Dimensionining and tolerancing*, Technical report PADL TM-19, Production Automation Project 1977, University of Rochester.

[39] Todd P., *A k-tree generalization that characterizes consistency of dimensioned engineering drawings,* SIAM J DISC MATH 1989, 2(2), 255-261.

[40] Owen J.C., *Algebraic solution for geometry from dimensional constraints,* ACM Symp. Found. of Solid Modeling 1991, Austin, TX.,397-407.

[41] D-Cubed, Ltd., 68 Castle Street, Cambridge, CB3 OAJ, England. The Dimensional Constraint Manager, June 1994, Version 2.7.

[42] Fudos I. and Hoffmann C.M., *A graph-constructive method to solving systems of geometric constraints,* ACM Transactions on Graphics 1997, 16(2), 179-216.

[43] Buchberger B., *Grobner Bases: An algorithmic method in polynomial ideal theory*, in Multidimensional Systems Theory, N.K. Bose, Editor, 1985, D. Reidel Publishing Company, 184-232.

[44] Wu W.T., *Basic principles of mechanical theorem proving in elementary geometries,* Journal of Automated Reasoning 1986, 2, 221-252.

[45] Hoffmann C.M., Lomonosov A., and Sitharam M., *Finding solvable subsets of constraint graphs*, L. G. Smolka, editor, 1997, Springer Verlag. 463-477.

[46] Fudos I., Kavousianos X., Markouzis D. and Tsiatouhas Y. - *Placement and Routing in Computer Aided Design of Standard Cell Arrays* - Computer Aided Design and Applications, vol. 5(1-4), pp 325-337

[47] Shah J.J. and Mantyla M., *Parametric and Feature-based CAD/CAM* 1995, John Wiley & Sons Inc.

[48] Thompson W.B., Owen J.C., James de St Germain H., Stark S.R. and Henderson T.C., *Feature-based reverse engineering of mechanical parts,* IEEE Transactions on Robotics and Automation 1999, 12(1), 57-66, .

[49] Lee J.Y. and Kim K., *A feature-based approach to extracting machining features,* Computer-Aided Design 1998, 30(13), 1019-1035.

[50] Stamati V. and Fudos I., *A parametric feature-based CAD system for reproducing traditional pierced jewellery,* Computer Aided Design 2005, 37(4), 431-449.

[51] Nyirenda P. J., Mulbagal M. and Bronsvoort W. F., *Definition of freeform surface feature classes,* Computer Aided Design & Applications 2006, 3(5), 665-674.

[52] Fontana M., Giannini F. and Meirana M., *A free form feature taxonomy*, In Proceedings of EUROGRAPHICS '99, 1999,107-118.

[53] Dobson G.T., Waggenspack Jr W.N. and Lamousin H.J., *Feature based models for anatomical data fitting,* Computer Aided Design 1995, 27(2), 139-146.

[54] Gumhold S., Wang X. and MacLeod R., *Feature extraction from point clouds*, Proceedings of the 10th International Meshing Roundtable, 2001.

[55] Hoffmann C.M. and Joan-Arinyo R., *On user-defined features,* Computer Aided Design 1998, 30(5), 321-332.

[56] PTC, *PRO/ENGINEER*, http://www.ptc.com.

[57] Autodesk, *AUTOCAD*, http://www.autodesk.com/autocad.

[58] IRONCAD, *IRONCAD*, http://www.ironcad.com.

[59] Dassault Systems, *CATIA*, http://www.3ds.com/products-solutions/plm-solutions/catia/ overview.

[60] Dassault Systems, *Solidworks*, http://www.3ds.com/products-solutions/ solidworks.

[61] Siemens - UGS PLM Software, *Solid Edge*, http://www.solidedge.com.

[62] Alibre Inc., *Alibre Design*, http://www.alibre.com.
[63] Autodesk, *3D Studio Max*, http://www.autodesk.com/3dsmax.
[64] Autodesk, *Maya*, http://www.autodesk.com/maya.
[65] Varady T., Martin R.R. and Cox J., *Reverse engineering of geometric models - an introduction,* Computer Aided Design 1997, 29(4), 253-330.
[66] Werghi N., Fisher R., Robertson C. and Ashbrook A., *Object reconstruction by incorporating geometric constraints in reverse engineering,* Computer Aided Design 1999, 31(6), 363-399.
[67] Au C.K. and Yuen M.M.F., *Feature-based reverse engineering of mannequin for garment design,* Computer-Aided Design 1999, 31(12), 751-759.
[68] Fisher R.B., *Applying knowledge to reverse engineering problems,* Computer Aided Design 2004, 36, 501-510.
[69] Cantzler, H., *Improving architectural 3D reconstruction by constrained modeling*, Institute of Perception, Action and Behaviour, School of Informatics, University of Edinburgh, 2003, PhD Thesis.
[70] Gao C.H., Langbein F.C., Marshall A.D. and Martin R.R., *Local topological beautification of reverse engineered models,* Computer-Aided Design 2004, 36(13), 1337-1355.
[71] Thompson W.B., James de St Germain H., Henderson T.C. and Owen J.C., *Constructing high-precision geometric models from sensed position data*, Proceedings of the 1996 ARPA Image Understanding Workshop, 1996,987-994.
[72] James de St. Germain H., Stark S.R., Thompson W.B. and Henderson T.C., *Constraint optimization and feature-based model construction for reverse engineering*, ARPA Image Understanding Workshop, 1997.
[73] Stamati V. and Fudos I., *A feature based approach to re-engineering objects of freeform design by exploiting point cloud morphology*. Proceedings of the 2007 ACM symposium on Solid and physical modeling 2007, Beijing China, 347-353
[74] Agathos A., Pratikakis I., Perantonis S., Sapidis N. and Azariadis P., *3D Mesh segmentation methodologies for CAD applications,* Computer-Aided Design and Applications, 2007, 4(6), 827-842.
[75] Cyberware, *Cyberware Rapid 3D Scanners - Desktop 3D Scanner Samples,* 1999, http://www.cyberware.com/products/ scanners/desktopSamples.html

In: Computer-Aided Design...
Editors: C.M. De Smet et al, pp. 109-138
ISBN 978-1-60456-860-8

Chapter 5

POWER MANAGEMENT AND POWER CONTROL IN WIRELESS NETWORKS*

***Rong Zheng*[†], *Jennifer C. Hou*[‡] *and Ning Li*[§]**
Department of Computer Science, University of Illinois
at Urbana-Champaign, Urbana, IL 61801

Abstract

With the proliferation of portable computing platforms and small wireless devices, wireless networks have received more and more attention as a means for providing data communications among devices regardless of their physical locations. However, due to the slow advancement in battery technology, battery power continues to be a constrained resource in wireless networks and thus energy conservation remains to be an important issue. In this book chapter, we provide a taxonomy of power management and power control algorithms and protocols for wireless networks.

We start with a description of energy consumption characteristics of wireless devices, and identify the power consumed in the wireless transmitters essentially consists of two parts: power consumed by the radio electronic and power consumed in the RF output. To save power, one can either turn off the radio electronic and put wireless devices into the power saving mode at appropriate times, or adjust the RF output power (and hence the wireless transmission range) subject to maintaining network connectivity and bi-directionality. The former techniques are termed as power management, while the latter power control. For each category, we then state the performance objectives, present representative, state-of-the-art algorithms and protocols in both wireless infrastructure and infrastructureless (a.k.a. ad hoc) networks, and discuss their advantages and drawbacks.

Key Words: Energy conservation, power management, power control, wireless networks.

*This work was supported by NSF under Grant No. CNS 0221357. Any opinions, findings, and conclusions or recommendations expressed in this chapter are those of the authors and do not necessarily reflect the views of the funding agency.

[†]E-mail address: zheng4li@cs.uiuc.edu
[‡]E-mail address: jhou@cs.uiuc.edu
[§]E-mail address: nli@cs.uiuc.edu

1. Introduction

With the proliferation of portable computing platforms and small wireless devices, wireless networks have received more and more attention as a means for providing data communications among devices regardless of their physical locations. Wireless networks have the advantage of allowing untethered communication. This in turn implies the reliance on portable power sources such as batteries. However, due to the slow advancement in battery technology, battery power continues to be a constrained resource and thus energy conservation remains to be an important issue. Even in cases when wireless devices possess self-power capability and can extract energy from the environment by, for example, converting solar power or mechanical vibration into electronic power [47], it is desirable to keep the energy-dissipation level below 100 microwatts in order to eliminate frequent battery replacement. In a typical scenario, it has been estimated that 3000 instructions could be executed for the same energy cost of sending a bit at the distance of 100 meters by radio. Therefore, it is important to reduce the energy consumption on the wireless interfaces of portable devices.

Most modern wireless devices can be put to different power states to conserve energy. The power consumption in the low-power state is, in general, an order of magnitude lower than that in the idle and active (transmitting or receiving) states. As a matter of fact, as indicted in several experimental results [14], the power consumed in the idle state is only slightly smaller than that in the active state. This is because a wireless device in the idle state has to continuously listen to the wireless medium for potential communication. Because of this observation, several techniques have been proposed to reduce the power consumption of wireless devices by selectively putting them into the low-power states. This is termed as power management. Alternatively, the energy incurred in transmission can also be reduced by using different transmission power levels and/or coding/modulation mechanisms. This is termed as power control. Ideally, power control explores a continuous control space and is more theoretically attractive. However, in reality wireless devices are only capable of changing power levels and/or coding/modulation in a discrete fashion.

It has been widely recognized that energy conservation trades off performance in standalone systems. One example is that users experience a significant delay to bring up a laptop from the hibernation mode. Similar observations can be made in applying power management and power control techniques in wireless systems. Many research endeavors explore the energy-performance design space to devise better energy-conservation protocols subject to several performance constraints. In particular, an intelligent energy conservation mechanism should leverage information from the various layers of the protocol stack. For example, QoS requirements of applications such as the delay bound can be used to guide power management/control decisions. Knowledge of communication patterns also helps to conserve energy without degrading performance.

This book chapter presents an overview of power management and power control techniques in wireless networks, with the emphasis on the energy conservation and performance tradeoff. In what follows, we first give a succinct overview of energy consumption characteristics of wireless devices and the commonly used energy model. We then focus on the protocol aspects of power management and power control techniques in wireless networks.

2. Energy Characteristics of Wireless Devices

Power consumption of wireless interfaces, in general, consists of two parts: power consumed by the radio electronics (such as the frequency synthesizers and mixers) and power consumed in the RF output. The overall power consumption is determined by the modulation scheme used, the data transmission rate, the transmit power level and the operation modes (e.g., transmit, receive, idle and sleep). Table 1 shows the power consumption of various wireless devices in different modes.

Shih *et al.* [53] have characterized the average power consumption of the radio in the active states as

$$P_{active} = N_{tx}[P_{tx}(T_{on-tx} + T_{st}) + P_{out}T_{on-tx}] + N_{rx}[P_{rx}(T_{on-rx} + T_{st})], \qquad (1)$$

where $N_{tx/rx}$ is the average rate (i.e., the average number of times per second) at which the transmitter/receiver is used, $P_{tx/rx}$ is the power consumed by the transmitter/receiver, P_{out} is the output transmit power, $T_{on-tx/rx}$ is the transit/receive on-time (i.e., the actual data transmission/reception time), and T_{st} is the start-up time of the transceiver. With the use of the free-space propagation model (which is appropriate for short-range communication), P_{out} can be approximated by $\epsilon_{amp} \cdot r \cdot d^2$, where $\epsilon_{amp} \propto (2^b - 1)(J/bit/m^2)$ is the energy consumed to deliver one symbol (corresponding to b bits) information over one unit distance with an acceptable SNR (under the assumption of Additive White Gaussian Noise channel), r is the data rate and d is the distance of the transmission. ϵ_{amp} is affected by the modulation scheme chosen. For example, multi-level modulation such as M-PSK/M-QAM can achieve higher bandwidth efficiency and hence $T_{on-rx/tx}$ can be reduced at the cost of increased P_{tx} and P_{out}. As an example, for short range transmission at the GHz carrier frequency, the energy consumption of a communication subsystem is dominated by the radio electronics, which is of the order of 10-100mW. The output transmit power, on the other hand, is only about 0dBm (1mW) for bit error rate (BER) as low as 10^{-5} at 1Mbps. Moreover, the power consumed for receiving packets can be greater than the power consumed for transmitting packets for short transmission distances, since more circuitry is required to receive/decode signals. Lastly, the start-up overhead associated with switching from the sleep mode to the active mode is not negligible in both latency interval and energy dissipation. A typical start-up time is of the order of $100\mu s$. This implies that the control granularity of switching between modes should not be too small.

To account for the energy consumption in the idle state and low power state, Eq. (1) is modified to

$$P_{radio} = P_{active} + T_{idle}P_{idle} + T_{sleep}P_{sleep}, \qquad (2)$$

where T_{idle} and T_{sleep} are the percentage of time in the idle and low-power states. P_{idle} and P_{sleep} are, respectively, the power consumed in the idle and sleep states. Typically $P_{sleep} << P_{rx}$. By Eq. (2), we conclude that to reduce power consumption of the communication subsystems, one can reduce either the communication-time power consumption P_{active} or the idle-time power consumption by reducing the idle period T_{idle}.

Table 1. Transmit, Receive and Sleep Mode Power Consumption of Different Wireless Devices

Device	Transmit	Receive	Idle	Sleep
Cisco Aironet	1.48W	1.0W	830mW	75mW
ORiNOCO 11b	1.43W	925mW	925mW	45mW
Mica mote	36mW	13.5mW	13.5mW	$< 1\mu A$

3. Power Management

3.1. Overview

A power management policy in wireless networks has to make the following decisions:

- Which set of nodes should perform power management,
- When a power-managed node switches to the low-power state, and
- When a node in the low-power state switches to the active state.

The first decision is contingent upon the power sources of, and the role of, the devices. For example, in wireless local area networks (WLANs), access points (APs) are in general fixed and wall-powered. As a result, there is very little incentive to perform power management on APs.

The second decision is controlled by power management policies. The most common policy is *a timeout policy* [12, 27, 72], i.e., a device switches to the low power state if it becomes idle for a pre-determined period of time. Another group of policies [41, 46, 54] base their decision on certain assumptions of the stochastic properties of communication events and formulate power management as a constrained optimization problem.

The mechanism that determines when a node switches from the low-power state to the active state is termed as the *wake-up mechanism*. The decision can either be local, i.e., a power-saving wireless device brings up its wireless interface on its own, or in response to requests by other devices through certain signaling methods. There are mainly three types of wake-up mechanisms, i.e. event-driven wake-up, scheduled rendezvous, and asynchronous wake-up. In event-driven wake-up mechanisms[53], a power-saving wireless device is waken up by internal or external events, for example, a local application needs to access wireless I/O, a wireless wake-up signal is received from other nodes, or certain sound with matched signatures is detected by the acoustic sensing module. In scheduled rendezvous approaches [21], low-power sleeping nodes wake up periodically at the same time to communicate with one another. This requires network-wide time synchronization. The third category is asynchronous wake-up [60, 71] in which wireless devices follow carefully devised time schedules to wake up from low-power states. The schedules do not have to be synchronized but must ensure sufficient overlap periods to allow message exchanges.

Next we discuss several power management protocols in both infrastructured wireless networks and infrastructureless networks and illustrate how the three decisions are made in each protocol.

3.2. Power Management with Infrastructure Support

In this section, we discuss power management schemes that operate in infrastructured networks (such as wireless LANs with APs or cellular networks). In this type of networks, there exists a central entity that serves as a gateway to access the global network. Gateways service multiple wireless devices at the same time and are in general wall-powered. In contrast, wireless devices are mostly battery powered. This creates an asymmetry in the up-link (wireless devices to gateways) and down-link (gateways to wireless devices) communication. In particular, data transmission from wireless devices to a gateway does not usually incur delay for waking up the corresponding gateway. The reverse is, however, not true if a wireless device is in the power saving mode.

We consider up-link and down-link power management separately. However, it should be noted that power management states at a wireless device is a combined result of both up-link and down-link power management, with the following precedence constraints: active (transmission or receiving) > sleep > power-off. If the up-link power management policy decides that a wireless device should enter the low-power state while the down-link policy requires it to be active, the wireless device should remain active.

3.2.1. Up-link Power Management

Up-link communication originates at wireless devices, and is usually initiated by local processes that access the network I/O of a wireless device. As the wireless device has full knowledge of the timing of network I/O activities, power management decisions can be made purely based on the host information. A power-saving device can switch to the active state whenever an wireless network I/O is accessed.

Most research efforts address the problem of when to put the devices to the low-power states and which low-power state the devices should be put into. There are two major challenges: (1) future wireless network I/O activities are in general not known a priori, and (2) as changing power states incurs extra delay and energy, the benefit of changing power states may not fully compensate for the extra delay and energy thus incurred. Consider a device whose state transition delay is T_o (including shutdown and wake-up delays) and the transition energy is E_o. Suppose its power in the active and low-power states are P_a and P_s respectively. There exists a minimum idle period, called the *break-even time* (T_{be}), for which the energy incurred in leaving the device in the active state and the energy consumed in switching the device to the low-power state are equal. Specifically, $P_a \times T_{be} = E_o + P_s \times (T_{be} - T_o)$ or $T_{be} = (E_o - P_s \times T_o)/(P_a - P_s)$[36].

Time-out Policy A time-out policy specifies a time-out value τ. If the device is idle for τ, it is put to the low-power state. Time-out policies with the use of fixed time-out values have been widely used in many commercial products[29, 19, 12, 28]. It can be readily proved that if a policy using $\tau = T_{be}$ consumes at most twice the energy of an ideal "oracle" policy that has perfect information of future I/O requests. The value of T_{be} is a device dependent quantity. One major drawback of time-out policies is the energy wasted during the time-out period if the time-out value is not fine-tuned. The time-out value can be dynamically adjusted by measuring the ratio of τ and the previous idle period. If the ratio is relatively small, the policy increases τ; otherwise, it decreases τ.

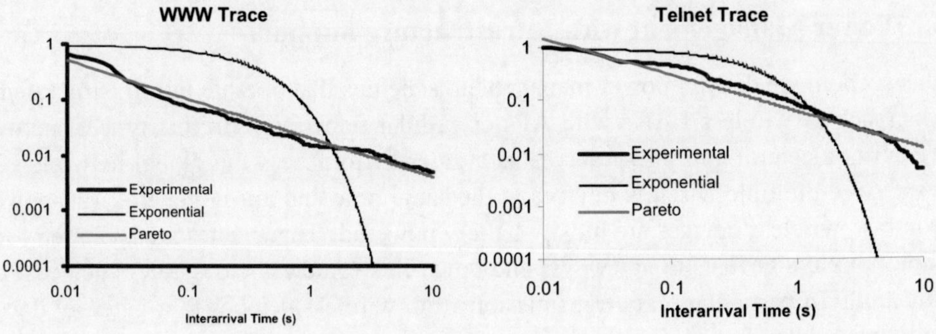

Figure 1. Requests for wireless communication are best modeled by a Pareto distribution in WLANs.

Stochastic Policy Stochastic policies model request arrivals and device power-state changes as a stochastic process. The problem of minimizing the power consumption thus becomes a stochastic optimization problem. Several stochastic models have been proposed for requests and power state transitions, including discrete-time Markov (DM) processes[41], continuous-time Markov models[46], continuous-time semi-Markov models[61] and non-stationary processes[9]. In particular, it has been observed in [54] that requests for wireless communication are best modeled by a Pareto distribution (Fig. 1). A time-index semi-Markov (SM) model is then proposed to model the request process. The power management policies based on the stochastic models target to minimize the performance penalty (usually in the form of delay) under the energy consumption constraint, and can be formulated as a linear programming problem. The interested reader is referred to [36] for a detailed survey of stochastic power management policy.

3.2.2. Down-link Power Management

To communicate with a wireless device, a gateway has to wait for the device to enter the active states; otherwise, it buffer the packets temporarily. In addition, certain mechanisms have to be employed to wake up the power-saving receiver. In an infrastructured network, power state transition at a wireless device is orchestrated by the gateway and carried out by the wireless device.

IEEE 802.11 Power Saving Mode in Infrastructured Networks IEEE 802.11 MAC [21] is one of the most widely used medium access protocols in wireless LANs. In addition to specifying services that support data delivery between stations, LAN access control and confidentiality, IEEE 802.11 also specifies the function to perform power management in both the infrastructured network (also called BSS) and independent basic service set (IBSS, a.k.a ad hoc mode).

In IEEE 802.11 PSM, a node can be in one of the two power modes: the active mode when it can receive and transmit frames at any time and the power-save mode (PS) when it is mainly in the sleep state. Transition from the PS mode to the active mode is subject to the rules described next. In an infrastructured network, a wireless device informs the AP of

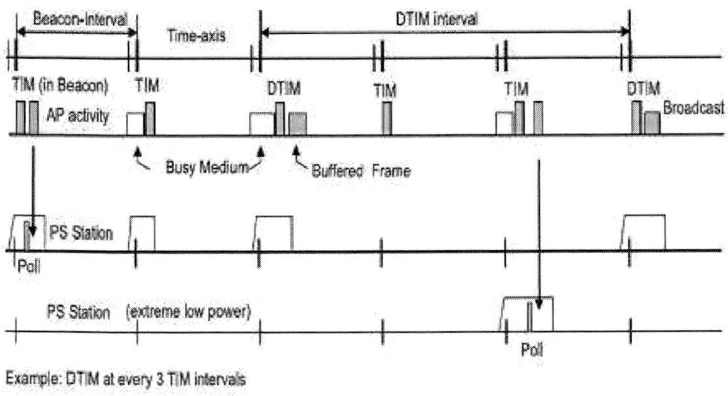

Figure 2. Basic Operation of IEEE 802.11 PSM in BSS.

the change of its power management modes by setting the corresponding control bit in the MAC header. The AP buffers packets to a wireless device in the power saving mode and only transmits them at designated times. Beacon messages are transmitted periodically in every beacon interval by the AP carrying a *traffic indication map* (TIM) of wireless stations for which it has buffered messages. In BSS, each wireless station has an associated id (AID) with the AP when it first joins the network. TIM contains a bit map of AIDs.

Upon determining (from the TIM in the beacon messages) that a packet destined for a wireless device is currently buffered at the AP, the device operating in the PS mode sends a PS-Poll frame to the AP, which responds with the buffered packets immediately or acknowledges the PS-Poll and responds with the corresponding packet at a later time. The *More Data* field in the MAC header of a packet indicates the presence of more buffered packets. If any device in its BSS is in the power saving mode, the AP buffers all broadcast and multicast packets and delivers them to all the devices immediately following the next beacon frame containing a delivery TIM (DTIM) transmission. An AP can use an aging function to delete pending packets that have been buffered for an excessive period of time.

The operations of IEEE 802.11 PSM with the AP support are illustrated in Fig. 2. The top line represents the time axis, with the beacon interval shown together with a DTIM interval (for announcing broadcast/multicast transmissions) of three beacon intervals. The second line shows the AP activities. The third and fourth lines depict the activities of two devices operating in different modes. Both devices power-on their receivers whenever they need to listen for a TIM. The first device, for example, powers up its receivers and receives a TIM in the first beacon which indicates a buffered packet destined for it. The device then generates a PS-Poll frame, which elicits transmission of the buffered packet from the AP. When an AP is informed that the device changes to the active mode, it sends the buffered packet to it without waiting for PS-Poll.

IEEE 802.11 PSM with AP supports provides a minimalist support for power-saving wireless devices to receive packets. However, it leaves out most of the decisions for the wireless devices to determine whether it should perform power management and if so, when it should solicit buffered packets from the AP. To a power-saving device, such decisions would have an impact on its energy consumption as well as the delay and packet delivery performance.

3.2.3. Power Management for Interactive Applications

Waking up power-saving wireless devices incur extra delays, which may not be desirable for interactive applications, such as web browsing, multimedia applications and distributed file systems. End-to-end delay for these applications directly affects the user perspective of the system performance. The wake-up latency could be of the order of 100 ms (the same order as the beacon interval length in IEEE 802.11 PSM), and is comparable to or larger than the round trip time of connections between most continental American sites on the Internet. Therefore, power management decisions should take into account of application specifics and exploit the knowledge of I/O access patterns of applications.

Kravets *et al.* [27] investigate the energy and delay impact of a power-aware transport protocol. In ideal circumstances, applications inform the protocol of when the network interface should be turned off. When such information is not available, a pre-determined timeout period is used. The empirical studies indicate that a sleep interval of 500ms achieves the most energy savings and reduces energy for Web browsing by 30-80% as compared to no power management. The performance gain is, however, achieved at the cost of increasing the delay by 300-700ms. The authors also present an adaptive implementation of their algorithm in which the sleep interval is set to 250ms in the presence of network activities, and exponentially backs off up to 5 minutes in the lack of activities.

Krashinsky *et al.* [26] discover that the fixed beacon interval structure in IEEE 802.11 PSM can be wasteful in energy while incurring significant delay. Specifically, let b be the length of a beacon interval. If a station listens for TIM every beacon interval, the wake-up delay is of the order of b (as a packet that arrives right after the beacon message has to be buffered until the next beacon interval). Let the round trip time to the remote server be rtt. Then a slow-down of at least $\frac{rtt+b}{rtt}$ is incurred due to power management. Since web traffic usually consists of short-lived TCP connections, the in-bound traffic is not heavy enough to keep the wireless interface active throughout a beacon interval in the power-saving mode. The authors propose a bounded slow-down (BSD) scheme that probes the round trip time between the request and the response progressively. Upon transmission of a request, the node remains on for t_s time, where t_s is set to b/p initially, and $p+1$ is the slow-down ratio. If there is no response by the end of the active period, it implies $rtt > b/p$ and a wireless device can sleep for a beacon interval. If the device received no response upon waking up, t_s increases exponentially. The solution explores the dependency in two-way traffic but is only applicable to out-bound requests initiated by the wireless device.

Anand *et al.* [2] demonstrate that IEEE 802.11 PSM is not well-suited for latency-sensitive applications. They propose a self-tuning power management (STPM) that adapts its behavior to the patterns and intent of applications, the characteristics of the network interface, and the energy usage of the platform. STPM is implemented as a Linux kernel module. It takes (i) the hints of network usage from applications and (ii) power characteristics of the network interface, and determines the most economical (measured by a weighted function of energy cost and performance) power mode to use. STPM is shown to achieve better energy-efficiency for a wide range of network access patterns. It requires modification of applications to provide hints to the power management module.

3.3. Power Management without Infrastructure Support

In infrastructureless networks, communication peers assume similar roles in performing power management. From the perspective of a wireless device, transmissions to or from a neighbor are subject to power states of its peer or itself. Essentially, power management is a distributed coordination problem. Distributed power management decisions can be made at different time granularity and can leverage information from different layers of the network protocol stack.

3.3.1. Packet Level Approaches

Packet-level approaches make power management decisions on a per-packet basis. The PAMAS power-saving medium access protocol [56] turns a node's radio off when it overhears a packet that is not addressed to it. This can be done by decoding the MAC headers of request-to-send/clear to send (RTS/CTS) or data packets. PAMAS is well-suited for radios in which processing a received packet is expensive as compared to listening to an idle medium. In the case of an idle medium, a node must remain on all the time for incoming transmission. Therefore, the effectiveness of PAMAS is limited to reducing the power consumed in processing unnecessary packets.

Another disadvantage of packet-level power management schemes is that the start-up time and the extra energy incurred in bringing a wireless device from the low-power state to the active state are usually non-negligible. Therefore, in designing such power management schemes, one has to ensure that the extra wake-up energy cost thus incurred can be compensated by the power saving that results from putting nodes to the sleep state, i.e., the packet transmission time is larger than the *break-even time* (Section 3.2.).

3.3.2. MAC Layer Approaches

In the MAC layer, power management decisions are made based on single-hop information.

IEEE 802.11 PSM in Ad Hoc Mode and Its Improvements In the ad hoc mode, all power-saving nodes in the network are synchronized to wake up periodically to listen to beacon messages. Broadcast/multicast messages or unicast messages to a power-saving node are first buffered at the transmitter and announced via an ad hoc traffic indication message (ATIM) inside a small ATIM window at the beginning of the beacon interval. All nodes are required to be active during the ATIM window. If a node receives a directed ATIM frame in the ATIM window (i.e., it is the designated receiver of a unicast message), it sends an acknowledgment and stays awake for the entire beacon interval waiting for data packets to be transmitted. Immediately after the ATIM window, a node can transmit buffered broadcast/multicast and unicast data frames addressed to nodes that are known to be active (e.g., by reception of acknowledgments to ATIM frames). Otherwise, the node switches to the sleep state to conserve energy. The behavior of IEEE 802.11 PSM is illustrated in Fig. 3. Compared with IEEE 802.11 PSM in BSS, exchanges of ATIM/ACKs establishes a

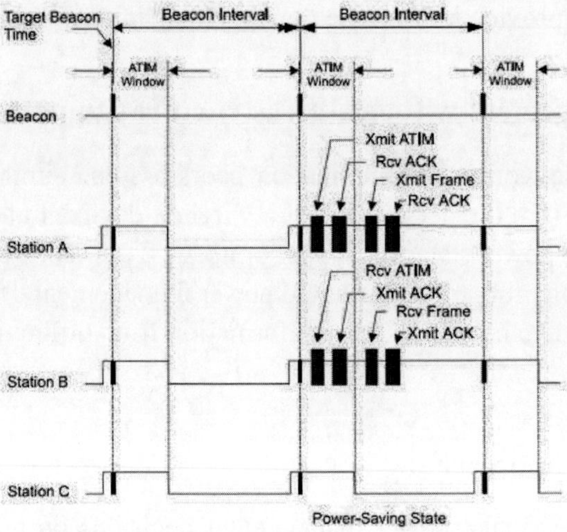

Figure 3. Basic Operations of IEEE 802.11 PSM in IBSS.

temporary "contract" between a pair of nodes to remain active for the entire beacon interval. There are several deficiencies in the design of IEEE 802.11 PSM:

- **Periodic power management decision points**. Under low to medium traffic load, nodes spend a significant amount of time in the idle state as IEEE 802.11 PSM mandates a node to stay active for the entire beacon interval. This leads to energy waste as power consumption in the idle state is usually comparable to that incurred in the transmitting and receiving states.

- **Signaling overhead to wake up power-saving nodes**. First, in IEEE 802.11 PSM an ATIM window is set aside in each beacon interval to announce the presence of pending packets. No data packets can be transmitted inside the ATIM window. Second, ATIM frame-ACK hand-shake is limited to a pair of sender and receiver, i.e., it establishes a *link* state. However, power management is a *nodal* state. In the worst case in which there exist n nodes in a single hop network each of which has a packet to transmit to every other node, the total number of ATIM frames to be transmitted are $O(n^2)$. As n goes larger, ATIM frames may collide with one another.

- **Clock synchronization**. IEEE 802.11 PSM requires nodes to be synchronized to exchange ATIM/ACK messages. It is not well-suited in multi-hop ad hoc networks, as distributed clock synchronization is a non-trivial issue [13]. In particular, IEEE 802.11 PSM does not work well in the presence of network dynamics. For example, two partitioned sub-networks may have non-overlapping ATIM windows. As a result, even when they are geographically adjacent to each other, the time for neighbor discovery is unbounded.

Several research efforts have been made to address these problems. Jung *et al.* [24] propose a scheme that adjusts the ATIM window size dynamically to accommodate varying traffic load in wireless LANs. The number of pending packets destined for a receiver is piggy-backed in data packets. If this number is zero, the receiver can go to sleep; otherwise, if there are still packets pending at the end of a beacon interval, both the sender and the receiver stay up in the next beacon interval. The major difficulty in realizing such a scheme is that it is non-trivial to adjust the size of an ATIM window individually and maintain consistent information among neighboring nodes. Also, switching to the low-power state as soon as there is no buffered packet destined for a receiver without consideration of future arrivals can potentially lead to significant packet losses and higher delay.

When IEEE 802.11 PSM is applied to multihop wireless networks, the wake-up delay is incurred at each hop. Hu and Hou [20] propose a traffic prediction mechanism, called *LISP*, that improves the performance of IEEE 802.11 PSM in multi-hop networks. Conceptually, nodes seek the correlation between ATIM-ACKs and incoming traffic and stay awake in beacon intervals in which packets are anticipated to arrive *from upstream*, thus reducing the end-to-end delay in multihop communication. Specifically, there are two phases in the traffic prediction process: learning and prediction. In the learning phase, a node makes a conjecture and attempts to confirm it. If in the ATIM window of a beacon interval, a node A overhears from its neighbor node B an ATIM_ACK packet addressed for some other node, node A conjectures itself to be the next hop node. If in the next beacon interval, node A indeed receives an ATIM packet from node B, it confirms the conjecture and enters the prediction phase. Otherwise, node A resets its state and starts all over again. In the prediction phase, node A predicts that node B will forward one or more packets to itself and will stay awake through the current beacon interval. Meanwhile, node A transmits a pseudo-ACK packet announcing this fact. All of node A's neighbors that receive this pseudo-ACK packet will take it as if it were a ATIM_ACK packet and run the same traffic prediction process accordingly. Via simulation, the authors show that LISP achieves a performance improvement of 65%–75% over IEEE 802.11 PSM with respect to the end-to-end delay, and 6% and 178% over IEEE 802.11 with and without PSM with respect to energy efficiency.

To relax the synchronization requirement in IEEE 802.11 PSM, Tseng *et al.* [60] consider the use of asynchronous wake-up schedules. In asynchronous wake-up mechanisms, each node follows its own pre-determined schedule with interleaved active and sleep intervals. To allow communication among neighboring nodes, their schedules should have common overlapping active period. Three asynchronous wake-up schemes are considered in [60]: dominating-awake-interval, periodically-fully-awake-interval and quorum-based. In all the schemes, the wake-up pattern is repeated every T interval. In the dominating-awake-interval scheme (Fig. 4(a)), each node wakes up for more than half of the time, thus guaranteeing wake-up overlap between any two nodes. The duty cycle (defined as the percentage of time a node is active) is, however, more than 50% in this case. In the periodically-fully-awake-interval scheme (Fig. 4(b)), a node's wake-up pattern interleaves between the low-power intervals and the fully-awake intervals. In a low power interval, a node only wakes up in a small, active window at the beginning of each frame, while in a fully-awake interval, the length of the active window is extended to the entire frame. In the quorum-based scheme (Fig. 4(c)), the wake-up interval is determined using a quorum structure. A node arbitrarily picks one column and one row of entries in the $n \times n$ array to stay awake, and the duty cycle k of a node is $(2n-1)/n^2$.

Zheng *et al.* [71] formalize the conditions that asynchronous wake-up schedules need to satisfy in order to ensure common overlapping active periods. They formulate the problem

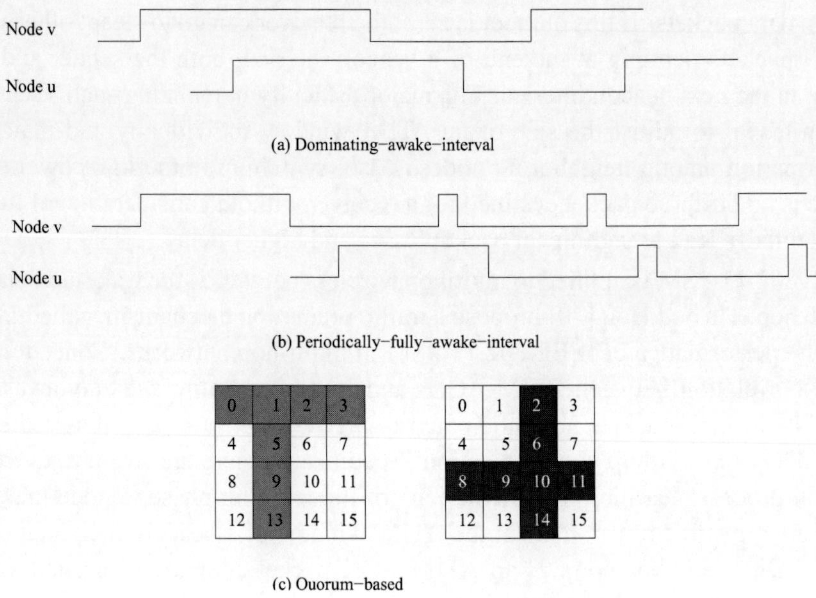

Figure 4. The schedules generated by the dominating-awake-interval, periodically-fully-awake-interval and quorum-based asynchronous wakeup schemes. The shaded blocks in (c) correspond to active slots.

of designing asynchronous wake-up schedules as an optimization problem and derive the lower bound on the duty cycle for schedules of length T. The low bound can be achieved asymptotically using difference set [3]. An example is given in Fig. 5. It should be noted that asynchronous wake-up schedule is not limited to IEEE 802.11 PSM like power management schemes.

Energy-efficient MAC Protocols in Sensor Networks Wireless sensor networks (WSNs) can be considered as a special case of multi-hop wireless networks. As compared to general multi-hop wireless networks, sensor networks possess the following unique characteristics:

1. *Data-centric*: Sensor networks are largely data-centric, with the objective of delivering data (collected by sensors), in a timely fashion, to destinations that require such data. Data that contains information of different qualities represents different values to destinations. As a result, the overall system objective is no longer to maximize the raw data throughput, but to maximize the amount of useful information carried to destinations.

2. *Application-oriented*: While traditional wired and wireless networks are expected to cater to a variety of applications, sensor networks are usually deployed to perform specific tasks. The specific algorithms/protocols and performance metrics used in sensor networks thus depend on the characteristics and requirements of applications. For instance, for mission-critical applications, it is very important to ensure that the end-to-end latency be kept below certain threshold.

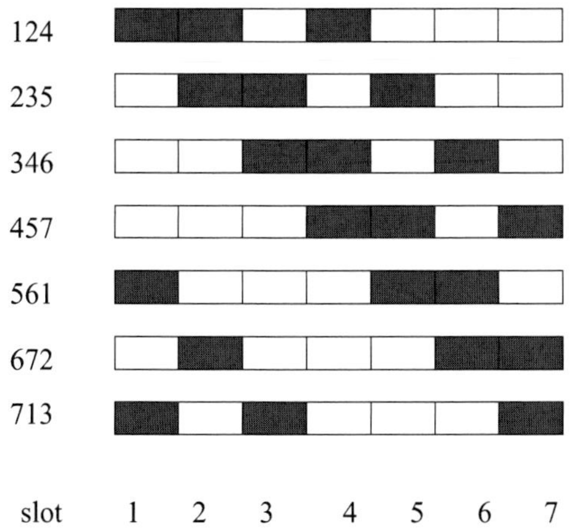

Figure 5. The optimal asynchronous wakeup schedule with $T = 7$. A node is active in solid slots. Any two schedules share a common active slot. The shaded blocks correspond to active slots, while the white blocks to power-saving slots.

3. *Collaborative*: Because of the application-oriented nature of sensor networks, how nodes collaborates with each other to realize the global system objective outweigh the objective of achieving fairness of individual connections. This is in sharp contrast to conventional wired and wireless networks in which provisioning of fairness to users is an important design criterion.

Schurger *et al.* [52] propose a protocol, called *Sparse Topology and Energy Management (STEM)*, in WSNs. STEM uses asynchronous beacon packets in a second control channel to wake up intended receivers. After the transmission has ended (e.g., after a timeout), the node turns its radio off in the data channel. Sleeping nodes with packets destined for them are awakened on demand, but decisions about when a node should go back to sleep are based on the local information. STEM does not provide mechanisms for indicating the power management state of a node. Instead, the power management state is only maintained on a per-link basis between nodes with active communication. Therefore, it is possible that an initiator node will incur a delay from waking up a receiver node, even if the receiver is already awake due to recent communication with a third node.

In S-MAC (Sensor-MAC) [69], a message passing mechanism is used to modify the network allocation vector (NAV) for virtual channel reservation in MAC protocols of the IEEE 802.11 type. The length of a NAV is determined by the duration of a burst of messages. The virtual reservation serves for two purposes: (1) it mandates the receiver to remain on throughout the transmission of the burst, and (2) it prevents other nodes from transmitting during this interval. Though message passing may be desirable for some of the applications in sensor networks, it can be rather inefficient for more generic ad hoc networks. Additionally, the reservations may cause some nodes to be starved.

3.3.3. Network Level Approaches

In the network layer, power management can take advantage of topological information. Approaches based on the notion of connected dominating sets [68, 8] use neighborhood or topology information to determine the set of nodes that form a connected dominating set (CDS) for the network, where a node is either a member of the CDS or a direct neighbor of at least one of the members. Nodes in the CDS serve as the "routing backbone" and remain active all the time to maintain global connectivity. All the other nodes can choose to sleep if necessary.

In the geographical adaptive fidelity (GAF) framework [68], each node is associated with a "virtual grid." The location information needed to identify which virtual grid a node belongs to is provided by GPS or other equivalent localization systems. All the nodes in the same grid are considered equivalent in forwarding packets, and coordinate with each other to determine who can sleep and for how long. The election mechanism ensures the presence of at least one active node in each grid.

Span [8] is a distributed and randomized protocol in which nodes make local decisions on whether they should sleep or join a forwarding backbone. Nodes that choose to stay awake and maintain network connectivity/capacity are called *coordinators*. A non-coordinator node elects itself as a coordinator if any two of its neighbors cannot communicate with each other directly or indirectly through one or two existing coordinators. The information needed for coordinator election is exchanged among neighbors via HELLO messages. The coordinator announcement is broadcast locally, deferred by an interval that reflects the residual power of a node.

3.3.4. Cross-layer Approaches

Zheng and Kravets [72] propose an on-demand power management framework for multi-hop wireless networks. In this framework, power management decisions are driven by data transmission in the network. Only nodes on the communication path along which a connection is routed are kept active while all the other nodes can switch to the power-save mode. Specifically, on-demand power management exploits the knowledge about route setup in on-demand routing protocols such as DSR [22] and AODV [42], and instruments transitions from the power-save mode to the active mode accordingly. For example, when a node receives a *route discovery* or *route reply* message (used in on-demand routing protocols), it takes the message as an indication that likely data packets will subsequently follow. The node then sets a soft state timer, called the *keep-awake timer*, and remains awake. The time-out value of the keep-awake timer depends on the type of messages the node receives. Upon expiration of the keep-alive timer, a node switches from the active mode to the power-save mode. On-demand power management can be implemented on top of IEEE 802.11 PSM (or other asynchronous wakeup mechanisms) as a high level mechanism to determine which nodes should perform power management. The station transition diagram is shown in Fig. 6.

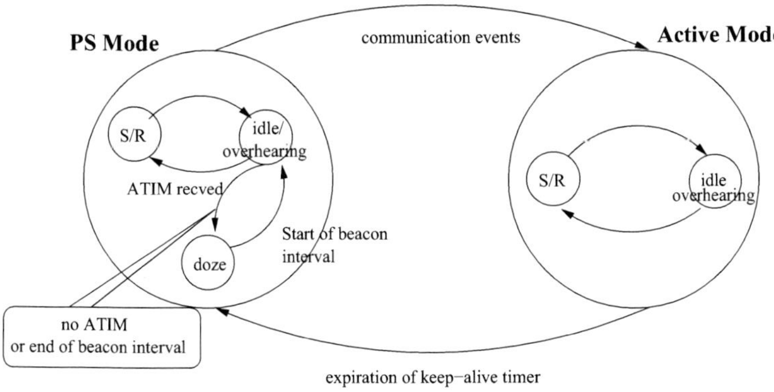

Figure 6. State transition diagram for power management modes enhanced with IEEE 802.11 physical states.

4. Control of Transmission Power

4.1. Overview

As discussed in Section 2., power consumed by wireless transmitters consists of two parts: power consumed by the radio electronic and power consumed in the RF output. In Section 3., we have discussed how to reduce the power consumed by the radio electronic by putting wireless devices in the low power state whenever desirable. In this section, we discuss how to save power from the other direction — use of different coding schemes and/or adjustment of the RF output power (and hence the transmission range) to reduce the power incurred in transmission. We will also discuss energy-efficient broadcasting that can be laid on top of the power control mechanisms.

4.2. Use of Channel Coding to Reduce Transmission Power

The energy required to transmit a packet can be reduced by lowering the transmission power and transmitting the packet over a longer period of time. However, it is not desirable to make the transmission times arbitrarily long. Choosing the most energy-efficient coding scheme while satisfying the delay requirement thus becomes a constrained optimization problem.

Prabhakar *et al.* [44] propose a lazy scheduling mechanism for energy-efficient transmission over a wireless link. Let $w(\tau)$ denote the energy required to transmit one packet over a duration τ. It is assumed that $w(\tau)$ is a non-negative, strictly decreasing convex function with respect to τ. This assumption holds for the Additive White Gaussian noise (AWGN) channel using optimal channel coding. The Shannon channel capacity is given by $C = \frac{1}{2}log_2(1 + \frac{P}{N})$, where P and N are the average signal and noise power level. For any given $0 < \alpha < 1$, information can be reliably transmitted at the rate $R = \alpha C$. Let $s = 1/R$ and hence the energy per bit $\epsilon = sP = sN(2^{\frac{2}{\alpha s}} - 1)$. Consequently, $w(\tau) = \epsilon B$ (B is the size of the packet). The authors argue that ϵ is a monotonically decreasing convex function for a typical range of s. Under this assumption, an energy efficient schedule should allow each packet to be transmitted over a time interval that is as long as possible.

However, if all packets need to be transmitted in T units of time, a head-of-line blocking in the transmission queue will violate the delay constraint. This problem is relatively simple if the arrival time of packets are known and an optimal offline solution can be derived. When future arrivals are not known a priori, an online scheduling algorithm proceeds as follows. The transmission time of a packet that starts being transmitted at time $t < T$ when there is a backlog of b packets is set to the expected value of a random variable

$$\tau(b,t) = max_{k\in\{1,\ldots,M\}}\frac{1}{k+b}\sum_{i=1}^{k} D_i, \tag{3}$$

where b is the current backlog and D_i's are the inter-arrival times of the M packets that will arrive in (t,T) (M is a random variable). D_i's need to estimated online.

Yu *et al.* [70] extend the above work in two aspects. First, the case that $w(\tau)$ is a non-monotonic decreasing function is considered. Second, the authors apply the design strategy to data gathering applications in wireless sensor networks. Compared to transmission over a wireless link, the delay constraint is an end-to-end constraint. The problem can thus be formulated as follows: Given a data aggregation tree T consisting of n sensor nodes, energy function $w_i(\tau)$ for each link and latency constraint, Γ, find a schedule of packet transmission, so as to minimize

$$f(\tau) = \sum_{i=1}^{n} w_i(\tau_i) \tag{4}$$

such that for every p_i in T, $L_i = \sum_{j:V_j\in p_j}\tau_j \leq \Gamma$, where p_i is a path from a sensor node which gathers data to the sink.

The authors devise several offline algorithms and a distributed online approximation algorithm. The optimal packet transmission problem is a convex problem with linear constraints and can be solved by extending the MoveRight algorithm in [15]. If the packet transmission time τ only takes discrete values, an offline algorithm based on dynamic programming is proposed. To account for the effects of MAC layer contention, the dynamic programming algorithm is modified with the assumption that only children of a sensor node interfere with each other on the data aggregation tree. Lastly, in the online approximation, a sensor node i keeps the following information: i) a flag r if the node has the highest positive energy gradient in subtree T_i rooted at i; ii) τ_i the time cost for transmitting to its parent and iii) τ_d the cumulative time cost for data gathering till i (excluding τ_i). A sink node periodically disseminates a feedback packet to its children with its local value τ_d and the difference between Γ and τ_d, denoted as δ. For ease of presentation, let τ_d' denote the field τ_d in the feedback packet. If $\delta < 0$, node i decreases its transmission time by β (a user-specified value) and sends the feedback packet to all its children. If $r = 1$ and $\delta \leq \epsilon$ (i.e., the node itself has the largest gradient and there is some slack in the transmission time), the transmission time is increased by ϵ and the feedback packet is suppressed. Otherwise, the feedback packet is updated by setting $\delta = \delta + (\tau_d' - \tau_i - \tau_d)$ and $\tau_d' = \tau_d$ and then forwarded to all children. This process guarantees that in each round, at most one node increases its transmission time per path. Under fixed traffic load, the distributed algorithm terminates.

4.3. Topology Control

Adjustment of the RF output power (and hence the wireless transmission range) is another approach to reducing the power incurred in transmission. Once the wireless transmission range is determined, the neighbor relation of each node (and hence the topology) is also determined. Hence this approach is usually termed as *topology control*. In addition to saving power, topology control can also alleviate MAC layer contention, increase spatial reuse (i.e., the number of concurrent transmissions), and improve the network capacity [17, 18]. However, the decision on the wireless transmission range a node has to be coordinated among nodes. If the range is not properly determined, nodes that are originally reachable from each other may no longer be able to communicate and the network may be partitioned. That is, topology control should be performed with the objective of determining the minimal possible transmission power while maintaining the network connectivity.

Another issue to be addressed is to maintain bi-directional links when topology control is used in conjunction with MAC protocols that require bi-directional message exchanges. One example is IEEE 802.11 MAC with the RTS/CTS floor acquisition mechanism. In the RTS/CTS mechanism, the wireless medium is reserved by exchanging RTS/CTS packets. A node A that intends to send data packets broadcasts an RTS packet. Upon receipt of the RTS packet, the intended receiver B sends a CTS packet if it is not silenced by other on-going communication activities. Upon receipt of the CTS packet, the sender node A then proceed with its data transmission. Upon overhearing the duration field in the RTS/CTS packets, a node sets up a network allocation vector (NAV) and does not contend for channel use during the transmission of data packets. If unidirectional links are created in the process of topology control, the RTS/CTS mechanism may not operate correctly, as depicted in Fig. 7(a). Existence of uni-directional links may render a higher probability of collision. An example is given in Fig. 7 (b) where node B attempts to reserve the wireless medium with a CTS packet that cannot reach node C (because of node B's use of a smaller transmission power). As a result, node C does not hear node B's CTS packet and commence its transmission that will collide with the transmission from node A to node B [43].

There are several solutions to the above problem. Gomez *et al.* [16] propose that control packets such as RTS/CTS are transmitted with the (common) maximum transmission power, while data packets can be transmitted with a smaller power. This preserves the channel reservation mechanism in IEEE 802.11 but at the expense of sacrificing the gain in spatial reusablility. Jung *et al.* [23] find that using a smaller transmission power for data messages reduces the carrier sensing range and thus increases packet collision. They propose to increase the transmission power periodically during the transmission of a data packet. This may be difficult to be implemented using the off-the-shelf hardware.

Several topology control algorithms that aim to determine the minimum wireless transmission power while maintaining the network connectivity and link bi-directionality [49, 48, 63, 38, 4, 34, 33, 25] have been proposed in the literature. In what follows, we summarize a set of representative algorithms.

Common Power (COMPOW) topology control Narayanaswamy *et al.* [39] develop a topology control protocol, called *COMPOW*, that requires that all the nodes use a common minimum transmission power [39]. The authors argue that if each node uses the smallest

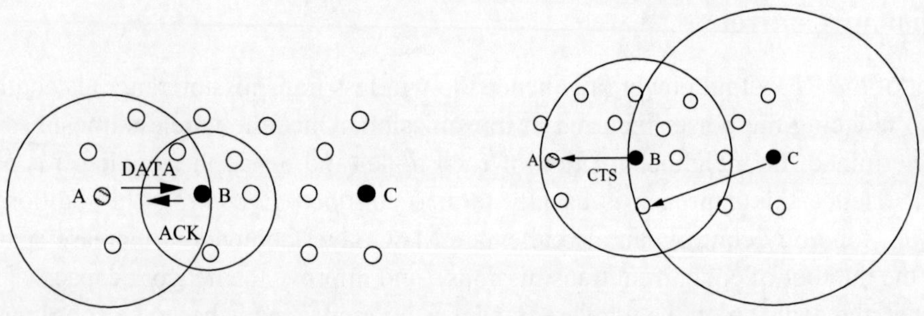

(a) Node A uses a larger transmission power than node B. Node B can successfully receive node A's data packets but node A cannot hear node B's ACK

(b) Node C uses a larger transmission range but its transmission collides with node A's transmission at node B.

Figure 7. Problems with uni-directional links created in topology control.

common power required to maintain the network connectivity, the traffic carrying capacity of the entire network is maximized, the battery life is extended, and the link bi-directionality requirement is met. In *COMPOW*, each node runs several routing daemons in parallel, one for each power level. Each routing daemon maintains its own routing table by exchanging control messages at the specified power level. By comparing the entries in different routing tables, each node can determine the smallest common power which ensures that the maximal number of nodes are connected. Specifically, let $N(P_i)$ denote the number of entries in the routing table corresponding to the power level P_i. Then the adequate power level for data packets is simply set to the smallest power level P_i for which $N(P_i) = N(P_{max})$.

The major drawback of *COMPOW* is its significant message overhead, since each node runs multiple daemons, each of which has to exchange link state information with the counterparts at other nodes. Another drawback of *COMPOW* is that it tends to use higher power in the case that nodes are not evenly distributed on a region, e.g., nodes are distributed in the cluster fashion. The requirement of a common (minimum) transmission power may unnecessarily lead to a larger transmission power for all nodes. This is undesirable from the perspective of both spatial reusability and energy efficiency. Finally, since the common power is collaboratively determined by the all nodes inside the network, global reconfiguration is required in the case of node joining/leaving. The latter two drawbacks have been lifted to some extent in [38].

Relay-region and enclosure-based approach (R&M) Rodoplu *et al.* [50] introduce the notion of *relay region* and *enclosure* for the purpose of power control. For any node i that intends to transmit to node n, node n is said to lie in the *relay region* of a third node j, if node i will consume less power when it chooses to relay through node j instead of transmitting directly to node n. The *enclosure* of node i is then defined as the union of the complement of relay regions of all the nodes that node i can reach by using its maximal transmission power. It is shown that the network is strongly connected if every node maintains links with nodes in its enclosure and the resulting topology is a minimum power topology. Fig. 8 illustrates the relay regions and enclosure of a node.

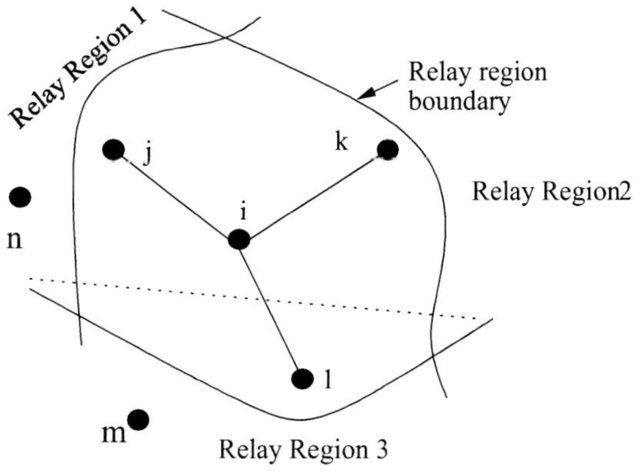

Figure 8. Enclosure of node i. Relay regions corresponding to node j, k, and l form the enclosure of node i.

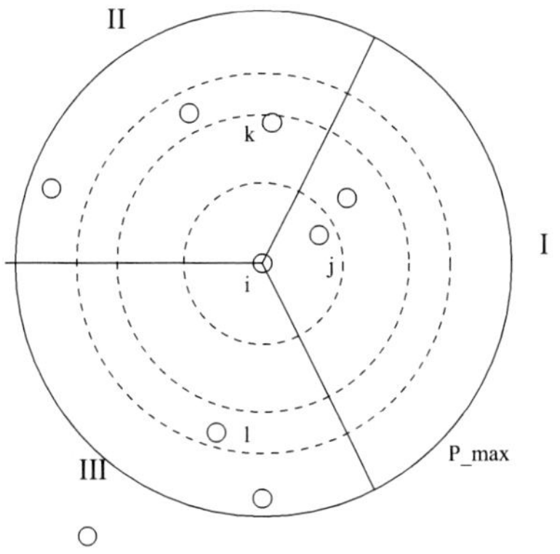

Figure 9. Neighbor discovery in the cone-based algorithm, $\alpha = \frac{2\pi}{3}$. Node i adjusts its transmit power to P_{max} to reach all neighbors in all cones.

A two-phase distributed protocol is then devised to find the minimum power topology for a static network. In the first phase, each node i executes local search to find the enclosure graph. This is done by examining neighbor nodes that a node can reach by using its maximal power and keeping only those who do not lie in the relay regions of previously found nodes. In the second phase, each node runs the distributed Bellman-Ford shortest path algorithm upon the enclosure graph, using power consumption as the cost metric. When a node completes the second phase, it can either start data transmission or enter the sleep mode to conserve power.

To deal with limited mobility, each node periodically executes the distributed protocol to find the enclosure graph. This algorithm assumes that there is only one data sink (destination) in the network, which may not hold in practice. Also, an explicit propagation channel model is needed to compute the *relay region*.

Cone-based topology control CBTC(α) [63, 31] is a two-phase algorithm in which each node finds the minimum power p such that transmitting with p ensures that it can reach some node in every cone of degree α (Fig. 9). The algorithm has been analytically shown to preserve network connectivity if $\alpha < 5\pi/6$. It can also ensure that every link between nodes is bi-directional.

Several optimizations to the basic algorithm are discussed. These include: (i) a *shrink-back* operation can be added at the end of the execution of the base algorithm to allow a boundary node to broadcast with less power, if doing so does not reduce the cone coverage; (ii) if $\alpha < 2\pi/3$, asymmetric edges can be removed while maintaining the network connectivity; and (iii) if there exists an edge from node u to node v_1 and from node u to node v_2, respectively, the longer edge can be removed while preserving connectivity, as long as $d(v_1, v_2) < \max\{d(u, v_1), d(u, v_2)\}$.

An event-driven strategy is proposed to reconfigure the network topology in the case of mobility. Each node is notified when any neighbor leaves/joins the neighborhood and/or the angle changes. The mechanism used to realize this requires state to be kept at, and message exchanges among, neighboring nodes. A node then determines, based on the state information, whether it needs to rerun the topology control algorithm.

Topology control using local minimum spanning tree Li *et al.* [33] propose a topology control algorithm, called *local minimum spanning tree (LMST)*, for multi-hop wireless networks with limited mobility. In LMST, each node broadcasts periodically a Hello message using its maximal transmission power. The node id and position of the node are contained in the Hello message. After gathering the location information of all neighbors that a node u can reach by the maximum transmission power (called the *visible neighborhood* $NV_u(G)$), node u builds its local minimum spanning tree $T_u = (V(T_u), E(T_u))$ of G_u which spans all the nodes within its neighborhood, where $G_u = (V_u, E_u)$ is an induced subgraph of G such that $V_u = NV_u$. After node u builds a minimum spanning tree to span its visible neighborhood, it selects *only* one-hop neighbors on the LMST as its direct neighbors. The neighbor relation defined above is not symmetric and thus the links can be unidirectional (Fig. 10). Bi-directionality can be enforced by either adding reverse edges of existing unidirectional links or removing all the uni-direction links. Once the neighboring set is determined, each node can determine the specific power levels it needs to reach each of its neighbor based on measurement of the receiving power of Hello messages.

LMST ensures that (i) the topology constructed under LMST preserves network connectivity, (ii) the (logical) node degree of any node in the resulting topology is bounded by 6; and (iii) the resulting topology can be converted into one with only bi-directional links (after removal of uni-directional links).

Topology control based on the notion of RNG Borbash and Jennings [4] utilize the notion of *relative neighborhood graph (RNG)* for topology initialization of wireless networks. Let the transmission power required for the communication between nodes u and v be denoted as $w(u, v)$. The neighbor relation in a RNG is defined as follows: in a RNG [59, 58], a bi-directional link exists between nodes u and v (denoted as $u \overset{RNG}{\longleftrightarrow} v$), if and only if there does not exist a third node p such that $w(u, p) < w(u, v)$ and $w(p, v) < w(u, v)$. With the

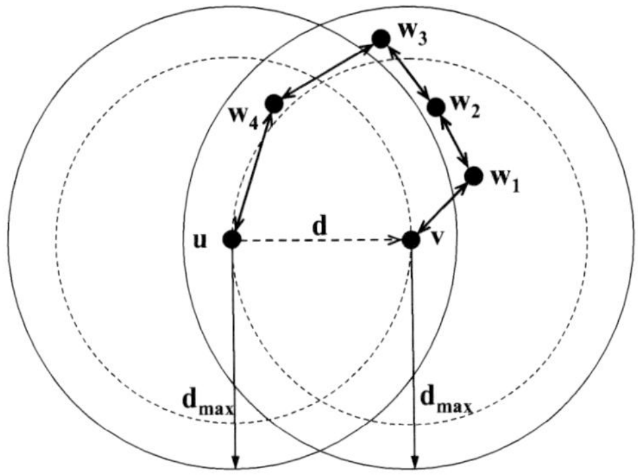

Figure 10. A scenario that demonstrates that links in the topology derived under LMST may be uni-directional.

use of a similar information collection procedure as in LMST, each node has the knowledge on the local neighborhood, and can make its local decision to derive the network topology based on RNG. The network topology thus derived has been reported to exhibit good overall performance in terms of power usage, low interference, and reliability.

Note that most of the aforementioned topology control algorithms (except [50]) assume the uniform maximum transmission ranges among wireless nodes. This assumption does not always hold in practice, as even devices of the same type may have slightly different maximal transmission power, let alone the fact that there exist heterogeneous wireless networks in which devices have dramatically different capabilities. Li and Hou [32] show that most of the topology control algorithms cannot be directly applied to heterogeneous wireless multi-hop networks in which the maximal transmission power of each node may be different. (Examples which show that CBTC($\frac{2}{3}\pi$), RNG, and LMST may lead to network disconnectivity in heterogeneous wireless networks are given in Figures 11–13 (a)–(b).) They then extend RNG and LMST to two localized topology control algorithms for heterogeneous networks with non-uniform transmission ranges: Directed Relative Neighborhood Graph (DRNG) and Directed Local Spanning Subgraph (DLSS) (Figures 11–13 (c)). It is proved (1) the topology derived under DRNG or DLSS preserves network connectivity; (2) the out-degree of any node in the topology by DLSS or DRNG is bounded by a constant; and (3) the topology generated by DRNG or DLSS preserves network bi-directionality, i.e., if the original topology by having every node use its maximal transmission power is bi-directional, then the topology generated by either DRNG or DLSS is also bi-directional after some simple operations.

4.4. Energy-Efficient Broadcast

Energy-efficient broadcast protocols [55, 64, 66, 30, 6] aim to construct energy-efficient multicast and broadcast trees by selectively pruning the original network connectivity graph (after the topology control phrase).

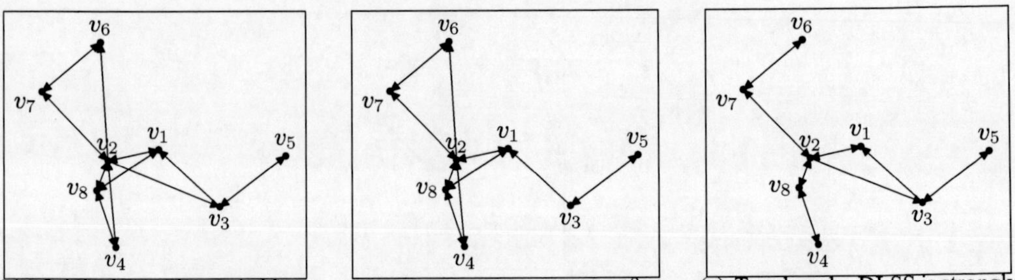

(a) Original topology (without topology control) is strongly connected.

(b) Topology by $CBTC(\frac{2}{3}\pi)$ without optimization is not strongly connected: there is no path from v_1 to v_3.

(c) Topology by DLSS is strongly connected.

Figure 11. An example that shows $CBTC(\frac{2}{3}\pi)$ may render disconnectivity in heterogeneous networks. There is no path from v_1 to v_3 due to the loss of edge (v_2,v_3), which is discarded by v_2 since v_1 and v_4 have already provided the necessary coverage.

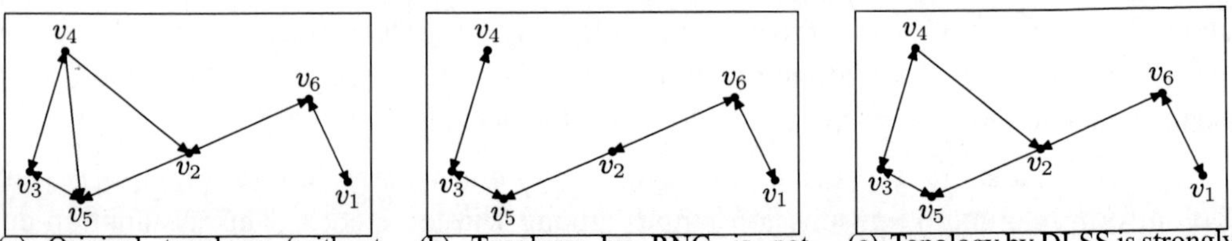

(a) Original topology (without topology control) is strongly connected.

(b) Topology by RNG is not strongly connected: there is no path from v_5 to v_2.

(c) Topology by DLSS is strongly connected.

Figure 12. An example that shows RNG may render disconnectivity in heterogeneous networks. There is no path from v_5 to v_2 due to the loss of edge (v_4,v_2), which is discarded since $|(v_4, v_5)| < |(v_4, v_2)|$, and $|(v_2, v_5)| < |(v_4, v_2)|$.

Centralized heuristics The *Broadcast Incremental Power* (BIP) algorithm [65] constructs energy-efficient, source-based broadcast/multicast trees in wireless ad hoc networks. It is assumed that each node can adjust its transmission power, and energy is consumed only during transmissions. To build an energy-efficient broadcast/multicast tree, the algorithm begins by determining nodes that the source can reach with the smallest transmission power. At each step thereafter, one new node with the minimum additional cost is added to the tree. When the tree construction completes, an additional procedure called *sweep* is taken to eliminate unnecessary transmissions and further reduce the total energy consumption. BIP is perhaps the first algorithm to exploit the trade-off between reaching more nodes in a single hop by using larger power and relaying messages through several hops by using lower power. As analyzed in [62], like other greedy heuristics, BIP may render "bad" results under certain cases.

The *Iterative Maximum-Branch Minimization* (IMBM) algorithm [30] is another effort to construct power-efficient broadcast trees. It starts with a basic broadcast tree in which the source directly transmits to all nodes. Then it attempts to approximate the minimum-energy broadcast tree by iteratively replacing the maximum branch with less-power, more-

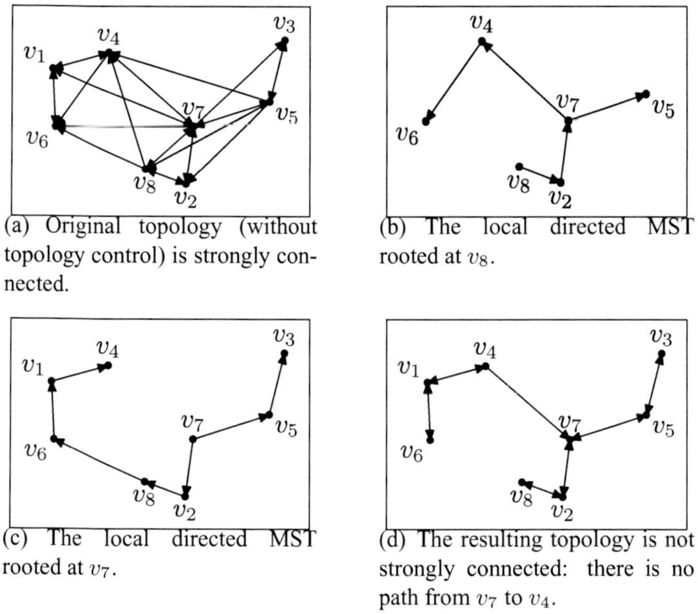

(a) Original topology (without topology control) is strongly connected.

(b) The local directed MST rooted at v_8.

(c) The local directed MST rooted at v_7.

(d) The resulting topology is not strongly connected: there is no path from v_7 to v_4.

Figure 13. An example that shows the algorithm in which each node builds a local directed minimum spanning tree and only keeps the one-hop neighbors may result in disconnectivity.

hop alternatives.

Both BIP and IMBM operate under the assumption that the transmission power of each node is unconstrained, i.e., every node can reach every other node. Both algorithms are centralized and require: (a) the source node knows the position/distance of every other node; and (b) each node knows its downstream, on-tree neighbors so as to propagate broadcast messages. As a result, it may be difficult to extend both algorithms into distributed versions, as a significant amount of information is required to be exchanged among nodes.

Distributed heuristics Wieselthier *et al.* [67] propose and evaluated two distributed versions of BIP: *Distributed-BIP-All* and *Distributed-BIP-Gateways*. In Distributed-BIP-All, each node calculates its local BIP tree and broadcasts the tree to all one-hop neighbors. Then each node forms the global tree by combining the local trees in certain temporal manner. The major drawback of Distributed-BIP-All is that many unnecessary transmissions are incurred when the global tree is constructed. Distributed-BIP-Gateways is proposed to overcome this disadvantage by selecting gateways to form local BIP trees that can reach all neighbors within two hops. After the global tree is constructed, the *sweep* operation (which is essentially a centralized procedure) can be applied. The performance of both distributed versions without the sweep operation is degraded 30%-50% as compared to that of BIP.

Cagali *et al.* [5] propose the *Embedded Wireless Multicast Advantage* (EWMA) algorithm. EWMA uses the link-based minimum spanning tree (MST) as the initial solution and adjusts the transmission range for each node to reduce the total cost. A distributed version that involves construction of a MST in a decentralized manner is also proposed. Simulations show that both EWMA and its distributed version outperform BIP. A possible drawback of the distributed version of EWMA is that it may not perform well under frequent topological changes as it relies on information that is multiple hops away to construct the MST.

Ahluwalia *et al.* [1] propose a clustering-based algorithm that takes the following three steps. A distributed clustering algorithm is first used to divide the entire network into clusters. Then a clustering sweep procedure is used to further reduce the transmission range. Finally a distributed MST construction algorithm is applied to join all the clusters together. Simulation results show its performance is degraded 18% as compared to BIP. This algorithm has the same drawback as EWMA, as it also relies on information that is multiple hops away to construct the MST.

Optimization based schemes The scheme proposed in [37] is built upon an alternate search based paradigm in which the minimum-cost broadcast/multicast tree is constructed by a search process. Two procedures are devised to check the viability of a solution in the search space. Preliminary experimental results show that this method renders better solutions than BIP, though at a higher computational cost.

Liang [35] show that the minimum-energy broadcast tree problem is NP-complete, and propose an approximate algorithm to provide a bounded performance guarantee for the problem in the general setting. Essentially the minimum-energy broadcast tree problem is reduced to an optimization problem on an auxiliary weighted graph, which is solved to give an approximate solution for the original problem. They also propose another algorithm that yields better performance under a special case.

Das *et al.* [10] propose an evolutionary approach using genetic algorithms. The same authors also present in [11] three different integer programming models which can be used to find the solutions to the minimum-energy broadcast/multicast problem. The major drawback of optimization based schemes are, however, that they are centralized and require the availability of global topological information.

All aforementioned approaches so far are subject to the power consumption model used, and the resulting broadcast tree might be totally different for slightly different models. This limits the applicability of both algorithms in realistic scenarios in which the power consumption model may be time-varying.

Flooding-based schemes Santivánez *et al.* [51] show that flooding is a good solution for the sake of scalability and simplicity. Several flooding techniques for wireless networks have been proposed [40, 45, 57], each with respect to certain optimization criterion. However, none of them take advantage of the feature that the transmission power of a node can be adjusted.

Localized Schemes A localized algorithm depends only on local information and is thus more robust to topological changes. Cartigny *et al.* [7] propose a localized algorithm, called RBOP [7] that is built upon the notion of *relative neighborhood graph* (RNG). In RBOP, the broadcast is initiated at the source and propagated, following the rules of neighbor elimination, on the topology represented by RNG. Simulation results show that the performance degradation could be as high as 100% as compared to BIP.

5. Conclusion

In this book chapter, we have provided a taxonomy of power management and power control algorithms and protocols for wireless networks. We start by giving a description of energy consumption characteristics of wireless devices, and identify that the power consumed in wireless transmitters consists of two parts: power consumed by the radio electronic and power consumed in the RF output. Power management refers to the mechanisms of turning off the radio electronic and putting wireless devices into the low-power states at appropriate times, while power control refers to those that either use different coding schemes and/or adjust the RF output power (and hence the wireless transmission range) to reduce the power consumed in transmission. For each category of techniques, we have stated important performance objectives, presented representative algorithms and protocols in both wireless infrastructured and infrastructureless (a.k.a. ad hoc) networks, and discussed their advantages and drawbacks.

Although the choice on the power management/control techniques to use depends on the environment characteristics and constraints, the performance requirements of applications, and the availability and costs of hardware devices, the technical discussion made in this book chapter serves as the starting points to understand, compare, reason about the pros and cons of, and research on the various, state-of-the-art power management and control techniques.

References

[1] A. Ahluwalia, E. Modiano, and L. Shu. On the complexity and distributed construction of energy-efficientbroadcast trees in static ad hoc wireless networks. In *Proc. 36th Annual Conference on Information Sciences and Systems (CISS)*, pages 807–813, Mar. 2002.

[2] M. Anand, E. Nightingale, and J. Flinn. Self-tuning wireless network power management. In *Proc. of Mobicom)*, September 2003.

[3] I. Anderson. *Combinatorial Designs and Tournaments*, chapter 2. Oxford University Press, 1998.

[4] S. A. Borbash and E. H. Jennings. Distributed topology control algorithm for multihop wireless networks. In *Proc. 2002 World Congress on Computational Intelligence (WCCI 2002)*, Honolulu, Hawaii, US, May 2002.

[5] M. Čagalj, J.-P. Hubaux, and C. Enz. Minimum-energy broadcast in all-wireless networks: NP-completeness and distribution issues. In *Proc. ACM International Conference on Mobile Computing and Networking (MOBICOM) 2002*, Atlanta, Georgia, US, Sept. 2002.

[6] M. Cagalj and J.-P. Hubaux. Minimum-energy broadcast in all-wireless networks: NP-completeness and distribution issues. In *Proc. of the 8th Int'l Conference on Mobile Computing and Networking (Mobicom'02)*, 2002.

[7] J. Cartigny, D. Simplot, and I. Stojmenović. Localized minimum-energy broadcasting in ad-hoc networks. In *Proc. IEEE INFOCOM 2003*, San Francisco, California, US, Apr. 2003.

[8] B. Chen, K. Jamieson, H. Balakrishnan, and R. Morris. Span: An energy-efficient coordination algorithm for topology maintenance in ad hoc wireless networks. In *Proc. of MobiCom*, July 2001.

[9] E. Chung, L. Benini, and G. D. Micheli. Dynamic power management for non-stationary service requests. In *Design, Automation and Test in Europe*, pages 77–81, 1999.

[10] A. K. Das, R. J. Marks, M. El-Sharkawi, P. Arabshahi, and A. Gray. The minimum power broadcast problem in wireless networks: an ant colony system approach. In *Proc. IEEE International Symposium on Circuits and Systems*, Scottsdale, Arizona, US, May 2002.

[11] A. K. Das, R. J. Marks, M. El-Sharkawi, P. Arabshahi, and A. Gray. Minimum power broadcast trees for wireless networks: integer programming formulations. In *Proc. IEEE INFOCOM 2003*, San Francisco, California, US, Apr. 2003.

[12] F. Douglis, P. Krishnan, and B. Marsh. Throwarting the power-hungry disk. In *Proc. of Winter 1994 USENIX Conference*, 1994.

[13] J. Elson, L. Girod, and D. Estrin. Fine-grained network time synchronization using reference broadcasts. In *under review*, 2002.

[14] L. M. Feeney and M. Nilsson. Investigating the energy consumption of a wireless network interface in an ad hoc networking environment. In *Proc. of IEEE INFOCOM*, April 2001.

[15] A. E. Gamal, C. Nair, , E. Uysal, and S. Zahedi. Energy-efficient scheduling of packet transmission over wireless networks. In *Proc. of IEEE INFOCOM*, 2002.

[16] J. Gomez, A. Campbell, M. Naghshineh, and C. Bisdikian. Conserving transmission power in wireless ad hoc networks. In *Proc. of IEEE Conference on Network Protocols (ICNP'01)*, Nov. 2001.

[17] P. Gupta and P. R. Kumar. Critical power for asymptotic connectivity in wireless networks. In *Stochastic Analysis, Control, Optimization and Applications: A Volume in Honor of W.H. Fleming*, 1998.

[18] P. Gupta and P. R. Kumar. The capacity of wireless networks. *IEEE Transactions on Information Theory*, IT-46(2):388–404, 2000.

[19] D. Helmbold, D. Long, and B. Sherrod. A dynamic disk spin-down technique for mobile computing. In *Int'l Conf. on Mobile Computing and Networking (MobiCom)*, 1999.

[20] C. Hu and J. Hou. LISP: A link-indexed statistical traffic prediction approach to improving IEEE 802.11 PSM. In *Proc. of ICDCS*, 2004.

[21] IEEE Computer Society. IEEE standard 802.11: wireless LAN medium access control (MAC) and physical layer (PHY) specifications. The institute of Electrical and Electronics Engineers, New York, NY, 1997.

[22] D. B. Johnson and D. A. Maltz. Dynamic source routing in ad hoc wireless networks. draft-ietf-manet-dsr-04.txt, 2001.

[23] E. Jung and N. Vaidya. A power control MAC protocol for ad-hoc networks, 2002.

[24] E.-S. Jung and N. Vaidya. An energy efficient MAC protocol for wireless LANs. In *Proc. of IEEE INFOCOM*, 2002.

[25] V. Kawadia and P. Kumar. Power control and clustering in ad hoc networks. In *Proc. IEEE INFOCOM 2003*, San Francisco, California, US, Apr. 2003.

[26] R. Krashinsky and H. Balakrishnan. Minimizing energy for wireless web access with bounded slowdown. In *Proc. of MobiCom*, 2002.

[27] R. Kravets and P. Krishnan. Application-driven power management for mobile communication. *Wireless Networks*, 6(4), 2000.

[28] P. Krishnan, P. M. Long, and J. S. Vitter. Adaptive disk spindown via optimal rent-to-buy in probabilistic environments. *Algorithmica*, 23(1), 1999.

[29] A. R. Lebeck, X. Fan, H. Zeng, and C. Ellis. Power aware page allocation. In *ASPLOS*, 2000.

[30] F. Li and I. Nikolaidis. On minimum-energy broadcasting in all-wireless networks. In *Proc. 26th Annual IEEE Conference on Local Computer Networks*, 2001.

[31] L. Li, J. Y. Halpern, P. Bahl, Y.-M. Wang, and R. Wattenhofer. Analysis of a cone-based distributed topology control algorithm for wireless multi-hop networks. In *Proc. ACM Symposium on Principles of Distributed Computing*, pages 264–273, Newport, Rhode Island, US, Aug. 2001.

[32] N. Li and J. C. Hou. Topology control in heterogeneous wireless networks: problems and solutions. In *Proc. IEEE INFOCOM 2004*, March 2004.

[33] N. Li, J. C. Hou, and L. Sha. Design and analysis of an MST-based topology control algorithm. In *Proc. IEEE INFOCOM 2003*, San Francisco, California, US, Apr. 2003.

[34] X.-Y. Li, G. Calinescu, and P.-J. Wan. Distributed construction of planar spanner and routing for ad hoc networks. In *Proc. IEEE INFOCOM 2002*, New York, New York, US, June 2002.

[35] W. Liang. Constructing minimum-energy broadcast trees in wireless ad hoc networks. In *Proc. ACM Symposium on Mobile Ad Hoc Networking and Computing (MOBIHOC) 2002*, pages 194–205, Lausanne, Switzerland, June 2002.

[36] Y. Lu and G. D. Micheli. Comparing system-level power management policies, 2001.

[37] R. J. Marks, A. K. Das, M. El-Sharkawi, P. Arabshahi, and A. Cray. Minimum power broadcast trees for wireless networks: optimizing using the viability lemma. In *Proc. IEEE International Symposium on Circuits and Systems*, pages 273–276, Scottsdale, Arizona, US, May 2002.

[38] S. Narayanaswamy, V. Kawadia, R. S. Sreenivas, and P. R. Kumar. Power control in ad hoc networks : Theory, architecture, algorithm and implementation of the COMPOW protocol. In *European Wireless Conference*, 2002.

[39] S. Narayanaswamy, V. Kawadia, R. S. Sreenivas, and P. R. Kumar. Power control in ad-hoc networks: Theory, architecture, algorithm and implementation of the COMPOW protocol. In *Proc. of European Wireless 2002, Next Generation Wireless Networks: Technologies, Protocols, Services and Applications*, pages 156–162, Florence, Italy, Feb. 2002.

[40] K. Obraczka and K. Viswanath. Flooding for reliable multicast in multi-hop ad hoc networks. *Wireless Networks*, 7:627–634, 2001.

[41] G. A. Paleologo, L. Benini, A. Bogliolo, and G. D. Micheli. Policy optimization for dynamic power management. In *Design Automation Conference*, pages 182–187, 1998.

[42] C. E. Perkins, E. M. Royer, and S. Das. Ad hoc on demand distance vector (AODV) routing. draft-ietf-manet-aodv-07.txt, 2000.

[43] N. Poojary, S. V. Krishnamurthy, and S. Dao. Medium access control in a network of ad hoc mobile nodes with heterogeneous power capabilities. In *IEEE International Conference on Communications (ICC)*, pages 872–877, 2001.

[44] B. Prabhakar, E. Uysal, and A. E. Gamal. Energy-efficient transmission over a wireless link via lazy packet scheduling. In *Proc. of IEEE INFOCOM*, 2001.

[45] A. Qayyum, L. Viennot, and A. Laouiti. Multipoint relaying for flooding broadcast messages in mobile wireless networks. In *Proc. the 35th Annual Hawaii International Conference on System Sciences*, pages 3898–3907, Hawaii, US, Jan. 2002.

[46] Q. Qiu and M. Pedram. Dynamic power management based on continuous-time markov decision processes. In *Design Automation Conference*, pages 555–561, 1999.

[47] J. M. Rabaey, A. J. L. d Silva Jr., D. Patel, and S. Roundy. Picoradio supports ad hoc ultra-low power wireless networking. In *Computer Magazine*, July 2000.

[48] R. Ramanathan and R. Rosales-Hain. Topology control of multihop wireless networks using transmit power adjustment. In *Proc. IEEE INFOCOM 2000*, pages 404–413, Tel Aviv, Israel, Mar. 2000.

[49] V. Rodoplu and T. H. Meng. Minimum energy mobile wireless networks. In *Proceedings of the 1998 IEEE International Conference on Communications (ICC)*, 1998.

[50] V. Rodoplu and T. H. Meng. Minimum energy mobile wireless networks. *IEEE J. Select. Areas Commun.*, 17(8):1333–1344, Aug. 1999.

[51] C. A. Santiván, B. McDonald, I. Stavrakakis, and R. Ramanathan. On the scalability of ad hoc routing protocols. In *Proc. IEEE INFOCOM 2002*. New York, New York, US, June 2002.

[52] C. Schurgers, V. Tsiatsis, S. Ganeriwal, and M. Srivastava. Topology management for sensor networks: Exploiting latency and density. In *Proceedings of The Third ACM International Symposium on Mobile Ad Hoc Networking and Computing*, 2002.

[53] E. Shih, S.-H. Cho, N. Ickes, R. Min, A. Sinha, A. Wang, and A. Chandrakasan. Physical layer driven algorithm and protocol design for energy-efficient wireless sensor networks. In *Proceedings of the Seventh Annual ACM/IEEE International Conference on Mobile Computing and Networking (MobiCom)*, 2001.

[54] T. Simunic, L. Benini, P. W. Glynn, and G. D. Micheli. Dynamic power management for portable systems. In *ACM Mobile Computing and Networking (MobiCom)*, pages 11–19, 2000.

[55] S. Singh, C. S. Raghavendra, and J. Stepanek. Power-aware broadcasting in mobile ad hoc networks. In *Proc. PIMRC '99*, Osaka, Japan, Sept. 1999.

[56] S. Singh, M. Woo, and C. S. Raghavendra. PAMAS: Power aware multi-access protocol with signalling for ad hoc network. *ACM Computer Communication Review*, pages 5–26, July 1998.

[57] I. Stojmenović, M. Seddigh, and J. Zunic. Dominating sets and neighbor elimination-based broadcasting algorithms in wireless networks. *IEEE Trans. Parallel Distrib. Syst.*, 13(1):14–25, Jan. 2002.

[58] K. J. Supowit. The relative neighborhood graph, with an application to minimum spanning trees. *Journal of the ACM*, 30(3):428–448, July 1983.

[59] G. Toussaint. The relative neighborhood graph of a finite planar set. *Pattern Recognition*, 12:261–268, 1980.

[60] Y.-C. Tseng, C.-S. Hsu, and T.-Y. Hsieh. Power-saving protocols for IEEE 802.11-based multi-hop ad hoc networks. In *Proceedings of the The 21st Annual Joint Conference of the IEEE Computer and Communications Societies*, 2002.

[61] T. Šimunić, L. Benini, and G. D. Micheli. Event-driven power management of portable systems. In *International Symposium on System Synthesis*, pages 18–23, 1999.

[62] P. J. Wan, G. Calinescu, X. Y. Li, and O. Frieder. Minimum-energy broadcast routing in static ad hoc wireless networks. In *Proc. IEEE INFOCOM 2001*, volume 2, pages 1162–1171, Anchorage, Alaska, US, Apr. 2001.

[63] R. Wattenhofer, L. Li, P. Bahl, and Y.-M. Wang. Distributed topology control for power efficient operation in multihop wireless ad hoc networks. In *Mobile Computing and Networking*, 2001.

[64] J. E. Wieselthier, G. D. Nguyen, and A. Ephremides. On the construction of energy-efficient broadcast and multicast trees in wireless networks. In *Proc. IEEE INFOCOM 2000*, volume 2, pages 585–594, Tel Aviv, Israel, Mar. 2000.

[65] J. E. Wieselthier, G. D. Nguyen, and A. Ephremides. On the construction of energy-efficient broadcast and multicast trees in wireless networks. In *Proc. IEEE INFOCOM 2000*, volume 2, pages 585–594, Tel Aviv, Israel, Mar. 2000.

[66] J. E. Wieselthier, G. D. Nguyen, and A. Ephremides. The energy efficiency of distributed algorithms for broadcasting in ad hoc networks. In *Proc. IEEE 5th International Symposium on Wireless Personal Multimedia Communications (WPMC)*, pages 499–503, Oct. 2002.

[67] J. E. Wieselthier, G. D. Nguyen, and A. Ephremides. The energy efficiency of distributed algorithms for broadcasting in ad hoc networks. In *Proc. IEEE 5th International Symposium on Wireless Personal Multimedia Communications (WPMC)*, pages 499–503, Oct. 2002.

[68] Y. Xu, J. Heidemann, and D. Estrin. Geography-informed energy conservation for ad hoc routing. In *Proc. of MobiCom*, July 2001.

[69] W. Ye, J. Heidemann, and D. Estrin. An energy-efficient MAC protocol for wireless sensor networks. In *Proceedings of the The 21st Annual Joint Conference of the IEEE Computer and Communications Societies*, 2002.

[70] Y. Yu, V. K. Prasanna, and B. Krishnamachari. Exploring energy-latency tradeoffs for data gathering in wireless sensor networks. In *Proc. of IEEE INFOCOM*, 2004.

[71] R. Zheng, J. C. Hou, and L. Sha. Asynchronous wakeup for ad hoc networks. In *Proceedings of the Fourth ACM International Symposium on Mobile Ad Hoc Networking and Computing (MobiHoc)*, 2003.

[72] R. Zheng and R. Kravets. On-demand power management for ad hoc network. In *Proc. of IEEE INFOCOM*, 2003.

In: Computer-Aided Design...
Editors: C.M. De Smet et al, pp. 139-153
ISBN: 978-1-60456-860-8

Chapter 6

VERTICAL HANDOFF SCHEMES FOR INTERWORKING OF 3G CELLULAR NETWORKS AND WIRELESS LAN

Maode Ma
School of Electrical and Electronic Engineering,
Nanyang Technological University, Singapore

Abstract

The combination of cellular wireless technology and wireless LAN technology offers great possibility of achieving anywhere, anytime Internet access. Wireless LAN technology can provide high bandwidth data transmission within a small coverage while cellular wireless network including 3G cellular wireless networks can serve relative low bandwidth data transmission in a wider area. The integration of these two wireless technologies will enhance the Internet access ability of mobile users to achieve "Always Best Connected". Loosely coupled architecture seems to be prospective to implement. One of the important issues in loosely coupled approach is the handoff between wireless LAN and 3G cellular networks. This chapter presents an overall view on various techniques to perform the vertical handoff. We describe several state-of-the-art schemes to implement the vertical handoff and seamless connection processes in quite detail. The objective of this review is to present a general picture on the topic and the relevant techniques for further research.

1. Introduction

Recent development on the wireless technologies has indicated that wireless local area networks, wireless LAN, based on IEEE 802.11.x standards and third-generation, 3G, cellular wireless networks such as CDMA2000 or UMTS (i.e. WCDMA) could be integrated together to offer Internet access to end users. The two technologies can offer functions that are complementary to each other. The 802.11.x standards based wireless LANs support data rates from 1 Mbps to 54 Mbps. However, by 802.11.x standard, one access point (AP) in a wireless LAN can only cover an area of a few thousand square meters. It is perfectly applied for enterprise networks and public hot-spots such as hotels and airports. On the contrary, wireless cellular networks built with 3G standards can only support peak data transmission rates from

64Kbps to nearly 2 Mbps with a much wider area of coverage that enables ubiquitous connectivity. It is reasonable and feasible to combine these two technologies to make Internet access much easier and more convenient. The implementation of the integration of 3G cellular wireless networks and 802.11.x standard based wireless LANs is a challenging task. Its difficulty lies in the objective of the integration, which is to achieve the seamless interoperation between the two types of the wireless networks with QoS level and other requirements maintained at the same time, from the perspectives of both the end-users and the operators. There are basically two proposals as the solutions to the architecture of the integration. One is the tight coupling. The other is the loose coupling. Although there is no final decision on whether the future integrated network would use either of these techniques or some other one, much focus of the research is currently on the loose coupling approach due to its feasibility.

The loose coupled architecture for the integration of 3G cellular networks and wireless LANs has shown a lot of advantages [1-3]. And it is the preferred architecture for the integration. However, to implement such architecture in order to realize the integration, there are a lot of issues to be addressed. One of the important issues is the mobility management in such heterogeneous wireless networks. In order to maintain the network connectivity, efficient and seamless handoff schemes are needed to handle two types of transfer. One of them is the switch between two different APs or base stations (BS) in a homogeneous wireless network, which is referred as horizontal handoff. The other is the switch between two different wireless networks, which is featured as vertical handoff. The horizontal handoff is the traditional handoff received a lot of discussions while the vertical handoff deserves extensive research due to its need of extra supports in both the terminal side and the network side. Vertical handoff is a critical issue to maintain the connectivity in a heterogeneous wireless network. There are a number of challenges in vertical handoff including the strategy to decide a vertical handoff, the scheme to keep connectivity during handoff, and the architecture to support the handoff scheme.

The rest of the chapter will be organized as follows. Section 2 will review the strategies on vertical handoff decision making. Section 3 will present various approaches and corresponding architectures to handle the mobility management during the vertical handoff. And the last section will conclude the paper with a summary.

2. Vertical Handoff Decision Strategies

The handoff decision is to decide whether a handoff should be performed, where a mobile user should be transferred to, and when to perform the handoff. The decision is going to be formed based on different metrics and strategies. Handoff metrics are the quantities to provide an indication to show whether a handoff is needed. Horizontal handoff needs only signal strength and channel availability for consideration. However, other new metrics should be considered when a vertical handoff decision is making. They could include QoS provided by the target wireless network, cost of the service in the target network, the target network system states (including the parameters like traffic load and bandwidth availability, which show medium access control (MAC) and upper layers states, and the physical layer states shown by the parameters like channel bit error rate and inter-channel interference, etc.), dynamic states and profile of mobile nodes, and the user preferences. The reason to include the new parameters in a vertical handoff decision lies in its differences from the traditional horizontal handoff. And it makes the vertical handoff decision making more complex.

We identify that a handoff decision process could be divided into three phases in general. The first one is the discovery phase, in which based on the two basic parameters, signal strength and channel availability, reachable wireless networks can be found. The second phase can be referred as evaluation phase, which is for the mobile nodes to evaluate all of other parameters to decide whether a handoff to one of reachable candidate networks is worthwhile. The handoff decision could be immediately made and got into the handoff execution phase if the handoff criteria could be met by all of the parameters. If all the real-time state independent parameters can meet the criteria, the decision could be delayed to execute the handoff until all of the real-time state dependent parameters meet the criteria. Otherwise, there will be no decision to make.

The strategies on horizontal handoff decision had received a lot of research focuses during the development of wireless cellular networks. Traditionally, the horizontal handoff decision algorithms employ thresholds to compare the values of basic metrics from different points of attachment and then decide whether to make the handoff after a stability period. Almost all of typical legacy algorithms make decisions with the major basic parameter of the strength or power of the received signals, which are reviewed in [4]. Recently, other techniques such as hypothesis testing, dynamic programming, and pattern recognition techniques based on neural networks or fuzzy logic systems have been taken into consideration to evaluate whether the parameters can meet the criteria in making handoff decision. These complicated algorithms are necessitated by the complexity of the handoff problem, especially, in the hybrid data or voice networks.

The vertical handoff decision making is more complicated than the horizontal handoff with more parameters and different scenarios to consider. It will experience every phase of general handoff decision making process. Moreover, the difficulty could come from the cases as following. When a mobile user moves from a cellular network into a wireless LAN, the vertical handoff may not be able to be triggered by signal decay of the current cellular system as in the process of horizontal handoff. Both the MAC layer sensing and traditional physical layer sensing for the wireless LAN are needed to perform to ensure smooth handoff and better QoS. On the other hand, when the mobile user moves out of a wireless LAN area, the connection will be lost if no handoff is operated so that prompt detection on the unavailability of the wireless LAN and quick switch the connection from the wireless LAN to the cellular network seamlessly is extremely important. The seamless vertical handoff should be able to not only avoid disconnections but also improve QoS whenever is possible or support user device independence (user can change their devices when continue their applications).

2.1. Simple Evaluation for Vertical Handoff

A solution to the vertical handoff with explicit two stages has been proposed in [5]. Its handoff decision stage is the evaluation phase, in which handoff target is chosen based on the predefined criteria. The decision on the handoff in both directions will be made based on two major parameters, which are signal level and the distance between mobile user and BS/AP. Moreover, the handoff decision scheme provides high priority to the handoff from UMTS network to the wireless LAN since wireless LAN can always provide high bandwidth service to the mobile users. Another solution proposed in [6] provides further differentiation on the vertical handoffs in different directions of vertical handoff with two different strategies. For a handoff from a cellular network to a wireless LAN, both MAC layer sensing and traditional physical layer sensing for the wireless LAN are performed to ensure better QoS. More specifically, physical layer sensing is used to detect the availability of the stable wireless LAN signal, while MAC layer sensing is used to detect the network conditions of the wireless LAN system such as access delay and available bandwidth. On the other hand, for a handoff from a wireless LAN to a cellular network, a fast Fourier transform based signal decay detection scheme and an adaptive threshold configuration approach are adopted.

The solution proposed in [7] utilizes context information as major parameter to make vertical handoff decisions in order to support required QoS during the handoff. The scheme operates above the transport layer to allow changes between networks with different protocol stacks. The vertical handoff decision scheme includes the context repository, which gathers and manages context information and the adaptability manager, which makes decision about adaptations to context changes including decisions about handoffs between different networks and responsibility for executing handoffs. Decisions can be made based on evaluation of context changes including user location changes and a selection of a new network to which the application's communication streams should be redirected. The evaluation of user location changes is performed with respect to the network grid map and the network coverage with the user device and network priorities. The evaluation is a rules-based process. The selection of a new network process selects a network that satisfies multiple objectives, which include satisfying the user's preference of devices, achieving the highest level of bandwidth for their respective applications while minimizing packet loss, delay, and jitter, and avoiding bandwidth fluctuations which may affect the applications.

The first two vertical handoff decision making solutions are similar to the traditional handoff schemes with simple consideration of the signal strength lever and distance. The only difference from traditional handoff is that different directions of vertical handoffs have been handled in different ways. The handoff from a cellular network to a wireless LAN has been given a higher priority to process in order to achieve better QoS service for the mobile users. The third scheme has employed more information on users as well as networks. The vertical handoff decision is based on a rules-based evaluation of context changes and a multiple-criteria selection of a new network. The handoff decision has considered maintaining QoS requirements of mobile users and real-time situation of the networks.

2.2. Quantitative Evaluation for Vertical Handoff

In order to make effective evaluation on the system parameters for the vertical handoff decision, a fuzzy logic based multiple criteria-decision scheme has been employed in [8]. This scheme takes multiple parameters such as signal quality, terminals available battery power, required bandwidth, and service priority as inputs of the fuzzy engine to find suitable candidate network and decide whether and when to execute the vertical handoff. The criteria used to make decision are the signal strength, network load, network cost, and bandwidth requirement. The fuzzy engine can make the vertical handoff decision based on the inputs and criteria in a reasonable processing time.

In [9], a utility function has been used to evaluate the system parameters for the vertical handoff decision. The utility function quantifies the QoS provided by the wireless network from the view of running applications on the mobile terminals. A virtue performance agent is assumed to periodically announce the available resources information at BSs. The utility function of wireless network *j* from the view of mobile users is composed of several normalized factors $f_{i,j}$ that are multiplied with their weights w_i of importance for application *i*. Different applications have different weight values for a particular factor. The maximum requirement and the minimum requirement for each factor should be defined by the corresponding application. And the application system parameters can be mapped to the factors. Those application system parameters may include effective bandwidth, charge model and cost, power consumption, moving speed and coverage, etc. The vertical handoff decision will be made relying on the utility ratios of the two wireless networks. After a reachable wireless network found for vertical handoff by signal strength, in the evaluation phase, the utility of the reachable wireless network will be evaluated. The network with higher utility than the current one will be considered as a target network. After a stability period, if it is consistently better than the current one, the vertical handoff will be executed. An improvement on this scheme can be found in [10], which is going to achieve the optimization for the vertical handoff decision when multiple reachable wireless networks and multiple services at each mobile user are present. A vertical handoff cost function is proposed to measure the benefit obtained for each application by handing off to a particular network. It is evaluated for each network *n* that covers the service area of a user. The network choice that results in the lowest calculated value of the cost function is the network that would provide the most benefit to the services of the user. The major element in the cost function is the QoS factor, which represents the QoS experienced by choosing to receive service *s* from network *n*. It is a multiplication of normalized value for the QoS parameter and a weight for the impact of the parameter on either the user or the network. The system parameters should be mapped to the QoS parameters and impact factors for different system parameters in order to use the cost function for the vertical handoff decision making. After multiple reachable wireless networks founded as target networks for vertical handoff in the discovery phase, in the evaluation phase of the vertical handoff decision process, for each service in a priority order at the mobile node, the cost function for each reachable network will be evaluated to find out the minimum value of the cost function. Then the service will be transferred to the target network with minimum value of the cost function. The evaluation continues until every service can find its desired target network.

The evaluation has become more complex due to the multiple metrics and criteria introduced into the vertical handoff process. In order to consider mores factors and objectives to get close optimal or optimal solution, complicated evaluation is necessary. The first approach can just provide a rough quantitative evaluation for the vertical handoff decision. The last two proposals can provide quite accurate evaluation based on the calculation of the utility function or the cost function. The last solution is the improvement to the second one in terms of that it can serve more complicated environment with multiple reachable networks and multiple services at one mobile user. There will be a tradeoff between accuracy and efficiency of the evaluation. If the evaluation algorithm is much complex to achieve high accurate outcomes resulting in longer execution time, it cannot keep the rapid pace of the system parameters' change. The high accurate evaluation results will always lag behind the real-time situation of the networks. Then any accurate results will be no use.

From this point of view, accurate evaluation algorithms with less complexity are necessary to develop for the vertical handoff decision making.

3. Mobility Management Schemes and Architectures

After a vertical handoff decision has been made, the mobility management scheme should maintain a connection's continuity after a vertical handoff. Mobile IP is the most widely studied approach for mobility handling. The mobile IP protocol is a network layer independent mobility protocol. It is a popular candidate to support smooth vertical handoff because vertical handoff involves changing the access interface, which typically results in changing the mobile nodes' IP address. Mobile IP provides IP layer mobility by enabling a mobile node that originates from its home network to be addressable by the same home IP address across different networks, in one of which that the mobile node is visiting, while maintaining a binding between the mobile node's home IP address and the care of address. Recently, there are some other proposals to support mobility at different layers including MAC, transport, and application layer. However, among them, the approaches at transport layer have shown much feasibility. In this section, the approaches at both network layer and transport layer will be presented in detail.

3.1. Approaches at Network Layer

IP is the default network layer protocol in the Internet. It routes packets from a source node to a destination node by allowing routers to forward packets from an incoming network interface to an outbound network interface based one a routing table. Mobile IP is designed to solve the problem of link disruption by allowing each mobile node to have two IP addresses with transparent maintaining the binding between them. One of the IP addresses is the static home address that is assigned at the home network and is used to identify communication endpoints. The other is a dynamic care-of address that represents the current location of the mobile node.

Mobility agents maintain the mobility binding. There are two types of them including home agents and foreign agents. A home agent, a designated router in the home network of the mobile node, maintains the mobility binding by a mobility-binding table, which maps a mobile node's home address with its care-of address in order to forward packets accordingly. A foreign agent is another specialized router in the foreign network that is the network the mobile node is currently visiting. The foreign agent maintains a visitor list, which contains information about the mobile nodes currently visiting that network.

In the following subsections, the solutions supported by the Mobile IPv4 will be presented. The first proposal is the initial proposal to support mobility in the interworking of 3G cellular network and wireless LAN. The subsequent three proposals can be considered as variants to improve the performance of the interworking networks in different ways based on Mobile IP technique.

3.1.1. Direct Mobile IP Solution

The goal of mobile IP service is to preserve user sessions when a user roams among heterogeneous networks of different providers. The system reported in [11] takes advantages of Mobile IPv4 to handle the vertical handoff in the interworking of CDMA2000 and wireless LAN networks. The system achieves this goal with the idea to implement Mobile IP at the wireless LAN gateway node.

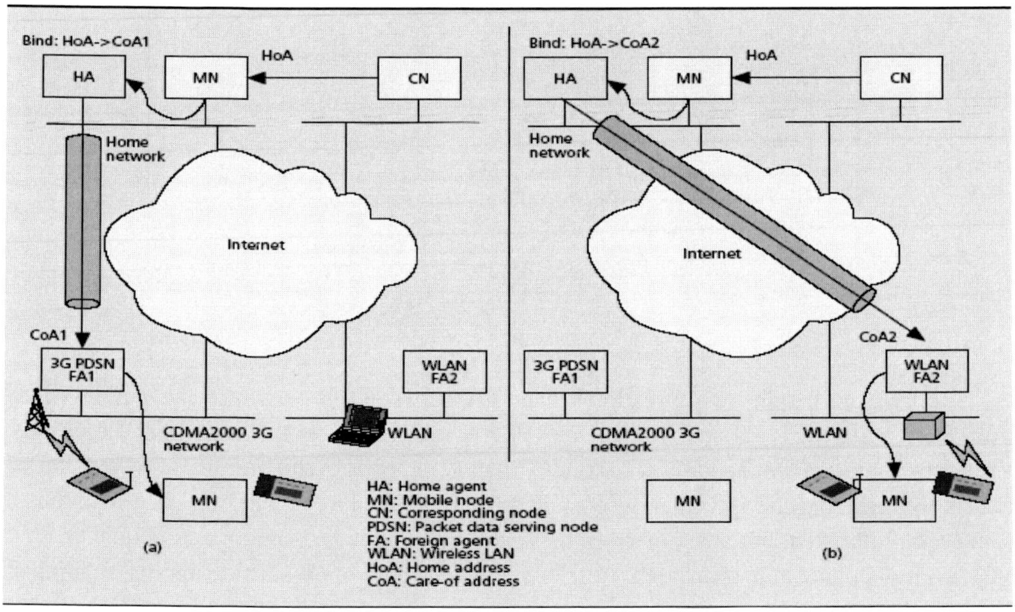

Figure 1. Vertical handoff by Mobile IP.

The CDMA2000 standard has incorporated Mobile IP to achieve inter-packet data serving node (PDSN) handoff. The PDSN in the CDMA2000 network functions as a foreign agent. Therefore, a natural way to implement vertical handoff between CDMA2000 and wireless LAN networks is to implement Mobile IP functionality in the wireless LAN gateway and mobile node. The architecture of the system is depicted in Figure 1. A mobile node performs session handoffs in two cases: when it loses signal on the wireless link currently in use or when it finds a better wireless link that can provide better performance. For example, a MN will switch from 3G to wireless LAN when it acquires wireless LAN, and switch from wireless LAN to 3G when it loses wireless LAN signal. To avoid service disruption and packet loss during handoff, the mobile node can exploit any overlapped 3G and wireless LAN coverage. It can keep both network interfaces active. While using the current network link (e.g., 3G), it can use the non-current network link (e.g., wireless LAN) to prepare a handoff in the background.

3.1.2. Connectivity Manager Solution

To provide an efficient and seamless roaming service to mobile users, a systematic IP–centric scheme has been proposed in [7]. The architecture of this scheme is shown in Figure 2. The distinct feature of this scheme is that a connection manager (CM) and virtual connectivity manager (VC) have been introduced to intelligently detect the conditions of the different types of networks and manage the availability of multiple networks.

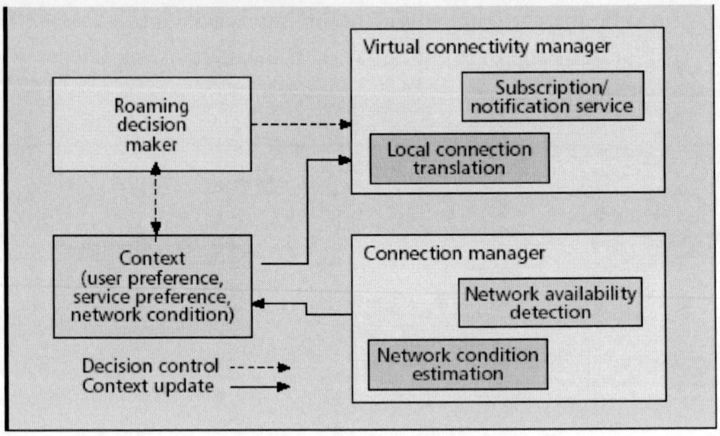

Figure 2. An architecture of seamless handoff between wireless LAN and cellular network.

The CM can handle two directional handoffs between 3G networks and wireless LAN: from 3G to wireless LAN and from wireless LAN to 3G networks. Meanwhile, the proposed VC is to maintain connection's continuity using an end-to-end argument when handoff occurs. By utilizing the information provided by the CM, the VC can not only maintain the connection unbroken, but also always achieve the best possible communication quality. In the VC, a local connection translation (LCT) is designed to maintain a mapping relationship between the original connection information and the current connection information for each active connection, making the mobility solution transparent to upper applications.

A roaming decision maker and a context database are introduced to act as the interconnection between CM and VC. The purpose of this context database is to make roaming context-aware. The context may consist of user/service preferences and technical parameters such as access delay, available bandwidth, and capabilities of the terminal. The roaming decision maker makes the roaming decision after taking the entire related context into consideration. The collaboration among these four components accomplishes efficient end-to-end mobility management for vertical handoff.

3.1.3. Gateway Solution

Mobile IP approach is a reasonable way to maintain the connectivity while handoff. However, mobile IP introduces serious latency and packet lost for roaming users to move between two networks frequently. A new approach, called gateway approach, is introduced in [12-13] to interconnect UMTS and wireless LAN to handle vertical handoff. Figure 3 shows the protocol architecture of the gateway approach. In this approach, a mobile user uses standard UMTS session management (SM) and GPRS mobility management (GMM) to access the UMTS network and uses the standard IP to connect to the wireless LAN. In the wireless LAN, the mobile users can use mobile IP to handle the mobility within the wireless LAN. For users to have interworking services, the control signals and data packets will be routed through the gateway. The gateway approach aims to separate the operations of the two networks making them to handle their single mode subscribers independently. If the two network operators have a roaming agreement, the gateway enables the intersystem roaming of the two networks. The merits of this approach are that the two networks can be operated independently and mobile IP is not necessary.

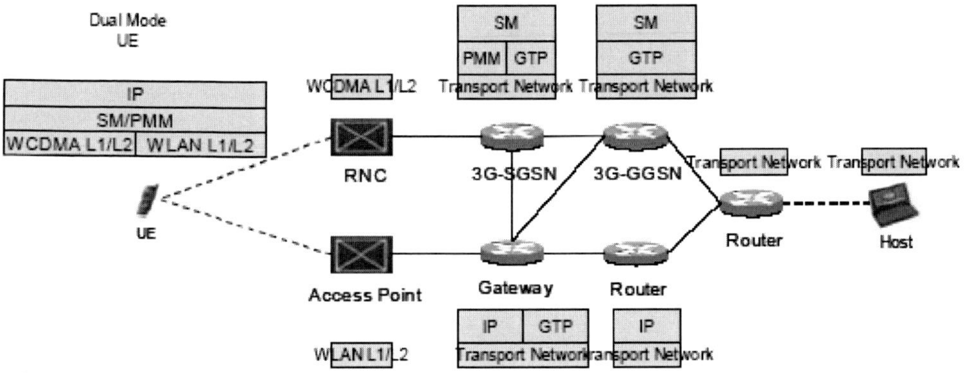

Figure 3. Protocol architecture of the gateway approach.

Figure 4 shows the detailed UMTS to wireless LAN and wireless LAN to UMTS handoff procedures. It is assumed that a mobile user is registered in a UMTS network and the UMTS network has a roaming agreement with wireless LAN operators. The first scenario is the handoff from UMTS to wireless LAN. Initially, the mobile user is sending or receiving packets through a UMTS network. At the step 1, a mobile user decides to handoff to a wireless LAN. The mobile user performs L1/L2 handoff procedures. At the step 2, the mobile user tries to obtain a gateway address in order to perform the intersystem handoff procedure by dynamic host configuration protocol (DHCP). The mobile user sends a message of DHCPDISCOVER to ask a gateway address in the visited network. The gateway responds it with its IP address. Once the gateway address obtained, the mobile user sends routing area update (RA update) to the gateway using its original IP address of the UMTS network. Then, the gateway sends a standard Update PDP Contexts Request to a GGSN to ask a GGSN changing its SGSN address-in-use. Once the GGSN receives PDP Context Request from the gateway, it knows that the mobile user wants to move to a wireless LAN. The gateway becomes the SGSN temporally. Packets to the mobile user should go to the gateway instead of the old SGSN. The GGSN sends a PDP/MM context standby command to the old SGSN.

After above steps, the mobile user can send packets out using its original IP address of the UMTS network. For the packets from the mobile user to Internet, they can be sent through the wireless LAN if the wireless LAN does not perform ingress filtering on these UMTS IP address. If the wireless LAN applies the ingress filtering on non-wireless LAN IP addresses, packets should go to the gateway and then to the Internet. For the packets to the mobile user, they should go to the UMTS network based on IP routing. The GGSN recognizes that the mobile user moves to the wireless LAN and it tunnels the packets to the gateway.

The second handoff scenario is that a wireless LAN user performs a handoff to a UMTS network. It is assumed that a mobile user is registered in a wireless LAN network and the wireless LAN has a roaming agreement with a UMTS network. The mobile user is also a subscriber of the UMTS network. Initially, a mobile user is sending or receiving packets through a wireless LAN. Once the mobile user decides to move to the UMTS network, it performs UMTS standard procedures. If it has already attached to the UMTS network and in the same RA, it can just start the service. If it is the first time to attach to the network, it should perform attach and PDP context activation and then can start the service. In the attach procedure, a mobile user uses the gateway as its access point name (APN) to inform the SGSN that it wants to use wireless LAN IP. During the PDP context activation procedure, the UMTS user uses the wireless LAN IP to request the PDP context. Once the gateway detects the IP is a wireless LAN IP and the security process is passed, it responds the mobile user with the same wireless LAN IP. The mobile user can use the same IP address that was used in the wireless LAN. Here, the gateway simulates the GGSN in a UMTS network. The SGSN will send outgoing packets to the gateway and incoming packets go through the gateway to the SGSN.

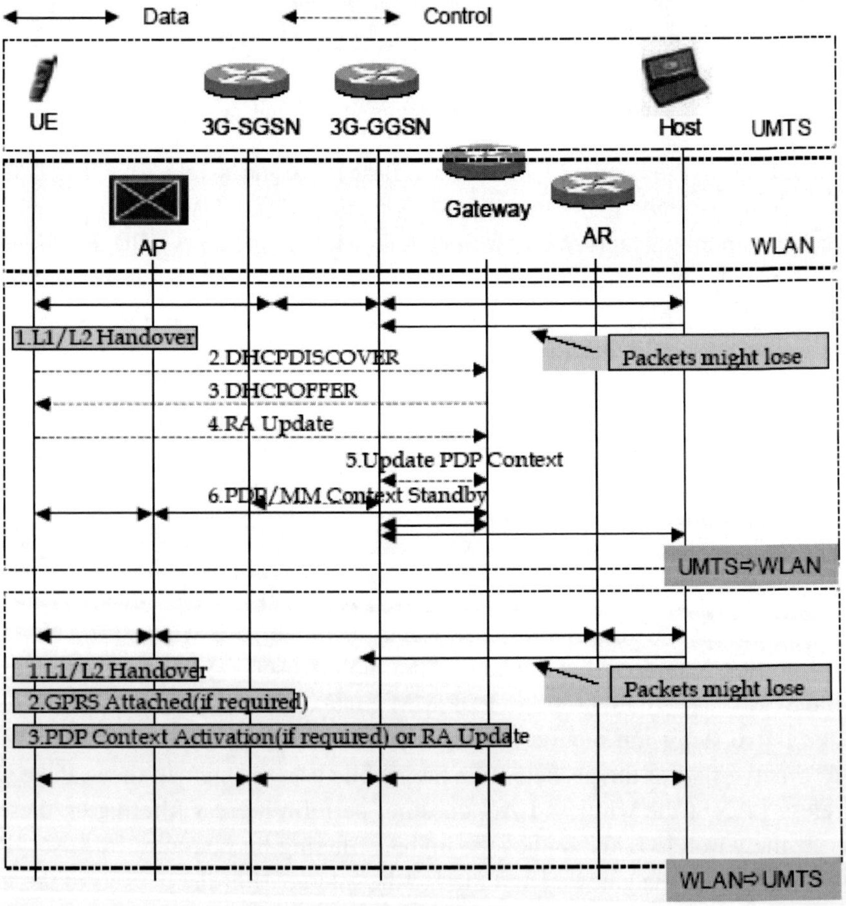

Figure 4. UMTS to wireless LAN and wireless LAN to UMTS handoff procedures.

Both incoming and outgoing packets go through the same path. If Internet hosts send packets to the wireless LAN mobile user, the packets will go through the wireless LAN, received by the gateway, sent to the SGSN and ended at the mobile user. The merits of this approach are that (1) handoff is faster and packet lost is less than mobile IP approach since all signaling messages are routed within the internal network; (2) mobile IP may not be necessary.

3.1.4. Dormant Solution

Non-dormant inter-technology roaming can be supported between wireless LAN and UMTS through home agent by using mobile IP. The mobile user is responsible for mobile IPv4 registration when it roams to UMTS from wireless LAN. Mobile IPv4 registration is performed after the mobile user establishes the GPRS Tunneling Protocol (GTP) tunnel to the Gateway GPRS Support Node (GGSN). If the mobile user roams back to the wireless LAN, it is responsible for performing "paging registration request" to mobility anchor point and mobile IPv4 registration to the home agent. To support dormant roaming, a new set of extensions is required in both wireless LAN and UMTS. Using a GTP tunnel for each mobile IPv4 registration during roaming is not feasible, and it degrades the wireless core network performance. It is benefit to support dormant roaming with a new set of required extensions in both wireless LAN and UMTS as reported in [14].

When a mobile user roams from UMTS to wireless LAN, it can figure out that it has changed its network from the beacons transmitted by AP in the wireless LAN. Then, the mobile user associates with AP and informs the AP that a mobile user will be in Power-save mode (dormant). The mobile user enters again into dormant mode. From this point on, the AP is responsible for the following actions: 1) Sending mobile IPv4 Registration Request message to the home agent (HA). 2) Receiving mobile IPv4 Registration Reply message from the HA. 3) If Layer 3 paging is supported, sending Paging Registration Request message to the paging agent, e.g. Paging Mobility Anchor Point (PMAP). 4) Receive Paging Registration Reply message from the PMAP. The proposed procedures are given in Figure 5.

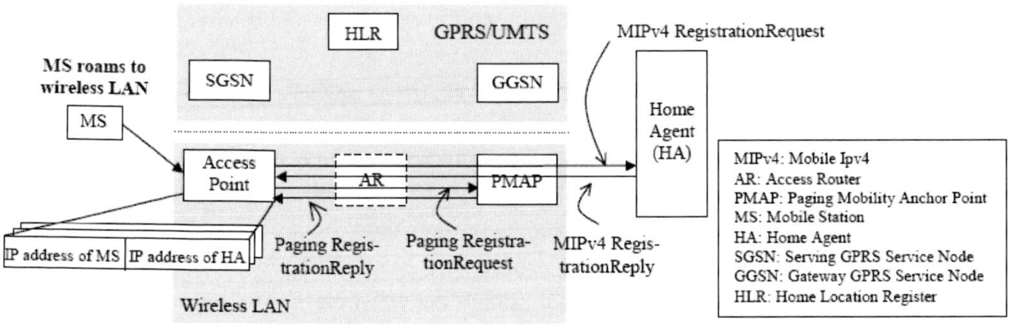

Figure 5. Dormant mode operation supports roaming from UMTS to wireless LAN.

When a mobile user roams from wireless LAN to UMTS, the mobile user does not need disassociating from its AP in the wireless LAN. When it moves to UMTS, the mobile user performs the location update to SGSN, which is a GPRS attached procedure. Then SGSN activates the location information and Mobile Mobility (MM) context in the Home Location

Register (HLR). Then, the mobile user can enter into dormant mode. It does not activate the GTP tunnel or perform any mobile IPv4 registration. The proposed procedures are given in Figure 6.

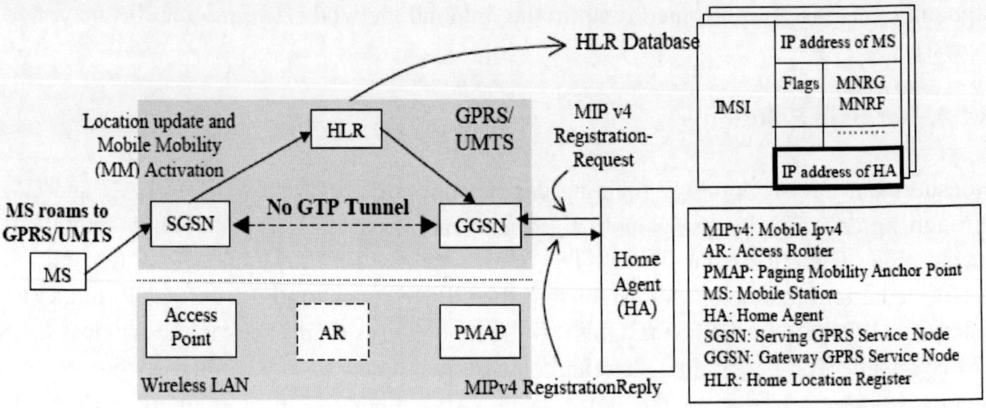

Figure 6. Dormant mode operation supports roaming from wireless LAN to UMTS.

3.2. Approaches at Transport Layer

Although Mobile IPv4 based approaches are prevalent technologies to provide some levels of mobility management after vertical handoff in the interworking architectures, it is shown that there are difficulties to maintain the continuity of ongoing data sessions during vertical handoff due to long handoff latency. Mobile users may experience QoS degradation or session disruption/termination during vertical handoffs so that seamless connectivity, which referred as the connectivity with low latency and negligible loss of data, cannot be guaranteed. However, since the transport layer is the lowest end-to-end layer in the Internet protocol stack, it is a natural candidate to support mobility management after vertical handoff. In addition, by the transport layer approach, no modification or addition of network components is required, which makes this approach universally applicable to all present and future network architectures. Moreover, a transport layer approach for mobility management enables the end nodes to adapt the flow and congestion control parameters quickly, thus offering the potential for significant performance enhancements.

One proposal is to use TCP protocol to handle mobility management after vertical handoffs in [15]. The scheme of using TCP protocol for mobility management works based on the different bandwidths of the two heterogeneous networks in the interworking architecture. Since wireless LAN and 3G cellular networks can provide different bandwidths to a mobile user, a drastic change in data rate may occur when the mobile user is transferred to the target network. Based on this fact, during handoffs, the scheme will make a TCP sender temporarily halt its data transmission to avoid a timeout and packet losses. When the handoff is completed, the sender will restore the transmission in the slow start state. The implementation of the scheme needs to have a radio resource control (RRC) module and some operations at both receiver and sender sides. The physical layer at a mobile node measures strength of signal and its velocity to report to the RRC module. The RRC module determines the vertical handoff time and notifies the impending handoff to the TCP layer. The scheme uses an optional field in TCP header to identify the handoff situation. The TCP receiver sends an acknowledgement (ACK) with setting the handoff field to the proper value according to the handoff type when a handoff is impending. It sends another ACK with setting to indicate the handoff is over in the handoff field as soon as the handoff completed so that the sender can resume the data transmission without waiting for a timeout. This ACK message to inform the sender of an impending handoff can be delivered multiple times to improve reliability. The TCP sender monitors the handoff field and adjusts its congestion window size. If it detects a horizontal handoff, the TCP sender stops the timeout timer and suspends data transmission until the handoff is completed. When the handoff is completed, the TCP sender resumes data transmission at the congestion avoidance state with the same congestion window size as before. If a vertical handoff is detected, the TCP sender stops the timeout timer and holds data transmission until the handoff is completed. The TCP sender resumes data transmission at the slow start state to estimate the available bandwidth.

Another proposal in [16] introduce a new scheme to support mobility management after vertical handoff using transport layer protocol Mobile SCTP, referred as mSCTP, which offers a point-to-point connection- oriented reliable delivery service for applications communicating over an IP network. It inherits many TCP functions and at the same time incorporates two major attractive new features, which are partial reliability and multihoming. Mobile SCTP has a partial reliability mechanism, by which it can configure a reliability level. And it can benefit real-time traffic transferred during periods of poor QoS due to path failures or network congestion. Multihoming enables an mSCTP session to be established over multiple interfaces identified by multiple IP addresses. mSCTP normally sends packets to a destination IP address designated the primary address. However, it can reroute packets to an alternative secondary IP address if the primary IP address becomes unreachable. Accordingly, the path between two mSCTP hosts using the primary addresses is the primary path. And a path between two SCTP hosts involving a secondary address is a secondary path. With this powerful feature, mSCTP can provide a simple but powerful framework for mobility support over IP networks.

The rationale behind the proposed scheme is that, due to the multihoming feature of mSCTP, from the association point of view it does not matter whether an endpoint's network interfaces belong to the same network or not. As long as it is possible for an interface to establish a connection to the Internet via an IP address, the interface can be added into the current association. Particularly, mSCTP's capabilities to add, delete, and change the IP addresses dynamically during an active SCTP association provides an end-to-end UMTS/WLAN vertical handover solution. Using the multihoming feature of SCTP, an mobile node can have two IP addresses during vertical handoff, one from the UMTS and the other from the wireless LAN. Similarly, a fixed server can also be configured either for single-homing, the fixed server with only one IP address to support handoff, or dual-homing, the fixed server with more than one (usually two) IP addresses to support handoff. For each of these configurations, the handoff procedure has three basic steps: 1) add IP address, 2) vertical handover triggering, 3) delete IP address. Since no addition or modification of network components is required, the proposed scheme has a network architecture that is much simpler than those required by network layer solutions.

4. Conclusion

Integrated wireless LAN and 3G cellular wireless network services will benefit both service providers and users. A loosely coupled network architecture that allows independent deployment and growth of each network will emerge as a preferred way to implement such services. One of the important issues on the topic of interworking of 3G cellular wireless network and wireless LAN is the mobility management, which includes vertical handoff decision making and vertical handoff management. Several strategies on the vertical handoff decision making have been overviewed in the first part of this paper. By using mobile IP, vertical handoff management can be implemented at the network layer. There are several schemes and architectures proposed to directly take the benefits of Mobile IP in order to allow internetworking roaming as reviewed. Another two proposals to implement mobility management at transport layer have been also presented. With the support of TCP and mSCTP protocols, the mobility management can be easily provided without extra network components needed. It shows that they are the natural candidates for the solution of the mobility management although Mobile IP solutions are prevalent in the current research focus. In this paper, a general view on the current progresses of the research topic on vertical handoff schemes could be formed. It is expected that with help of this article, more efficient and effective solutions can be further developed.

The current solutions and the further research on better solutions on the topic are the steps towards one goal, which is getting to close to a proposed concept "Always Best Connected" [17]. The future wireless technology will make the mobile users in any parts of the world to be seamlessly connected by the Internet through any types of wireless access networks including wireless LAN, 3G cellular wireless networks, and other high bandwidth wireless networks.

References

[1] H. Y. Lach, C. Janneteau, and A. Petrescu, "Network Mobility in Beyond-3G Systems", *IEEE Communications Magazine*, Vol. 41, Issue 7, July 2003, pg 52 – 57

[2] D. Findlay, H. Flygare, R. Hancock, T. Haslestad, E. Hepworth, D. Higgins, and S. McCann, "3G Interworking with Wireless LANs", *Proceedings of IEEE Third International Conference on 3G Mobile Communication Technologies 2002*, May 2002, pg 394- 399

[3] M. Buddhikot, G. Chandranmenon, S. Han, Y.W. Lee, S. Miller, and L. Salgarelli, "Integration of 802.11 and Third-generation Wireless Data Networks", *Proceedings of IEEE INFOCOM 2003,* Vol. 1, April 2003, pg 503 – 512

[4] G. P. Ppllini, "Trends in Handover Design," *IEEE Communications Magazine,* Vol.34, Issue 3, March 1996, pg 82-90

[5] H. Bing C. He, and L. Jiang, "Performance Analysis of Vertical Handover in a UMTS-wireless LAN Integrated Network", *Proceedings of the 14th IEEE International Symposium on Personal, Indoor and Mobile Radio communications 2003, PIMRC 2003.* Vol. 1, September 2003, pg 187 – 191

[6] Q. Zhang, C. Guo, Z. Guo, and W. Zhu, "Efficient Mobility Management for Vertical Handoff between WWAN and wireless LAN", *IEEE Communications Magazine,* Vol. 41, Issue 11, November 2003, pg 102 – 108

[7] S. Balasubramaniam and J. Indulska, "Handovers between Heterogeneous Networks in Pervasive Systems", *Proceedings of IEEE International Conference on Communication Technology 2003, ICCT2003*, Vol. 2, April 2003, pg 1056-1059

[8] H. Bing, C. He, and L. Jiang, "Intelligent signal processing of mobility management for heterogeneous networks", *Proceedings of the 2003 International Conference on Neural Networks and Signal Processing 2003*, Vol. 2, December 2003, pg. 1578 - 1581

[9] W. T. Chen, J. C. Liu, and H. K. Huang, "An adaptive scheme for vertical handoff in wireless overlay networks", *Proceedings of Tenth International Conference on Parallel and Distributed Systems 2004*, July 2004, pg 541 – 548

[10] F. Zhu, and J. McNair, "Optimizations for Vertical Handoff Decision Algorithms", *Proceedings of IEEE Conference of Wireless Communications and Networking,* Vol. 2, March 2004, pg 867 – 872

[11] M. Buddhikot, G. Chandranmenon, S. Han, Y. W. Lee, S. Miller, and L. Salgarelli, "Design and Implementation of a wireless LAN/cdma2000 Interworking Architecture", *IEEE Communications Magazine*, Vol. 41, Issue 11, November 2003, pg 90 – 100

[12] S. L. Tsao, and C. C. Lin, "VGSN: A Gateway Approach to Interconnect UMTS/wireless LAN Networks", *Proceeding of the 13th IEEE International Symposium on Personal, Indoor and Mobile Radio Communications 2002*, Vol. 1, September 2002, pg 275 - 279

[13] S. L. Tsao, and C. C. Lin, "Design and Evaluation of UMTS-wireless LAN Interworking Strategies", *Proceedings of of 56th IEEE Vehicular Technology Conference 2002*,. VTC 2002-Fall, Vol. 2, September 2002, pg 777 – 781

[14] B. Sarikaya, and T. Ozugur, "Dormant mode operation support for roaming from wireless LAN to UMTS",. *Proceedings of IEEE ICC 2003,* Vol. 2, May 2003, pg 1038 – 1042

[15] S. E. Kim, and J. A. Copeland, "TCP for Seamless Vertical Handoff in Hybrid Mobile Data Networks", *Proceedings of IEEE Globecom 2003,* Vol. 2, December 2003, pg 661-665

[16] L. Ma, F. Yu, V. C. M. Leung, and T. Randhawa, "A new method to support UMTS/WLAN vertical handover using SCTP", *IEEE Wireless Communications*, Vol. 11, Issue 4, August 2004, pg 44 – 51

[17] E. Gustafsson, and A. Jonsson, "Always Best Connected", *IEEE Wireless Communications*, Vol. 10, Issue 1, February 2003, pg 49 – 55

In: Computer-Aided Design…
Editors: C.M. De Smet et al, pp. 155-183
ISBN: 978-1-60456-860-8

Chapter 7

NCTUNS TOOL FOR INNOVATIVE NETWORK EMULATIONS

Shie-Yuan Wang*[1] *and Yu-Ming Huang
Department of Computer Science
National Chiao Tung University, Hsinchu, Taiwan

Abstract

Network emulation is an important research approach. It allows real-world traffic to interact with simulated traffic and experience various user-specified packet delaying, dropping, reordering, and duplication treatments. With emulation, one can test the function and performance of a real-world network device under various simulated network conditions without the need to get, know, or modify its internal protocol stack. Due to these capabilities, emulation is widely used to test network protocols and network devices. In this chapter, we introduce NCTUns, an innovative network simulator and emulator. We explain the novel simulation methodology used by it, present its new kernel-module-based design and implementation, and show its emulation capabilities and performance. Several examples are presented to illustrate its uses in wired and wireless network emulations. More information about this tool is available at its web site at http://NSL.csie.nctu.edu.tw/nctuns.html.

1. Introduction

Network emulation refers to the ability to simulate the characteristics of a real-world network in real time and let real-world packets pass through the simulated network to receive various treatments such as packet dropping, delaying, reordering, duplication, etc. (For brevity, in the rest of this chapter we will simply use "the simulated network" to denote "the network simulated in real time," which is the emulated network.) By emulation, real-world network devices can exchange their packets under various network conditions simulated by just one machine. The cost, effort, and time involved in setting up a large network to do real experiments can thus be significantly saved. Using emulation, one can evaluate the

[1] E-mail address: shieyuan@csie.nctu.edu.tw

performance of real-world network devices under various network conditions without the need to get, know, or modify its internal protocol stack. This capability is important as sometimes it is impossible, difficult, or expensive to acquire the source code of the protocol stack used in a network device.

Traditional emulation tools operate by allowing real-world packets to pass through an emulated link that gives packets special treatments based on simple statistics distributions. NCTUns is an innovative network simulator and emulator with many unique advantages. In addition to supporting the above common usage, it supports innovative emulations in which real-world traffic passes through a simulated network to interact with simulated traffic. In NCTUns, a real-world network device can set up TCP connections with any host in the simulated network to exchange their information. In addition, packets generated from a simulated network can be directed to a router in the real world and then come back into the simulated network to test the functions and performance of a real-world router. These unique capabilities are difficult to achieve by traditional network emulators. In this chapter, we introduce NCTUns, explain the novel simulation methodology used by it, present its emulation design and implementation, and show its emulation capabilities and performance. We also use several examples to illustrate its uses in wired and wireless network emulations. In the following, we first introduce the NCTUns network simulator as it will be turned into an emulator for emulation purposes.

2. NCTUns Network Simulator

2.1. Development Status

Network simulators implemented in software are valuable tools for researchers to develop, test, and diagnose network protocols. Simulation is economical because it can carry out experiments without the actual hardware. It is flexible because it can, for example, simulate a link with any bandwidth and propagation delay. Simulation results are easier to analyze than experimental results because important information at critical points can be easily logged to help researchers diagnose network protocols.

Network simulators, however, have their limitations. A complete network simulator needs to simulate networking devices (e.g., hosts and routers) and application programs that generate network traffic. It also needs to provide network utility programs to configure, monitor, and gather statistics about a simulated network. Developing a complete network simulator is a large effort. Due to limited development resources, traditional network simulators usually have the following drawbacks:

First, simulation results are not as convincing as those produced by real hardware and software equipment. In order to constrain their complexity and development cost, most network simulators usually can only simulate real-world network protocol implementations with limited details, and this may lead to incorrect results.

Second, most traditional network simulators are not extensible in the sense that they lack the standard UNIX POSIX application program interface (API). As a result, existing and to-be-developed real-world application programs cannot run normally to generate traffic for a simulated network, nor can their performance be evaluated under various simulated network conditions. Instead, they must be rewritten to use the internal API provided by the simulator (if there is any) and be compiled with the simulator to form a single, large, and complex program.

To overcome these problems, Wang invented a kernel re-entering simulation methodology [1, 2] and used it to implement the Harvard network simulator [3]. Later on, Wang further improved the methodology and used it to design and implement the NCTUns network simulator and emulator [4]. By using the novel kernel re-entering simulation methodology, NCTUns provides many unique advantages over traditional network simulators and emulators. Since its public release on November 1, 2002, as of August 1, 2009, more than 14,911 people from 132 countries in the world have registered at its web site (http://NSL.csie.nctu.edu.tw/nctuns.html) and downloaded it.

NCTUns is open-source and runs on the Linux operating system. It can simulate many different types of networks. After many years of development, it has become a high-quality and useful tool and has received many academic honors. For example, both ACM MobiCom 2002 [5] and MobiCom 2003 [6] international conferences select it as a research demonstration. The IEEE Network Magazine reports this tool in its July 2003 issue [7]. The IEEE MASCOTS 2004 international conference selects it as a tutorial [8]. The IEEE vehicular technology society selects it as a tutorial at its workshop [9]. The IEEE INFOCOM 2005 conference selects it as a demonstration [10]. The SPECTS 2005 international conference selects it as a tutorial [11]. In addition, Wiley publishes a paper to present the capabilities of NCTUns on wireless resource management [12].

2.2. Kernel Re-entering Simulation Methodology

Tunnel network interface is the key facility in the kernel re-entering simulation methodology. A tunnel network interface, available on most UNIX machines, is a pseudo network interface that does not have a physical network attached to it. The functions of a tunnel network interface, from the kernel's point of view, are no different from those of an Ethernet network interface. A network application program can send or receive packets through a tunnel network interface, just as if these packets were sent to or received from a normal Ethernet interface.

Each tunnel interface has a corresponding device special file in the /dev directory. If an application program opens a tunnel interface's special file and writes a packet into it, the packet will enter the kernel. To the kernel, the packet appears to come from a real network and will go up through the kernel's TCP/IP protocol stack as an Ethernet packet would do. On the other hand, if the application program reads a packet from a tunnel interface's special file, the first packet in the tunnel interface's output queue in the kernel will be dequeued and copied to the application program. To the kernel, the packet appears to have been transmitted onto a real link and this pseudo transmission is no different from an Ethernet packet transmission.

Using tunnel network interfaces, one can easily simulate the single-hop TCP/IP network depicted in Figure 1 (a), where a TCP sender application program running on host 1 sends its TCP packets to a TCP receiver application program running on host 2. One can set up the simulated network with two operations. First one configures the kernel routing table of the simulation machine so that tunnel network interface 1 is chosen as the outgoing interface for the TCP packets sent from host 1 to host 2, and tunnel network interface 2 is chosen for the

TCP packets sent from host 2 to host 1. Second, the simulation engine process simulates the characteristics of these two links. For the link from host i to host j (i = 1 or 2 and j = 3 – i), the simulation engine opens tunnel network interface i's and j's special files in /dev and then executes a while loop. In each step of this loop, it simulates a packet's transmission on the link from host i to host j by reading a packet from the special file of tunnel interface i, waiting the link's propagation delay time plus the packet's transmission time on the link (in simulation time), and then writing this packet to the special file of tunnel interface j.

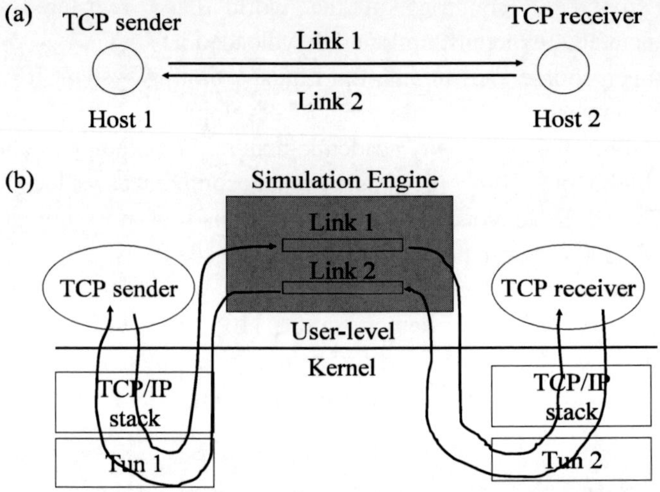

Figure 1. (a) A single-hop TCP/IP network to be simulated. (b) The way the single-hop TCP/IP network is simulated in NCTUns.

While the simulation engine process is running, the simulated network is constructed and alive. Figure 1 (b) depicts this simulation scheme. Since replacing a real link with a simulated link occurs outside the kernel, the kernels on both hosts do not know that their packets actually are exchanged on a virtual simulated network. The TCP sender and receiver programs, which run on top of the kernels, do not know the fact either. As a result, all existing real-world application programs can run on the simulated network, all existing real-world network utility programs can be applied to the simulated network, and the TCP/IP network protocol stack used in the simulation is the real-world working implementation. Note that in this methodology all nodes in a simulated network share the kernel of the simulation machine. Therefore, although two TCP/IP protocol stacks are depicted in Figure 1, actually they are the same one – the protocol stack of the simulation machine.

2.3. Features

The NCTUns network simulator has many useful and unique features. Here we describe each of them.

A. **It directly uses the real-world Linux's TCP/IP protocol stack to generate high-fidelity simulation results.** By using the novel kernel re-entering simulation methodology, the protocol stack of a real-world UNIX (e.g., FreeBSD or Linux) kernel is directly used to generate high-fidelity simulation results.

B. **It can use any existing and to-be-developed UNIX application program as a traffic generator program without any modification**. Any real-world program can be run on a simulated network to generate realistic network traffic and be evaluated. This capability enables a researcher to test the functions and performance of a distributed application or system (e.g., an Internet online game or auction system) under various network conditions. Another important advantage of this feature is that application programs developed during simulation studies can be directly used and deployed on real-world UNIX machines after simulation studies are finished. This capability eliminates the time and effort required to port a simulation prototype to a real-world implementation if traditional network simulators were used.

C. **It can use any real-world UNIX network configuration and monitoring tools.** For example, the UNIX route, ifconfig, netstat, tcpdump, traceroute, commands can all be run on a simulated network to configure and monitor the simulated network.

D. **The setup and usage of a simulated network and application programs are exactly the same as those used in real-world IP networks.** For example, in NCTUns each layer-3 interface has an IP address assigned to it and application programs use these IP addresses to communicate with each other. A person who is familiar with real-world IP network configurations and operations can learn and operate NCTUns in a few minutes. NCTUns is a good educational tool by which students learn how to configure and operate a real-world IP network.

E. **It simulates various networks**. NCTUns currently supports fixed Internet (including IPv4 and IPv6), wireless LAN networks (including the ad hoc mode and infrastructure mode), wireless sensor networks, wireless mesh networks, military tactics mobile ad hoc networks, optical networks (including traditional circuit-switching mode and more advanced Optical Burst Switching mode), GPRS cellular networks, DVB/RCS satellite networks, IEEE 802.16(d)(e)(j) WiMAX networks, IEEE 802.11p/1609 wireless vehicular networks, etc.

F. **It simulates various network devices.** For example, Ethernet hubs, switches, routers, hosts, IEEE 802.11(b) mobile stations and access points, WAN (Wide Area Network, for purposely delaying/dropping/reordering packets), Wall (wireless signal obstacle), GPRS base station, GPRS phone, GPRS GGSN, GPRS SGSN, optical circuit switch, optical burst switch, QoS DiffServ interior and boundary routers, wireless mesh routers, military agent nodes, etc.

G. **It simulates various protocols**. For example, IEEE 802.3 CSMA/CD MAC, IEEE 802.11(b) CSMA/CA MAC, IEEE 802.11(e) (MAC-layer QoS), learning bridge protocol, spanning tree protocol, IP, Mobile IP, Diffserv (IP-layer QoS), RIP, OSPF, UDP, TCP, RTP/RTCP/SDP, HTTP, FTP, Telnet, etc.

H. **Its simulation speed is high**. By combining the kernel re-entering simulation methodology with the discrete-event simulation methodology, a simulation job can be finished quickly.

I. **Its simulation results are repeatable**. NCTUns modifies the UNIX kernel to precisely control the scheduling order of the simulation engine process and application processes. As such, if the chosen random number seed for a simulation case is fixed, the simulation results of the case will be the same across different simulation runs even though some other activities (e.g., disk I/O) may occur on the simulation machine during simulation.

J. It provides a highly-integrated and professional GUI environment. The GUI can help a user (1) draw network topologies, (2) configure the protocol modules used inside a node, (3) specify the moving paths of mobile nodes, (4) plot network performance graphs, (5) play back the animation of a logged packet transfer trace, etc. All these operations can be easily and intuitively done with the GUI. Figure 2 shows the GUI environment of NCTUns.

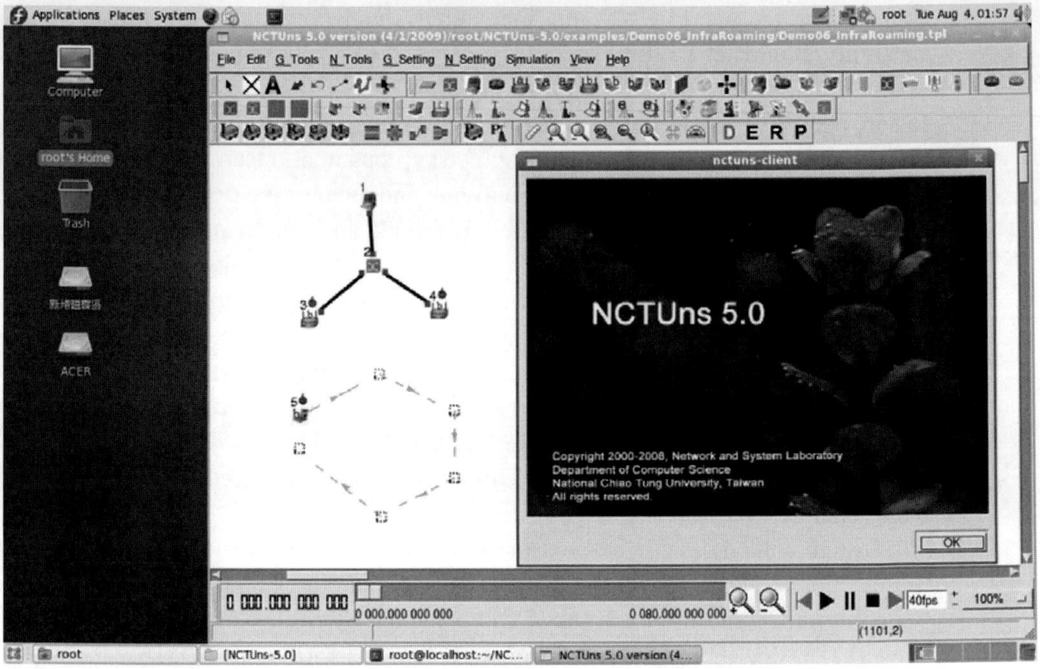

Figure 2. The GUI environment of NCTUns.

Its simulation engine adopts an open-system architecture and is open source. By using a set of module APIs provided by the simulation engine, one can easily implement a new protocol module and integrate it into the simulation engine. NCTUns uses a simple and effective syntax to describe the settings and configurations of a simulation job. These descriptions are generated by the GUI and stored in a suite of files. Normally the GUI will automatically transfer these files to the simulation engine for execution. However, if one wants to evaluate new types of networks that the GUI does not support, one can bypass the GUI and generate the suite of description files by himself/herself using any text editor (or by running a script program). The non-GUI-generated suite of files can be manually fed to the simulation engine for execution.

It supports more realistic wireless signal propagation models. In addition to providing the simple (transmission range = 250 m, interference range = 550 m) model that is commonly used in other network simulators, NCTUns provides over thirty more realistic models in which a received bit's BER (Bit Error Rate) is calculated based on the used modulation and coding schemes, the bit's received power level, and the noise power level around the receiver. Large-scale path loss and small-scale fading effects are also simulated.

Every node in a simulated network is equipped with a command console. One can launch application programs or execute UNIX commands during simulation in the command console of a simulated node. The allowed operations are exactly the same as what one can operate in the command console of a real-world network device. For example, one may run the "netstat" command in the command console of a simulated node to obtain the packet transfer statistics of an interface used by that simulated node. As another example, one can use the "ping" and "traceroute" program to test whether the routing path between the local node and a remote node is properly set up in the simulated network. This capability allows researchers to flexibly issue commands during simulation based on the current needs.

It supports the tcpdump packet capturing and filtering tool. The tcpdump program is a user-level packet filtering and capturing tool. It passes filtering rules to the kernel and displays the information of captured packets. The Berkeley-Packet-Filter (BPF) module in the kernel performs packet-filtering operations. When a packet is sent or received at an interface, the device driver of the interface passes the packet to the BPF module for evaluation. If the BPF module accepts this packet, it associates a timestamp with the packet. The BPF module gives each captured incoming packet a timestamp to record when it is received by the interface. The module also gives each captured outgoing packet a timestamp to record when it is transmitted onto a link. The tcpdump program can display the header and payload of captured packets. In NCTUns, the tcpdump program can monitor any network interface in a simulated network to capture desired packets.

3. Emulator Architecture

NCTUns network simulator can be easily turned into a network emulator by performing the following operations. First, an as-fast-as-possible simulation should be turned into a real-time simulation by synchronizing the virtual clock with the real time. This is required because the simulated network should appear as a real network to real-world devices when they are exchanging their packets over the simulated network. Second, several routing entries need to be added to the system routing table on real-world devices so that their packets can be transmitted to the simulation machine. Third, several packet-filtering rules need to be installed and several routing entries need to be added to the system routing table on the simulation machine. Doing so will allow incoming real-world packets to be captured and then directed to the simulated network. Conversely, packets generated from the simulated network can be captured and then sent to real-world devices. Finally, the headers of the captured packets need to be translated so that they can be forwarded between the simulated network and the real-world devices.

Regarding the first operation of real-time synchronization, NCTUns periodically synchronizes its simulation clock with the system's real time clock so that they differ by at most 1 ms at any time. Regarding the second operation of setting relevant routing entries on real-world machines, NCTUns automatically computes and outputs them for the user's references. Regarding the third operation of setting relevant packet-filtering rules and routing entries on the simulation machine, NCTUns automatically computes and installs them when an emulation case starts. Thus, no human intervention is needed. Finally, regarding necessary packet header translations, NCTUns implements an emulation module (kernel module) to receive captured packets and perform header translations.

To conduct an emulation case, one needs to first construct the simulated network that real-world packets will pass through. Using the GUI of NCTUns can easily do this job. Second, one needs to specify how an external machine interfaces with the simulated network. That is, when the packets generated by a real-world machine arrive at the simulation machine, to which part of the simulated network should they enter? To help a user easily specify this relationship, an external host/router icon is provided in the GUI of NCTUns. This node icon represents its corresponding external machine in the real world. By drawing a link between this node icon and a node icon in the simulated network in the GUI, one can clearly specify how the external machine in the real world connects to the simulated network. To avoid confusion, in the rest of this chapter, when we say "**external host**," we mean the one in the GUI. On the other hand, when we say "**external machine**," we mean the corresponding external machine in the real world.

3.1. Kernel Emulation Module

Packet header translations for emulation can be implemented as a user-level daemon or as a kernel module. Initially, NCTUns implemented a user-level daemon to support emulation. Starting the 5.0 version, NCTUns now implements a kernel emulation module to support emulation more efficiently. The main advantage for the module approach is that this approach can reduce memory copy operation overhead between the kernel and user space. In the module approach, when a packet arrives from an external machine and is received by the network device driver in the kernel, it is captured by the kernel module and directly forwarded to a tunnel interface in the kernel. If this operation is instead implemented as a user-level daemon, when the packet is received by the kernel, the kernel will need to copy the packet from the kernel space to the user space so that the daemon can get the packet and change the packet header. Later on, the daemon will need to write the packet into the kernel to enqueue it at a tunnel interface. Due to these two copy operations, the user-level daemon approach generates poorer performances than the kernel emulation module approach.

In NCTUns, when the simulation starts, the emulation module will be loaded into the kernel automatically and it will read a configuration file which contains all the filtering rules. During the simulation, the emulation module performs header translations for all packets that are either originated from or destined to the external machine. It functions like a NAT (network address translator) to translate IP addresses between the simulated network and the real world. Figure 3 shows that an emulation module is running to serve external machines (hosts) in the real world. Packets generated by this external machine are transmitted through an Ethernet link to reach the simulation machine. These packets are intercepted, filtered by the emulation module, and the headers of these packets are translated, then, the kernel forwards them into the corresponding tunnel interface and injects them into the simulation network. These packets then are transmitted over a link, pass a switch, are transmitted over another link, and finally reach their destination host all by simulation. Figure 4 shows the operations for the opposite direction when the simulated host sends back a packet to the external machine in the real world.

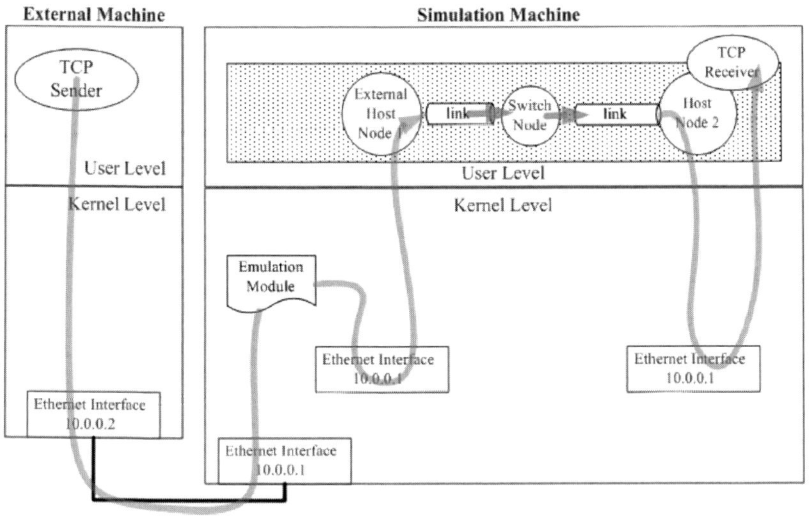

Figure 3. The emulation module captures packets for the traffic direction from the external machine to the simulation machine.

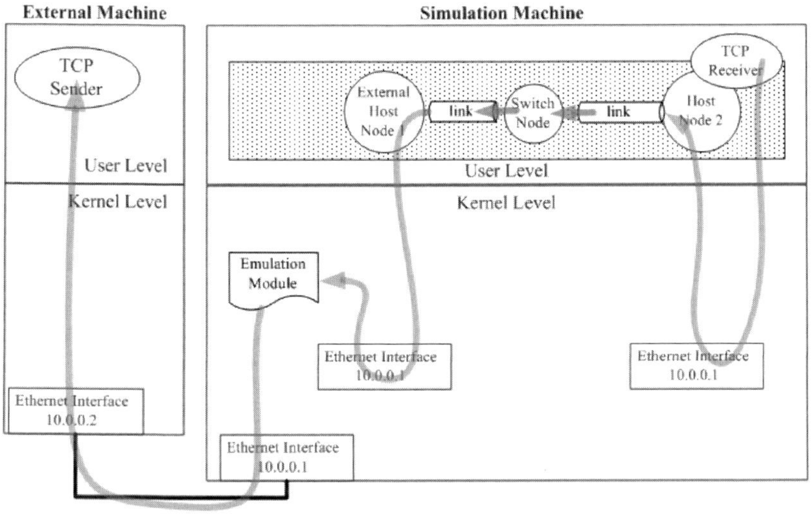

Figure 4. The emulation module captures packets for the traffic direction from the simulation machine to the external machine.

3.2. Capturing Packets in the Kernel

Emulation module needs a mechanism to filter and capture packets. This is accomplished through the help of another module in the kernel. Here, we describe how an emulation module filters and captures packets received from an interface in the kernel of the Linux operating system.

In Linux, the kernel uses the *netfilter* [13] mechanism to filter and capture packets. Netfilter is a set of hooks inside the Linux kernel that allows kernel modules or functions to register their callback functions with the network stack. When a packet traverses a hook, the hook's associated callback function will be called. Based on netfilter, *iptables* is a generic hook that is used for applications that need to capture packets from the kernel.

Figure 5 shows the architecture of these modules. The netfilter module maintains a global structure that has five lists each of which is associated with a hook number. Every hook number corresponds to a packet filtering point inside the network stack. This figure shows the filtering scenario when a packet coming from network interface 1 is forwarded at the IP layer to network interface 2. On the forwarding path, the packet will pass through three filtering points, which are IP_PRE_ROUTING, IP_FORWARD, and IP_POST_ROUTING, respectively. When a packet passes through the IP_FORWARD filtering point, it means that the IP layer is being used to forward the packet. When a packet passes through IP_PRE_ROUTING, it means that the kernel is filtering the packet before routing it. When a packet passes through IP_POST_ROUTING, it means that the kernel is filtering the packet after routing it. In total, there are five filtering points in the IP network stack. In this figure, only three filtering points are shown. The other two filtering points are IP_LOCAL_IN and IP_LOCAL_OUT and their corresponding hook numbers are 1 and 3, respectively. IP_LOCAL_OUT represents the filtering point where the kernel sends out a packet generated by the local host. In contrast, IP_LOCAL_IN represents the filtering point where the kernel receives a packet whose destination is the local host.

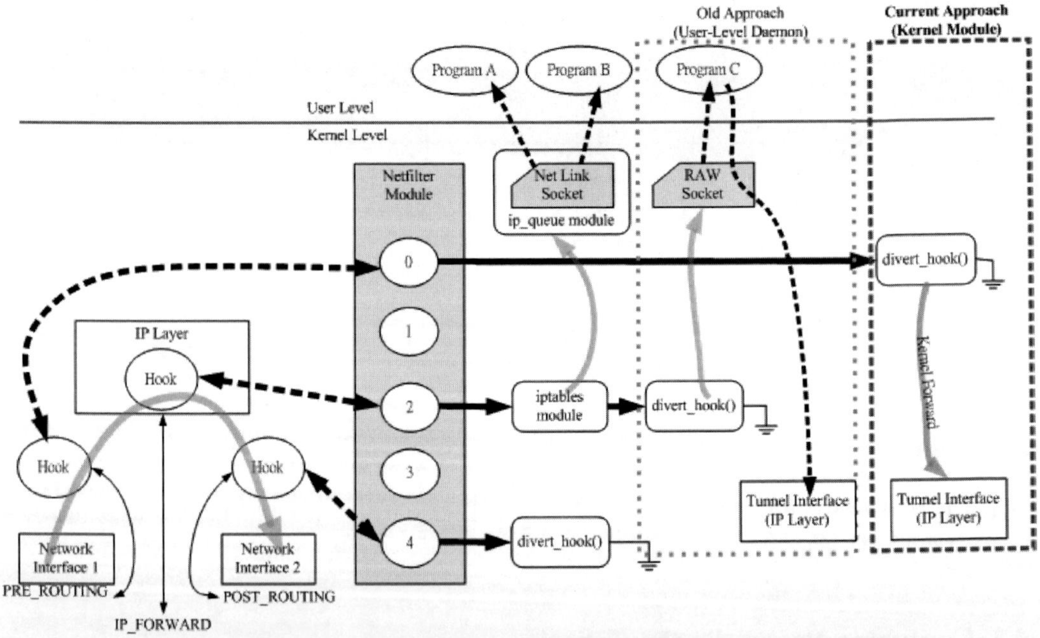

Figure 5. The packet filtering and capturing mechanism used in the Linux kernel.

When a packet passes through a filtering point, the kernel will send the packet to the netfilter module, which is depicted as a gray box in this figure. The netfilter module will relay this packet to those functions that have been registered in the corresponding filtering point (hook number). For example, when a packet passes through the IP_FORWARD filtering point, the kernel will send it to the netfilter module. The netfilter module will first relay the packet to the iptables module in the list of hook number 2. If the iptables module does not capture the packet, the packet will be sent back to the netfilter module. In this case, the netfilter module will continually relay the same packet to the next registered function, which is divert_hook() in this figure. Suppose that divert_hook() does not capture this packet, the packet will be sent back to the netfilter module again. At this time, the netfilter module will discover that no more registered function exists in the list of hook number 2. The netfilter module will then send the packet back to the network stack (the IP layer) and the packet will continually go through its original path.

4. Emulation Module Design

Besides capturing packets in the kernel, the emulation module needs to forward packets in the right direction. Here we describe how to forward packets between an external host in the real world and the simulated network. Due to space limitation, the emulation module design for supporting external routers is not presented.

4.1. Routing Entries Installation

In Figure 3, the external machine is equipped with a Fast Ethernet interface and this interface is configured with an IP address 10.0.0.2. The simulation machine's Fast Ethernet interface is configured with an IP address 10.0.0.1. In the simulated network, the external host (node 1) represents the external machine and has a tunnel interface with an assigned IP address 1.0.1.1. (In NCTUns, the IP address format is 1.0.subnetID.hostID [4].) If the TCP sender running on the external machine wants to communicate with the TCP receiver running on the simulated host (node 2), it should use 1.0.1.2 as the destination IP address of the packet. On the other hand, if the TCP sender running on the simulated host (node 2) wants to establish a TCP connection with the TCP receiver running on the external machine, it should use 1.0.1.1 as the destination IP address of the packet. That is, no matter whether the destination node of a packet is a simulated host or an external machine, the destination IP address used should be its assigned IP address in the simulated network.

Assume that the external machine wants to send packets to the simulated host and it is a Linux machine. One can execute the following command to add a routing entry on the external machine:

```
# route add -net 1.0.0.0/16 gw 10.0.0.1
```

This command indicates that all outgoing packets whose destination IP addresses are 1.0.X.X should be sent to the gateway whose IP address is 10.0.0.1. Since the simulation machine is configured with the IP address 10.0.0.1, any packet that is generated by the external machine and destined to the simulated network will be sent to the simulation machine. These packets will be filtered and captured by IP filter 0 depicted in Figure 3 and directed to the emulation module.

4.2. IP Address Translation

In Figure 3, the TCP sender running on the external machine establishes a TCP connection with the TCP receiver running on the simulated host, which binds 1.0.1.2 as its source IP address in the simulated network. The TCP sender thinks that the TCP connection is established between 10.0.0.2 (its own IP address in the real world) and 1.0.1.2 (the destination node's IP address in the simulated network). When the TCP sender sends its packets to 1.0.1.2, these packets will be captured and delivered to the emulation module and their source IP addresses will be modified from 10.0.0.2 to 1.0.1.1. This is because the external host (node 1) represents the external machine and the IP address of node 1 is 1.0.1.1. All packets generated by the external machine should be treated as though they were generated and sent out from node 1. If the address translation is not performed, the simulated network will not know which node the 10.0.0.2 IP address belongs to. With this translation, the TCP receiver will think that the TCP connection is established between 1.0.1.1 and 1.0.1.2. The TCP receiver will return a TCP ACK packet with its destination IP address set to 1.0.1.1.

In Figure 4, when the TCP ACK packet arrives at the external host (node 1), IP filter 0 will capture the packet and deliver it to the emulation module. Then, the emulation module will change the destination IP address 1.0.1.1 to 10.0.0.2, which is the IP address of the external machine in the real world. In the mean time, the source IP address of the TCP ACK packet is still kept the same (1.0.1.2). With this design, the ACK packet can reach the external machine and the TCP sender on the external machine will not know that the IP addresses of its packets have been translated.

5. Usage Examples

In the following, we illustrate how to use NCTUns to support emulations that involves real-world external hosts, external ad hoc mode mobile hosts, external infrastructure mode mobile hosts, and external routers, respectively.

5.1. External Host

External hosts can be connected to a simulated network in several ways. In the following, we present two emulation examples.

A. Example 1

Figure 6 shows the network topology used in the first example. In this figure, node 4 represents an external host in the real world (which is called an external machine interchangeably when there is no ambiguity) while all other nodes and links (inside the large dashed circle) are simulated in real time by another machine (which is called the simulation machine). This figure indicates that the external host (i.e., the external machine) is connected to the simulated network via the simulated switch (node 3). In this figure, the bandwidth and delay of the link between the external host (node 4) and the simulated switch is simulated. The bandwidth and delay of this simulated link need not be the same as those of the physical link that connects the simulation machine and the external machine together. To let real-world packets be exchanged between the two machines as fast as possible, the bandwidth and delay of the used physical link should be as high as possible and as low as possible, respectively. After packets generated by the external machine arrive at the simulation machine, they will be injected to the simulated network from the external host in the simulated network (i.e., node 4). These packets will then be transmitted over the simulated link to reach the simulated switch.

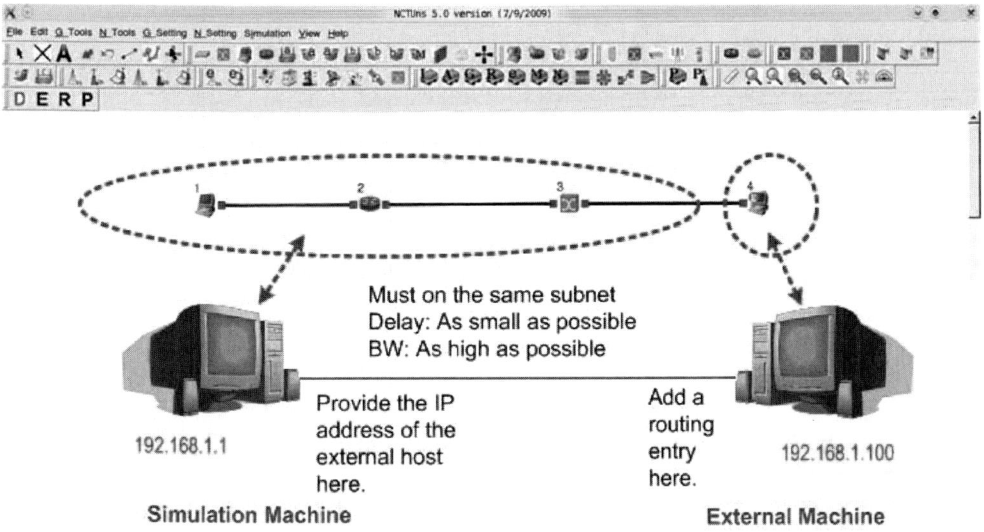

Figure 6. The network topology and physical setup used in the first example.

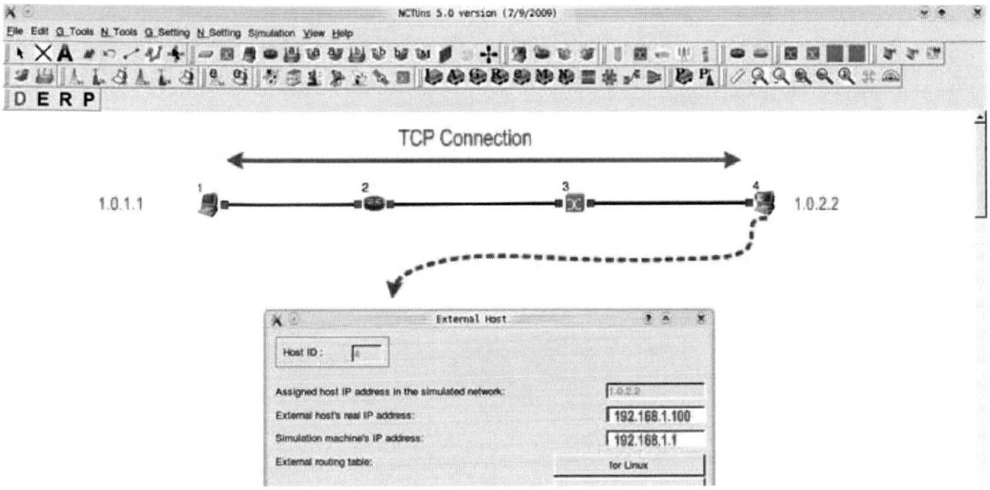

Figure 7. The GUI dialog box of the external host.

Suppose that in the simulated network the IP address assigned to the simulated host on the left (node 1) is 1.0.1.1 and the IP address assigned to the external host on the right (node 4) is 1.0.2.1. Also suppose that in the real world the simulation machine's IP address is 192.168.1.1 and the external machine's IP address is 192.168.1.100. Figure 7 shows that the above information is provided to NCTUns through the GUI dialog box of the external host. NCTUns will automatically set up relevant packet filtering rules and routing entries on the simulation machine. One only needs to set up a routing entry on the external machine to let its packets be directed to the simulation machine.

Suppose that the external machine wants to set up a greedy TCP connection to the simulated host. In such a case, the “rtcp -p 8000” command can be specified in the simulated host’s GUI dialog box. This will cause NCTUns to run up a TCP receiver program that binds on port number 8000 on the simulated host during emulation. After starting the emulation, one can execute the “stcp -p 8000 1.0.1.1” command on the external machine to run up a TCP sender program. Doing so will set up a TCP connection between the external machine and the simulated host and user data will begin to be transferred from the external machine to the simulated host.

B. Example 2

The top of Figure 8 shows the second example, where two external machines (node 3 and node 4) are connected to the simulated network. The right external machine connects itself to the simulated switch (node 2) while the left one connects itself to the simulated router (node 1). The two external machines want to exchange their TCP packets through the simulated network. Suppose that the IP address assigned to the left external host is 1.0.1.1 and the IP address assigned to the right external host is 1.0.2.1 in the simulated network. Suppose that the three machines (i.e., the two external machines and the simulation machine) are physically connected together via a high-speed network (e.g., a 100 Mbps Fast Ethernet or a Gigabit Ethernet) and each of them uses a different IP address in the 192.168.1.0/24 subnet. The bottom of Figure 8 shows this physical setup.

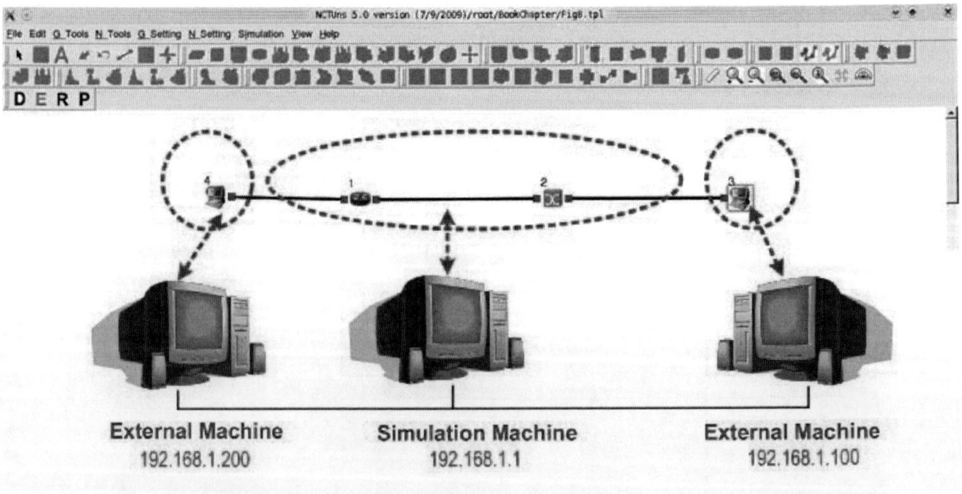

Figure 8. The network topology and physical setup used in the second example.

Suppose that one wants to set up a TCP connection between the two external machines and let their packets be exchanged over the simulated network. One can first start the emulation and keep it running. Then one executes the “rtcp -p 8000” command on the left external machine to run up a TCP receiver program. Then one executes “stcp –p 8000

1.0.1.1" on the right external machine to run up a TCP sender program. Doing so will set up a real-world TCP connection between the two external machines. User data will begin to be transferred from the right external machine to the left external machine over the simulated network.

When many external machines need to connect to the simulation machine, the simulation machine may not have that many number of network interfaces, each connecting to an external machine. To overcome this problem, a multi-port high-speed Ethernet switch (e.g., a 24-port Gigabit Ethernet switch) can be used to connect all external machines and the simulation machine together. In such a configuration, the simulation machine needs just one interface regardless of the number of external machines. Using this approach, one must take cares to ensure that the aggregate traffic from all external machines to the simulation machine will not exceed the bandwidth of the link from the switch to the simulation machine. Otherwise, the packets from external machines may be dropped or delayed in the switch, causing emulation results to be less accurate.

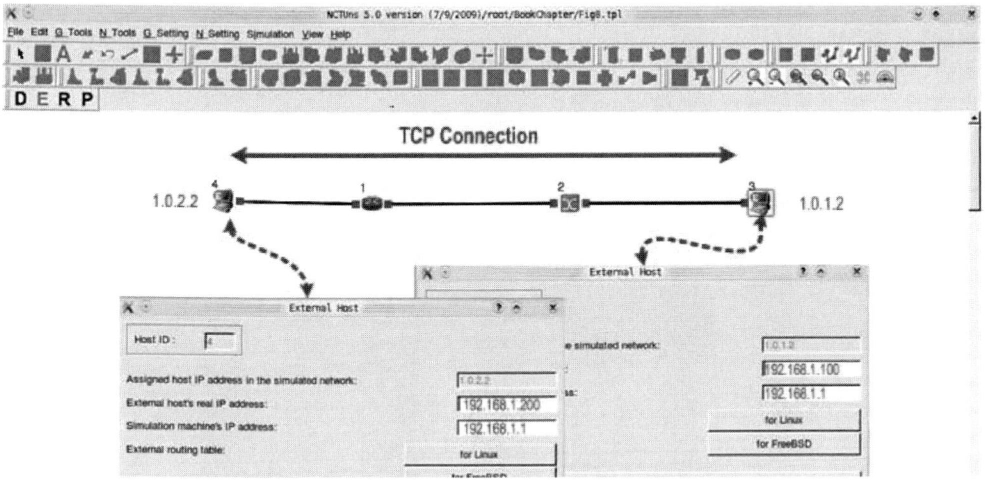

Figure 9. The GUI dialog boxes of the two external hosts.

5.2. External Ad Hoc Mode Mobile Host

An external ad hoc mode mobile host in the real world (called an external mobile machine here) can participate in a NCTUns emulation. In the simulated network one can specify the moving path of an external mobile host that represents an external mobile machine. However, the corresponding external mobile machine need not move in the real world. Actually, it can be a fixed host that uses an Ethernet link to connect to the simulated network (simulation machine).

The external mobile machine's IEEE 802.11 MAC protocol is simulated in the simulated network. It is not used to exchange packets between the external mobile machine and the simulation machine. When packets generated by the external mobile machine arrive at the simulation machine, they are directed to the emulation module. The emulation module will re-direct these packets into the simulation network. Then they will be wirelessly transmitted to other nodes in the simulated network using the (simulated) IEEE 802.11 MAC protocol.

Since the external mobile host in the simulated network represents the external mobile machine, its mobility is simulated by NCTUns rather than by the user physically moving the external mobile machine around the simulation machine in the real world. With these capabilities, one can easily evaluate the performance of the applications and higher-layer protocols running on the external mobile machine (e.g., a PDA or a cellular phone) under various simulated network and mobility conditions.

Figure 10 shows an emulation example in which one external ad hoc mode mobile host (node 3, which represents an external mobile machine in the real world) communicates with a simulated mobile host on the right (node 2) via another simulated mobile host in the middle (node 1). Initially, the external mobile host on the left can exchange packets with the simulated mobile host on the right via the middle mobile host. However, as time proceeds, the mobile host on the left begins to move away from the simulated mobile host (not in the real world but in the simulated network) and eventually it is out of the transmission range of the middle mobile host. At this time, it can no longer communicate with the simulated mobile host on the right via the middle mobile host. Later on, when the external mobile host moves into the transmission ranges of node 1 or node 2, it can communicate with node 2 again.

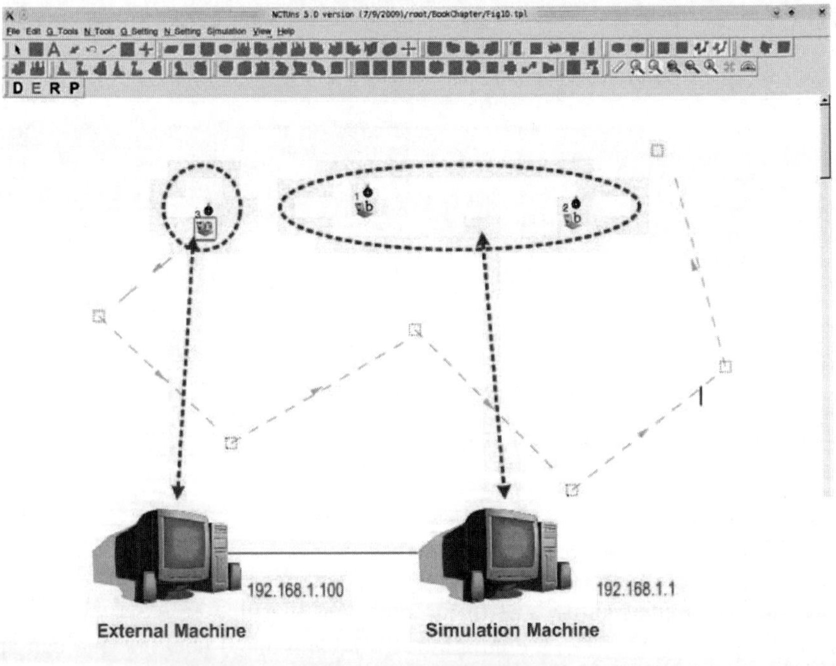

Figure 10. The network topology and physical setup used in the external ad hoc mode mobile host emulation example.

The physical setup for this emulation case is shown at the bottom of Figure 10. One simulation machine and one external mobile machine (which need not be mobile) are used and they can be connected via an Ethernet link or an IEEE 802.11(b) wireless network. Actually, any kind of networks can be used to connect these two machines together, including optical networks or IEEE 802.16(d)(e)(j) WiMAX networks). It does not matter which type of network link is used between the simulation machine and the external mobile machine as long as their IP packets can be exchanged on the used network. As in the external host emulation example, the simulation machine and the external mobile machine should be on the same subnet (if they are not, tunneling techniques may be used). Assuming that the simulation machine's IP address is 192.168.1.1 and the external mobile machine's IP address is 192.168.1.100 and they are physically connccted via a Fast Ethernet cable. Then on the external mobile machine, one can execute the following command to add the required routing entry to the system routing table.

route add 1.0/16 192.168.1.1 (FreeBSD version)

route add -net 1.0.0.0/16 gw 192.168.1.1 (Linux version)

After adding the required routing entry, the external mobile machine can begin to exchange packets with a simulated mobile host. If a node (either a simulated host or an external mobile machine) wants to send packets to another node (either a simulated host or an external mobile machine), it should use the IP address assigned to that node in the simulated network. Assume that in the simulated network node 1, node 2, and node 3 are assigned 1.0.1.1, 1.0.1.2, and 1.0.1.3 IP address, respectively. If the external mobile machine wants set up a greedy TCP connection to the simulated host on the right (node 2), the "rtcp –p 8000" command can be specified in the GUI dialog box of the simulated host and the "stcp –p 8000 1.0.1.2" command can be executed on the external mobile machine. On the other hand, if the simulated host wants to set up a greedy TCP connection to the external mobile machine, the "rtcp –p 8000" command can be executed on the external mobile machine and the "stcp –p 8000 1.0.1.3" command can be specified in the GUI dialog box of the simulated host. Figure 11 shows the information that needs to be specified in the GUI dialog box of the external mobile host for this example.

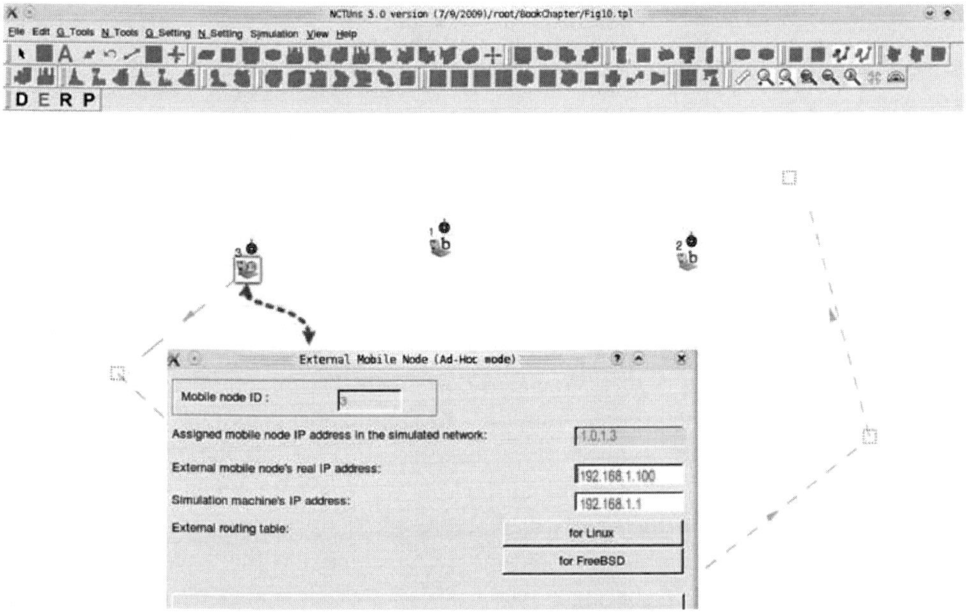

Figure 11. The GUI dialog box of the external ad hoc mode mobile host.

5.3. External Infrastructure Mode Mobile Host

An external infrastructure mode mobile host in the simulated network represents an external infrastructure mode mobile machine in the real world. The usage of external infrastructure mode mobile host is similar to that of external ad hoc mode mobile host. The only exception is that in the GUI dialog box of the external infrastructure mode mobile host, one needs to provide the gateway IP address for this mobile host in the simulated network. When the packets generated by the external mobile machine arrive at the simulation machine, they will be transmitted by the external mobile host that represents the external mobile machine and received by the simulated access points. With the gateway IP address information, the access point can correctly forward these packets to a simulated router (which is the gateway for these packets) for further forwarding in the simulated network.

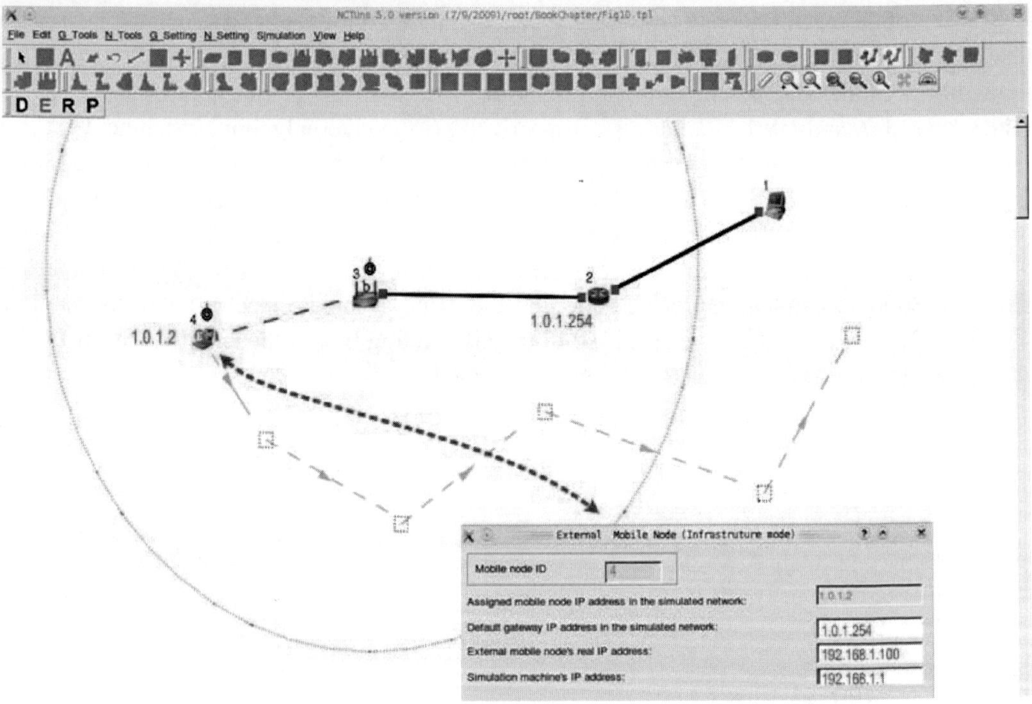

Figure 12. The GUI dialog box of the external infrastructure mode mobile host.

Figure 12 shows an emulation example in which one external infrastructure mode mobile host (node 4) communicates with a simulated host (node 1) via a simulated wireless access point (node 3) and a simulated router (node 2). The mobile host is assigned 1.0.1.2 address in the simulated network and the gateway IP address specified for this mobile host is 1.0.1.254. Suppose that the simulated host on the right (node 1) wants to set up a TCP connection to the external mobile machine in the real world (represented by node 4), the "rtcp –p 8000" command can be executed on the external mobile machine and the "stcp –p 8000 1.0.1.2" command can be specified in the GUI dialog box of this simulated host. In the simulated network, initially the host (node 1) can communicate with the external infrastructure mode mobile host. However, as time proceeds, the external mobile host will eventually leave the coverage area (the dashed circle in red color) of the wireless access point and no longer can communicate with that host. Since the external mobile host represents an external mobile machine in the real world, the external mobile machine will experience the same condition as described above while exchanging data with the simulated host.

5.4. External Router

An external router machine in the real world can interact with a simulated network and it is represented by an external router in the simulated network. This is a useful function as traffic originated from the simulated network can be directed to the external router machine, experience the router machine's packet scheduling and buffer management processing, and then return back to the simulated network. With this capability, one can easily test the router machine's functionality (e.g., one can generate and send virus and network-attack packets from the simulated network to the external router machine to see whether it can detect or filter them out).

Figure 13 shows an emulation example where three simulated hosts (node 2, node 3, and node 4) are connected to an external router (node 1) in the simulated network. On top of this topology, two greedy TCP connections are set up. The first one originates at node 2 and ends at node 4 while the second one originates at node 3 and ends at node 4. The packets of these two TCP connections need to pass through the external router. For the packets generated by node 2, when they arrive at node 1, they need to leave the simulated network and enter the real world to reach the external router machine through one of its port. They will be routed by the external router machine and leave it through a different port. They will then reach the simulation machine and re-enter into the simulated network at node 1. Finally, node 1 will transmit them to node 4 on the simulated link between node 1 and node 4. The packets generated by node 3 experience a similar scenario.

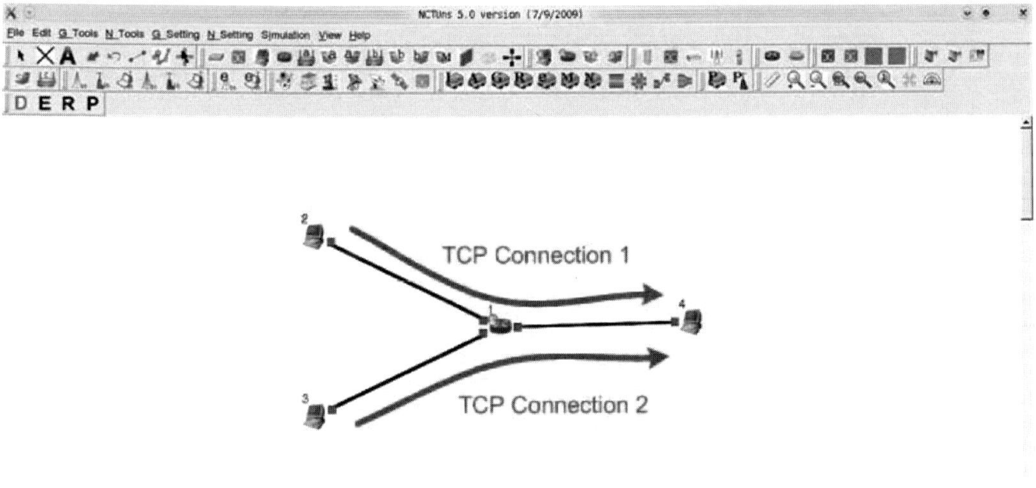

Figure 13. The network topology used in the external router emulation example.

The physical network setup for running this emulation is shown in Figure 14. The simulation machine simulates all hosts and links. It has three network interfaces each of which connects to one port of the external router machine via an Ethernet link. The bandwidth and delay of the links in the simulated network can be different from those of the three Ethernet links that physically connect the simulation machine and the external router machine.

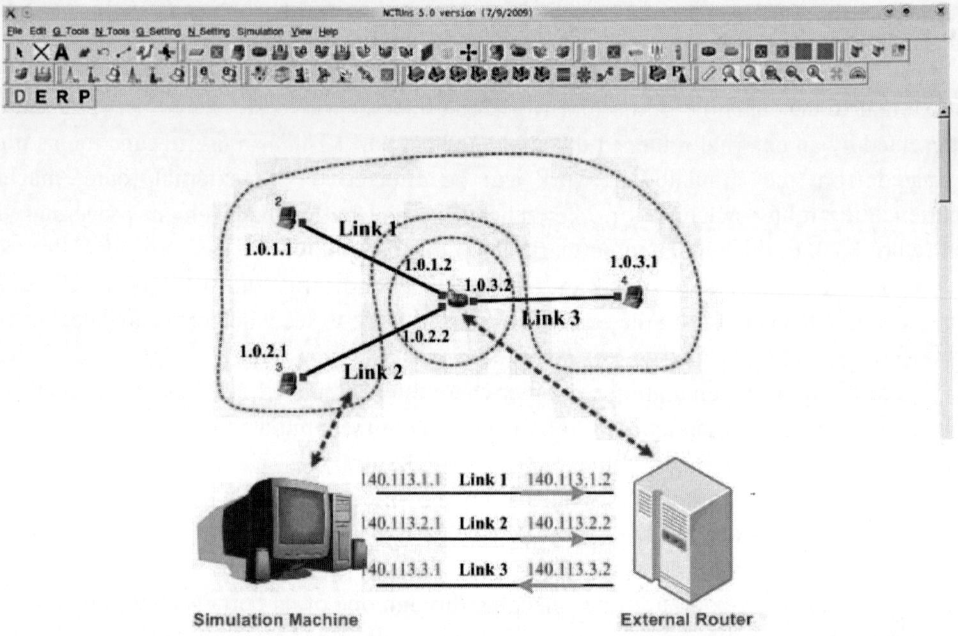

Figure 14. The network configuration and physical setup used in the external router emulation example.

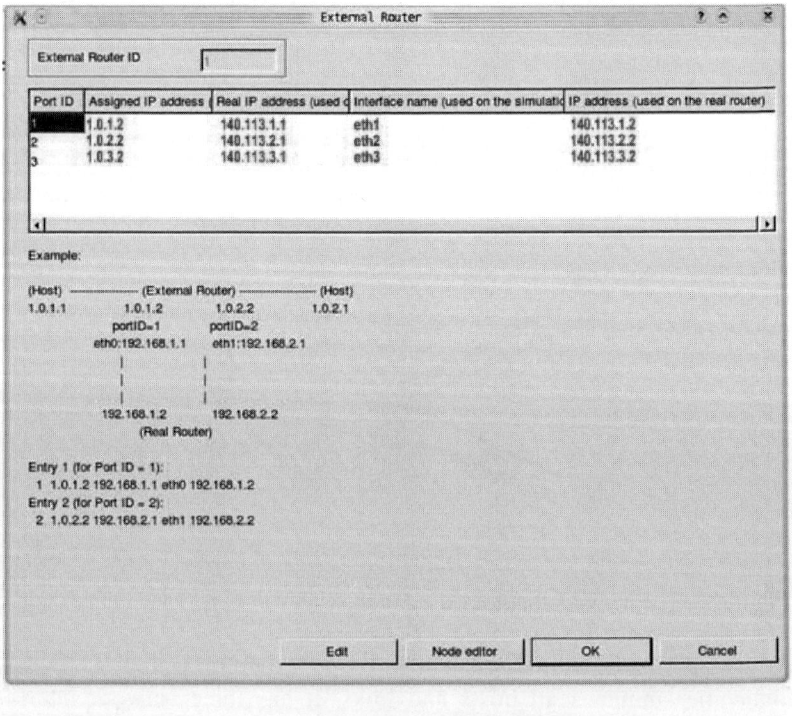

Figure 15. The GUI dialog box of the external router.

The simulation machine needs some information about the external router machine. One needs to provide such information in the GUI dialog box of an external router in the simulated network, which is shown in Figure 15. For each port of the external router machine in the real world, one needs to provide the association among the following information entities: its assigned IP address in the simulated network (this information is automatically provided by the GUI in the second column of this association table after the port ID column), the real IP address of the network interface on the simulation machine that connects to this port via a link, the name (e.g., eth1) of the above interface (on the simulation machine), and the real IP address used by this port on the external router machine. Assume that the names of the interfaces configured with the 140.113.1.1, 140.113.2.1, and 140.113.3.1 addresses on the simulation machine are eth1, eth2, and eth3, respectively. Then the association table should contain the following entries: (1, 1.0.1.2, 140.113.1.1, eth1, 140.113.1.2) for port 1, (2, 1.0.2.2, 140.113.2.1, eth2, 140.113.2.2) for port 2, and (3, 1.0.3.2, 140.113.3.1, eth3, 140.113.3.2) for port 3. Figure 15 illustrates the settings.

On the external router machine in the real world, some routing entries need to be added to the routing table so that packets originated from the simulated network can be redirected back to the simulated network. The rules for generating these routing entries are as follows. For every host with 1.0.X.Y as its assigned IP address in the simulated network, one can use the following routing commands (FreeBSD version) to add the needed routing entries: "route add 200.Z.X.Y -interface NICNAME" or "route add 200.Z.X.Y GatewayIPaddress." Here Z is a variable taken from the set of all subnet IDs used in the simulated network, NICNAME is the name of the interface on the external router machine (e.g., fxp0 or eth0), and GatewayIPaddress is the IP address of the interface on the simulation machine to which the external router machine would like to send these packets. Note that "200" should be used because the emulation module changes the first number of the destination IP address of every packet (e.g., Ss.Sh.Ds.Dh) going to the external router machine to 200 (200.Ss.Ds.Dh) so that it can come back to the simulated network correctly.

Using the above example to illustrate, assume that link 1 is subnet 1, link 2 is subnet 2, and link 3 is subnet 3 in the simulated network, and the IP address of node 2 is 1.0.1.1, the IP address of node 3 is 1.0.2.1, and the IP address of node 4 is 1.0.3.1, respectively. Further assume that the IP address of the external router on link 1 is 1.0.1.2, the IP address of the external router on link 2 is 1.0.2.2, and the IP address of the external router on link3 is 1.0.3.2. Suppose that in the real world the real IP address used by the external router port configured with 1.0.1.2 in the simulated network is 140.113.1.2, the real IP address used by the external router port configured with 1.0.2.2 in the simulated network is 140.113.2.2, and the real IP address used by the external router port configured with 1.0.3.2 in the simulated network is 140.113.3.2. Further suppose that on the simulation machine the IP address of the interface simulating link1 is 140.113.1.1 in the real world, the interface simulating link2 is 140.113.2.1, and the interface simulating link3 is 140.113.3.1. These address settings are illustrated in Figure 14.

For this example, on the external router machine in the real world one can execute the following routing commands (Linux version) to add the required routing entries.

```
route add 200.1.1.1 gw 140.113.1.1
route add 200.2.1.1 gw 140.113.1.1
route add 200.3.1.1 gw 140.113.1.1
```

```
route add 200.1.2.1 gw 140.113.2.1
route add 200.2.2.1 gw 140.113.2.1
route add 200.3.2.1 gw 140.113.2.1

route add 200.1.3.1 gw 140.113.3.1
route add 200.2.3.1 gw 140.113.3.1
route add 200.3.3.1 gw 140.113.3.1
```

With these commands, all packets that originate from subnet 1, 2, or 3 and go to 1.0.1.1 will be sent back to 140.113.1.1 via link1. Similarly, all packets that originate from subnet 1, 2, or 3 and go to 1.0.2.1 will be sent back to 140.113.2.1 via link2, and all packets that originate from subnet 1, 2, or 3 and go to 1.0.3.1 will be sent back to 140.113.3.1 via link3.

If there are multiple hosts on a subnet in the simulated network, it is more efficient and convenient to use subnet routing rather than host routing to specify these routing entries. The following routing commands can be executed to add these subnet routing entries (Linux version):

```
route add -net 200.1.1.0/24 gw 140.113.1.1
route add -net 200.2.1.0/24 gw 140.113.1.1
route add -net 200.3.1.0/24 gw 140.113.1.1

route add -net 200.1.2.0/24 gw 140.113.2.1
route add -net 200.2.2.0/24 gw 140.113.2.1
route add -net 200.3.2.0/24 gw 140.113.2.1

route add -net 200.1.3.0/24 gw 140.113.3.1
route add -net 200.2.3.0/24 gw 140.113.3.1
route add -net 200.3.3.0/24 gw 140.113.3.1
```

6. Traffic Mix Capability

We use a case here to show that a real-world TCP connection can contend with a simulated TCP connection for bandwidth in the simulated network. The real-world TCP connection is set up between an external host in the real world and a host in the simulated network. The simulated TCP connection on the other hand is set up between two hosts in the simulated network.

I. Emulation Setup

Figure 16 shows the tested network topology. One machine (simulation machine) is used to simulate the portion of the network inside the dashed circle in real time while another machine (external machine) acts as the external host. The simulation machine is a PC with Intel Core 2 Duo (3.0 GHz) CPU and 2 GB RAM, and the emulation machine is ASUS W7J notebook with Intel Centrino Duo T2400 (1.83 GHz) CPU and 1 GB RAM. A 100 Mbps Fast Ethernet network physically connects them together.

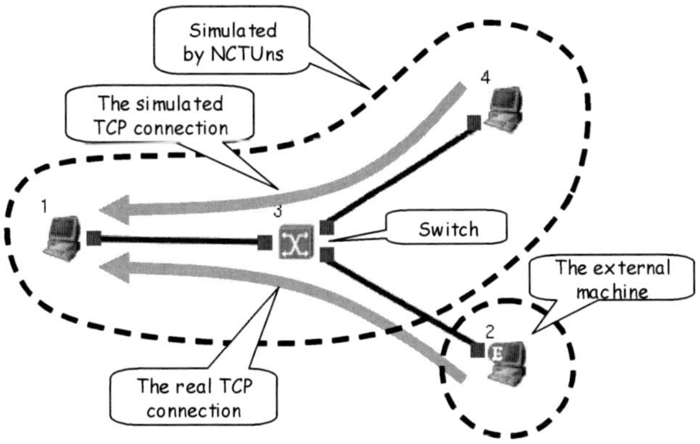

Figure 16. The network topology used in the traffic mix emulation test.

The link delay of all links in the simulated network is set to 25 ms and bandwidth of all links is set to 10 Mbps. We set up two greedy TCP connections in this test. The first one is between node 1 and node 4. We call this connection a simulated TCP connection because both of these nodes are simulated by NCTUns. The other connection is between node 1 and the external machine. We call this connection a real TCP connection because one of its endpoints is an external machine in the real world. During emulation, the two TCP connections contend for the bandwidth of the bottleneck link from the switch (node 3) to node 1.

II. Performance Results

Figure 17 shows the contending behavior of the real and the simulated TCP connections. We see that these two TCP connections compete with each other for the bandwidth of the

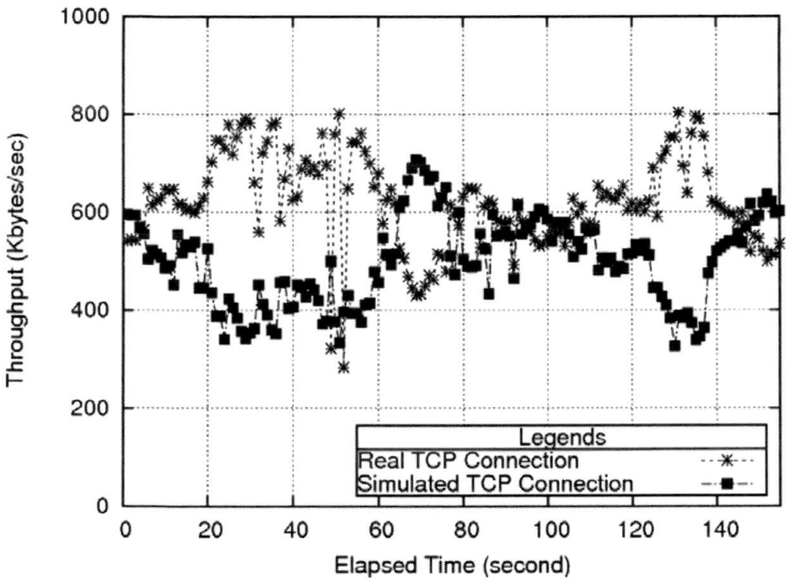

Figure 17. The contending behavior between a real TCP connection and a simulated TCP connection.

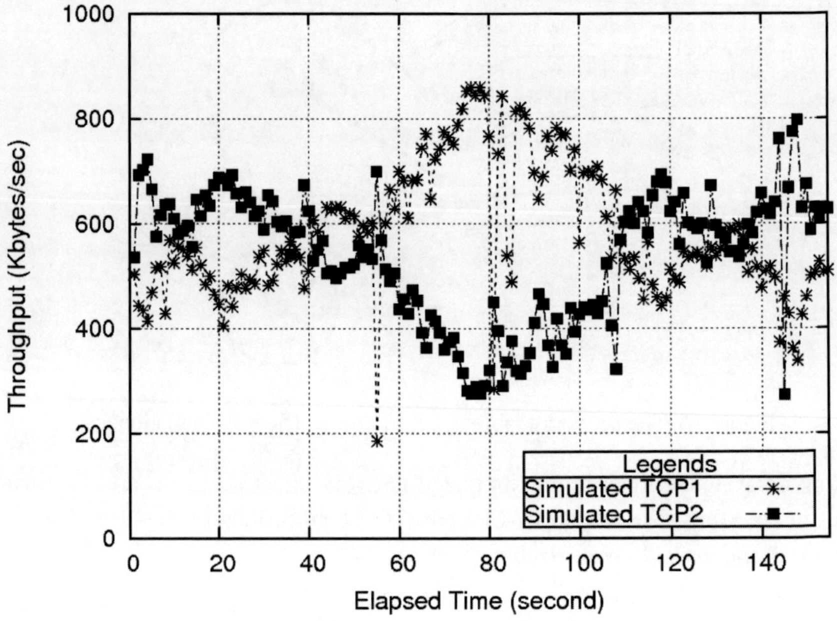

Figure 18. The contending behavior between two simulated TCP connections.

bottleneck link in the simulated network. This result shows that real-world and simulated traffic can coexist and dynamically contend in a simulated network created by NCTUns. For comparison purpose, we run a similar simulation case where the two contending TCP connections are both simulated. Figure 18 shows the contending behavior of the two simulated TCP connections. By comparing Figure 17 and Figure 18, we see that both figures show the same behavior. This result shows that NCTUns does not bias against a real-world or a simulated TCP connection when they contend in a simulated network.

7. Performance Evaluation

In the following, we conduct the following emulation test to evaluate the accuracy performance of the NCTUns network emulator.

I. Emulation Setup

Figure 19 shows the network topology used in this test. The portion of the network inside the dashed circle is simulated in real time by one machine (simulation machine). The external host on the right (node 2) represents an external host in the real world (external machine). The simulation machine is a PC with Intel Core 2 Duo (3.0 GHz) CPU and 2 GB RAM, and the emulation machine is ASUS W7J notebook with Intel Centrino Duo T2400 (1.83 GHz) CPU and 1 GB RAM. A 100 Mbps Fast Ethernet network physically connects them together. In this test suite, the clock synchronization time interval used by NCTUns to synchronize its simulation clock with the real clock is varied to evaluate its effects on the accuracy of NCTUns in emulating an end-to-end delay.

The delay for every link in the simulated network is set to 0.5, 1, 5, 10, and 50 ms such that the expected RTT (Round-Trip Time) between the external host and node 1 on the left is 10 (0.5*20), 20 (1*20), 100 (5*20), 200 (10*20), and 1000 (50*20) ms, respectively, where 20 is the number of links that a packet needs to traverse from the external host to node 1 and then go back to the external host. The bandwidth of all these links is set to 10 Mbps.

On the external machine in the real world, a "ping" program is run to measure the RTTs between the external machine and node 1. The "ping" program measures a RTT by sending an ICMP request packet to the target host, receiving an ICMP reply packet generated by the target host, and then computing the time elapsed between these two events. The time interval between two successive ICMP request packet transmissions is set to 0.5 second and the packet length is set to 64 bytes. The clock synchronization time interval is set to 0.1, 1, and 10 ms. The variance of measured RTTs and the difference between the average of measured RTTs and the expected RTT are reported.

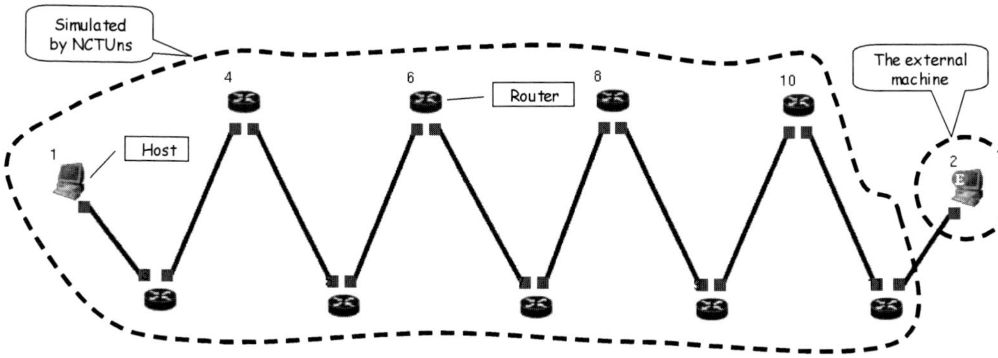

Figure 19. The network topology used in the performance evaluation emulation test.

II. Performance Results

Figure 20 shows the variance of the measured RTTs. We see that using a clock synchronization time interval of either 0.1 ms or 1 ms generates about the same level of accuracy, and using a clock synchronization time interval of 10 ms results in a much greater inaccuracy. This result suggests that using 1 ms as the clock synchronization time interval is a good choice considering both accuracy and time synchronization overhead.

Figure 21 shows the difference between the average of measured RTTs and the expected RTT. The expected RTT should be 20 times the delay of each link because an ICMP request/reply packet needs to traverse 20 links in a round trip. In Figure 21, we see that using a clock synchronization time interval of 10 ms results in a large difference between the average and the expected RTT. However, the difference is small for the cases using 1 and 0.1 ms as the clock synchronization time interval. For these two cases, the difference of the case using 0.1 ms is interestingly a little larger than the one using 1 ms. This accuracy degradation phenomenon may be caused by the excessive synchronous overhead when 0.1 ms is used as the clock synchronization time interval. By these analyses, the result again suggests that 1 ms should be used as the clock synchronization time interval.

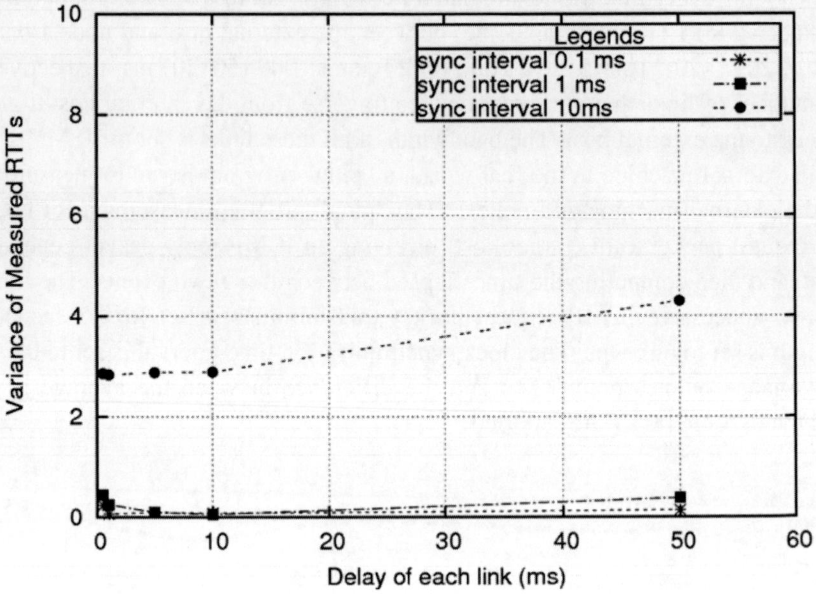

Figure 20. The variance of ping RTTs measured during the emulation test.

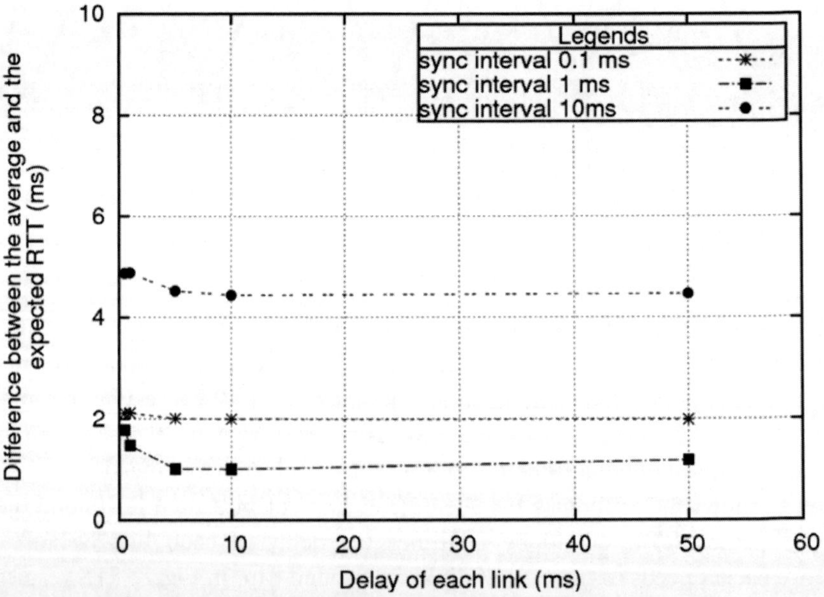

Figure 21. The difference between the average and the expected RTT under different clock synchronization time intervals.

The differences (about 1.2 ms extra delay) between the average of measured RTTs and the expected RTT are reasonable and can be explained. There are several reasons for the extra delay. First, an ICMP request packet generated by the external machine in the real world needs to be transmitted over the physical Fast Ethernet link to reach the simulation machine and its reply packet generated by node 1 needs to be transmitted over the same link to come back to the external machine. The transmission time of these two packet transmissions is 2 * 0.051 (64byte/100Mbps) = 0.0102 ms. Second, the emulation module needs to capture an ICMP packet from the kernel, translate the IP address and re-calculate the check sum of its header, and inject it into the simulated network. It also needs to perform reverse operations for the ICMP reply packet. These operations take about 0.05 ms. Third, in the simulated network an ICMP request packet needs to traverse 10 links to reach node 1 and its ICMP reply packet needs to traverse 10 links to come back to the external machine. Since the transmission time of an ICMP request/reply packet on each simulated link (10 Mbps) is about 0.051 ms, the total packet transmission time spent on these 20 links is about 1.02 (0.051*20) ms. In total, these delays sum up to 1.08 ms, which is close to the measured difference (1.2 ms).

Among the 1.2 ms delay difference, the 1.02 (0.051*20) ms delay is a natural result. This is because it will also occur in a real-world network whose network topology and link settings are the same as those of the simulated network. Regarding the 0.0102 ms delay, using a higher-bandwidth link such as a Gbps Ethernet link to connect the simulation and external machine together will further reduce it. The real extra delay caused by NCTUns emulation module is only about 0.1698 (1.2 – 1.02 – 0.0102) ms on the tested hardware platform. Using a higher-performance machine may further reduce this delay. However, due to the inaccuracy inherent in the used 1 ms clock synchronization interval, this 0.1698 ms extra delay may be unavoidable.

8. Related Work

The NIST Net [14] network emulator is a tool for evaluating the performance of the network protocol running on an IP host. It mainly operates at the IP layer. It can abstract and emulate the typical performance characteristics of a wide area network (e.g., congestion packet loss, congestion packet delay, and packet reordering, etc.). It can also emulate the characteristics of links built upon different underlying subnetwork technologies (e.g., the asymmetric bandwidth situations of xDSL and cable modems.). It is implemented as a Linux kernel module and users can install the module into a Linux system running on a PC-based machine. It allows users to specify several network conditions through which each packet needs to pass while it is forwarded by the PC-based router. Unlike NCTUns, NIST Net can only act as a simple black box giving passing packets some special treatments. One cannot simulate a network with various links and nodes in real time inside its black box.

Ns-2 [15], although it is primarily used as a network simulator, can be used as a network emulator as well. Ns-2 is a traditional network simulator and is implemented as a user-level program. Ns-2 with emulation has two modes: the opaque mode and protocol mode. In the opaque mode, the simulator acts as a router allowing real-world traffic to pass through. In the protocol mode, ns-2 can be used as an endpoint to generate network traffic. Both of these two modes are naturally and correctly supported in NCTUns. Although according to the user manual ns-2 network simulator can be turned into a network emulator, from the current mailing list discussions, it seems that most people are still using it as a simulator rather than an emulator. The most recent ns-2 package downloaded from its web site cannot support emulation correctly. No one responded to the emulation bug reported in its mailing list. It seems that the emulation function of ns-2 is no longer maintained and supported.

The PacketStorm IP network emulator [16] and the Hammer PacketSphere network emulator [17] use special devices and hardware to perform emulations. These emulators are commercial products. Their advantage may be on the performance because they can be equipped with various network interfaces, high-speed processors, larger memory, and more efficient operating system, etc. A general-purpose PC-based emulation machine on the other hand may not provide the same level of emulation performance because a general-purpose operating system such as FreeBSD or Linux is not specially designed for the emulation purpose. Commercial hardware-based emulators, however, are expensive and thus are not widely used in the network research community.

9. Conclusion

In this chapter we present the NCTUns network simulator and emulator and illustrate how researchers may use it to conduct innovative network emulations. Network emulation refers to the ability to simulate the characteristics of a real-world network in real time and let real-world packets pass through the simulated network to experience various conditions such as packet dropping, delaying, reordering, duplication, etc. Network emulation is an important approach as one can test, diagnose, and evaluate the function and performance of real-world network devices without the need to get, know, or modify its internal protocol stack. Such capability is important as sometimes it is impossible, difficult, or expensive to acquire the source code of the protocol stack used in a network device.

NCTUns supports emulation by simulating a desired network in real time, intercepting real-world packets and redirecting them into the simulated network, and letting them leave the simulated network to reach their destination hosts in the real world. The simulated network used in emulation can be arbitrarily large and composed of various types of networks. While in the simulated network, real-world packets can receive special treatments simply based on statistics distributions or they can interact and compete with packets originated from simulated nodes to experience more realistic and dynamic traffic conditions. In addition, during emulation a real-world network device can set up real network connections with any node in the simulated network to exchange their packets. These innovative capabilities make NCTUns an ideal network emulation tool.

References

[1] S.Y. Wang and H.T. Kung, "A Simple Methodology for Constructing Extensible and High-Fidelity TCP/IP Network Simulators," *IEEE INFOCOM'99*, March 21 - 25, 1999, New York, USA.

[2] S.Y. Wang and H.T. Kung, "A New Methodology for Easily Constructing Extensible and High-Fidelity TCP/IP Network Simulators," *Computer Networks*, Vol. 40, Issue 2, October 2002, pp. 257 - 278.

[3] S.Y. Wang, Harvard TCP/IP network simulator 1.0, available at http://www.eecs.harvard.edu/networking/simulator.html.

[4] S.Y. Wang, C.L. Chou, C.H. Huang, C.C. Hwang, Z.M. Yang, C.C. Chiou, and C.C. Lin, "The Design and Implementation of the NCTUns Network Simulator," *Computer Networks*, Vol. 42, Issue 2, June 2003, pp. 175 – 197.

[5] *ACM MobiCom 2002 conference* (The Eighth Annual International Conference on Mobile Computing and Networking), September 23 - 28, 2002, Atlanta, USA.

[6] *ACM MobiCom 2003 conference*, (The Ninth Annual International Conference on Mobile Computing and Networking), September 14 - 19, 2003, San Diego, USA

[7] S.Y. Wang, "NCTUns," In the column "Software Tools for Networking," *IEEE Networks*, Vol. 17, No.4, July 2003.

[8] *IEEE MASCOTS 2004 conference* (12th Annual Meeting of the IEEE International Symposium on Modeling, Analysis, and Simulation of Computer and Telecommunication Systems), Volendam, The Netherlands, October 4 - 7, 2004. (available at http://www.mascots-conf.org/)

[9] The workshop on "Wireless Systems and Network Topologies," *IEEE Vehicular Technology Society*, September 1 - 3, 2004, Taipei, Taiwan.

[10] IEEE INFOCOM 2005 conference (24th international conference on computer communication), March 13 - 17, 2005, Miami, USA.

[11] *The Society for Modeling and Simulation International, 2005 International Symposium on Performance Evaluation of Computer and Telecommunication Systems*, July 24 – 28, 2005, Philadelphia, USA.

[12] S.Y. Wang and Y.B. Lin, "NCTUns Network Simulation and Emulation for Wireless Resource Management," *Wiley Wireless Communications and Mobile Computing*, Vol. 5, issue 8, December 2005.

[13] The netfilter/iptables project, http://www.netfilter.org/

[14] Nist Net, http://snad.ncsl.nist.gov/itg/nistnet

[15] S. McCanne and S. Floyd, *ns-LBNL Network Simulator*, http://www.isi.edu/ nsnam/ns/

[16] *PacketStorm Communications*, Inc., http://www.PacketStorm.com

[17] Empirix Inc., http://www.empirix.com

EXPERT COMMENTARIES

In: Computer-Aided Design...
Editors: C.M. De Smet et al, pp. 187-285

ISBN: 978-1-60456-860-8

Expert Commentary A

SCULPTURED SURFACES GENERATION FOR ADVANCED *CAD/CAM* APPLICATIONS

Stephen P. Radzevich*

Professor, Mechanical Engineering; Professor, Manufacturing EngineerinEATON, Automotive, Innovation Center, 26201 Northwestern Highway, Southfield, MI 48076

Abstract

Many products are designed with aesthetic sculptured surfaces to enhance their aesthetic appear, an important factor in customer satisfaction, especially for automotive and consumer-electronics products. In other cases, products have sculptured surfaces to meet functional requirements. Examples of functional surfaces can be easily found out in aero-, gas- and hydrodynamic applications (turbine blades), optical (lamp reflector) and medical (parts of anatomical reproduction) applications, manufacturing surfaces (molding die, die face), *etc*. Functional surfaces interact with environment or with other surface. Due to this, functional surfaces also can be called *dynamic surface*.

Functional surfaces don't possess the property to slide over itself. This causes significant complexity in machining of sculptured surfaces. Application of multi-axis *NC* machine is the only way for efficient machining of sculptured surfaces.

Reduction of the machining time is a critical issue when machining sculptured surfaces on multi-axis *NC* machines. In order to decrease the machining cost of a sculptured surface the machining time must be as short as possible. Definitely, this is the case where the sentence "Time is money!" works. Generally speaking, the optimization of surface generation on multi-axis *NC* machine results in time savings. It is the right point to recall the words[1] "*gaining time is gaining everything*!"

The text below is the author's attempt to cover briefly the modern theory of surface generation with focus on optimal machining of sculptured surfaces on multi-axis *NC* machine.

* E-mail addresses: stephenpradzevich@eaton.com, radzevich@hotmail.com. Phone: 248/226-6831, Fax: 248/226-6499.

[1] John Shebbeare, 1709-1788.

1. Introduction

Machining of surfaces can be interpreted as the transformation of a work into the machined part. The shape and actual design parameters are the major characteristics of the machined part surfaces. They strongly depend upon the parameters of the surface generating process. This text is focused just on those parameters of the surface machining process that can be expressed in terms of surface geometry and of kinematics of relative motion of the cutting tool. Therefore the topic covered below can be referred to as the *sculptured surface generation*.

For a long time, scientific developments in the field of surface generation were aiming solution to those problems that are relatively simple in nature. No problem that could be referred to as the problem of ***synthesis*** of optimal sculptured surface generation was understood.

In the late 1970th early 1980th, the idea of synthesis of optimal sculptured surface machining operation was, in a manner of speaking, mentioned for the first time.

Literature on theory of surface generation on multi-axis *NC* machine is quite sparse. In all of the recently published books on the topic, the problem of surface generation is treated from the stand-point of ***analysis***, and not of ***synthesis*** of optimal surface generation.

The present text is an attempt to present a well-balanced and intelligible account of some of the geometric and algebraic procedures, to give a well-rounded picture.

Investigation, analysis, comparison, and application of various procedures for handling the several types of particular problems constituting the synthesis of optimal surface generation on multi-axis *NC* machine are considered in the chapter. Much attention is paid to the reviewing and/or establishing definitions, concepts, and notations, with recapitulation of familiar methods of sculptured surface analysis[2]. In the text below, first contact is established with fundamental concepts of sculptured surface geometry, and known results in the theory of multi-parametric motion of a rigid body in E_3 space.

It is postulated here that the surface to be machined is the primary element of the machining process. Rest elements of the machining operation, say the generating surface of the cutting tool and kinematics of their relative motion are considering as the secondary elements and, thus optimal parameters of them have to be determined in terms of design parameters of the sculptured surface to be machined.

To the best of our knowledge, the author was the first who have formulated the problem of synthesizing of optimal sculptured surface machining as early as in late 1970th the early 1980th. At the beginning, the problem was understood mostly intuitively. The first principal achievements in this field[3] allowed expressing of the optimal parameters of kinematics of the sculptured surface machining on multi-axis *NC* machine in terms of geometry of the part surface and of the generating surface of the form cutting tool.

Few years later, a principal solution to the problem of profiling of the form cutting tool[4] had been derived. This solution yields determination of the generating surface of the form

[2]It is the right point to recall here the old Chinese proverb: *The beginning of wisdom is call things with there right names.*

[3]Radzevich, S.P., *A Method of Sculptured Surface Machining on Multi-Axis NC Machine*, Pat. No.1185749, USSR, B23C 3/16, Filed: October 24, 1983, and: Radzevich, S.P., *A Method of Sculptured Surface Machining on Multi-Axis NC Machine*, Pat. No.1249787, USSR, B23C 3/16, Filed: November 27, 1984.

[4]Radzevich, S.P., *A Method of Design of a Form Cutting Tool for Sculptured Surface Machining on Multi-Axis NC Machine*. – Patent application No.4242296/08 (USSR), Filed: March 03, 1987.

cutting tool as the $\mathbb{R}$-mapping of the sculptured surface to be machined. With the help of the $\mathbb{R}$-mapping, optimal parameters of the generating surface of the form cutting tool could be expressed in terms of design parameters of the sculptured surface to be machined. Taking into account that the optimal parameters of kinematics of surface machining are already specified in terms of the surfaces P and T, the three solutions above allow an analytical representation of the entire surface generation process just in terms of design parameters of the sculptured surface P. This means that the necessary input information for solving of the problem of synthesizing of optimal surface machining operation is limited just to design parameters of the sculptured part surface to be machined. This input information is the minimal feasible. Use of no other approaches allows development of sculptured surface machining operation just on the premises of the geometry of the surface to be machined. Use of no other approaches allows solution to the problem of synthesizing of optimal machining of sculptured surface on multi-axis *NC* machine. It is of importance to stress the readers' attention here that the decrease of the required input information indicates that the theory is getting closer to be ideal.

The concept, which the chapter strictly follows to, is widely known as the *Occam's razor principle*.

Occam's razor principle states that the explanation of any phenomenon should make as few assumptions as possible, eliminating, or "shaving off", those that make no difference in the observable predictions of the explanatory hypothesis of theory. The principle is often expressed in Latin as: *Entia non sunt multiplicanda praeter necessitatem*, which translates to: *Entities should not be multiplied beyond necessity*.

In compliance with the fundamental Occam's razor principle, the *DG/K*-based method of sculptured surface generation is developed. Using the method, one can compute optimal values of all the major parameters of sculptured surface machining on multi-axis *NC* machine. Previous experience in the field is appreciated but it is not mandatory required for solving of the problem of synthesizing of the optimal machining operation.

The first attempt to summarize the obtained results of the research in the field had been undertaken by the author as early as in 1991. That year, the author's first book [43] in the field of surface generation was courageously introduced to the Engineering Community. Ten years later, much more comprehensive summarization had been carried out [24]. Essentials of the *DG/K*-based method of surface generation are disclosed in much in these two monographs.

It is postulated in this research that the sculptured surface to be machined is a primary element of the machining process. It is also assumed below that the rest of major elements of the machining process [say, (a) design of the form cutting tool to be applied for the machining operation, (b) the optimal work orientation on the worktable of the multi-axis *NC* machine, (c) coordinates of the optimal start-point of the surface machining, (d) equations of the optimal tool-paths, *etc.*] can be drawn up from the equation of the sculptured surface. This is the major reason for why the consideration below begins from the analytical representation of the sculptured surface to be machined.

2. Analytical Representation of Sculptured Surfaces

Enormous amount of kinds and types of parts is manufacturing in various industries. Every part is bounded with two or more surfaces[5]. Each of the part surfaces is a smooth regular surface or it can be composed with a certain number of patches of smooth regular surfaces that are properly linked to each other.

Two definitions those immediately below are of critical importance for further discussion.

Definition 1.1: *Sculptured surface P is a smooth regular surface, the major parameters of local topology of which in differential vicinity of any two infinitely closed to each other points differ from each other.*

It is instructive to point out here, that sculptured surface P does not allow sliding "*over itself*".

While machining a sculptured surface, cutting tool rotates about it axis and moves relative to the sculptured surface P. While rotating with a certain angular velocity ω_T or while performing relative motion of another kind, cutting edges of the cutting tool generate a certain surface. We refer to the surface that is represented by consecutive positions of cutting edges as to *the generating surface of cutting tool* [23], [24], [30], [43]:

Definition 1.2: *The generating surface of a cutting tool is a surface that can be represented as the set of consecutive positions of the cutting edges in their motion relative to the stationary coordinate system, embedded to the cutting tool itself.*

In most practical cases, the generating surface T allows sliding "*over itself*". Enveloping surface to consecutive positions of the surface T that performs such a motion is congruent to the surface T itself.

While machining a part, the surface T is conjugate to the sculptured surface P.

In order to be machined on a *NC* machine, as well as for *CAD/CAM* applications, a formal (analytical) representation of the sculptured surface is the required prerequisite. Analytical representation of the sculptured surface (further: the surface P) is based on analytical representation of surfaces in geometry, specifically, (a) in differential geometry of surfaces, and (b) in engineering geometry of surfaces. The second is based in much on the first.

A sculptured surface could be uniquely specified in terms of two independent variables. Therefore, we give a surface P (Figure 1), in most cases, by expressing its rectangular coordinates X_P, Y_P and Z_P, as functions of two Gaussian coordinates U_P and V_P in a certain closed interval [48]:

$$\mathbf{r}_P = \mathbf{r}_P(U_P, V_P) = \begin{bmatrix} X_P(U_P, V_P) \\ Y_P(U_P, V_P) \\ Z_P(U_P, V_P) \\ 1 \end{bmatrix}, \ (U_{1.P} \le U_P \le U_{2.P}; \ \ V_{1.P} \le V_P \le V_{2.P}) \qquad (1)$$

---

[5] Perhaps, ball of a ball-bearing is one of just few examples of part surfaces, which are bounded with the only surface that is the sphere.

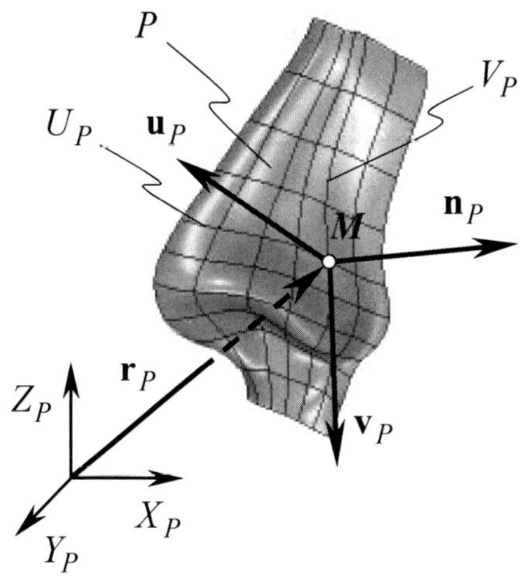

Figure 1. Principal elements of local topology of sculptured surface.

Here is designated

$\mathbf{r}_P$	is position vector of a point of the sculptured surface P
U_P and V_P	are curvilinear (Gaussian) coordinates of the point of the surface P
X_P, Y_P, Z_P	are Cartesian coordinates of the point of the surface P
$U_{1.P}$, $U_{2.P}$	are the boundary values of the closed interval of the U_P parameter
$V_{1.P}$, $V_{2.P}$	are the boundary values of the closed interval of the V_P parameter

The parameters U_P and V_P must enter independently, which means that the matrix

$$\mathbf{M} = \begin{bmatrix} \frac{\partial X_P}{\partial U_P} & \frac{\partial Y_P}{\partial U_P} & \frac{\partial Z_P}{\partial U_P} \\ \frac{\partial X_P}{\partial V_P} & \frac{\partial Y_P}{\partial V_P} & \frac{\partial Z_P}{\partial V_P} \end{bmatrix} \tag{2}$$

has rank 2. Positions where the rank is 1 or 0 are singular points; when the rank at all points is 1, then Eq. (1) represents a curve.

At this point, two important issues on sculptured surface geometry are necessary been considered. Both of them relate to intrinsic geometry in differential vicinity of a surface point.

The first fundamental form of sculptured surface P is the first of the two issues.

The first fundamental form $\Phi_{1.P}$ of smooth regular surface describes metric properties of the surface P. Usually, it is represented as the quadratic form

$$\Phi_{1.P} \quad \Rightarrow \quad ds_P^2 = E_P\, dU_P^2 + 2F_P\, dU_P\, dV_P + G_P\, dV_P^2 \tag{3}$$

Here, in Eq. (3) is designated:

s_P	is linear element of the sculptured surface P
E_P, F_P, G_P	are fundamental magnitudes of the first order

Equation (3) is known from many advanced sources.

In the theory of surface generation, matrix form of analytical representation of the first fundamental form $\Phi_{1.P}$ is proven be useful:

$$\Phi_{1.P} \;\Rightarrow\; ds_P^2 = [dU_P \quad dV_P \quad 0 \quad 0] \cdot \begin{bmatrix} E_P & F_P & 0 & 0 \\ F_P & G_P & 0 & 0 \\ 0 & 0 & 1 & 0 \\ 0 & 0 & 0 & 1 \end{bmatrix} \cdot \begin{bmatrix} dU_P \\ dV_P \\ 0 \\ 0 \end{bmatrix} \tag{4}$$

This kind of analytical representation of the first fundamental form $\Phi_{1.P}$ is proposed by Radzevich [22]. Practical advantage of Eq. (4) is due to it can be easily incorporated into computer programs using multiple coordinate system transformations that is vital for *CAD/CAM* applications.

For the computation of the fundamental magnitudes of the first order, the following equations can be used

$$E_P = \mathbf{U}_P \cdot \mathbf{U}_P\,,\; F_P = \mathbf{U}_P \cdot \mathbf{V}_P\,,\; G_P = \mathbf{V}_P \cdot \mathbf{V}_P \tag{5}$$

The first derivatives of $\mathbf{r}_P$ with respect to the Gaussian coordinates U_P and V_P are designated as $\frac{\partial \mathbf{r}_P}{\partial U_P} = \mathbf{U}_P$ and $\frac{\partial \mathbf{r}_P}{\partial V_P} = \mathbf{V}_P$. For the unit tangent vectors $\mathbf{u}_P$ and $\mathbf{v}_P$, the expressions $\mathbf{u}_P = \frac{\mathbf{U}_P}{|\mathbf{U}_P|}$ and $\mathbf{v}_P = \frac{\mathbf{V}_P}{|\mathbf{V}_P|}$ are valid. Vector $\mathbf{u}_P$ specifies the direction of the tangent to the U_P coordinate curve through the given point M on the surface P. Similarly, vector $\mathbf{v}_P$ specifies the direction of the tangent to the V_P coordinate curve through that same point M on P.

Fundamental magnitudes E_P, F_P, and G_P of the first order are scalar functions of U_P- and V_P-parameters of the surface P. In general form, these relationships can be expressed as $E_P = E_P(U_P, V_P)$, $F_P = F_P(U_P, V_P)$, and $G_P = G_P(U_P, V_P)$.

Fundamental magnitudes E_P and G_P are always positive ($E_P > 0$, $G_P > 0$), while the fundamental magnitude F_P can be equal zero ($F_P \geq 0$). Due to the first fundamental form represents length of a curve-line segment, thus it is always non-negative, *i.e.* the inequality $\Phi_{1.P} \geq 0$ always observes.

Discriminant H_P of the first fundamental form $\Phi_{1.P}$ can be computed from equation $H_P = \sqrt{E_P G_P - F_P^2}$. It is assumed that the discriminant H_P is always non-negative, *i.e.* $H_P = +\sqrt{E_P G_P - F_P^2}$.

The second fundamental form of the surface P is another of two mentioned above important issues.

The second fundamental form $\Phi_{2.P}$ describes curvature of a sculptured surface P. Usually, it is represented as the quadratic form

$$\Phi_{2.P} \Rightarrow -d\mathbf{r}_P \cdot d\mathbf{n}_P = L_P\, dU_P^2 + 2M_P\, dU_P\, dV_P + N_P\, dV_P^2 \tag{6}$$

Equation (6) is known from many advanced sources.

In the theory of surface generation, matrix form of analytical representation of the second fundamental form $\Phi_{2.P}$ is proven be useful:

$$\Phi_{2.P} \Rightarrow [dU_P \quad dV_P \quad 0 \quad 0] \cdot \begin{bmatrix} L_P & M_P & 0 & 0 \\ M_P & N_P & 0 & 0 \\ 0 & 0 & 1 & 0 \\ 0 & 0 & 0 & 1 \end{bmatrix} \cdot \begin{bmatrix} dU_P \\ dV_P \\ 0 \\ 0 \end{bmatrix} \tag{7}$$

This kind of analytical representation of the second fundamental form $\Phi_{2.P}$ is proposed by Radzevich [22]. Similar to Eq. (4), practical advantage of Eq. (7) is due to it can be easily incorporated into computer programs using multiple coordinate system transformations that is vital for *CAD/CAM* applications.

Here, in Eq. (7), the parameters L_P, M_P, N_P designate fundamental magnitudes of the second order.

For the computation of the fundamental magnitudes of the second order the following equations

$$L_P = \frac{\frac{\partial \mathbf{U}_P}{\partial U_P} \times \mathbf{U}_P \cdot \mathbf{V}_P}{\sqrt{E_P G_P - F_P^2}}, \quad M_P = \frac{\frac{\partial \mathbf{U}_P}{\partial V_P} \times \mathbf{U}_P \cdot \mathbf{V}_P}{\sqrt{E_P G_P - F_P^2}} = \frac{\frac{\partial \mathbf{V}_P}{\partial U_P} \times \mathbf{U}_P \cdot \mathbf{V}_P}{\sqrt{E_P G_P - F_P^2}}, \quad N_P = \frac{\frac{\partial \mathbf{V}_P}{\partial V_P} \times \mathbf{U}_P \cdot \mathbf{V}_P}{\sqrt{E_P G_P - F_P^2}} \tag{8}$$

can be used.

Fundamental magnitudes L_P, M_P, N_P of the second order are also scalar functions of U_P- and V_P- parameters of the sculptured surface P. These relationships in general form can be represented as $L_P = L_P(U_P, V_P)$, $M_P = M_P(U_P, V_P)$, and $N_P = N_P(U_P, V_P)$.

Discriminant T_P of the second fundamental form $\Phi_{2.P}$ can be computed from equation $T_P = \sqrt{L_P N_P - M_P^2}$.

Bonnet proved (1867) that the specification of the first and second fundamental forms determines a unique surface if the Gauss' characteristic equation and the Codazzi-Mainardi's relationships of compatibility are satisfied and those two surfaces that have identical first and second fundamental forms must be congruent[6] [1]. Six fundamental magnitudes E_P, F_P, G_P and L_P, M_P, N_P determine a surface uniquely, except as to position and orientation in space.

Specification of a surface in terms of the first and the second fundamental forms is usually called the natural kind of the surface parameterization. In general form, it can be represented by set of two equations

$$\left.\begin{array}{r}\text{Natural form of}\\ \text{the surface } P \text{ parameterization}\end{array}\right| \Rightarrow P = P(\Phi_{1.P}, \Phi_{2.P})\begin{cases}\Phi_{1.P} = \Phi_{1.P}(E_P, F_P, G_P)\\ \Phi_{2.P} = \Phi_{2.P}(E_P, F_P, G_P, L_P, M_P, N_P)\end{cases} \quad (9)$$

Equation (9) can be derived from Eq. (1). Both, Eq. (1) and Eq. (9) specify that same sculptured surface P.

3. Kinematics of Sculptured Surface Machining

A motion of the cutting tool relative to the work is necessary for machining of a given part surface. Relative motion of the work and the cutting tool always observes for all methods of machining of surfaces on machine tools.

The work and the cutting tool relative motions of different nature observe when machining a sculptured surface on multi-axis *NC* machine. Below, the generation motions, feed-rate motions, and orientation motions of the cutting tool are investigated.

For the development of the most efficient machining operation of a given sculptured surface, the optimal parameters of the relative motion of the work and of the cutting tool at every instant of machining are required been determined. An appropriate criterion of optimization is of critical importance in this concern.

Relative motion of the work and of the cutting tool can be represented as a superposition of a certain number of elementary motions, which are performing by the machine tool of a certain design. The mentioned elementary motions are the translations along and the rotations about various axes that are differently oriented relative to each other. Ultimately, a combination of a certain number of translations and of rotations can result in a complex relative motion of the work and of the cutting tool. All the elementary motions are timed (synchronized) with one another in a proper manner.

The analysis of kinematics of the multi-parametric sculptured surface generation is based on the presumption that any desired relative motion of the work and of the cutting tool can be performed on the *NC* machine.

Without loss of generality, the analysis of kinematics of sculptured surface generation can be substantially simplified if the principle of inversion of the relative motion is used.

---

[6]Two surfaces with the identical first and second fundamental forms might be also symmetrical. The interested reader is referred to special literature on differential geometry of surfaces on details about this specific issue.

3.1. Local Reference System

A reference coordinate system is necessary for the development of an analytical description of the instant motion of the cutter relative the work. A right-hand oriented Cartesian coordinate system is used below as the local reference system. Several approaches can be employed for to get the local coordinate system orthogonal.

A convenient way for establishing of an appropriate local reference system is to use a coordinate system that is naturally associated with the surface P. Darboux's trihedron fits the best the requirements those imposed by implementation of the *DG/K*-based method of sculptured surface generation.

Darboux's trihedron is associated with a point of interest on the sculptured surface. It can be defined by a triple of vectors, given by the normal unit vector $\mathbf{n}_P$ to the surface P and two mutually orthogonal principal unit tangent vectors $\mathbf{t}_{1.P}$ and $\mathbf{t}_{2.P}$ to the surface such that $\mathbf{n}_P = \mathbf{t}_{1.P} \times \mathbf{t}_{2.P}$.

Unit tangent vectors $\mathbf{u}_P$ and $\mathbf{v}_P$ can be used for the computation of the unit normal vector $\mathbf{n}_P$ to the surface P at the point of interest M:

$$\mathbf{n}_P = \mathbf{u}_P \times \mathbf{v}_P \tag{10}$$

When order of multipliers in Eq. (10) is chosen properly, then the unit normal vector $\mathbf{n}_P$ is pointed outward the bodily side of the surface P.

For the computation of unit vectors $\mathbf{t}_{1.P}$ and $\mathbf{t}_{2.P}$, the vectors of principal directions $\mathbf{T}_{1.P}$ and $\mathbf{T}_{2.P}$ are helpful. The tangent vectors $\mathbf{T}_{1.P}$ and $\mathbf{T}_{2.P}$ are defined by the ratio $\dfrac{dU_P}{dV_P}$, which can be computed as the solution to the quadratic equation

$$\begin{vmatrix} E_P\, dU_P + F_P\, dV_P & F_P\, dU_P + G_P\, dV_P \\ L_P\, dU_P + M_P\, dV_P & M_P\, dU_P + N_P\, dV_P \end{vmatrix} = 0 \tag{11}$$

Once the tangent vectors of the principal directions are computed, then for the computation of the unit tangent vectors $\mathbf{t}_{1.P}$ and $\mathbf{t}_{2.P}$ simple equations $\mathbf{t}_{1.P} = \dfrac{\mathbf{T}_{1.P}}{|\mathbf{T}_{1.P}|}$ and $\mathbf{t}_{2.P} = \dfrac{\mathbf{T}_{2.P}}{|\mathbf{T}_{2.P}|}$ can be used.

The unit vectors $\mathbf{t}_{1.P}$, $\mathbf{t}_{2.P}$, and $\mathbf{n}_P$ (Figure 2) comprise a right-hand oriented trihedron (otherwise direction of one of the parametric curves is required to be reversed), which is associated with the surface P in natural way [20].

The unit vectors $\mathbf{t}_{1.P}$, $\mathbf{t}_{2.P}$, and $\mathbf{n}_P$ allow composing of the moving orthogonal Cartesian coordinate system $x_P y_P z_P$ with the origin the point K of contact of the sculptured surface P and the generating surface T of the cutting tool. The point K is referred to as the cutter-contact-point (further CC-point). Axis of the local coordinate system $x_P y_P z_P$ are directed along the corresponding unit vectors $\mathbf{t}_{1.P}$, $\mathbf{t}_{2.P}$, and $\mathbf{n}_P$. Thus, the moving coordinate system $x_P y_P z_P$ is established at every point of the sculptured surface P.

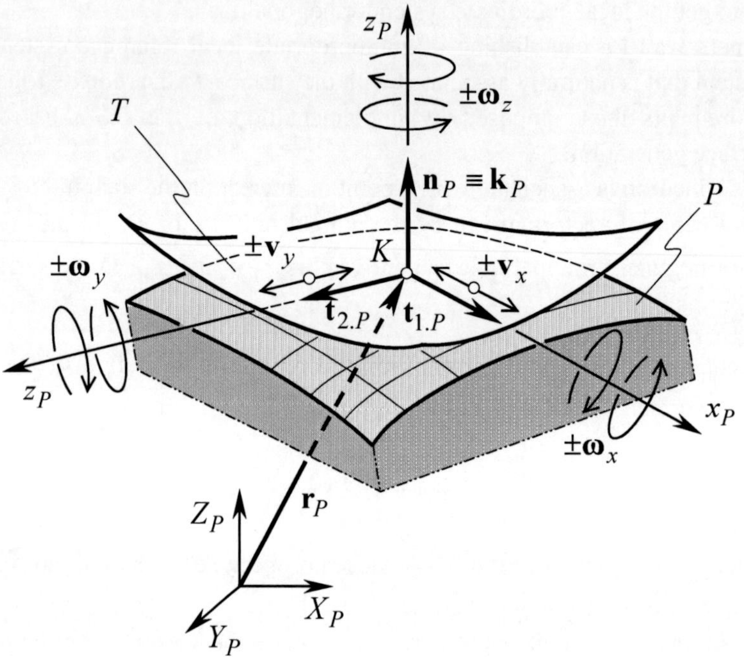

Figure 2. Instant kinematics of sculpture surface generation [20].

Most of equations those used for the analytical description of the sculptured surface machining process are getting significantly simpler in Darboux's trihedron.

3.2. Elementary Relative Motions

Instant motion of the cutting tool relative the work can be interpreted as an instant screw motion. The instant screw motion of the cutting tool can be decomposed on not more then six elementary motions, *i.e.* on three translations along and onto three rotations about axes of the local coordinate system $x_P y_P z_P$. Not all of six elementary relative motions are feasible. The translational motion of the cutting tool along z_P – axis is not feasible. This motion is eliminated from the instant kinematics of sculptured surface generation. There are two reasons[7] for the elimination of this translation motion from the instant kinematics of sculptured surface generation.

First, when the elementary motion of the cutting tool is performing in the $+\mathbf{n}_P$ direction this causes interruption of the surface generating process. Interruption of the surface

[7] Further the reader's attention will be stressed on special cases of sculptured surface machining when the motion of the cutting tool along z_P axis is allowed.

generating process is not allowed. Second, when the elementary motion of the cutting tool is performing in the $-\mathbf{n}_P$ direction this causes unavoidable interference of the surfaces P and T. Any interference of the surfaces P and T is not allowed. Hence, speed of the translational motion of the cutting tool along the common perpendicular has been equal to zero (Figure 2)

$$\mathbf{V_n} = \frac{\partial z_P}{\partial t} \cdot \mathbf{k}_P = 0 \tag{12}$$

Here time is designated as t.

Let's designate speed of the translational motions of the cutting tool along x_P and y_P axes as $\mathbf{V_u}$ and $\mathbf{V_v}$ correspondingly. Then $\boldsymbol{\omega}_\mathbf{u}$, $\boldsymbol{\omega}_\mathbf{v}$, and $\boldsymbol{\omega}_\mathbf{n}$ designate rotations about axes of the local coordinate system $x_P y_P z_P$.

In compliance with the principal instant kinematics of sculptured surface generation (Figure 2) [20], the cutting tool instant screw motion relative to the sculptured surface P can be decomposed onto not more than five elementary instant relative motions. This set of five feasible elementary relative motions is comprised by two translations

$$\mathbf{V_u} = \frac{\partial x_P}{\partial t} \cdot \mathbf{u}_P = \frac{\partial^2 \mathbf{r}_P}{\partial U_P \, \partial t}; \; \mathbf{V_v} = \frac{\partial y_P}{\partial t} \cdot \mathbf{v}_P = \frac{\partial^2 \mathbf{r}_P}{\partial V_P \, \partial t} \tag{13}$$

along axes of the local reference system $x_P y_P z_P$, and by three rotations

$$\boldsymbol{\omega}_\mathbf{u} = \frac{\partial \varphi_\mathbf{u}}{\partial t} \cdot \mathbf{u}_P; \; \boldsymbol{\omega}_\mathbf{v} = \frac{\partial \varphi_\mathbf{v}}{\partial t} \cdot \mathbf{v}_P; \; \boldsymbol{\omega}_\mathbf{n} = \frac{\partial \varphi_\mathbf{n}}{\partial t} \cdot \mathbf{n}_P \tag{14}$$

about axes of the local reference system $x_P y_P z_P$.

Here the angles of rotation of the cutting tool about the axes of the coordinate system $x_P y_P z_P$ are designated as $\varphi_\mathbf{u}$, $\varphi_\mathbf{v}$, and $\varphi_\mathbf{n}$ correspondingly.

3.2.1. Generating Motions of the Cutting Tool

After been machined on multi-axis *NC* machine, the sculptured surface is represented as a set of tool-paths. Generation of the sculptured surface by consequent tool-paths is a principal feature of machining of sculptured surfaces on multi-axis *NC* machine. Motion of the cutting tool along tool-path can be considered as a permanent following motion, while the side-step-motion of the cutting tool (in the direction that is orthogonal to the tool-path) can be considered as a discrete following motion.

The surface P can be generated as an enveloping surface to consecutive positions of the moving surface T when the surfaces P and T make either linear or point contact.

When linear contact of the surfaces observes, then a one-degree-of-freedom relative motion of the cutting tool is sufficient for generating of the surface P. Such relative motion is referred to as the *one-parametric motion* of the cutting tool. When the surfaces make point contact, then a two-degree-of-freedom relative motion of the cutting tool is required for generation of the entire surface P. Such relative motion is referred to as the *two-parametric motion* of the cutting tool. Number of available degrees of freedom can exceed two degrees. This results in that a *multi-parametric motion* of the cutting tool observes.

Known methods of the development of machining operations don't allow solution to the problem of synthesis of the most efficient (*i.e.* of the optimal) machining operations. Use of known methods returns a variety of solutions to the problem, efficiency of each of which is not the highest possible. For the computation of parameters of relative motion, known methods implement the equation of contact[8] $\mathbf{n}_P \cdot \mathbf{V}_\Sigma = 0$. Here $\mathbf{V}_\Sigma$ denotes speed of the resultant motion of the cutting tool relative the work.

Evidently, the infinite number of the vectors $\mathbf{V}_\Sigma$ satisfies the equation of contact $\mathbf{n}_P \cdot \mathbf{V}_\Sigma = 0$. All of them are within the tangent plane to the sculptured surface P. This is the principal reason for why implementation of known methods returns infinite number of solution to the problem under consideration. No doubt, performance of a sculptured surface generation depends on direction of the vector $\mathbf{V}_\Sigma$. For a certain direction of $\mathbf{V}_\Sigma$ performance of a sculptured surface machining is better, while for another direction of $\mathbf{V}_\Sigma$ it is poor. This yields intermediate conclusions that (a) the optimal direction of $\mathbf{V}_\Sigma$ exists, (b) this direction satisfies the equation of contact $\mathbf{n}_P \cdot \mathbf{V}_\Sigma = 0$, and indeed (c) the optimal parameters of the direction of $\mathbf{V}_\Sigma$ can be computed.

For the computation of the optimal parameters of the instant relative motion $\mathbf{V}_\Sigma$ of the work and of the cutting tool, an appropriate criterion of optimization is necessary. The major purpose of the criterion of the optimization is to select the optimal direction of the vector $\mathbf{V}_\Sigma$ from the infinite number of feasible directions that satisfy the equation of contact $\mathbf{n}_P \cdot \mathbf{V}_\Sigma = 0$.

In order to satisfy the equation of contact, vector $\mathbf{V}_\Sigma$ of the resultant relative motion of the cutting tool must be within the tangent plane to the surfaces P and T at the CC-point K. This is the geometrical interpretation of the equation of contact.

Consider the local reference system $x_P y_P z_P$ with the origin at CC-point K (Figure 3). In the coordinates system $x_P y_P z_P$ vector $\mathbf{V}_\Sigma$ can be described analytically by vector equation

$$\mathbf{V}_\Sigma = \frac{\partial x_P}{\partial t} \cdot \mathbf{u}_P + \frac{\partial y_P}{\partial t} \cdot \mathbf{v}_P + \frac{\partial z_P}{\partial t} \cdot \mathbf{n}_P \tag{15}$$

In that same local coordinate system, the equality $\mathbf{n}_P = \mathbf{k}_P$ observes. Substituting Eq. (15) and relationship $\mathbf{n}_P = \mathbf{k}_P$ along with Eq. (12) into equation of contact $\mathbf{n}_P \cdot \mathbf{V}_\Sigma = 0$, one can obtain

$$\mathbf{n}_P \cdot \mathbf{V}_\Sigma = \frac{\partial z_P}{\partial t} = 0 \tag{16}$$

[8]To the best of the author's knowledge, the condition of contact in the form that slightly differs from the equation of contact $\mathbf{n}_P \cdot \mathbf{V}_\Sigma = 0$ is known at least since the monograph by Willis, R., *Principles of Mechanism, Designed for the Use of Students in the Universities and for Engineering Students Generally*, London, John W. Parker, West Stand, Cambridge: J. & J.J. Deighton, 1841, 446p. In the present form $\mathbf{n}_P \cdot \mathbf{V}_\Sigma = 0$, equation of contact is known from late 1940th early 1950th, and it has to be credited to V.A Shishkov [47].

In order to satisfy the equation of contact, projection of the vector $\mathbf{V}_\Sigma$ of the resultant motion on the direction of common perpendicular to the surfaces P and T is required been equal to zero. This is a proof to the statement that the vector $\mathbf{V}_\Sigma$ is within the common tangent plane to the surfaces P and T.

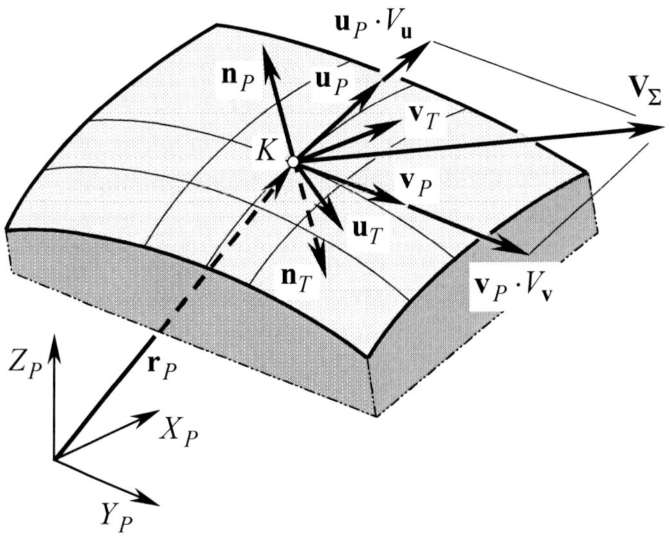

Figure 3. Feasible relative motions of the cutting tool.

It is of importance to point out here that the condition $pr_\mathbf{n}\mathbf{V}_\Sigma < 0$ can be considered as the condition of roughing. Portions of the surface T that perform such motion remove stock while machining the work. Condition $pr_\mathbf{n}\mathbf{V}_\Sigma = 0$ that is equivalent to the condition of contact $\mathbf{n}_P \cdot \mathbf{V}_\Sigma = 0$, corresponds to generating of the sculptured surface being machining. Finally, the condition $pr_\mathbf{n}\mathbf{V}_\Sigma > 0$ relates to portions of the surface T that are departing from the machined surface P.

Equation of contact $\mathbf{n}_P \cdot \mathbf{V}_\Sigma = 0$ determines instant kinematics of sculptured surface generation not uniquely. In addition to the infinite number of feasible directions for the vector $\mathbf{V}_\Sigma$, one more reason can affect indefiniteness of the equation of contact.

Location and orientation of the common perpendicular $\mathbf{n}_P$ is uniquely specified by geometry of the surface P. Usually (but not mandatory) it can't be changed. However, in special cases of machining, the orientation of the common perpendicular $\mathbf{n}_P$ can be changed for manufacturing purposes. For example, when machining a thin-wall part, an elastic deformation can be applied to the work [24]. If the elastic deformation is used for manufacturing purposes, then the equation of contact must be satisfied for the deformed stage of the surface being machining. Besides the capability of changing of orientation of the unit normal vector to the surface is limited, however such the capability exists and it affects the generation of the surface P. The last is of principal importance in particular cases of sculptured surface machining.

Capabilities to alternate the orientation of the unit normal vector $\mathbf{n}_T$ to the generating surface T of a cutting tool are significantly wider, especially when implementing cutting tools of special design with variable shape and parameters of the surface T for machining of a given sculptured surface [21], [22], [30], [42].

When machining a sculptured surface on multi-axis *NC* machine, the cutting tool is performing a continuous following motion along every tool-path [23], [24], [43]. Therefore, the generating motion can be considered as a continuous following motion of the cutting tool relative the work. This motion results in that the *CC*-point is traveling along the tool-path.

After the machining of a certain tool-path is complete, then the cutting tool is feeding across the tool-path in a new position. Machining of another tool-path begins from the new position of the cutting tool. Hence, the feed motion of the cutting tool can be represented as a discontinuous following motion of the cutting tool relative the work. This motion results in that the *CC*-point travels across the tool-path.

Generating motion of the cutting tool can be described analytically. For this purpose, the elementary motions those that comprise the principal instant kinematics of surface generation are used (Figure 2). The elementary relative motions are properly timed (synchronized) with one another in order to comprise the desired instant generation motion of the cutting tool (Figure 4).

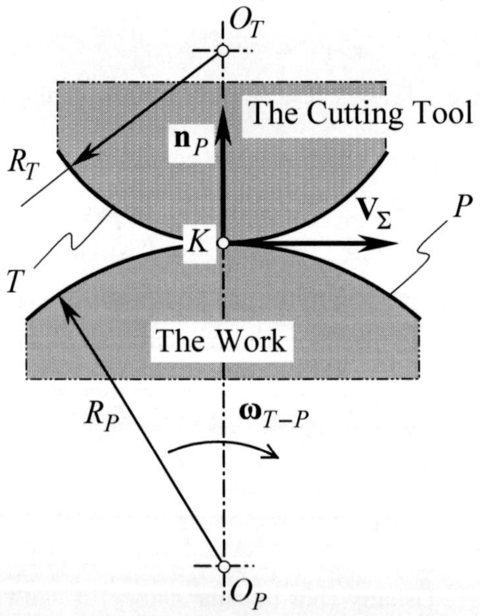

Figure 4. Generating motions of the cutting tool.

The following equations

$$|\mathbf{V_u}| = |\boldsymbol{\omega}_\mathbf{v}| \cdot R_{P.\mathbf{u}} \text{ and } |\mathbf{V_v}| = |\boldsymbol{\omega}_\mathbf{u}| \cdot R_{P.\mathbf{v}} \tag{17}$$

can be easily composed on the premises of analysis of the instant kinematics of sculptured surface generation.

Here $R_{P.\mathbf{u}}$ and $R_{P.\mathbf{v}}$ designate the normal radii of curvature of the sculptured surface P. The radii of curvature $R_{P.\mathbf{u}}$ and $R_{P.\mathbf{v}}$ are measured in the plane sections through the unit tangent vectors $\mathbf{u}_P$ and $\mathbf{v}_P$ correspondingly. For the computation of the parameter $R_{P.\mathbf{u}}$ Euler's equation

$$R_{P.\mathbf{u}} = \left[\frac{\cos^2 \varphi}{R_{1.P}} + \frac{\sin^2 \varphi}{R_{2.P}} \right]^{-1} \tag{18}$$

can be used.

Here, in Eq. (18), $R_{1.P}$ and $R_{2.P}$ designate principal radii of curvature[9] of the sculptured surface P, and φ designates the angle that the unit tangent vector $\mathbf{u}_P$ makes with the first principal direction $\mathbf{t}_{1.P}$ on the part surface. Principal radii of curvature $R_{1.P}$ and $R_{2.P}$ are the roots of the quadratic equation

$$\begin{vmatrix} L_P \cdot R_P - E_P & M_P \cdot R_P - F_P \\ M_P \cdot R_P - F_P & N_P \cdot R_P - G_P \end{vmatrix} = 0 \tag{19}$$

Similarly, the normal radius of curvature $R_{P.\mathbf{v}}$ can be computed.

Equations (17) yield generalization of the following kind

$$|\mathbf{V}_\Sigma| = |\boldsymbol{\omega}_{T-P}| \cdot R_{P.\Sigma} \tag{20}$$

where

$\mathbf{V}_\Sigma$	is vector of the resultant motion of *CC*-point along the tool-path
$\boldsymbol{\omega}_{T-P}$	is vector of instant rotation of the surface T about an axis that is perpendicular to the normal plane through the vector $\mathbf{V}_\Sigma$
$R_{P.\Sigma}$	is radius of normal curvature of the surface P in the direction of $\mathbf{V}_\Sigma$

After the relative motion of the cutting tool in the direction of the unit normal vector $\mathbf{n}_P = \mathbf{k}_P$ is eliminated from further analysis, then the vector $\mathbf{V}_\Sigma$ yields the following representation in projections on axes of the local coordinate system $x_P y_P z_P$

$$\mathbf{V}_\Sigma = \frac{\partial x_P}{\partial t} \cdot \mathbf{u}_P + \frac{\partial y_P}{\partial t} \cdot \mathbf{v}_P \tag{21}$$

In order to satisfy the conditions [see Eq. (17)], the both additives in Eq. (21) have to cause a continuous following motion of the *CC*-point over the sculptured surface P. Otherwise, the relative motion of the work and of the cutting tool can't be identified as the generating motion of the cutting tool. The condition [see Eq. (17)] is satisfied if

---

[9]Algebraic values of the radii of principal curvature $R_{1.P}$ and $R_{2.P}$ relate to each other as $R_{2.P} > R_{1.P}$.

$$\frac{\partial x_P}{\partial t}\cdot \mathbf{u}_P = \boldsymbol{\omega}_{\mathbf{v}} \times (R_{P.\mathbf{u}} \cdot \mathbf{n}_P) \text{ and } \frac{\partial y_P}{\partial t}\cdot \mathbf{v}_P = \boldsymbol{\omega}_{\mathbf{u}} \times (R_{P.\mathbf{v}} \cdot \mathbf{n}_P) \tag{22}$$

Taking into account this result, Eq. (21) casts into

$$\mathbf{V}_{\Sigma} = \boldsymbol{\omega}_{\mathbf{v}} \times (R_{P.\mathbf{u}} \cdot \mathbf{n}_P) + \boldsymbol{\omega}_{\mathbf{u}} \times (R_{P.\mathbf{v}} \cdot \mathbf{n}_P) \tag{23}$$

Generating motion of the cutting tool satisfies both the equation of contact $\mathbf{n}_P \cdot \mathbf{V}_{\Sigma} = 0$ and Eq. (23) at every instant of machining of the sculptured surface on multi-axis *NC* machine.

The relative motion $\mathbf{V}_{\mathbf{n}}$ of the cutting tool (Figure 2) is eliminated from further analysis not completely. Taking into consideration the tolerance on accuracy of machining of the sculptured surface, the motion $\mathbf{V}_{\mathbf{n}}$ along the unit normal vector $\mathbf{n}_P$ is feasible if it is performing within the tolerance $\delta = \delta^{+} + \delta^{-}$. More over, due to deviations of the desired cutting tool motion from the actual cutting tool motion, the motion $\mathbf{V}_{\mathbf{n}}$ always observes is actual machining operations. In case of necessity, the motion $\mathbf{V}_{\mathbf{n}}$ can be incorporated into the principal instant kinematics of surface generation.

The principal instant kinematics of surface generation is comprised of five elementary relative motions. Thus, the surface P can be represented as an enveloping surface to consecutive positions of not more then five-parametric motions of the generating surface T of the cutting tool.

3.2.2. Motions of Orientation of the Cutting Tool

As it has been already mentioned above, machining of a sculptured surface on multi-axis *NC* machine is the most general case of surface generation. This is due to that two surfaces, namely the sculptured surface P and the generating surface T of the cutting tool make point contact at every instant of the machining operation.

Among various kinds of feasible relative motions of the cutting tool, one more motion of special kind can be distinguished. When performing relative motion of this kind, *CC*-point doesn't change it position on the sculptured surface P being machining. This motion affects only orientation of the cutting tool relative to the work. Motions of this kind are referred to as the *orientation motions of the cutting tool* [28].

When performing the orientation motion, *CC*-point can remain it location on both, on the sculptured surface P as well as on the generating surface T of the cutting tool. The orientation motion of this kind is referred to as the *orientation motion of the first kind*.

When machining a sculptured surface, *CC*-point can remain its location on the sculptured surface P and change its location on the generating surface T of the cutting tool. The orientation motion of this kind is referred to as the *orientation motional motion of the second kind*.

Speed of the orientation motions of the cutting tool is a function of variation of the principal curvatures of the surface P at the current *CC*-point, and of speed of the generating motion. Orientation motions of the cutting tool don't directly affect on stock removal capacity of the cutting tool, or on generation of the surface P itself. These motions change orientation of the cutting tool relative the work as well as relative direction of the generating motion of the cutting tool. As it will be shown later, the orientation motions of the cutting tool can be used as a tool for improving performance of machining of a sculptured surface on multi-axis *NC* machine. This is the main reason for the orientation motions of the cutting tool deserve been investigated more in details.

In order to identify all feasible orientation motions of the cutting tool, it is helpful to consider all feasible groups of relative motions of the cutting tool. All groups of the relative motions are represented with the singular relative motions and with the combined relative motions. The singular relative motions are represented with a single elementary relative motion of the cutting tool. The combined relative motions are comprised of two and/or more elementary relative motions of the cutting tool.

There are only five groups of elementary relative motions of the cutting tool. Number of elementary relative motions at every group of relative motions is equal to the number of combinations of 5 elementary motions by i elementary motions. Here $i = 1, 2, \ldots, 5$. The total number N of relative motions in the principal instant kinematics of surface generation can be computed from the equation

$$N = \sum_{i=1}^{5} N_i = \sum_{i=1}^{5} C_5^i = 31 \quad (24)$$

The performed analysis of all of 31 relative motions reveals that only few elementary relative motions and there combinations can be distinguished as the orientational motions of the cutting tool [23], [24], [28], [30], [43]. They are:

The 1st group of the motions: $\{\boldsymbol{\omega}_{\mathbf{n}}\}$

The 2nd group of the motions: $\{\boldsymbol{\omega}_{\mathbf{u}}, \mathbf{V}_{\mathbf{v}}\}$, $\{\boldsymbol{\omega}_{\mathbf{v}}, \mathbf{V}_{\mathbf{u}}\}$

The 3rd group of the motions: $\{\boldsymbol{\omega}_{\mathbf{u}}, \boldsymbol{\omega}_{\mathbf{n}}, \mathbf{V}_{\mathbf{v}}\}$, $\{\boldsymbol{\omega}_{\mathbf{v}}, \boldsymbol{\omega}_{\mathbf{n}}, \mathbf{V}_{\mathbf{u}}\}$

The 4th group of the motions: $\{\boldsymbol{\omega}_{\mathbf{u}}, \mathbf{V}_{\mathbf{v}}, \boldsymbol{\omega}_{\mathbf{v}}, \mathbf{V}_{\mathbf{u}}\}$

The 5th group of the motions: $\{\boldsymbol{\omega}_{\mathbf{u}}, \mathbf{V}_{\mathbf{v}}, \boldsymbol{\omega}_{\mathbf{n}}, \boldsymbol{\omega}_{\mathbf{v}}, \mathbf{V}_{\mathbf{u}}\}$.

Ultimately, one can come up with a set of the orientation motions of the cutting tool. One of the motions is the singular orientation motion and six others are the combined orientation motions of the cutting tool.

The orientation motions of the first kind are represented with the only singular orientation motion $\{\boldsymbol{\omega}_{\mathbf{n}}\}$.

The orientation motions of the second kind are represented with six relative motions. The orientation motion $\{\boldsymbol{\omega}_{\mathbf{u}}, \mathbf{V}_{\mathbf{v}}, \boldsymbol{\omega}_{\mathbf{n}}, \boldsymbol{\omega}_{\mathbf{v}}, \mathbf{V}_{\mathbf{u}}\}$ is the most general one among them. Other orientation motions can be considered as particular orientation motions of the combined orientation motion $\{\boldsymbol{\omega}_{\mathbf{u}}, \mathbf{V}_{\mathbf{v}}, \boldsymbol{\omega}_{\mathbf{n}}, \boldsymbol{\omega}_{\mathbf{v}}, \mathbf{V}_{\mathbf{u}}\}$.

Elementary motions that comprise a combined orientation motion of the cutting tool are timed (synchronized) with one another. The rotational elementary motion $\boldsymbol{\omega}_{\mathbf{u}}$ about x_P axis is timed with the translational motion $\mathbf{V}_{\mathbf{v}}$ along y_P axis. Similarly, the rotational elementary motion $\boldsymbol{\omega}_{\mathbf{v}}$ about y_P axis is timed with the translational motion $\mathbf{V}_{\mathbf{u}}$ along x_P axis. Timing of the elementary motions results in that the surface T is rolling with sliding over the sculptured surface P. Timing of that kind of the elementary motions can be achieved when the following condition is satisfied.

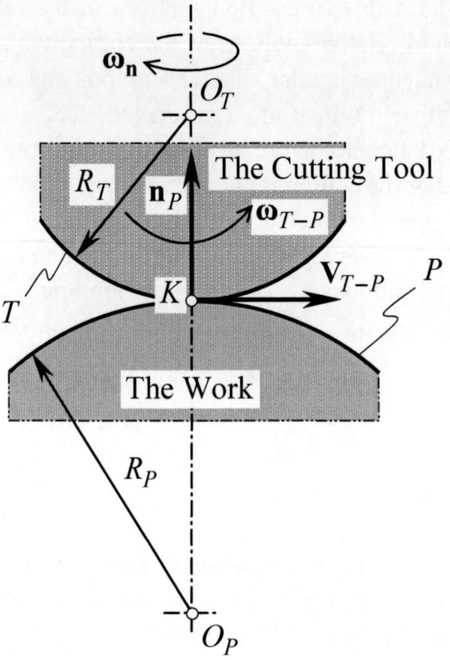

Figure 5. Motions if orientation of the cutting tool.

Orientational motion of the second kind can be considered as a superposition of the instant translational motion with a certain instant speed $\mathbf{V}_{T-P}$, and of the instant rotation $\boldsymbol{\omega}_{T-P}$ of the cutting tool (Figure 5). In order to be an orientational motion of the cutting tool, the following equality

$$|\mathbf{V}_{T-P}| = |\boldsymbol{\omega}_{P-T}| \cdot R_T \tag{25}$$

is necessary being satisfied.

Here is designated

$\boldsymbol{\omega}_{T-P}$ is vector of the instant rotation of the cutting tool about the axis O_T that crosses the vector $\mathbf{V}_{T-P}$ at right angle

R_T radius of curvature of the surface T in the normal plane section through the vector $\mathbf{V}_{T-P}$

Vector $\mathbf{V}_{T-P}$ can be represented in the form similar to Eq. (21)

$$\mathbf{V}_{T-P} = \frac{\partial x_P}{\partial t} \cdot \mathbf{u}_P + \frac{\partial y_P}{\partial t} \cdot \mathbf{v}_P \tag{26}$$

In order to satisfy the necessary condition [see Eq. (25)], it is required the both additives in Eq. (21) result in the *CC*-point is performing continuous following motion over the surface P. Otherwise, the relative motion can't be distinguished as the orientational motion of the cutting tool. The condition [see Eq. (25)] is satisfied if

$$\frac{\partial x_P}{\partial t} \cdot \mathbf{u}_P = \boldsymbol{\omega}_{\mathbf{v}} \cdot R_{T.\mathbf{u}} \text{ and } \frac{\partial y_P}{\partial t} \cdot \mathbf{v}_P = \boldsymbol{\omega}_{\mathbf{u}} \cdot R_{T.\mathbf{v}} \tag{27}$$

Here, in Eq. (27)

$R_{T.\mathbf{u}}$ and $R_{T.\mathbf{v}}$	are normal radii of curvature of the generating surface T of the cutting tool in the plane sections through the unit vectors $\mathbf{u}_P$ and $\mathbf{v}_P$ correspondingly
$\boldsymbol{\omega}_{\mathbf{u}}$ and $\boldsymbol{\omega}_{\mathbf{v}}$	are rotations about the directions of $\mathbf{u}_P$ and $\mathbf{v}_P$

Equations (27) yield representation of the combined orientation motion of the cutting tool $\mathbf{V}_{orient}$ in the form

$$\{\boldsymbol{\omega}_{\mathbf{u}}, \mathbf{V}_{\mathbf{v}}, \boldsymbol{\omega}_{\mathbf{v}}, \mathbf{V}_{\mathbf{u}}\} \Rightarrow \begin{cases} \boldsymbol{\omega}_{orient} = \boldsymbol{\omega}_{\mathbf{u}} + \boldsymbol{\omega}_{\mathbf{v}} \\ \mathbf{V}_{orient} = \boldsymbol{\omega}_{\mathbf{u}} \times (R_{T.\mathbf{v}} \cdot \mathbf{n}_P) + \boldsymbol{\omega}_{\mathbf{v}} \times (R_{T.\mathbf{u}} \cdot \mathbf{n}_P) \end{cases} \tag{28}$$

On the premises of the performed analysis, a scientific classification of the orientation motions of the cutting tool is developed. The interested reader may wish to go to [23], [24], [28], [30], [43] for details in this concern.

When representing a sculptured surface P as an enveloping surface to consecutive positions of the five-parametric motion of the generating surface T, the orientation motions of the cutting tool can be omitted from the consideration.

Orientation motions of the cutting tool make machining of a sculptured surface more agile. If proper parameters are assigned the orientation motions of the cutting tool could increase the performance of the machining operation.

The developed approach yields computation of the optimal parameters of all the motions of the cutting tool relative to the work. Solution to the problem of synthesis of the optimal kinematics of generation of a sculptured surface on multi-axis *NC* machine can be drawn up from the analysis of kinematics of multi-parametric motion of the cutting tool relative the work.

3.2.3. Coordinate Systems Transformations: their Impact on Fundamental Forms of the Surfaces

While moving, the surfaces P and T occupy various positions that are different from those in which the surfaces initially are described analytically. For the purposes of analytical representation of the moving sculptured surface and of the moving generating surface of the cutting tool appropriate operators of the coordinate system transformations are used.

For analytical description of translation along coordinate axes, the operators of translation $\mathbf{Tr}(a_x, X)$, $\mathbf{Tr}(a_y, Y)$ and $\mathbf{Tr}(a_z, Z)$ are used. The operators yield matrix representation in the form

$$\mathbf{Tr}(a_x, X) = \begin{bmatrix} 1 & 0 & 0 & a_x \\ 0 & 1 & 0 & 0 \\ 0 & 0 & 1 & 0 \\ 0 & 0 & 0 & 1 \end{bmatrix}, \ \mathbf{Tr}(a_y, Y) = \begin{bmatrix} 1 & 0 & 0 & 0 \\ 0 & 1 & 0 & a_y \\ 0 & 0 & 1 & 0 \\ 0 & 0 & 0 & 1 \end{bmatrix}, \ \mathbf{Tr}(a_z, Z) = \begin{bmatrix} 1 & 0 & 0 & 0 \\ 0 & 1 & 0 & 0 \\ 0 & 0 & 1 & a_z \\ 0 & 0 & 0 & 1 \end{bmatrix} \tag{29}$$

Here a_x, a_y, a_z are signed values that denote distance of translation along corresponding axis.

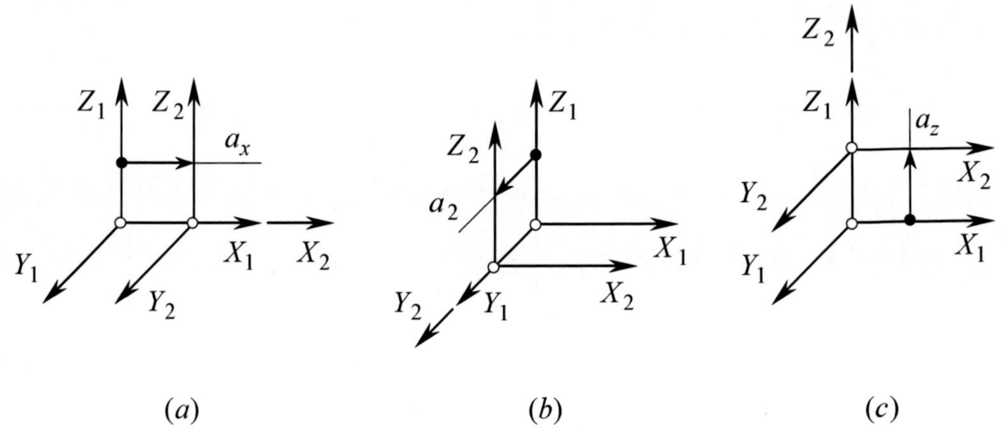

Figure 6. To analytical description of the operators of translation $\mathbf{Tr}(a_x, X)$, $\mathbf{Tr}(a_y, Y)$, $\mathbf{Tr}(a_z, Z)$ along coordinate axis.

Consider two coordinate systems $X_1Y_1Z_1$ and $X_2Y_2Z_2$ shifted along X_1 axis on a_x (Figure 6,a).

Let's a point M in the coordinate system $X_2Y_2Z_2$ is given by the position vector $\mathbf{r}_2(M)$. In the coordinate system $X_1Y_1Z_1$ that same point M can be specified by the position vector $\mathbf{r}_1(M)$. Then the position vector $\mathbf{r}_1(M)$ can be expressed in terms of the position vector $\mathbf{r}_2(M)$ by the equation $\mathbf{r}_1(M) = \mathbf{Tr}(a_x, X) \cdot \mathbf{r}_2(M)$. Equations similar to that above are valid for other operators $\mathbf{Tr}(a_y, Y)$ and $\mathbf{Tr}(a_z, Z)$ of the coordinate system transformation (Figure 6,b,c).

Suppose that a point P on a rigid body goes through a translation describing a straight path from P_1 to P_2 with a change of coordinates of (a_x , a_y , a_z). This motion can describe with a resultant translation operator $\mathbf{Tr}(a, \mathbf{A})$

$$\mathbf{Tr}(a,\mathbf{A}) = \begin{bmatrix} 1 & 0 & 0 & a_x \\ 0 & 1 & 0 & a_y \\ 0 & 0 & 1 & a_z \\ 0 & 0 & 0 & 1 \end{bmatrix} \tag{30}$$

The operator $\mathbf{Tr}(a,\mathbf{A})$ can be interpreted as the operator of translation along an arbitrary axis $\mathbf{A}$.

The operator $\mathbf{Tr}(a,\mathbf{A})$ of translation of that kind can be expressed in terms of the operators $\mathbf{Tr}(a_x,X)$, $\mathbf{Tr}(a_y,Y)$ and $\mathbf{Tr}(a_z,Z)$ of elementary translations

$$\mathbf{Tr}(a,\mathbf{A}) = \mathbf{Tr}(a_z,Z)\cdot\mathbf{Tr}(a_y,Y)\cdot\mathbf{Tr}(a_x,X) \tag{31}$$

Evidently, the axis $\mathbf{A}$ is always the axis through the origin.

Rotation of a coordinate system about a coordinate axis is another major kind of linear transformations used in the theory of surface generation.

For analytical description of rotation about coordinate axis the operators of rotation $\mathbf{Rt}(\varphi_x,X)$, $\mathbf{Rt}(\varphi_y,Y)$ and $\mathbf{Rt}(\varphi_z,Z)$ are used. The operators yield representation in the form of homogenous matrices

$$\mathbf{Rt}(\varphi_x,X) = \begin{bmatrix} \cos\varphi_y & 0 & -\sin\varphi_y & 0 \\ 0 & 1 & 0 & 0 \\ \sin\varphi_y & 0 & \cos\varphi_y & 0 \\ 0 & 0 & 0 & 1 \end{bmatrix} \tag{32}$$

$$\mathbf{Rt}(\varphi_y,Y) = \begin{bmatrix} 1 & 0 & 0 & 0 \\ 0 & \cos\varphi_x & \sin\varphi_x & 0 \\ 0 & -\sin\varphi_x & \cos\varphi_x & 0 \\ 0 & 0 & 0 & 1 \end{bmatrix} \tag{33}$$

$$\mathbf{Rt}(\varphi_z,Z) = \begin{bmatrix} \cos\varphi_z & \sin\varphi_z & 0 & 0 \\ -\sin\varphi_z & \cos\varphi_z & 0 & 0 \\ 0 & 0 & 2 & 0 \\ 0 & 0 & 0 & 1 \end{bmatrix} \tag{34}$$

Here φ_x, φ_y, φ_z are signed values that denote angles of rotation about corresponding axis: φ_x is rotation around the $X-$ axis (pitch); φ_y is rotation around the $Y-$ axis (roll), and φ_z is rotation around the $Z-$ axis (yaw).

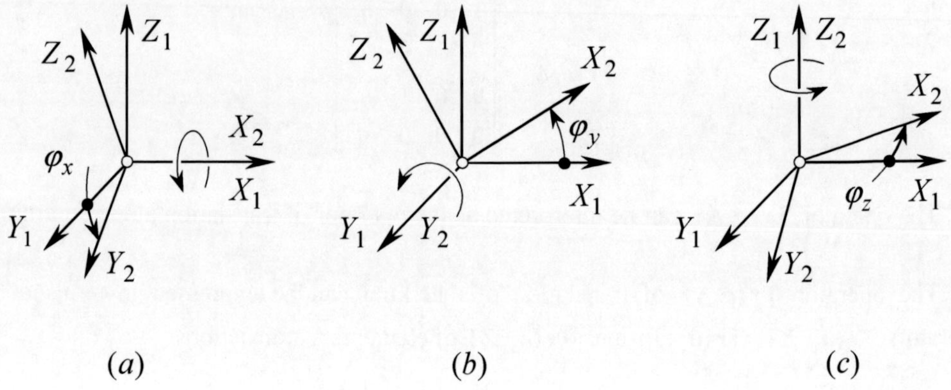

Figure 7. To analytical description of the operators of rotations $\mathbf{Rt}(\varphi_x, X)$, $\mathbf{Rt}(\varphi_y, Y)$, $\mathbf{Rt}(\varphi_z, Z)$ about coordinate axis.

Consider two coordinate systems $X_1Y_1Z_1$ and $X_2Y_2Z_2$ turned about X_1 axis through the angle φ_x (Figure 7,a). In the coordinate system $X_2Y_2Z_2$ a point M is given by the position vector $\mathbf{r}_2(M)$. In the coordinate system $X_1Y_1Z_1$ that same point M can be specified by the position vector $\mathbf{r}_1(M)$. Then the position vector $\mathbf{r}_1(M)$ can be expressed in terms of the position vector $\mathbf{r}_2(M)$ by the equation $\mathbf{r}_1(M) = \mathbf{Rt}(\varphi_x, X) \cdot \mathbf{r}_2(M)$. Equations similar to that above are valid for other operators $\mathbf{Rt}(\varphi_y, Y)$ and $\mathbf{Rt}(\varphi_z, Z)$ of the coordinate system transformation (Figure 7,b,c).

The operators of translations $\mathbf{Tr}(a_x, X)$, $\mathbf{Tr}(a_y, Y)$, $\mathbf{Tr}(a_z, Z)$ together with the operators of rotation $\mathbf{Rt}(\varphi_x, X)$, $\mathbf{Rt}(\varphi_y, Y)$, $\mathbf{Rt}(\varphi_z, Z)$ are used for composing of the operator $\mathbf{Rs}(1 \to 2)$ of the resultant coordinate system transformation. The operator $\mathbf{Rs}(1 \to 2)$ of the resultant coordinate system transformation analytically describes the transition from the initial coordinate system $X_1Y_1Z_1$ to the coordinate system $X_2Y_2Z_2$.

For example, the expression $\mathbf{Rs}(1 \to 5) = \mathbf{Tr}(a_x, X) \cdot \mathbf{Rt}(\varphi_z, Z) \cdot \mathbf{Rt}(\varphi_x, X) \cdot \mathbf{Tr}(a_y, Y)$ indicates that the transition from the coordinates system $X_1Y_1Z_1$ to the coordinate system $X_5Y_5Z_5$ is performed in the following four steps: (a) translation $\mathbf{Tr}(a_y, Y)$ followed by (b) rotation $\mathbf{Rt}(\varphi_x, X)$, followed by (c) second rotation $\mathbf{Rt}(\varphi_z, Z)$, finally followed by (d) the translation $\mathbf{Tr}(a_x, X)$. In the similar way the operator of resultant coordinate system transformations can be composed for any and all other cases.

Every coordinate system transformation results in corresponding change of equation of the surface P and/or the generating surface T of a cutting tool. Therefore, it is necessary to re-calculate coefficients of the first $\Phi_{1.P}$ and of the second $\Phi_{2.P}$ fundamental of the surfaces P as many times as the coordinate system transformation is performing. This routing and time-consuming operation can be eliminated if the operators of coordinate system transformations could be used directly to the fundamental forms $\Phi_{1.P}$ and $\Phi_{2.P}$. After been computed in an initial coordinate system, then the fundamental magnitudes E_P, F_P, G_P, L_P, M_P and N_P can be determined in any new coordinate system using for this purpose the operators of translation, of rotation and of resultant coordinate system transformation. Transformation of such kind of the fundamental magnitudes $\Phi_{1.P}$ and $\Phi_{2.P}$ becomes possible due to implementation of a formula, that is derived immediately below [27].

Let's consider a surface P that is given by equation $\mathbf{r}_P = \mathbf{r}_P(U_P, V_P)$, where $(U_P, V_P) \in G$.

For the analysis below, it is convenient to use the equation of the first fundamental form $\Phi_{1.P}$ of the surface P represented in matrix form [see Eq. (4)]

$$[\Phi_{1.P}] = \begin{bmatrix} dU_P & dV_P & 0 & 0 \end{bmatrix} \cdot \begin{bmatrix} E_P & F_P & 0 & 0 \\ F_P & G_P & 0 & 0 \\ 0 & 0 & 1 & 0 \\ 0 & 0 & 0 & 1 \end{bmatrix} \cdot \begin{bmatrix} dU_P \\ dV_P \\ 0 \\ 0 \end{bmatrix} \tag{35}$$

Similarly, equation of the second fundamental form $\Phi_{2.P}$ of the surface P can be given by equation (7)

$$[\Phi_{2.P}] = \begin{bmatrix} dU_P & dV_P & 0 & 0 \end{bmatrix} \cdot \begin{bmatrix} L_P & M_P & 0 & 0 \\ M_P & N_P & 0 & 0 \\ 0 & 0 & 1 & 0 \\ 0 & 0 & 0 & 1 \end{bmatrix} \cdot \begin{bmatrix} dU_P \\ dV_P \\ 0 \\ 0 \end{bmatrix} \tag{36}$$

The coordinate system transformation with the operator of linear transformation $\mathbf{Rs}(1 \to 2)$ transfers the equation $\mathbf{r}_P = \mathbf{r}_P(U_P, V_P)$ of the surface P initially given in $X_1Y_1Z_1$, to the equation $\mathbf{r}^*_P = \mathbf{r}^*_P(U^*_P, V^*_P)$ of that same surface P in a new coordinate system $X_2Y_2Z_2$. It is clear that $\mathbf{r}_P \neq \mathbf{r}^*_P$.

In the new coordinate system, the surface P is analytically described by the following expression

$$\mathbf{r}^*_P(U^*_P, V^*_P) = \mathbf{Rs}(1 \to 2) \cdot \mathbf{r}_P(U_P, V_P) \tag{37}$$

The operator of resultant coordinate system transformation $\mathbf{Rs}(1 \to 2)$ casts the column matrices of variables in Eq. (35) and Eq. (36) to the form

$$[dU^*_P \quad dV^*_P \quad 0 \quad 0]^T = \mathbf{Rs}(1 \to 2) \cdot [dU_P \quad dV_P \quad 0 \quad 0]^T. \tag{38}$$

Substitution of Eq. (38) into Eq. (35) and Eq. (36) yields expressions for $\Phi^*_{1.P}$ and $\Phi^*_{2.P}$ in the new coordinate system [27]

$$\left[\Phi^*_{1.P}\right] = \left[\mathbf{Rs}(1 \to 2) \cdot [dU_P \quad dV_P \quad 0 \quad 0]^T\right]^T \cdot \left[\Phi_{1.P}\right] \cdot \mathbf{Rs}(1 \to 2) \cdot [dU_P \quad dV_P \quad 0 \quad 0]^T \quad (39)$$

$$\left[\Phi^*_{2.P}\right] = \left[\mathbf{Rs}(1 \to 2) \cdot [dU_P \quad dV_P \quad 0 \quad 0]^T\right]^T \cdot \left[\Phi_{2.P}\right] \cdot \mathbf{Rs}(1 \to 2) \cdot [dU_P \quad dV_P \quad 0 \quad 0]^T \quad (40)$$

The following equation is valid for multiplication

$$\left[\mathbf{Rs}(1 \to 2) \cdot [dU_P \quad dV_P \quad 0 \quad 0]^T\right]^T = \mathbf{Rs}^T(1 \to 2) \cdot [dU_P \quad dV_P \quad 0 \quad 0] \quad (41)$$

Therefore,

$$\left[\Phi^*_{1.P}\right] = [dU_P \quad dV_P \quad 0 \quad 0]^T \cdot \left\{\mathbf{Rs}^T(1 \to 2) \cdot \left[\Phi_{1.P}\right] \cdot \mathbf{Rs}(1 \to 2)\right\} \cdot [dU_P \quad dV_P \quad 0 \quad 0] \quad (42)$$

$$\left[\Phi^*_{2.P}\right] = [dU_P \quad dV_P \quad 0 \quad 0]^T \cdot \left\{\mathbf{Rs}^T(1 \to 2) \cdot \left[\Phi_{2.P}\right] \cdot \mathbf{Rs}(1 \to 2)\right\} \cdot [dU_P \quad dV_P \quad 0 \quad 0] \quad (43)$$

It can be easily shown that the matrices $\left[\Phi^*_{1.P}\right]$ and $\left[\Phi^*_{2.P}\right]$ in Eqs. (42) and (43) represent quadratic forms with respect to dU_P and dV_P.

Operator of the resultant transformation $\mathbf{Rs}(1 \to 2)$ of the surface P having the first $\Phi_{1.P}$ and the second $\Phi_{2.P}$ fundamental forms from the initial coordinate system $X_1Y_1Z_1$ to the new coordinate system $X_2Y_2Z_2$ results in that in the new coordinate system the corresponding fundamental forms are expressed in the form [27]:

$$\left[\Phi^*_{1.P}\right] = \mathbf{Rs}^T(1 \to 2) \cdot \left[\Phi_{1.P}\right] \cdot \mathbf{Rs}(1 \to 2) \quad (44)$$

$$\left[\Phi^*_{2.P}\right] = \mathbf{Rs}^T(1 \to 2) \cdot \left[\Phi_{2.P}\right] \cdot \mathbf{Rs}(1 \to 2) \quad (45)$$

Equations (44) and (45) reveal that after the coordinate system transformation is completed, the first $\Phi^*_{1.P}$ and the second $\Phi^*_{2.P}$ fundamental forms of the surface P in the coordinate system $X_2Y_2Z_2$ are expressed in terms of the first $\Phi_{1.P}$ and the second $\Phi_{2.P}$ fundamental forms initially represented in the coordinate system $X_1Y_1Z_1$. In order to do that, the corresponding fundamental form either $\Phi_{1.P}$ or $\Phi_{2.P}$ is required been pre-multiplied by $\mathbf{Rs}(1 \to 2)$ and after that it been post-multiplied by $\mathbf{Rs}^T(1 \to 2)$.

Implementation of Eq. (44) and Eq. (45) significantly simplifies formulae transformations.

Equations similar to those above Eqs. (44) and (45) are valid for the generating surface T of the cutting tool.

4. Analytical Description of the Geometry of Contact of the Sculptured Surface and of the Generating Surface of the Form Cutting Tool

Priority of the sculptured surface to be machined over the rest elements of the machining process is the corner stone concept of the *DG/K*-based method of surface generation. Synthesis of optimal sculptured surface machining operation is based on the premises of this fundamental concept.

A method for the analytical description of the geometry of contact of the surfaces P and T is required for the synthesizing of the optimal operation of the sculptured surface generation. The problem of analytical description of the geometry of contact of two smooth regular surfaces in the first order of tangency is a sophisticated one. The interested reader is referred to [23], [31], [32], [35] for details on known methods for analytical description of the geometry of contact of smooth regular surfaces are developed by now.

It is convenient to begin the analysis from the analytical description of local relative orientation of the surfaces P and T (in differential vicinity of the point of contact K of the surfaces). In sculptured surface machining on multi-axis *NC* machine, point of contact of the surfaces P and T is often referred to as the *cutter-contact point* (farther *CC*-point).

4.1. Local Relative Orientation of the Surfaces *P* and *T*

A sculptured surface P and the generating surface T of the cutting tool are the conjugate surfaces in nature. This means that during the machining operation the surfaces P and T are in permanent tangency to one another (Figure 8). The requirement to be permanently in tangency to each other imposes a kind of restrictions on the relative configuration (location and orientation) of the surfaces, and on their relative motion. In the theory of surface generation, a quantitative measure of the surfaces P and T relative orientation is established.

Relative orientation of the surfaces P and T is specified by the angle μ of the surfaces local[10] relative orientation. By definition, angle μ is equal to the angle that the unit tangent vector $\mathbf{t}_{1.P}$ of the first principal direction of the surface P makes with the unit tangent vector $\mathbf{t}_{1.T}$ of the first principal direction of the surface T. That same angle μ can be also determined as the angle that make the unit tangent vectors $\mathbf{t}_{2.P}$ and $\mathbf{t}_{2.T}$ of the second principal directions of the surfaces P and T at a point K of their contact. This immediately yields equations for the computation of the angle μ [23], [24], [30], [39], [43]:

$$\tan\mu = \frac{|\mathbf{t}_{1.P} \times \mathbf{t}_{1.T}|}{\mathbf{t}_{1.P} \cdot \mathbf{t}_{1.T}} \equiv \frac{|\mathbf{t}_{2.P} \times \mathbf{t}_{2.T}|}{\mathbf{t}_{2.P} \cdot \mathbf{t}_{2.T}} \tag{46}$$

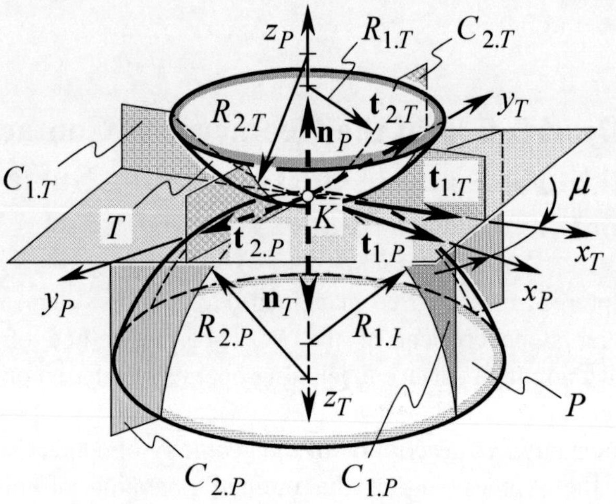

Figure 8. To the second order analysis: tangent quadrics to the surfaces P and T.

Determination of the angle μ of the surfaces P and T local relative orientation is illustrated in Figure 8. Evidently, the angle μ is measured in the common tangent plane to the surfaces P and T at the *CC*-point K

$$(\mathbf{r}_{tp} - \mathbf{r}_K) \cdot \mathbf{u}_P \cdot \mathbf{v}_P = 0 \tag{47}$$

Here,

$\mathbf{r}_{tp}$	is position vector of a point of the common tangent plane
$\mathbf{r}_K$	is position vector of the contact point K

In case of point contact of the surfaces P and T, actual value of the angle μ is computed at the point K of contact of the surfaces. If the surfaces P and T are in line contact, then the actual value of the angle μ can be computed at every point of the line of contact[11].

The unit vectors of principal directions $\mathbf{t}_{1.P}$, $\mathbf{t}_{1.T}$ and $\mathbf{t}_{2.P}$, $\mathbf{t}_{2.T}$ can be computed following one of two approaches. The first approach for the computation employs solution to Eq. (11). The second approach is disclosed below.

Actual value of the coordinate angle ω_P can be computed from one of the following equations [2], [24], [30]

[10]The surfaces orientation is *local* in nature because it relates only to differential vicinity of the point K of contact of the surfaces P and T.

[11]It is worthy pointing out here that for a line contact, relative orientation of the surfaces P and T is predetermined in global sense. However, actual value of the angle μ of the surfaces *local* relative orientation at different points of the characteristic E is different.

$$\sin\omega_P = \frac{\sqrt{E_P G_P - F_P^2}}{\sqrt{E_P G_P}}, \quad \cos\omega_P = \frac{F_P}{\sqrt{E_P G_P}}, \quad \tan\omega_P = \frac{\sqrt{E_P G_P - F_P^2}}{F_P} \tag{48}$$

Equations similar to those above are also valid for the computation of angle ω_T of the generating surface T of the cutting tool.

Directions along the unit tangent vectors $\mathbf{u}_P$ and $\mathbf{v}_P$, as well as directions along the unit tangent vectors $\mathbf{u}_T$ and $\mathbf{v}_T$ can be specified by the angles θ and ε. For the computation of actual values of the angles θ and ε the following equations can be used: $\cos\theta = \mathbf{u}_P \cdot \mathbf{u}_T$, and $\cos\varepsilon = \mathbf{v}_P \cdot \mathbf{v}_T$.

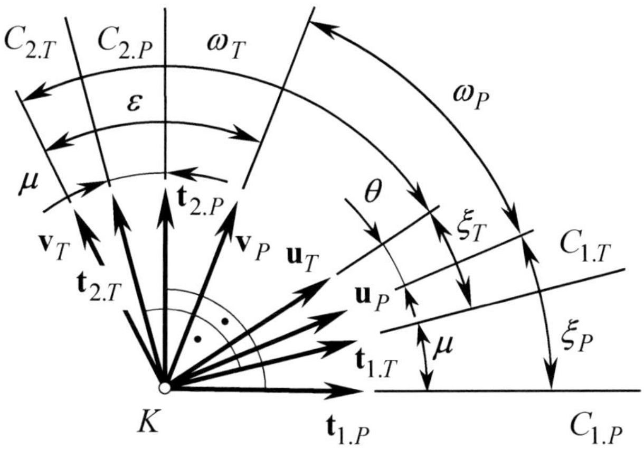

Figure 9. Local relative orientation of the surfaces P and T, represented in a common tangent plane.

Angle ξ_P (Figure 9) is the angle that the first principal direction $\mathbf{t}_{1.P}$ on the surface P makes with the unit tangent vector $\mathbf{u}_P$ [23], [24], [43]

$$\sin\xi_P = \frac{\eta_P}{\sqrt{\eta_P^{\,2} - 2\eta_P\cos\omega_P + 1}}\sin\omega_P \tag{49}$$

where η_P designates the ratio $\eta_P = \dfrac{\partial U_P}{\partial V_P}$.

Equation for the computation of actual value of the angle ξ_P yields representation in another form. Following the chain rule, $d\mathbf{r}_P$ can be represented in the form

$$d\mathbf{r}_P = \mathbf{U}_P\, dU_P + \mathbf{V}_P\, dV_P \tag{50}$$

By definition, $\tan\xi_P = \dfrac{\sin\xi_P}{\cos\xi_P}$. The functions $\sin\xi_P$ and $\cos\xi_P$ yield representation in the form

$$\sin\xi_P = \frac{|\mathbf{U}_P \times d\mathbf{r}_P|}{|\mathbf{U}_P|\cdot|d\mathbf{r}_P|} \text{ and } \cos\xi_P = \frac{\mathbf{U}_P \cdot d\mathbf{r}_P}{|\mathbf{U}_P|\cdot|d\mathbf{r}_P|} \tag{51}$$

Omitting elementary formulae transformation one can come up with the formula

$$\tan\xi_P = \frac{\sqrt{E_P G_P - F_P^2}}{\eta_P \cdot E_P + F_P} \tag{52}$$

for the computation of actual value of the angle ξ_P.

Equations similar to those above Eqs. (49) and (52) are also valid for the computation of actual value of the angle ξ_T that the first principal direction $\mathbf{t}_{1.T}$ on the generating surface T makes with the unit tangent vector $\mathbf{u}_T$.

The performed analysis yields the following equations for computation of the principal directions $\mathbf{t}_{1.P}$, $\mathbf{t}_{2.P}$

$$\mathbf{t}_{1.P} = \mathbf{Rt}(\xi_P, \mathbf{n}_P)\cdot\mathbf{u}_P,\ \mathbf{t}_{2.P} = \mathbf{Rt}\left[\left(\xi_P + \frac{\pi}{2}\right), \mathbf{n}_P\right]\cdot\mathbf{u}_P \tag{53}$$

for the surface P, and similar equations for computation of the principal directions $\mathbf{t}_{1.T}$, $\mathbf{t}_{2.T}$

$$\mathbf{t}_{1.T} = \mathbf{Rt}(\xi_T, \mathbf{n}_P)\cdot\mathbf{u}_T,\ \mathbf{t}_{2.T} = \mathbf{Rt}\left[\left(\xi_T + \frac{\pi}{2}\right), \mathbf{n}_P\right]\cdot\mathbf{u}_T \tag{54}$$

for the generating surface T of the cutting tool.

4.2. Dupin's Indicatrix

For the development of analytical description of the geometry of contact of the surfaces P and T, Dupin's indicatrix is employed. Equation of Dupin's indicatrix $Dup(P)$ of the sculptured surface P is usually represented in the form [23], [24], [43]:

$$Dup\,(P) \;\Rightarrow\; \frac{L_P}{E_P}\cdot x_P^2 + \frac{2\cdot M_P}{\sqrt{E_P\cdot G_P}}\cdot x_P\cdot y_P + \frac{N_P}{G_P}\cdot y_P^2 = \pm 1 \tag{55}$$

It describes the distribution of normal curvature within differential vicinity of the point K on the surface P. The similar equation is valid for the generating surface T of the form cutting tool.

Like any other quadratic form, Eq. (55) of the Dupin's indicatrix of the sculpture surface P can be represented in matrix form:

$$Dup\,(P) \;\Rightarrow\; [x_P \quad y_P \quad 0 \quad 0]\cdot\begin{bmatrix} \frac{L_P}{E_P} & \frac{2M_P}{\sqrt{E_P\cdot G_P}} & 0 & 0 \\ \frac{2M_P}{\sqrt{E_P\cdot G_P}} & \frac{N_P}{G_P} & 0 & 0 \\ 0 & 0 & \mp 1 & 0 \\ 0 & 0 & 0 & 1 \end{bmatrix}\cdot\begin{bmatrix} x_P \\ y_P \\ 0 \\ 0 \end{bmatrix} = \pm 1 \qquad (56)$$

Equation of Dupin's indicatrix can be represented in the form $r_{Dup}(\varphi) = \sqrt{|R_P(\varphi)|}\cdot \operatorname{sgn} \Phi_{2.P}^{-1}$. The last equation reveals that position vector of a point of the indicatrix $Dup(P)$ in any direction is equal to square root of the radius of curvature in that same direction.

4.3. Rate of Conformity of the Surfaces *P* and *T* at the *CC*-point

Consider two surfaces P and T in the first order of tangency that make contact at a point K. Rate of conformity of the surfaces P and T can be interpreted as a function of radii of normal curvature R_P and R_T of the surfaces. The radii of normal curvature R_P and R_T are taken in a common normal plane section through the point K. For a given radius of normal curvature R_P of the surface P, the rate of conformity of the surfaces depends upon the corresponding value of radius of normal curvature R_T of the generating surface T.

In most cases of part surface generation, the rate of conformity of the surfaces P and T is not constant. It depends on orientation of the normal plane section through the point K, and changes as the normal plane section is turning about the common perpendicular $\mathbf{n}_P$. This statement immediately follows from the above made conclusion that the rate of conformity of the surfaces P and T yields interpretation in terms of radii of normal curvature R_P and R_T.

Figure 10 illustrates the change of the rate of conformity of the surfaces P and T due to turning of the normal plane section about the common perpendicular $\mathbf{n}_P$. Here, in Figure 10 just two-dimensional examples are shown, for which that same normal plane section of the surface P makes contact with different plane sections $T^{(i)}$ of the generating surface T.

In the example shown in Figure 10,a, radius of normal curvature $R_T^{(1)}$ of the convex plane section $T^{(1)}$ of the surface T is positive ($R_T^{(1)} > 0$). Convex normal plane section of the surface T makes contact with convex normal plane section ($R_P > 0$) of the surface P. The rate of conformity of the generating surface T to the part surface P in Figure 10,a is relatively low.

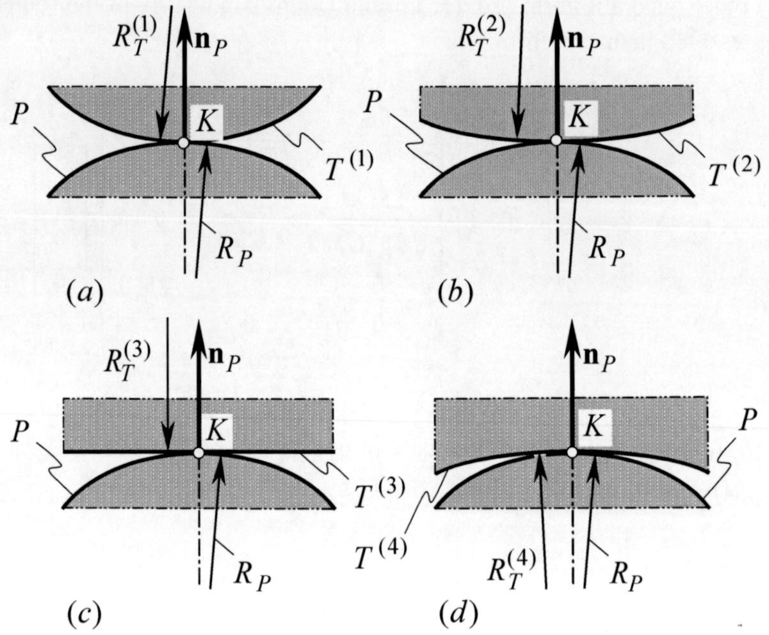

Figure 10. Plane sections of the surfaces P and T through the common perpendicular.

Another example is shown in Figure 10,b. Radius of normal curvature $R_T^{(2)}$ of the convex plane section $T^{(2)}$ of the surface T also is positive ($R_T^{(2)} > 0$). However, it value exceeds the value $R_T^{(1)}$ of radius of normal curvature in the first example ($R_T^{(2)} > R_T^{(1)}$). This results in that the rate of conformity of the surface T to the surface P (Figure 10,a) is higher compare to what is shown in Figure 10,b.

In the next example (Figure 10,c), the normal plane section $T^{(3)}$ of the surface T is represented with locally flatten section. Radius of normal curvature $R_T^{(3)}$ of the flatten plane section $T^{(3)}$ approaches the infinity ($R_T^{(3)} \to \infty$). Thus, the inequality $R_T^{(3)} > R_T^{(2)} > R_T^{(1)}$ is valid. Therefore, the rate of conformity of the surface T to the surface P in Figure 10,c is also getting higher.

Finally, for concave normal plane section $T^{(4)}$ of the surface T (Figure 10,d), radius of normal curvature $R_T^{(4)}$ is negative ($R_T^{(4)} < 0$). The rate of conformity of the surface T to the surface P is the highest of four examples considered in Figure 10.

Shown in Figure 10 examples qualitatively illustrate what it is feeling intuitively regarding the different rate of conformity of two smooth regular surfaces in the first order of tangency. Intuitively one can realize that in the examples shown in Figure 10,a through Figure 10,d the rate of conformity of two surfaces P and T is rising up.

The similar observes for a given pair of the surfaces P and T when different sections of the surfaces by a plane surface through the common perpendicular $\mathbf{n}_P$ are considering (Figure 11,a). While rotating the plane section about the common perpendicular $\mathbf{n}_P$ one can observe that, the rate of conformity of the surfaces P and T is different in different directions (Figure 11,b).

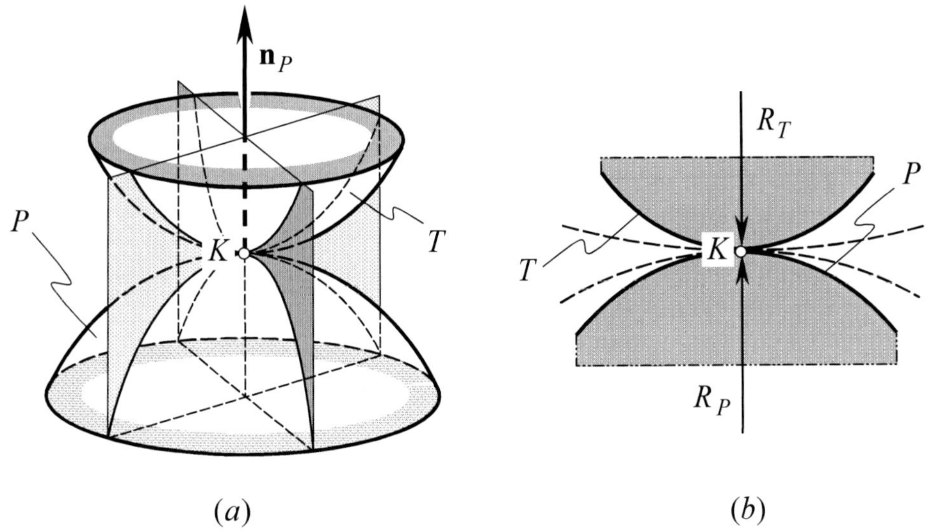

Figure 11. To analytical description of the geometry of contact of the surface P being machining and of the generating surface T of the cutting tool.

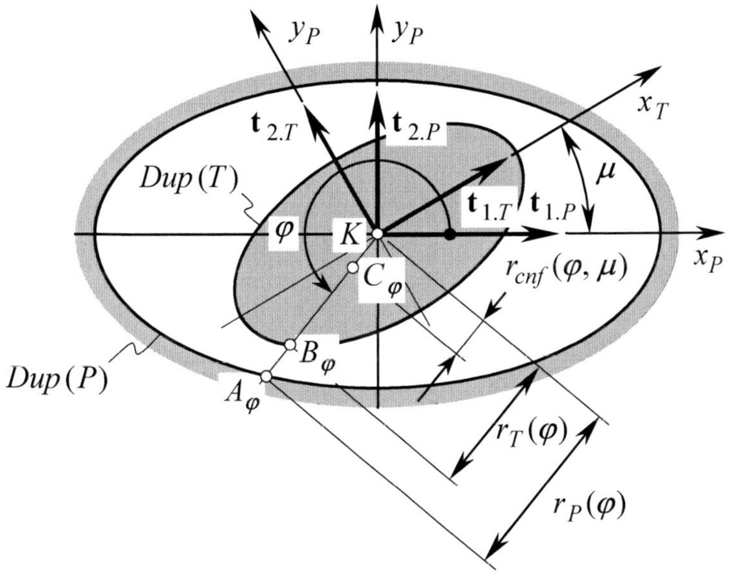

Figure 12. To derivation of equation of the indicatrix of conformity $Cnf_R(P/T)$ of two smooth regular surfaces P and T in the first order of tangency.

This section is aiming introduction of a quantitative measure of the rate of conformity of two surfaces. The rate of conformity of two surfaces P and T indicates how the surface T is close to the surface P in differential vicinity of the point K of their contact, say how much the surface T is *congruent* to the surface P in differential vicinity of the point K.

In order to develop a quantitative measure of the rate of conformity the surfaces P and T, it is convenient to implement Dupin's indicatrices $Dup(P)$ and $Dup(T)$ of the surfaces P and T respectively.

Dupin's indicatrix $Dup(P)$ indicates the distribution of radii of normal curvature of the surface P as it had been shown, for example, for a concave elliptic patch of the surface P (Figure 12). For a surface P equation of this characteristic curve [see Eq. (55)] in polar coordinates can be represented in the form:

$$Dup(P) \Rightarrow r_P(\varphi_P) = \sqrt{|R_P(\varphi_P)|} \tag{57}$$

where

r_P	is position vector of a point of the Dupin's indicatrix $Dup(P)$ of the surface P
φ_P	is polar angle of the indicatrix $Dup(P)$

The similar is true with respect to the Dupin's indicatrix $Dup(T)$ of the surface T as it had been shown, for instance, for a convex elliptical patch of the surface T (Figure 12). Equation of this characteristic curve in polar coordinates can be represented in the form

$$Dup(T) \Rightarrow r_T(\varphi_T) = \sqrt{|R_T(\varphi_T)|} \tag{58}$$

where

r_T	is position vector of a point of the Dupin's indicatrix $Dup(T)$ of the surface T
φ_T	is polar angle of the indicatrix $Dup(T)$

Equation of indicatrix of conformity $Cnf_R(P/T)$ of the surfaces P and T is postulated of the following structure:

$$Cnf_R(P/T) \Rightarrow r_{cnf}(\varphi, \mu) = r_P(\varphi)\,\text{sgn}\, R_P(\varphi) + r_T(\varphi, \mu)\,\text{sgn}\, R_T(\varphi, \mu) \tag{59}$$

Because of the position vector $r_P(\varphi)$ defines location of a point a_P of the Dupin's indicatrix $Dup(P)$, and the position vector $r_T(\varphi, \mu)$ defines location of a point a_T of the Dupin's indicatrix $Dup(T)$, then the position vector $r_{cnf}(\varphi, \mu)$ defines location of a point a_C (see Figure 12) of the indicatrix of conformity $Cnf_R(P/T)$ of the surfaces P and T. Therefore, the equality $r_{cnf}(\varphi, \mu) = Ka_C$ observes, and length of the straight line segment Ka_C is equal to the distance $a_P\, a_T$.

Here, in Eq. (59) are denoted

$r_P = \sqrt{\mid R_P \mid}$	is position vector of a point of the Dupin's indicatrix of the surface P
$r_T = \sqrt{\mid R_T \mid}$	is position vector of a corresponding point of the Dupin's indicatrix of the surface T

Here, in Eq. (59), the multipliers $\operatorname{sgn} R_P(\varphi)$ and $\operatorname{sgn} R_T(\varphi, \mu)$ are assigned to each of the functions $r_P(\varphi) = \sqrt{|R_P(\varphi)|}$ and $r_T(\varphi, \mu) = \sqrt{|R_T(\varphi, \mu)|}$ just for the purpose of remaining the corresponding sign of the functions, *i.e.* that same sign that the radii of normal curvature $R_P(\varphi)$ and $R_T(\varphi, \mu)$ have.

Omitting routing formulae transformations, one can come with the following equation of the indicatrix of conformity $Cnf_R(P/T)$ of the generating surface T of the form cutting tool to the sculptured surface P at the CC-point:

$$Cnf_R(P/T) \;\Rightarrow\; r_{cnf}(\varphi, \mu) = \sqrt{\left|\frac{E_P G_P}{L_P G_P \cos^2\varphi - M_P\sqrt{E_P G_P}\sin 2\varphi + N_P E_P \sin^2\varphi}\right|}\operatorname{sgn}\Phi_{2.P}^{-1} +$$

$$+\sqrt{\left|\frac{E_T G_T}{L_T G_T \cos^2(\varphi+\mu) - M_T\sqrt{E_T G_T}\sin 2(\varphi+\mu) + N_T E_T \sin^2(\varphi+\mu)}\right|}\operatorname{sgn}\Phi_{2.T}^{-1} \tag{60}$$

Equation (60) of the characteristic curve[12] $Cnf_R(P/T)$ is published in [8], and (in a hidden form) in [7].

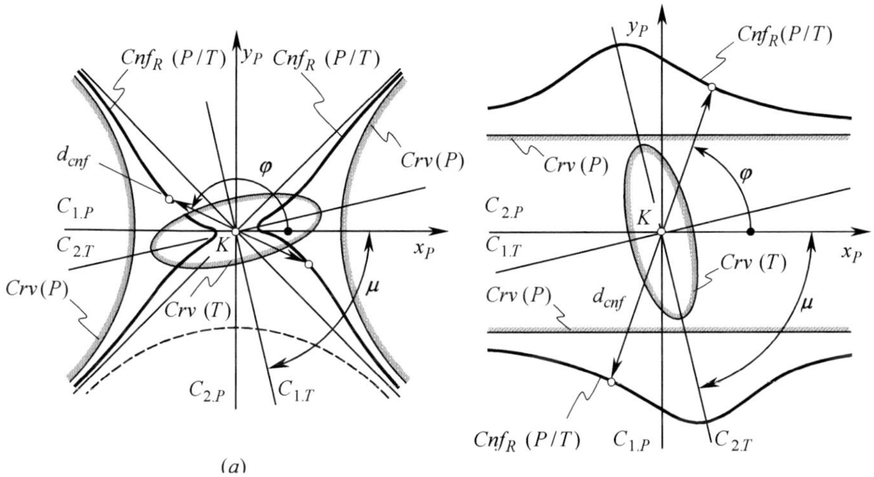

Figure 13. Examples of indicatrix of conformity $Cnf_R(P/T)$ for two smooth regular surfaces.

Analysis of Eq. (60) reveals that the indicatrix of conformity $Cnf_R(P/T)$ of the surfaces P and T at the point K is represented with a planar centro-symmetrical curve of the fourth order. In particular cases, this characteristic curve also possesses a property of mirror symmetry. Mirror symmetry of the indicatrix of conformity observes, for example, when the

[12]Equation of this characteristic curve is known from (a) Pat. No.1249787, USSR, *A Method of Sculptured Surface Machining on Multi-Axis NC Machine*, S.P.Radzevich, B23C 3/16, Filed: December 27, 1984, [8], and (in a hidden form) from (b) Pat. No.1185749, USSR, *A Method of Sculptured Surface Machining on Multi-Axis NC Machine*, S.P.Radzevich, B23C 3/16, Filed: October 24, 1983, [7].

angle μ of the surfaces P and T local relative orientation is equal $\mu = \pm\frac{\pi \cdot n}{2}$, where n designates an integer number.

Two illustrative examples of the indicatrix of conformity $Cnf_R(P/T)$ are shown in Figure 13. The first example (Figure 13,a) relates to the cases of contact of a saddle-like local patch of the part surface P and of a convex elliptic-like local patch of the generating surface T. The second one (Figure 13,b) is for the case of contact of a convex parabolic-like local patch of the part surface P and of a convex elliptic-like local patch of the generating surface T. For both cases (see Figure 13), the corresponding curvature indicatrices $Crv(P)$ and $Crv(T)$ of the surfaces P and T are depicted as well. The imaginary (phantom) branches of the Dupin's indicatrix $Dup(P)$ for the saddle-like local patch of the part surface P are shown in dashed line (see Figure 13,a).

Surfaces P and T can make contact geometrically while physical conditions of their contact could be violated. Violation of the physical condition of contact results in the surfaces P and T interferes into one another. Implementation of the indicatrix of conformity $Cnf_R(P/T)$ immediately uncovers the surfaces interference if any.

Value of the current diameter[13] d_{cnf} of the indicatrix of conformity $Cnf_R(P/T)$ indicates the rate of conformity of the surfaces P and T in the corresponding cross-section of the surfaces by normal plane through the common perpendicular. Orientation of the normal plane sections with respect to the surfaces P and T is defined by the corresponding central angle φ.

4.4. Directions of the Extremal Rate of Conformity of the Surfaces *P* and *T*

Directions, along which the rate of conformity of the surfaces P and T is extremal, *i.e.* it reaches either maximal it value or minimal it value, are of prime importance for implementation of the *DG*/*K*-based method of surface generation.

Directions of the extremal rate of conformity of the surfaces P and T (*i.e.* the directions pointed along the extremal diameters $d_{cnf}^{(\min)}$ and $d_{cnf}^{(\max)}$) can be found out from equation of the indicatrix of conformity $Cnf_R(P/T)$.

Two angles $\varphi_{\min}$ and $\varphi_{\max}$ specify two directions within the common tangent plane, along which the rate of conformity of the surface T to the surface P reaches it extremal values. These angles are the roots of equation

$$\frac{\partial}{\partial \varphi} r_{cnf}(\varphi, \mu) = 0 . \tag{61}$$

It is easy to prove that in general case of two sculptured surfaces in contact, the difference between the angles $\varphi_{\min}$ and $\varphi_{\max}$ is not equal to 0.5π. This means the equality

[13]Diameter of a centro-symmetrical curve can be defined as a distance between two points of the curve, measured along the corresponding straight line through the center of symmetry of the curve.

$\varphi_{\min} - \varphi_{\max} = \pm 0.5\pi n$ doesn't observe, and in most cases the relationship $\varphi_{\min} - \varphi_{\max} \neq \pm 0.5\pi n$ is valid (here n is an integer number). The condition $\varphi_{\min} = \varphi_{\max} \pm 0.5\pi\, n$ is satisfied only in cases when the angle μ of the surfaces P and T local relative orientation is equal to $\mu = \pm 0.5\pi n$, and thus the principal directions $\mathbf{t}_{1.P}$ and $\mathbf{t}_{2.P}$ of the surface P, and the principal directions $\mathbf{t}_{1.T}$ and $\mathbf{t}_{2.T}$ of the surface T either aligned to each other or they are directed in oppositely.

This enables one making the following statement: *in general case of two sculptured surfaces in contact, directions along which the rate of conformity of two smooth regular surfaces P and T is extremal are not orthogonal to each other.*

This conclusion is of critical importance for engineering applications.

4.5. Implementation of Plücker's Conoid

Plücker's conoid could be used as a characteristic surface for visualization of the distribution of normal curvature at a given point of the sculptured surface. One more characteristic curve for the analytical description of the geometry of contact of the sculptured part surface and the generating surface of the form cutting can be derived on the premises of Plücker's conoid[14] [11].

The characteristic surface $\mathbf{Pl}_R(P)$ is referred to as the *Plücker's conoid of the first kind,* while the characteristic surface $\mathbf{Pl}_k(P)$ is referred to as the *Plücker's conoid of the second kind.*

The conoids $\mathbf{Pl}_R(P)$ and $\mathbf{Pl}_k(P)$ are *inverse* to each other [$\mathbf{Pl}_R(P) = \mathbf{Pl}_k^{inv}(P)$, and vice versa].

Boundary curve of the Plücker's conoid contains all the necessary information on the distribution of normal curvature of the surface P in differential vicinity of the point K. Thus, without loss of accuracy, the Plücker's conoid itself could be replaced with it boundary curve. The boundary curve $\mathsf{Pl}_R(P)$ of the characteristic surface $\mathbf{Pl}_R(P)$ is referred to as the *Plücker's curvature indicatrix of the first kind* of the part surface P at the point K.

The Plücker's curvature indicatrix is represented therefore by the end-points of the position vector of length of $R_P(\varphi)$ that is rotating about and travels up-and-down the axis of the surface $\mathbf{Pl}_R(P)$. This immediately leads to equation of this characteristic curve:

$$\mathsf{Pl}_R(P) \;\Rightarrow\; \mathbf{r}_R(\varphi) = \begin{bmatrix} R_P(\varphi)\cos\varphi \\ R_P(\varphi)\sin\varphi \\ R_P(\varphi) \\ 0 \end{bmatrix} \tag{62}$$

where $R_P(\varphi)$ is given by the Euler's formula $R_P(\varphi) = (R_{1.P}^{-1}\cos^2\varphi + R_{2.P}^{-1}\sin^2\varphi)^{-1}$.

[14]*Plücker's conoid* is a ruled surface, which is bearing the name of famous German mathematician and physicist Julius Plücker (1802-1868) known for his research in the field of a new geometry of space [11].

Equation, similar to that above Eq. (62) is valid for the Plücker's curvature indicatrix $\mathsf{Pl}_k(P)$ of the second kind:

$$\mathsf{Pl}_k(P) \;\Rightarrow\; \mathbf{r}_k(\varphi) = \begin{bmatrix} k_P(\varphi)\cos\varphi \\ k_P(\varphi)\sin\varphi \\ k_P(\varphi) \\ 0 \end{bmatrix} \tag{63}$$

where $k_P(\varphi) = k_{1.P}\cos^2\varphi + k_{2.P}\sin^2\varphi$.

The interested reader is referred to [19] on details of the Plücker's curvature indicatrices $\mathsf{Pl}_R(P)$ and $\mathsf{Pl}_k(P)$.

4.6. An_R (*P*) -indicatrix of the Surface *P*

Aiming simplification of the analytical description of local topology of two smooth regular surfaces in the first order of tangency, the Plücker's curvature indicatrix could be replaced with the planar characteristic curve of novel kind.

As it is following from Eq. (62), the first two elements $R_P(\varphi)\cos\varphi$ and $R_P(\varphi)\sin\varphi$ at the right-hand side portion of the above equation contain all the required information on the distribution of normal radii of curvature of P at K. Hence, instead of consideration of the Plücker's curvature indicatrix $Pl_k(P)$ [see Eq. (62)] could be implemented for the purpose of analytical description of the geometry of contact of two smooth regular surfaces, but a planar characteristic curve $\mathsf{An}_R(P)$ of simpler structure instead. Equation of this characteristic curve yields representation in the form

$$\mathsf{An}_R(P) \;\Rightarrow\; \mathbf{r}_{iR}(\varphi) = \begin{bmatrix} R_P(\varphi)\cos\varphi \\ R_P(\varphi)\sin\varphi \\ 0 \\ 0 \end{bmatrix} \tag{64}$$

This planar characteristic curve is referred to as the $\mathsf{An}_R(P)$ *indicatrix of the first kind* of the surface P.

The distribution of normal curvature of the surface P at K could be given by another planar characteristic curve:

$$\mathsf{An}_k(P) \;\Rightarrow\; \mathbf{r}_{ik}(\varphi) = \begin{bmatrix} k_P(\varphi)\cos\varphi \\ k_P(\varphi)\cos\varphi \\ 0 \\ 0 \end{bmatrix} \tag{65}$$

This planar characteristic curve [see Eq. (65)] is referred to as to the $\mathsf{An}_k(P)$– *indicatrix of the second kind* of the part surface P at K.

4.7. Relative Characteristic Curves

Aiming further simplification of analytical description of the geometry of contact of the surfaces P and T, the Plücker's relative indicatrix $Pl_R(P/T)$ could be replaced with the planar characteristic curve of a simpler structure. Therefore, equation of the two-dimensional $An_R(P/T)$ – relative indicatrix can be represented in the form

$$An_R(P/T) \quad \Rightarrow \quad \mathbf{R}_{iR}(\varphi) = \begin{bmatrix} (R_P + R_T)\cos\varphi \\ (R_P + R_T)\sin\varphi \\ 0 \\ 0 \end{bmatrix} \tag{66}$$

This planar characteristic curve is referred to as the $An_R(P/T)$ – *relative indicatrix of the first kind*. The $An_R(P/T)$ – relative indicatrix of the first kind analytically describes the distribution of summa of normal radii of curvature of the part surface P and of the generating surface T of the cutting tool at the point K.

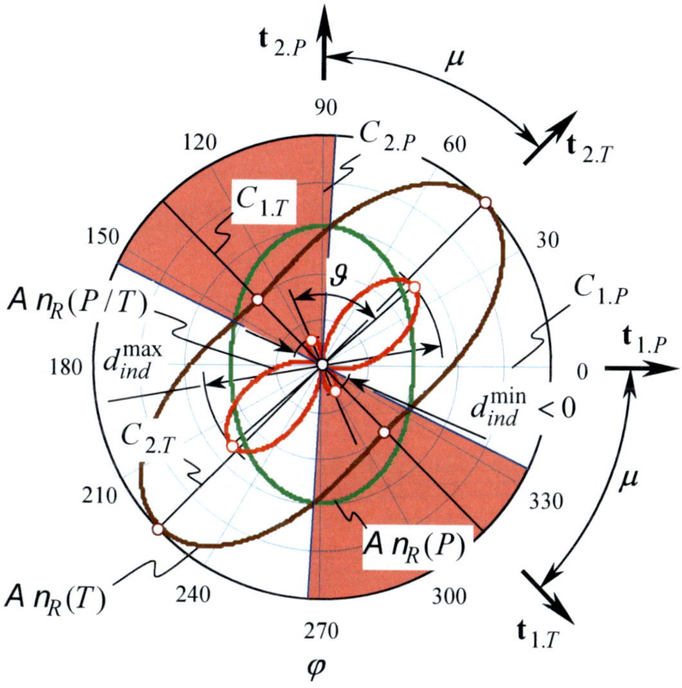

Figure 14. An example of the $An_R(P/T)$ – relative indicatrix of the surfaces P and T at K ($R_{1.P} = 2\,mm$, $R_{2.P} = 3\,mm$, $R_{1.T} = -2\,mm$, $R_{2.T} = -5\,mm$, $\mu = 45^\circ$) plotted together with the corresponding $An_R(P)$ – indicatrix and $An_R(T)$ – indicatrix.

An example of the $\mathrm{Anp}_R(P/T)$ – relative indicatrix of the surfaces P and T is shown in Figure 14. The characteristic curve $\mathrm{Anp}_R(P/T)$ is computed for the case of contact of the convex elliptic local patch of the surface P ($R_{1.P} = 3\,mm$, and $R_{2.P} = 15\,mm$) with the concave elliptic local patch of the surface T ($R_{1.T} = -2\,mm$, and $R_{2.T} = -5\,mm$). The surfaces P and T are turned through the angle $\mu = 45^\circ$ relative to one another around the common perpendicular $\mathbf{n}_P$. The corresponding $\mathrm{Anp}_R(P)$ – indicatrix, as well as the $\mathrm{Anp}_R(T)$ – indicatrix are also plotted in Figure 14. It is of importance to point out here that the direction of the minimal diameter $d_{ind}^{\min}$ and the direction of the maximal diameter $d_{ind}^{\max}$ of the characteristic curve $\mathrm{Anp}_R(P/T)$ do not align neither with the principal directions $\mathbf{t}_{1.P}$ and $\mathbf{t}_{2.P}$ on the part surface P, nor with the principal directions $\mathbf{t}_{1.T}$ and $\mathbf{t}_{2.T}$ on the generating surface T of the cutting tool. The extremal directions of the $\mathrm{Anp}_R(P/T)$ – relative indicatrix are not orthogonal to each other. In general case of the surfaces contact, they make a certain angle $\vartheta \neq 90^\circ$.

The following statement can be made at this point:

In general case of surface contact, directions of the extremal (i.e., of the maximal and of the minimal) rate of conformity of the surface P and T at the point K are not orthogonal to one another. The directions of the extremal rate of conformity of the surface P and T could be orthogonal to one another only in particular (degenerated) cases of the surfaces contact.

Shape and parameters of the $\mathrm{Anp}_R(P/T)$ – relative indicatrix depend upon algebraic values of the principal radii of curvature $R_{1.P}$, $R_{2.P}$ and $R_{1.T}$, $R_{2.T}$ of the surfaces P and T, as well as on the actual value of the angle μ of the surfaces P and T local relative orientation.

The characteristic curve $\mathrm{Anp}_R(P/T)$ is of simpler structure rather than the Plücker's relative indicatrix $Pl_R(P/T)$ itself. The $\mathrm{Anp}_R(P/T)$ – relative indicatrix is always a planar curve, while the Plücker's relative indicatrix $Pl_R(P/T)$ is a 3D curve. This makes the use of the characteristic curve $\mathrm{Anp}_R(P/T)$ more preferred rather then the Plücker's relative indicatrix $Pl_R(P/T)$.

The distribution of differences between normal curvatures of the surfaces P and T at K can be analytically described by a planar characteristic curve of another kind:

$$\mathrm{Anp}_k(P/T) \;\Rightarrow\; \mathbf{R}_{ik}(\varphi) = \begin{bmatrix} (k_P - k_T)\cos\varphi \\ (k_P - k_T)\sin\varphi \\ 0 \\ 0 \end{bmatrix} \tag{67}$$

The characteristic curve [see Eq. (67)] is referred to as the $\mathrm{Anp}_k(P/T)$ – *relative indicatrix of the second kind.*

The planar characteristic curves $\mathrm{A\,n}_R(P)$ and $\mathrm{A\,n}_R(P/T)$, as well as the characteristic curves $\mathrm{A\,n}_k(P)$ and $\mathrm{A\,n}_k(P/T)$ originate from the Plücker's conoid.

It is proven analytically that both planar characteristic curves, say the characteristic curve $\mathrm{A\,n}_R(P/T)$, as well as the indicatrix of conformity $Cnf_R(P/T)$ of two smooth regular surfaces P and T specify that same direction $\mathbf{t}_{cnf}^{\max}$ at which the rate of conformity of the surfaces P and T is the maximal possible. Both characteristic curves, $Cnf_R(P/T)$ and $\mathrm{A\,n}_R(P/T)$ are powerful tools in the theory of surface generation. They can be used for the analysis of the geometry of contact of two smooth surfaces P and T.

5. Form Cutting Tools of Optimal Design

Machining of a sculptured surface practically is performing with the help of the form cutting tool. The stock removal and generation of the surface P are the two major functions of the cutting tool. The shape and parameters of the generating surface T of the form cutting tool significantly affect the performance of the cutting. The last indicates the necessity of profiling of optimal form cutting tools for machining sculptured surfaces on multi-axis *NC* machine.

The novel $\mathbb{R}$-mapping based method for profiling of form cutting tools is disclosed in this section. The $\mathbb{R}$-mapping based method is the most general method for profiling of form cutting tools.

Optimal design of a form cutting tool can be developed on the premises of it generation surface T. Derivation of the generating surface T is the start-point of designing of the form cutting tool.

5.1. On the Principal Concept of Profiling of the Form Cutting Tools for Sculptured Surface Machining

The problem of profiling of the form cutting tool for machining of a sculptured surface on multi-axis *NC* machine got no profound investigation yet. Not profiling of the form cutting tool of optimal design but selection of a certain cutting tool among several available it designs (Figure 15) often recommended instead.

While machining a sculptured surface, cutting tool rotates about it axis of rotation and moves relative to the sculptured surface P. When rotating or when performing relative motion of another kind, cutting edges of the cutting tool generate a certain surface. The surface that is represented by consecutive positions of cutting edges is referred to as the *generating surface of the cutting tool* [23], [24], [43].

Number of surfaces those that satisfy the above definition is infinite. It is naturally to assume that not all of them equivalent to each other from the standpoint of performance of sculptured surface generation, and that some of them could be preferred. Moreover there exists an optimal generating surface of the form cutting tool for machining of a given sculptured surface. After been determined, the unique generating surface T is used on further steps of designing of an optimal form cutting tool for machining of a given surface P.

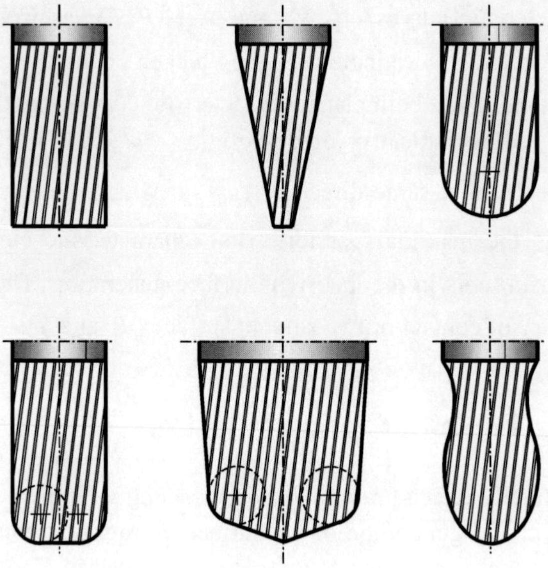

Figure 15. Milling cutters of conventional design for machining of sculptured surfaces on multi-axis NC machine.

Commonly, the generating surface T of the cutting tool doesn't exist physically, and it is represented as the set of consecutive positions of the cutting edges in their motion relative to the stationary coordinate system, associated to the cutting tool itself.

In most practical cases, the generating surface T allows sliding "*over itself*". Enveloping surface to consecutive positions of the surface T that performs such a motion is congruent to the surface T itself.

When machining a surface P, the surface T is conjugate to the sculptured surface P.

It is of critical importance to clarify from the very beginning what the term "*optimal cutting tool*" means. In the consideration below, the term "*optimal cutting tool*" means that the design parameters of a certain cutting tool are those implementation of which enables achieving the required extremum (minimum/minimum) of the pre-given criterion of optimization. Maximal productivity of the part surface machining, and minimal deviations of the actual part surface from the desired part surface are the perfect examples of the criteria of optimization.

In the theory of surface generation, only those criteria of optimization are applicable that could expressed in terms (a) of geometry of the part surface P, (b) of geometry of the generating surface T of the cutting tool, and (c) of the kinematics of the machining operation.

It is the right point now to consider a general example of sculptured surface generation that supports in much the just made conclusion.

Consider generation of a sculptured surface P with the form cutting tool having arbitrarily shaped the generation surface T. Cross-section of the surfaces P and T by the plane through the unit normal vector $\mathbf{n}_P$ is shown in Figure 16. This plane section is perpendicular to the tool-path on the surface P at the point K. In Figure 16, S_T designates width of the tool-path. In all the examples considered, the width S_T of the tool-path remains identical to each other. Radius of normal curvature R_P of the surface P at the point K remains the same. The scallop's height on the machined surface P is designated as h_P.

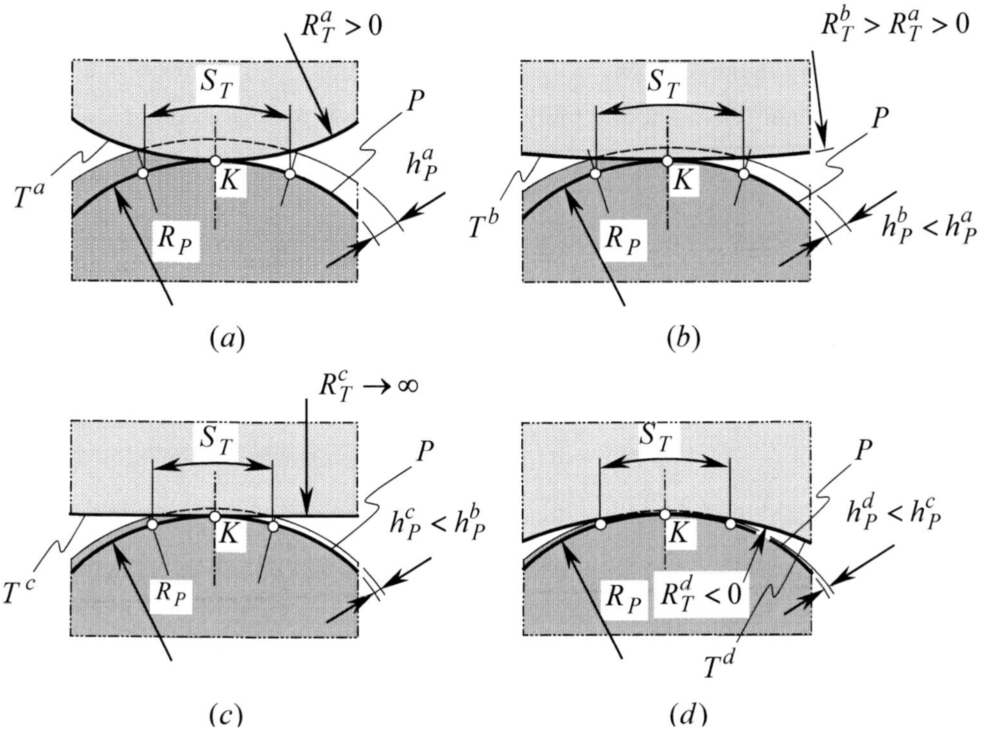

Figure 16. Various rate of conformity of the generating surface T of the form cutting tool to the sculptured surface P in the plane section through the unit normal vector $\mathbf{n}_P$.

The surface P can be generated with the machining surface T^a of the cutting tool (Figure 16,a). Radius of curvature of the generating surface T^a is of a certain positive value $R_T^a > 0$. Due to point contact of the surfaces P and T^a observes, not the desired surface P but an approximation to it is generated instead. For the pre-specified width S_T of the tool-path, scallops height is equal to a certain value h_P^a. It is required that the scallop's height be smaller than the tolerance $[h]$ on accuracy of machining of the surface P.

That same sculptured surface P can be generated with the machining surface T^b of the cutting tool (Figure 16,b). Radius of curvature of the generating surface T^b in this case exceeds the value of the radius of curvature of the surface T^a in the previous case ($R_T^b > R_T^a$). Due to the surfaces P and T^b make point contact, then scallops on the generated surface observe. Under such scenario, a certain reduction of the scallops height occurs ($h_P^b < h_P^a$). The scallop height reduction is due to the surface T^b is getting closer to the surface P in differential vicinity of the point K rather than the surface T^a does. Locally, the surface T^b is more congruent to the surface P rather than the surface T^a. Say, the rate of conformity of the surface T^b to the surface P is greater rather than the rate of conformity of the surface T^a to that same surface P.

Further, that same sculptured surface P can be generated with the machining surface T^c of the cutting tool (Figure 16,c). At the point K, the surface T^c is flattened, and therefore radius of curvature R_T^c is equal to infinity ($R_T^c \to \infty$). Evidently that value of the radius of curvature R_T^c exceeds value of the radius of curvature R_T^b. Again, the surfaces P and T^c make contact at a point. Because of $R_T^c > R_T^b$, than the scallop's height h_P^c is smaller than the scallop's height h_P^b. The scallop height reduction in this case is due the increase of the rate of conformity of the generating surface T^c of the tool to the part surface P compare to what observes with respect to the surfaces P and T^b.

Ultimately, let's consider generation of the surface P with the concave generating surface T^d of the cutting tool (Figure 16,d). Radius of curvature R_T^d of the cutting tool surface T^d is negative ($R_T^d < 0$). In this case the rate of conformity of the generating surface T^d of the cutting tool to the part surface P is the biggest of all considered cases (Figure 16). Thus, scallops of the smallest height h_P^d observe on the generated surface P.

Summarizing the analysis of Figure 16, the following conclusion can be formulated: *Increase of the rate of conformity of the generating surface T of the cutting tool to the sculptured surface P causes corresponding reduction of height of residual scallop on the machined sculptured surface P.*

This conclusion is of critical importance for the development of a method of profiling of form cutting tools, as well as for the entire theory of surface generation.

The rate of conformity of the surface T to the surface P can be used as a mathematical criterion of efficiency of a machining operation. This issue is of prime importance to bypass all the major bottlenecks in designing of the optimal form-cutting-tool those, imposed by initial indefiniteness of the problem.

5.2. ℝ–Mapping of the Part Surface *P* on the Generating Surface *T* of the Form Cutting Tool

The rate of conformity of the generating surface T of the form cutting tool to the sculptured part surface P significantly affects efficiency of the machining operation. The higher the rate of conformity results in (a) the higher productivity of the machining operation, (b) the smaller residual scallops on the machined part surface, (d) the shorter machining time *etc* [23], [24], [43], [45].

In order to come up with the optimal design of a form cutting tool, the generating surface of the tool must be conformal to the sculptured surface to be machined as much as possible. For this purpose, the cutting tool surface T can be generated as a kind of mapping of the part surface P to be machined. The required kind of mapping of the surface P onto the generating surface T had been proposed initially by Radzevich[15] [17], [37], [38], [43]. It is referred to as the $\mathbb{R}$–mapping of the sculptured part surface P onto the generating surface T of the cutting tool.

Consider the generating surface T of a form cutting tool that make contact with a sculptured part surface P at the point K. A pencil of planes can be constructed using the unit normal vector $\mathbf{n}_P$ as the directing vector of the axis of the pencil of planes. The maximal rate of conformity of the generating surface T of the tool to the sculptured surface P observes when for every plane of the pencil of planes the equality

$$R_T = -R_P \tag{68}$$

is valid.

When the equality [see Eq. (68)] is satisfied, than the surfaces P and T make either surface-kind of contact or a kind of locally-surface contact (either locally-surface contact of the first kind, or locally-surface contact of the second kind [23], [24], [43]).

Actually, deviations in configuration of the cutting tool with respect to the sculptured part surface P are unavoidable. Because of this, Eq. (68) can't be satisfied. This forces the replacement of Eq. (68) with an equality of the sort

$$R_T = R_T(R_P) \tag{69}$$

instead.

The function $R_T(R_P)$ can be expressed in terms of deviations/tolerances of the actual configuration of the cutting tool with respect to the sculptured surface.

Ultimately, the problem of profiling of a form cutting tool of the optimal design reduces to the determination of the generating surface T that is maximally conformal to the given surface P, and that satisfies Eq. (69).

Switching from use of the function $R_T = -R_P$ to use of a function $R_T = R_T(R_P)$ instead results in that the ideal locally-extremal contact of the surfaces P and T is replaced with a kind of there quasi-kinds of contact. Recall that quasi-kinds of contact of the surfaces P and T yields that same range of agile-ability of *NC* machining operation as point contact of the surfaces possess'. Moreover, productivity of surface generation when maintaining the quasi-kind of contact of the surfaces P and T practically is identical to the productivity of surface generation when surface-kind of contact of the surfaces is maintaining.

It is convenient to derive equation of the generating surface T of the form cutting tool in it natural parameterization. For this purpose, it necessary to express the first $\Phi_{1.T}$ and the second $\Phi_{2.T}$ fundamental forms of the generating surface T in terms of the fundamental magnitudes E_P, F_P, G_P and L_P, M_P, N_P of the sculptured surface P.

When two surfaces P and T are given, then one can easily compute the rate of conformity of the surfaces at the given *CC*-point. In the case under consideration, the problem of another sort arises. This problem could be interpreted as an inverse problem to the problem

[15]Radzevich, S.P., *A Method for Designing of the Optimal Form-Cutting-Tool for Machining of a Given Sculptured Surface*

of computation of the actual rate of conformity of the surface T to the surface P in the prescribed direction on P. The $\mathbb{R}$−mapping of surfaces is capable of establishing the required correspondence between points of the surfaces P and T.

The $\mathbb{R}$−mapping establishes a functional relationship between principal radii of curvature of the surface P and of the generating surface T of the cutting tool in differential vicinity of the *CC*-point K.

The equation $R_T = R_T(R_P)$ can be split up onto the set of two equations:

$$\begin{cases} M_T = M_T(M_P;\ G_P) \\ G_T = G_T(M_P;\ G_P) \end{cases} \tag{70}$$

Here M_P and M_T designate the mean curvatures, and G_P and G_T are the Gaussian curvatures of the surfaces P and T at a *CC*-point respectively.

In order to come up with the function $R_T = R_T(R_P)$, functions F_1, F_2, and F_3 those that specify rate of conformity of the surfaces P and T are implemented. The functions F_1, F_2, and F_3 are referred as the *rate of conformity functions*.

For satisfaction of the set of two Eqs. (70), the following equalities are necessary been satisfied:

$$L_T N_T - M_T^2 = \mathsf{F}_1(L_P N_P - M_P^2) \tag{71}$$

$$E_T N_T - 2F_T M_T + G_T L_T = \mathsf{F}_2(E_P N_P - 2F_P M_P + G_P L_P) \tag{72}$$

$$E_T G_T - F_T^2 = \mathsf{F}_3(E_P G_P - F_P^2) \tag{73}$$

These expressions analytically describe the vital link between optimal values of the design parameters of the form cutting tool and between parameters of the actual process of sculptured surface machining. Equations (71) through (73) allow incorporating into the design of the actual cutting tool all of important features of machining operation: cutting tool performance, tool wear, rigidity of a cutting tool, *etc*.

The rate of conformity functions F_1, F_2, and F_3 can be determined, for instance, using the proposed [10] experimental method of simulation of machining of a sculptured surface.

Three Eqs. (71) through (73) are necessary but not sufficient for the determining of six unknown fundamental magnitudes E_T, F_T, G_T of the first $\Phi_{1.T}$ and L_T, M_T, N_T of the second $\Phi_{2.T}$ fundamental forms of the generating surface T of the form cutting tool. The equations of compatibility could be incorporated into the analyses in order to complete Eqs. (71) through (73) to a set of six equations of six unknowns.

---

on Multi-Axis NC Machine. – Pat. №4242296/08 (USSR), Filed: March 31, 1987г.

Every smooth regular generating surface T of the form cutting tool mandatory satisfies the Gauss' equation of compatibility that follows from his famous *theorema egregium* [2], [23], [24], [48]:

$$\tilde{G}_T(E_T G_T - F_T^2) = \left[\frac{\partial^2 F_T}{\partial U_T \partial V_T} - \frac{1}{2}\left(\frac{\partial^2 E_T}{\partial V_T^2} + \frac{\partial^2 G_T}{\partial U_T^2}\right)\right] \cdot (E_T G_T - F_T^2) + \tag{74}$$

$$+ \begin{vmatrix} 0 & \frac{\partial F_T}{\partial V_T} - \frac{1}{2}\frac{\partial G_T}{\partial U_T} & \frac{1}{2}\frac{\partial G_T}{\partial V_T} \\ \frac{1}{2}\frac{\partial E_T}{\partial U_T} & E_T & F_T \\ \frac{\partial F_T}{\partial U_T} - \frac{1}{2}\frac{\partial E_T}{\partial V_T} & F_T & G_T \end{vmatrix} - \begin{vmatrix} 0 & \frac{1}{2}\frac{\partial E_T}{\partial V_T} & \frac{1}{2}\frac{\partial G_T}{\partial U_T} \\ \frac{1}{2}\frac{\partial E_T}{\partial V_T} & E_T & F_T \\ \frac{1}{2}\frac{\partial G_T}{\partial U_T} & F_T & G_T \end{vmatrix}$$

Another two equations of compatibility are by Mainardy-Codacci [2], [23], [24], [48]:

$$\frac{\partial L_T}{\partial V_T} - \frac{\partial M_T}{\partial U_T} = L_T \Gamma_{12}^1 + M_T \cdot (\Gamma_{12}^2 - \Gamma_{11}^1) - N_T \Gamma_{11}^2 \tag{75}$$

$$\frac{\partial M_T}{\partial V_T} - \frac{\partial N_T}{\partial U_T} = L_T \Gamma_{22}^1 + M_T \cdot (\Gamma_{22}^2 - \Gamma_{12}^1) - N_T \Gamma_{12}^2 \tag{76}$$

Here, in Eqs. (74) through (76), the Christoffel's symbols Γ_{jk}^{i} of the second kind are used.

The set of three Eqs. (71) through (73) together with three equations of compatibility [Eq. (74) through (76)] completely describe the $\mathbb{R}$-mapping of two smooth regular surfaces, *i.e.* they describe the generating surface T of the cutting tool of optimal design as the $\mathbb{R}$-mapping of the sculptured surface P.

Thus, the fundamental magnitudes of the first $\Phi_{1.T}$ and of the second $\Phi_{2.T}$ fundamental forms of the generating surface T of the form cutting tool can be determined using the $\mathbb{R}$-mapping of the sculptured part surface P onto the generating surface T of the cutting tool.

5.3. Reconstruction of the Generating Surface *T* of the Form Cutting Tool

For the conversion of the natural parameterization of the surface T to it representation in a Cartesian coordinate system the set of two Gauss-Weingarten's equations in tensor notation

$$\left.\begin{array}{r}\text{The Generating Surface } T \\ \text{of the Form Cutting Tool}\end{array}\right| \Leftarrow \begin{cases} \mathbf{r}_{ij} = \Gamma_{ij}^{k} \mathbf{r}_P + b_{ij} \mathbf{n}_P \\ \mathbf{n}_i = -b_{ik} g^{kj} \mathbf{r}_j \end{cases} \tag{77}$$

is required been solved.

Solution to the set of Eqs. (77) returns a matrix equation of the generating surface T of the form cutting tool for machining of a given sculptured part surface P on multi-axis *NC* machine. Initial conditions of integration of Eqs. (77) are necessary been selected properly.

Here, in Eqs. (77) is designated: $\mathbf{r}_i = \dfrac{\partial \mathbf{r}_T}{\partial U_T}$; $\mathbf{r}_{ij} = \dfrac{\partial^2 \mathbf{r}_T}{\partial U_T \partial V_T}$; $\mathbf{n}_i = \dfrac{\partial \mathbf{n}_T}{\partial U_T}$; $b_{ij} = \mathbf{r}_{ij} \cdot \mathbf{n}_T = -\mathbf{n}_i \mathbf{r}_j - \mathbf{n}_j \cdot \mathbf{r}_i$; and g_{ij} is metric tensor of the generating surface T of the form-cutting-tool of optimal design; g^{ij} is contra-variant tensor of the generating surface T of cutting tool.

For solving of the set of Eqs. (77) the known methods [5] are used.

5.4. An Algorithm for the Computation of the Design Parameters of the Form Cutting Tool

Computation of the major design parameters of the generating surface T of the form cutting tool for machining of a given sculptured surface on multi-axis *NC* machine is illustrated with the flow-chart (Figure 17).

1. Compose an equation of the smooth regular sculptured surface P. When the part surface P is comprised of two or more portions, then a set of equations of all n surface patches $P_i\big|_{i=1}^{n}$ is required been composed
2. Compute the first derivatives of equation(s) of the sculptured part surface P
3. Compute the fundamental magnitudes E_P, F_P, and G_P of the first order of the surface P
4. Compute the second derivatives of equation(s) of the part surface P
5. Compute the fundamental magnitudes L_P, M_P, and N_P of the second order of the surface P

The results (3) and (5) could be interpreted as the natural parameterization of the sculptured surface P

6. Compose a set of three equations those that describe the desired rate of conformity of the generating surface T of the form cutting tool to the sculptured surface P
7. Determine the rate of conformity functions F_1, F_2, and F_3
8. Use of the $\mathbb{R}$–mapping of the sculptured surface P onto the generating surface T of the form cutting tool returns a set of three equations [Eq. (71), Eq. (72), Eq. (73)]
9. Incorporate into consideration the Gauss' equation of compatibility [Eq. (74)]
10. Incorporate into consideration two Mainardi-Codazzi's equations of compatibility [Eq. (75), Eq. (76)] – ultimately, this yields a set of six equations [Eq. (71) through Eq. (76)] of six unknowns E_T, F_T, G_T and L_T, M_T, N_T
11. Compute the fundamental magnitudes E_T, F_T, and G_T of the first, and L_T, M_T, and N_T of the second order of the generating surface T of the form-cutting-tool

The result (11) allows interpretation as the natural parameterization of the generating surface T of the form-cutting-tool.

12. Solve the set of two Gauss-Weingarten's equation in tensor notation. Output: Matrix equation of the generating surface T of the from cutting tool in a Cartesian coordinates
13. Incorporate into consideration initial conditions for integration of the set of two Gauss-Weingarten's equations.

Examples of the computation of the design parameters of the form cutting tool can be found out, for example in [18], [23], [24], [40] *etc.*

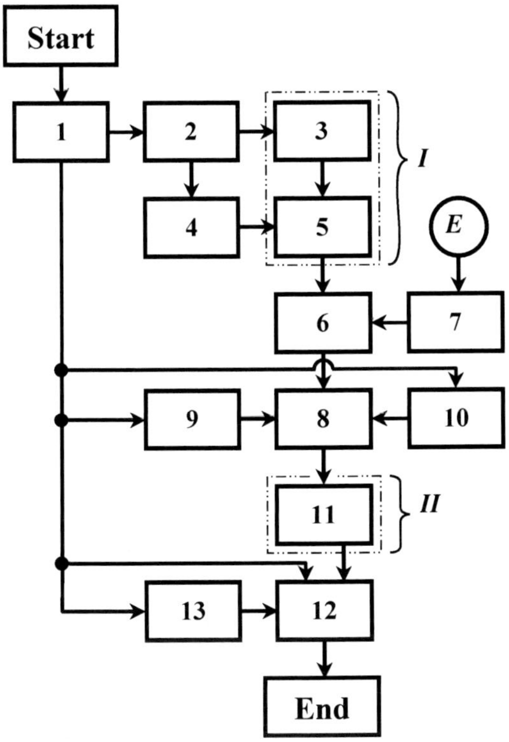

Figure 17. Flow-chart of the algorithm for the computation of the major design parameters of the form cutting tool of optimal design for machining of a given sculptured surface P on multi-axis NC machine.

For machining of a sculptured surface P of any geometry, the discussed above generalized solution [see Eq. (77)] yields an approximation of the surface T with optimal topology by a surface of revolution, and so finding a form-cutting-tool having all necessary combinations of $k_{1.T}$ and $k_{2.T}$.

5.5. Selection of the Form Cutting Tools of Rational Design

Versatility of known designs of form cutting tools for sculptured surface machining on multi-axis *NC* machine is not limited to the designs schematically shown in Figure 15. Form cutting tools of other designs can be implemented as well.

The machining surface T of the milling cutter is shaped in the form of a surface of revolution. For better performance of the milling cutter, it is highly desired to have the principal radii of curvature of the generating surface of the milling cutter equal to (or almost equal to) the extremal values of principal radii of curvature of the part surface taken with the opposite sign. For this purpose, the interval of variation of the radius of curvature of the generating curve of the milling cutter surface T, as well as configuration of the generating curve with respect to the cutting tool axis of rotation are necessary been determined in compliance with the interval of variation of principal radii of curvature of the part surface P. It is practical to assign constant gradient of alteration of radius of curvature of the generating curve.

For the constant gradient of the alteration, the linear relationship between the radius of curvature ρ_T of the generating curve, and between the length of it arc L_T is required been observed. Therefore, in the case under consideration, the equality $\rho_T = c \cdot L_T$ is valid. Here, the constant parameter c specifies the intensity of alteration of the radius of curvature ρ_T.

In polar coordinates, equation of the generating curve can be represented in the following way.

Consider equation of the generating curve in the form $r_T = r_T(\psi)$. Here, r_T designates position vector of a point of the generating curve, and ψ designates the parameter of the generating curve. Omitting routing formulae transformations, the equation for the generating curve

$$R_T = R_{T.0} \exp(c \cdot \psi) \tag{78}$$

can be derived. Here, position vector of a certain zero point is designated as $R_{T.0}$.

When rotating the generating curve Eq. (78) about a tool axis O_T, the generating surface T of the cutting tool is generated.

Equation of the generating surface T is analytically described by equation

$$\mathbf{r}_T(\psi, \delta) = \begin{bmatrix} (r_t + R_o e^{c \cdot \psi} \cos\psi) \cdot \sin\delta \\ (r_t + R_o e^{c \cdot \psi} \cos\psi) \cdot \cos\delta \\ r_t \tan\varphi + R_o e^{c \cdot \psi} \sin\psi \\ 1 \end{bmatrix} \tag{79}$$

The disclosed approach makes it possible to generate the generating surface T of the cutting tool[16] having either convex generating curve (Figure 18,a), or concave generating curve (Figure 18,b), as well as the generating curve with a point of inflection (Figure 18,c), say the point M of tangency of two logarithmic spiral curves[17]. In addition, it makes possible

[16]Pat. No. 1.271.680 (USSR). *A Form Cutting Tool for Machining of Sculptured Surface on Multi-Axis NC Machine.*/S.P. Radzevich, Int. Cl. B 23 C 5/10, Filed: August 09, 1984.

[17]Pat. No. 1.355.378 (USSR). *A Form Cutting Tool for Machining of Sculptured Surface on Multi-Axis NC Machine.*/S.P. Radzevich, Int. Cl. B 23 C 5/10, Filed: April 14, 1986.

creating of the generating surface of the cutting tool having internal tangency with the part surface to be machined. In the last case, the work is located inside the cutting tool [38]. The similar approach is applicable to design of finishing tools[18] for reinforcement of sculptured surface using the method of surface plastic deformation.

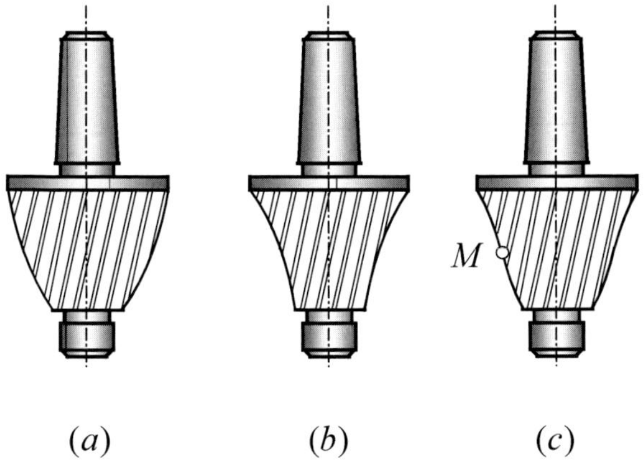

Figure 18. Form milling cutters (SU Pat. No. 1.271.680, SU Pat. No. 1.355.378) for machining of a sculptured surface on multi-axis NC machine.

Use of the milling cutter of the discussed design allows increase of productivity of surface machining, as well as enhanced quality of the machined surface.

5.6. Form Cutting Tools Having Continuously Changeable the Generating Surface

The generating surface T of the most known designs of the form cutting tools is a rigid surface. No changes to the shape and to the parameters of the surface T are feasible. However, for machining of sculptured surfaces on multi-axis *NC* machines form cutting tools of special designs are used as well. Cutting tools of the discussed design have continuously movable blades [21], [33], [34] and others. The continuous motion of the cutting tool blades is under *NC* control. Wooden parts, as well as parts made of plastics, light alloys etc can be machined with form cutting tool of the design.

Equation of the generating surface T of the form cutting tools of design under consideration always contains at least one parameter, which is under *NC* control.

Evidently, that the continuously changeable generating surface T of the form cutting tool can't be formed as an envelope to consecutive positions of the part surface P that is performing a motion relative a coordinate system $X_T Y_T Z_T$ of the form cutting tool. Unknown kinematics of the surface generation is the major reason for this: That same sculptured surface can be machined with that same cutting tool under different kinematics of surface generation.

[18] Pat. №1428563 (USSR). *A Tool for Finishing of Sculptured Surface on Multi-Axis NC Machine.*/S.P. Radzevich, Int. Cl. B 24 B 39/00, Filed: February 11, 1986.

For the development of design of the form cutting tool having continuously changeable the generating surface T, as well as for the determining of optimal kinematics of surface generation implementation of the $\mathbb{R}$–mapping of surfaces is vital.

6. Conditions of Proper Sculptured Surface Generation

Due to peculiarities of shape (a) of the sculptured surface to be machined, (b) of the generating surface of the cutting tool, and (c) of kinematics of the machining operation, actual shape of the machined part surface could deviate from the desired it shape. When a portion of stock on the part surface remained uncut, then an under-cut observes. When the cutting tool removes material beneath the part surface, then the over-cut observes. Both the under-cut and the over-cut are allowed if and only if the resultant deviations of the machined part surface from the desired part surface are within the tolerance on accuracy of the part surface.

In order to ensure precise machining of the given part surface, it is necessary (a) to properly orient the work on the worktable of multi-axis *NC* machine, and (b) to satisfy a set of conditions of proper part surface generation.

6.1. Optimal Work-Piece Orientation on the Worktable of Multi-axis *NC* Machine

There are many feasible configurations of a given sculptured part surface on the worktable of multi-axis *NC* machine. It is naturally to assume that not all of them are equivalent to each other, and that certain particular orientation of the sculptured surface is the most preferred for machining purposes, say this configuration is optimal in certain sense.

Consider general case of machining of a sculptured surface on multi-axis *NC* machine. Optimal work-piece orientation is generally defined as orientation of the work-piece so as to minimize the number of setups in multi-axis *NC* machining of a given sculptured surface P, or to allow the maximal number of surfaces to be machined in a single setup.

To find the optimal work-piece orientation Gauss' maps of the sculptured surface and of the generating surface of the cutting tool are used.

As early as in 1987, Radzevich[19] have picked up the Gauss' idea to sculptured surface orientation problem [9], [23], [36], [43], [44]. The proposed method of finding the optimal work-piece orientation maintains minimal difference of the angle between the normal to sculptured part surface P at its central point and a milling tool axis at its optimal position, in order to minimize the number of setups in rough machining.

If the actual work-piece orientation is far from been optimal, this leads to decreased tool performance or to a situation in which the surface P can not be machined in one setup.

Consider configuration of a sculptured surface P on the worktable of a three-axis *NC* machine (Figure 19). The shadowed planar region $A_{xy}B_{xy}CB^{*}A^{*}$ appears in Figure 19. This means that for the given configuration the portion $ABCB^{*}A^{*}$ of the sculptured surface P can't be machined in that setup.

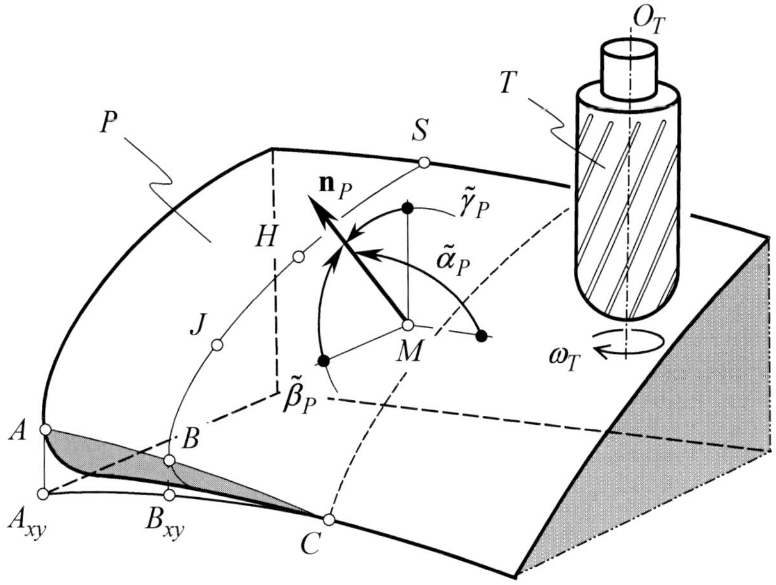

Figure 19. An arbitrary orientation of a sculptured surface P on the worktable of multi-axis NC machine.

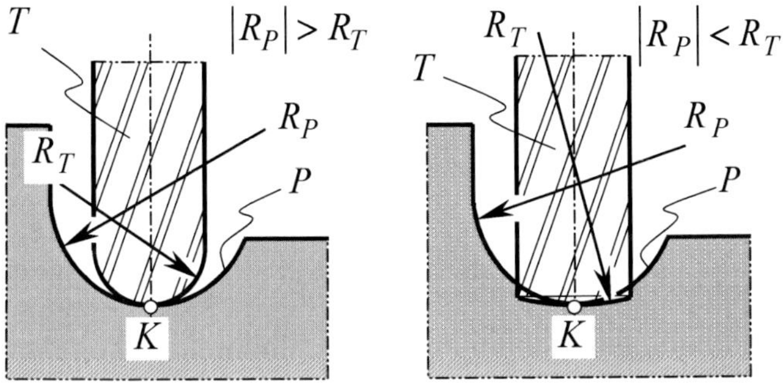

(*a*) (*b*)

Figure 20. Examples of satisfaction (a), and of violation (b) of the third necessary condition of proper PSG.

Gauss introduced the notion of mapping of surface normals onto the surface of a unit sphere by means of parallel normals, in which a point on a map is the result of the intersection of the surface normal vector, translated so as to emanate from the center of a unit sphere, with the surface of the unit sphere [4].

For the computation of parameters of orientation of the area-weighted mean normal vector $\widetilde{\mathbf{N}}_P$, the following formulae

[19]Pat. No.1442371, (USSR). *A Method of Optimal Work-Piece Orientation on the Worktable of Multi-Axis NC Machine*, /S. P. Radzevich. Int. Cl. B23q15/007, Filed: February 17, 1987.

$$\tilde{\mathbf{N}}_P = \frac{\iint\limits_P \sqrt{E_P G_P - F_P^2}\,\mathbf{N}_P(U_P;V_P)dU_P dV_P}{S_P} \tag{80}$$

In cases when the several part surfaces P_i are to be machined on a multi-axis *NC* machine in one setup, Eq. (80) yields the more general formula

$$\tilde{\mathbf{N}}_P = \frac{\sum\limits_{i=1}^{k} \iint\limits_{P_i} \sqrt{E_P G_P - F_P^2}\,\mathbf{N}_P(U_P;V_P)dU_P dV_P}{\sum\limits_{i=1}^{k} S_{Pi}} \tag{81}$$

where k is the total number of the part surfaces P_i to be machined in one setup.

In the latter case, not the area-weighted mean normal to the part surface P is considered, but the area-weighted mean normal to the several surfaces P_i. The last is referred to as the so-called *area-weighted mean normal* to all part surfaces P_i. In this case, instead of a central point of the surface a central point of the entire part to be machined is considered. Definitely, this is a considerably more general approach.

In the initial orientation of the work-piece, the angles that the area-weighted mean normal to the surface P makes with the coordinate axes of the *NC* machine are denoted as α, β, γ. The resultant coordinate system transformation using Euler's angles can be analytically represented with the operator $\mathbf{Eu}\,(\psi, \theta, \varphi)$ of Eulerian transformation [24].

In the optimal work-piece orientation, it is possible to rotate the part surface P about the area-weighted mean normal $\tilde{\mathbf{N}}_P$. Under such a rotation, the optimal orientation of the work-piece is preserved, but the orientation of part surface P relative to the *NC* machine coordinate axes changes. This feasible rotation of the surface P can be used for satisfaction additional requirements to the part surface orientation on the worktable of the multi-axis *NC* machine.

For example, workspace of the multi-axis *NC* machine is the bounded plane or volume within which the cutting tool and the work-piece can be positioned and through which controlled motion can be invoked. When *NC* instructions are generated by a part programmer, the geometry of the work-piece must be transformed into a coordinate system that is consistent with the workspace origin and coordinate reference frame. That is why after the work-piece is turned to a position at which its area-weighted mean normal has an optimal orientation, it is necessary to rotate it about the weighted normal to a position in which the projection of the part surface P (or of the part surfaces P_i) to be machined is within the largest closed contour traced by the cutting tool on the plane of the *NC* machine worktable. In addition, the vertical position of the work-piece must conform to the capabilities of the *NC* machine to move in the vertical direction.

The interested reader may wish to go to [36], [44] for details on computation of the optimal work-piece orientation on the worktable of multi-axis *NC* machine.

6.2. A Set of Necessary and Sufficient Conditions of Proper Part Surface Generation

Once the optimal (or at least a feasible) workpiece orientation is defined, it is necessary to establish the rest of necessary and sufficient conditions of proper part surface generation (further *conditions of proper PSG*) [14], [15], [22], [23], [24], [43].

The first condition of proper part surface generation. Cutting tool of a certain design is necessary for the machining of a given sculptured surface on multi-axis *NC* machine. Cutting tool of any design can be designed on the premises of the generating surface T of the cutting tool. This means that existence of the generating surface T of the cutting tool is a prerequisite for the feasibility of machining of a given sculptured part surface.

Evidently, no machining operation of a sculptured surface P can be performed without cutting tool of an appropriate design. This allows the statement:

Existence of the generating surface T of a form cutting tool, which is conjugate to a given part surface P to be machined (to be generated) is the first necessary condition of proper PSG.

The second condition of proper part surface generation. When machining a part, the generating surface T of the form cutting tool must be in contact with the part surface P to be machined. The surfaces P and T can be either in permanent contact with one another, or they could make contact just in a certain instant of time. In the first case, generation of the sculptured surface P is referred to as the *continuous surface generation*. In the second case, generation of the sculptured surface P is referred to as the *instantaneous surface generation.*

In the instant of surface generation, the sculptured surface P and the generating surface T of the cutting tool must be in tangency to each other. For the analytical interpretation of this requirement, the so-called *equation of contact* $\mathbf{n}_{P/T} \cdot \mathbf{V}_{\Sigma} = 0$ is required been satisfied. Here, in the equation of contact, $\mathbf{n}_{P/T}$ designates a common unit normal vector (the unit vector $\mathbf{n}_{P/T}$ can be interpreted either as the $\mathbf{n}_{P/T} \equiv \mathbf{n}_P$ or as the $\mathbf{n}_{P/T} \equiv -\mathbf{n}_T$), and $\mathbf{V}_{\Sigma}$ designates vector of a resultant relative motion of the surfaces P and T.

The above mentioned equality $\mathbf{n}_P + \mathbf{n}_T = 0$ in common sense of engineering application is equivalent to the equality $\mathbf{n}_P \cdot \mathbf{n}_T = -1$. Any of these two equations can be interpreted as the analytical representation of the second necessary condition of proper *PSG*. Other forms of the equalities can be drawn up as well.

The second necessary condition of proper *PSG* can be formulated in the following way:

The unit normal vectors to the sculptured part surface P to be machined and to the generating surface T of a form cutting tool at each point of the surfaces contact must be aligned to each other and be directed oppositely.

Usually, it is not difficult to satisfy the second condition of proper *PSG* when developing software for machining a sculptured surface on multi-axis *NC* machine.

The third condition of proper part surface generation. To ensure proper contact of the surfaces P and T without penetration of one of the surfaces into another surface, it is also necessary to satisfy certain correspondence of their normal radii of curvature at every cross-section of the surfaces by a plane through the common perpendicular. Evidently, no problem arises when two convex surfaces P and T are required been put in contact. It is also evident that it is not feasible to put in contact two concave surfaces P and T, or two surfaces one of which is concave and another one is saddle-like surface. These cases are evident, and thus they don't need in careful analysis.

The problem of critical importance for the machining of a sculptured surface on multi-axis *NC* machine is to establish necessary and sufficient conditions of proper contact of the surfaces P and T in the vicinity of an arbitrary point K when: (a) one of the surfaces P and T is a convex surface and another one is a concave surface, (b) one of the surfaces P and T is a convex surface and another one is a saddle-like the surface, and finally (c) both of the surfaces P and T are the saddle-like the surfaces. Analytical interpretation of the condition of contact of the surfaces is the most critical for the machining of a sculptured surface on multi-axis *NC* machine.

For the analysis of the actual correspondence between the radii of normal curvature of the surfaces, the normal cross-sections of all possible kinds of contact of the surfaces P and T have been analyzed [23], [24], [43].

When the proper correspondence observes between the radii of normal curvature R_P of the sculptured surface P and of the radii of normal curvature R_T of the generating surface T of the form cutting tool (*i.e.*, when the inequality $|R_P| > R_T$ observes), then the sculptured surface P can be generated with the surface T in the vicinity of every point K of their contact (Figure 20,a). Otherwise, when the inequality $|R_P| < R_T$ is valid, an interference of the surfaces P and T occurs and thus surface P can't be generated in the differential vicinity of the point K (Figure 20,b).

The inequality $|R_P| > R_T$ can be used for the analytical description of satisfaction of the third necessary condition of proper *PSG*.

To verify the satisfaction/violation of the third necessary condition of proper *PSG*, the indicatrix of conformity $Cnf_R\ (P/T)$ of the surfaces P and T can be implemented.

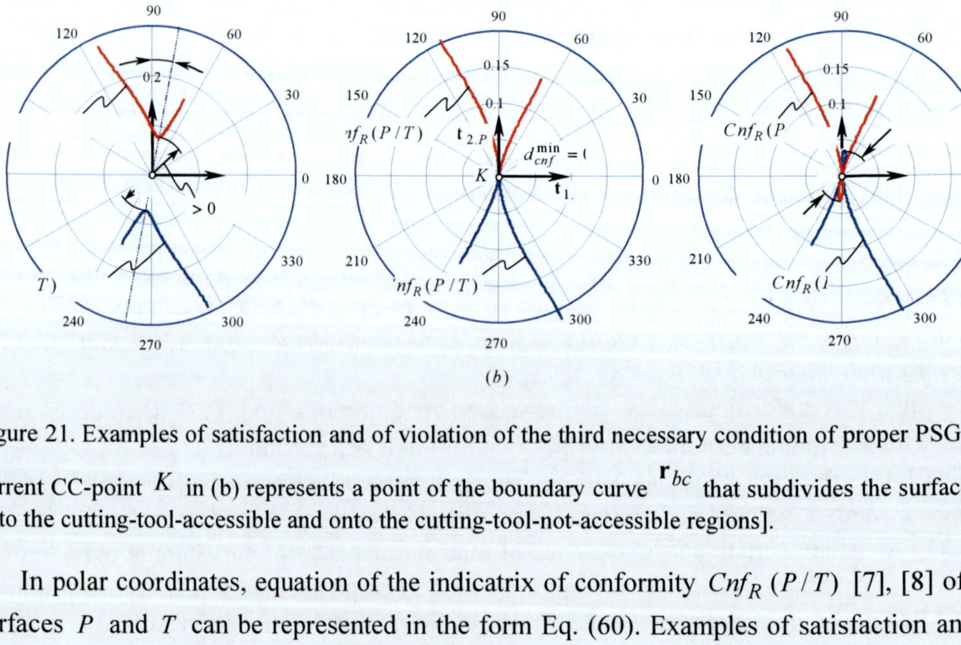

Figure 21. Examples of satisfaction and of violation of the third necessary condition of proper PSG [the current CC-point K in (b) represents a point of the boundary curve $\mathbf{r}_{bc}$ that subdivides the surface P onto the cutting-tool-accessible and onto the cutting-tool-not-accessible regions].

In polar coordinates, equation of the indicatrix of conformity $Cnf_R\ (P/T)$ [7], [8] of the surfaces P and T can be represented in the form Eq. (60). Examples of satisfaction and of violation of the third necessary condition of proper *PSG* is illustrated in Figure 21.

When the third necessary condition of proper *PSG* is satisfied, then all the diameters $d_{cnf} = 2r_{cnf}$ of the indicatrix of conformity $Cnf_R\,(P/T)$ are non-negative. Thus, within the common tangent plane in any direction through the point K the inequality $r_{cnf} \geq 0$ is satisfied. The set of two equations $\operatorname{sgn} r_{cnf} = 0$ or $\operatorname{sgn} r_{cnf} = +1$ is equivalent to the inequality $r_{cnf} \geq 0$. When the third necessary condition of proper *PSG* is satisfied either the equations $\operatorname{sgn} r_{cnf} = 0$ or the equation $\operatorname{sgn} r_{cnf} = +1$ is valid.

When the minimal diameter $d_{cnf}^{(\min)}$ of the indicatrix of conformity $Cnf_R\,(P/T)$ of the surfaces P and T is non-negative, say when the inequality $d_{cnf}^{(\min)} \geq 0$ observes, all other diameters d_{cnf} of this characteristic curve are non-negative as well. Therefore, the third necessary condition of proper *PSG* is satisfied when the minimal diameter $d_{cnf}^{(\min)}$ is equal to or exceeds zero [$d_{cnf}^{(\min)} \geq 0$].

The above analysis enables the following formulation for:

The condition of proper contact of a sculptured surface P to be machined and of the generating surface T of the form cutting tool without their mutual penetration, i.e. without their mutual interference in differential vicinity of the point of contact, is the third necessary condition of proper PSG.

Many examples of satisfaction/violation of the third necessary condition of proper *PSG* can be found out in practice.

The fourth condition of proper part surface generation. When no local interference of the surfaces P and T observes, the surfaces can interfere into each other out of local vicinity of the point K of their contact. This kind of interference of the surfaces is referred to as the *global interference* of the surfaces P and T.

In order to verify satisfaction/violation of the global interference of the sculptured surface P and of the generating surface T of the form cutting tool, equation $\mathbf{r}_P = \mathbf{r}_P(U_P, V_P)$ of the part surface P, and equation $\mathbf{r}_T = \mathbf{r}_T(U_T, V_T)$ of the generation surface T are required been represented in a common reference system. For the satisfaction of the fourth necessary condition of proper *PSG*, no real solutions to the set of two equations

$$\begin{cases} \mathbf{r}_P = \mathbf{r}_P(U_P, V_P) \\ \mathbf{r}_T = \mathbf{r}_T(U_T, V_T) \end{cases} \tag{82}$$

must be observing out of point(s) at which the surfaces P and T make contact of regular kind.

The fourth necessary condition of proper PSG is satisfied if and only if no global interference of the sculptured part surface P to be machined and of the generating surface T of the form cutting tool observes.

The fifth condition of proper part surface generation. Mechanism's and machine's components usually are bounded not by the only surface P to be machined, but by several surfaces.

In order to machine the part, the form cutting tool has to reproduce all the corresponding generating surfaces T_i. For the machining of the neighboring surface $P_{i\pm1}$, the form cutting tool has to be capable of generating corresponding surface $T_{i\pm1}$. Various kinds of relative configuration of the neighboring generating surfaces T_i and $T_{i\pm1}$ are feasible.

For the analytical description of the fifth necessary condition of proper *PSG*, the following set of two equations:

$$\begin{cases} \mathbf{r}_T^{(i)} = \mathbf{r}_T^{(i)}(U_T^{(i)}; V_T^{(i)}) \\ \mathbf{r}_T^{(i\pm1)} = \mathbf{r}_T^{(i\pm1)}(U_T^{(i\pm1)}; V_T^{(i\pm1)}) \end{cases} \tag{83}$$

is considered.

Here $\mathbf{r}_T^{(i)}$ and $\mathbf{r}_T^{(i\pm1)}$ designate position vectors of the surfaces T_i and $T_{i\pm1}$ and $U_T^{(i)}$, $V_T^{(i)}$ and $U_T^{(i\pm1)}$, $V_T^{(i\pm1)}$ are the curvilinear (Gaussian) coordinates of a point on the surfaces T_i and $T_{i\pm1}$ correspondingly.

The fifth necessary condition of proper *PSG* is satisfied if and only if the set of two Eqs. (83) has no real solution.

The fifth necessary condition of proper PSG could be satisfied if and only if the neighboring portions of the generating surface of the form cutting tool do not intersect each other, and no one of them is located within the generating body of the cutting tool beneath the other neighboring surface portion.

In other words, in order to satisfy the fifth necessary condition of proper *PSG*, no transition surfaces are allowed to be observed on the machined part surface P.

The sixth condition of proper part surface generation. When machining a sculptured surface, point contact of the surfaces P and T usually observes. Due to point contact of the surfaces, the so-called *discrete* generation of the sculptured surface often occurs. Representation of the generating surface T by distinct cutting edges of the form cutting tool is the other reason for the discrete generation of the sculptured surface takes place.

In an instant of time, it is physically impossible generating the sculptured surface P by a single moving point. When the discrete surface generation occur, the nominal smooth regular sculptured surface $P^{(n)}$ and the actually machined surface $P^{(a)}$ are not identical to each other. The actual part surface $P^{(a)}$ can be interpreted as the nominal sculptured surface $P^{(n)}$ that is covered by cusps and/or may have other deviations from $P^{(n)}$.

The sixth necessary condition of proper *PSG* is formulated as follows:

The actual part surface P with cusps, if any, must remains within the tolerance on surface accuracy.

Cusps on the machined sculptured surface P are required being within the tolerance on the surface accuracy.

Then maximal height h_Σ of cusps must not exceed the tolerance $[h]$ on the sculptured surface accuracy.

The sixth necessary condition of proper *PSG* is satisfied if and only if the following condition

$$\mathbf{n}_P^{(n)} \cdot h_\Sigma = \mathbf{r}_P^{(a)} - \mathbf{r}_P^{(n)} \leq \mathbf{r}_P^{(t)} = \mathbf{n}_P^{(n)} \cdot [h] \tag{84}$$

is satisfied at every point of the nominal sculptured surface P.

Here, in Eq. (84), position vector of a point of a nominal sculptured surface $P^{(n)}$ is designated as $\mathbf{r}_P^{(n)}$; position vector of the corresponding point[20] of the actual part surface $P^{(a)}$ is designated as $\mathbf{r}_P^{(a)}$, position vector of a point of the surface of tolerance $P^{(t)}$ is designated as $\mathbf{r}_P^{(t)}$, and, finally unit normal vector to surface $P^{(n)}$ is designated as $\mathbf{n}_P^{(n)}$.

If the sixth necessary condition of proper *PSG* is satisfied, then the actual part surface $P^{(a)}$ is entirely located within the nominal sculptured part surface $P^{(n)}$ and the surface of tolerance $P^{(t)}$.

Fulfillment of the set of six conditions of proper part surface generation is necessary and sufficient to insure machining of the part surface in compliance with the requirements indicated in the part blueprint.

6.3. Global Verification of Satisfaction of the Conditions of Proper Sculptured Surface Generation

When machining a sculptured surface on multi-axis *NC* machine, it is of importance to know whether the entire part surface can be machined, or it can't be machined on the given machine. It is also of importance to detect the sculptured surface regions, those that are not accessible by the cutting tool of a given design. In other words, it is necessary to detect regions on the sculptured surface P, which the cutting tool can't reach without being obstructed by another portion of the part. Certainly, such the regions (if any) are due to not just to geometry of the sculptured surface P, but to geometry of the generating surface T of the cutting tool as well. Summarizing, the problem of this sort can be referred to as the *problem of global machinability* of a given sculptured surface with the given cutting tool on the multi-axis *NC* with a certain articulation.

On the premises of the above discussed results the problem of global machinability is solved. A solution to the problem can be derived by means of implementation (a) of spherical indicatrices of machinability $Mch(P/T)$ [44], (b) of focal $\boldsymbol{R}$ –surfaces [13], [41], (c) of two-dimensional $\mathbb{K}$-mapping of the sculptured surface to be machined and of the generating surface of the cutting tool [24], [29], [42].

There is much room for the improvements in this area.

---

[20]Two points on the surfaces $\mathbf{r}_P^{(n)}$ and $\mathbf{r}_P^{(a)}$ are corresponding to each other if they share a common straight line, which aligned with the perpendicular $\mathbf{n}_P^{(n)}$ to the surface $\mathbf{r}_P^{(n)}$.

7. Predicted Accuracy of the Machined Sculptured Surface

Accuracy of the machined part surfaces is a critical issue for many reasons. Use of the *DG/K*-based method of surface generation makes it possible to predict the accuracy of the machined sculptured surface.

7.1. Components of the Resultant Deviation of the Machined Surface from the Desired Surface

There are two major reasons those cause deviation of the machined sculptured surface from the desired it shape.

First, the generating surface of the cutting tool usually is represented discretely by a set of distinct cutting edges. The discrete representation of the surface T of the cutting tool causes deviations h_{fr} of the actually machined part surface P_{ac} from the desired (say, from the nominal) part surface P_{nom} (Figure 22,a).

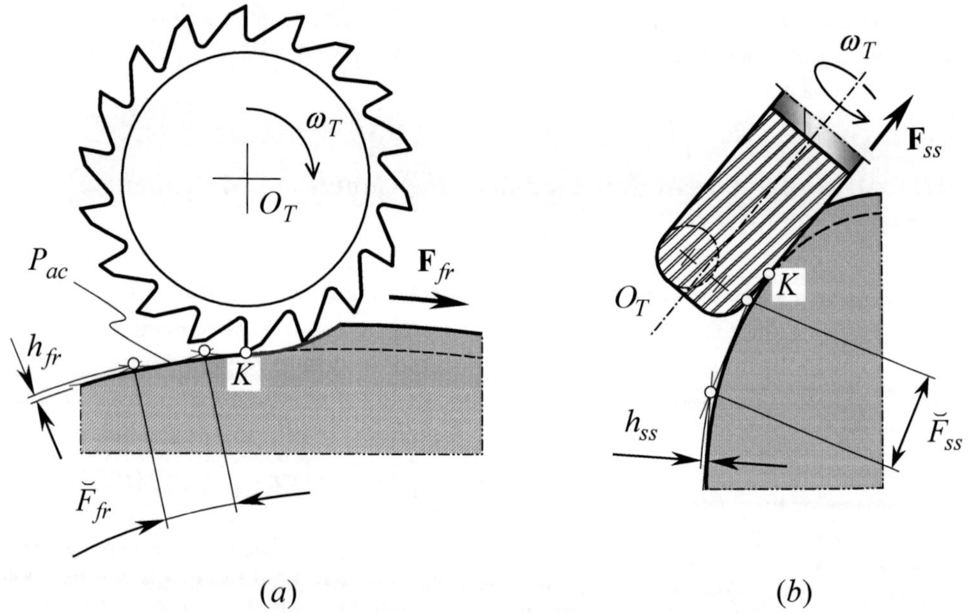

Figure 22. Two kinds of the deviation of the machined sculptured surface from the desired part surface, those caused by the limited number of cutting edges of the cutting tool (a), and those caused by point kind of contact of the surfaces P and T (b).

Second, point contact of the part surface and of the generating surface of the cutting tool usually observes when machining a sculptured surface on multi-axis *NC* machine. Point contact of the surfaces P and T causes deviations h_{ss} of the actually machined part surface P_{ac} from the desired part surface P_{nom} (Figure 22,b).

Sources for the deviations of the machined part surface from the desired part surface are not limited to two mentioned major reasons. Deviations of the surfaces P and T configuration also affect the resultant accuracy of the machined sculptured surface P_{nom}.

Resultant deviation h_{Σ} of the machined sculptured surface P_{ac} from the nominal surface P_{nom} is measured along the unit normal vector $\mathbf{n}_P$ to the nominal part surface P_{nom}, and is equal to the distance between the surfaces P_{ac} and P_{nom}. Value of the resultant deviation h_{Σ} depends upon the elementary deviations h_{fr} and h_{ss}.

Resultant deviation $h_{\Sigma,i}$ at a current $i-$point of the surface P is equal

$$h_{\Sigma,i} = h_{\Sigma,i}(h_{fr,i}, h_{ss,i}) \tag{85}$$

Here, in Eq. (85) the elementary deviations $h_{fr,i}$ and $h_{ss,i}$ have to be considered as functions (a) of coordinates of the point on the part surface P, (b) of the corresponding point of the generating surface of the cutting tool, and (c) the angle μ of the surfaces P and T local relative orientation. This relationship is expressed by two functions

$$h_{fr} = h_{fr}(U_P, V_P, U_T, V_T, \mu) \tag{86}$$

$$h_{ss} = h_{ss}(U_P, V_P, U_T, V_T, \mu) \tag{87}$$

Maximal resultant deviation $h_{\Sigma}^{\max}$ of the surface P_{ac} from the surface P_{nom} can be used for the quantitative evaluation of accuracy of the machined sculptured surface.

If the principle of superposition of the elementary deviations h_{fr} and h_{ss} is assumed been valid, then for the computation of the resultant deviation h_{Σ} the following equation

$$h_{\Sigma} = a_h \cdot h_{fr} + b_h \cdot h_{ss} \tag{88}$$

can be used.

Here a_h and b_h designate certain constants for a given point K. The constants a_h and b_h are within the intervals $0 \le a_h \le 1$ and $0 \le b_h \le 1$.

The resultant deviation of surface generation h_{Σ} is getting its maximal value of $h_{\Sigma}^{\max}$ when the equality $a_h = b_h = 1$ observes. In this particular case, the deviation $h_{\Sigma}^{\max}$ can be computed from the equation

$$h_{\Sigma}^{\max} = h_{fr}^{\max} + h_{ss}^{\max} \tag{89}$$

Generally, the function $h_{\Sigma} = h_{\Sigma}(h_{fr}, h_{ss})$ is of complex nature.

The maximal value of the resultant deviation h_{Σ} is limited by the tolerance $[h]$ on accuracy of the surface machining.

7.2. Local Approximation of the Contacting Surfaces

Actual surfaces P and T can be given in a complex analytical form, that is not convenient for the computations. Solutions to many of geometrical problems can be easier derived from local consideration of the surfaces rather than from consideration of the entire surfaces.

For the local analysis, the surfaces are often represented by quadrics. As it is shown in our previous works [23], [24], [43], from the prospective of local approximation of surface patches helical canal surfaces are featuring important advantages over other candidates. A helical canal surface is a particular case of swept surface. Monge was the first to investigate helical canal surfaces, in 1850 [6].

Locally, the surface P is specified by the principal radii of curvature $R_{1.P}$ and $R_{2.P}$ at the point K, and by the surface torsion τ_P. Helical canal surfaces can fit the principal curvatures and torsion of the local patch of sculptured surfaces, as well as of the generating surfaces of cutting tools.

Further simplification is possible due to torsion of the surfaces P and T usually is of negligibly small value. If torsion is assumed equal to zero then the helical canal surface reduces to torus surface. For the purposes of local surface approximation, implementation of torus surfaces is of significant practical importance.

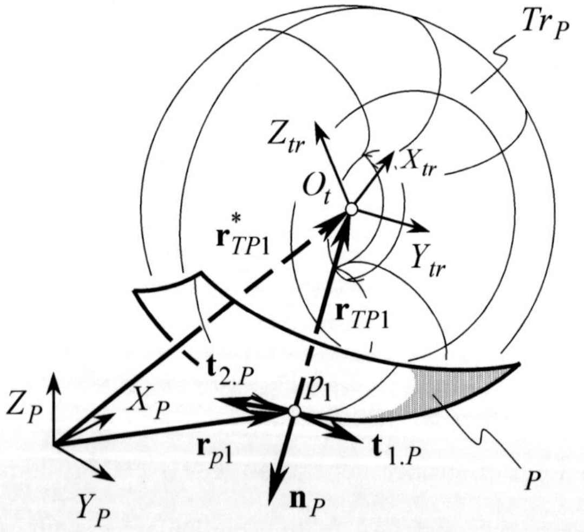

Figure 23. To the construction of the torus surface T_{P1} at the point p_1 of the part surface P.

Local approximation of the part surface P by the torus surface Tr_P is illustrated in Figure 23. Position vector of an arbitrary point p_1 of the surface P is designated as $\mathbf{r}_{p1}$. Here, in Figure 23, the surfaces P and Tr_P share common unit tangent vectors $\mathbf{t}_{1.P}$ and $\mathbf{t}_{2.P}$

of the surfaces principal directions, as well as they share common unit normal vector $\mathbf{n}_P$. The vectors $\mathbf{t}_{1.P}$, $\mathbf{t}_{2.P}$ and $\mathbf{n}_P$ together with the computed values of the principal radii of curvature $R_{1.P}$ and $R_{2.P}$ yield computation of the position vector $\mathbf{r}_{TP1}$. The last vector together with the position vector $\mathbf{r}_{p1}$ of the point p_1 allow computation of the position vector $\mathbf{r}^*_{TP1}$ in the coordinate system $X_P Y_P Z_P$ associated with the surface P.

For further consideration it is of importance to stress the readers' attention here that not every point of the approximating torus surface can be used for the local approximation of the surfaces P and T. Only points that are within the circle either of the biggest meridian, or of the smallest it meridian can be used for this purpose.

A torus surface can be expressed in terms of radius r_{tr} of its generating circle, and in terms of radius R_{tr} of its directing circle. Depends on the actual ratio between the radii r_{tr} and R_{tr}, the torus radius r_{tr} can be equal to the first principal radius of curvature $R_{1.P}$ of the part surface ($r_{tr} = R_{1.P}$), while the torus radius R_{tr} in this case is equal to the difference $R_{tr} = R_{2.P} - R_{1.P}$. For another ratio between the radii r_{tr} and R_{tr}, the equalities $r_{tr} = R_{2.P} - R_{1.P}$ and $R_{tr} = R_{1.P}$ are valid.

A routine transformations yield the following expression for $\mathbf{r}_{tr}(\theta_{tr}, \varphi_{tr})$

$$\mathbf{r}_{tr}(\theta_{tr}, \varphi_{tr}) = \begin{bmatrix} -(R_{2.P} - R_{1.P})\cos\theta_{tr} + R_{1.P}\cos\varphi_{tr}\cos\theta_{tr} \\ -(R_{2.P} - R_{1.P})\sin\theta_{tr} + R_{1.P}\cos\varphi_{tr}\sin\theta_{tr} \\ R_{1.P}\sin\varphi_{tr} \\ 1 \end{bmatrix} \qquad (90)$$

Unit normal vector $\mathbf{n}_{tr}$ to the torus surface $\mathbf{r}_{tr}$ can be calculated by the formula $\mathbf{n}_{tr} = \mathbf{u}_{tr} \times \mathbf{v}_{tr}$, where $\mathbf{u}_{tr} = \mathbf{U}_{tr} / |\mathbf{U}_{tr}|$, and $\mathbf{v}_{tr} = \mathbf{V}_{tr} / |\mathbf{V}_{tr}|$, and the tangent vectors $\mathbf{U}_{tr}$ and $\mathbf{V}_{tr}$ are given by the equations $\mathbf{U}_{tr} = \partial\mathbf{r}_{tr} / \partial U_{tr}$ and $\mathbf{V}_{tr} = \partial\mathbf{r}_{tr} / \partial V_{tr}$.

Unit tangent vectors $\mathbf{t}_{1.tr}$ and $\mathbf{t}_{2.tr}$ can be employed for the specification of configuration of the torus surface $\mathbf{r}_{tr}$. At the point K, the unit tangent vectors $\mathbf{t}_{1.tr}$ and $\mathbf{t}_{2.tr}$ are identical to the unit tangent vectors $\mathbf{t}_{1.P}$ and $\mathbf{t}_{2.P}$ of the surface P.

It is of importance to stress here that (a) the patches of torus surfaces that locally approximate the surfaces P and T, (b) and the torus portion of the generating surface T of a cutting tool are completely different entities. The last is clearly illustrated in Figure 24 where a portion of filleted-end milling cutter is shown.

The major advantage of implementation of the torus surface for local approximation of the sculptured surface is due to a patch of the torus surface is capable of to provide perfect approximation for bigger surfaces area compare to the approximation by quadrics, use of which is valid just within differential vicinity of the surface point.

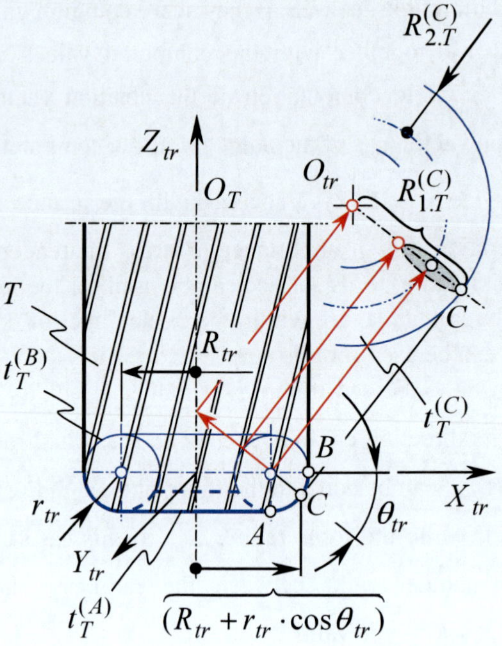

Figure 24. To the analysis of the local geometry of the generating surface T of a filleted-end milling cutter.

7.3. Configuration of the Approximating Torus Surfaces

When a sculptured surface P and the generating surface T of a cutting tool contact each other at a certain point K, then the approximating torus surfaces are also contacting each other at that same point K. Moreover, unit tangent vectors $\mathbf{t}_{1.P}$ and $\mathbf{t}_{2.P}$ of the surface P at K and the unit tangent vectors $\mathbf{t}_{1.T}$ and $\mathbf{t}_{2.T}$ of the surface T at K are identical to the corresponding unit tangent vectors of the approximating torus surfaces Tr_P and Tr_T. The last is convenient for the development of analytical description of local configuration of the approximating torus surfaces.

Assume that the sculptured surface P and the generating surface T of the cutting tool are in proper tangency at a certain point K (Figure 25). The Darboux trihedron that is comprised of the vectors $\mathbf{t}_{1.P}$, $\mathbf{t}_{2.P}$ and $\mathbf{n}_P$ is implemented here for the purpose of construction of the local left-hand-oriented Cartesian coordinate system $x_P y_P z_P$ having origin at the point K.

Location and orientation of the sculptured surface P as well as location and orientation of the generating surface T in the coordinate system $X_{NC}Y_{NC}Z_{NC}$ associated with the machine tool is known. Therefore, corresponding operators of the coordinate system transformations, say (a) the operator $\mathbf{Rs}(NC \mapsto P)$ of the resultant transformation from the coordinates system $X_{NC}Y_{NC}Z_{NC}$ to the coordinate system $X_P Y_P Z_P$, and further (b) the operator $\mathbf{Rs}(P \mapsto K_P)$ of the resultant transformation from the coordinates system $X_P Y_P Z_P$

to the local coordinate system $x_P y_P z_P$ can be composed. Ultimately, the operator $\mathbf{Rs}(NC \mapsto K_P)$ of the resultant coordinate systems transformation can be composed.

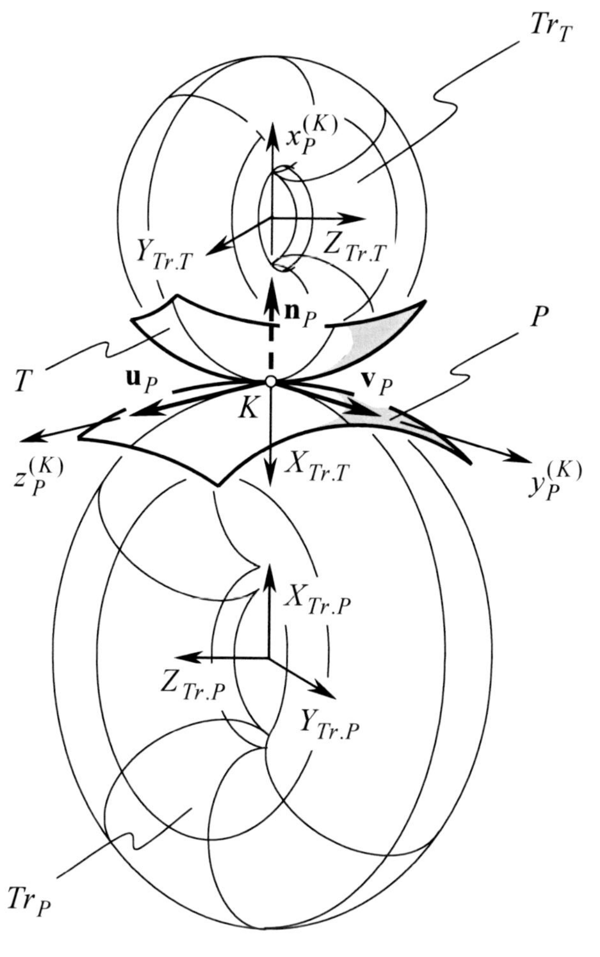

Figure 25. An example of relative disposition of the of approximating torus surfaces Tr_P and Tr_T.

The similar operators $\mathbf{Rs}(NC \mapsto T)$, $\mathbf{Rs}(T \mapsto K_T)$ and $\mathbf{Rs}(NC \mapsto K_T)$ of the consequent coordinate systems transformations are composed for the generating surface T of the cutting tool. Ultimately, the operators of the direct $\mathbf{Rs}(K_T \mapsto K_P)$ and of the inverse $\mathbf{Rs}(K_P \mapsto K_T)$ coordinate system transformations can be composed as well. The operators $\mathbf{Rs}(K_T \mapsto K_P)$ and $\mathbf{Rs}(K_P \mapsto K_T)$ complement the earlier composed operators of the coordinate systems transformation to a closed loop of the coordinate system transformation.

The derived operators of the coordinate systems transformations yield representation of the surfaces $\mathbf{r}_P$, $\mathbf{r}_T$ and of all major elements of there geometry in a common coordinate system. Implementation of the local coordinate system $x_P y_P z_P$ for this purpose is preferred.

7.4. Predicted Elementary Surface Deviations

For the computation of the resultant deviation $h_\Sigma = a_h \cdot h_{fr} + b_h \cdot h_{ss}$, actual values of the elementary deviations h_{fr} and h_{ss} are necessary. Equation for the computation of the elementary deviation h_{fr} is similar to that for the computation of the deviation h_{ss}.

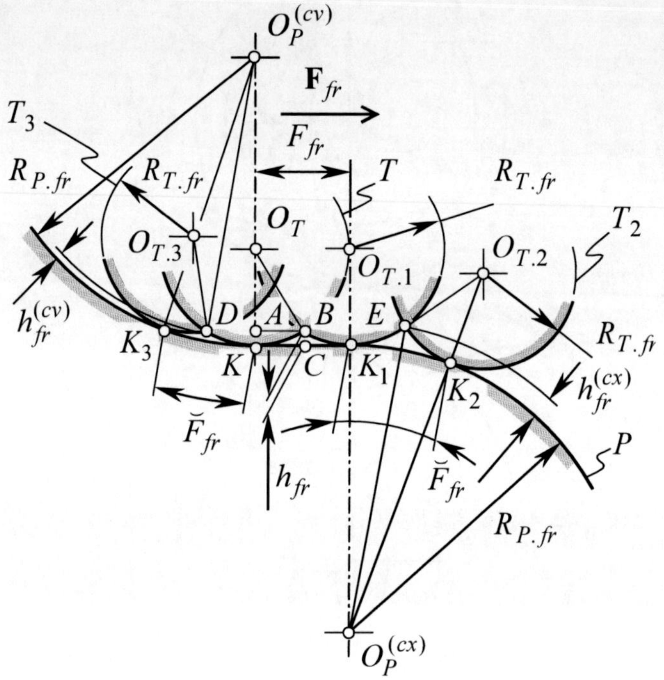

Figure 26. To the computation of the elementary deviation h_{fr} (the waviness) on the sculptured part surface P.

Consider, for example, computation of the elementary deviation h_{fr}. Figure 26 illustrates a cross-section of a sculptured surface P by a plane through the unit normal vector $\mathbf{n}_P$ and through the feed-rate vector $\mathbf{F}_{fr}$. Depends on the chosen point of interest on the surface P, the cross-section of the surface P could have either straight profile KK_1, or convex profile K_1K_2, or concave profile K_2K_3.

For the computation of the elementary deviation h_{fr} the approximate equation

$$h_{fr} \cong \frac{R_{P.fr} \cdot (R_{P.fr} + R_{T.fr}) \cdot \left(1 - \cos \dfrac{\breve{F}_{fr}}{2 \cdot R_{P.fr}}\right)}{R_{P.fr} - (R_{P.fr} + R_{T.fr}) \cdot \cos\left(\dfrac{\breve{F}_{fr}}{2 \cdot R_{P.fr}}\right)} \tag{91}$$

is derived by Radzevich [23], [24], [25], [26], [43].

Here, in Eq. (91), radii of normal curvature of the surfaces P and T are designated as $R_{P.fr}$ and $R_{T.fr}$ respectively, and the arc segment $\breve{F}_{fr}$ designates the feed-rate per tooth of the cutting tool.

The radii $R_{P.fr}$ and $R_{T.fr}$ are measured in the direction of the feed-rate vector $\mathbf{F}_{fr}$. For the computation of the radius of normal curvature $R_{P.fr}$, the equation

$$R_{P.fr} = \frac{E_P G_P}{G_P L_P \sin^2 \xi + M_P \sqrt{E_P G_P} \sin 2\xi + E_P N_P \cos^2 \xi} \tag{92}$$

is derived in [25], [26]. Here angle ξ specifies the direction of the feed-rate vector $\mathbf{F}_{fr}$ relative to the principal directions $\mathbf{t}_{1.P}$ and $\mathbf{t}_{2.P}$ of the sculptured surface P.

An equation similar to Eq. (87)

$$R_{T.fr} \cong \frac{E_T G_T}{G_T L_T \sin^2(\xi + \mu) + M_T \sqrt{E_T G_T} \sin 2(\xi + \mu) + E_T N_T \cos^2(\xi + \mu)} \tag{93}$$

is derived [25], [26] for the computation of the radius of normal curvature $R_{T.fr}$.

In Eq. (92), the angle μ of the surfaces P and T local relative orientation indicates that the surface T is analytically represented in that same local coordinates system $x_P y_P z_P$ as the part surface P is.

It is assumed in Eq. (92) that the radius of normal curvature of the surface of cut is approximately equal to the corresponding radius of normal curvature of the generating surface T of the cutting tool.

In particular cases, Eq. (91) can be significantly simplified. For example, when a flat portion of a part surface P is machined with the milling cutter of diameter d_T, then the cusp height is equal to

$$h_{fr} = R_{T.fr} - \sqrt{R_{T.f}^2 - 0{,}25\, \breve{F}_{T.f}^2} \tag{94}$$

The last equation is well known from practice.

For the computation of the elementary surface deviation h_{ss}, a plane through the unit normal vector $\mathbf{n}_P$ and through the vector $\mathbf{F}_{ss}$ of side-step of the cutting tool is employed. The plane through the vectors $\mathbf{n}_P$ and $\mathbf{F}_{ss}$ is orthogonal to the plane through the vectors $\mathbf{n}_P$ and $\mathbf{F}_{fr}$ [23], [24], [25], [26], [43].

Derivation of equation for the computation of the elementary deviation h_{ss} is similar in much to the derivation of Eq. (91). Therefore, without going into details of derivation, just the final equation for the computation of the elementary deviation h_{ss} is represented below

$$h_{ss} \cong \frac{R_{P.ss} \cdot (R_{P.ss} + R_{T.ss}) \cdot \left(1 - \cos \frac{\breve{F}_{ss}}{2 \cdot R_{P.ss}}\right)}{R_{P.ss} - (R_{P.ss} + R_{T.ss}) \cdot \cos\left(\frac{\breve{F}_{ss}}{2 \cdot R_{P.ss}}\right)} \tag{95}$$

where

$$R_{P.ss} = \frac{E_P G_P}{G_P L_P \cos^2 \xi + M_P \sqrt{E_P G_P} \sin 2\xi + E_P N_P \sin^2 \xi} \tag{96}$$

$$R_{T.ss} \cong \frac{E_T G_T}{G_T L_T \cos^2 (\xi + \mu) + M_T \sqrt{E_T G_T} \sin 2(\xi + \mu) + E_T N_T \sin^2 (\xi + \mu)} \tag{97}$$

Here, in Eq. (95), radii of normal curvature of the surfaces P and T are designated as $R_{P.ss}$ and $R_{T.ss}$ respectively, and the arc segment $\breve{F}_{ss}$ designates the side-step of the cutting tool. The radii $R_{P.ss}$ and $R_{T.ss}$ are measured in the direction of the side-step vector $\mathbf{F}_{ss}$.

7.5. Total Displacement of the Cutting Tool with Respect to the Sculptured Surface

No absolute accuracy observes in machining of sculptured surfaces on multi-axis *NC* machine. Displacements of the generating surface T of the cutting tool with respect to the desired part surface P are unavoidable. Both the *NC* machine and the cutting tool are the major sources of unavoidable deviations of the machined part surface from the desired sculptured surface. Actual relative motion of the cutting tool is performing with certain deviations of it parameters with respect to the desired relative motion of the cutting tool. The last is also a source of significant surface deviations.

Problems of two kinds arise in this concern.

First, it is of importance to know how much the displacement of the cutting tool donates to the resultant deviation of the actually machined part surface from the desired part surface. Second, in order to avoid the cutter penetration into the part surface P, it is of critical importance to determine the maximal allowed dimensions of the cutting tool in order to avoid violation of the necessary conditions of proper surface generation.

For solving of the problems of both kinds, computation of the *closest distance of approach* (*CDA*) of the surfaces P and T is necessary.

It is convenient to begin the analysis from the ideal case, when the surfaces P and T are in proper tangency at a certain point K (Figure 27).

The left-hand-oriented local Cartesian coordinate system $x_P y_P z_P$ is associated with the sculptured surface P (Figure 27). Similarly, the left-hand-oriented local Cartesian coordinate system $x_T y_T z_T$ is associated with the generating surface T of the cutting tool.

A left-hand-oriented Cartesian coordinate system $X_{NC} Y_{NC} Z_{NC}$ is associated with the multi-axis *NC* machine.

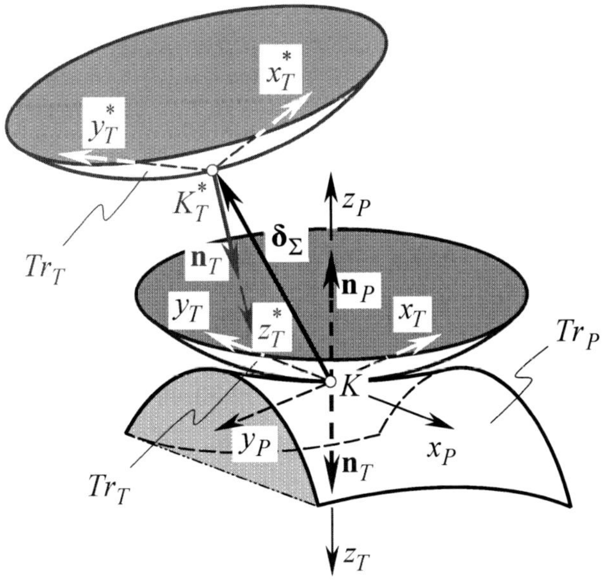

Figure 27. Actual configuration of local patches of the torus surfaces Tr_P and Tr_T.

Configuration of the sculptured surface P as well as configuration of the generating surface T of the cutting tool in the coordinate system $X_{NC}Y_{NC}Z_{NC}$ is known. Therefore, corresponding operators of the coordinate system transformations, say (a) the operator $\mathbf{Rs}(NC \mapsto P)$ of the resultant transformation from the coordinate system $X_{NC}Y_{NC}Z_{NC}$ to the coordinate system $X_P Y_P Z_P$, and further (b) the operator $\mathbf{Rs}(P \mapsto K_P)$ of the resultant transformation from the coordinate system $X_P Y_P Z_P$ to the local coordinate system $x_P y_P z_P$ can be composed. The operators $\mathbf{Rs}(NC \mapsto P)$ and $\mathbf{Rs}(P \mapsto K_P)$ of the resultant coordinate system transformations are expressed in terms of the operators of elementary coordinate system transformations. Ultimately, the operator $\mathbf{Rs}(NC \mapsto K_P)$ of the resultant coordinates systems transformation can be composed as well.

The similar operators $\mathbf{Rs}(NC \mapsto T)$, $\mathbf{Rs}(T \mapsto K_T)$ and $\mathbf{Rs}(NC \mapsto K_T)$ of the consequent coordinate systems transformations are composed for the generating surface T of the cutting tool. Ultimately, the operators of the direct $\mathbf{Rs}(K_T \mapsto K_P)$ and of the inverse $\mathbf{Rs}(K_P \mapsto K_T)$ coordinate system transformations can be composed as well. It is of importance to note here one more time that the equality $\mathbf{Rs}(K_T \mapsto K_P) = \mathbf{Rs}^{-1}(K_P \mapsto K_T)$ always observes. The operators $\mathbf{Rs}(K_T \mapsto K_P)$ and $\mathbf{Rs}(K_P \mapsto K_T)$ complement the earlier composed operators of the coordinate systems transformation to the closed loop of the coordinate systems transformations.

The operators of the coordinate systems transformations yield representations of the surfaces $\mathbf{r}_P$ and $\mathbf{r}_T$ in a common coordinate system.

When the generating surface T of the cutting tool is in proper tangency with the sculptured surface P (Figure 27), then origins of the both local coordinate systems $x_P y_P z_P$

and $x_T y_T z_T$ coincide with the point of contact K of the surfaces P and T. In reality, the surfaces P and T don't make proper contact. Actually, the surfaces are either slightly apart of each other, or the surface T penetrates into the surface P. This is due to the unavoidable deviations of configuration of the cutting tool with respect to the part surface P.

The deviations cause a displacement of the local coordinate system $x_T y_T z_T$ from it desired position to the actual position $\overset{*}{x}_T \overset{*}{y}_T \overset{*}{z}_T$. Deviations of this kind are unavoidable.

The resultant linear displacement $\boldsymbol{\delta}_\Sigma$ of the cutting tool with respect to the part surface P can be expressed in terms of the elementary linear displacements δ_x, δ_y and δ_z of the cutting tool along the axes x_P, y_P, z_P

$$\boldsymbol{\delta}_\Sigma = \begin{bmatrix} \delta_x \\ \delta_y \\ \delta_z \\ 1 \end{bmatrix} \tag{98}$$

In addition to the linear displacements δ_x, δ_y and δ_z, the elementary angular displacements θ_x, θ_y and θ_z of the local coordinate system $x_T y_T z_T$ with respect to the local coordinate system $x_P y_P z_P$ observe.

The resultant angular displacement $\boldsymbol{\theta}_\Sigma$ of the cutting tool with respect to the part surface P can be expressed in terms of the elementary angular displacements of the cutting tool through the angles θ_x, θ_y and θ_z about the axes x_P, y_P, z_P

$$\boldsymbol{\theta}_\Sigma = \begin{bmatrix} \theta_x \\ \theta_y \\ \theta_z \\ 1 \end{bmatrix} \tag{99}$$

Ultimately, the local coordinate system $x_T y_T z_T$ associated with the cutting tool moves to a position $\overset{*}{x}_T \overset{*}{y}_T \overset{*}{z}_T$.

Because of the displacements $\boldsymbol{\delta}_\Sigma$ and $\boldsymbol{\theta}_\Sigma$ always observe, either a gap between local patches of the surfaces P and T occur, or the surfaces interfere P and T into each other.

The resultant linear $\boldsymbol{\delta}_\Sigma$ and the resultant angular $\boldsymbol{\theta}_\Sigma$ displacements can be expressed in terms of the corresponding elementary displacements of all the local coordinate systems between the point $K_P \equiv K$ and the point K_T. Here K_P and K_T designate origins of the local coordinate systems $x_P y_P z_P$ and $\overset{*}{x}_T \overset{*}{y}_T \overset{*}{z}_T$. No closed loop of the consequent coordinate systems transformations can be constructed at this point. The loop of the consequent coordinate systems transformations is not closed yet. In order to make the loop close, it is necessary to compose the operator $\mathbf{Rs}(\overset{*}{K}_T \mapsto K_P)$ of the resultant coordinate systems transformation, and the operator $\mathbf{Rs}(K_P \mapsto \overset{*}{K_T}) = \mathbf{Rs}^{-1}(\overset{*}{K_T} \mapsto K_P)$ of the inverse coordinate systems transformation. For the composing of the operators $\mathbf{Rs}(\overset{*}{K_T} \mapsto K_P)$ and $\mathbf{Rs}(K_P \mapsto \overset{*}{K_T})$, the earlier developed operators $\mathbf{Rs}(P \mapsto K_P)$ and $\mathbf{Rs}(P \mapsto K_T)$ are helpful:

$$\mathbf{Rs}(\overset{*}{K_T} \mapsto K_P) = \mathbf{Rs}^{-1}(P \mapsto K_T) \cdot \mathbf{Rs}(P \mapsto K_P) \tag{100}$$

In the ideal case of surface generation when no displacement of the surface T with respect to the surface P occur, the surfaces P and T make contact at a point K. Actually, it is allowed to interpret the ideal surfaces contact in the way that the point K_P of the part surface P, and the point K_T of the cutting tool surface T are snapped into a common point K. Therefore, the identity $K_P \equiv K_T \equiv K$ is valid for the ideal case of surface generation.

The closest distance of approach between the surfaces P and T is identical to the closest distance of approach between the approximating torus surfaces Tr_P and Tr_T, and it is identical to zero when $K_P \equiv K_T \equiv K$. The closest distance of approach between the surfaces P and T can be interpreted as the distance between the points K_P and K_T. Therefore, for the ideal case of surfaces generation the equality $K_P K_T = 0$ is valid.

In reality, the generating surface T of the cutting tool is displaced with respect to the part surface P. The total linear displacement of the surface T with respect to the surface P is equal to the magnitude of the vector $\boldsymbol{\delta}_\Sigma$ [see Eq. (98)]. The total angular displacement of the surface T with respect to the surface P is equal to magnitude of the vector $\boldsymbol{\theta}_\Sigma$ [see Eq. (99)]. The closest distance of approach of the surfaces P and T is not equal to zero. It can be either positive, or it can be negative. In the first case the cutting tool surface T is located apart of the part surface P. In the second case the cutting tool surface T interfere into the part surface P.

It is of critical importance to realize that the following theorem

Theorem: *The closest distance of approach of two smooth regular surfaces is perpendicular to both the surfaces simultaneously.*

is correct. The theorem is proved analytically. We are not going into details of proof of the theorem here. The interested reader may wish to exercise in this concern on his/her own.

The closest distance of approach of the surfaces P and T is not equal to the distance between the points $\overset{*}{K_T}$ and $K\ (\equiv K_P)$. In-perpendicularity of the straight-line segment $K\overset{*}{K_T}$ to the surfaces P and T is the major reason for the equality doesn't observe.

The analysis below is based in much on the presumption that the configuration of the local coordinate system $\overset{*}{x_T}\overset{*}{y_T}\overset{*}{z_T}$ with respect to the local coordinate system $x_P y_P z_P$ is known. The configuration is specified by the operator $\mathbf{Rs}(\overset{*}{K_T} \mapsto K_P)$ of the resultant coordinate system transformation [see Eq. (100)]. Use of the operator $\mathbf{Rs}(\overset{*}{K_T} \mapsto K_P)$ together with the earlier discussed in this sub-section operator $\mathbf{Rs}(K_P \mapsto K_T)$ yield introduction of the matrix $\mathbf{Ds}(T/P)$ of the displacement of the generating surface T of the cutting tool with respect to the part surface P. The displacement matrix $\mathbf{Ds}(T/P)$ specifies the actual configuration of the local coordinate system $\overset{*}{x}_T\overset{*}{y}_T\overset{*}{z}_T$ associated with the cutting tool with respect to the local coordinate system $x_T y_T z_T$ associated with the cutting tool in it ideal configuration with respect to the part surface P.

Actually, matrix $\mathbf{Ds}(T/P)$ of the resultant displacements can be composed in the following way. Consider all "n" elements and joints between the elements, those that are involved in the closed loop of the consequent coordinate systems transformations. Elementary displacement of every element and at every joint donate to the resultant displacement of the cutting tool with respect to the part surface P. The elementary $i-$th displacement can be interpreted as the displacement of the actual elementary coordinate system $X_i^{ac}Y_i^{ac}Z_i^{ac}$ with respect to the nominal location of the corresponding elementary coordinate system $X_iY_iZ_i$. Implementation of the generalized formula for the resultant coordinate system transformations yields derivation of the matrix $\mathbf{ds}_i(ac_i \mapsto nom_i)$ of a particular elementary displacement

$$\mathbf{ds}_i(ac_i \mapsto nom_i) = \begin{bmatrix} \cos\theta_{xx}^{(i)} & \cos\theta_{xy}^{(i)} & \cos\theta_{xz}^{(i)} & \delta_x^{(i)} \\ \cos\theta_{xy}^{(i)} & \cos_{yy}^{(i)} & \cos\theta_{yz}^{(i)} & \delta_y^{(i)} \\ \cos\theta_{xz}^{(i)} & \cos\theta_{yz}^{(i)} & \cos_{zz}^{(i)} & \delta_z^{(i)} \\ 0 & 0 & 0 & 1 \end{bmatrix} \tag{101}$$

In particular cases, the $i-$th displacement can be either just liner, or just angular. Encompassing all the elementary displacements between the local coordinate systems $\overset{*}{x}_T\overset{*}{y}_T\overset{*}{z}_T$ and $x_P y_P z_P$, the following equation for the computation of the matrix $\mathbf{Ds}(T/P)$ of the resultant displacements can be obtained

$$\mathbf{Ds}(T/P) = \prod_{i=1}^{n} \mathbf{ds}_i(ac_i \mapsto nom_i) \tag{102}$$

Here, ac_i and nom_i designate the actual and the nominal location of the $i-$th coordinate system.

When the operators $\mathbf{Rs}(\overset{*}{K}_T \mapsto K_P)$ and $\mathbf{Rs}(K_P \mapsto K_T)$ are known, then the displacement matrix $\mathbf{Ds}(T/P)$ can be expressed in terms of the operators $\mathbf{Rs}(\overset{*}{K}_T \mapsto K_P)$ and $\mathbf{Rs}(K_P \mapsto K_T)$ of the resultant coordinate systems transformations

$$\mathbf{Ds}(T/P) = \mathbf{Rs}(K_P \mapsto K_T) \cdot \mathbf{Rs}(\overset{*}{K}_T \mapsto K_P) \tag{103}$$

Ultimately, the displacement matrix $\mathbf{Ds}(P/T)$ can be expressed in terms of the elementary linear and angular displacements of the local coordinate system $\overset{*}{x}_T\overset{*}{y}_T\overset{*}{z}_T$ with respect to the desired location of the local coordinate system $x_T y_T z_T$

$$\mathbf{Ds}(P/T) = \begin{bmatrix} \cos\theta_{xx} & \cos\theta_{xy} & \cos\theta_{xz} & \delta_x \\ \cos\theta_{xy} & \cos\theta_{yy} & \cos\theta_{yz} & \delta_y \\ \cos\theta_{xz} & \cos\theta_{yz} & \cos\theta_{zz} & \delta_z \\ 0 & 0 & 0 & 1 \end{bmatrix} \tag{104}$$

For the inverse transformation, the displacement matrix $\mathbf{Ds}(P/T)$ can be used. The matrix $\mathbf{Ds}(P/T)$ can be either composed similar to the displacement matrix $\mathbf{Ds}(T/P)$ is composed [see Eq. (103)], or it can be computed from the formulae $\mathbf{Ds}(P/T) = \mathbf{Ds}^{-1}(T/P)$.

All the elements of the displacements matrix $\mathbf{Ds}(T/P)$ can be expressed in terms of the actual elementary displacements of all the elements that comprise the closed loop of the consequent coordinate systems transformations. The elementary displacements include (a) the linear and the angular displacements in all mechanical joints, (b) all the deflections caused by elasticity of material of the components involved into the closed loop of the consequent coordinate systems transformations, (c) all the thermal extensions of the components involved into the closed loop of the consequent coordinate systems transformations *etc.*

The displacements of the surface T with respect to the surface P are not known. Theoretically, components of all of the above listed matrices of the actual elementary displacements can be determined through the direct measurements of the system comprised of "*Work/NC machine tool/Cutting tool*". Actually, it is not practical to perform such complex measurements.

Under such scenario not the displacement matrix $\mathbf{Ds}(T/P)$ can be employed for the computation of the actual configuration of the generating surface T of the cutting tool with respect to the part surface P, but the tolerances matrix $\mathbf{Tl}(T/P)$ can be used instead. The tolerances matrix $\mathbf{Tl}(T/P)$ is composed similar to the displacements matrix $\mathbf{Ds}(T/P)$ is composed. The only difference is that not the elementary displacements $\mathbf{ds}_i(ac_i \mapsto nom_i)$ of the surface T with respect to the surface P are employed for the computations but the corresponding tolerances $\mathbf{tl}_i(ac_i \mapsto nom_i)$ are used instead

$$\mathbf{Tl}(T/P) = \prod_{i=1}^{n} \mathbf{tl}_i(ac_i \mapsto nom_i) \tag{105}$$

Based on the last statement, the following approximate equality

$$\mathbf{Ds}(T/P) \cong \mathbf{Tl}(T/P) \tag{106}$$

occur.

The required elementary tolerances for comprising of the tolerance matrix $\mathbf{Tl}(T/P)$ can be determined much easier. Therefore, if the displacements matrix $\mathbf{Ds}(T/P)$ is not known the tolerance matrix $\mathbf{Tl}(T/P)$ can be used instead.

The approximating torus surface Tr_T is associated with the local coordinate system $x_T^* y_T^* z_T^*$.

Once the displacements matrix $\mathbf{Ds}(T/P)$ is composed, then the equation $\mathbf{r}_{tr.T}(\theta_{tr.T}, \varphi_{tr.T})$ [see Eq. (90)] of the approximating torus surface Tr_T can be represented in the local coordinate system $x_P y_P z_P$

$$\mathbf{r}_{tr.T}^{(P)}(\theta_{tr.T}, \varphi_{tr.T}) = \mathbf{Ds}(T/P) \cdot \mathbf{r}_{tr.T}(\theta_{tr.T}, \varphi_{tr.T}) \tag{107}$$

Equation $\mathbf{r}_{tr.P}(\theta_{tr.P}, \varphi_{tr.P})$ of the approximating torus surface Tr_P is initially determined in the local coordinate system $x_P y_P z_P$. Equation (107) describes analytically the approximating torus surface Tr_T in that same local coordinate system $x_P y_P z_P$. This yields making a conclusion that the actual configuration of the torus surfaces Tr_P and Tr_T is determined.

Generally, the problem of the computation of the closest distance of approach between two smooth regular surfaces is a challenging one. For the purpose of computation of the deviation δ_P of the actual part surface P_{ac} with respect to the desired part surface P_{nom}, the problem under consideration can be reduced to the problem of computation of the *CDA* between two torus surfaces.

Consider the surfaces P and T that initially are given in a common coordinate system $X_{NC} Y_{NC} Z_{NC}$ (Figure 28) associated with the *NC* machine. The surfaces P and T are locally approximated by portions of torus surfaces Tr_P and Tr_T respectively.

The points K_P and K_T^* are chosen as the first guess points on the surfaces Tr_P and Tr_T. For the analysis below, it is convenient to re-label the points K_P and K_T^* to p_i and t_i correspondingly.

For a given configuration of the torus surfaces Tr_P and Tr_T, the *CDA* between these surfaces can be used as a first approximation to the *CDA* between the surfaces P and T themselves. The *CDA* between the torus surfaces Tr_P and Tr_T is measured along the common perpendicular to these surfaces. Unit normal vector $\mathbf{n}_{Tr.P}$ to the torus surface Tr_P is within a plane through the axis of rotation of the surface Tr_P.

For the computation of the *CDA* between the torus surfaces Tr_P and Tr_T (Figure 28) a recursive algorithm is developed. The cycle of the recursive computations is repeated as many times as it is necessary for making the deviation of the computation of the *CDA* between the surfaces P and T smaller then the maximal allowed value.

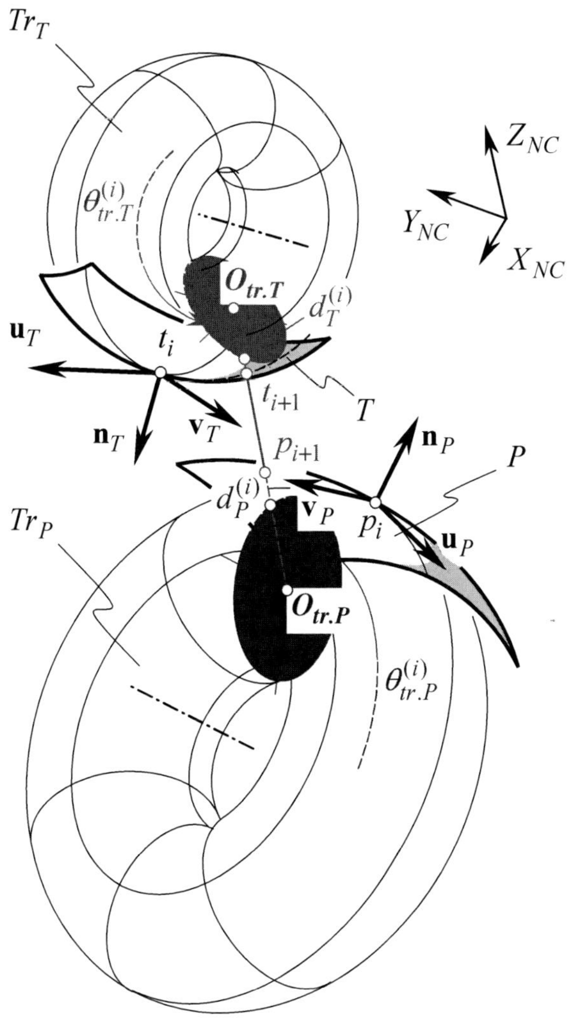

Figure 28. To the computation of the CDA of the surfaces P and T.

7.6. Efficient Ways for Increasing Accuracy of the Machined Sculptured Surface

The resultant deviation of the machined sculptured surface P_{ac} from the desired surface P_{nom} depends mostly upon two components. Height h_{Σ} of the residual cusps on the machined part surface is the first component. The deviation δ_P of the surfaces is the second component. Therefore, the resultant deviation δ_{Σ} of the machined part surface from the desired surface can be expressed by a simple formula

$$\delta_{\Sigma} = h_{\Sigma} + \delta_P \tag{108}$$

Both the components h_Σ and δ_Σ are necessary been reduced in order to increase the resultant accuracy of the machined part surface. However, the *DG*/*K*-based approach allows control only over the component h_Σ. As an example consider two possible way for the intensive increase of accuracy of the machined sculptured surface.

For the most intensive reduction of the resultant deviation h_Σ of the machined sculptured surface gradient of the function $h_\Sigma = h_\Sigma(R_{P.fr}, R_{P.ss}, R_{T.fr}, R_{T.ss}, \breve{F}_{fr}, \breve{F}_{ss}, \ldots)$ can be implemented. Following this approach, for the most intensive reduction of h_Σ the parameters of the machining operation alternating in compliance with the function $\mathbf{grad}\, h_\Sigma$.

Another way for the reduction of h_Σ is based on the following analysis. The resultant height of cusps h_Σ is a function of two elementary surface deviations, say it is a function of the height of waviness h_{fr} and of height of the elementary surface deviation h_{ss}. Various ratios between the feed-rate $|\mathbf{F}_{fr}|$ and the side-step $|\mathbf{F}_{ss}|$ results in different total cusps height h_Σ. It is naturally to assume that the resultant cusps height h_Σ is getting it minimal value under certain ratio between the feed-rate and the side-step. This ratio is referred to as the *optimal ratio* between the feed-rate and the side-step.

Maximal elementary surface deviation h_{ss} is smaller then the resultant tolerance $[h]$ on accuracy of the part surface. The deviation h_{ss} is equal to a portion of the tolerance $[h]$, say $h_{ss} = c \cdot [h]$. Here "c" designates the local parameter of distribution of the tolerance $[h]$. Actual value of the parameter c is within the interval $0 \le c \le 1$. At a current point of the surface P there exists the optimal value of the parameter c. Therefore, current value of the parameter c can be expressed in terms of Gaussian coordinates of the sculptured surface P, *i.e.* $c = c(U_P, V_P)$.

If it is assumed that $h_\Sigma = h_{fr} + h_{ss}$, then the equality $h_{fr} = (c-1)\cdot[h]$ is valid for the elementary deviation h_{fr}. Ultimately, the height of cusps h_Σ can be expressed as a function of the parameter c, say $h_\Sigma = h_\Sigma(c)$. When the parameter c is of optimal value, the following equality

$$\frac{\partial h_\Sigma(c)}{\partial c} = 0 \tag{109}$$

observes.

The condition [see Eq. (109)] is the necessary condition for the minimum of the function $h_\Sigma = h_\Sigma(c)$. In addition, the inequality

$$\frac{\partial^2 h_\Sigma(c)}{\partial c^2} > 0 \tag{110}$$

is required been observed.

For the computation, a computer code is developed [46] where an example of the results of the computations is available.

7.7. Principle of Superposition of the Elementary Deviations

Resultant cusps height h_{Σ} depends upon the two components namely of the waviness height h_{fr}, and of the elementary surface deviation h_{ss}. For simplicity, equation

$$h_{\Sigma} = h_{fr} + h_{ss} \tag{111}$$

is often used for this purpose. For more accurate computations, Eq. (88) is used instead.

All the approximate equations, say Eq. (111), as well as Eq. (88) and Eq. (89) are derived on the premises of the principle of superposition of the elementary surface deviations. Actually, implementation of the principle of superposition is valid only for linear functions. Analysis of the earlier derived Eq. (99) for the computation of the elementary deviation h_{fr} and of Eq. (95) for the computation of the elementary deviation h_{ss} reveals that the functions $h_{fr} = h_{fr}(R_{P.fr}, R_{T.fr}, \breve{F}_{fr}, \ldots)$ and $h_{ss} = h_{ss}(R_{P.ss}, R_{T.ss}, \breve{F}_{ss}, \ldots)$ are the substantionally non-linear functions. In this concern, the question "*Under which conditions implementation of the principle of superposition of the elementary surface deviations is valid*?" naturally arises.

In order to answer this practical question, comparison of results of computation of the resultant cusps height that are performed using Eq. (111) [or using more general Eq. (88)] with the results of precise computations is vital.

The above analysis allows making the final conclusion with respect to the principle of superposition of the elementary surface deviations: *Principle of superposition of the elementary surface deviations* h_{fr} *and* h_{ss} *is valid if and only if the inequality* $\tilde{h}_{\Sigma} - h_{\Sigma} \leq [\Delta h_{\Sigma}]$ *observes.*

Here, $[\Delta h_{\Sigma}]$ designates the tolerance on accuracy of computation of height of the resultant cusps.

8. Optimal Sculptured Surface Machining

Machining of the part surface in the most economical way is the main goal when designing a manufacturing process [23], [24], [43]. Selection of appropriate criterion of optimization is critical for the implementation of the *DG/K*-method of surface generation.

8.1. Criteria of the Optimization

In order to solve the problem of designing of the most efficient machining of a sculptured surface an appropriate criterion of optimization is necessary.

Various criteria of optimization are used in industry for the optimization of parameters of surface machining.

Productivity of surface machining and productivity of surface generation are the important criteria of the optimization. Highest productivity of machining of sculptured surface causes shortest machining time. Because of high cost of multi-axis *N*C machine, the economical conditions of sculptured surface machining are those ensuring shortest machining time.

In sculptured surface machining three aspects of the surface generation process are distinguished. They are: (a) the local surface generation, (b) the regional surface generation, and (c) the global surface generation [23], [24], [43].

The local analysis of the part surface generation encompasses generation of the surface P just in differential vicinity of the point K of contact of the part surface P and of the generating surface T of the cutting tool. Generation of the part surface within a single tool-path is investigated from prospective of the regional surface generation. Ultimately, partial interference of the neighboring tool-paths coordinates of the start-point for the surface machining, and impact of shape of the contour of the surface P patch are investigated from prospective of the global surface generation. Consequently, three kinds of productivity of surface machining are distinguished. They are (a) local productivity of surface generation, (b) regional productivity of surface generation, and (c) global productivity of surface generation.

When machining a sculptured surface all major parameters of the machining operation vary in time. This makes reasonable consideration of instantaneous (current) values of the surface generation process.

Instantaneous productivity of surface generation $P_{sg}(t)$ is determined by current values of the feed-rate $\breve{F}_{fr} = |\mathbf{F}_{fr}|$ and of the side-step $\breve{F}_{ss} = |\mathbf{F}_{ss}|$ (here t designates time). Usually, the vector $\mathbf{F}_{fr}$ and the vector $\mathbf{F}_{ss}$ are orthogonal to each other ($\mathbf{F}_{fr} \perp \mathbf{F}_{ss}$). In general case, the vectors $\mathbf{F}_{fr}$ and $\mathbf{F}_{ss}$ are at a certain angle θ to each other.

Instantaneous productivity of surface generation can be computed by the formula [25], [26]

$$P\ (t) = |\mathbf{F}_{fr} \times \mathbf{F}_{ss}| \tag{112}$$

Equation (112) casts into [25], [26]

$$P\ (t) = \breve{F}_{fr} \cdot \breve{F}_{ss} \cdot \sin\theta \tag{113}$$

Equations (112) and (113) reveal that increase of the feed-rate $\breve{F}_{fr}$, as well as increase of the side-step $\breve{F}_{ss}$ lead to increase of the instantaneous productivity of surface generation $P\ (t)$. Deviation of the angle θ from $\theta = 90^\circ$ results in corresponding reduction of the instantaneous productivity of surface generation $P\ (t)$.

When machining a part surface, the rate of increase of the machined surface area reflects the surface generation output. It is easy to conclude that productivity of surface generation

P_{sg} depends on coordinates of the current point of contact K on both the surfaces P and T, on the angle μ of the surfaces P and T local relative orientation, and on the direction of the relative motion of the surfaces P and T at the point K

$$P_{sg} = P_{sg}(U_P, V_P, U_T, V_T, \mu, \varphi) \tag{114}$$

The mean surface generation output $\tilde{P}_{sg}$ can be analytically expressed by the formula

$$\tilde{P}_{sg} = \frac{S_{sg}}{t_\Sigma} \tag{115}$$

where S_{sg} designate the machined part surface area.

Instantaneous surface generation output P_{sg} is another characteristic of surface machining performance. By definition, the instantaneous surface generation output P_{sg} is equal

$$P_{sg} = \frac{d\,S_{sg}}{dt} \tag{116}$$

Mean chip-removal output is used for the analysis of efficiency of a machining operation in global, say for the whole part surface P. The mean chip-removal output $\tilde{P}_{mr}$ can be used as an index. By definition, it is equal

$$\tilde{P}_{mr} = \frac{V_{mr}}{t_\Sigma} \tag{117}$$

Here, in Eq. (117) is designated

V_{mr}	total volume of the stock to be removed
t_Σ	total time required for the stock removal

For the local analysis of efficiency of a machining operation, instantaneous chip-removal output is used. The instantaneous chip-removal output P_{mr} also can be used as an index. By definition, it is equal

$$P_{mr}(t) = \frac{d\,v_{mr}}{d\,t} \tag{118}$$

When a sculptured surface P and the generating surface T of the cutting tool are in point contact with each other, maximal allowed displacements of the cutting tool are constrained by the corresponding limit values $[\breve{F}_{fr}]$ and $[\breve{F}_{ss}]$. These limits specify in much parameters of the elementary surface cell on the machined part surface.

The limit values $[\breve{F}_{fr}]$ and $[\breve{F}_{ss}]$ of the cutting tool displacements $\breve{F}_{fr}$ and $\breve{F}_{ss}$ can be computed. For this purpose the tolerance $[h]$ on accuracy of surface machining has been taken into consideration.

Milling cutters are widely used for machining of sculptured surfaces on multi-axis *NC* machines. Use of milling cutters causes waviness of the machined surface P. It is required to keep the waviness height h_{fr} under the corresponding portion $[h_{fr}]$ of the total tolerance $[h]$. The limit feed-rate displacement $[\breve{F}_{fr}]$ strongly depends on the allowed value of the partial tolerance $[h_{fr}]$.

For the computation of the instantaneous value of the feed-rate $[\breve{F}_{fr}]$ per tooth of the cutting tool the approximate formulae [23], [24], [43], [44]

$$[\breve{F}_{fr}] \cong 2R_{P.fr} \arccos \frac{R^2_{P.fr} + R_{T.fr} \cdot (R_{P.fr} + [h_{fr}] \cdot \operatorname{sgn} R_{P.fr})}{(R_{P.fr} + R_{T.fr}) \cdot (R_{P.fr} + [h_{fr}] \cdot \operatorname{sgn} R_{P.fr})} \tag{119}$$

can be used. Equations (92) and (93) are used here for the computation of the radii of normal curvatures $R_{P.fr}$ and $R_{T.fr}$. It is assumed in this equation that the inequality $\breve{F}_{fr} << R_{P.fr}$ is valid, and therefore $\breve{F}_{fr} \cong AB = F_{fr}$. It is assumed also that $[h_{fr}]^2$ is a reasonably small value, and therefore it can be omitted from further analysis.

In the most practical cases, the feed-step displacement $\breve{F}_{ss}$ affects the surface generation output P_{sg} the most. Computation of the limit side-step displacement $[\breve{F}_{ss}]$ is similar in much to the computation of the limit feed-rate displacement $[\breve{F}_{fr}]$. Without going into details of derivation of equations, it is allowed in this case just to rewrite the equation

$$[\breve{F}_{ss}] \cong 2R_{P.ss} \arccos \frac{R^2_{P.ss} + R_{T.ss} \cdot (R_{P.ss} + [h_{ss}] \cdot \operatorname{sgn} R_{P.ss})}{(R_{P.ss} + R_{T.ss}) \cdot (R_{P.ss} + [h_{ss}] \cdot \operatorname{sgn} R_{P.ss})} \tag{120}$$

for the computation of the limit side-step displacement $[\breve{F}_{ss}]$. This equation is derived in the way similar to the way Eq. (119) has been derived. Equations (96) and (97) are used here for the computation of the radii of normal curvatures $R_{P.ss}$ and $R_{T.ss}$.

Greatest part surface area coverage is an important output when machining a sculptured surface on multi-axis *NC* machine. Determining of conditions under which the productivity of surface generation is maximal is a critical issue in sculptured surface machining. Use of the *DG/K*-method of surface generation enables an analytical solution to this challenging engineering problem.

The productivity of surface generation $P_{sg}^{\max}$ reaches its maximal rate if and only if the instantaneous productivity of surface generation $P_{sg}^{\max}(t)$ is maximal at every point of contact K of the surfaces P and T. For the computation of conditions of the maximal instantaneous productivity of surface generation, the modified equation

$$P_{sg}^{\max}(t) = [\breve{F}_{fr}]\cdot[\breve{F}_{ss}]\cdot\sin\theta \tag{121}$$

can be used.

As it follows from Eq. (121), in order to increase the instantaneous surface generation output $P_{sg}^{\max}(t)$, the feed-rate displacement $\breve{F}_{fr}$ as well as the side-step displacement $\breve{F}_{ss}$ are required been of maximal rate at every point K of contact of the surfaces P and T.

The performed analysis reveals that width of the limit side-step shift increases when the rate of conformity of the surface T to the surface P is getting greater. The similar conclusion can be derived with respect to the limit feed-rate shift $[\breve{F}_{fr}]$.

Because of the instantaneous productivity of surface generation $P_{sg}^{\max}(t)$ is a function of the limit feed-rate shift $[\breve{F}_{fr}]$ and of the limit side-step shift $[\breve{F}_{ss}]$, this statement immediately yields a conclusion: *The bigger the rate of conformity of the generating surface T of the cutting tool to the sculptured surface P, the bigger instantaneous productivity of surface generation $P_{sg}^{\max}(t)$.*

It can be proven analytically, that the function $P_{sg}^{\max}(t)$ is a kind of functions of conformity of two smooth regular surfaces. All functions of conformity have extremes under the same values of the input arguments. Therefore, not just the function $P_{sg}^{\max}(t)$ can be used for solving the problem of synthesis of optimal machining operations, but any corresponding function of conformity of the surfaces P and T can be used instead. For example, the function $P_{sg}^{\max}(t)$ of the instantaneous productivity of surface generation can be substituted with the indicatrix of conformity $Cnf_R(P/T)$ of the surfaces P and T at the point K. Such the substitution is reasonable because the analytical expression for the indicatrix of conformity $Cnf_R(P/T)$ is simpler compare to the analytical expression for the function $P_{sg}^{\max}(t)$. The indicatrix of conformity $Cnf_R(P/T)$ can be considered as a kind of geometrical analogue of the instantaneous productivity $P_{sg}^{\max}(t)$ of surface generation.

8.2. Synthesis of Optimal Operations of Sculptured Surface Machining

Synthesis of optimal surface machining operation means here development of a procedure of computation of the optimal parameters of a surface machining operation.

Solution to the problem of synthesizing of optimal surface machining operation can be solved in three consequent steps. The local surface generation is synthesized on the first step.

Then, on the second step, the regional synthesis is performed on the premises of the results of the computations obtained on the first step. Ultimately, solution to the problem of the global synthesis of optimal surface machining operation is derived on the final third step.

Local surface generation is considering just within an elementary surface cell on the machined part surface.

For the illustration purposes, indicatrix of conformity of the sculptured surface and of the generating surface of the cutting tool is used below as a geometric analogue of the criterion of optimization. Chip removal output, productivity of surface generation or an economical criterion of optimization can be used for this purpose as well.

For the analytical representation of the indicatrix of conformity $Cnf_R(P/T)$ of two smooth regular surfaces P and T Eq. (60) is used. Equation (60) yields a generalized form for the diameter d_{cnf} of the indicatrix of conformity $Cnf_R(P/T)$

$$d_{cnf} = d_{cnf}(U_P, V_P, U_T, V_T, \mu, \varphi) \tag{122}$$

For a point within the generating surface T of the cutting tool being capable of making optimal contact with the part surface P at the selected point of interest, the necessary conditions of contact

$$\frac{\partial d_{cnf}}{\partial U_T} = 0 \text{ and } \frac{\partial d_{cnf}}{\partial V_T} = 0 \tag{123}$$

have to be satisfied.

In addition to the necessary conditions [Eqs. (123)], the sufficient conditions for the $d_{cnf}^{\min}$

$$\begin{vmatrix} \dfrac{\partial^2 d_{cnf}}{\partial U_T^2} & \dfrac{\partial^2 d_{cnf}}{\partial U_T \partial V_T} \\ \dfrac{\partial^2 d_{cnf}}{\partial U_T \partial V_T} & \dfrac{\partial^2 d_{cnf}}{\partial V_T^2} \end{vmatrix} > 0 \text{ and } \frac{\partial^2 d_{cnf}}{\partial U_T^2} > 0 \tag{124}$$

are required been satisfied as well.

Solution to the set of two Eqs. (123) under the conditions [see Eqs. (124)] returns Gaussian coordinates U_T^{opt} and V_T^{opt} of the optimal point K_T within the generating surface T of the cutting tool.

For the highest possible productivity of surface generation, it is necessary that at the point of interest K_P, the generation surface T of the cutting tool contacts the part surfaces P with its optimal point K_T. Once the points K_P and K_T are snapped together, further their designation is substituted with K (*i.e.* $K_P \equiv K_T \equiv K$).

Point contact of surfaces imposes strong restrictions on feasible motions of the surface T relative to the surface P. The only motion is allowed for the surfaces P and T while they are in contact at the fixed point K. Depends upon parameters of the actual surfaces P and T

at the point K, the cutting tool surface T is allowed either to rotate about the common unit normal vector $\mathbf{n}_P$, or just to turn through a certain angle about this unit normal unit vector. No other relative motions are feasible for the surfaces P and T in the case under consideration.

Current configuration of the surfaces P and T at the *CC*-point is specified by the angle μ of their local relative orientation. Equation (122) is helpful for the computation of the optimal value μ^{opt} of the angle of the surfaces P and T local relative orientation. The angle μ^{opt} can be computed as a solution to the equation

$$\frac{\partial d_{cnf}}{\partial \mu} = 0 \tag{125}$$

The computed solution to Eq. (125) must satisfy the sufficient condition

$$\frac{\partial^2 d_{cnf}}{\partial \mu^2} > 0 \tag{126}$$

for the minimal of $d_{cnf}^{\min}$.

Solution to Eq. (125) under the condition [see Eq. (126)] specifies the optimal local configuration of the cutting tool with respect to the part surface being machining. In compliance with the derived solution, the cutting tool is required been turned about the unit normal vector $\mathbf{n}_P$ through a certain angle to its optimal configuration relative the surface P that is specified by the computed angle μ^{opt}.

Direction along which current diameter d_{cnf} is measured makes a certain angle φ with the first principal direction $\mathbf{t}_{1.P}$ of the sculptured surface P. For the minimal diameter $d_{cnf}^{\min}$, the equality

$$\frac{\partial d_{cnf}}{\partial \varphi} = 0 \tag{127}$$

is satisfied. Here, for Eq. (127), the sufficient condition for the maximum of the diameter $d_{cnf}^{\min}$

$$\frac{\partial^2 d_{cnf}}{\partial \varphi^2} > 0 \tag{128}$$

also observes.

Solution to Eq. (127) under condition [see Eq. (128)] returns the optimal value φ^{opt} of the angle φ.

Vector $\mathbf{F}_{fr}$ of the cutting tool feed-rate motion is at the angle $\xi^{opt} = \varphi^{opt} + 90°$. Ultimately, the computed angle ξ^{opt} specifies the optimal direction of the instant motion of the cutting tool relative the work. The vector $\mathbf{F}_{fr}$ also defines the direction at which the point K travels over the generating surface of the cutting tool.

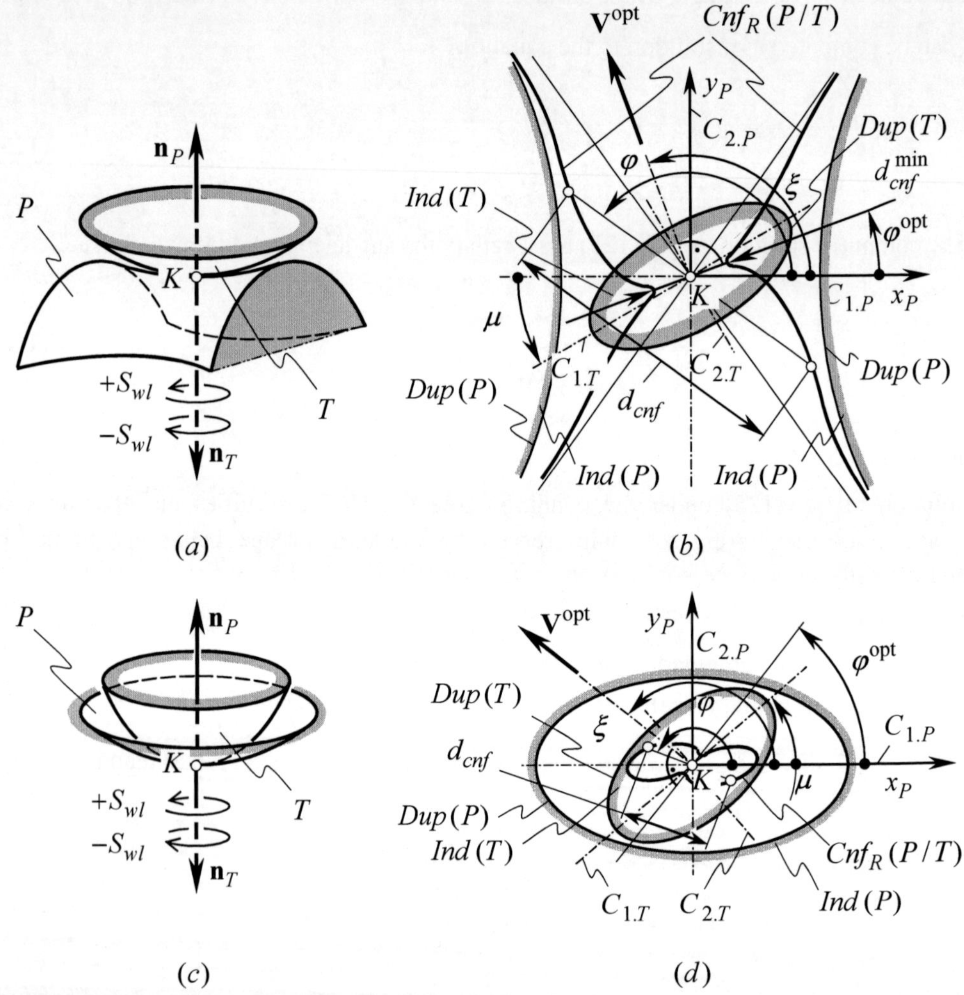

Figure 29. Two examples of the solutions to the problem of synthesis of local sculptured surface generation.

Two examples in Figure 29 illustrate the results of solutions to the problem of synthesis of local surface generation.

When a saddle-like local patch of the sculptured surface P is machined with the convex portion of the generating surface T of the cutting tool (Figure 29,a), solution to the problem of synthesis of local surface generation is shown in Figure 29,b. Here, the minimal diameter d_{cnf}^{min} of the indicatrix of conformity $Cnf_R(P/T)$ is at the optimal angle φ^{opt} to the first principal cross-section $C_{1.P}$ of the surface P at the point K. Optimal direction of the vector $\mathbf{V}^{\text{opt}}$ of the surfaces P and T relative motion makes the angle $\xi^{\text{opt}} = \varphi^{\text{opt}} + 90^{\circ}$ with the first principal direction $\mathbf{t}_{1.P}$. The vector $\mathbf{V}^{\text{opt}}$ is identical to the vector $\mathbf{F}_{fr}^{\text{opt}}$ of the optimal feed-rate motion of the cutting tool ($\mathbf{V}^{\text{opt}} \equiv \mathbf{F}_{fr}^{\text{opt}}$).

Similarly, when a convex local patch of the sculptured surface P is machined with the convex portion of the generating surface T of the cutting tool (Figure 29,c), solution to the problem of synthesis of local surface generation is shown in Figure 29,d. Optimal direction of the vector $\mathbf{V}^{\text{opt}}$ of the surfaces P and T relative motion makes the angle $\xi^{\text{opt}} = \varphi^{\text{opt}} + 90^{\circ}$ with the first principal cross-section $C_{1.P}$.

When solving a problem of synthesis of local surface generation some peculiarities could observe.

Particular cases of contact of the surfaces P and T could observe when solving the problem of synthesis of local surface generation. One such a problem is caused by a possibility of two alternative optimal configurations of the cutting tool which actually are equivalent to each other. An example of two equivalent optimal configurations of the cutting tool is depicted in Figure 30.

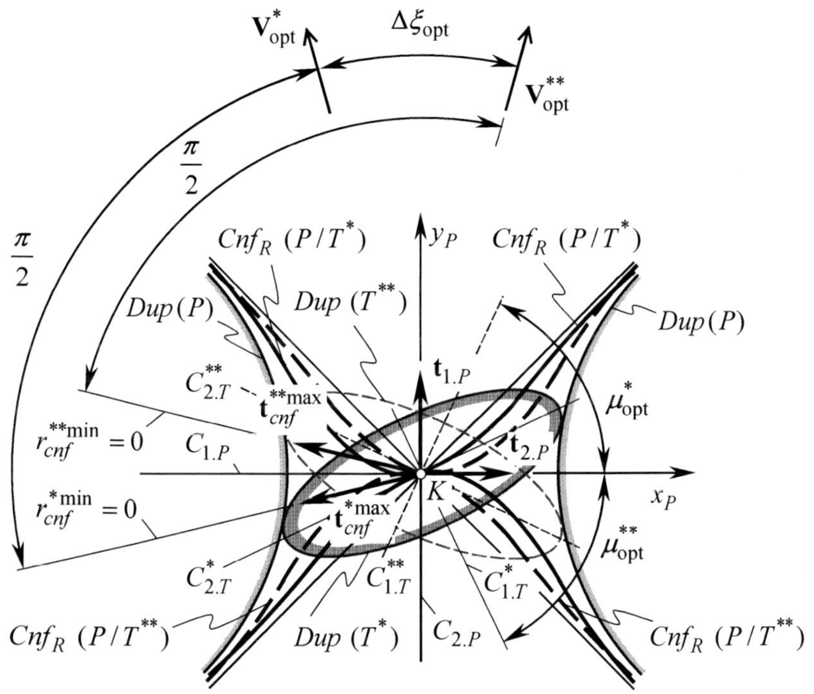

Figure 30. An example of alternative configurations of the cutting tool.

The example in Figure 30 relates to generation of the saddle-like local portion of the sculptured surface P with the convex portion of the generating surface T of the cutting tool.

Minimal radius of the indicatrix of conformity $Cnf_R(P/T^*)$ of the surface P and the cutting tool surface in it first optimal configuration T^* is equal to zero ($r_{cnf}^{*\min} = 0$). The first principal plane-section $C_{1.T}^*$ of the cutting tool surface T^* is at the optimal angle μ_{opt}^* of the surfaces P and T^* local relative orientation. Vector $\mathbf{V}_{\text{opt}}^*$ of the optimal direction of motion of the generating surface T^* of the cutting tool relative the part surface P is orthogonal to the direction along which the minimal radius $r_{cnf}^{*\min}$ of the indicatrix of conformity $Cnf_R(P/T^*)$ is measured. This direction is the direction of maximal rate of conformity of the generating surface of the cutting tool to the sculptured part surface. It is labeled as $\mathbf{t}_{cnf}^{*\max}$.

On another hand, that same saddle-like local portion of the sculptured surface P can be generated with that same convex portion of the generating surface T of the cutting tool under the different configuration of the cutting tool. Minimal radius of the indicatrix of conformity $Cnf_R(P/T^{**})$ of the surface P and the cutting tool surface T^{**} in it second optimal configuration is also equal to zero ($r_{cnf}^{**\min} = 0$). The first principal plane-section $C_{1.T}^{**}$ of the cutting tool surface T^{**} is at the optimal angle μ_{opt}^{**} of the surfaces P and T^{**} local relative orientation. Vector $\mathbf{V}_{\text{opt}}^{**}$ of the optimal direction of motion of the generating surface T^{**} of the cutting tool relative the part surface P is orthogonal to the direction along which the minimal radius $r_{cnf}^{**\min}$ of the indicatrix of conformity $Cnf_R(P/T^{**})$ is measured. This direction is the direction of maximal rate of conformity of the generating surface of the cutting tool to the sculptured part surface. It is labeled as $\mathbf{t}_{cnf}^{**\max}$.

Ultimately, Figure 30 reveals that two optimal directions of the cutting tool relative motion are feasible. The first optimal direction $\mathbf{V}_{\text{opt}}^*$ is specified by the angle $\xi_{\text{opt}}^* = \varphi_{\text{opt}}^* + 90^\circ$. The second optimal direction $\mathbf{V}_{\text{opt}}^{**}$ is specified by the angle $\xi_{\text{opt}}^{**} = \varphi_{\text{opt}}^{**} + 90^\circ$. Due to lack of space, the angles ξ_{opt}^*, φ_{opt}^* and ξ_{opt}^{**}, $\varphi_{\text{opt}}^{**}$ are not depicted in Figure 30. The directions $\mathbf{V}_{\text{opt}}^*$ and $\mathbf{V}_{\text{opt}}^{**}$ are at a certain angle $\Delta\xi_{\text{opt}}$ to each other.

Problems of this sort can be easily solved by implementation of the *DG*/*K*-base method of surface generation.

The derived solution to the problem of synthesis of optimal local surface generation returns the optimal parameters of surface generation process that is valid just within a surface cell on the machined part surface. This solution is the key input for the synthesis of optimal regional surface generation. Synthesis of the optimal regional surface generation is targeting solution to the problem of the most efficient generation along a tool-path on a sculptured surface.

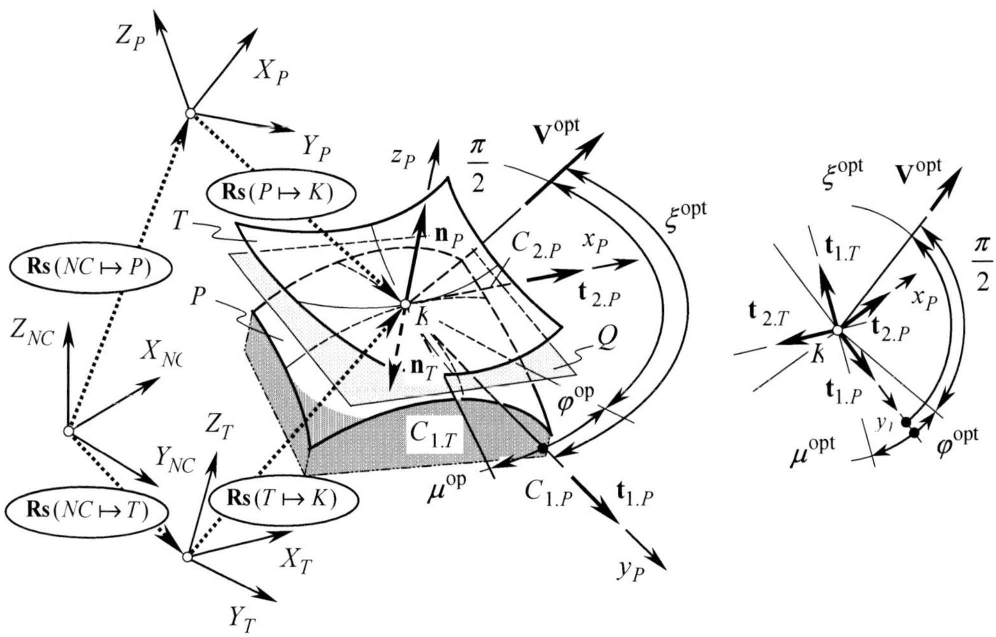

Figure 31. Configuration and relative motion of the surfaces P and T in the Cartesian coordinate system $X_{NC}Y_{NC}Z_{NC}$ associated with the multi-axis NC machine.

Consider generation of a sculptured surface P with the generating surface T of the form cutting tool (Figure 31). At a given *CC*-point K within the part surfaces P, Gaussian coordinates U_T and V_T of the point of contact within the generating surface T of the cutting tool are of optimal values U_T^{opt} and V_T^{opt}. The optimal angle μ^{opt} of the surfaces P and T local relative orientation is measured between the principal directions $\mathbf{t}_{1.P}$ and $\mathbf{t}_{1.T}$. The direction of minimal value of the diameter $d_{cnf}^{\min}$ of the characteristic curve $Cnf_R(P/T)$ is at the angle φ^{opt} with respect to the principal direction $\mathbf{t}_{1.P}$. The optimal direction of traveling of the cutting tool over the sculptured surface P is specified by the angle $\xi^{\text{opt}} = \varphi^{\text{opt}} + 90°$.

Local Cartesian coordinate system $x_P y_P z_P$ is associated with part surface P.

In the local coordinate system $x_P y_P z_P$, vector $\mathbf{V}^{\text{opt}}$ of the optimal direction of the cutter travel relative the surface P can be expressed in matrix form

$$\mathbf{V}^{\text{opt}} = \begin{bmatrix} \sin \xi^{\text{opt}} \\ \cos \xi^{\text{opt}} \\ 0 \\ 1 \end{bmatrix} \tag{129}$$

Use of the operator $\mathbf{Rs}(K \mapsto NC)$ allows representation of the vector $\mathbf{V}^{\text{opt}}$ in the coordinate system $X_{NC}Y_{NC}Z_{NC}$:

$$\mathbf{V}_{NC}^{\text{opt}} = \mathbf{Rs}(K \mapsto NC) \cdot \mathbf{V}^{\text{opt}} = \begin{bmatrix} \left(\frac{\partial x_P}{\partial U_P}(t) \cos \varphi^{\text{opt}}(t) - \frac{\partial x_P}{\partial V_P}(t) \sin \varphi^{\text{opt}}(t) \right) \\ \left(\frac{\partial y_P}{\partial U_P}(t) \cos \varphi^{\text{opt}}(t) - \frac{\partial y_P}{\partial V_P}(t) \sin \varphi^{\text{opt}}(t) \right) \\ \left(\frac{\partial z_P}{\partial U_P}(t) \cos \varphi^{\text{opt}}(t) - \frac{\partial z_P}{\partial V_P}(t) \sin \varphi^{\text{opt}}(t) \right) \\ 1 \end{bmatrix} \tag{130}$$

Finally, the closed form solution to the problem of the optimal tool-paths[21] can be represented in the form [12], [23], [24], [43]:

$$[\mathbf{r}_{tp}^{\text{opt}}](t) = \begin{bmatrix} \int_{t_1}^{t_2} \left(\frac{\partial X_P}{\partial U_P}(t) \cos \varphi^{\text{opt}}(t) - \frac{\partial X_P}{\partial V_P}(t) \sin \varphi^{\text{opt}}(t) \right) \cdot dt \\ \int_{t_1}^{t_2} \left(\frac{\partial Y_P}{\partial U_P}(t) \cos \varphi^{\text{opt}}(t) - \frac{\partial Y_P}{\partial V_P}(t) \sin \varphi^{\text{opt}}(t) \right) \cdot dt \\ \int_{t_1}^{t_2} \left(\frac{\partial Z_P}{\partial U_P}(t) \cos \varphi^{\text{opt}}(t) - \frac{\partial Z_P}{\partial V_P}(t) \sin \varphi^{\text{opt}}(t) \right) \cdot dt \\ 1 \end{bmatrix} \tag{131}$$

At a current *CC*-point, the maximal allowed speed of travel of the cutting tool along the optimal tool-path is restricted by the limit value of the feed-rate per tooth $[\breve{F}_{fr}]$ of the cutting tool. From the prospective of just geometrical and kinematical consideration, the maximal speed of the cutting tool travel is bigger when concave portion of the surface P is machining, and it is smaller when machining a convex portion of the surface P. However, when the chip removal output is included into consideration, the maximal speed of the cutting tool travel is smaller when concave portion of the surface P is machining, and it is bigger when machining a convex portion of the surface P.

In some particular cases of sculptured surface generation, equation for the optimal tool-paths simplifies to the differential equation

[21]The author would like to mention here that many proficient researchers came up with the decision that no closed-form-solution to the problem of optimal tool-paths is feasible at all.

$$[\mathbf{r}_{tp}^{\text{opt}}] \;\Rightarrow\; \begin{vmatrix} E_P\, dU_P + F_P\, dV_P & F_P\, dU_P + G_P\, dV_P \\ L_P\, dU_P + M_P\, dV_P & M_P\, dU_P + N_P\, dV_P \end{vmatrix} = 0 \tag{132}$$

Equation (132) for the optimal tool-paths is applicable, for instance, when machining a sculptured surface P either with a ball-end milling cutter, or with a flat-end milling cutter, *etc.* Under such scenario, the angle μ of the surfaces P and T local relative orientation vanishes. It is getting indefinite: no principal directions can be identified neither on a sphere, nor on the plane surface. Therefore, the optimal tool-paths align with lines of curvature on the surface P.

When machining a part surface, coordinate system $X_T Y_T Z_T$ that is associated with the cutting tool, is rotating like a rigid body. This rotation is performing about a certain instant axis of rotation. Angular velocity of the rotation of the coordinate system $X_T Y_T Z_T$ is equal to $|\mathbf{\Omega}| = \sqrt{k_{tp}^2 + \tau_{tp}^2}$. The axis of instant rotation aligns with the Darboux's vector $\mathbf{\Omega} = k_{tp}\,\mathbf{t}_{tp} + \tau_{tp}\,\mathbf{b}_{tp}$ (here k_{tp} and τ_{tp} denote curvature and torsion of the trajectory of *CC*-point, and $\mathbf{t}_{tp}$ and $\mathbf{b}_{tp}$ is the unit tangent vector and the bi-normal vector to the trajectory of *CC*-point at a current point K). The Darboux's vector is located in the rectifying plane to the trajectory of *CC*-point. It can be expressed in terms of the normal vector $\mathbf{n}_{tp}$ and of the tangent vector $\mathbf{t}_{tp}$ to the trajectory of *CC*-point

$$\mathbf{\Omega} = \sqrt{k_{tp}^2 + \tau_{tp}^2}\,(\mathbf{t}_{tp}\cos\theta + \mathbf{n}_{tp}\sin\theta) \tag{133}$$

where θ is the angle that make the Darboux's vector $\mathbf{\Omega}$ and the tangent vector $\mathbf{t}_{tp}$ to the trajectory at *CC*-point.

It is instructive to note, that velocity $|\mathbf{\Omega}|$ is a function of full curvature of the trajectory of *CC*-point.

Synthesis of optimal global surface generation is the final sub-problem of the general problem of synthesis of optimal surface generation. Solution to the problem of optimal global surface generation is based in much on the derived solutions to the problems of optimal local and of optimal regional surface generation.

Minimal machining time is the major goal of the problem of synthesis of optimal global surface generation. In order to solve the problem under consideration, it is necessary:

(a) To minimize interference of the neighboring tool-paths of the cutting tool over the part surface being machining
(b) To determine the optimal parameters of entering of the cutting tool into contact with the part surface, and of its departing from the contact. This sub-problem is referred to as the *boundary problem* of surface generation, and
(c) To determine location of the optimal start-point of the surface machining.

The sub-problems (a) through (c) are discussed below.

The machined sculptured surface actually is represented as a set of tool-paths that cover the nominal surface P. At a current surface point, width of the tool-path is equal to the side-step $\breve{F}_{ss}$ computed at that same *CC*-point. The tool-path width is varying along the trajectory of the *CC*-point over the sculptured surface, as well as across the trajectory. Because of this, neighboring tool-paths partially interfere into each other. Ultimately, some portions of the part surface P are double-covered by the tool-paths. Partial interference of the neighboring tool-paths causes reduction of the surface generation output. For the synthesis of optimal surface generation operation the interference of the neighboring tool-paths is required been minimized.

Trajectory of the *CC*-point over the sculptured surface is a $3D$ curve. For the analysis below it is convenient to operate with the natural parameterization of the trajectory: $l_{tr} = l_{tr}(r_{tr}, \tau_{tr})$. Here, length l_{tr} of arc of the trajectory measured from a certain point within the trajectory. The length l_{tr} is expressed in terms of radius of curvature r_{tr} at a current trajectory point, and of torsion τ_{tr} of the trajectory at that same point.

At the current *CC*-point, the tool-path width can be expressed in terms of length of the $i-$th trajectory

$$\breve{F}_{ss}^{(i)} = \breve{F}_{ss}^{(i)}[l_{tr}^{(i)}] \tag{134}$$

During the time dt, the cutting tool travels along the $i-$th trajectory at a distance dl_{th}. A sculptured surface portion

$$dS_{tr}^{(i)} = \breve{F}_{ss}^{(i)}[l_{tr}^{(i)}] \cdot dt \tag{135}$$

is generated in this motion of the cutting tool.

Area of a single $i-$th tool-path is equal

$$S_{tr}^{(i)} = \int_{[l_{tr}^{(i)}]} \breve{F}_{ss}^{(i)}[l_{tr}^{(i)}] \cdot dt \tag{136}$$

Total area of all the tool-paths can be computed from the formula

$$S_{tr} = \sum_{i=1}^{n} S_{tr}^{(i)} = \sum_{i=1}^{n} \int_{[l_{tr}^{(i)}]} \breve{F}_{ss}^{(i)}[l_{tr}^{(i)}] \cdot dt \tag{137}$$

Here n denotes the total number of tool-paths that are necessary to cover the entire part surface.

Due to partial interference of the neighboring tool-paths, the total area S_{tr} exceeds the area S_{sg} of the actually generated part surface P, *i.e.* the inequality $S_{tr} > S_{sg}$ always observes. The rate of interference of the neighboring tool-paths is evaluated by the coefficient of interference K_{int}

$$K_{\text{int}} = \frac{S_{tr} - S_{sg}}{S_{sg}} = \frac{\sum_{i=1}^{n} \int_{[l_{tr}^{(i)}]} \breve{F}_{ss}^{(i)}[l_{tr}^{(i)}] \cdot dt - S_{sg}}{S_{sg}} \tag{138}$$

Coefficient of interference K_{int} is a function: (a) of design parameters of the part surface being machining, (b) of design parameters of the generating surface of the cutting tool, and (c) of parameters of kinematics of the surface machining operation. So, it can be minimized ($K_{\text{int}} \to \min$) using for this purpose conventional methods of minimization of analytical functions.

Generation of a part surface within the area next to the surface border differs from that when machining of boundless surface is investigated. Shape and parameters of the surface contour affects the efficiency of surface generation process. Prior to search for a solution to the boundary problem, it is necessary to determine the part surface region within which the boundary effect is significant.

The part surface region within which the impact of the boundary effect is significant. Consider a sculpture surface P having tolerance $[h]$ on accuracy of the surface machining. The surface of tolerance $S_{[h]}$ is at the distance $[h]$ from the surface P. The actual machined part surface is located within the surfaces P and $S_{[h]}$.

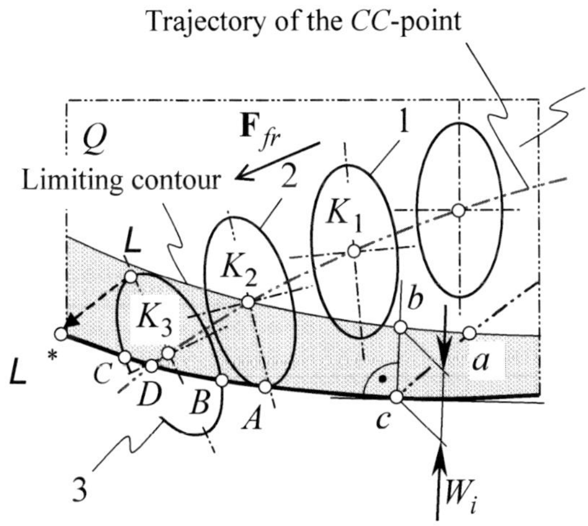

Figure 32. On boundary effect when machining a sculptured surface P.

The generating surface T of the cutting tool is contacting the nominal part surface P at a certain point K_1 (Figure 32). The surface T intersects the surface of tolerance $S_{[h]}$. The line 1 of intersection of the surfaces $S_{[h]}$ and T is a kind of a closed ellipse-like curve. The curve has no common points with the part surface boundary. Therefore, no boundary effect observes in this location of the cutting tool.

At the point K_2 within the trajectory of *CC*-point the cutting tool surface T also intersects the surface of tolerance $S_{[h]}$. The line 2 of intersection is also a kind of closed ellipse-like curve. However, in this location of the cutting tool the curve 2 make tangency with the part surface boundary at the point A. This indicates that starting at the point K_2, the boundary affects the efficiency of surface generation. The impact of the boundary is getting stronger toward the point D on the part surface boundary curve.

At a certain point K_3 of the trajectory of *CC*-point the line of intersection 3 of the surfaces $S_{[h]}$ and T is not a closed line. It intersects the part surface boundary at the points B and C.

Departing of the cutting tool from the interaction with the surface P is over when the limit point L on the biggest diameter of the curve 3 reaches the part surface boundary curve at the point L^*.

The point K_2 is constructed for the point A of the part surface boundary curve. For every point A_i of the part surface boundary curve a point K_i, that is similar to the point K_2 can be constructed. All the points K_i specify the so-called *limit contour*. It is necessary to take into account the impact of the boundary effect for those arcs of *CC*-point trajectories, which are located between part surface boundary curve and the limit contour.

Width bc of the part surface boundary affected region is not constant. Width W_i at a current point c is measured along the perpendicular to the part surface boundary curve. The point c is the end-point of the arc ac of the trajectory of *CC*-point. Feed-rate per tooth $\breve{F}_{fr}$ of the cutting tool could be either constant within the arc ac of the trajectory of *CC*-point, or it can vary in compliance with current width of the tool-path.

Particular features of impact of the boundary effect could observe:

(a) When the stock thickness is bigger, this causes longer trajectories of the cutting tool to enter in contact with the part surface.
(b) Bigger tolerance $[h]$ on accuracy of the machined part surface results in longer trajectories of the cutting tool to exit from contact with the part surface.
(c) Smaller the area of the nominal part surface P, more significant the impact of the boundary effect on the efficiency of the machining operation.
(d) Impact of the boundary effect could be more significant when machining *long* surfaces.

Location of the point from which machining of the sculptured surface begins also affects the resultant surface generation output. One can conclude from this that the optimal location of the start-point exists and it can be found out. Much room for the investigation is left in the synthesis of optimal global part surface generation [23], [24], [43].

8.3. An Example of Implementation of the *DG/K*-based Method of Sculptured Surface Machining

The *DG/K*-based approach for surface generation can be used for the development of novel advanced methods of sculptured surface machining on multi-axis *NC* machine.

Consider machining of a sculptured surface on multi-axis *NC* machine (Figure 33).

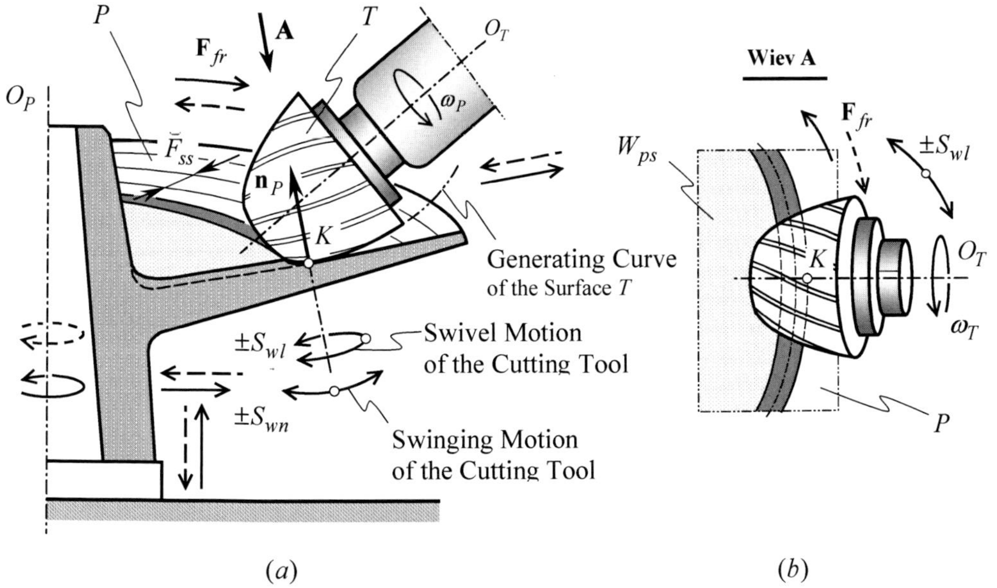

Figure 33. Optimization of machining of a sculptured part surface on multi-axis NC machine [SU Pat. No.1185749], [SU Pat. No.1249787].

Prior to machine the part surface, the workpiece have to be properly oriented on the worktable of the *NC* machine [SU Pat. No.1442371].

For the machining of the sculptured surface P a form milling cutter is used. Parameters of geometry of the generating surface T of the cutting tool are computed on the basis of the method of design of a form cutting tool for sculptured surface machining on multi-axis *NC* machine [SU Pat. No.4242296/08].

When machining the sculptured surface P (Figure 33), the cutting tool is rotating about its axis O_T with a certain angular velocity ω_T. The cutting tool is traveling with the optimal feed-rate $\mathbf{F}_{fr}$ along the optimal tool-paths. The optimal tool-paths are given by Eq. (131). After machining of a tool-path is accomplished, then the cutting tool moves across the trajectory of the *CC*-point in the direction of side-step $\mathbf{F}_{ss}$ at a distance $\breve{F}_{ss}$. In the new position of the cutting tool machining of the next tool-path begins.

For the most efficient surface machining, width of the tool-path must be maximal possible at every instance of the surface machining. In order to maintain the maximal width of the tool-path, two more motions are performing by the cutting tool. These two motions are the motions of orientation of the cutting tool. One of the orientation motions is swiveling[22] of the cutting tool [7]. Another orientation motion[23] is swinging $\pm S_{wn}$ of the cutting tool [8].

It is convenient to consider the swinging motion of the cutting tool before considering its swivel motion.

The swinging motion $\pm S_{wn}$ is the orientation motion of the second kind of the cutting tool.

Consider cross-section of the part surfaces and of the generating surface of the cutting tool with a plane surface through the common perpendicular $\mathbf{n}_P \equiv -\mathbf{n}_T$ at a *CC*-point K. Figure 34 reveals the nature of the swinging motion $\pm S_{wn}$ is the orientation motion of the second kind of the cutting tool.

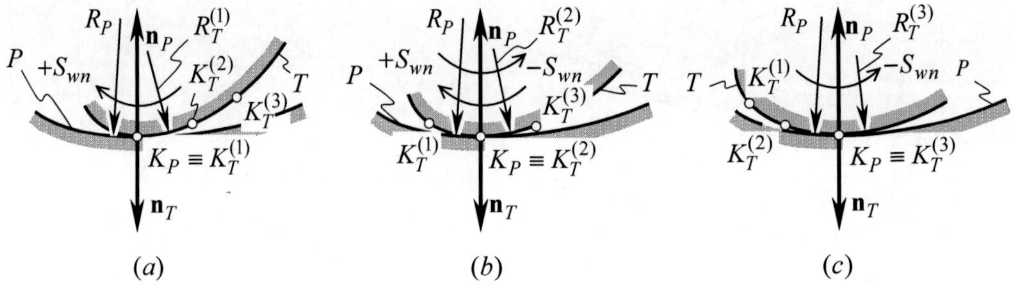

Figure 34. Swinging motion $\pm S_{wn}$ of the cutting tool: the orientation motion of the second kind of the cutting tool [SU Pat. No.1249787].

For precise positioning of the cutting tool, swinging motion is performing at a certain angle to the direction specified by $\mathbf{t}_{cnf}^{\max}$ [SU Pat. No. 1336366]. Oblique trajectory of the swinging motion reduces the impact of the deviations those inherited to multi-axis *NC* machine of the particular design[24] [16].

The swivel motion $\pm S_{wl}$ is the orientation motion of the first kind of the cutting tool. This orientation motion results in rotation $\omega_{\mathbf{n}}$ (or turning through a creation angle) of cutting tool about common perpendicular $\mathbf{n}_P \equiv -\mathbf{n}_T$. Evidently, speed of the orientation motion $\pm S_{wl}$ is equal to $\omega_{\mathbf{n}} = \partial \mu / \partial t$. The swivel motion is performing by the cutting tool simultaneously with its swinging motion.

The resultant relative motion of the part and of the cutting tool could be decomposed onto several rotations and translations. The rotations and translations (they are not labeled in Figure 33) are performing by corresponding servo-drives of a multi-axis *NC* machine.

---

[22] SU Pat. No.1185749, *A Method of Sculptured Surface Machining on Multi-Axis NC Machine.*/S.P. Radzevich, Int. Cl. B23C 3/16, Filed: October 24, 1983.

[23] SU Pat. No.1249787, *A Method of Sculptured Surface Machining on Multi-Axis NC Machine.*/S.P. Radzevich, Int. Cl. B23C 3/16, Filed: December 27, 1984.

[24] SU Pat. No.1336366, *A Method of Sculptured Surface Machining on Multi-Axis NC Machine.*/S.P. Radzevich, Int. Cl. B23C 3/16, Filed: October 21, 1985.

Conclusion

A novel method of the optimal sculptured surface generation is briefly disclosed in the text. So far, the *DG/K*-based method is the only method capable of solving the problem of synthesis of optimal machining operation of sculptured surfaces on multi-axis *NC* machine.

The author would like to share the credit for any research success with his numerous doctoral students with whom he tested the proposed ideas and applied them in the industry. The contributions of many friends, colleagues, and students in overwhelming numbers – cannot be acknowledged individually, much as we would like to. We remain grateful to our benefactors even though their kindness and help must go unrecorded.

Notation

$An_k(P/T)$	Andrew's indicatrix of normal curvature of the surfaces P and T
$An_R(P/T)$	Andrew's indicatrix of normal radii of curvature of the surfaces P and T
CC – point	cutter contact point
$Cnf_k(P/T)$	indicatrix of conformity of the part surface P and of generating surface T of the cutting tool at the current contact point K (normal curvatures)
$Cnf_R(P/T)$	indicatrix of conformity of the part surface P and of generating surface T of the cutting tool at the current contact point K (radii of normal curvature)
$\mathbf{Cp}_i[i \mapsto (i \pm 1)]$	couple of elementary coordinate system transformation
$\mathbf{Ds}(P/T)$	matrix of the resultant displacement of the cutting tool with respect to the part surface P
$Dup(P)$	Dupin's indicatrix of the surface P
$Dup(T)$	Dupin's indicatrix of the generating surface T of the cutting tool
E	a characteristic line
E_P, F_P, G_P	fundamental magnitudes of the first order of the surface P
E_T, F_T, G_T	fundamental magnitudes of the first order of the generating surface T of the cutting tool
$\mathbf{Eu}(\psi, \theta, \varphi)$	operator of the Eulerian transformation
$\breve{F}_{fr}$	feed-rate per tooth of the cutting tool
$[\breve{F}_{fr}]$	limit feed-rate per tooth of the cutting tool
$\mathbf{F}_{fr}$	Vector of the feed-rate motion of the cutting tool
$\breve{F}_{ss}$	magnitude of the side-step of the cutting tool
$[\breve{F}_{ss}]$	limit magnitude of the side-step of the cutting tool
$\mathbf{F}_{ss}$	vector of the side-step motion of the cutting tool
F_1, F_2, F_3	the rate of degree of conformity functions
G_P, G_T	full (Gaussian) curvature of the surface P, and of the generating surface T of the cutting tool

H_P	discriminant of the first fundamental form of the surface P
H_T	discriminant of the first fundamental form of the generating surface T of the cutting tool
K	point of contact of the surfaces P and T (or a point within the line of contact of the surfaces P and T)
L_P, M_P, N_P	fundamental magnitudes of the second order of the surface P
L_T, M_T, N_T	fundamental magnitudes of the second order of the generating surface T of the cutting tool
$Mch(P/T)$	indicatrix of machinability of the surface P with the cutting tool T
M_P, M_T	mean curvature of the surface P, and of the generating surface T of the cutting tool
P	sculptured part surface to be machined
P_{mr}	chip (material) removal output
P_{sg}	part surface generation output
$\mathbf{Rs}(A \mapsto B)$	operator of the resultant coordinate system transformation, say from the coordinate system A to the coordinate system B
$\mathbf{Rt}(\varphi_x, X)$	operator of rotation through an angle φ_x about X – axis
$\mathbf{Rt}(\varphi_y, Y)$	operator of rotation through an angle φ_y about Y – axis
$\mathbf{Rt}(\varphi_z, Z)$	operator of rotation through an angle φ_z about Z – axis
$R_{1.P}$, $R_{2.P}$	the first and the second principal radii of curvature of the surface P
$R_{1.T}$, $R_{2.T}$	the first and the second principal radii of curvature of the generating surface T of the cutting tool
T	the generating surface of the cutting tool
T_P	discriminant of the second fundamental form of the surface P
T_T	discriminant of the second fundamental form of the generating surface T of the cutting tool
$\mathbf{Tl}(P/T)$	resultant matrix of tolerances on relative configuration of the cutting tool with respect to the part surface P
$\mathbf{Tr}(a_x, X)$	operator of translation at a distance a_x along X – axis
$\mathbf{Tr}(a_y, Y)$	operator of translation at a distance a_y along Y – axis
$\mathbf{Tr}(a_z, Z)$	operator of translation at a distance a_z along Z – axis
U_P, V_P	curvilinear (Gaussian) coordinates of a point of the surface P
U_T, V_T	curvilinear (Gaussian) coordinates of a point of the generating surface T of the cutting tool
$\mathbf{U}_P$, $\mathbf{V}_P$	tangent vectors to the curvilinear coordinate lines on the surface P
$\mathbf{U}_T$, $\mathbf{V}_T$	tangent vectors to the curvilinear coordinate lines on the generating surface T of the cutting tool
$\mathbf{V}_\Sigma$	vector of the resultant motion of the generating surface T of the cutting tool with respect to the sculptured surface P
X_{NC}, Y_{NC}, Z_{NC}	Cartesian coordinates of a point in the coordinate system associated with the multi-axis *NC* machine
X_P, Y_P, Z_P	Cartesian coordinates of a point of the surface P
X_T, Y_T, Z_T	Cartesian coordinates of a point of the generating surface T of the cutting tool

$\mathbf{ds}_i[i \mapsto (i \pm 1)]$	matrix of an elementary $i-$th displacement of the cutting tool with respect to the part surface P
$[h]$	tolerance on accuracy of the machined part surface P
h_{fr}	height of the surface waviness
h_{ss}	height of the surface cusps in the direction of vector $\mathbf{F}_{ss}$ of the side-step motion
h_{Σ}	resultant deviation of the machined surface from the desired part surface
$k_{1.P}$, $k_{2.P}$	the first and second principal curvatures of the surface P
$k_{1.T}$, $k_{2.T}$	the first and second principal curvatures of the generating surface T of the cutting tool
$\mathbf{n}_P$	unit normal vector to the surface P
$\mathbf{n}_T$	unit normal vector to the generating surface T of the cutting tool
r_{cnf}	position vector of a point of the indicatrix of conformity $Cnf_R(P/T)$
$\mathbf{r}_P$	position vector of a point of the surface P
$\mathbf{r}_T$	position vector of a point of the generating surface T of the cutting tool
$\mathbf{tl}_i[i \mapsto (i \pm 1)]$	matrix of the $i-$th element of the resultant tolerance on configuration of the cutting tool with respect to the part surface P
$\mathbf{t}_{1.P}$, $\mathbf{t}_{2.P}$	unit tangent vectors of the principal directions on the surface P
$\mathbf{t}_{1.T}$, $\mathbf{t}_{2.T}$	unit tangent vectors of the principal directions on the generating surface T of the cutting tool
$\mathbf{u}_P$, $\mathbf{v}_P$	unit tangent vectors to the curvilinear coordinate lines on the surface P
$\mathbf{u}_T$, $\mathbf{v}_T$	unit tangent vectors to the curvilinear coordinate lines on the generating surface T of the cutting tool
$x_P y_P z_P$	local Cartesian coordinate system with the origin at the point of contact of the surfaces P and T

Greek Symbols

$\Phi_{1.P}$, $\Phi_{2.P}$	the first and the second fundamental forms of the surface P
$\Phi_{1.T}$, $\Phi_{2.T}$	the first and the second fundamental forms of the generating surface T of the cutting tool
μ	angle of the surfaces P and T local relative orientation
ω_P	coordinate angle on the part surface P
ω_T	coordinate angle on the part generating surface T of the cutting tool

Subscripts

cnf	conformity
max	maximal
min	minimal
opt	optimal

References

[1] Bonnet, P.O., *Journ. Ec. Polytech*, xiii, 31, 1867.

[2] doCarmo, M.P., *Differential Geometry of Curves and Surfaces*, Englewood Cliffs, NJ: Prentice-Hall, 1976, 503p.

[3] Faux, L.D., Pratt, M.J., (1987), *Computational Geometry for Design and Manufacture,* Ellis Horwood Limited Publishers, Chichester, John Wiley & Sons, NY, 331p.

[4] Gauss, K.-F., *Disquisitions Generales Circa Superficies Curvas,* Goettingen (1828). (English translation: *General Investigation of Curved Surfaces*, by J.C.Moreheat & A.M.Hiltebeitel, Princeton, 1902, reprinted with introduction by Courant, Raven Press, Hewlett, New York, 1965, 119 p.).

[5] Jeffreys, H., *Cartesian Tensors*, Cambridge, University Press, 1961, 93p.

[6] Monge, G., *Application de l'analyse à la géométrie*, Bachelier, 1850.

[7] Pat. No. 1185749, *A Method of Sculptured Surface Machining on Multi-Axis NC Machine.*/S.P. Radzevich, Int. Cl. B23c 3/16, Filed: October 24, 1983.

[8] Pat. No. 1249787, *A Method of Sculptured Surface Machining on Multi-Axis NC Machine.*/S.P. Radzevich, Int. Cl. B23c 3/16, Filed: December 27, 1984].

[9] Pat. No.1442371, (USSR), *A Method of Optimal Work-Piece Orientation on the Worktable of Multi-Axis NC Machine.* /S.P. Radzevich, Int. Cl. B23q15/007, Filed: February 17, 1987.

[10] Pat. №1449246 (USSR). *A Method of Experimental Simulation of Machining of a Sculptured Surface on Multi-Axis NC Machine.*/S.P. Radzevich. Filed: February 17, 1987, Int. Cl. B 23 C, 3/16.

[11] Plűcker, J., (1865), *On a New Geometry of Space*, Phil. Trans. R. Soc. London, Vol. 155, pp.725-791.

[12] Radzevich, S.P., "A Closed-Form Solution to the Problem of Optimal Tool-Path Generation for Sculptured Surface Machining on Multi-Axis *NC* Machine", *Mathematical and Computer Modeling*, Vol. 43, Issue 3-4, February 2006, pp. 222-243.

[13] Radzevich, S.P., "A Cutting-Tool-Dependent Approach for Partitioning of Sculptured Surface", *Computer-Aided Design*, Vol. 37, № 7, July 2005, pp.767-778.

[14] Radzevich, S.P., "A Generalized Analytical Representation of the Conditions of Proper Part Surface Generation. Part 1", In: *Improvement of Efficiency of Metal Cutting*, Volgograd, *VolgPI*, 1987, pp.70-79.

[15] Radzevich, S.P., "A Generalized Analytical Representation of the Conditions of Proper Part Surface Generation. Part 2", In: *Improvement of Efficiency of Metal Cutting*, Volgograd, *VolgPI*, 1988, pp.56-73.

[16] Radzevich, S.P., *A Method of Sculptured Surface Machining on Multi-Axis NC Machine*, Pat. No.1336366, USSR, B23C 3/16, Filed: October 21, 1985.

[17] Radzevich, S.P., *A Method for Designing of the Optimal Form-Cutting-Tool for Machining of a Given Sculptured Surface on Multi-Axis NC Machine.* – Pat. №4242296/08 (USSR), Filed: March 31, 1987г.

[18] Radzevich, S.P.: "A Novel Method for Mathematical Modeling of a Form-Cutting-Tool of the Optimum Design", *Applied Mathematical Modeling*, Vol. 00, 2007, pp.000-000.

[19] Radzevich, S.P., "A Possibility of Application of Plücker's Conoid for Mathematical Modeling of Contact of Two Smooth Regular Surfaces in the First Order of Tangency", *Mathematical and Computer Modeling*, Vol. 42, 2004, pp.999-1022.

[20] Radzevich, S.P., "A Universal Principal Kinematic Scheme of Sculptured Surface Generation", In: *Research in the Field of Cutting Tools and Metal Cutting*, Tula, *TulPI*, 1986, pp.112-119.
[21] Radzevich, S.P., *Advanced Methods of Sculptured Surface Machining*, Moscow, *VNIITEMR*, 1988, 56p.
[22] Radzevich, S.P., "Conditions of Proper Sculptured Surface Machining", *Computer-Aided Design*, Vol. 34, Number 10, 1 September, 2002, pp.727-740.
[23] Radzevich, S.P., *Differential-Geometric Method of Surface Generation*, Doctoral Thesis, Tula, *TulPI*, 1991, 300p.
[24] Radzevich, S.P., *Fundamentals of Surface Generation. Monograph*, Kiev, Rastan, 2001, 592p.
[25] Radzevich, S.P., "Generation of Actual Sculptured Part Surface on Multi-Axis *NC* Machine. Part 1", *Izvestiya VUZov. Mashinostroyeniye*, No. 5, 1985, pp.138-142.
[26] Radzevich, S.P., "Generation of Actual Sculptured Part Surface on Multi-Axis *NC* Machine. Part 2", *Izvestiya VUZov. Mashinostroyeniye*, No. 9, 1985, pp.141-146.
[27] Radzevich, S.P., "Impact of Linear Transformations on the Principal Fundamental Forms of the Surfaces *P(T)*", In: *Proceeding of Dneprodzerzhinsk State Technical Univresity: Engineering*, Vol. 1, Dneprodzerzhinsk, *DSTU*, 1995, pp.49-54.
[28] Radzevich, S.P., "Investigation and Classification of the Relative Motions of Orientation of the Cutting Tool", In: *Research in the Field of Cutting Tools and Metal Cutting*, Tula, TulPI, 1989, pp.82-89.
[29] Radzevich, S.P., "*K*-mapping of Sculptured Part Surfaces and of the Machining Surface of a Cutting Tool", Proceedings of National Technical University of the Ukraine "Kiev Polytechnic Institute", Series: *Machine-Building*, Vo. 33, 1998, pp.232-240.
[30] Radzevich, S.P., *Kinematic Geometry of Surface Machining*, *CRC* Press, 2008, ... p.
[31] Radzevich, S.P., "Mathematical Modeling of Contact of Two Surfaces in the First Order of Tangency", *Mathematical and Computer Modeling*, Vol. 39, 2004, pp.1083-1112.
[32] Radzevich, S.P., *Methods for Investigation of the Conditions of Contact of Surfaces, Monograph*, Kiev, UkrNIINTI, №759–Uk88, 1987, 103p.
[33] Radzevich, S.P., *Methods of Milling of Sculptured Surfaces*, Moscow, *VNIITEMR*, 1989, 72p.
[34] Radzevich, S.P., *New Achievements in the Field of Sculptured Surface Machining on Multi-Axis NC Machine*, Moscow, *VNIITEMR*, 1987, 48p.
[35] Radzevich, S.P., "On Analytical Description of the Geometry of Contact of Surfaces in Highest Kinematic Pairs", *Theory for Mechanisms and Machines*, St. Petersburg Polytechnic Institute, Vol.3, No.5, 2005, pp.3-14.
[36] Radzevich, S.P., "Optimal Sculptured Surface Orientation on the Worktable of Multi-Axis *NC* Machine", *Izvestiya VUZov. Mashinostroyeniye*, No. 2, 1990, pp.140-145.
[37] Radzevich, S.P., "Profiling of the Form Cutting Tools for Sculptured Surface Machining on Multi-Axis *NC* Machine", in Proceedings of the Conference: *Advanced Designs of Cutting Tools for Agile Production and Robotic Complexes, Moscow*, *MDNTP*, 1987, pp.53-57.
[38] Radzevich, S.P., "Profiling of the Form Cutting Tools for Machining of Sculptured Surface on Multi-Axis *NC* Machine", *Stanki I Instrument*, 1989, No.7, pp.10-12.

[39] Radzevich, S.P., "Relative Orientation of the Sculptured Surface and of the Generating Surface of the Cutting Tool at the *CC*-Point", Problems of Engineering and Reliability of Machines, No.3, 1990, pp.76-82.

[40] Radzevich, S.P., "□-Mapping Based Method for Designing of Form Cutting Tool for Sculptured Surface Machining", In: *Mathematical and Computer Modeling*, Vol.36, No.7-8, 2002, pp.921-938.

[41] Radzevich, S.P., "***R*** -Surfaces: A Novel Tool for Partitioning of a Sculptured Surface", *Mathematical and Computer Modeling*, 2007. (In press).

[42] Radzevich, S.P., "Selection of the Cutting Tool of Optimum Design for Sculptured Surface Machining on Multi-Axis *CNC* Machine", in: *Automation & Assembly Summit 2005*, April 18-20, 2005, St. Louis, Missouri, *SME* Technical Paper TP05PUB71.

[43] Radzevich, S.P., *Sculptured Surface Machining on Multi-Axis NC Machine. Monograph*, Kiev, Vishcha Shkola, 1991, 192p.

[44] Radzevich, S.P., Goodman, E.D., "Computation of Optimal Workpiece Orientation for Multi-Axis *NC* Machining of Sculptured Part Surfaces", ASME *J. of Mechanical Design*, June 2002, Vol.124, №2, pp.201-212.

[45] Radzevich, S.P., Goodman, E.D., "Efficiency of Multi-Axis *NC* Machining of Sculptured Part Surfaces", Proceedings of the Sculptured Surfaces Machining Conference: *Machining Impossible Shapes SSM'98*, November 9-11, 1998, Chrysler Technology Center, Auburn Hills, Michigan, USA, pp.42-58.

[46] Radzevich, S.P., *et al*, "On the Optimization of Parameters of Sculptured Surface Machining on Multi-Axis *NC* Machine", In: *Investigation into the Surface Generation*, Kiev, *UkrNIINTI*, No.65-Uk89, pp.57-72.

[47] Shishkov, V.A., *Generation of Surfaces Using Continuously Indexing Method*, Moscow, Mashgiz, 1951, 152p.

[48] Struik, D.J., *Lectures on Classical Differential Geometry*, 2nd Edition, Addison-Wesley Publishing Company Inc., Massachusetts, 1961, 232p.

Bibliography

Amirouche, F.M.L., *Computer-Aided Design and Manufacturing*, Englewood Cliffs, N.J., Prentice Hall, 1993, 538p.

Burke, W.L., *Applied Differential Geometry*, Cambridge University Press, Cambridge, 1985.

Chao-Hwa Chang, Melkanoff, M.M., *NC Machine Programming and Software Design*, Prentice Hall, 1989, 589p.

Choi, B.K., Jerard, R.B., *Sculptured Surface Machining. Theory and Application*, Kluwer Academic Publishers, Dordrecht/Boston/London, 1998, 368p.

Eisenhart, L.P., *A Treatise on the Differential Geometry of Curves and Surfaces*, London, Dover Publications, Inc., 1909; New York, reprint 1960, 474p.

Faux, L.D., Pratt, M.J., *Computational Geometry for Design and Manufacture,* Ellis Horwood Limited Publishers, Chichester, John Wiley & Sons, NY, 1987, 331p.

Farin, G.E., *Curves and Surfaces for CAGD. A Practical Guide*, Morgan Kaufmann Publishers, San Francisco, 2001, 499p.

Ferguson, R.S., *Practical Algorithms for 3D Computer Graphics*, A K Peters, Natick, Massachusetts, 2001, 539p.

Gasson, P.C., *Geometry of Spatial Forms*, Ellis Horwood, Chichester, 1983, 601p.

Hausdorf, F., *Grundzüge der Mengenlehre*, Leipzig: Veit & Comp. 1914, New York: Reprint Chelsea, 1949.

Held, M., *On the Computational Geometry of Pocket Machining*, Springer-Verlag, 1991.

Hilbert, D., Cohn-Vossen, S., *Geometry and the Imagination*, Chelsea Publishing Company, NY, 1952, 357p.

Hopf, H., *Lectures on Differential Geometry in the Large*, 1955 - ?, 155p. (Typewritten, Copy: The Library of Brown Universirty, USA).

http://www.minitech.com/software/Rhino/Rhino_cl.htm.

Koenderink, J.J., *Solid Shape*, The MIT Press, Cambridge, Massachusetts, 1990, 699p.

Olling, G.J., Choi, B.K., Jerard, R.B., Eds., *Machining Impossible Shapes*, Kluwer Academic Publishers, Boston, USA, 1998, 386p.

Ligun, A.A., Shumeiko, A.A., Radzevich, S.P., Goodman, E.D., "Asymptotically Optimal Disposition of Tangent Points for Approximation of Smooth Convex Surfaces by Polygonal Functions", *Computer Aided Geometric Design*, Vol. 14, 1997, pp. 533-546.

Marciniak, K., *Geometric Modeling for Numerically Controlled Machining,* Oxford University Press, N.Y., 1991, 245p.

Mortenson, M.E., *Geometric Modeling*, John Wiley & Sons, NY, 1985, 763p.

Patrikalakis, N.M., and Maekawa, T., *Shape Interrogation for Computer Aided Design and Manufacturing*, New York, Springer Verlag, 2002, 410p.

Piegl, L., Tiller, W., *The NURBS Book. (Monographs in Visual Communications)*, Springer, New York, 1995, 646p.

Pottmann, H., Wallner, J., (Eds.), *Bringing Line Geometry Together with CAGD: Computational Line Geometry*, Springer, Berlin, 2001, 563 p.

Radzevich, S.P., *A Method of Sculptured Surface Machining on Multi-Axis NC Machine*, Pat. No.1367300, USSR, B23C 3/16, Filed: January 30, 1986.

Radzevich, S.P., *A Method of Sculptured Surface Machining on Multi-Axis NC Machine*, Pat. No.2050228, Russia, B23C 3/16, Filed: December 25, 1990.

Radzevich, S.P., *A Method of Reinforcement of Sculptured Surface on Multi-Axis NC Machine*. Pat. No.1533174 USSR, Int. Cl. B24B 39/00, Filed: December 2, 1987.

Radzevich, S.P., *Classification of Surfaces*, Monograph, Kiev, UkrNIINTI, No. 1440-Ук88, 1988, 185p.

Radzevich, S.P., "$\mathcal{R}$-surfaces: A Novel Tool for Partitioning of a Sculptured Surface", *Mathematical and Computer Modeling*, 2007. (In press).

Sarma, R., Dutta, D., "The Geometry and Generation of *NC* Tool Path", *ASME Journal of Mechanical Design,* June, Vol.119, 1997, pp. 253-258.

Struik, D.J., *Lectures on Classical Differential Geometry*, 2nd Edition, Addison-Wesley Publishing Company Inc., Massachusetts, 1961, 232p.

Yamaguchi, F., *Curves and Surfaces in Computer Aided Design*, Springer-Verlag, Berlin, Heidelberg, New York, London, Paris, Tokyo, 1988, 378p.

In: Computer-Aided Design...
Editors: C.M. De Smet et al, pp. 287-318
ISBN 978-1-60456-860-8

Expert Commentary B

On the Fusion of Multi-Sensor Images: The Multiresolution Approaches

Zheng Liu and Jinzhong Yang
Institute for Aerospace Research, Ottawa, Canada

Abstract

The advance of multi-sensor imaging systems enables the capability of producing multiple image modalities across the electromagnetic spectrum bands. These multi-modality images should be combined together to generate a composite image, which is able to display plenty of information captured by the system. The technique named image fusion is developed for this purpose. Varies of image fusion approaches have been presented in the literature, a popular category of which is the multiresolution image fusion (MRIF). This chapter reviews the state of the art of the MRIF algorithms and the performance assessment issue in image fusion. The mechanism and applications of the MRIF are described. However, there is not a universal solution for all applications. The image fusion algorithm must be carefully selected or tailored based on the specific requirements of an application. This chapter discusses these relevant issues as well.

1. Introduction

With the development of imaging sensors, it is possible for heterogeneous image modalities to perform across different wavebands of the electromagnetic spectrum [1, 2]. The information acquired from these wavebands should be combined together to produce an enhanced single view of a scene with extended information content. This process is generally achieved by the so-called image fusion technique. The application of image fusion has found in a wide range of applications including multi-focus imagery, concealed weapon detection (CWD), intelligent robots, surveillance systems, medical diagnosis, remote sensing, non-destructive testing (NDT), etc. [3–14].

The multiresolution analysis (MRA) approach is one of the most important tools to implement multi-sensor image fusion [15]. The MRA algorithms represent an image in a transform domain spanned by a set of basis functions. Image features, like edges and lines, can be easier to access and manipulate in such a transform domain. The multiresolution image fusion (MRIF) takes advantage of the MRA approach to find an optimal way to integrate these image features. The MRIF has been studied for several decades and some good reviews have been presented in the literature. A general review includes MRA-based approaches and non-MRA-based approaches has been given in [16, 17]. Specific review and tutorial on MRIF can be found in [18, 19].

Instead of providing only a general overview, this chapter will address all aspects of issues related to the study of multiresolution image fusion. This chapter describes the image fusion problems and the multiresolution solutions offered by researchers as well as the performance assessment issues involved in image fusion. It also provides readers a guideline on how to choose appropriate image fusion approaches for a specific application. However, the detailed implementation of related fusion algorithms will not be repeated herein. Readers are referred to the cited references.

The remainder of this chapter is organized as follows. The MRA-based image fusion techniques are described in section 2.. section 3. discusses the performance assessment issues in image fusion. The applications, which benefit from the MRA-based image fusion techniques, are presented in section 4.. Finally we conclude this chapter in section 5..

2. Image Fusion Based on Multiresolution Analysis (MRA)

2.1. What Does Image Fusion Do?

Image fusion combines multiple inputs into one single fused image that present more information than any individual inputs. There are two types of image fusion as illustrated in Figure 2. First type is the feature combination or integration. In Figure 1(a), different features (face and moon) from two input images are integrated into a new single image. The circle in the center represents the common feature in both inputs. This circle can be further sharped or enhanced through the fusion process. Both the face and moon is available in the fused image. Additional processing can be applied to the fused image to extract further information of the features. The second type shown in Figure 1(b) discriminates different features through fusion. Sensor one can discriminate A and B from C while sensor two distinguishes A and C from B. Herein, the letter A, B, and C have a more extensive meaning like image feature. The fusion of the two images eventually separates A, B, and C from each other. Usually, such kind of fusion is performed at an abstract level and the fused result is represented by a thematic map of the scene. The MRA approach usually works with this first type of image fusion, which is dedicated to the integration of image features from multiple inputs.

The entire procedure for multi-sensor image fusion is illustrated in Figure 2, which consists of four steps, i.e. pre-processing, registration, fusion, and post-processing. The performance assessment can be applied to guide the fusion process. The feedback from the performance assessment makes it possible to create an adaptive fusion process.

A simple example is given below to demonstrate how the MRA works for the image fusion. Two images, one with a horizontal and the other with a vertical square bar crossing at the center, are fused using six MRA-based fusion algorithms. The six algorithms are Laplacian pyramid (LAP), gradient-based pyramid (GRAD), ratio-of-lowpass pyramid (RoLP), forth order Daubechies wavelet (DB), shift-invariant discrete wavelet transform (SIDWT),

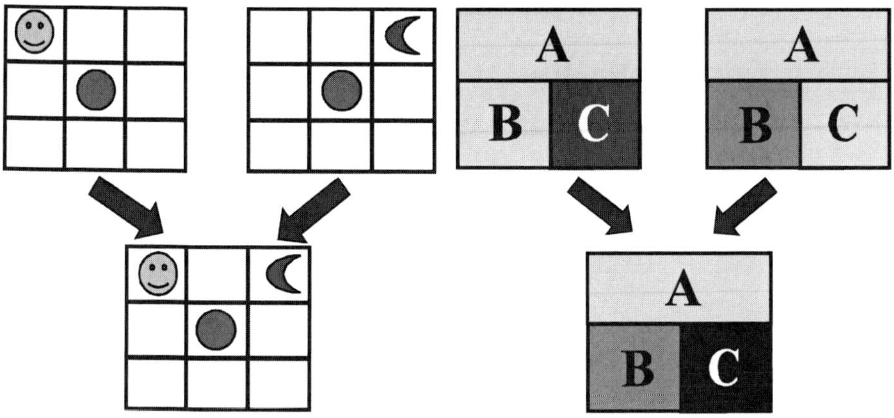

(a) Feature combination. (b) Feature classification.

Figure 1. The two categories of image fusion.

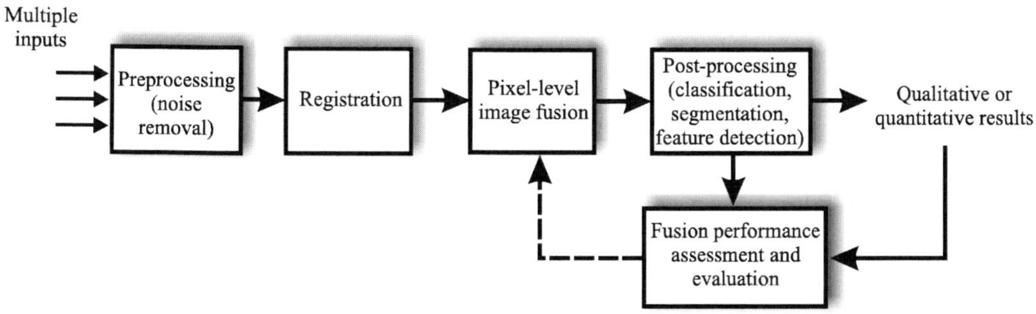

Figure 2. The procedure for multi-sensor image fusion.

and steerable pyramid (STEER) [3, 20–23]. The decomposition level is set to four and the fusion rule is to select the absolute maximum for the high- or band-pass sub-images (components) and to average the low-pass sub-images (components).

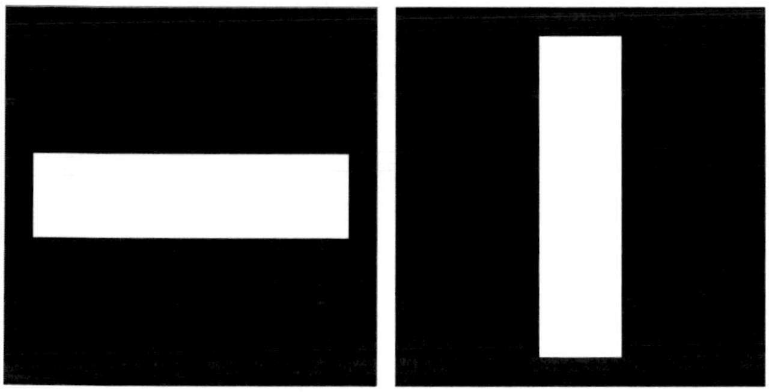

(a) Horizontal bar. (b) Vertical bar.

Figure 3. Two images are used for testing MRA-based image fusion.

To clearly show the results, we visualize the fused images in three dimensions in Fig-

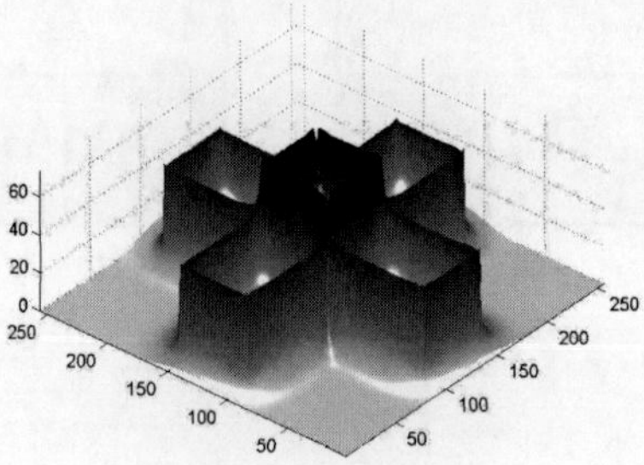

(a) LAP

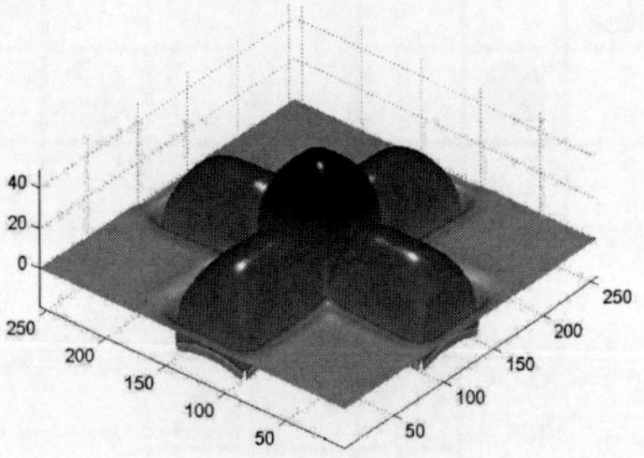

(b) GRAD

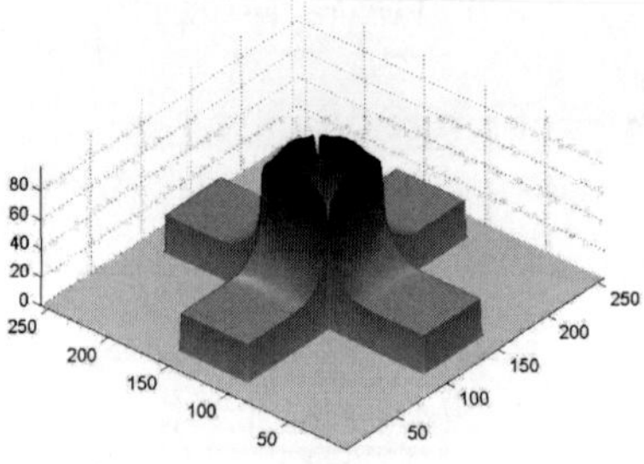

(c) RoLP

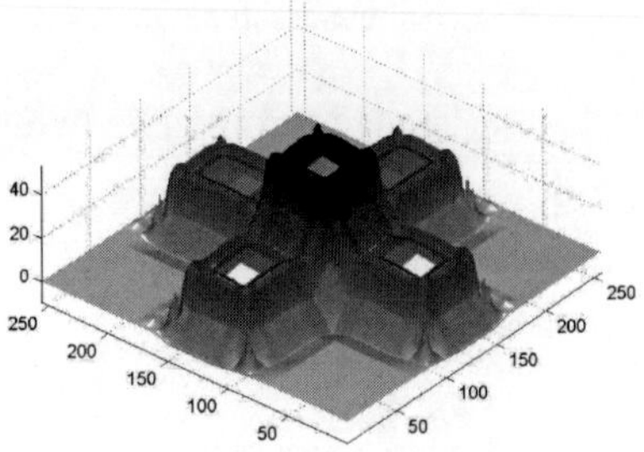

(d) DB

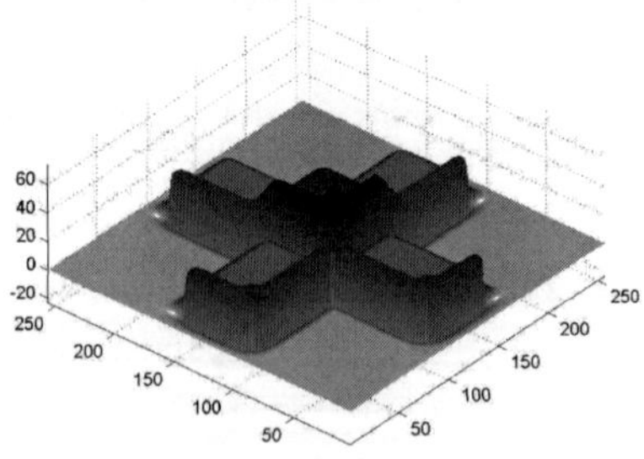

(e) SIDWT

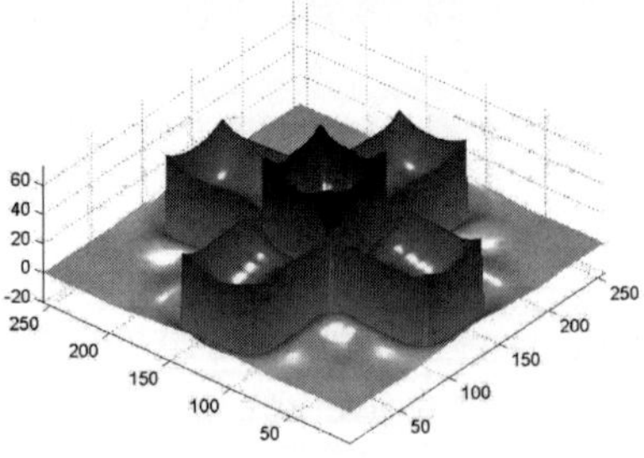

(f) STEER

Figure 4. The fusion results with different MRA-based fusion algorithms.

ure 4. In this example, Figure 4(a) and 4(f) give better results than others, in which a shaper edge is present. The fused result depends on how the features are represented by the MRA algorithms. In other words, the same features are treated differently in different MRA algorithms even though the same fusion rule is applied. To demonstrate how the fusion rule impacts the fusion result, the maximum selection rule is applied to all coefficients for the steerable pyramid based fusion, as shown in Figure 5, which can be compared with the result shown in Figure 4(f). To explore more examples of image fusion, the readers are referred to Rockinger's Matlab ® toolbox [24].

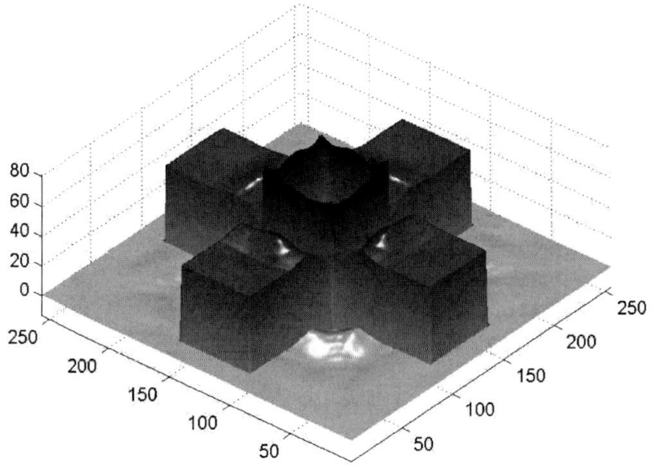

Figure 5. The fusion result with the steerable pyramid. The fusion rule is the maximum selection of both the low-pass and high-pass coefficients (see Figure 4(f) for comparison).

2.2. The State of the Art

A number of MRIF approaches have bee proposed since 1984 when Adelson, Burt and their colleague published their paper on using pyramids for image processing [20, 25]. Another important publication on MRIF is from Li and his coauthors [21], in which the discrete wavelet transform (DWT) was first introduced into image fusion area. The basic principle of MRIF can be described as to retain the salient image features from each individual inputs in the transform domain. Different MRIF methods vary with the basis functions of the transform domain and the fusion rules for the transformed coefficients.

The MRIF procedure is illustrated in Figure 6. The major steps of MRIF include image decomposition via MRA transform, coefficient combination according to specific fusion rules, and image reconstruction via inverse MRA transform. Specifically, the input image $I(x, y)$ is first transformed to another domain that is spanned by a set of basic functions $g_i(x, y)$, i.e.

$$I(x, y) = \sum_i y_i g_i(x, y) \tag{1}$$

where y_is are the transformed coefficients that can be obtained by projecting the image onto a set of projection functions, $h_i(x, y)$:

$$y_i = \sum_{x,y} h_i(x, y) I(x, y) \tag{2}$$

The fusion rule is then applied to each y_i based on the measurement of image features and characteristics of $g_i(x, y)$ to obtain a set of fused coefficients for each (x, y). the final fused image is obtained by applying inverse MRA transform to the fused coefficients.

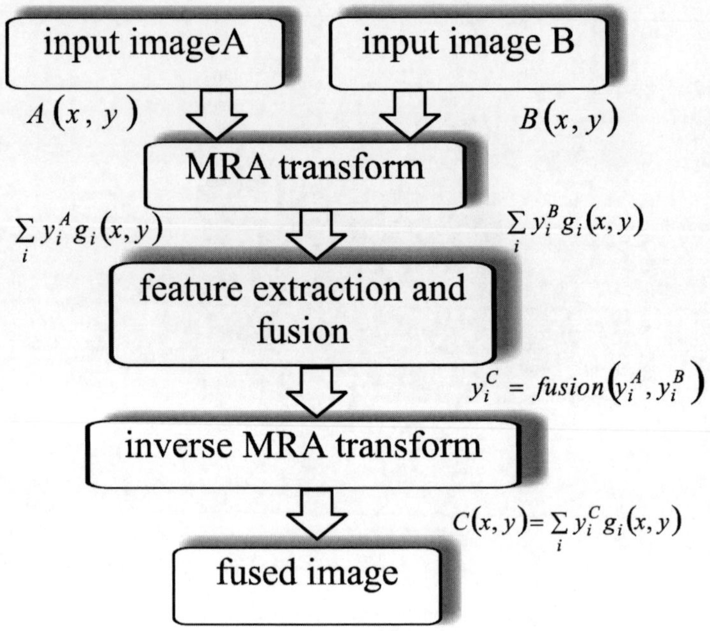

Figure 6. The procedure of MRA-based pixel level fusion.

2.2.1. MRIF Algorithms

The study of MRIF is twofold encompassing a multiresolution algorithm and a coefficient combination rule. A number of MRA algorithms have been investigated for the fusion of multi-sensor images so far. Normally the MRA algorithm can be roughly separated into two groups, the pyramid based methods and the wavelet based methods. These methods are summarized in Table 1 and 2 respectively. The readers are referred to [16, 18] for detailed information on these methods. Before choosing an MRA algorithm, two questions should be bore in mind, which are (1) "What are the advantages of this MRA algorithm compared with another?" and (2) "Is this algorithm suitable to this application or image types?" The answers to these questions are case by case. There are a number of factors that should be considered, e.g. reconstruction error, complexity of implementation, shift-invariant property, representation of directional features, etc. The final judgement should meet the minimal requirements of the application. Usually the choice of the MRA algorithms depends on the characteristics of the algorithm and the input images. Since an image is represented as a weighted sum of the basis functions, choosing these basis functions that resemble the image will facilitate the analysis. Nikolov et al. applied the multiscale edge representation proposed by Mallat and Hwang [26] to fuse CT and MR images of human brains [27]. Such a representation facilitates the access to edge information in images. Gradient map representation is another example to access the edges [28]. Shift-invariant property is another important consideration when choosing the MRA algorithm. The shift-invariant MRA algorithms, such as the steerable pyramid and shift-invariant discrete wavelet transform, exhibit the robustness to fuse images that are not perfectly registered [22].

Other image fusion approaches are briefly described in Table 3. Those methods marked with a star are not MRIF methods and will not be discussed in this chapter. The MRIF based

Table 1. The image pyramid based approaches.

MRA Algorithm	Fusion Rule	Application	Reference
Laplacian pyramid	absolute value maximum selection	multi-focused images	[20]
Ratio of Low Pass pyramid	maximum absolute contrast selection	simulation	[29]
Gradient pyramid	1) based on match and salience measure; 2) weighted average	infrared and visible image, hyperspectral image	[3,30,31]
Morphological pyramid	maximum operation	CT and MRI images	[11]
Steerable pyramid	apply Laplacian pyramid	standard images for simulation and multi-sensor images	[23]
Gradient map	absolute value maximum selection	multi-sensor images	[28]

on support value transform is derived from support vector machine (SVM), which is also known as a maximum margin classifier mapping the input vectors to a higher dimensional space using a maximal separating hyperplane [42]. Zheng et al. implemented a least-square SVM (LS-SVM) for the multi-sensor image fusion [43]. Curvelet transform is claimed to have a better representation of edges than other MRA algorithms [44,45]. Noise reduction can be implemented in this transform domain and directional information is available in this multiresolution representation.

2.2.2. Fusion Rule

The fusion rule is to optimize the coefficient combination process in terms of certain feature measurement. The basic rule for coefficient combination is choosing maximum absolute value in the high-frequency (high- and band-pass) bands and averaging in the low-frequency (low-pass) band. The coefficients with larger absolute value from the high frequency bands normally correspond to image features like edges, lines, or boundaries, and thus will be retained in the fused image. More sophisticated fusion rules perform coefficient combination in an area or a region around the pixel in consideration, some of which even include the corresponding areas or regions across the frequency bands or resolution scales [18,51,52]. Figure 7 illustrates the pixel, window, and region based image fusion approaches in the sense of fusion rules. The detailed description of these approaches is summarized in Table 4.

The concept of match measure and salience measure originated from Burt's work on gradient pyramid based image fusion [3], where the match measure determined the selection or averaging operation and the salience measure decided the coefficient choice in the selection operation. Wilson et al. introduced the contrast sensitivity measure to weight the coefficient sets [30,31]. Li et al. choose the coefficient based on a 3-by-3 or 5-by-5 win-

Table 2. The wavelet-based approaches.

MRA Algorithm	Fusion Rule	Application	Reference
Orthogonal wavelet	absolute value maximum selection	multi-focus image and multi-sensor images	[21]
Steerable dyadic wavelet	maximum local oriented energy	different channels of landsat TM images	[32]
Discrete wavelet frame	Fusion rule is the same as [3].	Video sequences	[22,33,34];
	activity measure, region-based rule, grouping approach	multi-focus images, millimeter wave images, infrared images	[35]
Contrast-based wavelet	absolute value maximum selection	infrared and visual images	[36]
Complex wavelet	chain representation fusion	multi-focus images, CT and MR images	[37]
	region-based fusion determined by priority maps	multi-focus and multi-sensor images	[38]
Multiwavelet	pixel selection based on the image's feature map	SPOT images	[39,40]
Nonseparable wavelet	averaging the low-pass sub-image; window-based selection for high-pass sub-images	visible and infrared images, remote sensing images	[41]

dow [21], where the pixel with the maximum absolute value in the window represented the activity of the pixel located at the center. Li et al. also introduced a consistency verification as a rectification of the selection process. Zhang and Blum used average value in a region that were contoured and segmented using the Canny edge detector [35]. This approach is considered to be more robust to noise. Koren et al. proposed a fusion rule based on the local oriented energy [32]. Cross-band selection and coefficient grouping methods were proposed by Petrovic and Xydeas [52], and Zhang and Blum [35], respectively. This fusion rule is similar to the region-based combination rule, since a single pixel at a lower resolution corresponds to several pixels (region) at a higher resolution. Yang and Blum recently proposed to use the hidden Markov model (HMM) to capture the correlation of the coefficients across the resolution scales to improve the fusion confidence [55]. However, the significant difference of these rules in terms of the fusion quality has not yet been fully explored.

The aforementioned rules only consider the saliency of features. Most of them did not address the problem resulted from noise that is easily regarded as part of salient features and is integrated into the fused image. To address the noise introduced by imaging sensors, Blum proposed a robust image fusion method based on statistical theory of minmax robustness [54]. This method was incorporated into the MRA framework. However, more

Table 3. Other approaches (The one marked with a star is not a MRA-based method).

MRA Algorithm	Fusion Method and Rule	Application	Reference
Support value transform	Choose max and weighted average	multi-focus and multi-sensor images	[43]
Curvelet transform		remote sensing images	[44,45]
Neural networks★	probabilistic neural network and radial basis function network	multi-focus images	[46]
Independent component analysis (ICA)★	weighted combination scheme	simulated and multi-sensor images	[47]
Pulse-coupled neural network★	use image segment to guide the fusion process	multi-focus and multi-sensor images	[48]
DCT-based method★	maximum selection of the AC coefficients; averaging the DC coefficients	multi-focus images	[49]
Pseudo-Wigner distribution ★	pixel selection	multi-focus images only	[50]
Cooperative neural fusion algorithm★	based on cooperative modular neutral network	simulated images	[]

Table 4. The summary of fusion rules in transform domain.

	Description	Reference
Pixel-based rule	absolution value maximum selection (AVMS) for high-pass components; averaging for low-pass components	[53]
	maximum selection based on local oriented energy	[32]
	apply Laplacian pyramid fusion for the sub-images	[23]
Region-based rule	match and salience measure	[3]
	maximum absolute value in a window	[21]
Grouping-based rule	associating decomposition coefficients across the frequency bands	[35]
Others	Minmax approach	[54]
	expectation maximum (EM) method	[55,56]
	principal component analysis (PCA) for approximation coefficients and AVMS for detail coefficients	[57]

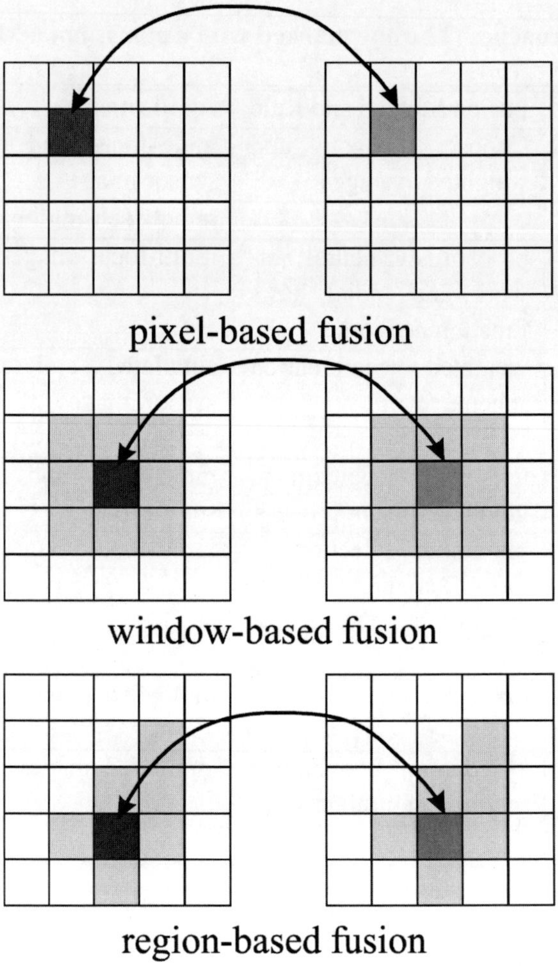

Figure 7. The different fusion rules.

experiments should be carried out to verify the effectiveness of this sophisticated approach. Another solution to tackle this problem is the so-called “adaptive” fusion method, which use the feedback of performance assessment to guide the fusion process. This method will be described in section 2.2.4..

2.2.3. Color-based Approaches

It has been demonstrated that the human visual system (HVS) is much more sensitive to colors than grayscales. This implies a color representation of the fused image is preferable for better visualization. However, the color information normally is not available in all input sources, for example, most thermal sensors only produce grayscale images. In practice, many image fusion systems only produce fused images with grayscale representation. In order to capitalize on the colors, a category of image fusion approaches, referred as to the color composite fusion, has been developed to produce a false color representation of the fused image by combining the input images or their processed correspondents in a color space [16, 58–61]. The false color fused image also implies that the input images could be either color or grayscale images.

The color composite fusion technique is often applied in combination with the MRA procedure to achieve a better false color representation. A wide employment of this technique has been found in the field of remote sensing [45, 62–65]. The MRA-based algorithms, such as the wavelet transform or the curvelet transform, are applied to decompose a high-resolution panchromatic image and the R, G, and B components of the multispectral images into multiscale representations. The fusion is performed by adding the multiscale coefficients of the high-resolution image to each component of the multispectral images. The new R, G, and B components are then obtained by taking inverse transform on the composite multiscale coefficients. Another color composite fusion method based on opponent-color processing has been developed in the field of night-time surveillance [59–61]. The opponent-color processing creates the relationship between the sensor opponent-color contrast and the human opponent-color perception. It was applied to fuse a low-light visual image and a thermal IR image by generating three channels of grayscale images that are assigned to the red, green, and blue (RGB) color space for a composite false color image. Xue and Blum [66] extended the opponent-color processing to the multiresolution space by incorporating the discrete wavelet frame (DWF) for fusion. The color composite fusion approaches with the MRA procedure are summarized in Table 5.

Table 5. The color-based approaches.

MRA Algorithm	Fusion Rule	Application	Reference
Orthogonal wavelet or shift invariant wavelet	R,G,B additive	remote sensing	[62, 63]
Nonseparable wavelet	R,G,B additive	remote sensing	[65]
Curvelet transform or contourlet transform	R,G,B additive	remote sensing	[45, 64]
discrete wavelet frame	oponent-color processing	law enforcement or night time surveillance	[66]

2.2.4. The Adaptive Approaches

Zhang suggested applying different fusion rules to segmented regions in [67]. The idea to applying a number of fusion rules to one region and select the "best" one based on an energy function. However, there is no evidence that can support the effectiveness of that energy function. Trying different fusion rules does not really implement an adaptive process. The idea of segmenting image into regions does make sense. The algorithm should be adaptive to the image itself. Wang et al. proposed a dynamic fusion method [68]. The input images are first segmented into regions. These regions aggregate into single target region, superposed target region, and background region. Three different fusion rules were applied to the coefficients in these regions. The importance thing is how well these regions are segmented.

Zheng et al. implemented a adaptive algorithm guided by an image quality index (IQI) [57]. The quality index for image fusion is proposed by Piella et al. in [69]. Zheng et al. assigned two parameters adjusted for an optimal fusion process; one is wavelet decomposition level (L_d) and the other is the wavelet length (L_w). The process actually implements a selection of appropriate L_d and L_w value in terms of an evaluation metric. This is an adjustment of the MRA algorithm instead of the fusion rule.

Another attempt is reported by Petrovic et al. for the fusion of still images and video sequences [70]. Instead of control the multiresolution decomposition level, the proposed method optimized the decision map for the low-pass sub-image with a evaluation metric. It is fair to assess the fusion results with an evaluation metric that is not employed as the optimization metric during the fusion process. However, such assessment is not available in that report [70].

There are a number of parameters that affect the final fusion result in terms of certain evaluation metric. How important are these parameters, such a decomposition level, filter size, fusion rule for the low-pass component, to mention just a few? In other words, which is the key factor that should be optimized with the highest priority? And what is the "significant" improvement? So far, there is still no answer to such question yet.

Conventionally, further analysis or post-processing is applied on the fused image. Is it possible to apply the analysis during the fusion process so that we can retain the information that are expected in the fusion result? The adaptive fusion scheme is trying to provide such a solution. The key issue is how to determine and adapt the parameters to a specific scenario. This direction is the future of image fusion technique. Even though the fusion is carried out at pixel level, higher level information from image region and feature will be incorporated in the fusion process for an optimal performance. The adaptive fusion will need such information to implement the adaptive process.

3. Performance Assessment

3.1. Background

The methods for performance assessment can be classified into two categories. One is reference-based method; the other is the blind method. Before going into the details, we must make clear about the concept. The reference-based method is a comparison with the final result. The blind assessment does not. It counts on how well the information/features are transferred to the fusion result. In other words, most of the blind assessment evaluate the fusion operation, the process itself, instead of a fused result. The blind assessment does not tell how well the fused image matches a true scene. The blind assessment is a relative measure of fusion result. Therefore, it does not make any sense to talk to fusion performance without considering the requirements of a specific application. Each metric can only provide a single measurement for the link between the input and fused images. The first question to answer is what is expected in the fusion result. This may vary with the

[0]See Section 3. for details.

requirements of different applications and determine which metric is used. The second is to confirm the availability of expected results either subjectively or objectively.

3.2. Reference-based Assessment

The reference-based assessment is straightforward, since the "perfect" reference is available. A comparison between the fused image and the reference image can be carried out. There are a number of metrics available for image comparison. The commonly used approaches include root mean square error (RMSE), normalized least square error (NLSE), the peak signal to noise ratio (PSNR), and correlation (CORR). The definition of these metrics are given in equation (3)-(6), where $I(x, y)$ and $F(x, y)$ stand for the reference and input (fused) image respectively and L is the maximum pixel value. The size of the two images is M-by-N. The advantage of the these methods is the simplicity and computational efficiency. However, there is the possibility that images with a similar RMSE value may exhibit a quite different appearance [71]. It is a disadvantage of the RMSE method.

$$RMSE = \sqrt{\frac{\sum_{x=1}^{M}\sum_{y=1}^{N}\left[F(x,y) - I(x,y)\right]^2}{MN}} \tag{3}$$

$$NLSE = \sqrt{\frac{\sum_{x=1}^{M}\sum_{y=1}^{N}\left[F(x,y) - I(x,y)\right]^2}{\sum_{x=1}^{M}\sum_{y=1}^{N}\left[F(x,y)\right]^2}} \tag{4}$$

$$PSNR = 10\log_{10}\left(\frac{L^2}{\frac{1}{MN}\sum_{x=1}^{M}\sum_{y=1}^{N}\left[F(x,y) - I(x,y)\right]^2}\right) \tag{5}$$

$$CORR = \frac{2\sum_{x=1}^{M}\sum_{y=1}^{N}F(x,y)\,I(x,y)}{\sum_{x=1}^{M}\sum_{y=1}^{N}R(x,y)^2 + \sum_{x=1}^{M}\sum_{y=1}^{N}I(x,y)^2} \tag{6}$$

More sophisticated methods include difference entropy (DE) and mutual information (MI). The difference entropy between two images reflects the difference between the average amount of information they contained. It is defined as:

$$DE = \left|\sum_{g=0}^{L-1} P_F(g)\log_2 P_F(g) - \sum_{g=0}^{L-1} P_I(g)\log_2 P_I(g)\right| \tag{7}$$

where $P_I(g)$ and $P_F(g)$ are the probability of pixel value g for the reference and input image respectively. The mutual information between the input and reference images is defined on the normalized joint gray level histogram $h_{FI}(u, v)$ and normalized marginal histogram of the two images i.e. $h_F(u)$ and $h_I(v)$:

$$MI = \sum_{v=1}^{L}\sum_{u=1}^{L} h_{FI}(u,v)\log_2\frac{h_{FI}(u,v)}{h_F(u)\,h_I(v)} \tag{8}$$

The notation for the equation (3) to (7) is given in Table 6.

A closely related topic is image quality assessment, which is based on the comparison with a reference. Wang and Bovik proposed an universal image quality index (UIQI) in [71]. The universal image quality index is based on the evidence that human visual

Table 6. The notation for equation (3)-(7).

$I(x,y)$	reference image
$F(x,y)$	fused image
L	maximum pixel value
$P_I(g)$	probability of value g of the reference image
$P_F(g)$	probability of value g of the fused image
$h_{IF}(u,v)$	normalized joint histogram of the reference image and he fused image
$h_I(u)$	normalized marginal histogram of the reference image
$h_F(v)$	normalized marginal histogram of the fused image

system is highly adapted to structural information and a measurement of the loss of structural information can provide a good approximation of the perceived image distortion. The definition of the UIQI is [71]:

$$Q = \frac{4\sigma_{ab}\mu_a\mu_b}{\left(\sigma_a^2+\sigma_b^2\right)\left({\mu_a}^2+{\mu_b}^2\right)} = \frac{\sigma_{ab}}{\sigma_a\sigma_b}\cdot\frac{2\mu_a\mu_b}{{\mu_a}^2+{\mu_b}^2}\cdot\frac{2\sigma_a\sigma_b}{\sigma_a^2+\sigma_b^2} \tag{9}$$

where μ_a and μ_b are the average values of image $a(x,y)$ and $b(x,y)$, σ_a , σ_b, and σ_{ab} are the variance and covariances respectively. There are:

$$\mu_a = \frac{1}{MN}\sum_{x=1}^{M}\sum_{y=1}^{N} a\left(x,y\right) \tag{10}$$

$$\mu_b = \frac{1}{MN}\sum_{x=1}^{M}\sum_{y=1}^{N} b\left(x,y\right) \tag{11}$$

$$\sigma_a^2 = \frac{1}{MN-1}\sum_{x=1}^{M}\sum_{y=1}^{N}\left(a\left(x,y\right)-\mu_a\right)^2 \tag{12}$$

$$\sigma_b^2 = \frac{1}{MN-1}\sum_{x=1}^{M}\sum_{y=1}^{N}\left(b\left(x,y\right)-\mu_b\right)^2 \tag{13}$$

$$\sigma_{ab} = \frac{1}{MN-1}\sum_{x=1}^{M}\sum_{y=1}^{N}\left(a\left(x,y\right)-\mu_a\right)\left(b\left(x,y\right)-\mu_b\right) \tag{14}$$

This equation has been modified to produce the structural similarity index measure (SSIM), which is better adapted to more general conditions [72]. The SSIM is defined as [72]:

$$SSIM\left(a,b\right) = \left[l\left(a,b\right)\right]^{\alpha}\left[c\left(a,b\right)\right]^{\beta}\left[s\left(a,b\right)\right]^{\gamma} \tag{15}$$

where there are:

$$l(a,b) = \frac{2\mu_a\mu_b + C_1}{\mu_a^2 + \mu_b^2 + C_1} \quad (16)$$

$$c(a,b) = \frac{2\sigma_a\sigma_b + C_2}{\sigma_a^2 + \sigma_b^2 + C_2} \quad (17)$$

$$s(a,b) = \frac{\sigma_{ab} + C_3}{\sigma_a\sigma_b + C_3} \quad (18)$$

In equation (15), three components are clearly defined to measure the degree of linear correlation between image a and b. The first one, $l(a,b)$, measures how the mean luminance is between the two images while the second $c(a,b)$ estimates the contrast. The third one $s(a,b)$ is the correlation of structure. The parameter α, β, and γ can be used to adjust the relative importance of the three components.

By setting $\alpha = \beta = \gamma = 1$ and $C_3 = C_2/2$, equation (15) becomes:

$$SSIM(a,b) = \frac{(2\mu_a\mu_b + C_1)(2\sigma_{ab} + C_2)}{\left(\mu_a^2 + \mu_b^2 + C_1\right)\left(\sigma_a^2 + \sigma_b^2 + C_2\right)} \quad (19)$$

In above equation, two constant values C_1 and C_2 are defined to avoid the instability when the denominators are very close to zero. These two values are further determined by two subjectively selected values K_1, K_2, and the dynamic range of the pixel values, i.e. $C_1 = (K_1L)^2$ and $C_2 = (K_2L)^2$. For a 8-bit gray-scale image, L is selected as 255.

3.3. Blind Assessment

In a practical application, the "perfect" reference is not always available. It would be better if the assessment can be accomplished without any reference image. The fused image only needs to refer to the input images to evaluate itself. Qu et al. considered mutual information (MI) and simply used the summation of the MI between the fused image (F) and inputs (A and B) to represent the difference in quality. The expression of MI-based fusion performance measure M_F^{AB} is [73]:

$$M_F^{AB} = \sum_{i,j} h_{AF}(i,j)\log_2 \frac{h_{AF}(i,j)}{h_A(i)\,h_F(j)} + \sum_{i,j} h_{BF}(i,j)\log_2 \frac{h_{BF}(i,j)}{h_B(i)\,h_F(j)} \quad (20)$$

where $h_{AF}(i,j)$ indicates the normalized joint grey level histogram of images A and F, $h_K(i,j)$ ($K = A, B$, and F) is the normalized marginal histogram of image A, B, or F. However, the MI metric still needs a reference value to compare with. We cannot tell in advance if a fused image with a given MI value is good or not; a reference point is a must. Furthermore, the MI-based approach is insensitive to impulsive noise and is subject to great change in the presence of additive Gaussian noise.

Another strategy of blind assessment without reference was proposed by Xydeas et al. in [74–76]. Their method aimed at measuring the amount of visual information transferred from the input images to the fused image. With the assumption that the edge information is closely related to the visual information, the metric is defined in terms of edge strength and orientation. The Sobel edge operator is used in the implementation to extract the strength and orientation information for each pixel. Unfortunately, the Sobel edge detection that is based on the measurement of the intensity gradient depends on image contrast and spatial magnification and hence one does not know in advance what level of edge strength corresponds to a significant feature [77, 78]. A subjective method was developed to carry out a qualitatively validation process [76].

Recently, Piella and Heijmans defined a fusion quality index based on Wang and Bovik's work on universal image quality index (UIQI) (see equation (9)) [69]. The quality measurement is applied to local regions using a sliding window of size 8 by 8 from top left to bottom right of the image. The overall quality is given by the average $Q = \sum_{k=1}^{K} Q_b/M$, where K is the total number of image blocks. The formula can be rewritten in another form like:

$$Q_0\left(a, b\right) = \frac{1}{|W|} \sum_{w \in W} Q_0\left(a, b\left|w\right.\right) \tag{21}$$

where a and b are two images for comparison while w stands for the sliding window. W is the family of all windows and $|W|$ is the cardinality of W. Piella and Heijmans defined three fusion quality indexes based on the UIQI concept [69, 79]:

$$\begin{aligned} Q\left(a, b, f\right) &= \frac{1}{|W|} \sum_{w \in W} \left[\lambda\left(w\right) Q_0\left(a, f\left|w\right.\right) + \left(1 - \lambda\left(w\right) Q_0\left(b, f\left|w\right.\right)\right)\right] && (22) \\ Q_w\left(a, b, f\right) &= \sum_{w \in W} c\left(w\right) \left[\lambda\left(w\right) Q_0\left(a, f\left|w\right.\right) + \left(1 - \lambda\left(w\right) Q_0\left(b, f\left|w\right.\right)\right)\right] && (23) \\ Q_E\left(a, b, f\right) &= Q_w\left(a, b, f\right) Q_w\left(a', b', f'\right)^{\alpha} && (24) \end{aligned}$$

where f stands for the fused image of a and b, and the variance measure $\lambda\left(w\right)$ can be expressed as:

$$\lambda\left(w\right) = \frac{s\left(a\left|w\right.\right)}{s\left(a\left|w\right.\right) + s\left(b\left|w\right.\right)} \tag{25}$$

where there are $C\left(w\right) = \max\left(s\left(a\left|w\right.\right), s\left(b\left|w\right.\right)\right)$ and $c\left(w\right) = C\left(w\right) / \left(\sum_{w' \in W} C\left(w'\right)\right)$. Herein, $s\left(a\left|w\right.\right)$ and $s\left(b\left|w\right.\right)$ are the local salience of image a and b respectively. One choice is using variance of image a and b within the window w of size 8 by 8. Equation (22) gives a general definition of fusion quality index. The value Q_0 measures the difference between the inputs and the fused image, weighted by the variance measurement. a', b', and f' are the corresponding edge map of image a, b, and f respectively. The weighted fusion quality index actually carries out a maximum selection operation to emphasize the overall importance of each block. In equation (24), the edge-dependent fusion quality index tries to include the effect of edges, their contribution being controlled by the parameter α. Piella and Heijmans also implemented a weighted sum or a scaled weighted sum of the similarity measure UIQI or SSIM [69,79]. The success of Piella's metrics depends on the performance of UIQI or SSIM.

Instead of using $\lambda\left(w\right)$ as the weighting coefficient, Cvejic et al. suggested a new measure $sim\left(a, b, F|w\right)$, which took into account the similarity between the input image block and the fused image block [80]. It is defined as:

$$sim\left(a,b,F|w\right)=\begin{cases}0 & if \quad \frac{\sigma_{af}}{\sigma_{af}+\sigma_{bf}}0\\ \frac{\sigma_{af}}{\sigma_{af}+\sigma_{bf}} & if \quad 0\leq\frac{\sigma_{af}}{\sigma_{af}+\sigma_{bf}}\leq 1\\ 1 & if \quad \frac{\sigma_{af}}{\sigma_{af}+\sigma_{bf}}1\end{cases} \tag{26}$$

And the new metric is:

$$Q_b=\sum_{w\in W} sim\left(a,b,F|w\right)Q\left(a,F|w\right)+\left(1-sim\left(a,b,F|w\right)\right)Q\left(b,F|w\right) \tag{27}$$

However, the advantage of the proposed method was not fully demonstrated in their publication [80].

Chen at al. considered the regional information for blind assessment in [81]. The metric they defined is as:

$$Q=\frac{\sum_{l=1}^{L}\left(\lambda\left(a^{W_l}\right)D\left(a^{W_l},F^{W_l}\right)+\lambda\left(b^{W_l}\right)D\left(b^{W_l},F^{W_l}\right)\right)}{\sum_{l=1}^{L}\left(\lambda\left(a^{W_l}\right)+\lambda\left(b^{W_l}\right)\right)} \tag{28}$$

where $\lambda\left(a^{W}\right)$ is the local region saliency, which is expressed as the summation of edge strength $G_a\left(x,y\right)$ [81]:

$$\lambda\left(a^{W}\right)=\sum_{(i,j)\in W} G_a\left(i,j\right)^{\alpha} \tag{29}$$

And $D\left(a^{W_l},F^{W_l}\right)$ is the similarity measure in the location region W_l, which is measured by the mean squared value of a contrast sensitivity function (CSF) filtered image $\hat{f}_a^W\left(x,y\right)$. The local error image $f_a^W\left(x,y\right)$ is obtained from the difference between the input and fused image. Three CSF filters were tested in their experiments [81].

Zheng et al. proposed to use the ratio of spatial frequency (SF) error as a metric for image fusion [82]. A reference SF is calculated from the SFs of the input images. According to [82], there is:

$$RF_R=\sqrt{\frac{1}{MN}\sum_{x=1}^{M}\sum_{y=1}^{N}\left[Grad^H\left(I_R\left(x,y\right)\right)\right]^2} \tag{30}$$

where $Grad^H\left(I_R\left(x,y\right)\right)$ is the horizontal reference gradient at point (x,y). The ratio of SF error is defined as: $rSFe=(SF_F-SF_R)/SF_R$.

Liu et al. proposed blind assessment metrics based on image phase congruency, which provide an absolute measure of image features [83, 84]. The input images and fused one are compared through their feature maps, phase congruency map, maximum and minimum moment. An example is given in Figure 8. How the features are presented in the image's feature maps is illustrated. Three metrics were proposed in [84]. One is defined as:

$$P'_{blind}=\left(P_p\right)^{\alpha}\left(P_M\right)^{\beta}\left(P_m\right)^{\gamma} \tag{31}$$

When there are two input images, we will obtain three values, e.g. P_p, P_M, and P_m respectively, which is defined as the maximum one of C_{ab}^k:

$$P_p = max\left(C^p_{1f}, C^p_{2f}, C^p_{mf}\right) \tag{32}$$
$$P_M = max\left(C^M_{1f}, C^M_{2f}, C^M_{mf}\right) \tag{33}$$
$$P_m = max\left(C^m_{1f}, C^m_{2f}, C^m_{mf}\right) \tag{34}$$

and there is:

$$C^k_{ab} = \frac{\sigma^k_{ab} + C_k}{\sigma^k_a \sigma^k_b + C_k} \tag{35}$$

Herein, C^k_{ab} stands for the correlation coefficients between two sets a and b. The symbol $\{k|p, M, m\}$ refers to the phase congruency map and its principal moments. The subfix 1, 2, m, and f correspond to the two inputs, their maximum-selected map, and the result derived from the fused image. The exponential parameters α, β, and γ can be adjusted based on the importance of the three components. In our experiments, all the three values are set to one and the small constant value C_k is selected as 0.0001.

To implement a local comparison, each pixel is compared within a 11-by-11 block in the image and only the points with a phase congruency value larger than 0.1 are used in the calculation. Assume there are total K blocks in the image, the final result is obtained by:

$$P'_{blind} = \frac{1}{K}\sum_{k=1}^{K} P'_{blind}(k) \tag{36}$$

3.4. Summary of Fusion Performance Assessment

It should be mentioned that the proposed approaches are subject to the presence of noise, which is introduced during the image acquisition. The evaluation metrics cannot identify and remove the noise automatically. In the MRA-based pixel-level fusion, the fusion rule is to keep the coefficients with a larger absolute value, which corresponds to the image feature like lines, edges, and boundaries. The input images come with the "features" (noise) that may not be part of the perfect result; however, the coefficient selection process may eventually retains such "feature" in the fused result. We will still get a confirm from our metric that that "feature" is available in the fused image. In that sense, the assessment metric is a tool to evaluate how the information (feature) is transferred to the fused result. This does not assure a perfect result unless the features are totally complementary. That is the limitation of all approaches that are based on feature measurement in the fused image. The only solution to this problem is the optimization of fusion process rather than the assessment metric. An example is given in Figure 9. Image in Figure 9(a) has a two-pixel-wide line across the center with a gray scale value of five. The second image is the blurred version of the first image by applying the averaging operation. The maximum gray scale value is around 1.2. The two images can represent a segment from a bigger picture captured by two image modalities. The MRA-based fusion generates a result shown in Figure 9(c) [1].

[1]The grayscale is adjusted ($[0, 0.2]$)to show the details of the result.

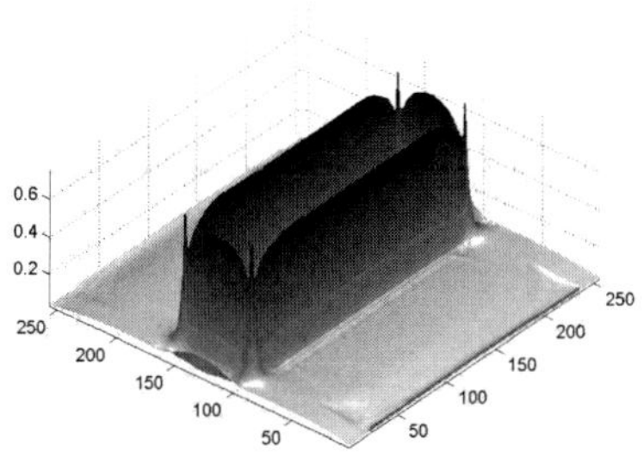

(a) Phase congruency map.

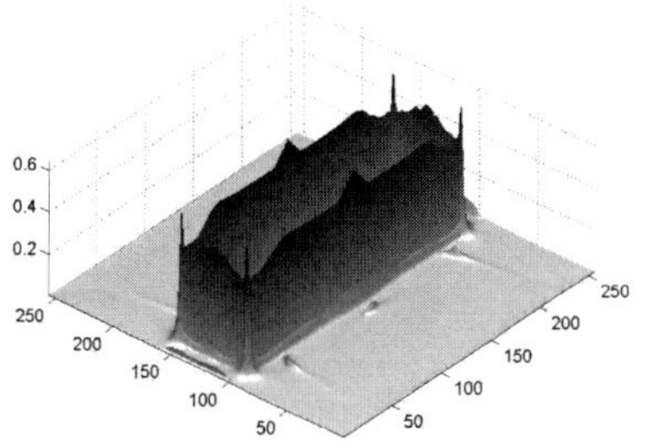

(b) Maximum moment.

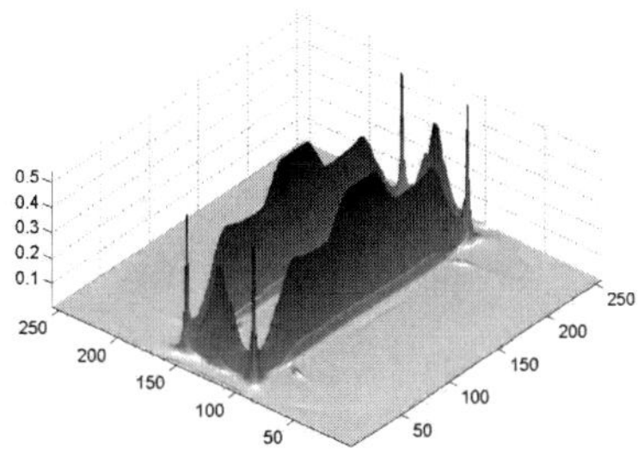

(c) Minimum moment.

Figure 8. The principal moments of phase congruency of the image in Figure 3(a).

If the evaluation metric is to assess whether the features from the two images are fused in the final result. The conclusion could be that the image in Figure 9(a) is "better" than the one in Figure 9(b). A good implementation of fusion will not introduce any noises or artifacts to the result, but the algorithm must be intelligent enough to identify what should be retained. More sophisticated fusion algorithms considers not only an isolated pixel but also its surroundings and correspondences in other frequency bands. However, no suppression operation has been taken into account when the situation in Figure 9 happens. Therefore, the objective evaluation metric cannot be implemented through finding a perfect result as the reference. This is the ultimate goal of fusion. The assessment of the fusion is carried out by evaluating how the features are transferred from the inputs to the fused result. A comparative study of currently available metrics will be helpful.

For the study of fusion performance assessment, the best way to do the assessment is through the application itself. What is the purpose of using image fusion for this application? Has this goal been achieved in terms of the established criteria? Using an assessment metric can provide a quantitative evaluation result, but the metric selected must be suitable to this application. There will not be one metric that works for all applications. Sometimes, multiple metrics may provide a better estimation. However, there will be a problem on how to validate the effectiveness of these metrics. How to identify a good metric? What does the difference between 0.6700 and 0.6500 tell us about the fusion performance? Do the difference 0.0200 make any sense to an application? Subjective methods taking human factor

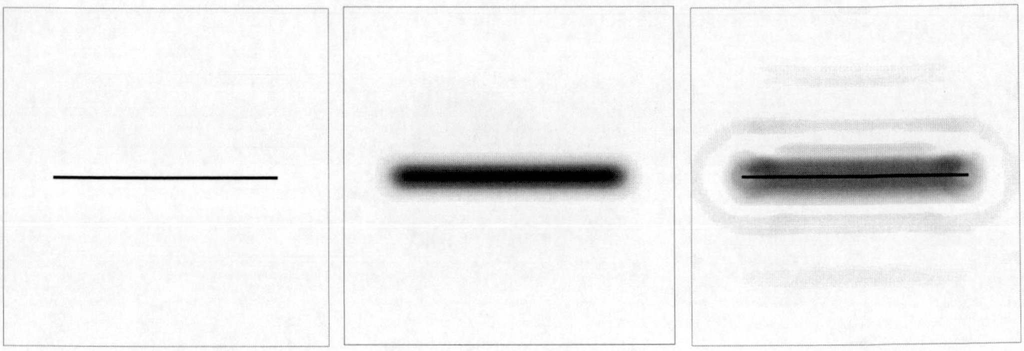

(a) Salient feature. (b) Weak feature. (c) The fused result.

Figure 9. The example of fusing a strong and a weak feature.

into account may be a solution [85].

4. The Applications

The multi-sensor images from different applications have been fused to achieve a better understanding of those applications. When we talk about an application, we may be more interested in what are the problems in the application and what can be solved with the image fusion technique. The purpose of this section is not to cover all the image fusion applications from different fields and study each case, such as forensic and non-destructive testing (NDT) [14, 86]. We try to get an understand of how the MRA-based combinative image fusion is applied in different scenarios. It should be aware that there are fusion algorithms other than MRA-based approaches available for various applications.

4.1. Surveillance Application

The vision technique beyond visible spectrum becomes essential to advanced surveillance systems. The performance of the systems can be enhanced through taking full advantage of the information captured across the electromagnetic spectrum. This makes the surveillance systems more robust and reliable under different conditions, such as a noisy and cluttered background, poor lighting, smoke, and fog. An example shown in Figure 10 is typical application and this pair of images have been widely used in image fusion research by numerous researchers [38, 85, 87–90]. Herein, we want to clarify two questions. The first is how the fused image is used. If the purpose is to detect the human body, the infrared image should be good enough to accomplish the task. There is no need to touch the visible image. If the fused image will be presented to an end user for his/her prompt response, the fusion with a visible image does contribute to this. However, the direct pixel-level fusion does not contribute much to this purpose.

Various fusion algorithms have been applied to this pair of images [38, 85, 87–90]. In [87], Toet et al. studied how the image fusion improved the situational awareness. The baseline is that a person can be identified together with the background reference features.

(a) Visible image.

(b) Infrared image.

Figure 10. The multi-sensor images of an UN camp [24].

The awareness of the relative position of the person in the scene was investigated among a group of observers. All the others work are lack of such study.

The use of a "cut and paste" version of the visible and IR image as the "perfect" reference is questionable [88]. If this is true, a "cut and paste" operation can be good enough and it does not make any sense to fuse them. The only requirement is that the person can

(a) Direct pixel-level fusion result.

(b) A modified fusion result.

Figure 11. The image fusion results of multi-sensor UN camp images [90].

be jointly detected from the source images. The purpose of image fusion is to provide an image that most suitable for further (automatic) analysis and human perception. However, the visible and IR images use a different pixel intensity table. The pixel-level fusion, which mixes the two intensity tables, can never obtain a result like the "perfect" one. A modified fusion approach was recently proposed in [90] by Liu and Laganière. The result is shown in Figure 11. That approach tried to present the fused image in the range of the visible spectrum, which is exactly as what people see from the scene.

Another application for surveillance is the concealed weapon detection [9,91]. Herein, one concept needs to bc clarify. When the "multi-sensor detection" is concerned, it means all the sensors can detect the concealed weapon and they work together to achieve an improved probability of detection rate. The fusion with a visible image is to provide the operators a composite image for their prompt response. This is a kind of visualization. An example is shown in Figure 12. The millimeter wave (MMW) image can reveal the region of concealed weapon while the visible image provides the information of facial pattern. Different from the application in Figure 11, the concealed weapon is not visible since it is underneath the clothing.

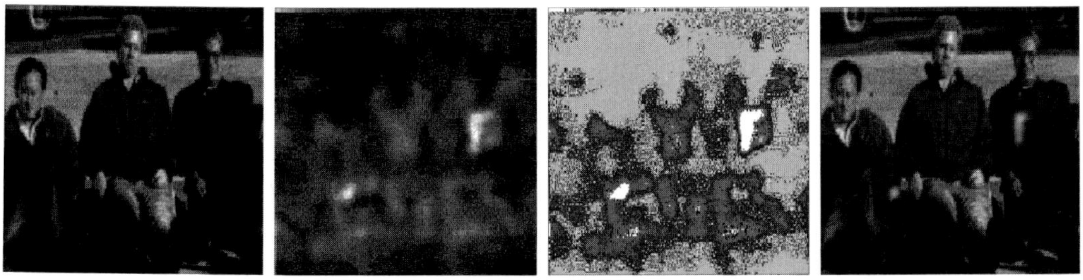

Figure 12. Concealed weapon detection from a MMW image. From left to right: visible image, MMW image, segmented MMW image, the synthesized image [84].

The infrared camera has been widely employed for surveillance applications. The fusion with video sequences captured by a CCD or CMOS camera for object detecting and tracking has been reported in many publications [92]. However, MRA-based pixel-level fusion does not contribute a lot for that purpose and we will not discuss those topics herein.

4.2. Biomedical Imaging

Laliberté et al. experimented with the fusion algorithms implemented in Rockinger's Matlab® for retinal images, which are of different modalitics (color,fluorescein angiogram), different resolutions, and taken at different times [93]. The authors claimed that their fused images contain more information and have a better contrast than the source images. Li et al. fused the fluorescence image and transmission image of cells with wavelet-based fusion algorithms [94]. They found the weighted algorithm was most suitable to their application. The fused image facilitated the determination of Acridine Orange distribution and the analysis of physiological state of cells.

4.3. Night Vision for Transportation

Krebs' study showed that fused imagery reliably produced performance better than or equivalent to that produced by either format of single-band imagery [95]. However, this paper did not report any study on the performance of different fusion algorithms. Tao et al. proposed a nonlinear scheme to enhance visible image and then fused with a thermal image for assisting drivers in poor lighting conditions [96]. The contributions from the enhancement and image fusion are not explicitly identified. In another study carried out by Bender et al. [97], they evaluated a series o image fusion in a head-tracked vision system, which is a driving system for wheeled and tracked military vehicles. One observation is that the low-contrast scene texture provided by the image-intensified CCD sensor required a higher relative weighting to be adequately translated into the fused image [97]. This means the region-based adaptive fusion is preferred for a real application.

4.4. Remote Sensing

Bretschneider et al. reviewed the image fusion methods for remote sensing in [98]. The MRA-based image fusion is one of the methods applied in fusing multispectral low-resolution remotely sensed image with a more highly resolved panchromatic image. The purpose is to obtain a high-resolution multispectral image which combines the spectral characteristic of he low-resolution data. A comprehensive comparison of the wavelet-based fusion approaches for panchromatic and multispectral images was carried out by Amolins et al. [99]. This literature provides a good reference for applying MRA-based approaches to the application of remote sensing. Simone et al. used the discrete wavelet together with the salience computation method to fuse multi-frequency and multi-polarization images [100]. An improvement of classification accuracy was achieved. Li et al. merged Landsat TM (thematic mapper) and SPOT (Satellite Pour l'Observation de la Terre) panchromatic images with discrete wavelet frame [101], but no evidence was provided on how the further analysis benefited from the fusion process. Teggi et al. used the *a tròus* algorithm to fuse the TM and panchromatic images to get a fused image more suitable for automatic classification. Zhao et al. developed a spatially adaptive wavelet fusion approach to combine polarimetric component images [102]. Due to the characteristic of polarization imaging, the fusion method is somewhat novel compared with conventional processing method.

5. Conclusion

It is worth pointing out at the end of this chapter that more attention must be paid to the application requirement itself, when image fusion technique is applied. Once the application requirements are specified, the assessment criteria can be set up accordingly. The available assessment metrics can be used to pre-select algorithms and post-evaluate the results as well. The adaptive fusion scheme is a promising method to identify the useful information that should be fused in the final result. A comparative study of different algorithms and assessment metrics under certain scenario will be helpful to understand the advantages of each fusion algorithm. Although the image fusion is implemented in the pixel level, a guidance from a higher level will be helpful to optimize the fusion process, because the images are interpreted by our human beings at a higher level.

Acknowledgements

Dr. A. Toet is acknowledged for providing the images used in this Chapter.

References

[1] "`http://www.physics.gatech.edu/academics/tutorial/phys2122/Chapter{\%}2034/ir.htm`," August 2007.

[2] I. Moria and J. P. Heather, "Review of image fusion technology in 2005," in *Proceedings of SPIE*, G. Raymond Peacock et al., Ed., Bellingham, WA, 2005, vol. 5782, pp. 29–45.

[3] P. J. Burt and R. J. Kolczynski, "Enhanced image capture through fusion," in *Proceedings of International Conference on Image Processing*, 1993, pp. 248–251.

[4] M. A. Slamani, L. Ramac, M. Uner, P. Varshney, D. D. Weiner, M. Alford, D. Derris, and V. Vannicola, "Enhancement and fusion of data for concealed weapons detection," in *Proceedings of SPIE*, 1997, vol. 3068, pp. 20–25.

[5] M. K. Uner, L. C. Ramac, P. K. Varshney, and M. Alford, "Concealed weapon detection: An image fusion approach," in *Proceedings of SPIE*, 1996, vol. 2942, pp. 123–132.

[6] P. K. Varshney, L. Ramac, M. A. Slamani, M. G. Alford, and D. Ferris, "Fusion and partitioning of data for the detection of concealed weapons," in *Proceedings of the International Conference on Multisource-Multisensor Information Fusion*, 1998.

[7] P. K. Varshney, H. Chen, and M. Uner, "Registration and fusion of infrared and millimetre wave images for concealed weapon detection," in *Proceedings of International Conference on Image Processing*, 1999, vol. 13, pp. 532–536.

[8] J. K. Aggarwal, *Multisensor Fusion for Computer Vision*, vol. 99 of *NATO ASI Series F: Computer and Systems Science*, 1993.

[9] Z. Xue, R.S. Blum, and Y. Li, "Fusion of visual and IR images for concealed weapon detection," in *Proceedings of ISIF 2002*, 2002, pp. 1198–1205.

[10] G. L. Foresti and L. Snidaro, "A distributed sensor network for video surveillance of outdoors," in *Multisensor Surveillance Systems*, G. L. Foresti, C. S. Regazzoni, and P. K. Varshney, Eds. Kluwer Academic Publishers, 2002.

[11] G. K. Matsopoulos, S. Marshall, and J. N. H. Brunt, "Multiresolution morphological fusion of MR and CT images of the human brain," *IEE Proceedings on Vision, Image and Signal Processing*, vol. 141, no. 3, pp. 137–142, 1994.

[12] I. Koren, A. Laine, and F. Taylor, "Enhancement via fusion of mammographic features," in *Proceedings of International Conference on Image Processing*, 1998, pp. 722–726.

[13] C. Pohl and J. L. Van Genderen, "Multi-sensor image fusion in remote sensing: Concepts, methods and applications," *International Journal of Remote Sensing*, vol. 19, no. 5, pp. 823–854, 1998.

[14] X. E. Gros, Z. Liu, K. Tsukada, and K. Hanasaki, "Experimenting with pixel-level NDT data fusion techniques," *IEEE Transaction on Instrumentation and Measurement*, vol. 49, no. 5, pp. 1083–1090, October 2000.

[15] S. G. Mallat, "A theory for multiresolution signal decomposition: The wavelet representation," *IEEE Transactions on Pattern Analysis and Machine Intelligence*, vol. 11, no. 7, pp. 674–693, 1989.

[16] R. S. Blum, Zhiyun Xue, and Zhong Zhang, "An overview of image fusion," in *Multi-Sensor Image Fusion and Its Applications*, Rick S. Blum and Zheng liu, Eds., chapter 1, pp. 1–35. Taylor and Francis, 2005.

[17] M. I. Smith and J. P. Heather, "Review of image fusion technology in 2005," in *Proceedings of SPIE*, 2005, vol. 5782, pp. 29–45.

[18] G. Piella, "A general framework for multiresolution image fusion: from pixels to regions," *Information Fusion*, vol. 4, no. 4, pp. 259–280, December 2003.

[19] G. Pajares and J. M. de la Crus, "A wavelet-based image fusion tutorial," *Pattern Recognition*, vol. 37, pp. 1855–1872, 2004.

[20] E. H. Adelson, C. H. Anderson, J. R. Bergen, P. J. Burt, and J. M. Ogden, "Pyramid methods in image processing," *RCA Engineer*, vol. 29, no. 6, pp. 33–41, 1984.

[21] H. Li, B. S. Manjunath, and S. K. Mitra, "Multisensor image fusion using the wavelet transform," *Graphical Models and Image Processing*, vol. 57, no. 3, pp. 235–245, 1995.

[22] O. Rockinger, "Image sequence fusion using a shift-invariant wavelet transform," in *Proceedings of International Conference on Image Processing*, 1997, vol. 3, pp. 288–301.

[23] Z. Liu, K. Tsukada, K. Hanasaki, Y. K. Ho, and Y. P. Dai, "Image fusion by using steerable pyramid," *Pattern Recognition Letters*, vol. 22, pp. 929–939, 2001.

[24] "`http://www.imagefusion.org`," August 2007.

[25] P. J. Burt and E. H. Adelson, "The laplacian pyramid as a compact image code," *IEEE Transactions on Communications*, vol. COM-31, no. 4, pp. 532–540, 1983.

[26] S. G. Mallat and W. L. Hwang, "Singularity detection and processing with wavelets," *IEEE Transactions on Information Theory*, vol. 38, no. 2, pp. 617–643, 1992.

[27] S. G. Nikolov, D. R. Bull, C. N. Canagarajah, M. Halliwell, and P. N. T. Wells, "Fusion of 2-D image using their multiscale edges," in *Proceedings of International Conference on Pattern Recognition*, 200, pp. 41–44.

[28] V. Petrovic and C. S. Xydeas, "Gradient-based multiresolution image fusion," *IEEE Transactions on Image Processing*, vol. 13, no. 2, pp. 228–237, Feburary 2004.

[29] A. Teot, "Image fusion by a ratio of low-pass pyramid," *Pattern Recognition Letters*, vol. 9, pp. 245–253, 1989.

[30] T. A. Wilson, S. K. Rogers, and M. Kabrisky, "Perceptual-based image fusion for hyperspectral data," *IEEE Transaction on Geoscience and Remote Sensing*, vol. 35, no. 4, pp. 1007–1017, July 1997.

[31] T. A. Wilson, S. K. Rogers, and L. R. Myers, "Perceptual-based hyperspectral image fusion using multiresolution analysis," *Optical Engineering*, vol. 34, no. 11, pp. 3154–3164, November 1995.

[32] I. Koren, A. Laine, and F. Taylor, "Image fusion using steerable dyadic wavelet transform," in *Proceedings of International Conference on Image Processing*, 1995, pp. 232–235.

[33] O. Rockinger, "Pixel level fusion of image sequences using wavelet frames," in *Proc. 16th Leeds Annual Statistical Research Workshop*. 1996, pp. 149–154, Leeds University Press.

[34] O. Rockinger and T. Fechner, "Pixel-level image fusion: The case of image sequences," in *SPIE*, 1998, vol. 3374, pp. 378–388.

[35] Z. Zhang and R. S. Blum, "Image fusion for a digital camera application," in *Proceedings of 32nd Asilomar Conference on Signals Systems, and Computers*, Monterey, CA, 1998, pp. 603–607.

[36] T. Pu and G. Q. Ni, "Contrast-based image fusion using discrete wavelet transform," *Optical Engineering*, vol. 39, no. 8, pp. 2075–2082, August 2000.

[37] S. Nikolov, P. Hill, D. Bull, and N. Canagarajah, "Wavelets for image fusion," in *Wavelets in signal and image analysis, Computational Imaging and Vision Series*, A. Petrosian and F. Meyer, Eds., pp. 213–244. Kluwer Academic Publishers, Dordrecht, The Netherlands, 2001.

[38] J. J. Lewis, R. J. O'Callaghan, S. G. Nikolov, and D. R. Bull, "Pixel- and region-based image fusion with complex wavelets," *Information Fusion*, vol. 8, pp. 119–130, 2007.

[39] H. Wang, J. Peng, and W. Wu, "Fusion algorithm for multisensor images based on discrete multiwavelet transform," *IEE Proceedings on Vision, Image Signal Process*, vol. 149, no. 5, pp. 283–289, October 2002.

[40] H. H. Wang, "A new multiwavelet-based approach to image fusion," *Journal of Mathematical Imaging and Vision*, vol. 21, pp. 177–192, 2004.

[41] B. Liu and J. Peng, "Image fusion method based on nonseparable wavelet," *Machine Vision and Applications*, vol. 16, pp. 189–196, 2005.

[42] C. J. C. Burges, "A tutorial on support vector machines for pattern recognition," in *Data Mining and Knowledge Discovery*, chapter 2, pp. 121–167. Kluwer Academic Publishers, Boston, USA, 1998.

[43] S. Zheng, W. Shi, J. Liu, G. Zhu, and J. Tian, "Multisource image fusion method using support value transform," *IEEE Transactions on Image Processing*, vol. 16, no. 7, pp. 1831–1839, July 2007.

[44] F. Nencini, A. Garzelli, S. Baronti, and L. Aparone, "Remote sensing image fusion using the curvelet transform," *Information Fusion*, vol. 8, pp. 143–156, 2007.

[45] M. Choi, R. Y. Kim, M. Nam, and H. O. Kim, "The curvelet transform for image fusion," in *Proceedings of ISPRS Congress Youth Forum*, 2004, vol. XXXV part B8, pp. 59–64.

[46] S. Li, J. T. Kwok, and Y. Wang, "Multifocus image fusion using artifical neural networks," *Pattern Recognition Letters*, vol. 23, pp. 985–997, 2002.

[47] N. Mitianoudis and T. Stathaki, "Pixel-based and region-based image fusion schemes using ICA bases," *Information Fusion*, vol. 8, pp. 131–142, 2007.

[48] M. Lin, W. Cai, and Z. Tan, "A region-based multi-sensor image fusion scheme using pulse-coupled neural network," *Pattern Recognition Letters*, vol. 27, pp. 1948–1956, 2006.

[49] J. Tang, "A contrast based image fusion technique in the dct domain," *Digital Signal Processing*, vol. 14, pp. 218–226, 2004.

[50] S. Gabarda and G. Cristobal, "Multifocus image fusion through pseudo-wigner distribution," *Optical Engineering*, vol. 44, no. 4, pp. 047001–1–9, 2005.

[51] Z. Zhang, *Investigations of Image Fusion*, Ph.D. thesis, Lehigh University, 1999.

[52] V. Petrovic and C. Xydeas, "Multiresolution image fusion using cross band feature selection," in *Proceedings of SPIE*, 1999, vol. 3719, pp. 319–326.

[53] P. J. Burt, "The pyramid as a structure for efficient computation," in *Multiresolution Image Processing and Analysis*, A. Rosenfold, Ed., pp. 6–35. Springer-Verlag, 1984.

[54] R. S. Blum, "Robust image fusion using a statistical signal processing approach," *Information Fusion*, vol. 6, pp. 119–128, 2005.

[55] J. Yang and R. S. Blum, *A Statistical Signal Processing Approachto Image Fusion Using Hidden Markov Models*, chapter 8, pp. 265–287, Signal Processing and Communications. Taylor and Francis, 2005.

[56] J. Yang, *Statistical Signal Processing Approaches to Image Fusion*, Ph.D. thesis, Lehigh University, September 2006.

[57] Y. Zheng, E. A. Essock, and B. C. Hansen, "Advanced discrete wavelet transform fusion algorithm and its optimization by using the metric of image quality index," *Optical Engineering*, vol. 44, no. 3, pp. 037003 (12 Pages), March 2005.

[58] W.J. Carper, T. M. Lillesand, and R. W. Kiefer, "The use of intensity-hue-saturation transformations for merging spot panchromaticc and multispectral image data," *Photogrammetric Engineering Remote Sensing*, vol. 56, pp. 459–467, 1990.

[59] E. D. Savoye, M. C. Seibert, J. E. Carrick, J. P. Racamato, D. A. Fay, A. N. Gove, and A. M. Waxman, "Color night vision: Opponent processing in the fusion of visible and ir imagery," *Neural Networks*, vol. 1, no. 10, pp. 1–6, 1997.

[60] D. A. Fay, A. M. Waxman, M. Aguilar, D. B. Ireland, J. P. Racamato, W. D. Ross, W. W. Streilein, and M. I. Braun, "Fusion of multi-sensor imagery for night vision: Color visualization, target learning and search," in *Proceedings of ISIF 2000*, 2000, pp. TuD3: 3–10.

[61] A. Toet and J. Walraven, "New false color mapping for image fusion," *Optical Engineering*, vol. 35, no. 3, pp. 650–658, 1996.

[62] J. Nunez, X. Otazu, O. Fors, A. Prades, V. Pala, and R. Arbiol, "Multiresolution-based image fusion with additive wavelet decomposition," *IEEE Transactions on Geoscience and Remote Sensing*, vol. 37, no. 3, pp. 1204–1211, 1999.

[63] D. A. Yocky, "Multiresolution wavelet decomposition image merger of landsat thematic mapper and spot panchromatic data," *Photogrammetric Engineering Remote Sensing*, vol. 62, pp. 1067–1074, 1996.

[64] Y. Zheng, J. Song, W. Zhou, and R. Wang, "False color fusion for multi-band sar images based on contourlet transform," *ACTA Automatica Sinica*, vol. 33, no. 4, pp. 337–341, 2007.

[65] Z. Li, Z. Jing, X. Yang, and S. Sun, "Color transfer based remote sensing image fusion using non-separable wavelet frame transform," *Pattern Recognition Letters*, vol. 26, no. 13, pp. 2006–2014, 2005.

[66] Z. Xue and R. S. Blum, "Concealed weapon detection using color image fusion," in *Proceedings of 6th International Conference of Information Fusion*, 2003, vol. 1, pp. 622–627.

[67] Y. Zhang, "Adaptive region-based image fusion using energy evaluation model for fusion decision," *Singal, Image and Video Processing*, 2007.

[68] Z. Wang, Z. Qin, and Y. Liu, "A framework of region-based dynamic image fusion," *Journal of Zhejiang University Science A*, vol. 8, no. 1, pp. 42–48, 2007.

[69] G. Piella and H. Heijmans, "A new quality metric for image fusion," in *Proceedings of International Conference on Image Processing*, Bacelona, 2003.

[70] V. Petrovic and T. Cootes, "Objectively adaptive image fusion," *Information Fusion*, vol. 8, pp. 168–176, 2007.

[71] Z. Wang and A. C. Bovik, "A universal image quality index," *IEEE Signal Processing Letters*, vol. 9, no. 8, pp. 81–84, 2002.

[72] Z. Wang, A. C. Bovik, H. R. Sheikh, and E. P. Simoncelli, "Image quality assessment: From error visibility to structural similarity," *IEEE Transactions on Image Processing*, vol. 13, no. 4, pp. 600–612, April 2004.

[73] G. Qu, D. Zhang, and P. Yan, "Information measure for performance of image fusion," *Electronics Letters*, vol. 38, no. 7, pp. 313–315, 2002.

[74] C. S. Xydeas and V. Petrovic, "Objective image fusion performance measure," *Electronics Letters*, vol. 36, no. 4, pp. 308–309, 2000.

[75] C. S. Xydeas and V. Petrovic, "Objective pixel-level image fusion performance measure," in *Proceedings of SPIE*, 2000, vol. 4051, pp. 89–98.

[76] V. Petrovic and C. Xydeas, "Objective evaluation of signal-level image fusion performance," *Optical Engineering*, vol. 44, no. 8, pp. 087003–1–8, August 2005.

[77] P. Kovesi, "Image features from phase congruency," *Videre: A Journal of Computer Vision Research*, vol. 1, no. 3, 1999.

[78] P. Kovesi, "Image features from phase congruency," Tech. Rep., University of Western Australia, 1995.

[79] G. Piella, "New quality measures for image fusion," in *Proceedings of International Conference on Information Fusion*, Stockholm, Sweden, 2004.

[80] N. Cvejic, A. Loza, D. Bull, and N. Canagarajah, "A similarity metric for assessment of image fusion algorithms," *International Journal of Signal Processing*, vol. 2, no. 3, pp. 178–182, 2005.

[81] H. Chen and P. K. Varshney, "A human perception inspired quality metric for image fusion based on regional information," *Information Fusion*, vol. 8, pp. 193–207, 2007.

[82] Y. Zheng, E. A. Essock, B. C. Hansen, and A. M. Haun, "A new metric based on extended spatial frequency and its application to dwt based fusion algorithms," *Information Fusion*, vol. 8, pp. 177–192, 2007.

[83] Z. Liu, D. S. Forsyth, and R. Laganiere, "A feature-based metric for the quantitative evaluation of pixel-level image fusion," *Computer Vision and Image Understanding*, 2007.

[84] Z. Liu, *Investigations on Multi-Sensor Image System and Its Surveillance Applications*, Ph.d. thesis, University of Ottawa, Ottawa, Ontario, Canada, September 2007.

[85] T. Dixon, J. Noyes, T. Troscianko, E. F. Canga, D. Bull, and N. Canagarajah, "Psychophysical and metric assessment of fused images," in *Proceedings of 2nd Symposium on Applied Perception in Graphics and Visualization*, 2005, pp. 43–50.

[86] C. Y. Wen and J. K. Chen, "Multi-resolution image fusion technique and its application to forensic science," *Forensic Science International*, vol. 140, pp. 217–232, 2004.

[87] A. Toet, J. K. IJspeert, A. M. Waxman, and M. Aguilar, "Fusion of visual and thermal imagery improves situational awareness," *Displays*, vol. 18, pp. 85–95, 1997.

[88] N. Cvejic, D. R. Bull, and C. N. Canagarajah, "Mctric for multimodal image sensor fusion," *Electronics Letters*, vol. 43, no. 2, pp. 95–96, January 2007.

[89] G. Piella and H. Heijmans, "multiresolution image fusion guided by a multimodal segmentation," in *Proceedings of Advanced Concepts for Intelligent Vision System*, Ghent, Belgium, September 2002, pp. S00–1–8.

[90] Z. Liu and R. Laganiere, "Context enhancement through infrared vision: A modified scheme," *Signal, Image, and Video Processing*, 2007.

[91] H. M. Chen, S. Lee, R. M. Rao, M. A. Slamani, and P. K. Varshney, "Imaging for concealed weapon detection," *IEEE Singal Processing Magazine*, vol. 22, no. 2, pp. 52–61, March 2005.

[92] G. L. Foresti, G. S. Regazzoni, and P. K. Varshney, *Multisensor Surveillance Systems: The Fusion Perspective*, Kluwer Academic Publishers, 2003.

[93] F. Laliberte, L. Gagnon, and Y. Sheng, "Registration and fusion of retinal images - an evaluation study," *IEEE Transactions on Medical Imaging*, vol. 22, no. 5, pp. 661–673, May 2003.

[94] Q. Li, C. Dai, X. Yu, and S. Wang, "Study of image fusion methods suitable for biomedical image," in *Proceedings of SPIE*, 1998, vol. 3548, pp. 158–165.

[95] W. K. Krebs, J. S. McCarley, T. Kozek, G. M. Miller, M. J.Sinai, and F. S. Werblin, "An evaluation of a sensor fusion system to improve drivers nighttime detection of road harzards," in *Proceedings of the 43rd Annual Meeting Human Factors and Ergonomics Society*, 1999, pp. 1333–1337.

[96] L. Tao, H. Ngo, M. Zhang, A. Livingston, and V. Asari, "A multi-sensor image fusion and enhancement system for assisting drivers in poor lighting conditions," in *Proceedings of the 34th Applied Imagery and Pattern Recognition Workshop*, October 2005.

[97] E. J. Bender, C. E. Reese, and G. S. van der Wal, "Comparison of additive image fusion vs. feature-level image fusion techniuqes for enhanced night driving," in *Proceedings of SPIE*, C. Bruce Johnson, Divyendu Sinha, and Philip A. Lapante, Eds., 2003, vol. 4796, pp. 140–151.

[98] T. Bretschneider and O. Kao, "Image fusion in remote sensing," in *Proceedings of the Online Symposium for Electronics Engineers*, 2000, pp. 1–8.

[99] K. Amolins, Y. Zhang, and P. Dare, "Wavelet based image fusion techniques - an introduction, review and comparison," *Journal of photgrammetry and Remote Sensing*, vol. 62, pp. 249–263, 2007.

[100] G. Simone, A. Farina, F. C. Morabito, S. B. Serpico, and L. Bruzzone, "Image fusion techniques for remote sensing application," *information Fusion*, vol. 3, pp. 3–15, 2002.

[101] S. Li, J. T. Kwok, and Y. Wang, "Using the discrete wavelet frame transform to merge landsat TM and SPOT panchromatic images," *Information Fusion*, vol. 3, pp. 17–23, 2002.

[102] Y. Zhao, Q Pan, and H. Zhang, "New polarization imaging method based on spatially adaptive wavelet image fusion," *Optical Engineering*, vol. 45, no. 12, pp. 123202–1–7, December 2006.

In: Computer-Aided Design...
Editors: C.M. De Smet et al, pp. 319-350
ISBN 978-1-60456-860-8

Expert Commentary C

Computer Aided Geometric Design with Powell-Sabin Splines

Hendrik Speleers[1,2], *Paul Dierckx*[1] *and Stefan Vandewalle*[1]

[1]Katholieke Universiteit Leuven, Department of Computer Science, Belgium
[2]Fund for Scientific Research Flanders, Belgium

Abstract

Powell-Sabin splines are bivariate C^1-continuous quadratic splines defined on an arbitrary triangulation. Their construction is based on a particular split of each triangle in the triangulation into six smaller triangles. In this article we give an overview of the properties of Powell-Sabin splines in the context of computer aided geometric design. These splines can be represented in a compact normalized B-spline basis with an intuitive geometric interpretation involving control triangles. Using these triangles one can interactively change the shape of the splines in a predictable way. We describe the simple subdivision rules for Powell-Sabin splines, and discuss some applications. We consider a new efficient spline visualization technique based on subdivision. We also look at two useful generalizations of the Powell-Sabin splines, i.e., QHPS splines and NURPS surfaces. The QHPS splines are a hierarchical variant of Powell-Sabin splines. They have very similar properties as the Powell-Sabin splines, and their hierarchical nature allows a local refinement of the spline in a very straightforward way. The NURPS surface is the rational extension of the Powell-Sabin spline. By means of weights they give extra degrees of freedom to the designer for the modelling of surfaces.

1. Introduction

The ability to represent complex surfaces on the computer is important in a broad range of applications [10]. Tensor product B-splines are today's most commonly used surface splines in computer aided geometric design (CAGD) packages. They are very attractive because of their compact representation, the ease of implementation and their efficiency. The B-spline control net of such a surface enables local adaptations in a geometrically intuitive way. A definite drawback, however, is that they are restricted to regular meshes on rectangular domains. Therefore, they are not well suited to represent strongly irregular objects defined on arbitrary domains.

Instead of using the tensor product representation on rectangular domains, one can also describe piecewise bivariate polynomial surfaces in terms of barycentric coordinates with respect to a triangular domain. These triangular patches in Bernstein form are called Bézier triangles [9]. In spite of the flexibility of a triangular mesh, the representation of complex smooth surfaces can require a large number of Bézier triangles. Imposing smoothness conditions between these patches results in a large number of non-trivial continuity relations between the coefficients.

A number of authors studied the construction of smooth bivariate spline functions on arbitrary triangulations. A major difficulty is to determine the dimension of such spline spaces. In general, it is not possible to express the dimension in terms of the number of vertices and triangles in the triangulation. There are some results for particular choices of polynomial degree and smoothness [1, 3, 13], and for particular constrained triangulations [11]. Yet, in general and especially for low degree polynomials the problem remains open. One can overcome this problem by using so-called macro-elements, where each triangle in the triangulation is split in a particular way. Well-known in the finite element literature is the C^1-continuous cubic Clough-Tocher spline space [5]. For C^1-continuous quadratic splines, Powell and Sabin [21] constructed an element by splitting all triangles into six subtriangles.

Powell-Sabin splines can be compactly represented in a normalized basis. Dierckx [6] discovered that the basis splines have an intuitive geometric interpretation by means of control triangles. Windmolders [34] was the first to investigate the use of Powell-Sabin splines in CAGD applications. Many new interesting properties and techniques have been developed since, e.g., a triadic subdivision scheme. We will overview them in the context of computer aided design and modelling. Section 2. is devoted to the Powell-Sabin spline space. It recalls some basic concepts of Powell-Sabin splines and the construction of a suitable normalized basis. In section 3. we describe a subdivision scheme for the splines, and we discuss some applications. The next sections cover two generalizations of Powell-Sabin splines. Section 4. discusses a hierarchical variant of the splines, called QHPS splines. They retain similar properties as the Powell-Sabin splines, but they are defined on a hierarchical triangulation. These splines are very useful in an adaptive local refinement strategy. In section 5. we consider NURPS surfaces, a rational extension of Powell-Sabin splines. They give the designer more degrees of freedom by means of extra weights.

2. Powell-Sabin Splines

In this section we detail the theory of Powell-Sabin splines. We first recall some general concepts of polynomials on triangles in their Bernstein-Bézier representation. Powell-Sabin splines are defined on arbitrary triangulations refined with a particular split. We discuss a normalized basis for this spline space, and we give an overview of their properties.

2.1. Polynomials on Triangles

Barycentric coordinates provide an elegant tool for defining points inside a triangle. Let $\mathcal{T}(V_1, V_2, V_3)$ be a non-degenerated triangle. An arbitrary point P in the plane of the triangle can be uniquely expressed in terms of the barycentric coordinates $\tau = (\tau_1, \tau_2, \tau_3)$ with respect to $\mathcal{T}$, such that

$$P = \sum_{i=1}^{3} \tau_i V_i, \quad \text{and} \quad \tau_1 + \tau_2 + \tau_3 = 1. \tag{2.1}$$

If the point P lies inside the triangle $\mathcal{T}$, then its barycentric coordinates are all positive. Consider two points in the plane of the triangle, i.e., P_1 and P_2. The barycentric direction $\delta = (\delta_1, \delta_2, \delta_3)$ of the vector $P_2 - P_1$ with respect to $\mathcal{T}$ is defined as the difference of the barycentric coordinates of both points. If the Euclidian distance $\|P_2 - P_1\| = 1$, then δ is called a unit barycentric direction.

Let Π_d denote the linear space of bivariate polynomials of total degree less than or equal to d. Any polynomial $p_d \in \Pi_d$ on triangle $\mathcal{T}$ has a unique Bernstein-Bézier representation [9],

$$p_d(\tau) = \sum_{i+j+k=d} b_{ijk} B^d_{ijk}(\tau), \tag{2.2}$$

with

$$B^d_{ijk}(\tau) = \frac{d!}{i!j!k!} {\tau_1}^i {\tau_2}^j {\tau_3}^k \tag{2.3}$$

the Bernstein polynomials on the domain triangle $\mathcal{T}$. The coefficients b_{ijk} are called Bézier ordinates, and the Bézier domain points ξ_{ijk} are defined as the points with barycentric coordinates $\left(\frac{i}{d}, \frac{j}{d}, \frac{k}{d}\right)$. By associating each Bézier ordinate b_{ijk} with the Bézier domain points ξ_{ijk}, we can display the Bernstein-Bézier representation schematically as in Figure 1(a) for the case $d = 2$. The piecewise linear interpolant of the Bézier control points, defined as (ξ_{ijk}, b_{ijk}), is called the Bézier control net. This control net is tangent to the polynomial surface $z = p_d(\tau)$ at the three vertices of the triangle, and it mimics the shape of the Bernstein-Bézier surface. Figure 1(b) shows such a surface together with its control points and control net.

Polynomials in their Bernstein-Bézier representation (2.2) can be evaluated using the recursive de Casteljau algorithm [4], i.e.,

$$p_d(\tau) = b^d_{0,0,0}(\tau), \tag{2.4a}$$

where

$$b^0_{i,j,k}(\tau) = b_{ijk}, \qquad i + j + k = d, \tag{2.4b}$$

$$b^r_{i,j,k}(\tau) = \tau_1\, b^{r-1}_{i+1,j,k}(\tau) + \tau_2\, b^{r-1}_{i,j+1,k}(\tau) + \tau_3\, b^{r-1}_{i,j,k+1}(\tau), \quad i + j + k = d - r, \quad \text{and} \quad r = 1, \ldots, d. \tag{2.4c}$$

This algorithm is numerically stable and has many interesting properties [9]. Besides for evaluation, the algorithm can also be used for computing derivatives and for obtaining continuity conditions on neighbouring triangular patches.

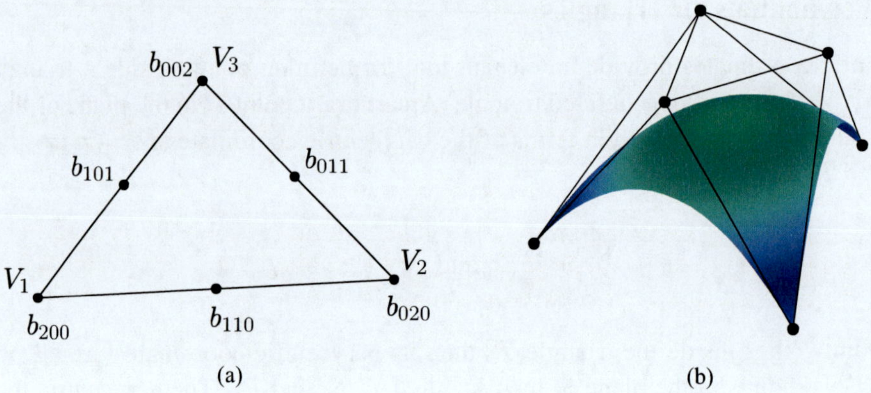

Figure 1. (a) Schematic representation of a quadratic bivariate polynomial by means of its Bézier ordinates b_{ijk}. (b) A quadratic Bernstein-Bézier polynomial with its control points and control net.

Representing complex surfaces requires the use of a large number of Bézier triangles. Preserving a certain degree of continuity between all patches results then in a large set of non-trivial relations between their Bézier ordinates. Therefore, one has looked for piecewise polynomials with inherent global continuity conditions.

2.2. The Powell-Sabin Spline Space

Consider a simply connected subset $\Omega \subset \mathbb{R}^2$ with polygonal boundary $\partial\Omega$. Assume a conforming triangulation Δ of Ω is given, consisting of t triangles $\mathcal{T}_j$, with $j = 1, \ldots, t$, and having n vertices V_k, with $k = 1, \ldots, n$. A triangulation is conforming if no triangle contains a vertex different from its own three vertices.

The Powell-Sabin (PS) refinement Δ^* of Δ partitions each triangle $\mathcal{T}_j$ into six smaller triangles in the following way:

1. Choose an interior point Z_j in each triangle $\mathcal{T}_j$, so that if two triangles $\mathcal{T}_i$ and $\mathcal{T}_j$ have a common edge, then the line joining Z_i and Z_j intersects the common edge at a point R_{ij} between its vertices.
2. Join each point Z_j to the vertices of $\mathcal{T}_j$.
3. For each edge of the triangle $\mathcal{T}_j$
   (a) which belongs to the boundary $\partial\Omega$: join Z_j to an arbitrary point on that edge;
   (b) which is common to a triangle $\mathcal{T}_i$: join Z_j to R_{ij}.

Figure 2(a) displays a triangulation with 8 triangles, and a corresponding PS refinement containing 48 triangles.

The space of piecewise quadratic polynomials on Δ^* with global C^1-continuity is called the Powell-Sabin spline space:

$$S_2^1(\Delta^*) := \left\{ s \in C^1(\Omega) : s|_{\mathcal{T}_j^*} \in \Pi_2,\ \mathcal{T}_j^* \in \Delta^* \right\}. \tag{2.5}$$

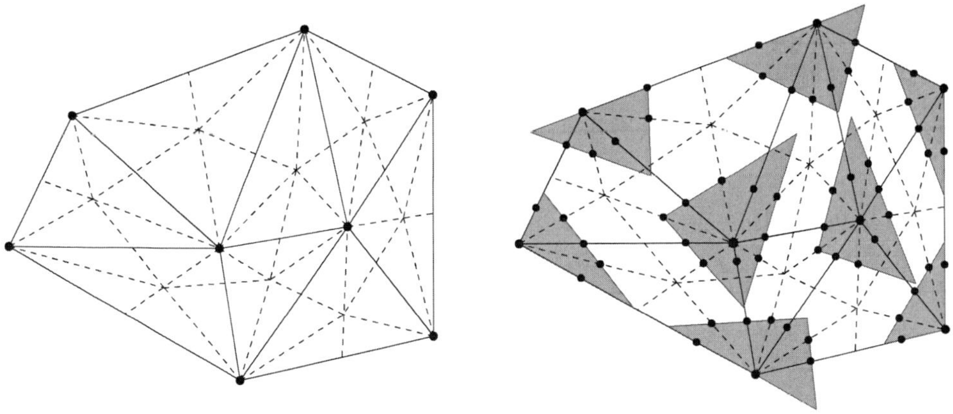

(a) (b)

Figure 2. (a) A PS refinement Δ^* (in dashed lines) of a given triangulation Δ (in solid lines). (b) The PS points (bullets) and a set of suitable PS triangles (shaded).

Each of the $6t$ triangles resulting from the PS refinement is the domain triangle of a quadratic Bernstein-Bézier polynomial. Powell and Sabin [21] proved that the following interpolation problem

$$s(V_k) = f_k, \quad \frac{\partial s}{\partial x}(V_k) = f_{x,k}, \quad \frac{\partial s}{\partial y}(V_k) = f_{y,k}, \qquad k = 1, \ldots, n, \tag{2.6}$$

has a unique solution $s(x, y) \in S_2^1(\Delta^*)$ for any given set of n $(f_k, f_{x,k}, f_{y,k})$-triplets. Hence, the dimension of the Powell-Sabin spline space $S_2^1(\Delta^*)$ equals $3n$.

2.3. A B-spline Representation

Dierckx [6] presented a geometric method to construct a normalized basis for the spline space $S_2^1(\Delta^*)$. Every Powell-Sabin spline can then be represented as

$$s(x, y) = \sum_{i=1}^{n} \sum_{j=1}^{3} c_{i,j} B_i^j(x, y). \tag{2.7}$$

To obtain the basis functions $B_i^j(x, y)$, we associate with each vertex V_i three linearly independent triplets $(\alpha_{i,j}, \beta_{i,j}, \gamma_{i,j})$, $j = 1, 2, 3$. These triplets are determined as follows:

1. For each vertex $V_i \in \Delta$ with Cartesian coordinates (x_i, y_i), find the corresponding PS points. These points are the immediately surrounding Bézier domain points of V_i in the PS refinement Δ^*. The vertex V_i itself is also a PS point. In Figure 2(b) the PS points are indicated as bullets.

2. For each vertex V_i, find a triangle $t_i(Q_{i,1}, Q_{i,2}, Q_{i,3})$ that contains all the PS points of V_i. These triangles t_i, $i = 1, \ldots, n$, are called PS triangles, and we denote their vertices as $Q_{i,j} = (X_{i,j}, Y_{i,j})$. Figure 2(b) shows a possible set of PS triangles.

3. The three linearly independent triplets $(\alpha_{i,j}, \beta_{i,j}, \gamma_{i,j})$, $j = 1, 2, 3$, are derived from the PS triangle t_i of vertex V_i as follows:

   - $\alpha_i = (\alpha_{i,1}, \alpha_{i,2}, \alpha_{i,3})$ are the barycentric coordinates of V_i with respect to t_i,
   - $\beta_i = (\beta_{i,1}, \beta_{i,2}, \beta_{i,3})$ and $\gamma_i = (\gamma_{i,1}, \gamma_{i,2}, \gamma_{i,3})$ are the unit barycentric directions with respect to t_i, in the x- and y-direction respectively.

   Practically, they can be computed as

$$\alpha_i = \left(\frac{1}{E} \begin{vmatrix} x_i & y_i & 1 \\ X_{i,2} & Y_{i,2} & 1 \\ X_{i,3} & Y_{i,3} & 1 \end{vmatrix}, \frac{1}{E} \begin{vmatrix} X_{i,1} & Y_{i,1} & 1 \\ x_i & y_i & 1 \\ X_{i,3} & Y_{i,3} & 1 \end{vmatrix}, \frac{1}{E} \begin{vmatrix} X_{i,1} & Y_{i,1} & 1 \\ X_{i,2} & Y_{i,2} & 1 \\ x_i & y_i & 1 \end{vmatrix} \right),$$

$$\beta_i = \left(\frac{Y_{i,2} - Y_{i,3}}{E}, \frac{Y_{i,3} - Y_{i,1}}{E}, \frac{Y_{i,1} - Y_{i,2}}{E} \right),$$

$$\gamma_i = \left(\frac{X_{i,3} - X_{i,2}}{E}, \frac{X_{i,1} - X_{i,3}}{E}, \frac{X_{i,2} - X_{i,1}}{E} \right),$$

   with

$$E = \begin{vmatrix} X_{i,1} & Y_{i,1} & 1 \\ X_{i,2} & Y_{i,2} & 1 \\ X_{i,3} & Y_{i,3} & 1 \end{vmatrix}.$$

The Powell-Sabin B-spline $B_i^j(x, y)$ is defined as the unique solution of the interpolation problem (2.6) with all $(f_k, f_{x,k}, f_{y,k}) = (0, 0, 0)$ except for $k = i$, where $(f_i, f_{x,i}, f_{y,i}) = (\alpha_{i,j}, \beta_{i,j}, \gamma_{i,j}) \neq (0, 0, 0)$. Figure 3 shows an example of three linearly independent Powell-Sabin B-splines corresponding to the same vertex.

Choice of PS triangles. The set of PS triangles is not uniquely defined for a given PS refinement. One possibility for their construction is to calculate triangles of minimal area, the so-called optimal PS triangles [6]. Computationally, this problem leads to a quadratic programming problem. An alternative (and easier to implement) solution is given in [31], where the sides of the PS triangle are found by connecting two neighbouring PS points.

From a practical point of view, other choices may be more appropriate. A particular choice of the PS triangles can, e.g., simplify the treatment of boundary conditions [28]. In such a case it is better to construct PS triangles at the boundary vertices with one side tangential and another normal to the boundary curve. For quasi-interpolation [20] the corners of each PS triangle are preferred to be chosen on edges of the triangulation.

2.4. Properties of the B-spline Basis

The Powell-Sabin B-splines have some nice properties, which are very useful in CAGD and approximation applications. In this section we review some of them. Later on, in section 3., we will discuss in more detail subdivision rules for Powell-Sabin splines in the representation (2.7).

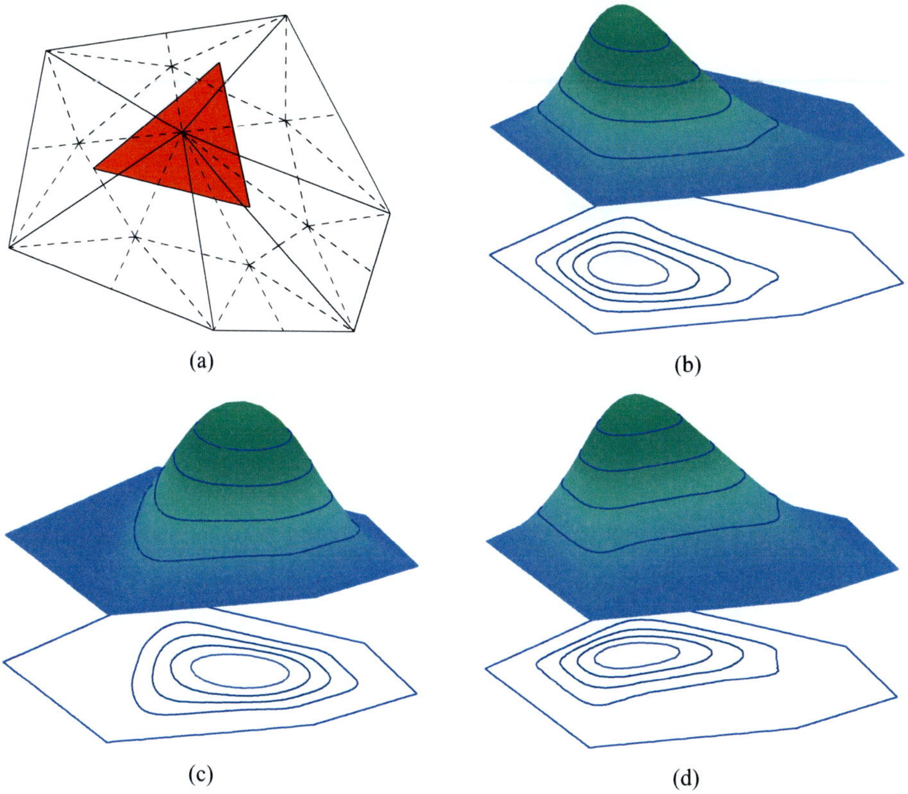

Figure 3. (a) A given triangulation with PS refinement. (b)-(d) The three Powell-Sabin B-splines $B_i^j(x, y)$ corresponding to the central vertex V_i and its PS triangle. The contour lines of the basis functions are depicted.

Local support. It is easy to see that each Powell-Sabin B-spline $B_i^j(x, y)$ has a local support, because the basis function is zero outside the molecule M_i of vertex V_i. The molecule (also called 1-ring) is defined as the union of all triangles in the triangulation that contain V_i.

Convex partition of unity. Dierckx showed in [6] that the proposed basis forms a convex partition of unity on the domain Ω, i.e.,

$$B_i^j(x, y) \geq 0, \quad \text{and} \quad \sum_{i=1}^{n} \sum_{j=1}^{3} B_i^j(x, y) = 1, \quad \text{for all } (x, y) \in \Omega. \tag{2.8}$$

The fact that each PS triangle t_i contains all PS points of vertex V_i guarantees the positivity of the basis functions.

Stability. Maes *et al.* [19] proved that the basis is L_∞-stable. For the max-norms

$$\|c\|_\infty = \max_{i,j} |c_{i,j}|, \quad \text{and} \quad \|s(x, y)\|_\infty = \max_{\Omega} |s(x, y)|,$$

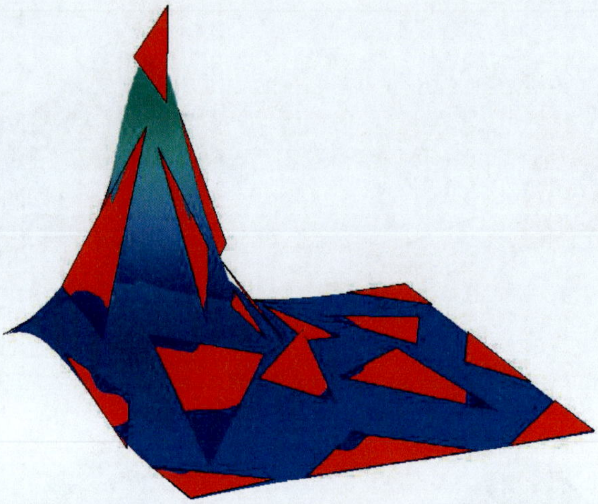

Figure 4. A Powell-Sabin spline and its PS control triangles.

they showed that for all choices of the coefficient vector c, one has that

$$K_1 \|c\|_\infty \leq \|s(x,y)\|_\infty \leq K_2 \|c\|_\infty, \tag{2.9}$$

where $K_2 = 1$, and K_1 depends only on the smallest angle θ_Δ in the triangulation Δ and on the size of the PS triangles. Moreover, the smaller the PS triangles the better (the larger) the stability constant. In [25] an adapted version of the proof is given, resulting in a sharper stability bound. The ratio K_2/K_1 yields an upper bound for the condition number of the basis. It reflects the influence of a change in the coefficients on the magnitude of the corresponding spline with respect to the L_∞-norm. In [26, 32] the stability of the Powell-Sabin spline basis is proven in the more general L_p-norm with $1 \leq p \leq \infty$.

A stable local basis provides spline approximations of smooth functions with an optimal order [16].

PS control triangles. Referring to the representation (2.7) for Powell-Sabin splines, we define control points as

$$\mathbf{c}_{i,j} = (Q_{i,j}, c_{i,j}). \tag{2.10}$$

These points lead to PS control triangles $T_i(\mathbf{c}_{i,1}, \mathbf{c}_{i,2}, \mathbf{c}_{i,3})$, which are tangent to the spline surface $z = s(x,y)$ at the vertices V_i. The projection of the control triangles T_i in the (x,y)-plane are simply the PS triangles t_i. Using these control triangles a designer can interactively change the shape of a given Powell-Sabin spline locally in a predictable way. From property (2.8) it follows that the graph of the spline (2.7) lies inside the convex hull of its control points $\mathbf{c}_{i,j}$.

Figure 4 shows a Powell-Sabin spline surface together with the corresponding control triangles. The spline is taken from [7] and represents a smooth approximation of the function $\left(\exp((x-0.52)^2 + (y-0.48)^2) - 0.95\right)^{-1}$ on the domain $[-1,1] \times [-1,1]$.

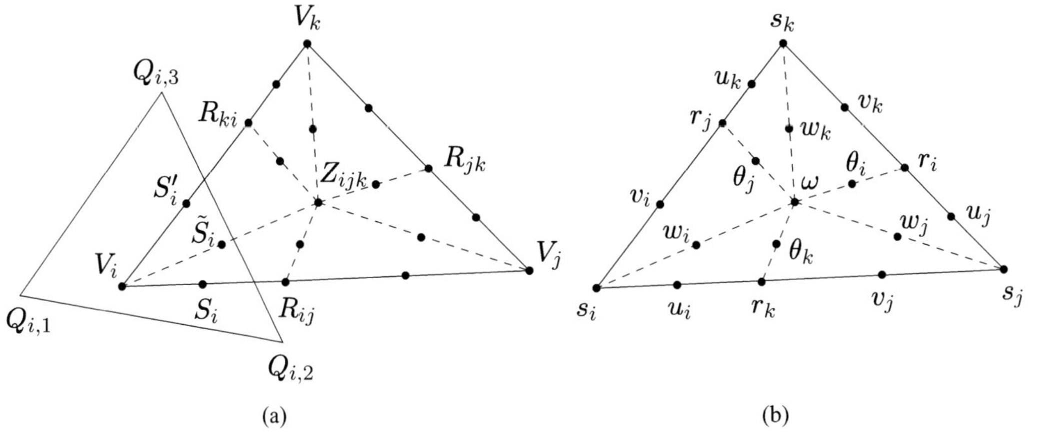

Figure 5. (a) PS refinement of a triangle $\mathcal{T}(V_i, V_j, V_k)$, together with the PS triangle $t_i(Q_{i,1}, Q_{i,2}, Q_{i,3})$ associated with vertex V_i. (b) Schematic representation of the Bézier ordinates of a Powell-Sabin spline.

Other bases for the Powell-Sabin spline space can be found in the literature [2, 17]. Their construction is based on so-called minimal determining sets. They are stable, but they do not form a convex partition of unity and they have no geometric interpretation via control triangles.

2.5. A Bernstein-Bézier Representation

For further manipulation (e.g. evaluation and differentiation) of a Powell-Sabin spline in the form (2.7), we can write the spline in a Bernstein-Bézier representation.

We consider a single domain triangle $\mathcal{T}(V_i, V_j, V_k) \in \Delta$ with its PS refinement $\in \Delta^*$. The other triangles in the triangulation can be treated in the same way. We assume that the points indicated in Figure 5(a) have the following barycentric coordinates:

$$\begin{array}{llll} V_i(1,0,0), & V_j(0,1,0), & V_k(0,0,1), & Z_{ijk}(z_i, z_j, z_k), \\ R_{ij}(\lambda_{ij}, \lambda_{ji}, 0), & R_{jk}(0, \lambda_{jk}, \lambda_{kj}), & R_{ki}(\lambda_{ik}, 0, \lambda_{ki}). & \end{array}$$

On each of the six triangles in Δ^* the Powell-Sabin spline is a quadratic polynomial, that can be represented in its Bernstein-Bézier formulation, i.e., with $d = 2$ in equations (2.2) and (2.3). The value of the corresponding Bézier ordinates is derived in [6]. The outcome is schematically represented in Figure 5(b), with

$$s_i = \alpha_{i,1}\, c_{i,1} + \alpha_{i,2}\, c_{i,2} + \alpha_{i,3}\, c_{i,3}, \tag{2.11a}$$

$$u_i = L_{i,1}\, c_{i,1} + L_{i,2}\, c_{i,2} + L_{i,3}\, c_{i,3}, \tag{2.11b}$$

$$v_i = L'_{i,1}\, c_{i,1} + L'_{i,2}\, c_{i,2} + L'_{i,3}\, c_{i,3}, \tag{2.11c}$$

$$w_i = \tilde{L}_{i,1}\, c_{i,1} + \tilde{L}_{i,2}\, c_{i,2} + \tilde{L}_{i,3}\, c_{i,3}. \tag{2.11d}$$

The values of $(\alpha_{i,1}, \alpha_{i,2}, \alpha_{i,3})$, $(L_{i,1}, L_{i,2}, L_{i,3})$, $(L'_{i,1}, L'_{i,2}, L'_{i,3})$ and $(\tilde{L}_{i,1}, \tilde{L}_{i,2}, \tilde{L}_{i,3})$ are found as the barycentric coordinates of the PS points V_i, S_i, S_i' and $\tilde{S}_i$, respectively, with respect to the PS triangle $t_i(Q_{i,1}, Q_{i,2}, Q_{i,3})$. These points are depicted in Figure 5(a). Analogously, we can compute the values of (s_j, u_j, v_j, w_j) and (s_k, u_k, v_k, w_k). The other Bézier ordinates are derived from the inherent continuity conditions of the Powell-Sabin spline, e.g.,

$$r_k = \lambda_{ij}\, u_i + \lambda_{ji}\, v_j, \tag{2.11e}$$

$$\theta_k = \lambda_{ij}\, w_i + \lambda_{ji}\, w_j, \tag{2.11f}$$

$$\omega = z_i\, w_i + z_j\, w_j + z_k\, w_k. \tag{2.11g}$$

In this Bernstein-Bézier representation the Powell-Sabin splines can be easily manipulated using the de Casteljau algorithm (2.4).

2.6. Parametric Powell-Sabin Surfaces

A parametric Powell-Sabin surface is defined as

$$\begin{cases} x = \sum_{i=1}^{n} \sum_{j=1}^{3} c_{i,j}^{x}\, B_i^j(u,v) \\ y = \sum_{i=1}^{n} \sum_{j=1}^{3} c_{i,j}^{y}\, B_i^j(u,v) \\ z = \sum_{i=1}^{n} \sum_{j=1}^{3} c_{i,j}^{z}\, B_i^j(u,v) \end{cases}, \quad (u,v) \in \Omega, \tag{2.12}$$

or, compactly,

$$\mathbf{s}(u,v) = \sum_{i=1}^{n} \sum_{j=1}^{3} \mathbf{c}_{i,j}\, B_i^j(u,v), \tag{2.13}$$

where the $\mathbf{c}_{i,j} = (c_{i,j}^x, c_{i,j}^y, c_{i,j}^z)$ are again called control points. Referring to (2.7), the graph of a Powell-Sabin spline is a particular case of the parametric Powell-Sabin surface, notably with $x = u$ and $y = v$.

A parametric surface $\mathbf{s}(u,v)$ lies within the convex hull of its control points. We can associate a control triangle $T_i(\mathbf{c}_{i,1}, \mathbf{c}_{i,2}, \mathbf{c}_{i,3})$ with each vertex V_i in the parameter domain. This triangle is tangent to the surface at $\mathbf{s}(V_i)$. Note that in the parametric setting the choice of the control points $\mathbf{c}_{i,j}$ is completely free, whereas for Powell-Sabin splines only the z-component of the control points can be chosen. Figure 6 depicts a torus modelled using a parametric Powell-Sabin surface with 16 control triangles.

Parametric Powell-Sabin surfaces can be easily manipulated by applying the algorithms for Powell-Sabin splines separately on the three components in (2.12).

3. Spline Subdivision

A natural question that comes up in many applications is how to represent a spline function on a refinement Δ^1 of the given triangulation Δ^0. A procedure to do that is called a subdivision scheme. Windmolders and Dierckx [35] considered the subdivision problem for uniform Powell-Sabin splines with a dyadic scheme. Recently, this was used to construct a tangent subdivision scheme for parameter free surfaces [30].

However, the dyadic refinement scheme is generally not applicable for non-uniform Powell-Sabin splines. Vanraes *et al.* [33] presented a global triadic subdivision scheme for

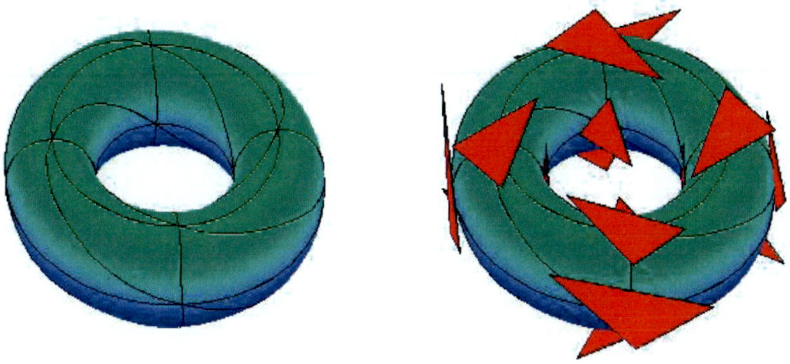

Figure 6. A torus modelled by a parametric Powell-Sabin surface. The control triangles and the triangular mesh lines are shown.

general Powell-Sabin splines, which was extended to a local adaptive scheme in [23]. First, we explain the refinement strategy for a given triangulation, and then we determine the corresponding PS control triangles of the new spline representation such that the original spline surface is preserved.

3.1. Refinement Rules of the Triangulation

General subdivision for Powell-Sabin splines is based on the so-called $\sqrt{3}$ refinement scheme [14, 15]. Such a refinement proceeds as follows:

1. Split every triangle into three subtriangles by inserting a new vertex V_{ijk} inside the old triangle $\mathcal{T}(V_i, V_j, V_k)$, and connect it to the surrounding old vertices. For example, in the Powell-Sabin case the new vertex will be located at the interior point Z_{ijk}.
2. Flip each edge adjacent to two refined triangles of the original triangulation in order to rebalance the new triangulation. These edges connect now two new vertices instead of two original vertices.

These two steps are illustrated in Figure 7. From the construction it follows that the refined triangulation $\Delta^{\sqrt{3}}$ does not preserve the original edges except at the boundary. However, if the new vertex V_{ijk} is chosen as the interior point Z_{ijk} of the original PS refinement, the new edges of $\Delta^{\sqrt{3}}$ still coincide with the edges of that PS refinement. When we apply the $\sqrt{3}$ refinement scheme twice, we obtain a triadic split, as shown in Figure 8. Every original edge is trisected and each original triangle is split into nine subtriangles.

In order to make subdivision possible, the interior points of the PS refinement $\Delta^{\sqrt{3},*}$ of the new triangulation $\Delta^{\sqrt{3}}$ must be chosen such that $\Delta^{\sqrt{3},*}$ contains the edges of the original PS refinement Δ^*. As can be seen in Figure 7(c), the new triangles in $\Delta^{\sqrt{3}}$ are bisected by an edge of Δ^*. If their interior points are chosen on such an edge, we obtain a valid PS refinement $\Delta^{\sqrt{3},*}$. Figure 9 depicts a $\sqrt{3}$ refined triangle where the corresponding PS refinement is indicated with dashed lines.

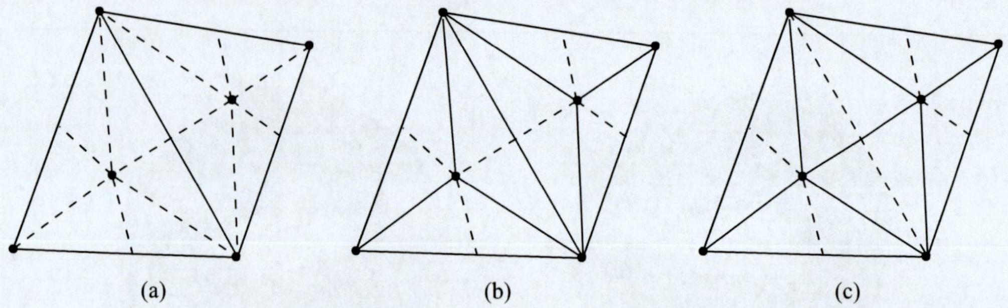

Figure 7. Principle of $\sqrt{3}$ refinement. (a) PS refinement of two neighbouring triangles. (b) Place a new vertex at the position of the interior points and connect with the triangle corners. (c) Flip the edge adjacent to the two refined triangles. The dashed lines are part of the PS refinement.

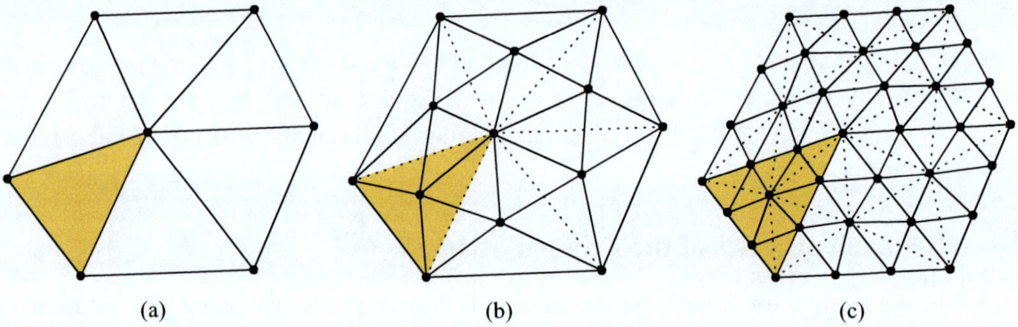

Figure 8. Applying the $\sqrt{3}$ refinement scheme twice results in a triadic refinement.

3.2. The Construction of Refined Control Triangles

In this section we explain how to derive the B-spline coefficients of the new Powell-Sabin spline on the (locally) refined triangulation, when the B-spline coefficients were given on the original triangulation.

For the vertices V_i in the original triangulation one can reuse the old PS triangles defined by their corner points $Q_{i,m}$, with $m = 1, 2, 3$. This is valid because any new PS point in the refined triangulation lies closer to the considered original vertex. However, it is better to determine a smaller PS triangle for improving the stability of the new Powell-Sabin spline. We will rescale the original PS triangle with an appropriate scalar ω_i. The value of ω_i can be found by comparing the positions of the old and new PS points (see [33]). The corners of the new PS triangle $t_i^{\sqrt{3}}$ (see Figure 9) are then given by

$$Q_{i,m}^{\sqrt{3}} = \omega_i\, V_i + (1 - \omega_i)\, Q_{i,m}, \qquad m = 1, 2, 3,$$

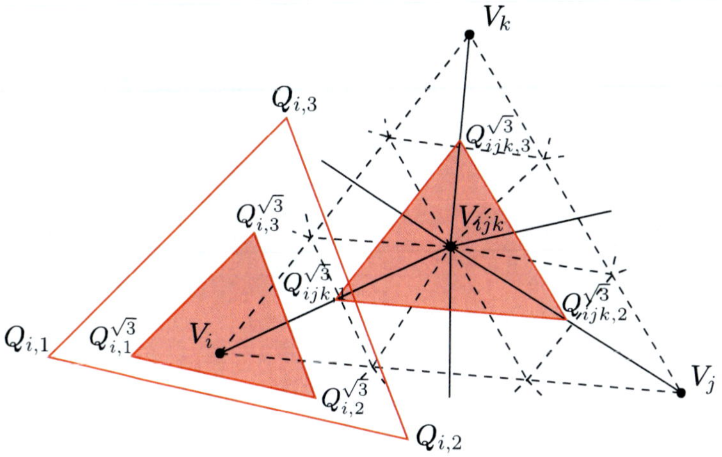

Figure 9. The PS triangles $t_i^{\sqrt{3}}(Q^{\sqrt{3}}_{i,1}, Q^{\sqrt{3}}_{i,2}, Q^{\sqrt{3}}_{i,3})$ and $t_{ijk}^{\sqrt{3}}(Q^{\sqrt{3}}_{ijk,1}, Q^{\sqrt{3}}_{ijk,2}, Q^{\sqrt{3}}_{ijk,3})$ associated with the vertices V_i and V_{ijk} in a $\sqrt{3}$ refined triangulation. The PS refinement is indicated with dashed lines.

and the corresponding coefficients $c^{\sqrt{3}}_{i,m}$ are calculated via the old coefficients $c_{i,m}$ as

$$c^{\sqrt{3}}_{i,1} = (\omega_i\alpha_{i,1} + 1 - \omega_i)\, c_{i,1} + \omega_i\alpha_{i,2}\, c_{i,2} + \omega_i\alpha_{i,3}\, c_{i,3}, \tag{3.1a}$$

$$c^{\sqrt{3}}_{i,2} = \omega_i\alpha_{i,1}\, c_{i,1} + (\omega_i\alpha_{i,2} + 1 - \omega_i)\, c_{i,2} + \omega_i\alpha_{i,3}\, c_{i,3}, \tag{3.1b}$$

$$c^{\sqrt{3}}_{i,3} = \omega_i\alpha_{i,1}\, c_{i,1} + \omega_i\alpha_{i,2}\, c_{i,2} + (\omega_i\alpha_{i,3} + 1 - \omega_i)\, c_{i,3}. \tag{3.1c}$$

The PS triangles $t^{\sqrt{3}}_{ijk}$ associated with the new vertices V_{ijk} in the $\sqrt{3}$ refined triangulation are defined by

$$Q^{\sqrt{3}}_{ijk,1} = (V_{ijk} + V_i)/2, \quad Q^{\sqrt{3}}_{ijk,2} = (V_{ijk} + V_j)/2, \quad \text{and,} \quad Q^{\sqrt{3}}_{ijk,3} = (V_{ijk} + V_k)/2,$$

as shown in Figure 9. The corresponding coefficients are computed as

$$c^{\sqrt{3}}_{ijk,1} = \tilde{L}_{i,1}\, c_{i,1} + \tilde{L}_{i,2}\, c_{i,2} + \tilde{L}_{i,3}\, c_{i,3}, \tag{3.2a}$$

$$c^{\sqrt{3}}_{ijk,2} = \tilde{L}_{j,1}\, c_{j,1} + \tilde{L}_{j,2}\, c_{j,2} + \tilde{L}_{j,3}\, c_{j,3}, \tag{3.2b}$$

$$c^{\sqrt{3}}_{ijk,3} = \tilde{L}_{k,1}\, c_{k,1} + \tilde{L}_{k,2}\, c_{k,2} + \tilde{L}_{k,3}\, c_{k,3}. \tag{3.2c}$$

Remark that $Q^{\sqrt{3}}_{ijk,1}$ simply corresponds to the point $\tilde{S}_i$ in Figure 5(a), and equation (3.2a) refers to equation (2.11d). Likewise, the triplets $(\tilde{L}_{j,1}, \tilde{L}_{j,2}, \tilde{L}_{j,3})$ and $(\tilde{L}_{k,1}, \tilde{L}_{k,2}, \tilde{L}_{k,3})$ can be computed as the barycentric coordinates of $Q^{\sqrt{3}}_{ijk,2}$ and $Q^{\sqrt{3}}_{ijk,3}$, respectively, with respect to the PS triangles of the vertices V_j and V_k.

The formulas (3.1)-(3.2) use only convex combinations of the old coefficients. As a consequence, this subdivision scheme is numerically stable.

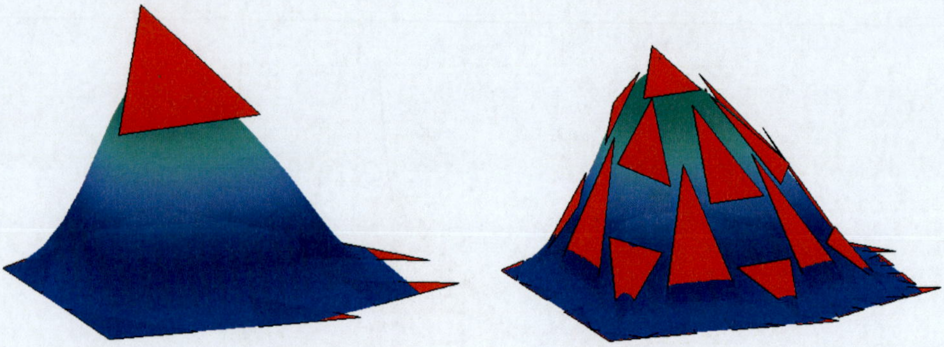

(a) (b)

Figure 10. (a) A Powell-Sabin spline with 7 control triangles. (b) The equivalent triadically subdivided spline.

Applying those rules twice, one obtains the control triangles of the new vertices in a triadically refined triangulation. Figure 10 illustrates the triadic subdivision scheme for a given Powell-Sabin spline.

3.3. Applications

In a broad range of application domains spline subdivision is of interest. In this section we discuss some applications of the PS subdivision scheme.

Visualization. A common application of spline subdivision is visualization. After a few subdivision steps, the PS control triangles mimic the shape of the Powell-Sabin spline quite well. These control triangles can be used to construct a wireframe that approximates the spline surface. The question is how to connect the PS control triangles efficiently into a single wireframe. We consider a few approaches.

The wireframe can be constructed by connecting the spline interpolation points $s(V_i)$, in the same way as the vertices V_i are connected in the domain triangulation. These points are the tangent points of the PS control triangles to the spline surface. This approach was suggested in [35]. Figure 11(a) shows such triangular meshes for the splines in Figure 10.

Another strategy is to use the Bézier control net, see Figure 1(b), of the Powell-Sabin spline in its Bernstein-Bézier representation [6]. This control net has the advantage that it forms a convex hull for the spline surface. It also converges more rapidly to the surface than the previous wireframe. However, many triangles are needed in this representation, as can be seen in Figure 11(b).

A fair compromise is the wireframe in Figure 11(c), constructed by connecting projections of some PS points into the PS control triangles in a particular way, as described below. We first build the mesh in the parameter domain, and then we project the points in this mesh into the corresponding PS control triangles. There are three types of patches in such a mesh, as illustrated in Figure 12. The first type is obtained by constructing for each vertex V_i the smallest envelope polygon that contains all PS points associated with V_i. Note

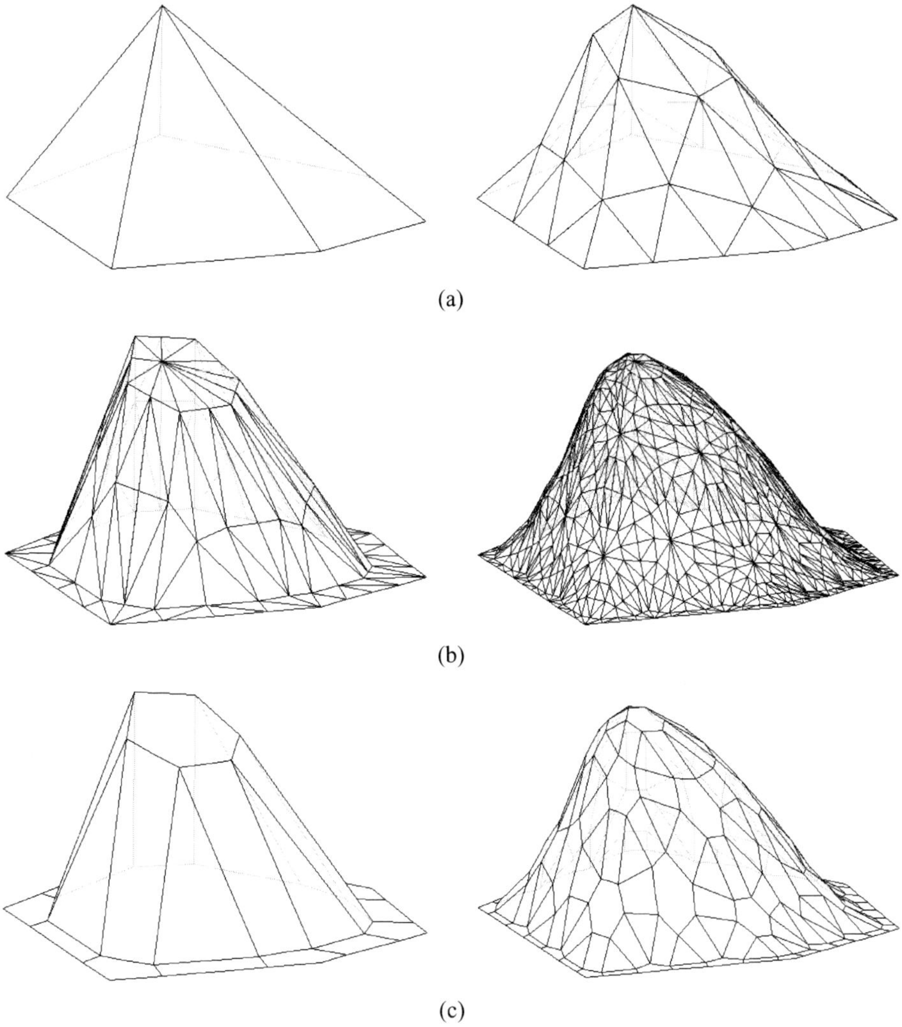

Figure 11. Different wireframes for visualizing the Powell-Sabin splines in Figure 10. The wireframe can be obtained (a) by connecting the spline interpolation points $s(V_i)$, (b) by using the Bézier control net, (c) by connecting the projections of certain PS points into the corresponding PS control triangles, as explained in section 3.3..

that the corners of such a polygon are particular PS points. Then, these corner points are connected into triangular and quadrilateral patches in the following way. For each triangle in the domain triangulation Δ we construct a triangular patch by connecting the three PS points in the interior of the considered triangle. We connect the adjacent PS points along each edge in Δ to form a quadrilateral patch. The wireframe is then defined by the projections of the corners of these patches into the corresponding PS control triangles. Note that these projections are just particular Bézier ordinates in the Bernstein-Bézier representation of the Powell-Sabin spline. For instance, the Bézier ordinate w_i is the projection of the PS point $\tilde{S}_i$ into PS control triangle T_i, as shown in Figure 5.

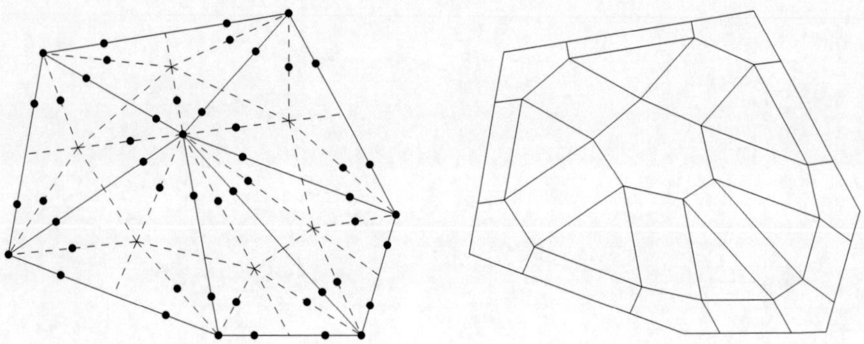

(a) (b)

Figure 12. (a) A triangulation with PS refinement and PS points. (b) The mesh used for constructing a wireframe.

As can be seen in the Figures 11(b)-(c), the edges of this wireframe coincide with particular edges in the Bézier control net. The number of used patches is about $1/8$ of the number needed for the Bézier control net. Let n, t and e be the number of vertices, triangles and edges, respectively, in the triangulation Δ. Then, the Bézier control net needs $24t$ patches. The wireframe of Figure 11(c) only needs $n+t+e$ patches, which amounts to about $3t$ using Euler's formulas. Because of the reduced number of patches, this wireframe is more visually pleasant than the Bézier control net. Note that at most four patches come together at each vertex in this wireframe. It could be disadvantageous that the patches in this wireframe are constructed of polygons with a different number of edges. Nevertheless, many graphical libraries, as OpenGL, can efficiently handle such set of polygons.

Modelling. The basis functions have a smaller support after subdivision. This gives the designer more local control for manipulating the spline surface. By the local nature of the $\sqrt{3}$ subdivision scheme, complex surfaces can be efficiently represented with a reasonable amount of memory [23].

Approximation. Subdivision is useful in data fitting and finite element applications. The original spline space is a subspace of the space obtained after subdivision. Hence, we are guaranteed of a better spline approximation in the refined space when a least squares data fitting strategy is applied [7], or a Ritz-Galerkin finite element method is used for the numerical solution of partial differential equations [24]. When we use an iterative method to solve the linear systems that arise in these methods, the subdivided version of the optimal spline approximation in the coarser spline space provides a good initial guess for the optimal solution in the finer space.

Geometric multigrid methods can be used to solve partial differential equations in a very efficient way. By means of a hierarchy of meshes, one can accelerate the convergence of a basic iterative method. Using the Powell-Sabin subdivision scheme, a nested sequence of triangulations can be easily created with natural intergrid transfer operators [26].

Multiresolution. Multiresolution techniques work with different levels of resolution. Wavelets are functions that split data into different frequency components. Each component is studied with a resolution matched to its scale. A common tool to develop wavelets is the lifting scheme, where subdivision can be used as the prediction step. Such wavelets, called Powell-Sabin spline wavelets, have been developed in [32,38]. They are particularly suitable for image/surface compression [18].

4. QHPS Splines

When an increased resolution is only required in a small part of the surface, the use of global subdivision may lead to excessive computational and storage costs. In such a case, a local (adaptive) subdivision scheme is recommended. Although the $\sqrt{3}$ refinement scheme described in section 3.1. can be applied locally, a naive use may introduce poorly shaped triangles at the boundary of the locally refined region. This problem can be dealt with by using a refinement propagation strategy [23]. When a triangle fails to satisfy a certain quality requirement, extra neighbouring triangles are refined. This results in an expansion of the refined region. By the edge flipping step in the $\sqrt{3}$ refinement method, a narrow triangle (with small angles) will be replaced by two better shaped triangles. At the boundary of the domain, artificial vertices outside the domain can be inserted into the triangulation. The proposed strategy is driven by one parameter that manages the trade-off between the mesh quality and the refinement localization.

Such a specialized shape-improvement strategy could be avoided if non-conforming triangulations were allowed. In this section we review the idea of [25], where Powell-Sabin splines are adapted towards certain non-conforming triangulations. In particular, we consider hierarchical triangulations which are obtained by partitioning an initial conforming triangulation with a triadic split. A hierarchical triangulation gives rise to a set of nested spline spaces. A hierarchical basis for such a space is constructed in a way that the basis functions of the coarser spaces are retained in the basis of the finer space. In a so-called quasi-hierarchical basis some of the coarse-level basis functions are replaced by finer-level basis functions [12].

This section discusses QHPS splines, which are a hierarchical variant of Powell-Sabin splines in a quasi-hierarchical basis representation [25].

4.1. The Hierarchical Powell-Sabin Spline Space

Consider a simply connected subset $\Omega \subset \mathbb{R}^2$ with polygonal boundary, and assume a conforming triangulation Δ^0 of Ω is given. We construct a hierarchical triangulation Δ_H on Ω by partitioning successively subsets of triangles with a triadic split, starting from the initial triangulation Δ^0. An example of such a triangulation is drawn in Figure 13(a) with solid lines. Here, Δ^0 is the triangulation of Figure 2(a).

The hierarchical triangulation has a total of n vertices. Of these vertices, n_{nc} are non-conforming (or hanging) vertices. They are located on interiors of triangle edges. The remaining ones, i.e. $n_c = n - n_{nc}$, are called conforming vertices. In Figure 13(a), Δ^0 consists of 8 triangles and 8 (conforming) vertices. The hierarchical triangulation in the figure consists of 16 triangles and 15 vertices ($n_c = 9$, $n_{nc} = 6$).

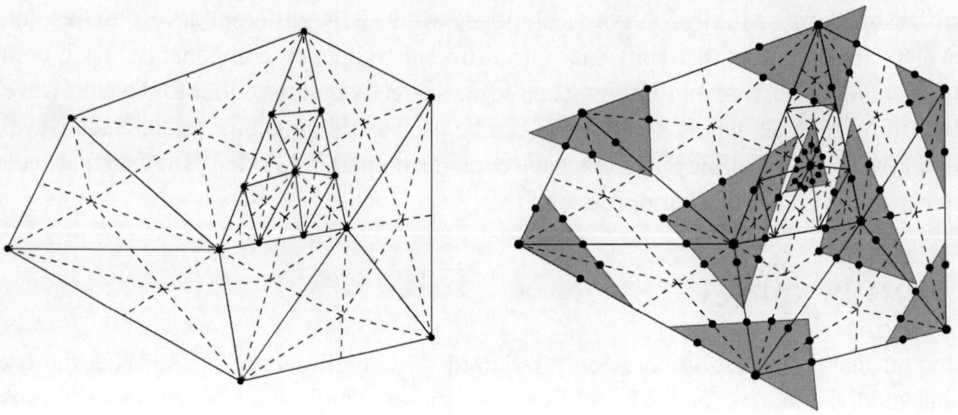

(a) (b)

Figure 13. (a) A HPS refinement Δ_H^* (in dashed lines) of a given hierarchical triangulation Δ_H (in solid lines). (b) The QHPS points (bullets) and a set of suitable QHPS triangles (shaded).

To each hierarchical triangulation Δ_H we can associate a hierarchical mesh structure $\boldsymbol{\Delta}_H$. It is the set of triangles $\mathcal{T}^k$ that are generated during the construction of Δ_H. The superscript k of a triangle $\mathcal{T}^k$ refers to the refinement level of that triangle, i.e., the minimal number of triadic refinement steps needed to construct the triangle. The triangles in $\boldsymbol{\Delta}_H$ that are part of Δ_H are called leaf triangles. We will denote $\boldsymbol{\Delta}_H^l$ as the subset of $\boldsymbol{\Delta}_H$ containing all triangles whose level is l or lower, and let Δ_H^l be its corresponding hierarchical triangulation. Note that these mesh structures are nested

$$\Delta^0 \subset \boldsymbol{\Delta}_H^1 \subset \boldsymbol{\Delta}_H^2 \subset \ldots \subset \boldsymbol{\Delta}_H. \tag{4.1}$$

We will use Powell-Sabin triadic splits, as in Figure 8(c), in the construction of a hierarchical triangulation Δ_H. The PS refinements needed in the splitting process generate a particular refinement of Δ_H which partitions each triangle in Δ_H into six subtriangles. This refinement is called the hierarchical Powell-Sabin (HPS) refinement Δ_H^* of Δ_H. Analogous to (4.1), the HPS refinement yields a nested structure of sets of triangles

$$\Delta^{0,*} \subset \boldsymbol{\Delta}_H^{1,*} \subset \boldsymbol{\Delta}_H^{2,*} \subset \ldots \subset \boldsymbol{\Delta}_H^*. \tag{4.2}$$

In Figure 13(a) such a HPS refinement is drawn in dashed lines.

The space of piecewise quadratic polynomials on Δ_H^* with global C^1-continuity is called the hierarchical Powell-Sabin spline space:

$$S_{2,H}^1(\Delta_H^*) = \left\{ s_H \in C^1(\Omega) : s_H|_{\mathcal{T}_j^*} \in \Pi_2,\ \mathcal{T}_j^* \in \Delta_H^* \right\}. \tag{4.3}$$

For this hierarchical spline space we considered a similar interpolation problem as (2.6) for Powell-Sabin splines [25] . Given a triplet $(f_k, f_{x,k}, f_{y,k})$ at each conforming vertex V_k in the hierarchical triangulation Δ_H, the interpolation problem

$$s_H(V_k) = f_k, \quad \frac{\partial s_H}{\partial x}(V_k) = f_{x,k}, \quad \frac{\partial s_H}{\partial y}(V_k) = f_{y,k}, \qquad k = 1, \ldots, n_c, \tag{4.4}$$

has a unique solution $s_H(x,y) \in S^1_{2,H}(\Delta^*_H)$. It follows that the dimension of the hierarchical Powell-Sabin spline space is equal to $3n_c$.

4.2. A Quasi-hierarchical Powell-Sabin Spline Basis

The construction of a normalized basis for the spline space $S^1_{2,H}(\Delta^*_H)$ is very similar to the geometric approach for the Powell-Sabin basis, described in section 2.3.. A hierarchical Powell-Sabin spline in its quasi-hierarchical representation is called a QHPS spline, and is denoted as

$$s_{QH}(x,y) = \sum_{i=1}^{n_c}\sum_{j=1}^{3} c_{i,j} B^j_{i,QH}(x,y). \tag{4.5}$$

We associate with each conforming vertex V_i in the hierarchical triangulation three linearly independent triplets $(\alpha_{i,j}, \beta_{i,j}, \gamma_{i,j})$, $j = 1,2,3$. The QHPS B-spline $B^j_{i,QH}(x,y)$ can then be determined as the solution of the interpolation problem (4.4) with all $(f_k, f_{x,k}, f_{y,k}) = (0,0,0)$ except for $k = i$, where $(f_i, f_{x,i}, f_{y,i}) = (\alpha_{i,j}, \beta_{i,j}, \gamma_{i,j}) \neq (0,0,0)$. The triplets $(\alpha_{i,j}, \beta_{i,j}, \gamma_{i,j})$ are computed as follows:

1. For each conforming vertex V_i in the hierarchical triangulation Δ_H, identify the corresponding QHPS points. Let k be the smallest level of all triangles in Δ_H that contain vertex V_i. Denote Δ^k_H as the triangulation, consisting of triangles of at most level k, that appears during the construction of Δ_H. The QHPS points of V_i are defined as the midpoints of all edges in the HPS refinement $\Delta^{k,*}_H$ ending in V_i. The vertex V_i is also a QHPS point. In Figure 13(b) the QHPS points are indicated as bullets.

2. For each conforming vertex V_i, construct a triangle $t_i(Q_{i,1}, Q_{i,2}, Q_{i,3})$ containing all the QHPS points of V_i. The triangles t_i, $i = 1,\ldots,n_c$, are called QHPS triangles. Figure 13(b) shows a possible set of QHPS triangles.

3. The three linearly independent triplets $(\alpha_{i,j}, \beta_{i,j}, \gamma_{i,j})$, $j = 1,2,3$, are derived from the QHPS triangle t_i of a vertex V_i as follows:

   - $\alpha_i = (\alpha_{i,1}, \alpha_{i,2}, \alpha_{i,3})$ are the barycentric coordinates of V_i with respect to t_i,
   - $\beta_i = (\beta_{i,1}, \beta_{i,2}, \beta_{i,3})$ and $\gamma_i = (\gamma_{i,1}, \gamma_{i,2}, \gamma_{i,3})$ are the coordinates of the unit barycentric directions, in x- and y-direction respectively, with respect to t_i.

Figure 14 illustrates how a QHPS B-spline associated with the central vertex in a given triangulation changes when some of the triangles are triadically refined. The same QHPS triangle is used in the three cases.

Note that if the hierarchical triangulation is obtained by global triadic splits, i.e., the final triangulation is conforming, then the QHPS B-splines are just the classical Powell-Sabin B-splines.

4.3. Properties of the QHPS B-spline Basis

The quasi-hierarchical B-splines have similar attractive properties as the classical Powell-Sabin B-splines. Unless stated otherwise, the proofs of the properties can be found in [25].

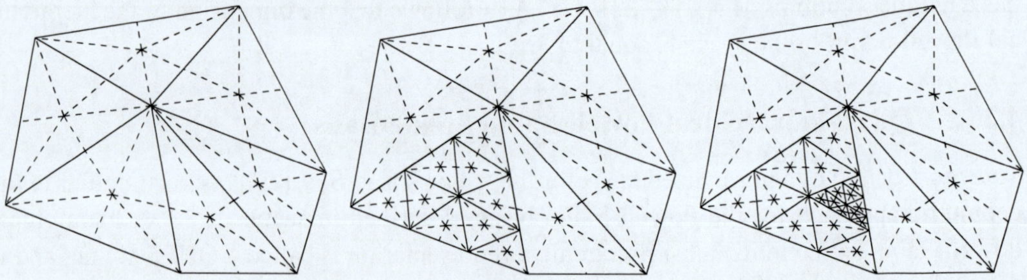

(a)

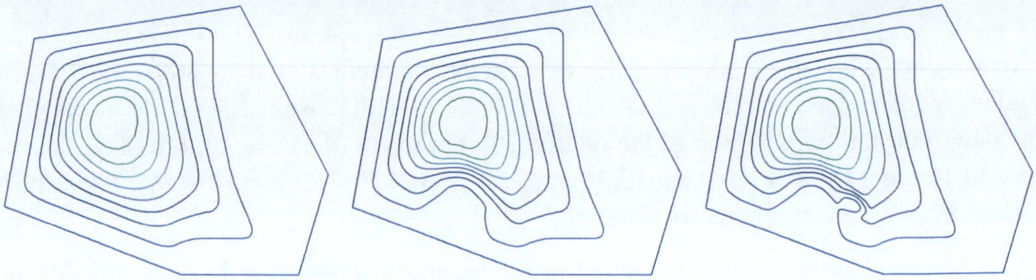

(b)

Figure 14. (a) Several triadically refined hierarchical triangulations. The HPS refinement is indicated with dashed lines. (b) Contour plots of a QHPS basis function associated with the central vertex for the corresponding meshes in (a). The first B-spline is the same as in Figure 3(b).

Local support. Each QHPS B-spline $B^j_{i,QH}(x, y)$ is zero outside the molecule M^k_i of the corresponding vertex V_i in Δ^k_H, with k the smallest level of any triangle in Δ_H containing V_i.

Convex partition of unity. The QHPS basis splines are positive, and they sum up to one.

Stability. The quasi-hierarchical basis is strongly L_∞-stable, i.e., the stability constants K_1 and K_2 in inequality (2.9) are both independent of the number of levels in the hierarchical triangulation. In [27] we investigated the L_p-stability of the basis. It turns out that the QHPS basis is, in general, weakly L_p-stable, i.e., the constants ${K_1}^{-1}$ and K_2 have at most a polynomial growth in the number of levels. However, this result can be improved for a broad class of hierarchical triangulations Δ_H. Suppose there exists an upper bound on the difference between the level numbers of any two triangles in Δ_H that lie inside the support of the same QHPS B-spline. If this bound is independent of the number of refinement levels in Δ_H, then the QHPS basis is strongly L_p-stable. More details can be found in [27]. Note that the classical Powell-Sabin B-splines are always strongly L_p-stable on a globally refined hierarchical triangulation.

QHPS control triangles. We can define control points as $\mathbf{c}_{i,j} = (Q_{i,j}, c_{i,j})$ and control triangles as $T_i(\mathbf{c}_{i,1}, \mathbf{c}_{i,2}, \mathbf{c}_{i,3})$. These triangles are tangent to the spline surface $z = s(x, y)$ at the vertices V_i, and the graph of the QHPS spline lies inside the convex hull of these control points.

Subdivision. The non-conformity of the hierarchical triangulation allows a local triadic refinement in a natural way. In addition, a QHPS spline can be locally subdivided on a given set of triangles, using the same triadic PS subdivision rules as explained in section 3.. The locality of the subdivision scheme ensures that a QHPS spline surface can be adaptively manipulated with a reasonable increase of dimension of the space.

In Figure 15(a) we subdivided the torus, shown in Figure 6, locally on two triangles, and we adapted the QHPS control triangles of the newly introduced vertices in Figure 15(b). Note that the support of each QHPS B-spline associated with one of these new vertices stays within its original triangle. This is a very interesting property for surface editing. The designer selects a triangle where the surface must be locally subdivided. Then, he/she can freely morph the surface while only the part within the selected triangle will be affected. The new QHPS surface in Figure 15(b) only consists of 18 control triangles, whereas a globally subdivided Powell-Sabin spline would need 144 control triangles to represent the same surface.

4.4. A Practical Implementation

In this section we show how the efficient algorithms for classical Powell-Sabin splines can be used for working with quasi-hierarchical Powell-Sabin splines.

A QHPS spline can be represented on each leaf triangle by a particular Powell-Sabin spline. To construct this Powell-Sabin spline, we have to determine the PS control triangles corresponding to the three corner vertices of the considered triangle. The PS control triangles associated with conforming vertices can be taken identical to the QHPS control triangles of the QHPS spline. We can use subdivision to compute the control triangles for the non-conforming vertices. The correct PS control triangles can be recursively obtained while moving through the hierarchical mesh structure. When the leaf triangle is reached, the corresponding Powell-Sabin spline on the considered triangle will then be fully defined. In this way, an algorithm for QHPS splines can be straightforwardly reduced to the equivalent algorithm for Powell-Sabin splines. We now present a generic QHPS algorithm [25]. It only needs an equivalent algorithm for classical Powell-Sabin splines.

Generic QHPS algorithm. Let $\mathbf{\Delta}_H$ be a hierarchical mesh structure, and Δ be a conforming triangulation. The generic algorithm *qhps_algorithm*($\mathbf{\Delta}_H$) for QHPS splines is based on the equivalent algorithm *ps_algorithm*(Δ) for classical Powell-Sabin splines. We suppose that each triangle in $\mathbf{\Delta}_H$ and Δ has access to the control triangles associated with its three corner vertices. For conforming vertices, their control triangles are already known in advance, i.e., the QHPS control triangles. For non-conforming vertices, their control triangles are computed during the algorithm.

function *qhps_algorithm(*hierarchical_structure $\mathbf{\Delta}_H$*)*

```
        for all triangles T in the initial triangulation Δ^0 of Δ_H:
            qhps_local_algorithm(T, Δ_H)
        endfor
    end

    function qhps_local_algorithm(triangle T, hierarchical_structure Δ_H)
        if T is not a leaf triangle:
          1. Let l be the level of T in the hierarchical structure.
          2. for all non-conforming vertices V_i of level (l + 1) situated at the interior of
             an edge of T:
                 Calculate the control triangle T_i by triadic PS subdivision, using the
                 control triangles of two corner vertices of T.
             endfor
          3. for all 9 subtriangles T_i of level (l + 1) in T:
                 qhps_local_algorithm(T_i, Δ_H)
             endfor
        else
            ps_algorithm(T)
        endif
    end
```

The algorithm requires that all triangles in the hierarchical mesh structure $\boldsymbol{\Delta}_H$ are stored in memory. It is recommended to manage these triangles in the following way. Use an array that contains the triangles in the initial triangulation Δ^0. A triangle that is refined keeps references to each of its nine subtriangles. That ensures that all triangles in $\boldsymbol{\Delta}_H$ are reachable. In order to navigate easily through the mesh structure it is also advisable that the triangles keep the references to their (at most three) neighbouring triangles.

Using a different Powell-Sabin spline on each leaf triangle in the hierarchical triangulation is usually not more time-consuming than considering a single Powell-Sabin spline on a larger set of triangles. Indeed, most of the algorithms for Powell-Sabin splines run over all triangles in the triangulation separately.

The QHPS splines can be evaluated and manipulated in a stable way. Only convex combinations are needed to convert the QHPS spline on each triangle to a Powell-Sabin spline, to represent these Powell-Sabin splines with Bernstein-Bézier polynomials, and to evaluate these polynomials via the de Casteljau algorithm.

5. NURPS Surfaces

Rational surfaces, such as rational Bézier and NURBS surfaces, are commonly used tools in commercial computer aided design and computer graphic packages. Rational surface representations give a designer extra degrees of freedom compared to their non-rational counterparts through the weights that are associated with the control points. These rational

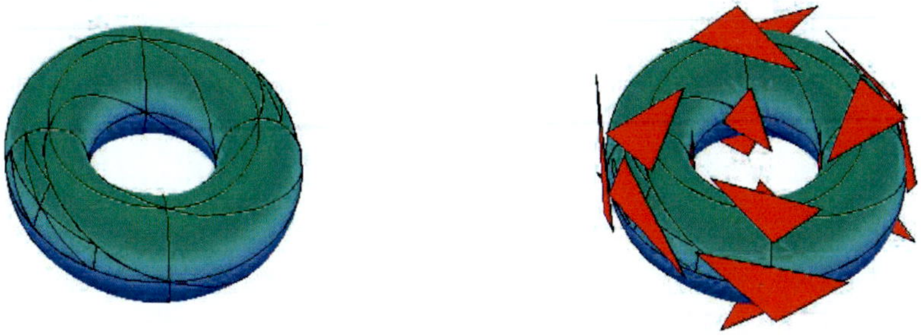

(a)

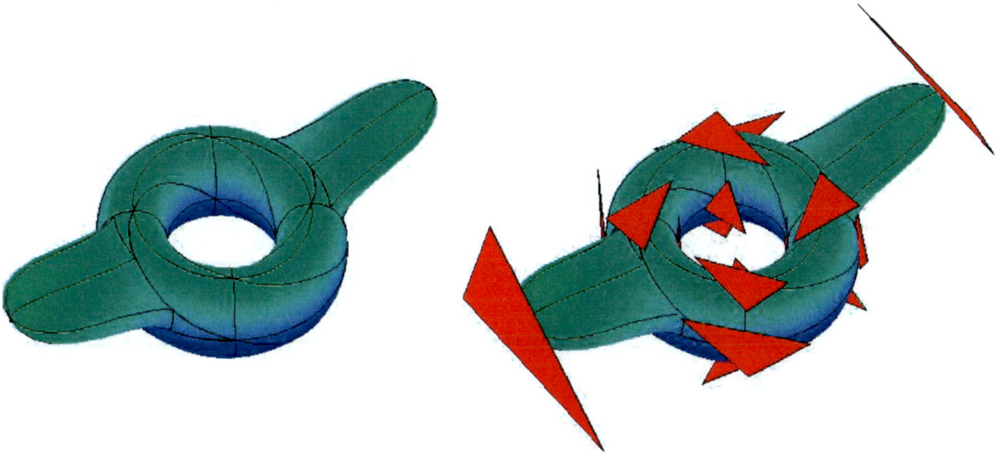

(b)

Figure 15. (a) Local QHPS subdivision applied on two triangles of the surface in Figure 6. The control triangles and the triangular mesh lines are shown. (b) Effect of moving the two new control triangles of the QHPS surface.

surfaces are able to exactly represent patches on quadric surfaces, e.g., patches on the cone and the sphere. In this section we discuss the rational extension of Powell-Sabin splines, called NURPS surfaces. For more details we refer to the papers [29, 36, 37].

5.1. Rational Powell-Sabin Surfaces

Consider a conforming triangulation Δ on a given domain $\Omega \subset \mathbb{R}^2$, with PS refinement Δ^*. A non-uniform rational Powell-Sabin (NURPS) surface $\mathbf{s}(u, v)$ is defined as

$$\mathbf{s}(u,v) = \sum_{i=1}^{n} \sum_{j=1}^{3} \mathbf{c}_{i,j}\, \phi_i^j(u,v), \quad (u,v) \in \Omega, \tag{5.1}$$

with $\mathbf{c}_{i,j} = (c^x_{i,j}, c^y_{i,j}, c^z_{i,j})$ the NURPS control points, and the blending functions

$$\phi_i^j(u,v) = \frac{w_{i,j} B_i^j(u,v)}{\sum_{i=1}^n \sum_{j=1}^3 w_{i,j} B_i^j(u,v)}. \tag{5.2}$$

Here, $B_i^j(u,v)$ are the normalized Powell-Sabin B-splines on Δ^*, and $w_{i,j}$ are positive weights. When all weights are constant, then (5.1) reduces to (2.13). The blending functions $\phi_i^j(u,v)$ in (5.2) have a local support and they form a convex partition of unity.

A NURPS surface in representation (5.1) can be seen as the 3D projection onto the Euclidian space of a 4D Powell-Sabin spline in the homogeneous space, i.e.,

$$\mathbf{s}(u,v) = \sum_{i=1}^{n} \sum_{j=1}^{3} \mathbf{c}^h_{i,j} B_i^j(u,v), \tag{5.3}$$

where the 4D homogeneous control points are given by

$$\mathbf{c}^h_{i,j} = (c^{hx}_{i,j}, c^{hy}_{i,j}, c^{hz}_{i,j}, c^{hw}_{i,j}) = (w_{i,j} c^x_{i,j}, w_{i,j} c^y_{i,j}, w_{i,j} c^z_{i,j}, w_{i,j}). \tag{5.4}$$

The next sections are devoted to some particular features of the NURPS surfaces. First, we discuss the use of the control points and the weights in shape modelling with NURPS surfaces. Then, we describe a subdivision scheme. We end with the NURPS representation of some quadric surfaces.

5.2. Modelling with NURPS Surfaces

A designer has two types of freedom in the construction of a NURPS surface: the coefficients $\mathbf{c}_{i,j}$ and the weights $w_{i,j}$. They can be determined in a geometrically intuitive way by means of control triangles and weight points.

Control triangles. Similar to the Powell-Sabin splines, the influence of the coefficients in (5.1) on the NURPS surface can be intuitively interpreted via control triangles [36]. With each vertex V_i in the triangulation Δ, one can define the control triangle $T_i(\mathbf{c}_{i,1}, \mathbf{c}_{i,2}, \mathbf{c}_{i,3})$. This triangle is tangent to the NURPS surface at the point

$$\mathbf{s}(V_i) = \hat{\alpha}_{i,1}\, \mathbf{c}_{i,1} + \hat{\alpha}_{i,2}\, \mathbf{c}_{i,2} + \hat{\alpha}_{i,3}\, \mathbf{c}_{i,3}, \tag{5.5}$$

where

$$\hat{\alpha}_{i,j} = \frac{w_{i,j}\alpha_{i,j}}{\sum_{k=1}^3 w_{i,k}\alpha_{i,k}}. \tag{5.6}$$

Here, $(\alpha_{i,1}, \alpha_{i,2}, \alpha_{i,3})$ are the barycentric coordinates of vertex V_i with respect to the PS triangle t_i.

Weight points. In [29] it is described how one can use so-called weight points as a design tool for handling the weights. Such a point is characterized by its position $\mathbf{p}_i$ and by a scaling factor K_i. The position is chosen as the tangent point of the control triangle T_i to the NURPS surface, i.e., $\mathbf{p}_i = \mathbf{s}(V_i)$.

The three weights $w_{i,j}$, with $j = 1, 2, 3$, are then uniquely defined by means of the barycentric coordinates $(\hat{\alpha}_{i,1}, \hat{\alpha}_{i,2}, \hat{\alpha}_{i,3})$ of $\mathbf{p}_i$ with respect to T_i, up to a positive factor K_i, via the formula

$$w_{i,j} = K_i \frac{\hat{\alpha}_{i,j}}{\alpha_{i,j}}. \tag{5.7}$$

A designer can freely move the weight point within the control triangle T_i. Since its position is the tangent point of T_i to the NURPS surface, the effect of the movement will be intuitive to the designer. This is illustrated in the first two pictures of Figure 16. One can use the scaling factor K_i to determine the relative importance of the considered three weights with respect to the other weights. Indeed, K_i can be interpreted as a weighted mean of these weights, i.e.,

$$K_i = \alpha_{i,1} w_{i,1} + \alpha_{i,2} w_{i,2} + \alpha_{i,3} w_{i,3}. \tag{5.8}$$

The larger the value of K_i, the more the NURPS surface will be attracted to the control triangle. A cusp can be simulated by reducing the scaling factor. The effect of changing the scaling factor is illustrated in the bottom two pictures of Figure 16. Similar effects can be obtained by rescaling (enlarging/reducing) the control triangles [37]. However, changing the factor K_i has the advantage that the designer can continue to work with the same control triangles.

Let $\mathbf{r}_{i,j}$ be the intersection point of the line $\mathbf{p}_i - \mathbf{c}_{i,j}$ and the edge of control triangle T_i opposite to $\mathbf{c}_{i,j}$, then

$$\mathbf{r}_{i,j} = \frac{\hat{\alpha}_{i,j'} \mathbf{c}_{i,j'} + \hat{\alpha}_{i,j''} \mathbf{c}_{i,j''}}{\hat{\alpha}_{i,j'} + \hat{\alpha}_{i,j''}}, \tag{5.9}$$

with $j' = 1 + (j \mod 3)$ and $j'' = 1 + (j' \mod 3)$. Using these points, the ratio of two weights can be geometrically interpreted as the ratio of two lengths, i.e.,

$$\frac{w_{i,j''}}{w_{i,j'}} = \frac{\alpha_{i,j'}}{\alpha_{i,j''}} \frac{\|\mathbf{r}_{i,j} - \mathbf{c}_{i,j'}\|}{\|\mathbf{r}_{i,j} - \mathbf{c}_{i,j''}\|}, \tag{5.10}$$

and, using formula (5.7), as a ratio of two triangular areas, i.e.,

$$\frac{w_{i,j''}}{w_{i,j'}} = \frac{\alpha_{i,j'}}{\alpha_{i,j''}} \frac{\mathcal{A}(\mathbf{p}_i, \mathbf{c}_{i,j}, \mathbf{c}_{i,j'})}{\mathcal{A}(\mathbf{p}_i, \mathbf{c}_{i,j''}, \mathbf{c}_{i,j})}. \tag{5.11}$$

5.3. NURPS Subdivision

We now adapt the subdivision scheme for Powell-Sabin splines towards NURPS surfaces. The construction of the refined triangulation $\Delta^{\sqrt{3}}$ and the choice of the PS triangles remain identical as described in section 3..

We can compute the control points of the subdivided NURPS surface via its homogeneous representation (5.3). For instance, the homogeneous control points $\mathbf{c}^{h,\sqrt{3}}_{ijk,m}$, with

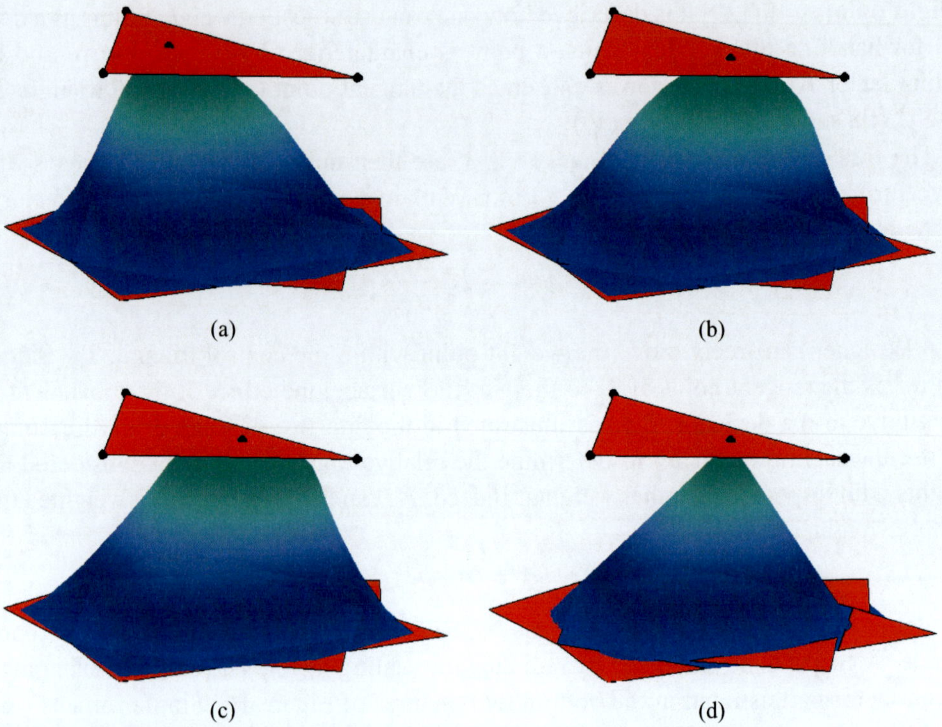

Figure 16. (a) Original NURPS surface. (b) The effect of moving the weight point $\mathbf{p}_i$ inside the control triangle. (c)-(d) Enlarging and reducing the scaling factor K_i. The considered weight point and control points are indicated with bullets.

$m = 1, 2, 3$, corresponding to the PS triangle $t_{ijk}^{\sqrt{3}}$, are then calculated as

$$\mathbf{c}_{ijk,1}^{h,\sqrt{3}} = \tilde{L}_{i,1}\,\mathbf{c}_{i,1}^{h} + \tilde{L}_{i,2}\,\mathbf{c}_{i,2}^{h} + \tilde{L}_{i,3}\,\mathbf{c}_{i,3}^{h}, \tag{5.12a}$$

$$\mathbf{c}_{ijk,2}^{h,\sqrt{3}} = \tilde{L}_{j,1}\,\mathbf{c}_{j,1}^{h} + \tilde{L}_{j,2}\,\mathbf{c}_{j,2}^{h} + \tilde{L}_{j,3}\,\mathbf{c}_{j,3}^{h}, \tag{5.12b}$$

$$\mathbf{c}_{ijk,3}^{h,\sqrt{3}} = \tilde{L}_{k,1}\,\mathbf{c}_{k,1}^{h} + \tilde{L}_{k,2}\,\mathbf{c}_{k,2}^{h} + \tilde{L}_{k,3}\,\mathbf{c}_{k,3}^{h}. \tag{5.12c}$$

The convex combinations are identical to the ones in formulas (3.2). Projecting the new control points (5.12) back to the Euclidian space yields

$$\mathbf{c}_{ijk,m}^{\sqrt{3}} = \left(\frac{c_{ijk,m}^{hx,\sqrt{3}}}{c_{ijk,m}^{hw,\sqrt{3}}}, \frac{c_{ijk,m}^{hy,\sqrt{3}}}{c_{ijk,m}^{hw,\sqrt{3}}}, \frac{c_{ijk,m}^{hz,\sqrt{3}}}{c_{ijk,m}^{hw,\sqrt{3}}} \right). \tag{5.13}$$

It is well known that working in the homogeneous space can lead to numerical instabilities. When the weights vary greatly in magnitude, the coordinates $c_{ijk,m}^{hr,\sqrt{3}}$, with $r = x, y, z$, can become extremely large. Then, the calculations do not operate in the convex hull of the rational control points anymore, and numerical stability is endangered.

Inspired by the idea behind the rational variant of the de Casteljau algorithm from Farin [8], we can improve the numerical stability by rearranging the calculations in or-

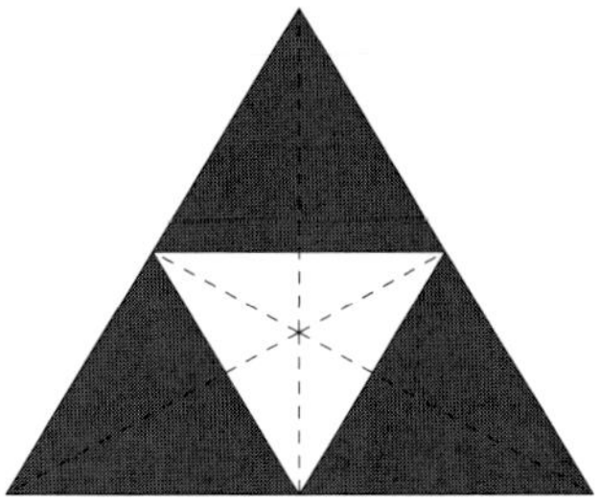

Figure 17. The domain triangle of a NURPS patch, together with its PS refinement and PS triangles.

der to avoid working in the homogeneous space. For instance, $\mathbf{c}_{ijk,1}^{\sqrt{3}}$ and its weight $w_{ijk,1}^{\sqrt{3}}$ are computed in a stable way as follows:

$$w_{ijk,1}^{\sqrt{3}} = c_{ijk,1}^{hw,\sqrt{3}} = \tilde{L}_{i,1}\, w_{i,1} + \tilde{L}_{i,2}\, w_{i,2} + \tilde{L}_{i,3}\, w_{i,3}, \tag{5.14a}$$

$$\hat{L}_{i,m} = \frac{w_{i,m}\, \tilde{L}_{i,m}}{w_{ijk,1}^{\sqrt{3}}}, \qquad m = 1, 2, 3, \tag{5.14b}$$

$$\mathbf{c}_{ijk,1}^{\sqrt{3}} = \hat{L}_{i,1}\, \mathbf{c}_{i,1} + \hat{L}_{i,2}\, \mathbf{c}_{i,2} + \hat{L}_{i,3}\, \mathbf{c}_{i,3}. \tag{5.14c}$$

Analogously, one can calculate the other control points in a numerically stable way.

5.4. Quadrics as NURPS Surfaces

In [37] closed formulas are derived for the control points of NURPS patches on a cylinder, a cone and a sphere. In this section we give another representation of such patches, resulting in a simpler choice of the control points. Further on, each triangular NURPS patch is defined on the equilateral domain triangle $\mathcal{T}(V_1, V_2, V_3)$ depicted in Figure 17, with the given PS refinement and PS triangles, defined by the points

$$\begin{aligned} Q_{1,1} &= V_1, & Q_{1,2} &= (V_1 + V_2)/2, & Q_{1,3} &= (V_1 + V_3)/2, \\ Q_{2,1} &= V_2, & Q_{2,2} &= (V_2 + V_3)/2, & Q_{2,3} &= (V_2 + V_1)/2, \\ Q_{3,1} &= V_3, & Q_{3,2} &= (V_3 + V_1)/2, & Q_{3,3} &= (V_3 + V_2)/2. \end{aligned}$$

The derivation of the corresponding control points is analogous to the one described in [37].

Cylinder. The cylinder

$$x^2 + y^2 = r^2, \quad 0 \le z \le h, \tag{5.15}$$

can be split into eight isometrical triangular segments. The control points and weights of the NURPS representation of such a patch is given in the following table.

i	$\mathbf{c}_{i,1}$	$w_{i,1}$	$\mathbf{c}_{i,2}$	$w_{i,2}$	$\mathbf{c}_{i,3}$	$w_{i,3}$
1	$(r,0,0)$	1	$(r,r,0)$	$\frac{\sqrt{2}}{2}$	$(r,0,\frac{h}{2})$	1
2	$(0,r,0)$	1	$(r,r,\frac{h}{2})$	$\frac{\sqrt{2}}{2}$	$(r,r,0)$	$\frac{\sqrt{2}}{2}$
3	$(r,0,h)$	1	$(r,0,\frac{h}{2})$	1	$(r,r,\frac{h}{2})$	$\frac{\sqrt{2}}{2}$

The entire cylinder, constructed with eight NURPS patches, is shown in Figure 18(a).

Cone. The cone

$$x^2 + y^2 = \left(\frac{h-z}{h} r\right)^2, \quad 0 \le z \le h, \tag{5.16}$$

can be split into four isometrical patches. The NURPS representation of such a patch is given in the following table.

i	$\mathbf{c}_{i,1}$	$w_{i,1}$	$\mathbf{c}_{i,2}$	$w_{i,2}$	$\mathbf{c}_{i,3}$	$w_{i,3}$
1	$(r,0,0)$	1	$(r,r,0)$	$\frac{\sqrt{2}}{2}$	$(0,0,h)$	1
2	$(0,r,0)$	1	$(0,0,h)$	1	$(r,r,0)$	$\frac{\sqrt{2}}{2}$
3	$(0,0,h)$	1	$(0,0,h)$	1	$(0,0,h)$	1

The complete cone is depicted in Figure 18(b).

Sphere. Using only NURPS patches, it is not possible to describe the entire sphere,

$$x^2 + y^2 + z^2 = 1. \tag{5.17}$$

Nevertheless, with $2n$ NURPS patches we can represent the sphere up to some small gaps. The maximal height of these gaps is equal to

$$h_g = \frac{2\sin^2\theta}{\cos^2\theta + 1}, \tag{5.18}$$

where $\theta = \pi/n$. Small gaps can be achieved by a small angle θ, but then a large number of patches has to be used. The control points of such a patch are shown in the table below.

i	$\mathbf{c}_{i,1}$	$w_{i,1}$	$\mathbf{c}_{i,2}$	$w_{i,2}$	$\mathbf{c}_{i,3}$	$w_{i,3}$
1	$(\cos\theta, -\sin\theta, 0)$	1	$\left(\frac{1}{\cos\theta}, 0, \tan^2\theta\right)$	$\cos^2\theta$	$(\cos\theta, -\sin\theta, 1)$	$\frac{\sqrt{2}}{2}$
2	$(\cos\theta, \sin\theta, 0)$	1	$(\cos\theta, \sin\theta, 1)$	$\frac{\sqrt{2}}{2}$	$\left(\frac{1}{\cos\theta}, 0, \tan^2\theta\right)$	$\cos^2\theta$
3	$(0,0,1)$	1	$(\cos\theta, -\sin\theta, 1)$	$\frac{\sqrt{2}}{2}$	$(\cos\theta, \sin\theta, 1)$	$\frac{\sqrt{2}}{2}$

An extension to a sphere with radius r is straightforward, i.e., by multiplying the coordinates of each control point with r. An incomplete NURPS representation of the sphere with twelve patches is given in Figure 18(c). The hole filling strategy in [34] can be used to close the gaps in the sphere approximately.

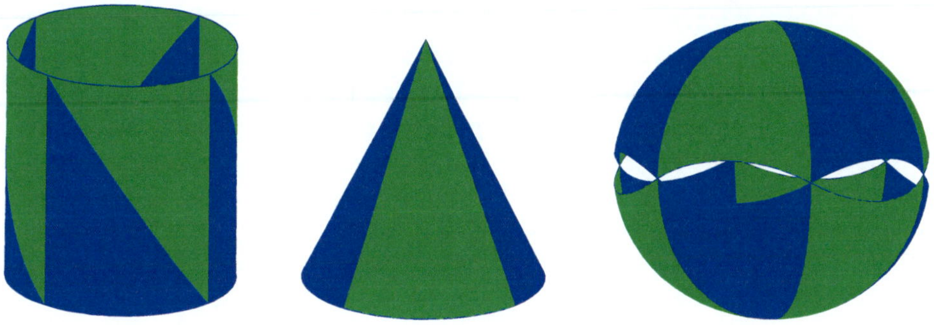

Figure 18. A NURPS representation of (a) a cylinder, (b) a cone, and (c) a sphere. The patches are defined on the domain triangle in Figure 17. Neighbouring patches are shaded in different colours.

6. Conclusion

Powell-Sabin splines are C^1-continuous piecewise quadratic polynomials defined on an arbitrary conforming triangulation. These splines can be compactly represented in a stable normalized basis. The basis functions can be chosen in a flexible way by means of PS triangles. This leads to a natural definition of PS control triangles, that allow an interactive change of the shape of Powell-Sabin splines in a predictable way.

Powell-Sabin splines can be refined using the $\sqrt{3}$ subdivision scheme. The control points of the subdivided spline can be easily calculated in a stable way. Applying the scheme twice results in a triadic refinement. Subdivision has many applications. The subdivision scheme can be applied for an efficient visualization of the Powell-Sabin splines. The increased resolution can also be used for obtaining a more detailed approximation or for a local manipulation of the spline shape.

QHPS splines are a hierarchical variant of Powell-Sabin splines in a quasi-hierarchical basis representation. They are defined on a hierarchical triangulation. Such a mesh is obtained, starting from an initial conforming triangulation, by partitioning successively a subset of triangles with a triadic split. The QHPS basis retains all advantages of the Powell-Sabin B-splines. In addition, a local refinement of the QHPS spline can be performed in a very natural way.

The rational extension of a Powell-Sabin spline surface is called a NURPS surface. In the rational representation a weight is associated with each control point. These weights can be used as extra degrees of freedom in the modelling of shapes by means of weight points. The position of the tangent points within the control triangles leads to an intuitive and graphical interpretation of the weights. NURPS surfaces are able to exactly represent patches of quadric surfaces, as the cylinder, the cone and the sphere. Note that the quasi-hierarchical setting is also applicable to the NURPS surfaces.

A generalization of Powell-Sabin splines to higher degrees and higher dimensions is not a trivial task. Some higher degree spline extensions on the Powell-Sabin split are considered in [2, 17]. Unfortunately, the proposed B-splines have no immediate geometric interpretation anymore, similar to PS triangles, and they are more difficult to implement. A generalization of the Powell-Sabin split in more dimensions is discussed in [22, 39]. Each simplex in a tessellation has to be split into a lot of smaller simplices. They must satisfy a particular set of geometric constraints in order to achieve C^1-continuity. At the moment it is not clear whether these constraints can always be satisfied for an arbitrary tessellation. Nevertheless, we can conclude that Powell-Sabin splines exhibit many nice properties that make them suitable for many CAGD applications.

References

[1] P. Alfeld and L.L. Schumaker. The dimension of bivariate spline spaces of smoothness r for degree $d \geq 4r + 1$. *Constr. Approx.*, **3**:189–197, 1987.

[2] P. Alfeld and L.L. Schumaker. Smooth macro-elements based on Powell-Sabin triangle splits. *Adv. Comp. Math.*, **16**:29–46, 2002.

[3] L.J. Billera. Homology of smooth splines: generic triangulations and a conjecture of Strang. *Trans. Amer. Math. Soc.*, **310**:325–340, 1988.

[4] W. Boehm and A. Müller. On de Casteljau's algorithm. *Comput. Aided Geom. Design*, **16**:587–605, 1999.

[5] R.W. Clough and J.L. Tocher. Finite element stiffness matrices for analysis of plates in bending. In *Proc. 1st Conference on Matrix Methods in Structural Mechanics*, pages 515–545, Wright Patterson Air Force Base, Ohio, 1965.

[6] P. Dierckx. On calculating normalized Powell-Sabin B-splines. *Comput. Aided Geom. Design*, **15**(1):61–78, 1997.

[7] P. Dierckx, S. Van Leemput, and T. Vermeire. Algorithms for surface fitting using Powell-Sabin splines. *IMA J. Numer. Anal.*, **12**:271–299, 1992.

[8] G. Farin. Algorithms for rational Bézier curves. *Comput. Aided Design*, **15**:73–77, 1983.

[9] G. Farin. Triangular Bernstein-Bézier patches. *Comput. Aided Geom. Design*, **3**:83–127, 1986.

[10] G. Farin. *Curves and Surfaces for CAGD: A Practical Guide*. Morgan Kaufmann Publishers, San Francisco, fifth edition, 2002.

[11] G. Farin. Dimensions of spline spaces over unconstricted triangulations. *J. Comput. Appl. Math.*, **192**:320–327, 2006.

[12] E. Grinspun, P. Krysl, and P. Schröder. CHARMS: a simple framework for adaptive simulation. *ACM Trans. Graphics*, **21**(3):281–290, 2002.

[13] D. Hong. Spaces of bivariate spline functions over triangulation. *Approx. Theory Appl.*, **7**:56–75, 1991.

[14] L. Kobbelt. $\sqrt{3}$-Subdivision. In *Computer Graphics Proceedings*, Annual Conference Series, pages 103–112. ACM SIGGRAPH, 2000.

[15] U. Labsik and G. Greiner. Interpolatory $\sqrt{3}$-subdivision. In *Proc. 21th European Conference on Computer Graphics*, volume 19 of *Computer Graphics Forum*, pages 131–138, Cambridge, 2000.

[16] M.J. Lai and L.L. Schumaker. On the approximation power of bivariate splines. *Adv. Comp. Math.*, **9**:251–279, 1998.

[17] M.J. Lai and L.L. Schumaker. Macro-elements and stable local bases for spaces of splines on Powell-Sabin triangulations. *Math. Comp.*, **72**:335–354, 2003.

[18] J. Maes and A. Bultheel. Stable multiresolution analysis on triangles for surface compression. *Electr. Trans. Numer. Anal.*, **25**:224–258, 2006.

[19] J. Maes, E. Vanraes, P. Dierckx, and A. Bultheel. On the Stability of normalized Powell-Sabin B-splines. *J. Comput. Appl. Math.*, **170**(1):181–196, 2004.

[20] C. Manni and P. Sablonnière. Quadratic spline quasi-interpolants on Powell-Sabin partitions. *Adv. Comput. Math.*, **26**:283–304, 2007.

[21] M.J.D. Powell and M.A. Sabin. Piecewise quadratic approximations on triangles. *ACM Trans. Math. Softw.*, **3**:316–325, 1977.

[22] T. Sorokina and A.J. Worsey. A multivariate Powell-Sabin interpolant. *Adv. Comput. Math.*, in press, 2007.

[23] H. Speleers, P. Dierckx, and S. Vandewalle. Local subdivision of Powell-Sabin splines. *Comput. Aided Geom. Design*, **23**(5):446–462, 2006.

[24] H. Speleers, P. Dierckx, and S. Vandewalle. Numerical solution of partial differential equations with Powell-Sabin splines. *J. Comput. Appl. Math.*, **189**(1-2):643–659, 2006.

[25] H. Speleers, P. Dierckx, and S. Vandewalle. Quasi-hierarchical Powell-Sabin B-splines. *Technical Report* **472**, Dept. Computer Science, K.U. Leuven, 2006.

[26] H. Speleers, P. Dierckx, and S. Vandewalle. Multigrid methods with Powell-Sabin splines. *Technical Report* **488**, Dept. Computer Science, K.U. Leuven, 2007.

[27] H. Speleers, P. Dierckx, and S. Vandewalle. On the L_p-stability of quasi-hierarchical Powell-Sabin splines. *Technical Report* **492**, Dept. Computer Science, K.U. Leuven, 2007.

[28] H. Speleers, P. Dierckx, and S. Vandewalle. Powell-Sabin splines with boundary conditions for polygonal and non-polygonal domains. *J. Comput. Appl. Math.*, in press, 2007.

[29] H. Speleers, P. Dierckx, and S. Vandewalle. Weight control for modelling with NURPS surfaces. *Comput. Aided Geom. Design*, **24**(3):179–186, 2007.

[30] E. Vanraes and A. Bultheel. A tangent subdivision scheme. *ACM Trans. Graphics*, **25**:340–355, 2006.

[31] E. Vanraes, P. Dierckx, and A. Bultheel. On the choice of the PS-triangles. *Technical Report* **353**, Dept. Computer Science, K.U. Leuven, 2003.

[32] E. Vanraes, J. Maes, and A. Bultheel. Powell-Sabin spline wavelets. *Int. J. Wav. Multires. Inf. Proc.*, **2**(1):23–42, 2004.

[33] E. Vanraes, J. Windmolders, A. Bultheel, and P. Dierckx. Automatic construction of control triangles for subdivided Powel-Sabin splines. *Comput. Aided Geom. Design*, **21**(7):671–682, 2004.

[34] J. Windmolders. *Powell-Sabin splines for computer aided geometric design*. PhD thesis, Dept. Computer Science, K.U. Leuven, 2003.

[35] J. Windmolders and P. Dierckx. Subdivision of uniform Powell-Sabin splines. *Comput. Aided Geom. Design*, **16**:301–315, 1999.

[36] J. Windmolders and P. Dierckx. From PS-splines to NURPS. In A. Cohen, C. Rabut, and L.L. Schumaker, editors, *Proc. of Curve and Surface Fitting, Saint-Malo 1999*, pages 45–54. Vanderbilt University Press, 2000.

[37] J. Windmolders and P. Dierckx. NURPS for special effects and quadrics. In T. Lyche and L.L. Schumaker, editors, *Proc. of Mathematical Methods for Curves and Surfaces, Oslo 2000*, pages 527 – 534. Vanderbilt University Press, 2001.

[38] J. Windmolders, E. Vanraes, P. Dierckx, and A. Bultheel. Uniform Powell-Sabin spline wavelets. *J. Comput. Appl. Math.*, **154**(1):125–142, 2003.

[39] A.J. Worsey and B. Piper. A trivariate Powell-Sabin interpolant. *Comput. Aided Geom. Design*, **5**:177–186, 1988.

In: Computer-Aided Design...
Editors: C.M. De Smet et al, pp. 351-376
ISBN 978-1-60456-860-8

Expert Commentary D

DESIGN OF SURVIVABLE VOIP NETWORKS USING THE VPN CONCEPT

***Dániel Orincsay*[*]*, Levente Tamási*[†]*, Balázs Gábor Józsa*[‡] *and Gábor Magyar*[§]**
Ericsson Research, Traffic Analysis and Network Performance Laboratory,
POB 107, H–1300 Budapest, Hungary[¶]

Abstract

This chapter addresses the issue of survivable Voice over IP (VoIP) network design. In the applied model the whole VoIP network is divided into two logical components: the access network and the transport network. The access network consists of VoIP end-points each representing a number of users, which connect to the transport network through edge routers serving as gateways. Since multiple edge routers may be available for any given VoIP node, one task of the design process is to assign gateways to the VoIP end-points. The edge routers have to be connected in a way that security and availability can be assured for the VoIP traffic. One obvious approach to fulfilling these requirements, which is assumed throughout the investigations, is to define a Virtual Private Network (VPN). Supposing a large volume of VoIP traffic, the cost of the VPN can be significant; thus, the other task of VoIP network design is to specify the transport VPN in the most economical way, while also taking the possible failures of transport network elements (i.e., routers and links) into consideration. Assuming a single network element failure at a time, the survivability of the VoIP network can be assured by assigning two gateways, namely a primary and a backup one, to each VoIP end-point, and calculating two disjoint paths between each pair of edge routers. To decrease the amount of backup reservations, a shared backup path protection scheme can be applied. The two tasks of survivable VoIP network design can be solved separately; however, in this chapter a novel solution is proposed in which the edge router assignment process takes both the objective function of VPN specification and the issues of survivability into consideration. Multiple methods realizing the novel approach are presented, which are based on the paradigms of evolutionary algorithms

[*]E-mail address: Daniel.Orincsay@ericsson.com
[†]E-mail address: Levente.Tamasi@ericsson.com
[‡]E-mail address: Balazs.Jozsa@ericsson.com
[§]E-mail address: Gabor.Magyar@ericsson.com
[¶]Tel: +36-1-437-7179, Fax: +36-1-437-7767

and simulated annealing. Moreover, a VPN specification algorithm is presented which utilizes the stepwise nature of the cost functions. The performance of the presented methods is evaluated with the help of simulations, using a well-known greedy algorithm as reference. It is shown that the proposed methods outperform the reference algorithm significantly in the simulation scenarios investigated.

Keywords: VoIP, VPN, survivable, network design, evolutionary algorithm, simulated annealing, shared protection

1. Introduction

Nowadays, the all-IP concept is favored by the infocommunication industry, which intends to conduct all types of traffic over the Internet protocol dominant in the networking area. As a part of all-IP, an increasing number of companies in the telephony sector commit themselves to using the voice over IP (VoIP) technology. Assuming a large VoIP network with a huge number of customers, it is necessary to take quality of service (QoS) as well as economic criteria into account during the design phase.

QoS requirements may be considered in various ways in the VoIP network. One possible approach is using a best effort IP service, the drawbacks of which are its incapability to provide *QoS guarantees* and the consequent fact that the service level can only be maintained by overprovisioning [1]. On the other hand, guaranteeing per flow QoS between all customer end-points, using e.g., the IntServ architecture, is both expensive and inefficient. In this chapter, a practically viable intermediate approach is followed: the VoIP network is divided into two logical components, with a pure IP based service used in the *access network* and QoS guaranteed in the *transport network*. The access network includes the *VoIP nodes*, i.e., the customer end-points that intend to use the VoIP service, while the transport network serves the purpose of carrying the aggregated VoIP traffic between the various access areas. The main parts of the transport network are the edge routers, the transit routers, and the connections between them. Since VoIP nodes may reach several edge routers so that the transmission paths fulfill the QoS requirements of the telephone service (e.g., limited maximal delay), it is necessary to select gateways for them towards the transport network.

Generally, it is more economical to apply a virtual private network (VPN) instead of deploying a brand-new physical network to realize the transport network for a VoIP service (see e.g., [2, 3]). The most important advantages of VoIP VPNs are cost efficiency, security, and scalability [4, 5]. Therefore, this chapter follows the VPN approach, which can be applied in different layers. One possibility is using a Layer 1 (L1) optical VPN (oVPN), in which case a network user rents separate optical connections from a service provider [6] and installs its own routers at their end-points. This results in total separation of the users' traffic at the physical level, similarly to leased lines. Another novel approach is using a Layer 2 (L2) VPN [7], which provides a data link layer service to customers over a wide area network (WAN) using multiprotocol label switching (MPLS); therefore, hosts connected by a wide area network appear to be on the same local area network (LAN). MPLS can also be used to realize a traditional Layer 3 (L3) IP VPN. The latter two approaches provide logical separation of users' traffic, i.e., at the physical level, the optical connections are shared, and the traffic of different customers is only separated at the MPLS level with the help of label switched paths (LSPs).

To sum up, there are several approaches to realizing a VoIP VPN. In all cases, however, the cost of the VPN depends on the capacity of the corresponding devices, i.e., the routers and the connections between them. The area of cost-optimal VPN design has been widely studied in the literature, with the topology, the set of traffic demands, and the cost functions of devices assumed as input parameters. However, during VoIP network design, the traffic distribution between the VPN nodes cannot be considered a fix input since it largely depends on the gateway assignments. Moreover, the possible failures of transport network elements should also be taken into consideration. Assuming a single network element failure at a time, the survivability of the VoIP network can be assured by (1) assigning two gateways, namely a primary and a backup one, to each VoIP end-point, and (2) applying a protection scheme in the transport network. The objects of the protection may be the connections of the transport network, which is referred to as *link protection* in the literature; however, during the current investigations, a *path protection* scheme is used which involves calculating two disjoint paths between each pair of edge routers. Therefore, in the case of a VPN element failure, the traffic handled by the corresponding router or link can be redirected onto backup paths unaffected by the failure. Moreover, in case the failed element is an edge router, the served VoIP end-points are reassigned to their respective backup gateways. In order to utilize the transport network resources efficiently, a *shared backup path protection* scheme [8, 9] is applied, which is the scheme preferred by the Internet Engineering Task Force (IETF). Since only one transport network element may fail at a time according to the applied model, the sharing of the backup reservations results in a significant decrease of the backup capacity needed compared to *dedicated protection* as well as various link protection schemes, e.g., *spare capacity assignment* and *joint capacity assignment* [9].

In summary, two interdependent tasks can be differentiated between in the case of survivable VoIP network design: (1) the assignment of each VoIP node to two VPN edge routers, which will serve as the primary and backup gateway of the particular VoIP node and (2) the design of the transport network covering the selected VPN nodes, including the calculation of two disjoint paths between all pairs of gateways. These two tasks can be solved independently by applying a number of existing methods, in which case the objective of the VPN transport network design is disregarded during the gateway assignment phase. However, it can be more efficient to have the cost and quality factors as well as the survivability issues concerning the transport network taken into consideration already in the first task. This approach is followed in this chapter by making several propositions with a view to solving the gateway assignment task of the survivable VoIP network design problem based on the principles of *evolutionary algorithms* [10] and *simulated annealing* [11]. Furthermore, in order to solve the VPN transport network design subproblem, a *core network design* algorithm (CND) is presented, which is applied after the gateway assignment phase. This heuristic algorithm exploits the *stepwise* nature of the cost functions of transport network devices and has been shown to be efficient in the area of cost-efficient VPN specification [12]. The numerical investigation of the proposed methods is performed by means of simulations, using the final cost of the survivable VoIP network given by CND as the main performance measure. During the investigations, a gateway assignment method based on a well-known greedy algorithm [13] is used as reference.

The rest of this chapter is organized as follows. The next section describes the network, traffic, and cost models used. It also includes the formulation of the survivable VoIP network design problem. In Section 3. novel methods are introduced aimed at solving the gateway assignment subproblem. Section 4. describes the core network design algorithm proposed for transport VPN design. Section 5. presents numerical results obtained from the performed simulations. Finally, the conclusions are drawn.

2. Problem Statement

This section introduces the interpretation of the survivable VoIP network design problem considered during the current investigations. First, the applied network, traffic, and cost models are discussed, followed by the formulation of the problem including the optimization objective.

2.1. Network Model

The VoIP network is modeled by a graph in the following way. A customer end-point that uses the VoIP service is called a *VoIP node*. The set of VoIP nodes is denoted by W. The possible routers of the VPN transport network to be composed are called *VPN nodes*. The set of VPN nodes is denoted by V.

Further, so-called *VoIP edges* are given which connect the VoIP-VoIP and VoIP-VPN node-pairs. The set of VoIP edges is denoted by F. Each VoIP edge $f \in F$ has a delay attribute $delay_f$ assigned representing its maximal one-way latency. Based on these edge delay values the delay value d_{wv} can be determined for each VoIP node $w \in W$ and VPN node $v \in V$ pair, representing a guarantee on the maximal latency between them. If a VPN node v is not available for a VoIP node w, value of d_{wv} is considered to be ∞. In the current interpretation, the QoS requirement that the routes between a VoIP node and its primary and backup gateway have to fulfill is the maximal access network latency d_{max}. Thus, a VPN node $v \in V$ is only considered as a *candidate gateway* for a given VoIP node $w \in W$ if the value of d_{wv} does not exceed d_{max}:

$$\Delta_w = \{v \in V : d_{wv} \leq d_{max}\} \qquad \forall w \in W, \tag{1}$$

where Δ_w denotes the candidate gateway set of VoIP node w. Since these delay requirements have to be fulfilled at both end-points of a VoIP call, and the VPN concept guarantees that latency limits are satisfied in the transport network, the maximum delay requirement of the voice service, i.e., a one-way delay of 150 ms as recommended by the ITU–T [14], can be assured.

Formally, the gateway assignments can be described as:

$$\begin{aligned} \delta^0_{wv} &= \begin{cases} 1 & \text{if the primary gateway of } w \text{ is } v \\ 0 & \text{otherwise} \end{cases} \qquad \forall w \in W, v \in V, \\ \delta^1_{wv} &= \begin{cases} 1 & \text{if the backup gateway of } w \text{ is } v \\ 0 & \text{otherwise} \end{cases} \qquad \forall w \in W, v \in V, \end{aligned} \tag{2}$$

subject to the following constraints:

$$\begin{aligned} \delta^0_{wv} &= 1 \Longrightarrow v \in \Delta_w, \\ \delta^1_{wv} &= 1 \Longrightarrow v \in \Delta_w, \end{aligned} \tag{3}$$

$$\begin{aligned} \sum_{v \in V} \delta^0_{wv} &= 1 \qquad \forall w \in W, \\ \sum_{v \in V} \delta^1_{wv} &= 1 \qquad \forall w \in W, \end{aligned} \tag{4}$$

$$\delta^0_{wv} + \delta^1_{wv} \leq 1 \qquad \forall w \in W, v \in V. \tag{5}$$

(3) represents the constraint that both the primary and the backup gateway of any given VoIP node w should be elements of the candiate gateway set of w. (4) means that each VoIP node should have both a primary and a backup gateway, while (5) assures the diversity of these two VPN nodes. Note that the gateway assignment subproblem is only feasible if each VoIP node has at least two candidate gateways:

$$|\Delta_w| \geq 2 \qquad \forall w \in W. \tag{6}$$

VPN nodes are connected by so-called *VPN edges*, the set of which is denoted by E. The use of VPN nodes as well as VPN edges is optional; typically only a subset of them is included in the final solution of the design. The bandwidth of VPN nodes and edges is limited; their particular capacity values are determined during the design phase using the corresponding cost functions (see Section 2.3.). While most VPN specification methods take the maximal capacity constraint of connections into account, the capacity aspect of routers is often neglected. However, during the design phase this latter factor also has to be considered, i.e., VPN nodes must be handled similarly to VPN edges. For this reason, the VPN nodes are substituted by virtual VPN edges for the investigations as shown in Figure 1. For instance, node u is decomposed into two nodes u_{in} and u_{out}, which belong to the incoming and outgoing traffic of the original node, respectively. Henceforth, node u_{out} is responsible for the traffic originated, while node u_{in} manages the traffic terminated by the original VPN node u. Further, since the traffic transferred by the original node u traverses the virtual edge between nodes u_{in} and u_{out}, the capacity constraint of the original router can be easily taken into consideration. Also note that connections in the transport VPN are assumed to be duplex in the sense that they can be used to transmit the amount of traffic corresponding to their capacities in both directions; therefore, two oppositely directed VPN edges with equal capacity values are used to represent one connection:

$$\begin{aligned} e = (u, v) \in E \Longrightarrow e' = (v, u) \in E \qquad & \forall e \in E, \\ cap_e = cap_{e'} \qquad & \forall e \in E, \end{aligned} \tag{7}$$

where e' denotes the opposite edge of e.

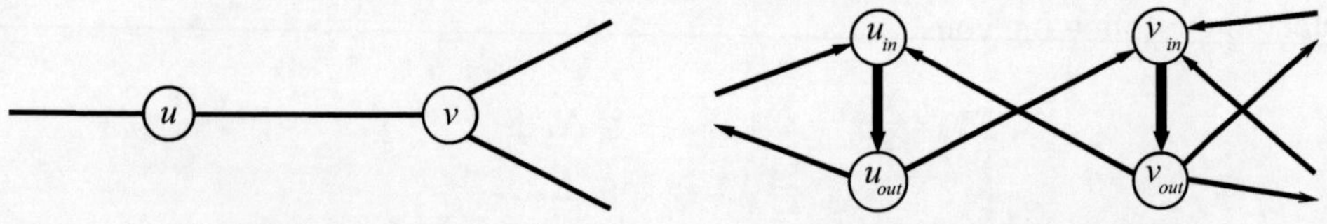

(a) Original VPN graph (b) Transformed VPN graph

Figure 1. Substituting the VPN nodes with virtual VPN edges.

2.2. Traffic Model

Although a VoIP node may refer to one particular customer owning a VoIP phone, it typically represents a private branch exchange (PBX) including a VoIP media gateway, which serves a number of users conducting a significant amount of VoIP calls. Due to the large number of VoIP nodes the generally applied approach of the *pipe model* [15] (also known as the *trunk model*), i.e., the source-destination pair based handling of traffic, is cumbersome. Therefore, the *hose model* [16] is followed, which defines only the sum incoming and outgoing traffic of a node. Considering that telephone calls are handled, the incoming and outgoing traffic are equal corresponding to the symmetric hose model. Thus, the traffic of any given VoIP node w is modeled by a bandwidth demand value tr_w that shows the amount of capacity needed to satisfy the calls generated (and received) by the VoIP users in the given node. This value can be derived from the number and calling habits of different VoIP users; however, this issue is related to the area of traffic modeling, and it is thus beyond the scope of the current investigations.

Although the hose model based design results in networks that can accommodate extreme traffic distributions as well, the high amount of spare capacity and the consequent extra price make it unacceptable in cost-sensitive situations. Therefore, in the case of the transport VPN the pipe model is applied, i.e., the traffic between a pair of VPN nodes $u, v \in V$ is modeled by bandwidth values Tr^0_{uv} and $Tr^y_{uv}, \forall y \in V$. Tr^0_{uv} represents the traffic between u and v under normal operation (and in the case of VPN edge failures, since they do not change the bandwidth requirements), while Tr^y_{uv} gives the traffic demand in the case of the failure of VPN node y. These values are estimated in the following way: first, the total hose traffic value of each edge VPN node v is calculated both for the case of normal operation and the failure of each VPN node y, denoted by TR^0_v and TR^y_v, respectively. This is performed by summing the hose traffic values of VoIP nodes according to the gateway assignments and considering the actual VPN node failure:

$$\begin{aligned} TR^0_v &= \sum_{w \in W} \delta^0_{wv} tr_w && \forall v \in V, \\ TR^v_v &= 0 && \forall v \in V, \\ TR^y_v &= \sum_{w \in W} (\delta^0_{wv} + \delta^0_{wy}\delta^1_{wv}) tr_w && \forall v, y \in V, v \neq y. \end{aligned} \tag{8}$$

For example, the total hose traffic for a given VPN node v in the case of the failure of a VPN node $y \neq v$ is calculated by summing the hose traffic values of those VoIP nodes w for which either of the following holds: (1) the primary gateway of w is v or (2) the primary gateway of w is y and the backup gateway is v. Considering that the total hose traffic values of gateways represent large numbers of users and the number of VPN nodes is relatively low, the pipe model is approximated by distributing the sum traffic of a particular VPN node among the other VPN nodes in direct proportion to their total hose traffic values, both in the case of normal operation and the failure of each VPN node:

$$
\begin{aligned}
Tr^0_{uv} &= \frac{TR^0_u \, TR^0_v}{\sum_{x \in V} TR^0_x} && \forall u, v \in V, \\
Tr^y_{uv} &= \frac{TR^y_u \, TR^y_v}{\sum_{x \in V} TR^y_x} && \forall u, v, y \in V. \qquad (9)
\end{aligned}
$$

2.3. Cost Model

The relationship between the cost and capacity values of VPN nodes and edges can be represented with the help of monotonic nondecreasing cost functions. In the simplest case, linear functions can be used. In this way, every required capacity unit has the same cost value, which gives the slope of the curve. In the overwhelming majority of cases, these approximations are inadequate to model real cost relations; however, it is a relatively frequent approach because of the simplicity of the computations involved.

In real-life situations, the various devices, i.e., the routers and the connections between them have discrete capacity values and consequently discrete cost amounts. These types of cost dependencies can be described with so-called *stepwise* functions [17, 18, 19, 20] (see Figure 2). Although this approach makes the VPN design subproblem mathematically complex [21], it can fulfill the high accuracy requirements arising in real-life situations. Moreover, in the applied model each VPN node v and VPN edge e has an individual cost function $cost_v$ and $cost_e$, respectively, which enables special cost modifying factors as well as policy reasons to be considered.

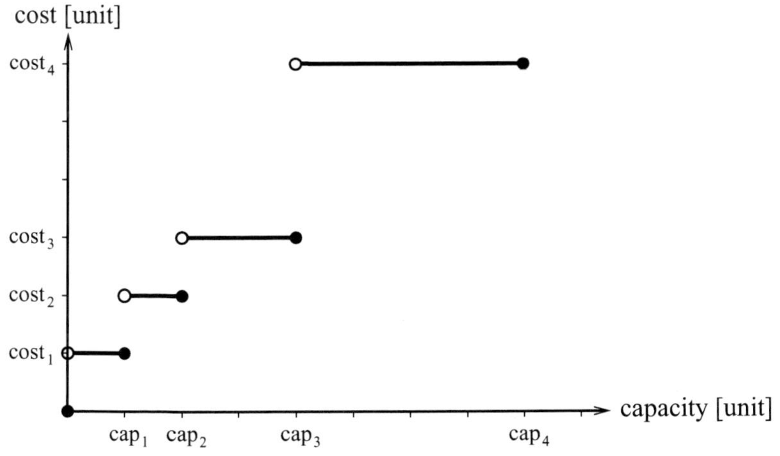

Figure 2. Stepwise cost function example.

Formally, a stepwise cost function can be described as:

$$cost_v(\alpha) = \begin{cases} cost_v^0 = 0 & \text{if } \alpha = cap_v^0 = 0 \\ cost_v^1 & \text{if } 0 < \alpha \leq cap_v^1 \\ cost_v^2 & \text{if } cap_v^1 < \alpha \leq cap_v^2 \\ \ldots \end{cases} \qquad \forall v \in V,$$

$$cost_e(\alpha) = \begin{cases} cost_e^0 = 0 & \text{if } \alpha = cap_e^0 = 0 \\ cost_e^1 & \text{if } 0 < \alpha \leq cap_e^1 \\ cost_e^2 & \text{if } cap_e^1 < \alpha \leq cap_e^2 \\ \ldots \end{cases} \qquad \forall e \in E. \tag{10}$$

Naturally, the cost functions of the two VPN edges corresponding to the same connection must be identical:

$$cost_e(\alpha) \equiv cost_{e'}(\alpha) \qquad \forall e \in E, \forall \alpha \in \mathbb{R}^+. \tag{11}$$

2.4. Problem Formulation

This section contains the description of the inputs and outputs of the two tasks of the survivable VoIP network design problem. The gateway assignment subproblem has the following input parameters: (1) the set of VoIP nodes W, (2) the set of possible VPN nodes V, (3) the set of delay values d_{wv} for all VoIP node $w \in W$ and VPN node $v \in V$ pairs (derived from the structure of VoIP nodes and edges) and the maximal access network latency d_{max}, and (4) the hose traffic values tr_w for all VoIP nodes $w \in W$.

As the output of the first subproblem, each VoIP node is assigned to a primary and a backup gateway, which determines a set of VPN nodes that are necessarily elements of the VPN transport network to be formed. This assignment can be used to calculate the traffic demands between pairs of VPN nodes as described in Section 2.2.. Therefore, the transport VPN design subproblem takes the following input parameters: (1) the set of VPN nodes V (both the gateways and the possible transit VPN nodes), (2) the set of possible VPN edges E, (3) the bandwidth values Tr_{uv}^0 and Tr_{uv}^y for all pairs of VPN nodes $u, v \in V$ and for all VPN nodes $y \in V$, and (4) the cost functions of VPN nodes and edges denoted by $cost_v$ and $cost_e$, respectively. As a result of the design process, the VPN transport network is specified, and the primary and backup paths to be established for the aggregated VoIP traffic demands are also provided. These can be represented with the following incidence functions:

$$\lambda_{uvx}^0 = \begin{cases} 1 & \text{if } x \in V \text{ is on the active path between } u, v \in V \\ 0 & \text{otherwise} \end{cases} \qquad \forall u, v, x \in V,$$

$$\mu_{uve}^0 = \begin{cases} 1 & \text{if } e \in E \text{ is on the active path between } u, v \in V \\ 0 & \text{otherwise} \end{cases} \qquad \forall u, v \in V, e \in E,$$

$$\lambda_{uvx}^1 = \begin{cases} 1 & \text{if } x \in V \text{ is on the backup path between } u, v \in V \\ 0 & \text{otherwise} \end{cases} \qquad \forall u, v, x \in V,$$

$$\mu_{uve}^1 = \begin{cases} 1 & \text{if } e \in E \text{ is on the backup path between } u, v \in V \\ 0 & \text{otherwise} \end{cases} \qquad \forall u, v \in V, e \in E. \tag{12}$$

The values of these functions have to satisfy the so-called *flow conservation constraint*; moreover, the active and backup paths have to be disjoint for all pairs of VPN nodes:

$$\sum_{e=(z,x)} \mu^0_{uve} - \sum_{e=(x,z)} \mu^0_{uve} = \begin{cases} -1 & \text{if } x = u \\ 0 & \text{if } x \neq u, x \neq v \\ 1 & \text{if } x = v \end{cases} \quad \forall u, v, x \in V,$$

$$\sum_{e=(z,x)} \mu^1_{uve} - \sum_{e=(x,z)} \mu^1_{uve} = \begin{cases} -1 & \text{if } x = u \\ 0 & \text{if } x \neq u, x \neq v \\ 1 & \text{if } x = v \end{cases} \quad \forall u, v, x \in V, \qquad (13)$$

$$\begin{aligned} \lambda^0_{uvx} + \lambda^1_{uvx} \leq 1 \qquad & \forall u, v, x \in V, x \neq u, x \neq v, \\ \mu^0_{uve} + \mu^1_{uve} \leq 1 \qquad & \forall u, v \in V, e \in E. \end{aligned} \qquad (14)$$

The active and backup paths can be used to calculate the exact capacity values of all devices, by determining the amount of active and backup reservations on the device. The active reservation can be computed as $\sum_{u,v \in V} \lambda^0_{uvx} Tr^0_{uv}$ for a VPN node $x \in V$, and as $\sum_{u,v \in V} \mu^0_{uve} Tr^0_{uv}$ for a VPN edge $e \in E$. Moreover, the backup reservations can be determined by using a so-called *backup reservation matrix* (BRM), which is similar to the *spare provisioning* matrix used in the literature. Both the rows and the columns of the BRM correspond to the transport network devices; thus, the matrix has $|V \cup E|$ rows and the same number of columns, where an element BRM_{ij} corresponds to the amount of backup reservation required on device $j \in V \cup E$ in case device $i \in V \cup E$ fails. Note that contrary to the shared backup path protection problem discussed in the literature, backup reservations also have to be made along the active paths of the demands, since the capacity required on the devices of the active path of a demand may increase if a VPN node fails. This phenomenon occurs if the following two conditions are fulfilled: (1) the failing VPN node is not an element of the active path of the particular demand, and thus the demand does not have to be rerouted, and (2) some of the VoIP nodes served by the failing VPN node are reassigned to one of the end-points of the demand. Moreover, when calculating the backup reservations needed for a VPN node failure along the backup path of a demand, the bandwidth value corresponding to the VPN node failure in question should be considered, i.e., the changes in the traffic demands should be taken into account. Therefore, the elements of the BRM can be calculated in the following way:

$$BRM_{ij} = \begin{cases} \sum\limits_{u,v \in V} \lambda^0_{uvi} \lambda^1_{uvj} Tr^i_{uv} + \sum\limits_{u,v \in V} (1 - \lambda^0_{uvi}) \lambda^0_{uvj} (Tr^i_{uv} - Tr^0_{uv}) & \text{if } i \in V, j \in V \\ \sum\limits_{u,v \in V} \mu^0_{uvi} \lambda^1_{uvj} Tr^0_{uv} & \text{if } i \in E, j \in V \\ \sum\limits_{u,v \in V} \lambda^0_{uvi} \mu^1_{uvj} Tr^i_{uv} + \sum\limits_{u,v \in V} (1 - \lambda^0_{uvi}) \mu^0_{uvj} (Tr^i_{uv} - Tr^0_{uv}) & \text{if } i \in V, j \in E \\ \sum\limits_{u,v \in V} \mu^0_{uvi} \mu^1_{uvj} Tr^0_{uv} & \text{if } i \in E, j \in E \end{cases} . \qquad (15)$$

In the case of a shared protection scheme, the amount of backup reservation on a device $j \in V \cup E$ can be calculated by finding the maximal element in column j of the BRM:

$\max_{i \in V \cup E} BRM_{ij}$. Therefore, the *capacity constraints* that the total load values (i.e., the sum of the active and backup reservations) of the transport network devices have to satisfy is as follows:

$$\begin{aligned} load_x &= \sum_{u,v \in V} \lambda^0_{uvx} Tr^0_{uv} + \max_{i \in V \cup E} BRM_{ix} \ \leq cap_x \quad \forall x \in V, \\ load_e &= \sum_{u,v \in V} \mu^0_{uve} Tr^0_{uv} + \max_{i \in V \cup E} BRM_{ie} \ \leq cap_e \quad \forall e \in E, \end{aligned} \tag{16}$$

where cap_x and cap_e denote the capacity values of the VPN nodes and edges, respectively. Note that the latter are subject to constraint (7), i.e., the capacity values of the two oppositely directed edges representing one connection are necessarily equal.

Aiming at minimizing the overall establishment cost of the VoIP network, which basically depends on the cost of the VPN transport network, the objective of the whole design process is to:

$$\min \left\{ \sum_{v \in V} cost_v(cap_v) + \frac{1}{2} \sum_{e \in E} cost_e(cap_e) \right\}, \tag{17}$$

subject to constraints (1) to (16). The total cost of edges are halved since two oppositely directed edges with equal capacity and cost values are used to model a single connection in the transport VPN.

3. Gateway Assignment

This section proposes several methods that are capable of solving the gateway assignment subproblem. Since it is related to the so-called *set-covering problem* widely studied in the literature [22, 23], the term *covering* is used throughout the descriptions of various algorithms referring to the situation when a VPN node is selected as a primary or backup gateway for a VoIP node.

3.1. Greedy Covering Algorithm (GC)

This section presents greedy algorithms that are based on a well-known greedy solution to the set covering problem (see e.g., [13]). The algorithms consist of two main steps, which are described in the following.

In the first step, VoIP nodes with only two candidate gateways each are identified. Since each of these VoIP nodes has access to only two VPN nodes fulfilling the delay requirements, their primary and backup gateways are fixed; therefore, the corresponding VPN nodes define a set of gateways that is a mandatory part of the solution. Then, for each mandatory VPN node v, all the VoIP nodes w for which it is a candidate gateway are checked for two conditions: (1) if the VoIP node has no primary gateway yet, the VPN node becomes its primary gateway:

$$\sum_{x \in V} \delta^0_{wx} = 0 \Longrightarrow \delta^0_{wv} \leftarrow 1, \tag{18}$$

and (2) if the VoIP node has a primary gateway, but no backup gateway, the VPN node becomes its backup gateway:

$$\sum_{x \in V} \delta^0_{wx} = 1 \wedge \delta^0_{wv} = 0 \wedge \sum_{x \in V} \delta^1_{wx} = 0 \Longrightarrow \delta^1_{wv} \leftarrow 1. \tag{19}$$

The second step of the algorithm is an iteration in which further VPN nodes are selected one by one based on a certain *utility value.* When a particular VPN node is selected, the two conditions described above are checked, and the appropriate assignments are made similarly to the first step. The iteration stops when each VoIP node has both a primary and a backup gateway. In the following, two utility value variants are presented.

3.1.1. VPN Node Number Based GC (GC-N)

In this variant the utility value corresponds to the number of VoIP nodes that can be covered by the given VPN node, considering the two conditions above. Formally, the sets of VoIP nodes that a VPN node v can be selected as a primary or backup gateway for is:

$$\begin{aligned} G^0_v &= \left\{ w \in W : v \in \Delta_w, \sum_{x \in V} \delta^0_{wx} = 0 \right\}, \\ G^1_v &= \left\{ w \in W : v \in \Delta_w, \sum_{x \in V} \delta^0_{wx} = 1, \sum_{x \in V} \delta^1_{wx} = 0, \delta^0_{wv} = 0 \right\}. \end{aligned} \tag{20}$$

Therefore, the utility value used by GC-N can be calculated is:

$$|G^0_v \cup G^1_v|. \tag{21}$$

Note that G^0_v and G^1_v change continuously based on the assignments performed. This approach aims at minimizing the number of selected VPN nodes; however, it does not take any cost factors into consideration.

3.1.2. VPN Node Cost Based GC (GC-C)

The utility value used by this variant is the number of VoIP nodes that the given VPN node can cover according to the two conditions above, divided by the cost value corresponding to the first step of its cost function:

$$\frac{|G^0_v \cup G^1_v|}{cost^1_v}. \tag{22}$$

The idea behind this utility value is to take the establishment costs of the VPN nodes also into account during the iteration.

3.2. Evolutionary Covering Algorithm (EC)

A common property of the greedy covering algorithms presented above is that they do not vary the existing gateway assignments. This approach is referred to as *construction method*, i.e., the algorithms stop when the first feasible solution is found. Therefore, they provide a fast solution to the first subproblem of the survivable VoIP network design problem; however, their drawback is that there is no possibility for sophisticated optimization.

This section proposes an algorithm that is based on the well-known paradigm of *evolutionary algorithms* (also called *genetic algorithms*) [10], which enables selection between more feasible solutions using complex *cost calculation methods* (see Section 3.4.). The representation of the gateway assignment subproblem applied in the evolutionary algorithm is the following. An *entity* defines a valid assignment, where two *genes* correspond to each VoIP node, and their values refer to the primary and backup gateway it is assigned to. For each VoIP node, the two VPN nodes have to be different and both have to be elements of the candidate gateway set of the given VoIP node. In each iteration of the evolutionary algorithm, either a *crossover* or a *killing* operation is performed based on the actual population size. In the case of crossover, each of the two parents is selected by choosing the entity with the lowest cost from a set of randomly selected entities (regarding the actual cost calculation method), and the child inherits each of its genes from either of its parents with equal probability. Similarly, the selection of entities that do not survive is performed by killing the oldest entity from a number of randomly selected entities, and killing the one with the highest cost (based on the cost calculation method used) from another set of randomly selected entities. In the case of both operations, the size of the set of randomly selected entities is given by a parameter k. Moreover, during all iterations, *mutation* is performed, i.e., one gene of an entity is changed randomly, which means that another candidate VPN node of the given VoIP node becomes its primary or backup gateway. Both the crossover and mutation operations are performed with respect to the necessary diversity of the primary and backup gateway of any given VoIP node. In order to create an appropriate *initial population*, the GC-C algorithm is applied in the following way. Several feasible solutions are sought by GC-C, excluding a VPN node from the initial set of VPN nodes; the excluded VPN node is altered in each iteration. Naturally, VPN nodes that are mandatory elements of the solution cannot be excluded. Using this method, several different feasible coverings consisting of VPN nodes with low establishment cost values can be generated to form the initial population. The evolutionary algorithm stops if the cheapest solution considering the actual cost calculation has not changed during the last n steps.

3.3. Simulated Annealing Based Covering Algorithm (SC)

This section proposes an algorithm for the gateway assignment subproblem based on the principle of *simulated annealing* [11]. The representation used is similar to the one presented in the previous section: a *state* defines a valid assignment, where two values correspond to each VoIP node. The two values, which describe the primary and backup gateway of the VoIP node, are necessarily different, and both have to be candidate gateways of the particular VoIP node. The *initial state* is based on a solution by GC-C, while *random changes* in the state are generated by changing either the primary or the backup gateway of a randomly selected VoIP node to another of its candidate VPN nodes, complying with the constraint that the primary and backup gateway have to be different for all VoIP nodes. States are evaluated using the same cost calculation methods as in the case of the evolutionary algorithm (see Section 3.4.). A state is accepted with a probability of $e^{\frac{C-C'}{T}}$, where C and C' denote the cost of the previous and current state, respectively, while T is the *temperature* of the previous state. This means that a state with a higher cost value can also be accepted by the algorithm; however, the probability of this event decreases heavily against both the cost difference and the current temperature. The *annealing schedule* takes the form of $T' = T \cdot \phi$, where T is the temperature in the previous iteration, T' is the current temperature, and ϕ denotes the *annealing factor*. The *initial temperature* is denoted by T_0. As seen in the case of the evolutionary algorithm, the simulated annealing algorithm terminates if the cost of the cheapest solution has not improved during the last n iterations.

3.4. Entity and State Cost Calculation Methods

The quality of the solutions by both EC and SC is heavily influenced by the cost calculation method used for evaluating the entities and states, respectively. Thus, several approaches are investigated, as it can be seen in the following paragraphs.

3.4.1. Cost Approximation Based Methods (EC-C, SC-C)

The main idea behind the *cost approximation* based methods is trying to foresee the final cost of the VPN transport network to be designed. First, the set of the aggregated VoIP traffic demands are routed several times, based on different random orders. *Suurballe's disjoint paths algorithm* [24] is applied for this purpose to calculate two disjoint paths between all pairs of edge VPN nodes, using an edge weight function that favors devices with low cost per unit traffic values. In each round, the actual capacity needed on the transport network elements is determined according to Section 2.4., considering the sharing of backup reservations. Finally, the algorithm considers the price of the cheapest configuration the cost of the entity or state.

3.4.2. Distance Weighted Traffic Based Methods (EC-D, SC-D)

When applying the *distance weighted traffic* based methods, the product of the maximal bandwidth requirement (computed over the normal operation and the failure of each VPN node) and the length of the possible shortest path (in terms of hop-count) is calculated for each aggregated VoIP traffic demand. Then the cost of the entity or state is specified as the sum of these products regarding the whole network:

$$\sum_{u,v \in V} Tr_{uv}^{max} D_{uv}, \tag{23}$$

where $Tr_{uv}^{max} = \max \left\{ Tr_{uv}^{0}, \max_{y \in V} Tr_{uv}^{y} \right\}$ denotes the maximal bandwidth requirement, while D_{uv} gives the length of the path with the minimal number of hops between $u, v \in V$. This metric aims at reducing the number of transit VPN nodes required, especially between edge VPN nodes where the bandwidth requirements can be high.

3.4.3. Suurballe Path Cost Weighted Traffic Based Methods (EC-S, SC-S)

The *Suurballe path cost weighted traffic* based methods are similar to the methods in the previous paragraph; however, they also consider the need for backup paths. For all pairs of VPN nodes, Suurballe's disjoint paths algorithm is performed using unit weights, which results in two disjoint paths with minimal sum hop-count. This sum hop-count, which is denoted by S_{uv} for a pair of VPN nodes $u, v \in V$, is multiplied by the maximal bandwidth requirement between the two VPN nodes. The cost of the entity or state is then calculated as the sum of these products considering all pairs of VPN nodes:

$$\sum_{u,v \in V} Tr_{uv}^{max} S_{uv}. \tag{24}$$

3.4.4. Two-Level Cost Metric Based Variants (EC-C2, EC-D2, EC-S2, SC-C2, SC-D2, SC-S2)

The two-level variants of the above cost metrics were also investigated in the following way. The number of the selected VPN edge routers serves as a primary metric, while the value computed by the cost approximation, distance weighted traffic, or Suurballe path cost weighted traffic methods is normalized by the initial value of the metric, scaled by an importance factor s, and used as a secondary metric:

$$|V^*| + s\frac{M}{M_0}, \tag{25}$$

where $V^* = \left\{v \in V : \sum_{w \in W} \delta_{wv}^0 + \sum_{w \in W} \delta_{wv}^1 \geq 1\right\}$ is the set of VPN nodes selected as either the primary or the backup gateway of at least one VoIP node, and M_0 and M denote the value of the corresponding one-level metric in the first and the current iteration, respectively. These metrics generally favor assignments where the number of gateways is low, however, they may also select a larger number of edge VPN nodes if the gain in the secondary metric is significant enough.

3.4.5. Traffic Weighted Interconnection Based Methods (EC-TI, SC-TI)

In the case of the *traffic weighted interconnection based* methods, each VPN edge between the currently selected VPN nodes is assigned a *weight* defined as the maximal bandwidth requirement (see Section 3.4.2.) between the two VPN nodes it connects. The weights of all VPN edges between the selected VPN nodes are summed, and this sum is divided by its maximal possible value corresponding to a fully meshed group of VPN nodes. The cost of the entity or state is defined as the number of selected VPN nodes divided by the above ratio:

$$\frac{|V^*|}{\frac{\sum_{u,v \in V^*,(u,v) \in E} Tr_{uv}^{max}}{\sum_{u,v \in V^*} Tr_{uv}^{max}}}. \tag{26}$$

The idea behind this metric is to favor assignments where VPN node pairs with higher maximal demands can transmit their traffic on direct links, while taking the number of selected VPN nodes into consideration at the same time.

4. Transport VPN Design

This section describes the core network design (CND) algorithm proposed as a solution to the transport VPN specification subproblem defined in Section 2.. The outline of the algorithm is given in Section 4.1., followed by a detailed description of its phases.

4.1. Algorithm Outline

The algorithm presented for transport VPN design is a heuristic method which outperformed [12] a reference algorithm based on the principle of *greedy randomized adaptive search procedures* (GRASP) [25], a method which was shown to be able to solve the location and dimensioning problems arising in the field of cost-optimal VPN specification efficiently [26]. Note that although CND is used to solve the transport VPN specification subproblem during the current investigations, it may be applied in the case of any underlying networking technology that supports explicit routing and bandwidth reservation (e.g., ATM or MPLS).

The process can be divided into three subsequential phases (see Figure 3). The algorithm starts with the initial capacity estimation (ICE) phase, whose task is to estimate the approximate capacity conditions. The main phase is the iterative routing optimization (IRO), which searches for an appropriate network configuration based on the initial estimations. Although this second phase already provides an economical solution to the VPN specification subproblem, a cheaper configuration can be reached with the help of the last phase called posterior capacity refinement (PCR).

Phase 1: initial capacity estimation (ICE)
Phase 2: iterative routing optimization (IRO)
Phase 3: posterior capacity refinement (PCR)

Figure 3. The three phases of the core network design (CND) algorithm.

Generally, two types of search methods can be differentiated between. The first two phases (ICE and IRO) perform global search, utilizing comprehensive information about the current network structure and the traffic demands. The purpose of this is to diminish the whole state space in a way that its remaining part approaches to the optimal solution. Then the third phase (PCR) performs a local search aimed at finding the most favorable solution in the reduced state space.

4.2. Initial Capacity Estimation

The main purpose of the initial capacity estimation (ICE) phase is to assess the necessary device capacities by analyzing the set of traffic demands. Thus, prior information can be provided for IRO by supplying a partially dimensioned network as an initial state. Therefore, the remaining task of IRO is to finalize the dimensioning of devices and the routing of demands. Although ICE typically does not give a feasible solution to the task, it specifies a favorable starting configuration based on a global picture of the transport VPN design subproblem.

The operation of ICE is based on an iteration (see Figure 4). In Step 1 the traffic demands to be accommodated are shuffled randomly. Then in Step 2 they are routed one after another (in the above order) using Suurballe's disjoint paths algorithm with the following edge weight function:

$$w_x = \frac{cost_x(load_x + Tr^0_{uv})}{load_x + Tr^0_{uv}} \qquad \forall x \in V,$$

$$w_e = \frac{cost_e(load_e + Tr^0_{uv})}{load_e + Tr^0_{uv}} \qquad \forall e \in E. \tag{27}$$

The denominator estimates the bandwidth reservation on the device if it is involved in one of the paths of the actual demand, while the numerator is the corresponding cost value of the device. This weight function favors devices with low cost per unit traffic values with a view to keeping the overall network cost at a low level. After the routing of each demand, the load and capacity values of devices are calculated, considering the amount of backup reservations as described in Section 2.4.; therefore, after the accommodation of the last demand, capacity values corresponding to a feasible accommodation are available, which are saved in Step 3 along with the total network cost. Steps 1, 2 and 3 are repeated a predefined number of times (see Step 4), which is set to 100 during the experiments. Finally in Step 5, those accommodations are determined whose total network cost is worse than the best cost value encountered during the above iterations at most by a predefined percentage (set to 10% during the simulations), and the capacity values of the devices are specified in a way that each device is assigned the lowest value of the ones saved in the selected iterations. This idea is based on the assumption that if several random accommodations with low total network cost values need a certain amount of capacity on a particular device, then it is probable that the optimal accommodation will also need as much bandwidth.

Step 1: Shuffle traffic demands.
Step 2: Route demands using Suurballe's disjoint paths algorithm, calculate load and capacity values after the routing of each demand.
Step 3: Store capacity values and total network cost corresponding to this feasible accommodation.
Step 4: If there are more iterations, go to Step 1.
Step 5: Select the accommodations with the lowest total network cost, and minimize device capacities over the above accommodations.

Figure 4. Steps of the initial capacity estimation (ICE) phase.

4.3. Iterative Routing Optimization

The main phase of the algorithm, namely the iterative routing optimization (IRO) phase is based on an algorithm that can accommodate a given set of traffic demands in a graph with capacity limits. During the current investigations, the algorithm proposed in [31] was used for this purpose. As it was shown in [31], this algorithm performs well in terms of *feasibility*, i.e., it generally finds a solution for a given problem instance, supposing that there is a valid solution. The algorithm was extended to handle the changes in the traffic demands caused by the failures of VPN nodes. Note that the routing optimization procedure applied can be substituted by any other method fulfilling the same task, which is an important advantage of IRO.

The steps of the IRO process are shown in Figure 5. In Step 1, IRO attempts to accommodate the traffic demand set considering the actual capacity constraints. If the algorithm terminates with success (Step 2), i.e., all demands are accommodated, IRO finishes. Otherwise, the capacity of a particular device is increased by one capacity step in the following way. In Step 3, the remaining demands that could not be fit into the graph under the actual capacity conditions are accommodated disregarding the capacity constraints, using a weight function which considers the cost of extending the particular device. The device to be extended in Step 4 is the one on which the capacity violation, i.e., the extra capacity required by the actual accommodation is the largest. After the capacity increase, Step 1 follows again with the updated capacity limits.

Step 1: Attempt to accommodate traffic demands.
Step 2: If successful, stop.
Step 3: Route remaining traffic demands disregarding the capacity constraints, and select device based on capacity violation.
Step 4: Increase device capacity, and go to Step 1.

Figure 5. Steps of the iterative routing optimization (IRO) phase.

4.4. Posterior Capacity Refinement

As it was discussed in Section 4.1., after the IRO phase a suitable solution to the VPN specification subproblem is already available. However, this result might be improved with the help of posterior capacity refinement (PCR). This greedy method is based on a local search procedure, which means that the process concentrates only on one part of the network at a time.

The idea behind PCR is to reduce the size of devices that are underutilized in the sense that if the bandwidth reservation on them was decreased by a relatively small amount, a device with lower capacity and consequently lower cost level would suffice. For example, if the reservation on a connection is 170 Mbps, then two 155 Mbps devices have to be installed in parallel, while if reservation on the particular connection could be reduced by about 10%, one 155 Mbps device would be sufficient, whose cost would be the half of the original. The demands corresponding to the remaining 10% of the original reservation should be redirected onto other connections utilizing their spare capacity, if possible.

Figure 6 shows the operation of the PCR method. In Step 1 the devices are sorted by their relative step utilization, i.e., the utilization of the capacity range belonging to the current cost value:

$$util_x = \begin{cases} 0 & \text{if } cap_x = cap_x^0 = 0 \\ \frac{load_x - cap_x^{i-1}}{cap_x^i - cap_x^{i-1}} & \text{if } cap_x > 0, \text{ where } cap_x = cap_x^i \end{cases} \quad \forall x \in V,$$

$$util_e = \begin{cases} 0 & \text{if } cap_e = cap_e^0 = 0 \\ \frac{load_e - cap_e^{i-1}}{cap_e^i - cap_e^{i-1}} & \text{if } cap_e > 0, \text{ where } cap_e = cap_e^i \end{cases} \quad \forall e \in E. \qquad (28)$$

The reason is that in the case of a device with a lower relative step utilization, it is more probable that if its capacity is decreased by one step, the traffic demands can still be satisfied under these tighter capacity conditions. Next in Step 2 the devices are shrunk one by one in the above order, and the accommodation of the traffic demands is attempted by IRO in Step 3. If, after the shrinking of a particular device, IRO results in a configuration that is cheaper than the best overall cost so far (Step 4), the process restarts from the sorting step. Otherwise, the solution before the capacity decrase step is restored in Step 5, and the device is removed from further optimization. The process is terminated if the overall cost could not be improved since the last sorting (Step 6).

Step 1: Sort devices by relative step utilization, and select first device.
Step 2: Shrink selected device.
Step 3: Perform IRO.
Step 4: If the result is the best so far, save it, and go to Step 1.
Step 5: Restore the solution before the capacity decrease step, remove device from further optimization.
Step 6: If there are more devices, select next device, and go to Step 2, otherwise stop.

Figure 6. Steps of the posterior capacity refinement (PCR) phase.

5. Results

In order to investigate the performance of the proposed algorithms, simulations were carried out using artificial problem instances. First, the automated method of problem instance generation is described; then, the performed simulation scenarios are presented, including the analysis of the numerical results.

5.1. Problem Instance Generation

During the simulations the aim was to create problem instances that provide a good representation of real-life situations. The first task was to generate the topology of the network, including the VoIP nodes and edges as well as the possible VPN nodes and edges. For the access network, a random VoIP graph generator method was applied that is based on the *Barabási–Albert model* [27, 28]. This approach is based on the *power laws* of Internet topology [29, 30], and is nowadays frequently used to model wide area communication networks. The topology of the transport VPN was generated using the random graph generator method presented in [31], which assures that the resulting topology is biconnected. Topologies of various sizes were examined; however, results are presented for networks with 500 VoIP nodes and 50 possible VPN nodes. The delay values of VoIP edges were specified randomly using a distribution that generates values proportionally to the lengths of edges, i.e., the distances between their end-points. The maximum access network latency d_{max} was set to 50 ms for the investigations, as was the guarantee on the maximal delay in the transport VPN. These values assure that the ITU–T recommendation for a maximal one-way delay of 150 ms is complied with.

The traffic demands of VoIP nodes were generated randomly in the following way. First, the maximal number of parallel calls was generated for each VoIP node in the interval $[1, 2N]$. The value of N refers to the average number of maximal parallel calls, and it was shifted from 64 to 256. Then the number of parallel calls had to be transformed into a bandwidth value based on the actual codec type and packetization overhead (RTP/UDP/IP header). Assuming the use of the ITU–T recommendation G.711 PCM codec, which can provide the highest voice quality, with silence suppression, an activity factor of 55%, and a packetization time of 5 ms, this resulted in a call bandwidth of 64 kbps. Thus, the investigated average VoIP node traffic (tr_w) interval was 4 to 16 Mbps. Note that the actual codec type only affects the bandwidth calculation; moreover, since the average VoIP node traffic interval is relatively wide, the results presented can apply to various codec types.

The cost functions of VPN edges were based on the Synchronous Transfer Mode (STM) standards referring to a physical layer approach as described in Section 1., while in the case of VPN nodes two different device sizes were assumed (see Table 1). As the cost values of these functions only represent ratios, they can be considered *cost units*. In the case of VPN edges, the capacity values 311 Mbps, 1244 Mbps and 5 Gbps refer to the situation when two connections of the same size are deployed in parallel. The cost function of VPN edges is based on the assumption that the deployment of two devices of similar capacity is reasonable, while it is worth installing a device of a larger capacity instead of installing three parallel devices of a given size.

Since in real-life situations the cost functions of devices may deviate from the average, each cost function was distorted randomly during the simulations. The original costs were multiplied or divided (with equal probability) by $1 + r$, where r is a random variable with a uniform distribution in the interval $[0, 1)$.

Table 1. The capacity and cost values of VPN nodes and edges

Capacity	Cost
1 Gbps	15
10 Gbps	45

Capacity	Cost
155 Mbps	10
311 Mbps	20
622 Mbps	30
1244 Mbps	60
2.5 Gbps	90
5 Gbps	180

In order to get accurate results, numerous network topologies and traffic distributions were examined for each network size resulting in a confidence interval size of 2% at a significance level of 95%.

5.2. Optimization of Parameters

The first simulation scenario targeted the optimization of the parameters of EC and SC. It turned out that in the case of EC the parameter value combination of $k = 3$ and $s = 500$, where k and s refer to the size of the sets of randomly selected entities and the importance factor of the secondary metric, respectively, can provide the most favorable results. In the case of SC, the combination of the initial temperature $T_0 = 10$, annealing factor $\phi = 0.9995$, and the importance factor $s = 500$ proved to be the best choice. Therefore, these parameter value combinations were used throughout the next simulation scenarios. The value of the parameter n used in the stop condition of the methods was fine-tuned independently for all variants of both algorithms.

5.3. Total Network Cost

The most important performance indicator is the total cost of the resulting network, which is shown in Figure 7 for the variants of the evolutionary algorithm EC. It can be seen in the figure that the algorithms EC-C and EC-C2 performed similarly. EC-TI provides low total network cost values in the case of lower average VoIP node traffic values, while the use of EC-D and EC-S results in more economical configurations in the traffic interval above 10 Mbps. EC-D2 and EC-S2 proved to be the best two algorithms as they provided favorable results in the case of all average VoIP node traffic values investigated. The improvement may reach 12-29% compared to EC-C and EC-C2.

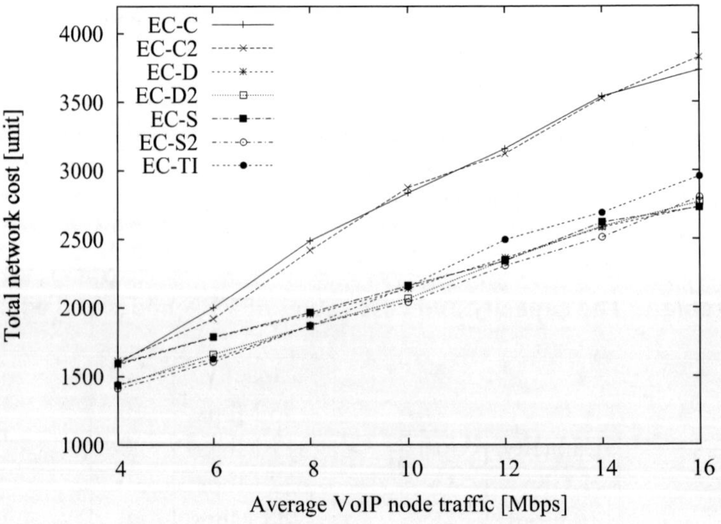

Figure 7. Total network cost using EC.

Figure 8 shows the results of applying the different variants of the simulated annealing based algorithm SC. It can be seen that the results provided by SC-C and SC-C2 converge in the higher traffic intervals, while about 10-15% improvement can be gained by applying SC-D2 in the average VoIP node traffic interval between 6 and 16 Mbps. Further improvement may be achieved by applying SC-S2 in the traffic interval above 10 Mbps; moreover, although SC-D proved to be more efficient than SC-TI in the case of lower average VoIP node traffic values by about 4%, the two algorithms provided similar total network cost values above 10 Mbps. The method based on the Suurballe path cost weighted traffic metric (SC-S) can be considered the best alternative, since it outperformed all other variants in the average VoIP node traffic interval between 8 and 16 Mbps.

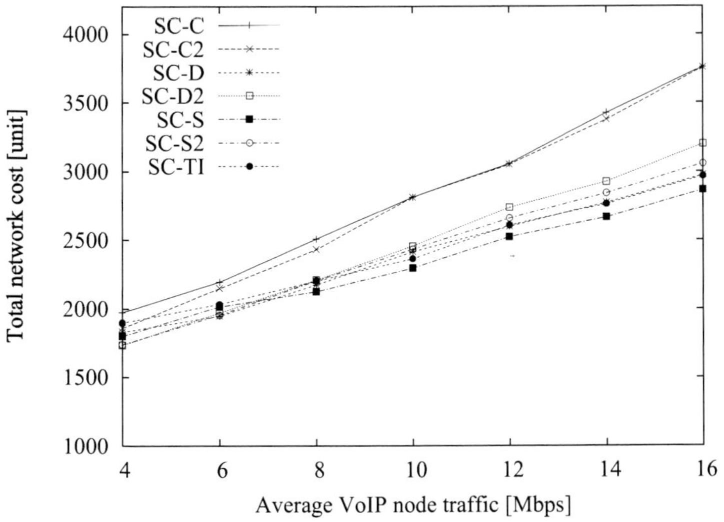

Figure 8. Total network cost using SC.

Figure 9 shows the total network cost for the two variants of the greedy covering algorithm GC as well as the two best variants of EC and SC. As it can be seen in the figure, GC-C provided network costs lower than the simplest algorithm GC-N by up to 4%. The sophisticated optimization algorithms EC and SC proved that more efficient results can be achieved by selecting from multiple feasible solutions, as they outperformed the greedy covering algorithms in almost all cases. While the two variants of the evolutionary algorithm EC achieved better results than the methods based on simulated annealing at lower average VoIP node traffic values, above 8 Mbps the gap between the results of EC and SC starts to close. However, EC-S2 proved to be the best algorithm overall providing an improvement of 13-31% compared to the greedy algorithms over the traffic interval investigated.

5.4. Number of VPN Nodes

Besides the cost of the VPN transport network, its size is also an important attribute, which can be described well by the number of VPN nodes. Thus, in this scenario the algorithms were compared focusing on this basic measure. Figure 10 presents the number of VPN nodes used in the final transport network differentiating between the edge and transit nodes for the two variants of the greedy covering algorithm GC as well as the best two variants

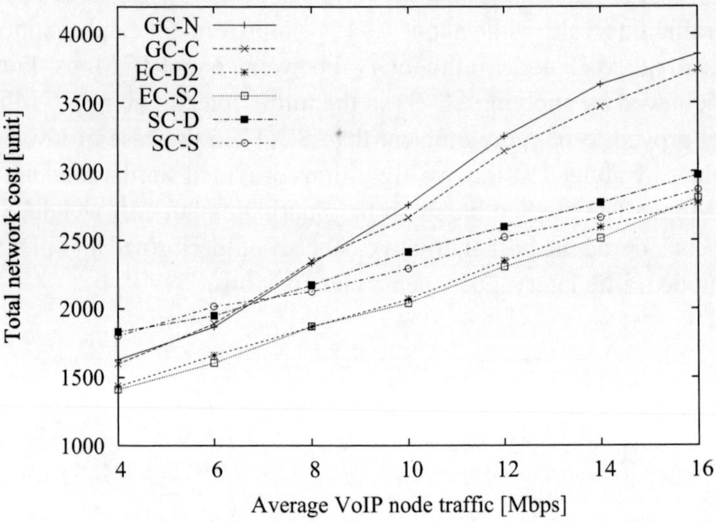

Figure 9. Total network cost using the different algorithms.

of EC and SC. Since these measures did not show relevant change against the change of average VoIP node traffic, results are presented only for the 10 Mbps value.

An important observation is that in the case of either variant of EC or SC, the number of edge VPN nodes is higher than in the case of either of the greedy algorithms, while the relation between the total network cost values of the algorithms is exactly the opposite. This means that the sophisticated selection of VoIP traffic aggregation points is more important than keeping their number as low as possible. Another point to note is that the number of edge VPN nodes is lower in the case of EC than SC, which is attributable to the fact that the two-level versions of the metrics take the number of gateways also into consideration. Moreover, in the case of the methods based on EC and SC, the ratio of transit VPN nodes is significantly smaller than in the case of the greedy algorithms. This can be explained by the fact that both the distance weighted traffic and the Suurballe path cost weighted traffic metric aim at diminishing the number of transit VPN nodes, by reducing the length of the shortest path and the sum hop-count of two disjoint paths between the edge VPN nodes with higher maximal bandwidth requirements, respectively.

5.5. Running Time

Although in the case of off-line network design the running time has only secondary importance, it is worth examining this factor also in order to make the investigations complete. Figure 11 depicts the values (including both phases) for the two versions of the greedy covering algorithm GC and the best two variants of EC and SC measured on a Linux-based PC with a 2.66 GHz Pentium 4 processor and 512 MB of RAM. As it can be seen, the GC algorithms were faster as they provided results within 8 minutes on average. Another important point to note is that the running time values of the two variants of the evolutionary covering algorithm EC were lower than those of the simulated annealing based covering algorithm SC. This can be partly attributed to the fact that the running time of the applied

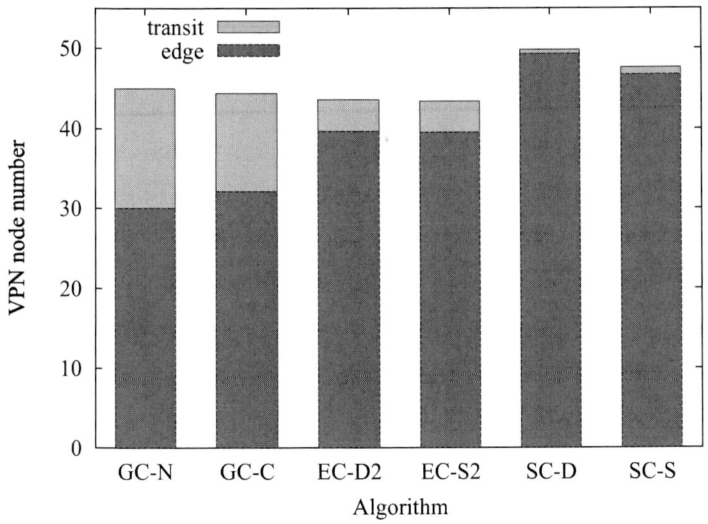

Figure 10. Number of edge and transit VPN nodes using the different algorithms.

VPN specification method depends heavily on the number of edge VPN nodes selected.

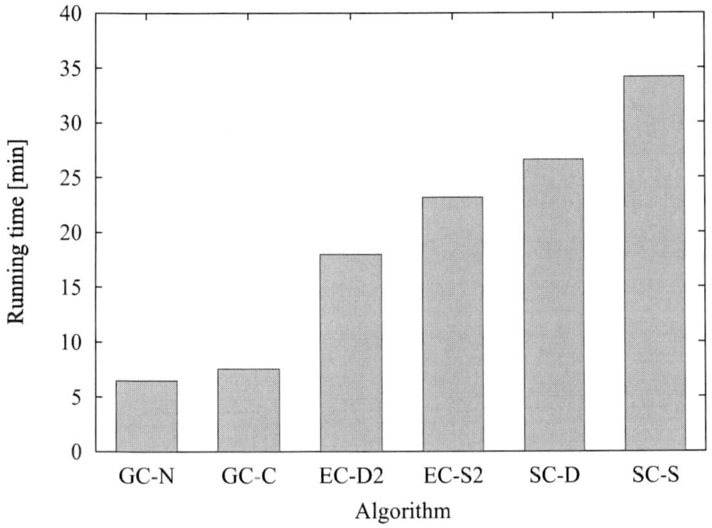

Figure 11. Running time values of the different algorithms.

6. Conclusion

This chapter addressed the topic of survivable VoIP network design. The whole design problem consists of two main tasks: the assignment of primary and backup gateways to VoIP nodes and the design of the VPN transport network. A novel approach was proposed aimed at improving the cost efficiency by taking both the objective of transport VPN design and the issues of survivability into consideration during the first task. Various algorithms based on the paradigms of evolutionary algorithms and simulated annealing were proposed, which perform the optimization of the gateway assignments using a number of cost calculation methods.

In order to evaluate the performance of the algorithms, numerous simulations were carried out using a large number of realistic problem instances. It turned out that significant reduction in total network cost can be achieved by applying sophisticated cost evaluation in the gateway assignment phase. The running time of the algorithms was acceptable considering the nature of off-line network design.

Possible future work in the area includes the investigation of situations where other types of traffic demands with high bandwidth requirements, e.g., video telephony, are also transmitted in the network.

References

[1] Taylor, S.; Wexler, J., "QoS: Is overprovisioning enough?," *Network World Wide Area Networking Newsletter*, September 2002.

[2] Krapf, E., "Avaya's VoIP over VPN," *Business Communications Review*, pp. 62–63, March 2002.

[3] VocalTec Communications Ltd., "The VocalTec Web Site," *http://www.vocaltec.com*, 2004.

[4] Dransfeld, H., "The Real Benefits of VoIP VPN," *http://www.ovum.com/go/content/020138.htm*, 2003.

[5] Netgear, Inc., "Security & Savings with Virtual Private Networks," *White Paper*, 2001.

[6] Reardon, M., "Tellium's Optical VPN: What Is It?," *http://www.lightreading.com/document.asp?doc_id=16724*, 2002.

[7] Anderson, L.; Rosen, E. C., "Framework for Layer 2 Virtual Private Networks (L2VPNs)," *Internet Draft*, IETF, *http://www.ietf.org/internet-drafts/draft-ietf-l2vpn-l2-framework-05.txt*, 2004.

[8] Grover, W. D.; Zheng, Y., "VP-Based ATM Network Design with Controlled Over-Subscription of Restoration Capacity," *In proc. of Design of Reliable Communications Networks (DRCN'98)*, Brugge, Belgium, May 1998.

[9] Grover, W. D.; Doucette, J.; Clouqueur, M.; Leung, D.; Stamatelakis, D., "New Options and Insights for Survivable Transport Networks," *IEEE Communications Magazine*, Vol. 40, No. 1, pp. 34-41, January 2002.

[10] Bäck, T.; Fogel, D. B.; Michalewicz, Z., "Handbook of Evolutionary Computation," *University Oxford Press*, New York, 1996.

[11] Kirkpatrick, S.; Gerlatt, C. D. Jr.; Vecchi, M. P., "Optimization by Simulated Annealing," *Science*, No. **220**, pp. 671–680, 1983.

[12] Józsa, B. G.; Orincsay, D.; Kern, A., "On the Use of Routing Optimization for Virtual Private Network Design," *In proc. of Optical Network Design and Modelling (ONDM'2003)*, Budapest, Hungary, pp. 865–880, February 2003.

[13] Daskin, M. S., "Network and Discrete Location," *Wiley*, New York, NY, USA, 1995.

[14] ITU–T, "Recommendation G.114 – One-way Transmission Time," $http://www.itu.int/itudocr/itu-t/aap/sg12aap/history/g.114/$ $g114_w w9.doc$, 2003.

[15] Cisco Systems, Inc., "Cisco IOS MPLS Quality of Service," *White Paper*, 2003.

[16] Kumar, A.; Rastogi, R.; Silberschatz, A.; Yener, B., "Algorithms for Provisioning Virtual Private Networks in the Hose Model," *In proc. of ACM SIGCOMM'01*, San Diego, CA, USA, August 2001.

[17] Harmatos, J.; Jüttner, A.; Szentesi, Á., "Cost-based UMTS Transport Network Topology Optimisation," *In proc. of International Conference on Computer Communications (ICCC'99)*, Tokyo, Japan, pp. 00111-1-8, 1999.

[18] Cinkler, T.; Henk, T.; Gordos, G., "Stochastic Algorithms for Design of Thrifty Single-Failure-Protected Networks," *In proc. of Design of Reliable Communications Networks (DRCN'2000)*, Munich, Germany, 2000.

[19] Chamberland, S.; Sansò, B., "Overall Design of Reliable IP Networks with Performance Guarantees," *Les Cahiers du GERAD,* Vol. 30-2000.

[20] Prytz, M.; Forsgren, A., "Dimensioning of a Multicast Network that Uses Shortest Path Routing Distribution Trees," *Technical Report, TRITA-MAT-02-OS01, Department of Mathematics, Royal Institute of Technology*, 2002.

[21] Garey, M. R.; Johnson, D. S., "Computers and Intractability: A Guide to the Theory of NP-Completeness," *Freeman*, San Francisco, CA, USA, 1979.

[22] Caprara, A.; Fischetti, M.; Toth, P., "Algorithms for the Set Covering Problem," *Annals of Operations Research*, Vol. 98, pp. 353–371, 2000.

[23] Beasley, J.; Chu, P., "A genetic algorithm for the set covering problem," *European Journal of Operational Research*, Vol. 94, pp. 392–404, 1996.

[24] Suurballe, J. W.; Tarjan, R. E., "A quick method for finding shortest pairs of disjoint paths," *Networks*, Vol. 14, pp. 325–336, 1984.

[25] Resende, M. G. C.; Ribeiro, C. C., "Greedy Randomized Adaptive Search Procedures," *In Glover, F.; Kochenberger, G. (Eds.), Handbook of Metaheuristics, Kluwer Academic Publishers*, pp. 219–249, 2002.

[26] Kumaran, K.; Srinivasan, A.; Wang, Q.; Lanning, S.; Ramakrishnan, K. G., "Efficient Algorithms for Location and Sizing Problems in Network Design," *In proc. of Global Communications Conference (GLOBECOM'2001)*, San Antonio, TX, USA, Vol. 4, pp. 2586–2590, November 2001.

[27] Barabási, A.; Albert, R., "Emergence of scaling in random networks," *Science*, pp. 509–512, October 1999.

[28] Albert, R.; Barabási, A., "Statistical Mechanics of Complex Networks," *Review of Modern Physics*, Vol. 74, pp. 47–97, January 2002.

[29] Faloutsos, M.; Faloutsos, P.; Faloutsos, C., "On Power-Law Relationships of the Internet Topology," *In proc. of ACM SIGCOMM'99*, August 1999.

[30] Bu, T.; Towsley, D., "On Distinguishing between Internet Power-Law Topology Generators," *In proc. of INFOCOM'2002*, June 2002.

[31] Józsa, B. G.; Király, Z.; Magyar, G.; Szentesi, Á., "An Efficient Algorithm for Global Path Optimization in MPLS Networks," *Optimization and Engineering,* Vol. 2, No. 3, pp. 321–347, 2001.

In: Computer-Aided Design...
Editors: C.M. De Smet et al, pp. 377-412
ISBN 978-1-60456-860-8

Expert Commentary E

COMPUTING WITH SUPERCONDUCTING CIRCUITS OF JOSEPHSON JUNCTIONS

Jie Han and Pieter Jonker
Quantitative Imaging Group, Faculty of Applied Sciences
Delft University of Technology, The Netherlands

Abstract

Superconducting circuits of Josephson junctions can be used for quantum information processing. A superconducting loop of three Josephson junctions has been proposed and demonstrated as a quantum bit or qubit [1]-[4]. A coherent superposition of two persistent-current states can be obtained when the two classical states are coupled via quantum tunneling through an energy barrier. The classical states of persistent currents can also be used as two binary bits [5]. Logic functions can be realized by coupling two or more bits, i.e. the circuit loops [6]. The interaction between loops is via magnetic interference of the superconductors.

In this chapter, superconducting circuits of Josephson junctions are investigated with as aim to possibly use them in locally-connected processor structures [7]. Both a classical SIMD computer architecture and an array-based quantum computer structure are presented that use the same basic circuit, the Josephson junctions. Our ideal is that the classical computer can serve as a pre-, post- and intermediate processor for the quantum computation that is performed in the heart of the Josephson circuit array. As such, it then establishes a heterogeneous quantum/classical computer for implementations of algorithms such as Shor's factoring algorithm which mixes classical computation steps with quantum computation steps in a single algorithm.

A quantum CNN (cellular nonlinear networks) architecture using the Josephson circuits is also proposed, presenting a novel computing paradigm for Josephson circuits [8]. Since classical computing architectures (SIMD arrays), quantum computing architectures and semi-quantum computing architectures (quantum CNNs) can be simultaneously studied on the same device, the Josephson circuit is a good vehicle for investigating the architectural issues of quantum and nanoelectronic computer systems, independently from the question of which device will be the ultimate implementation vehicle.

1. Introduction

The advances in nanotechnologies have raised design issues for novel computation structures based on nanoelectronic and quantum-effect devices [53]. Historically, parallel processing offered considerable performance advantages in many areas of computing. Several approaches have been explored and prototype systems were constructed. Due to the characteristics of many nanoelectronic devices, such as low power consumption, low drive capability and easy local interactions, parallel architectures that are highly regular and locally connected (typically the single instruction and multiple data (SIMD) computers [48], quantum cellular automata (QCA) [54] and cellular nonlinear networks (CNNs) [55]) have been studied as candidate architectures for nanocomputers.

SIMD computers consist of assemblies of identical, simple processor elements (PEs), usually each connected to its nearest neighbors in a linear or square array. Instructions are fed in a parallel stream to every PE and each instruction is executed simultaneously by PEs. Memories are distributed uniformly across the array such that each PE can access its local storage directly. SIMD systems have been successfully used in various areas of data processing (see, for examples, [48], [56] and [49]). The field of high performance image processing in particular has brought forward archetypical systems, such as the SPA (square processor array) CLIP4 [45], MPP [46], and currently the successful systems of LPA (linear processor array) IMAP-CE [57] and XETAL (SPA) [58]. Typically the QCA architecture has been studied as an implementation of arrays of electrostatically coupled quantum dots [54]. The architectural issues of a cellular array have been discussed in [59] for the implementations of quantum cellular automata (QCA) and resonant tunneling diodes (RTDs).

Cellular nonlinear networks (CNNs) represent a circuit architecture that is capable of high-speed parallel signal processing [55]. A CNN is usually an array of identical dynamical systems, or cells, and has mainly local interactions within a finite radius and analog signals as state variables. As a real-time signal processing architecture, CNNs have important applications in image processing and pattern recognition. Because of the local connectivity, which is independent of the number of cells, the CNN architecture is in principle scalable and reliable. The potential applications of CNNs using resonant tunneling diodes (RTDs) [60], single electron transistors (SETs) [61] and tunneling phase logic [62] have been investigated. A quantum CNN has been proposed for the use of quantum dots by exploring their local quantum dynamics and global interactions [63]. In this chapter, we present a quantum CNN architecture built on superconducting circuits of Josephson junctions [64].

Quantum computing has been extensively studied as a computing paradigm employing quantum mechanics [65]. A quantum computer performs a massively parallel processing on quantum mechanical superpositions of quantum bits or qubits. To perform a quantum computation, one must be able to prepare qubits in a desired initial state, to coherently preserve and manipulate superpositions of qubits' states, to couple qubits together, to measure their states, and to keep them relatively free from external interactions that induce noise and decoherence [66]. Essentially, any two-state quantum system that can be addressed, controlled, measured, coupled to its neighbors and decoupled from its environment, is potentially useful for quantum computing. Various physical systems have been proposed to realize a quantum computer [65]. Among these, mesoscopic superconducting circuits of Josephson junctions, produced by modern lithography, appear promising for integration in electronic circuits and for large-scale applications [67], [68]. Recently, the coherent superposition of two macroscopic persistent-current states on a superconducting Josephson circuit has been observed [69], and the coherent quantum dynamics of this Josephson flux qubit has been demonstrated [70]. The Josephson circuit has thus come up as a promising candidate for realizing a quantum computer. These superconducting circuits of Josephson junctions can also be designed to work in the classical domain. Classical processing circuits can be obtained by the same manufacturing process and can thus be used as supplementary or control circuitry affiliated with the circuits devoted to quantum processing [71], [72]. Boolean logic can further be obtained from the circuits, establishing a classical parallel computing architecture [73].

This chapter is organized as follows. In section 2, we first present a close look at the Josephson circuit. In section 3, we present a classical array architecture based on the Josephson circuits. We start the design with elementary logic gates and end up with a memory and PE array. In section 4, we discuss issues of quantum computing with the Josephson qubits and describe a feasibility study on how an architecture of a heterogeneous system based on the Josephson circuits could be set up to implement Shor's quantum factorization algorithm. Although the necessary classical computing could as well be done with conventional CMOS technology, the study on the Josephson circuits might bring insight that cannot easily be achieved with other, e.g. spin based, devices for quantum computers, because of the problems unsolved in combining them with conventional technologies. In section 5, we propose a quantum CNN architecture using the Josephson circuits. In this architecture, the quantum dynamics of the Josephson circuit are formulated as the state dynamics of a CNN cell. Each cell is thus a quantum dynamical system. The quantum states of neighboring cells interact with each other only via classical couplings, which distinguishes a quantum CNN architecture from a quantum computer. In section 6 some implementation issues are discussed. Section 7 concludes the chapter.

2. The Superconducting Circuit of Josephson Junctions

The Josephson circuit in principle consists of a loop with three Josephson junctions in series that encloses a magnetic flux that is provided by an external magnet (Figure 1 [67]). In particular when the enclosed magnetic flux is close to half a superconducting flux quantum Φ_0 ($=h/2e$, where h is Planck's constant), the system behaves as a particle in a double-well potential, where the classical states in each well correspond to persistent currents of opposite sign.

In the circuit, superconductors are coupled with Josephson junctions. The current through a Josephson junction is

$$I_J = I_0 \sin\gamma \tag{1}$$

with

$$I_0 = (4\pi e/h)E_J; \tag{2}$$

I_0 is the critical current of the Josephson junction, E_J is the Josephson energy and γ is the gauge-invariant phase difference. Two of the junctions in the loop have equal Josephson

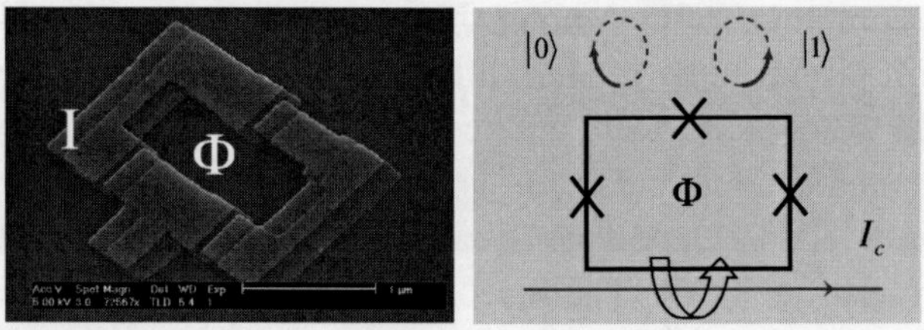

Figure 1. The superconducting circuit of Josephson junctions: a scanning electron microscope (SEM) picture (courtesy of J. E. Mooij) and a schematic representation [67].

energy E_J and the third has αE_J. If the applied magnetic flux is $f\Phi_0$ with $f \in [1/2 - f_c, 1/2 + f_c]$, where $f_c \leq 1/4$, this circuit has two stable persistent currents. Energy levels and persistent currents of the circuit as a function of applied flux Φ_{ext} are plotted in Figure 2 [68]. The amplitude of the persistent currents I_p is

$$I_p \approx 2\pi\alpha E_J/\Phi_0. \tag{3}$$

With $\alpha = 0.8$, I_c is about 0.5μA. The self-generated flux due to persistent currents is about $10^{-3}\Phi_0$ [68]. The states of the persistent currents can be changed by tuning the magnetic flux and magnetic interaction can be made by inductive coupling. The persistent currents can be used as classical binary bits when the applied flux is far away from the degeneracy point at $\Phi_0/2$. The issues of classical computing with the circuits are discussed in section 3.

When the enclosed flux is close to $\Phi_0/2$, the two classical states of the Josephson circuit are coupled via quantum tunneling through the barrier between the wells. The circuit is thus a macroscopic quantum system with two base states $|0\rangle$ and $|1\rangle$ with opposite circulating persistent currents, corresponding to the two lowest energy levels of the circuit, the ground state and the first excited state. The separation of the energy levels is controlled by varying the flux bias (Figure 2).

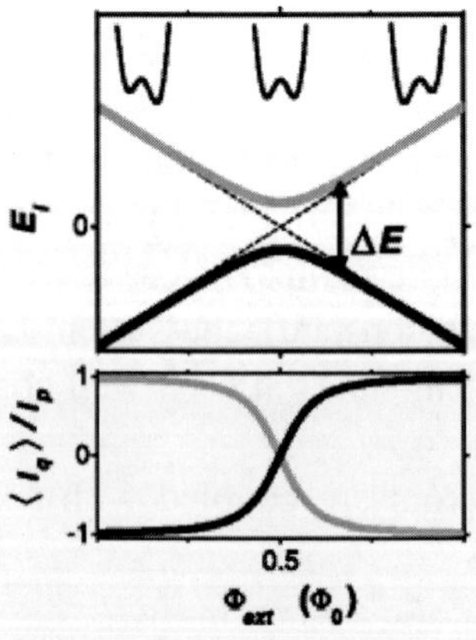

Figure 2. Energy levels and persistent currents of the Josephson circuit [69].

The quantum state of the circuit is given by:

$$|\Psi\rangle = \alpha\,|0\rangle + \beta\,|1\rangle\,, \tag{4}$$

with

$$|\alpha|^2 + |\beta|^2 = 1, \tag{5}$$

where α, β are complex numbers, and $|\alpha|$, $|\beta|$ are probability amplitudes. With regard to any measurement, this quantum system behaves as $|0\rangle$ or $|1\rangle$ with a probability of $|\alpha|^2$ or $|\beta|^2$.

The quantum dynamics of the circuit is described by the time-dependent Schrödinger equation:

$$i\hbar \frac{d\,|\Psi\rangle}{dt} = \mathbf{H}\,|\Psi\rangle\,, \tag{6}$$

with the Hamiltonian:

$$\mathbf{H} = I_p \Phi_0 (f - \frac{1}{2}) \boldsymbol{\sigma}_z - \frac{\lambda}{2} \boldsymbol{\sigma}_x, \tag{7}$$

where I_p is the classical magnitude of the persistent currents, f the magnetic flux in the loop in units of the flux quantum Φ_0, λ the energy level repulsion, and $\boldsymbol{\sigma}_{z,x}$ the Pauli matrices [68].

The quantum states of the circuit can be operated by resonant microwave modulation of the enclosed magnetic flux by a superconducting control line (as I_c in Figure 1). Measurement can be made with superconducting quantum interference devices (SQUIDs) [68]. Two or more Josephson circuits can be coupled through mutual inductance by means of the flux that the persistent currents generate. A wide variety of potential designs for the couplings are available. For instance, a coupling can be switched on or off via an external transporter attached with a SQUID loop, as proposed in [67]. The Josephson circuit is suitable for integrations in electronic circuits and scaling to large arrays. The issues of quantum computing with these circuits are discussed in section 4.

3. Classical Computing with Josephson Circuits

3.1. Circuit Topology and Simulations

In the classical regime, two or more Josephson circuits can be coupled through interactions of the magnetic field generated by external control currents or the persistent currents. Basically, two schemes are possible. One is to make a coupling directly through magnetic interference. The other is to make a coupling assisted with a superconductive flux transporter. The transporter is placed on top of the circuit loops and insulated by a thin layer. With the parameters suggested in [68], it has been shown that the coupling between circuit loops is stronger with the facility of a transporter, by evaluating the coefficients that describe the effective Hamiltonian and determine the interactions of the Josephson circuits [74]. To make a robust design, however, the layout and parameters of a circuit need to be carefully considered.

In this study, we propose a circuit topology with the use of a flux transporter for the coupling of two Josephson circuits, as shown in Figure 3. The inductive influences from control lines on top of the transporter are also considered. In order to independently manipulate a circuit, a control line should be strongly coupled with one loop while weakly coupled with the other. A circuit with more loops is proposed in Figure 4. This circuit is based on the

Table 1. The self and mutual inductances of the inverter circuit (pH).

	Transporter	Loop 1	Loop 2	Control line 1	Control line 2
Transporter	L_t=30	M_{t1}=9.7	M_{t2}=9.7	M_{tc1}=3.1	M_{tc2}=3.1
Loop 1	M_{t1}=9.7	L_1=11	M_{21}=-0.069	M_{l1c1}=2.3	M_{l1c2}=0.028
Loop 2	M_{t2}=9.7	M_{12}=-0.070	L_2=11	M_{l2c1}=0.028	M_{l2c2}=2.3
Control line 1	M_{tc1}=3.1	M_{l1c1}=2.3	M_{l2c1}=0.026	L_{c1}=4.3	M_{c1c2}=0.28
Control line 2	M_{tc2}=3.1	M_{l1c2}=0.026	M_{l2c2}=2.3	M_{c1c2}=0.28	L_{c2}=4.3

same topology as the one in Figure 3, and the couplings between neighbor loops are similar to the coupling of the circuit in Figure 3. We show in the next section the circuits in Figures 3 and 4 actually work as an inverter (NOT) and a not-majority voter (NMV).

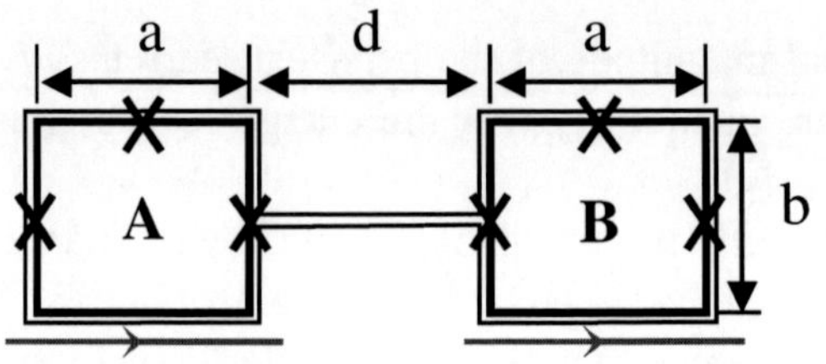

a = 6.2 um, b = 5.5 um, d = 5.0 um.

Figure 3. An inverter (NOT) circuit.

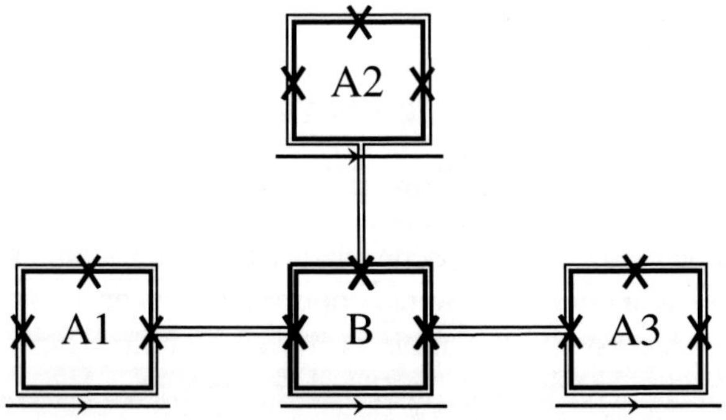

Figure 4. A not-majority voter (NMV) circuit.

The simulations of these circuits were carried out with a software package named FastHenry [75], which computes the frequency dependent self and mutual inductances and resistances between conductors of complex shape. The inductances obtained from the circuit in Figure 3 are shown in Table 1. As can be seen, the mutual inductance between a circuit loop and its control line is 2.3 pH[1], about two orders larger than the mutual induc-

[1]Here, pH = pico-Henry, a measure of inductance, not acidity.

Table 2. The self and mutual inductances of the NMV circuit (pH).

	Tran 1	Tran 2	Tran 3	Loop 1	Loop 2	Loop 3	Loop Out
Tran 1	L_{t1}=30	M_{t1t2}=8.9	M_{t1t3}=11	8.3	-0.099	-0.071	M_{ot1}=8.3
Tran 2	M_{t1t2}=8.9	L_{t2}=30	M_{t2t3}=11	-0.077	6.4	-0.079	M_{ot2}=6.5
Tran 3	M_{t1t3}=11	M_{t2t3}=11	L_{t3}=30	-0.070	-0.099	7.3	M_{ot3}=7.3
Loop 1	8.3	-0.089	-0.074	L_1=11	-0.023	-0.001	-0.065
Loop 2	-0.10	6.5	-0.10	-0.019	L_2=11	-0.019	-0.072
Loop 3	-0.073	-0.089	7.3	-0.001	-0.023	L_3=11	-0.064
Loop Out	M_{ot1}=8.3	M_{ot2}=6.5	M_{ot3}=7.3	-0.062	-0.066	-0.063	L_{out}=11

tance between the control line and the other loop, approximately 0.026 - 0.028 pH. The mutual inductance between the transporter and the loops is 9.7 pH, while the mutual inductance between the two loops is about 0.069 pH. The unnecessary couplings are thus effectively suppressed. The simulation result of the circuit in Figure 4 is shown in Table 2. For simplicity, the inductances of control lines are omitted. In this circuit, the mutual inductances of transporters are approximately 9 - 11 pH and the mutual inductances between the output loop and the transporters are approximately 6.5 - 8.5 pH. These variations are induced by the physical asymmetries due to the implementation and topology of the circuit. In a large-scale circuit, this will imply precision requirements on circuit design and fabrication process. Given the inductances, the magnetic interactions of the Josephson circuits can numerically be analyzed. This is presented in the next subsection.

3.2. Elementary Logic Gates

3.2.1. An Inverter and a Not-majority Voter

Consider first the circuit in Figure 3. Prepare an initial magnetic flux threading the two loops at $1/2\Phi_0$. The magnetic flux in the superconducting transporter is then Φ_0. If a flux change $\Delta\Phi_x$ due to external sources (e.g. the control currents) is introduced into a loop as an input, then a clockwise (or anti-clockwise, depending on the orientation of the flux change) persistent current is generated in the circuit. Since the transporter tends to keep the total flux unchanged (i.e. to keep it at multiples of a flux quantum) [76], there will be a current I_t generated on the transporter and it satisfies:

$$\Delta\Phi_x + I_t L_t + I_{c1} M_{t1} + I_{c2} M_{t2} = 0, \tag{8}$$

where L_t is the self inductance of the transporter, I_{c1} and I_{c2} are respectively the persistent currents on the two loops, M_{t1} and M_{t2} are the mutual inductances between the two loops and the transporter. The magnetic flux change in the second loop is then

$$\Delta\Phi_2 = I_{c1} M_{12} + I_t M_{t2} + I_{c2} L_2, \tag{9}$$

where M_{12} is the mutual inductance between the two loops and L_2 is the self inductance of loop 2. Because the persistent currents on the loops have similar amplitudes and opposite directions, we have $I_{c2} \approx -I_{c1}$, and, as can be seen in Table 1, $M_{t1} = M_{t2}$ and $M_{12} \approx 0$. Equation (8) becomes:

$$\Delta\Phi_x + I_t L_t \approx 0. \tag{10}$$

The magnetic flux change in the second loop is then:

$$\Delta\Phi_2 \approx I_t M_{t2} + I_{c2} L_2 \approx -(M_{t2}/L_t)\Delta\Phi_x + \Delta\Phi_p, \tag{11}$$

where $\Delta\Phi_p = I_{c2} L_2$ is the flux change induced by the persistent current on loop 2.

If $\Delta\Phi_x$ is relatively large compared to $\Delta\Phi_p$ (about $10^{-3}\Phi_0$), say, $\Delta\Phi_x = 0.1\Phi_0$ (corresponding to a control current of approximately 900μA), $\Delta\Phi_p$ is then negligible. This is usually true for operating in the classical realm. Taking the data in Table 1, we have then $\Delta\Phi_2 \approx -(1/3)\Delta\Phi_x$. This indicates that a fraction of the flux change in loop 1 due to external sources is transported to loop 2, but with a reversed orientation, the characteristic of an inverter.

Consider next the circuit in Figure 4. If a flux change $\Delta\Phi_{xi}$ $(i = 1, 2, 3)$ is introduced in each of the input loops and the magnetic flux generated by the persistent current on each loop is small compared to $\Delta\Phi_{xi}$, we have:

$$\Delta\Phi_{x1} + I_{t1} L_{t1} + I_{t2} M_{t1t2} + I_{t3} M_{t1t3} \approx 0, \tag{12}$$

$$\Delta\Phi_{x2} + I_{t2} L_{t2} + I_{t1} M_{t1t2} + I_{t3} M_{t2t3} \approx 0, \tag{13}$$

$$\Delta\Phi_{x3} + I_{t3} L_{t3} + I_{t1} M_{t1t3} + I_{t2} M_{t2t3} \approx 0, \tag{14}$$

where I_{t1}, I_{t2}, I_{t3} are the currents on transporters, L_{t1}, L_{t2}, L_{t3} are the self inductances of transporters, and M_{t1t2}, M_{t1t3}, M_{t2t3} are the mutual inductances between transporters. The flux change in the output loop is then given by:

$$\Delta\Phi_{out} \approx M_{ot1} I_{t1} + M_{ot2} I_{t2} + M_{ot3} I_{t3}, \tag{15}$$

where M_{ot1}, M_{ot2}, M_{ot3} are the mutual inductances between the output loop and transporters. Taking the data in Table 2, the flux change in the output loop is approximately $\Delta\Phi_{out} \approx -(1/8 \text{ - } 1/6)(\Delta\Phi_1 + \Delta\Phi_2 + \Delta\Phi_3)$. This indicates that a fraction of the total flux changes of input loops is transported to the output loop, but with an opposite direction.

If the initial magnetic flux in a Josephson circuit is lower or higher than $1/2\Phi_0$, a flux change can be introduced by using microwave pulses to activate or deactivate the circuit's state. A flux change is then induced in the loop by the reverse of a persistent current, i.e. $\Delta\Phi_x = 2I_{c1}M_{t1}$, and a flux change results in the second loop. This change can further be detected by applying microwave pulses, similar to the method used in manipulating the quantum processing circuits. This method may be applicable when classical and quantum computing are simultaneously implemented in the Josephson circuits.

Hence, the Josephson circuit has the states + (clockwise current), – (anticlockwise current), 0 (no current, i.e. suppressed by external control lines), digitally this can be associated with $+1$, -1 and 0, in Boolean Logic with TRUE, FALSE and Don't Care. Two or more circuits can be coupled through the interaction of magnetic field. For the circuit in Figure 3, as has been seen, any flux variation in a loop always causes a reverse change of the magnetic flux in the other loop, and so does the variation of a persistent current. Logically, this circuit functions as an inverter (or NOT gate), i.e. $B = NOT(A)$. For the circuit in Figure 4, the output loop obtains an "addition" of the flux changes of those it is coupled to, but with an opposite orientation. This circuit thus works on the principle of a not-majority voter (NMV), i.e. $B = NMV(A1, A2, A3)$. As revealed in the analysis, however, a major issue of the Josephson logic is the lack of a signal gain, which might suggest that only a limited number of logical gates is possible in a Josephson circuit module without signal restoration. A potential solution to this is to use an external magnetic field (via the control lines, for instance) to restore a signal, while this issue will not be adressed any further in our study.

3.2.2. A Universal Gate

Now we have an inverter and a NMV. By setting one of its inputs as an instruction bit, a NMV can be configured to a NAND or NOR gate. In Figure 5 we have $B = NAND(A2, A3)$ and in Figure 6 we have $B = NOR(A2, A3)$, as indicated in the truth table (Table 3). A NMV is hence a universal logic circuit, with which any logical function can be constructed. In addition, the topology of the NMV circuit can be configured to a fan-in or fan-out circuit (in a reversed manner though) by setting the instruction bits and control currents. In fact, the NMV circuit in Figure 4 can serve as a data processing unit, which can be used as a fundamental element in the construction of a large data processing network.

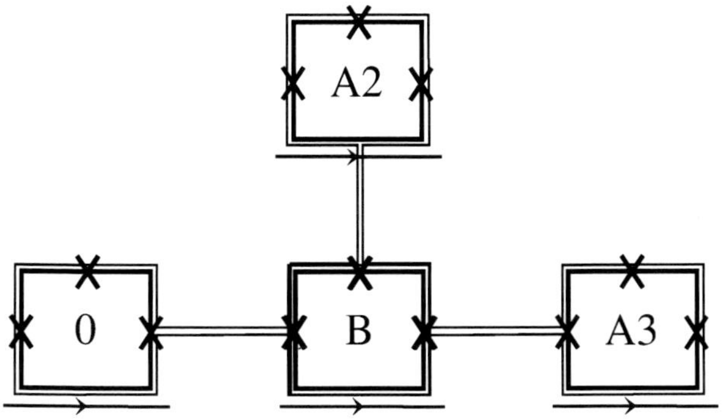

Figure 5. A NAND gate.

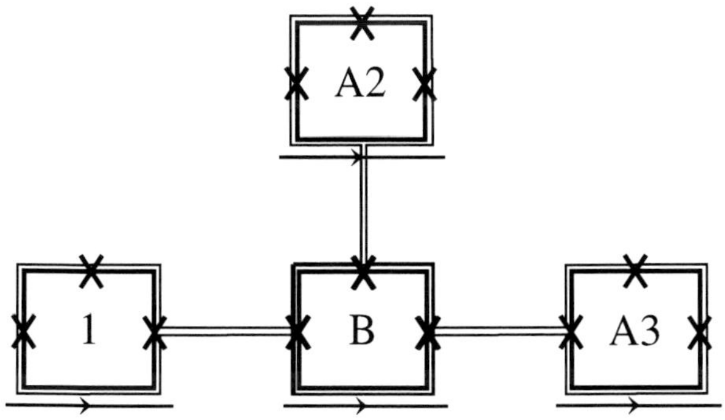

Figure 6. A NOR gate.

So far the circuits we discussed are coupled to their nearest neighbors, and long-range communication seems to be a hard task. With the use of a transporter, however, it may be

Table 3. True table of NAND and NOR from NMV.

$I/A1$	$A2$	$A3$	B	*Function*
0	0	0	1	$NAND$
0	0	1	1	
0	1	0	1	
0	1	1	0	
1	0	0	1	NOR
1	0	1	0	
1	1	0	0	
1	1	1	0	

possible to realize fast data propagating. Assume that a big transporter is put on the top of a chain, which consists of a number of Josephson loops (Figure 7). If each loop in the chain interacts equally with others, then all the loops switch simultaneously as soon as a flux variation is introduced into the input loop. In this way, a signal is propagated to all the cells in a chain at once. Similarly, the status of an array can be obtained by measurements with SQUIDs (Figure 8).

3.3. A Processor Element (PE) Design

A typical design of a processor element (PE) is usually an arithmetic and logic unit (ALU), registers and local memories. The memory ranges from a few bits up to megabytes. PEs are connected to a central controller that broadcasts instructions and has data buffers for inputs and outputs. In this section, we present the designs of a full adder (as a simple ALU), a memory array and a PE array structure, all based on the superconducting circuits of Josephson junctions.

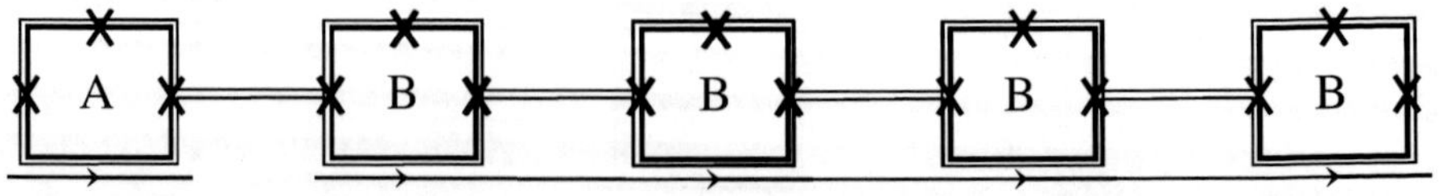

Figure 7. Fast data propagating in the Josephson circuits.

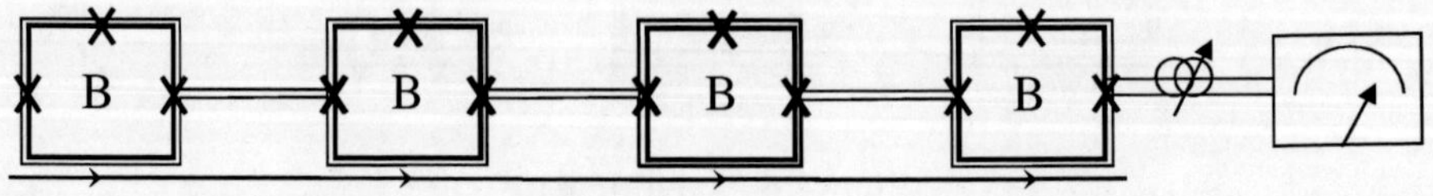

Figure 8. Gathering array status with SQUIDs.

3.3.1. An ALU Design

An ALU can be as simple as a full adder, a schematic drawing of which is shown in Figure 9. This adder consists of three NMV gates and two inverters, clocked by control currents. With appropriate configurations, it performs not only an arithmetic addition, but also many logical functions. To implement the adder, we map its functional blocks onto a Josephson circuit array and execute a desired function by configuring instruction bits and injecting input data into the array. A possible implementation is shown in Figure 10. Since instructions and input data can swiftly be switched into the array through fast propagating paths (as data buses), a Josephson array can readily be configured to perform desired computations.

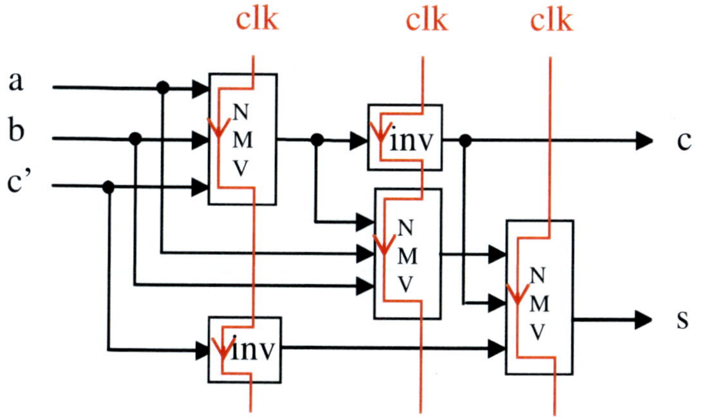

Figure 9. A schematic drawing of a full adder.

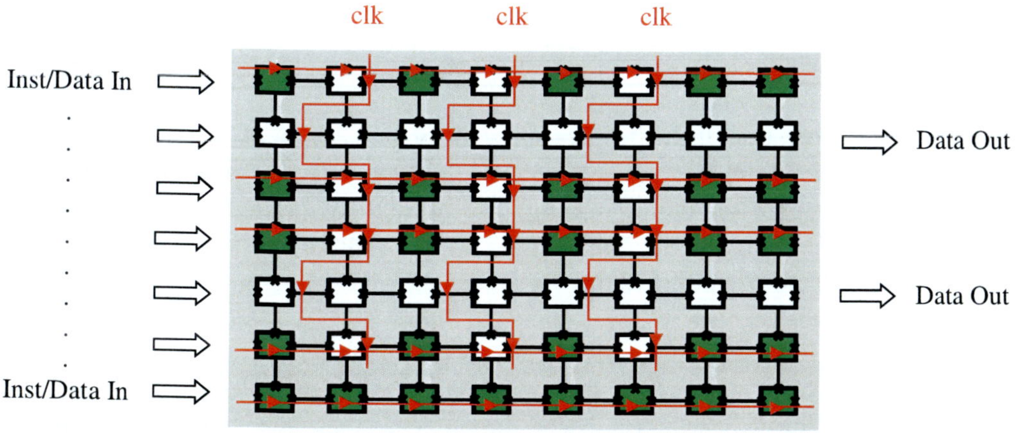

Figure 10. An implementation of the full adder in a Josephson circuit array.

3.3.2. A Memory Array

It is arguable that the most important component of modern computing systems is not the processor, but the memory. Fortunately, the Josephson circuit possesses natural properties to be a good memory cell, where a bit of information is stored as a persistent current. Writing and reading of information are carried out with the control currents. Figure 11 shows a 4 × 4 memory array implemented in the Josephson circuits with column (ca) and row (ra) addressing. A decoder for a row selection is shown as well.

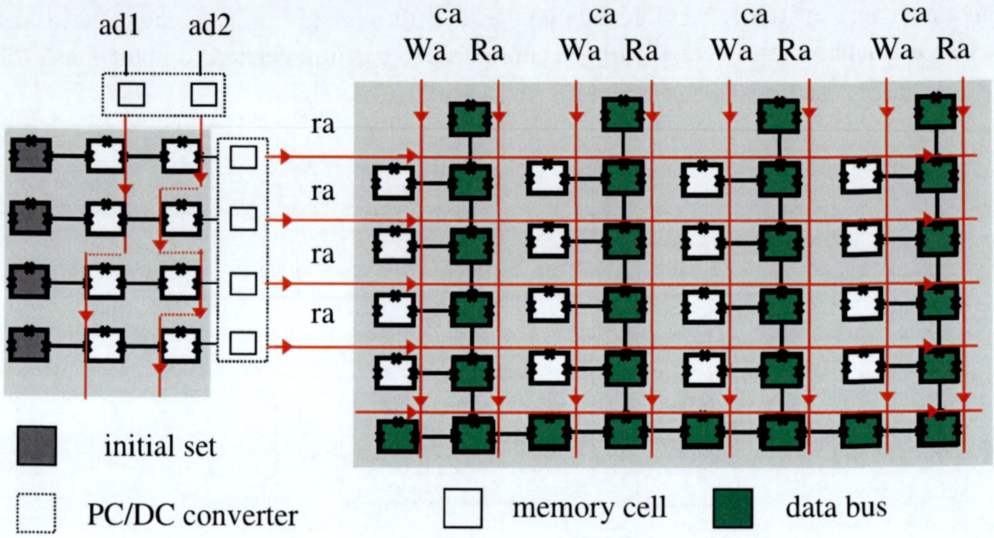

Figure 11. A 4×4 memory array with a 2-bit row decoder.

For a WRITE operation, a bit is fed into the array via the data buses and a cell is selected by a row address (ra) and a column WRITE address (Wa). The address lines are designed in such a way that a memory cell is selected only when both of its row address (ra) and column WRITE address (Wa) lines are active. A memory cell cannot independently be refreshed by either a row or a column address line. As soon as a cell is activated, the bit in the data buses is stored in. Other cells are not affected, because none or only one of their address lines is active.

For a READ operation, the cell adjacent to the being-accessed memory cell is selected by both of its row address (ra) and column READ address (Ra). Since other cells in the same column are suppressed during reading, this cell will get the stored information from its adjacent memory cell, without interacting with its neighbors in the same column. As soon as a bit is obtained, it is shifted out via the data bus.

A two-bit address decoder is as well shown in Figure 11. This decoder consists of rows of Josephson cells. In each row the left-most cell is fixed in an active state, and each cell is coupled to its nearest neighbors in the row. Address signals (ad1 and ad2) arrive at the PC/DC converters, by which the persistent currents (PCs) are translated into DC signals carried on control current lines. The control lines are inductively coupled to the cells in the decoder, and are designed in such a way that a cell is activated or suppressed by positioning its control line on one or the other side of the cell. The signal in the left-most cell is then passed through an activated cell while blocked by a suppressed one. By systematically arranging the control lines, as shown in Figure 11, it is possible that, for any address signal, there is only one row in the decoder, capable of passing a PC signal from one end to the other. The decoded information, i.e. the passed PC signal, is then transmitted into a PC/DC converter, by which it is translated to a DC signal that is transmitted into the memory array as a raw address (ra).

3.3.3. A PE Design

If the couplings among the Josephson circuits are well established, then each of them can be manipulated and addressed by the control currents, and, hence, data processing, storing and communicating can be realized in a Josephson array with the switchings of control currents. We present an implementation of such a Josephson processing network, an array of PEs attached with local memories, as schematically shown in Figure 12. Instructions and data are fed into the array while intermediate status and outputs are read out, possibly only via the edges of the array. The advantage of the structure is its extremely simple and regular topology. The manipulation of the array is accomplished by configuring the circuit states as inputs and instructions, and by applying the control currents as addressing and clock signals. The extreme simplicity in structure is thus accompanied by an enormously increased complexity in configuration or programming after fabrication.

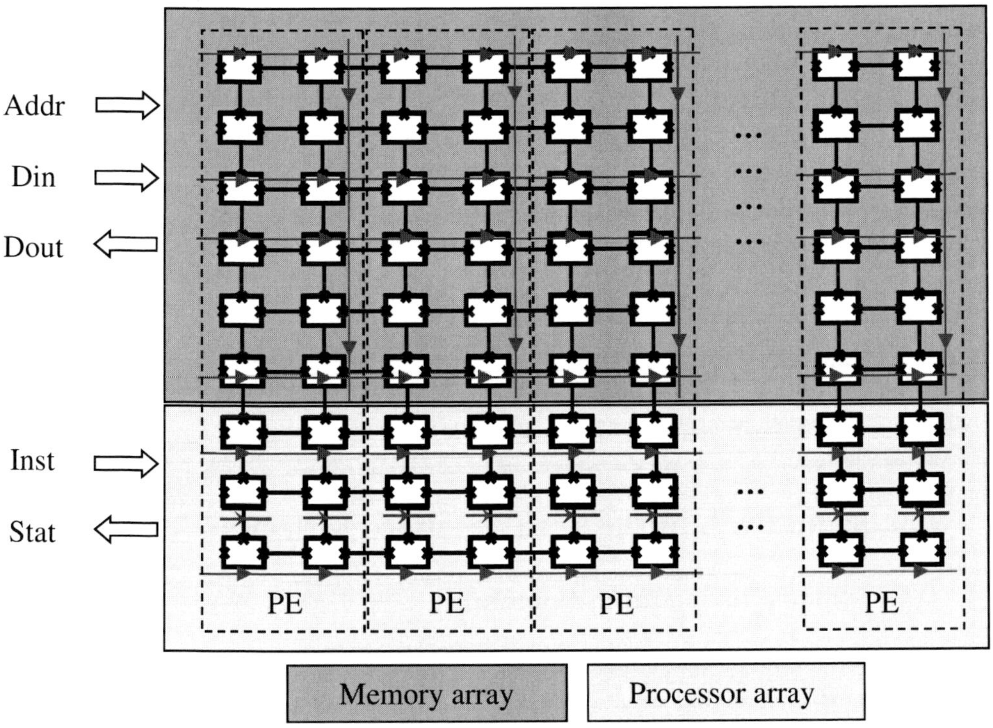

Figure 12. An implementation of a PE array on the Josephson circuits.

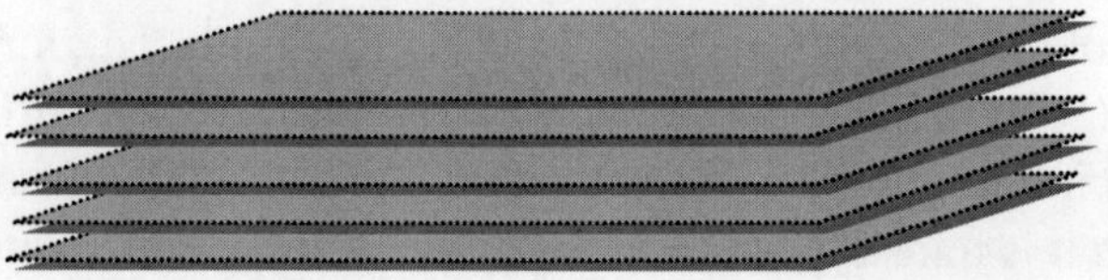

Figure 13. A multi-layer Josephson processing array.

Table 4. A comparison of the Josephson superconducting and CMOS technology.

	Gate length (μm)	Memory (MBits/cm^2)	On-chip clock (GHz)
CMOS in 2002	0.08	700	2.5
Josephson in 20??	4	25	100

Quantum-effect devices perhaps have more variability in their characteristics than conventional ones. We used a simulation tool, FastHenry, to facilitate the designs of elementary logic gates. In a large-scale network, however, more factors are involved, and an increased complexity in magnetic interference will result. Further fault-tolerant measures will be needed in order to cope with the inaccuracy induced by fabrication and the imprecision of magnetic field or microwave pulses applied during operation. In this regard, we envision a multi-layer Josephson array (Figure 13), in which redundancy schemes, e.g. consensus collecting or error correcting codes, can be incorporated.

Nevertheless, difficulties remain in the manipulation of a Josephson array, due to the electromagnetic interference among devices. It is unknown if a controller that provides effective control signals will be available. Furthermore, we compare the properties of the Josephson superconducting technology with those of current CMOS technology, as in Table 4. As can be seen, the proposed Josephson technology does not outperform CMOS in terms of device densities of logic and memory. This makes the hope to build a computer with the Josephson circuits rather gloomy. However, the Josephson memory, though bulky, appears to be a promising candidate for an ultra-fast memory structure, because of the properties of high switching speed, low power consumption and relatively simple and regular structure. It may be integrated with circuit components based on other technologies in a heterogeneous architecture or a System-on-Chip (SoC) based architecture.

4. Quantum Computing with Josephson Circuits

4.1. Introduction to Quantum Computing

Classical computation based on Boolean logic acts on classical bits, while a quantum computer composed of quantum logic gates performs operations on quantum bits or qubits. Each qubit represents an elementary unit of information. Corresponding to the classical bits of “0” and “1”, a qubit has a basis $\{|0\rangle, |1\rangle\}$ for computation. However, unlike a classical bit, which is one of the two distinguishable states “0” or “1”, a qubit exists as a superposition of basis states, represented mathematically as a complex linear combination of the two states $|0\rangle$ and $|1\rangle$, i.e.

$$|\Psi\rangle = a\,|0\rangle + b\,|1\rangle\,. \tag{16}$$

With regard to any measurement, the superposition above behaves like $|0\rangle$ with a probability $|a|^2$ and like $|1\rangle$ with a probability $|b|^2$, and we have

$$|a|^2 + |b|^2 = 1. \tag{17}$$

More generally, while a string of L classical bits exists in any of the Boolean states $x = 000\ldots0$ through $111\ldots1$, a string of L qubits exists in any state of the form

$$|\Psi\rangle = \sum_{x=00\ldots0}^{11\ldots1} c_x\,|x\rangle\,, \tag{18}$$

where c_x are complex numbers such that

$$\textstyle\sum_x |c_x|^2 = 1. \tag{19}$$

Consider a register composed of three physical bits, for instance. A classical 3-bit register can store one of eight different numbers, i.e. one of the eight possible binary configurations $000, 001, 010, \ldots, 111$ that represent the numbers 0 to 7. A quantum register composed of three qubits can store up to eight numbers at the same time, in the form of quantum superpositions as exhibited in equation (18). Mathematical operations can be executed at the same time on all of the numbers held in the register and the initial superpositions of numbers evolve into different superpositions during a computation. In a quantum computer, therefore, the same mathematical operation can be performed on, say, 2^L input numbers in a single computational step, and the result is a superposition of all of the corresponding outputs. It is this massive parallelism inherent in a quantum computation that suggests that a quantum computer may outperform any classical computer for solving some previously intractable problems.

A quantum computation can be defined as a unitary evolution of a quantum network that takes its initial state into some final states [77]. A quantum network is a quantum computing device consisting of quantum logic gates, and each quantum logic gate executes a unitary operation on one or more qubits. A quantum computer implements a unitary matrix operation on the quantum state of the quantum computer's register. Quantum computations are then always accomplished by building up quantum logic circuits out of quantum logic gates.

In the Josephson circuit, the persistent currents create a magnetic flux. The flux states obey all five functional requirements for a quantum bit: (1) The superconducting circuit is at a sufficiently low temperature that the flux qubits can easily be prepared in their ground states. (2) The flux states can be manipulated precisely with magnetic fields. (3) Two flux qubits can be readily coupled inductively, and the inductive coupling can be turned on and off. (4) The flux of the states can be detected and measured using a SQUID. (5) The flux states can be made insensitive to background charges and effectively decoupled from their environment [68].

All the ingredients for quantum computation are now available. The superconducting persistent current qubits can be initiated, manipulated, coupled to each other, read out and insulated from the environment. A quantum computer is thus in principle possible. As in the case of classical computers, certain sets of quantum logic gates are universal in the sense that any quantum computation can be performed by wiring members of them together. In the following we start with such a set of universal quantum gates, a single qubit rotation and a controlled-NOT gate, or CNOT, then present quantum sum and carry, quantum Fourier transform, and finally propose a draft structure of a quantum computer for an implementation of Shor's factoring algorithm [78].

4.2. Elementary Quantum Gates

An arbitrary single qubit rotation can be written as $e^{-i\sigma t} = \cos t\sigma - i \sin t\sigma$ for some Pauli matrix $\sigma = a\sigma_x + b\sigma_y + c\sigma_z$, where $a^2 + b^2 + c^2 = 1$. The persistent current qubit can be rotated precisely by apply a magnetic pulse for a certain duration (Figure 14, the unitary matrix describing the unitary transformation of states is also shown). For example, a pulse would be at 4 GHz and last for about 125 nsec.

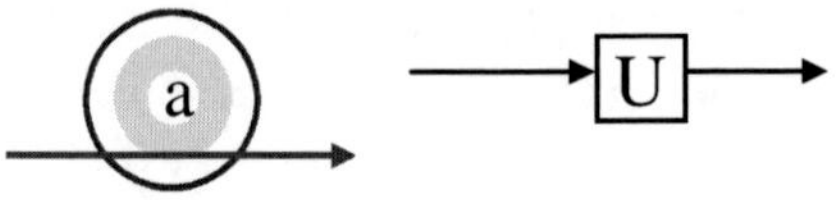

$$\begin{pmatrix} \alpha & \beta \\ \delta & \lambda \end{pmatrix}$$

Figure 14. Single qubit rotation.

A controlled-NOT is a two-qubit quantum logic gate that flips the second qubit if the first qubit is in state 1. That is, it takes $|00\rangle\ -> |00\rangle$, $|01\rangle\ -> |01\rangle$, $|10\rangle\ -> |11\rangle$, $|11\rangle\ -> |10\rangle$ (Figure 15). By exploring the magnetic interference of two qubits, a so-called controlled-rotation gate can be constructed, as shown in Figure 16. The target bit in a controlled-rotation gate can be precisely rotated according to the state of the control bit. This is characterized by a unitary matrix A_α. Given a π pulse, in particular, a controlled-NOT operation is obtained from a controlled-rotation gate. It has been shown that a controlled-rotation gate is universal for quantum computing and the controlled-NOT gates can be combined with single qubit rotation gates to realize any quantum logic function.

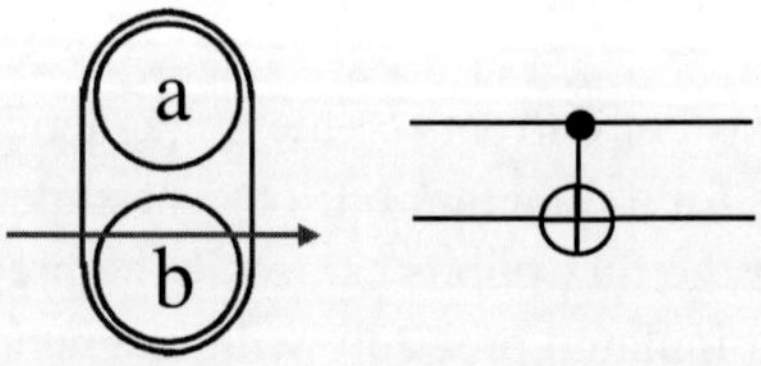

$$\begin{pmatrix} 1 & 0 & 0 & 0 \\ 0 & 1 & 0 & 0 \\ 0 & 0 & 0 & 1 \\ 0 & 0 & 1 & 0 \end{pmatrix}$$

Figure 15. A controlled-NOT (CNOT) gate.

Up to this moment, a single qubit has been measured [69] and the coherent quantum dynamics have been demonstrated [70] in the quantum transport laboratory of applied physics at the TU-Delft. A double-qubit circuit has been fabricated and experiments are being

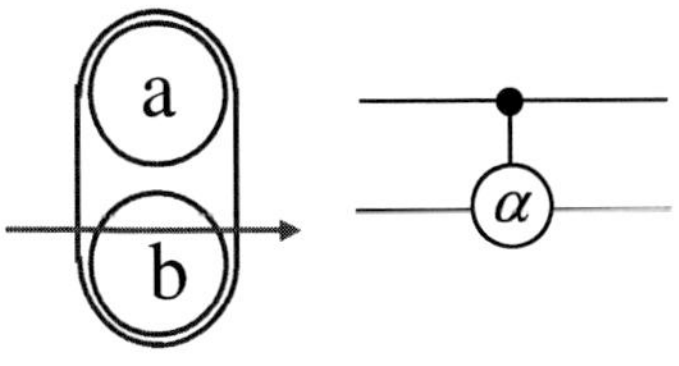

$$A_\alpha = \begin{pmatrix} 1 & 0 & 0 & 0 \\ 0 & 1 & 0 & 0 \\ 0 & 0 & i\cos\alpha & \sin\alpha \\ 0 & 0 & \sin\alpha & i\cos\alpha \end{pmatrix}$$

Figure 16. A controlled-rotation gate.

performed [79]. With a controlled operation, it becomes possible to implement a simple Deutsch-Jozsa (D-J) algorithm, which has been demonstrated in an NMR quantum computer [80].

The Deutsch-Jozsa (D-J) algorithm [81] determines whether an unknown function is constant or balanced. For a function $f(x)$ that transforms N bits of information to one bit, it is a constant function if output $f(x) = 0$ for all x, or $f(x) = 1$ for all x; it is a balanced function if output $f(x) = 0$ for exactly half of its inputs and $f(x) = 1$ for the remaining inputs. On a classical computer $2^{N-1}+1$ function calls are needed to determine with certainty whether a function is constant or balanced, while the D-J quantum algorithm determines whether an unknown function is constant or balanced using only one function call. This algorithm illustrates that a quantum computer can perform a computation in less steps than any classical computer. Since the simplest case of the algorithm can basically be carried out on a controlled-NOT gate, it can be the first step for the Josephson qubits to be in practice for a quantum computation.

4.3. Quantum Sum and Carry

Quantum computation performs unitary transformations and any unitary operation is reversible. This is the reason that quantum arithmetic cannot be directly deduced from its classical Boolean counterpart (it is obvious that most of classical logic gates are not reversible). Quantum arithmetic must be built from reversible logical components.

Before we turn to quantum sum and carry, we first present a 3-qubit quantum gate, the Toffoli gate or the controlled-controlled-NOT gate. The truth table of the Toffoli gate is shown in Table 5. The target bit c undergoes a NOT operation when the two control bits a and b are both in state 1, and is unaffected when the two control bits are in other states. The Toffoli gate can be constructed from the controlled-rotation and controlled-NOT gates [82], as depicted in Figure 17, where time flows from left to right.

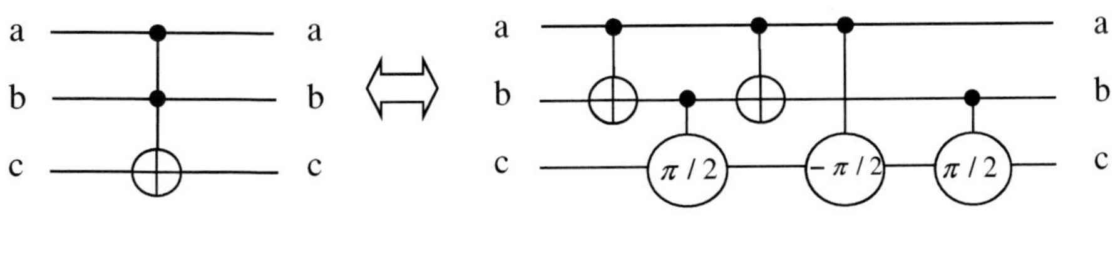

Figure 17. The Toffoli gate and its implementation.

Table 5. The truth table of Toffoli gate.

a	b	c	a	b	c
0	0	0	0	0	0
0	0	1	0	0	1
0	1	0	0	1	0
0	1	1	0	1	1
1	0	0	1	0	0
1	0	1	1	0	1
1	**1**	**0**	**1**	**1**	**1**
1	**1**	**1**	**1**	**1**	**0**

The addition of two quantum registers $|a\rangle$ and $|b\rangle$ can be written as $|a, b\rangle \quad - > |a, a+b\rangle$. As the input (a, b) can be reconstructed from the output $(a, a+b)$ and there is no loss of information in the process, this computation can be performed reversibly. The quantum sum of three qubits can be implemented with two CNOT gates while the quantum carry is obtained by using two Toffoli gates and one CNOT gate, as shown in Figure 18, where times goes from left to right. During a computation, a sequence of microwave pulses with different frequencies and durations is applied on each qubit. Those in resonance will switch their states. An implementation of such a process for the quantum carry is schematically shown in Figure 19.

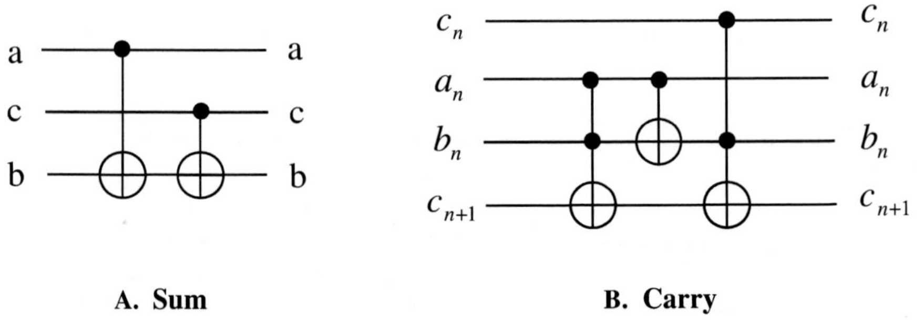

Figure 18. Quantum sum and carry.

Quantum sum and carry are basic elements for a quantum computation. Many functional quantum networks can be based on these two primitives. A modular exponentiation $U_{x,n}\,|a, 0\rangle \quad - > |a, x^a(\text{mod}\, n)\rangle$, probably the most significant part in Shor's quantum factoring algorithm, can be constructed from the networks of quantum sum and carry [83].

4.4. Quantum Fourier Transform

The discrete Fourier transform modulo q is a unitary transformation in q dimensions. Consider a number a with $0 \leq a < q$, we perform the transformation that takes the state $|a\rangle$ to

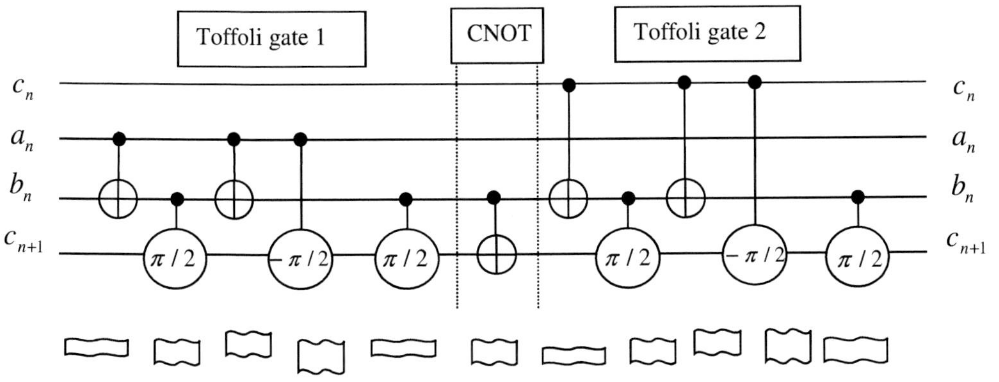

Figure 19. Quantum carry implemented by microwave pulses.

the state

$$\frac{1}{q^{1/2}}\sum_{c=0}^{q-1}\exp(2\pi iac/q)\,|c\rangle\,. \tag{20}$$

If we take $q = 2^l$, an integer can be represented in binary logic as $|a_{l-1}a_{l-2}...a_0\rangle$. For the quantum Fourier transform, we only need to use two types of quantum gates [66]. One of these gates is a single qubit rotation X_j, which operates on the jth bit of a quantum computer:

$$X_j = \frac{1}{\sqrt{2}}\begin{bmatrix} 1 & 1 \\ 1 & -1 \end{bmatrix}. \tag{21}$$

Another is a controlled-rotation gate $Y_{j,k}$, which operates on the bits in positions j and k with $j < k$:

$$Y_{j,k} = \begin{bmatrix} 1 & 0 & 0 & 0 \\ 0 & 1 & 0 & 0 \\ 0 & 0 & 1 & 0 \\ 0 & 0 & 0 & e^{i\theta_{k-j}} \end{bmatrix}, \tag{22}$$

where $\theta_{k-j} = \pi/2^{k-j}$. To perform a quantum Fourier transform, we apply the gates X_j in reverse order from X_{l-1} to X_0, and between X_{j+1} and X_j we apply all the gates $Y_{j,k}$ where $k > j$. A part of the transform is implemented as shown in Figure 20. By applying this sequence of transformations, we obtain a quantum state

$$\frac{1}{q^{1/2}}\sum_{c=0}^{q-1}\exp(2\pi iac/q)\,|b\rangle\,, \tag{23}$$

where b is the binary number obtained by reading the bits of c from right to left.

Since both the X and Y gates can be implemented by single qubit rotation or the controlled-rotation gates, we estimate that it would eventually be possible to realize the quantum Fourier transform with the Josephson qubits.

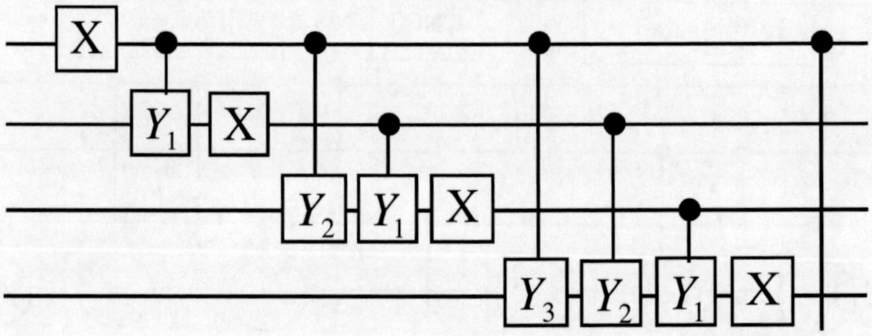

Figure 20. An implementation of quantum Fourier Transform.

Table 6. Factoring 21: (a) x=4 and (b) x=8.

A	x^A	$f(A)$
0	1	1
1	4	4
2	16	16
3	64	1
4	256	4
5	1024	16
6	4096	1

A	x^A	$f(A)$
0	1	1
1	8	8
2	64	1
3	512	8
4	4096	1
5	32768	8

4.5. A Draft Structure of a Quantum Computer

Although there is still a long way to go before a useful quantum computer comes into practice, people believe that it can solve problems that are intractable for present classical computers. One of these problems is the prime factorization of large numbers. For factoring an integer n, the best factoring algorithm available for classical computing takes a run time $\exp(c(\log n)^{1/3}(\log\log n)^{2/3})$ for some constant c. It is an exponential-time algorithm, which is inefficiently computable with the growing of integer n. The quantum algorithm for factoring by Shor takes $O((\log n)^2(\log\log n)(\log\log\log n))$ steps on a quantum computer, along with some polynomial (in $\log n$) processing time on a classical computer [78], [77].

To factor an odd number n, Shor's algorithm first finds the least integer r such that $x^r = 1(\mathrm{mod}\, n)$, i.e. the period of $f(A) = x^A$ for A from 0 to $n-1$, where x is random, with $x < n$ and $gcd(x, n) = 1$. Here, $gcd(a, b)$ is the greatest common divisor of a and b and it can be effectively computed with Euclid's algorithm on a classical computer. Then it finds factors of n by calculating $gcd(x^{r/2} - 1, n)$ and $gcd(x^{r/2} + 1, n)$ if r is even and $x^{r/2} \neq \pm 1 \bmod n$, otherwise, it repeats the algorithm.

For example, factoring $n = 21$. First we choose $x = 4$, and calculate $f(A) = 4^A \bmod 21$ for some A, then we obtain the period $r = 3$, as the data shown in Table 6 (a). Here r is not even, so we repeat the algorithm with $x = 8$. Calculating $f(A) = 8^A \bmod 21$, we obtain $r = 2$, as in Table 6 (b). Since r is even and $x^{r/2} = 8$, we calculate $gcd(x^{r/2} + 1, n)$ and $gcd(x^{r/2} - 1, n)$, and obtain $gcd(9, 21) = 3$ and $gcd(7, 21) = 7$, the two factors of 21.

To perform Shor's factoring algorithm, we start with two quantum registers, one of which is initiated to be in the superpositions $|a\rangle$ and the other is in the state $|0\rangle$. We compute $x^a(\mathrm{mod}\, n)$ in the second register and keep the first register in the $|a\rangle$ state, i.e. performing the modular exponentiation

$$U_{x,n}\,|a,0\rangle \quad -> |a, x^a(\mathrm{mod}\, n)\rangle$$

which can basically be built on a reversible network of quantum sum and carry [83]. Next, we perform the quantum Fourier transform on the first register to get period r. Finally, we calculate the factors of n with Euclid's algorithm by classical computing.

We see that in the realization of Shor's factoring algorithm classical computing is not dispensable; in addition, the experimental realization of a quantum network can be significantly simplified by using classical substitutions. An ultimate architecture for a quantum computer seems to be an integration of both quantum and classical components. As has been seen, the superconducting circuits of Josephson junctions can be designed to independently perform quantum and classical computing. We may eventually be able to build a heterogeneous Josephson array computer, with the quantum computing performed in the heart of the array and accompanied by classical computing components. A possible structure is shown in Figure 21.

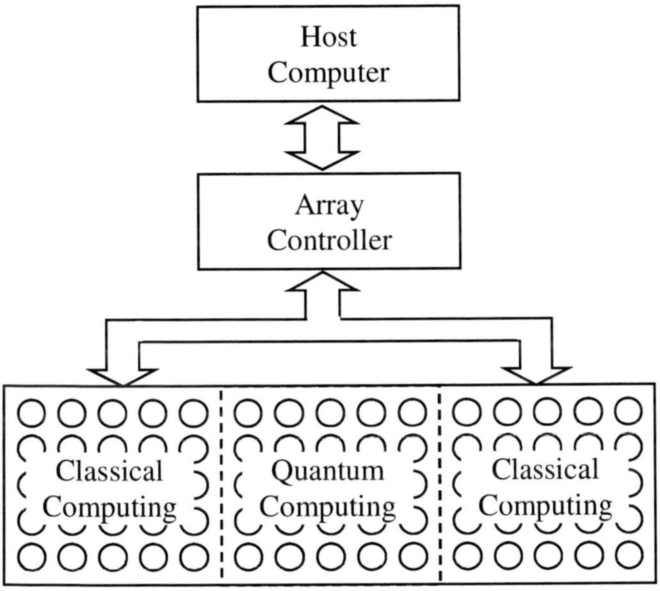

Figure 21. A draft structure of an array-based quantum computer.

Shor's factoring algorithm is probabilistic. Preliminary computations are needed for the quantum processing and the (intermediate) outputs of the quantum computing need to be processed classically in order to obtain appropriate results. This process has to be repeated if necessary. For the architecture in Figure 21, the classical processing network serves as such a pre- and post-processor for the quantum computing network in the center of the system. The interface between classical and quantum processing will be crucial for a practical implementation. Because classical and quantum computing based on the same device can now be studied simultaneously, which is impossible in certain circumstances, e.g. in the study of ensemble spin-based quantum computers, the array-based architecture of Josephson circuits is a good vehicle for studying the quantum computer paradigm, albeit that the possibility to realize such a quantum computer greatly depends on the progress in experiments on fundamental quantum devices and circuits.

5. Quantum Cellular Nonlinear Networks (CNNs) Using Josephson Circuits

5.1. Cellular Nonlinear Networks (CNNs)

A CNN is an N dimensional array of analog circuit cells with identical components and structures. Each cell is a dynamical system. It interacts directly with its neighbors within a radius and, indirectly, with other cells through a global interaction of continuous-time dynamics. The dynamics of a CNN is determined by a set of state dynamics of each cell in the array [55]. The state dynamics of a cell, indexed by k, is described by the CNN state equation:

$$\frac{dx_k}{dt} = f(x_k) + \sum_{i \in r} g_i(y_i) + \sum_{j \in r} h_j(u_j), \tag{24}$$

where x_k is the state variable, and y_i, u_j are inputs and outputs of neighboring cells within the area of effective interactions. The cell interactions, as can be seen, are implied in the linear or nonlinear functions (g_i and h_j in equation (24)) of the variables associated with neighbors (y_i and u_j in equation (24)). The state variable of a cell is thus completely determined by its inputs and the synaptic effect of neighboring interactions. The output of a cell is given as a function of the state variable:

$$u_k = q(x_k). \tag{25}$$

The CNN state equation (24) can be readily adapted to applications of image processing and pattern recognition [55], and the CNN architecture, when attached with local memories, can be used to construct a CNN universal machine, which is as universal as a Turing machine [84].

5.2. Formulating Josephson Quantum Dynamics as CNN State Dynamics

For a Josephson circuit based CNN (schematically shown in Figure 22), the cell dynamics are obtained as the quantum dynamics of the Josephson circuit. The state variable of a cell, indexed by k, is then:

$$|\Psi_k\rangle = \alpha_k |0\rangle + \beta_k |1\rangle \tag{26}$$

with

$$|\alpha_k|^2 + |\beta_k|^2 = 1. \tag{27}$$

The variable $|\Psi_k\rangle$ can be effectively represented by the unit three-dimensional sphere, often called the Bloch sphere. For the Bloch sphere representation, we have

$$\alpha_k = \cos\frac{\theta_k}{2} \tag{28}$$

and

$$\beta_k = e^{i\varphi_k}\sin\frac{\theta_k}{2} \tag{29}$$

where θ_k and φ_k are real numbers [65]. Let $A_k = \cos\frac{\theta_k}{2}$ and $B_k = \sin\frac{\theta_k}{2}$, then we have

$$\alpha_k = A_k, \tag{30}$$

and

$$\beta_k = B_k e^{i\varphi_k}, \tag{31}$$

where A_k, B_k are amplitude variables and φ_k is a phase variable.

A variety of methods is available for the coupling of Josephson circuits (e.g. to use flux transporters [67]). To a first analysis, however, we model the coupling as the interaction of flux generated by the superconducting currents through mutual inductance. Due to the neighboring couplings, the magnetic frustration of a cell k (as the one in the center of Figure 22) is changed over the initial frustration f_0 to

$$f_k = f_0 + \sum_{i \in r} M_{ik} I_i / \Phi_0, \tag{32}$$

where I_i is the persistent current of a neighbor circuit and M_{ik} is the mutual inductance.

The inductive couplings produce a magnetic flux change, which causes an energy shift in the circuit. If we assume that the coupling between cells is only via classical degrees of freedom, i.e., that there are no quantum entanglements among cells, a Josephson network is then an array of individual quantum systems. The magnetic frustration change of a circuit under interaction is dependent on the states of the circulating currents of neighbors. This change, incorporated in the Hamiltonian, can be described by including a coupling factor $F(A_i)$, a function of A_i, in equation (32). The Hamiltonian of a cell k becomes:

$$\mathbf{H}_k = I_p((f_0 - \frac{1}{2})\Phi_0 + \sum_{i \in r} F(A_i) M_{ik} I_i)\boldsymbol{\sigma}_z - \frac{\lambda}{2}\boldsymbol{\sigma}_x. \tag{33}$$

The dynamics of the Josephson network is simply described by a set of Schrödinger equations for each cell,

$$i\hbar\frac{d\,|\Psi_k\rangle}{dt} = \mathbf{H}_k\,|\Psi_k\rangle\,. \tag{34}$$

Taking equations (26), (27), (30), (31) and (33), the Schrödinger equation (34) can be written as a couple of equations for the amplitude variable A_k (or B_k, which is essentially equivalent to A_k) and the phase variable φ_k respectively:

$$\hbar\frac{dA_k}{dt} = -\frac{\lambda}{2}\sqrt{1 - A_k^2}\sin\varphi_k, \tag{35}$$

$$\hbar\frac{d\varphi_k}{dt} = I_p((f_0 - \frac{1}{2})\Phi_0 + \sum_{i\in r} F(A_i)M_{ik}I_i) + \frac{\lambda}{2}\frac{A_k}{\sqrt{1-A_k^2}}\cos\varphi_k. \tag{36}$$

As can be seen, equations (35) and (36) are analogous to the CNN state equation (24). The Josephson CNN cell dynamics are characterized by two variables A_k and φ_k. When a measurement is made, the phase information carried on φ_k is discarded, and the amplitude information carried on A_k is obtained as the probability amplitude. The output is therefore the probability that a cell behaves as one specific state of the persistent currents. The output equation is given by:

$$u_k = A_k^2. \tag{37}$$

Inputs are prepared in the form of the cells' initial states. Each cell is influenced by its neighbors through mutually inductive couplings. The mutual inductance between cells can simply be a function of their physical distance; the synaptic effect of couplings is therefore a weighted sum of neighboring couplings, as shown in Figure 22, where the grey levels of cells imply different coupling weights.

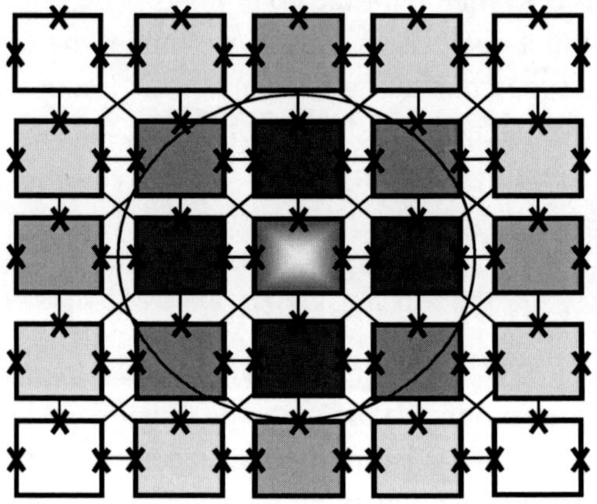

Figure 22. A quantum CNN using Josephson circuits.

5.3. Simulations

To illustrate how a Josephson circuit based CNN works, we present a study on a simple network.

Consider the network in Figure 22. Each cell is interacted with neighbors through the flux the persistent currents generate. The varying of the currents induces flux changes in the neighboring circuits, and therefore change the energies of those circuits. For the layout shown in Figure 22, the flux change in one cell will result in an opposite effect (i.e. a flux change with an opposite direction) on neighbors. The state of a cell can be manipulated by applying microwave pulses at a frequency equal to the energy splitting of the circuit; the microwave amplitude and pulse length determine the relative probability of the cell being in each base state.

Since every cell in the network has the same state equation as others (without loss of generality, we ignore boundary effects), the global properties of the network can be understood by studying the local properties of a single cell. We further assume that each cell interacts only with its nearest neighbors, i.e., that the interaction with far away cells is ignored. Thus we focus the study on a 3×3 network, as the one encircled in Figure 22.

We start the simulation with all cells being initially prepared in the ground state. To study the state dynamics under interaction, we apply microwave pulses to promote the states of a number of cells in the network to the first excited state, inducing the network to evolve due to interactions. Then we observe the changes of the state dynamics of cells. To a first approximation, we focus on the quantum dynamics of the cell $(2, 2)$, i.e. the cell in the center of the network, and assume that other cells are static either at the (initial) ground state or at the (promoted) first excited state.

In this simulation, the cells are operating at a magnetic field just below a half quantum flux $(0.5\Phi_0)$, namely, $0.496\Phi_0$ (i.e. $f_0 = 0.496$). Other circuit parameters are adopted from [70], as $a = 0.8$, $E_J = 260\ GHz$ and $\lambda = 3.4\ GHz$. The mutual inductances are obtained by FastHenry to be approximately $0.56\ pH$ for adjacent cells and $0.14\ pH$ for diagonally adjacent cells.

The actual state dynamics of cell $(2, 2)$ depends on the synaptic effects of the states of neighbors as well as its initial state. If the initial state of each cell (at $t = 0$) is prepared at the ground state, we have $|\Psi_{ij}(0)\rangle = |0\rangle$, i.e.,

$$A_{ij}(0) = 1, \ \ \varphi_{ij}(0) = 0, \ i, j \in [1, 2, 3],$$

If, at the same time, a number of the cells (except the cell $(2, 2)$) are excited to the first upper state, i.e., the states are inverted to as $|\Psi_{ij}(0)\rangle = |1\rangle$, the initial conditions for the network become then:

$$\begin{aligned} A_{ij}(0) &= 0, \ \ \varphi_{ij}(0) = 0, \ \ for\ chosen\ i, j, \\ A_{ij}(0) &= 1, \ \ \varphi_{ij}(0) = 0, \ \ otherwise. \end{aligned}$$

For example, consider the three distinct sets of initial conditions in Figure 23 (a1, a2, a3), shown in the form of $(A_{ij}(0), \varphi_{ij}(0))$. Because of the inverse of the persistent currents, the coupling factor $F(A_{ij}) = -2$ for each $A_{ij}(0) = 0$; and $F(A_{ij}) = 0$ for each $A_{ij}(0) = 1$. In all the cases, the initial states of cell $(2, 2)$ are the same, as $A_{22}(0) = 1$, $\varphi_{22}(0) = 0$. The neighbors of cell $(2, 2)$ are fixed in the state of $A_{ij}(t) = 0$ or 1, which can be interpreted as the pixel values of binary images [49]. In Figure 23, each cell is shaded by encoding its content to a grey-level image pixel: $(1, 0) = black$, $(0, 0) = white$ and $(0.7, \pi) = grey$.

The amplitude state dynamics of cell $(2, 2)$, $A_{22}(t)$, is plotted in Figure 24 (a1, a2, a3), for the three different sets of initial conditions. The minimum values of the amplitude variable, as can be seen, are approximately 0.84, 0.87 and 0.89, corresponding to different initial conditions. Although the variations of these values, due to the relatively weak coupling between cells, are rather small, they clearly indicate that the synaptic effects of different sets of neighboring couplings result in the different changes of cell dynamics, given the same initial states. The variation introduced by neighboring interaction can be strengthened by exploring other coupling methods (e.g. to use flux transporters).

Furthermore, the oscillation frequencies of the cell states are distinguishable. This means that a cell may be individually addressed and its state may be manipulated by microwave pulses during data processing. In other words, a CNN network based on Josephson circuits can be potentially programmable.

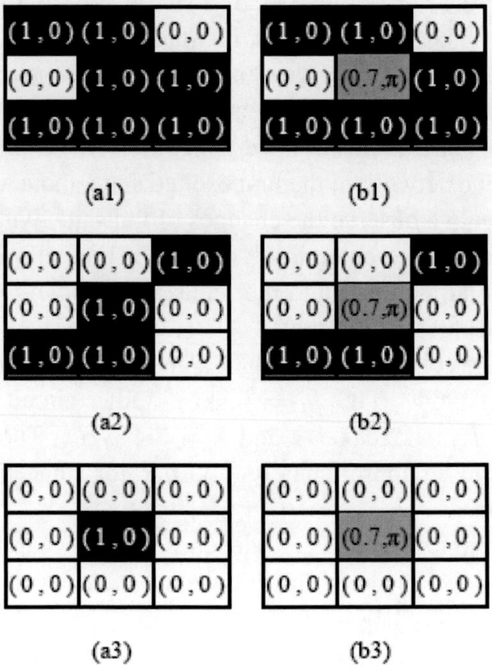

Figure 23. The six sets of initial conditions; cells are encoded as grey-level image pixels and shaded in the figure as $(1,0) = \mathit{black}$, $(0,0) = \mathit{white}$ and $(0.7,\pi) = \mathit{grey}$.

The dynamics of a cell also depends on its initial state. If cell $(2,2)$, for instance, is initially prepared at a superposition of the states $|0\rangle$ and $|1\rangle$ at $t = 0$, i.e. $|\Psi_{22}(0)\rangle = \frac{1}{\sqrt{2}}(|0\rangle - |1\rangle)$, the state variables are then $A_{22}(0) = \frac{1}{\sqrt{2}} \approx 0.7$, $\varphi_{22}(0) = \pi$. If the initial conditions of other cells are assumed to be unchanged, as shown in Figure 23 (b1, b2, b3), the amplitude state dynamics of cell $(2,2)$, $A_{22}(t)$, is plotted in Figure 24 (b1, b2, b3), for the three different sets of initial conditions. The minimum values of the amplitude variable, as can be seen, are approximately 0.20, 0.26 and 0.29, which distinguish these state dynamics, resulting from the different initial conditions in Figure 23 (b1, b2, b3).

It is interesting to notice that the oscillation frequencies obtained from Figure 24 (a1) and Figure 24 (b1), Figure 24 (a2) and Figure 24 (b2), Figure 24 (a3) and Figure 24 (b3), are identical. This indicate that, with the same configurations (circuit parameters, interaction conditions, etc.), a CNN network based on Josephson circuits will produce different output states, according to different inputs or initial states.

5.4. Summary and Issues

Quantum CNNs using superconducting circuits of Josephson junctions have been presented. The local quantum dynamics of the Josephson circuit is used as the state dynamics of CNNs by formulating the Schrödinger equation to a set of equations for an amplitude variable and a phase variable. The states of a cell are controlled by changing the enclosed magnetic flux of the circuit. Cells interact with their neighbors through the mutually inductive couplings. Output states are measured with superconducting magnetometers (SQUIDs). This quantum

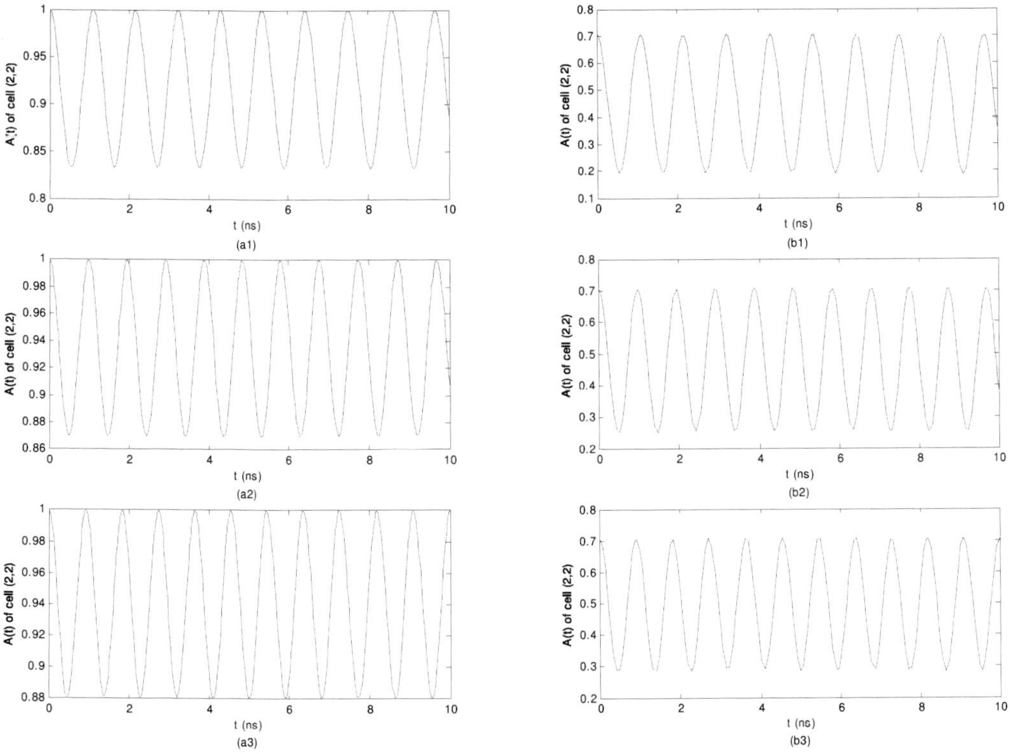

Figure 24. The state dynamics of cell (2,2) corresponding to the initial conditions of Figure 23.

CNN architecture presents a novel computing paradigm, other than quantum computing and classical computing based on binary logic, for the use of Josephson circuits.

The interactions of variables of cells are assumed to be only via classical degrees of freedom, i.e., no quantum entanglements among cells. This assumption distinguishes a quantum CNN architecture from a quantum computer. It is yet unknown if this assumption is feasible in an actual implementation.

Since any interaction with the external environment introduces decoherence to quantum coherent states, it would be difficult to keep the local coherent states away from decoherence under the circumstances that each Josephson circuit in an array is coupled with its neighbors and the control and measurement circuitry. In general, difficulties remain in the controlling of the states, in inserting inputs and measuring outputs of a large network, due to the decoherence problem. In the next section, a magnetic field gradient scheme is proposed for operations on integrated circuits of Josephson junctions.

6. Implementation Issues

As noted in previous sections, requirements for a Josephson circuit based system are that the cells can be prepared in well-defined quantum states, that the states can be precisely manipulated according to certain initial conditions (as inputs), and that the states can be measured and read out (as outputs).

The quantum state of a Josephson circuit is manipulated by radiation in resonance of the energy difference of the two base states. This energy difference is typically a few GHz. Microwave pulses can be injected into the circuits for control operations.

Josephson array oscillators consisting of parallel arrays of Josephson junctions have been studied as on-chip oscillators controlling quantum circuits of Josephson junctions [85]. The oscillators have a single frequency, and the frequency, as well as the amplitude, is tunable by independent variables. Oscillators based on RSFQ (rapid single flux quantum) technology have also been proposed for the driving and controlling of Josephson circuits [86], [87]. Measurement can be carried out by weakly coupling one or an ensemble of the Josephson circuits to a SQUID. These schemes aimed at an ultra-fast, high precision and on-chip control of integrated quantum circuits.

For the fabrication of integrated Josephson circuits, there are basically two strategies. One is to incorporate the superconducting control circuitry on a single chip as the Josephson circuits. The other is to develop a flip-chip, i.e., the working Josephson circuits are fabricated on one chip and the measurement and control circuitry are fabricated on another chip; the two chips can then be bonded to be inductively coupled [88].

In both methodologies, however, the mechanism of handles to address each individual cell (either in a quantum CNN or a quantum computation circuit), parameterize it, or input signals to it, have to be developed. In this section we present a magnetic bias scheme that makes it possible to individually address a cell. This scheme is inspired from the MRI (magnetic resonance imaging) technique [89].

Since the energy difference required for resonance in frequency is determined by the enclosed flux of a Josephson circuit, we would be able to control each individual cell if each of them has a unique magnetic flux. A gradient in the magnetic field will help to accomplish this.

A magnetic field gradient is a variation in the magnetic field with respect to position. A one-dimensional linear magnetic field gradient G_x along the x axis, for example, indicates that the magnetic field at position x is given by a linear equation:

$$B_x = B_0 + x \cdot G_x, \tag{38}$$

where B_0 is the magnetic field at the initial reference point. A linear magnetic field gradient G_y along the y axis similarly gives the magnetic field at position y.

Applying simultaneously the linear magnetic field gradient G_x and G_y to a two-dimensional array leads to a magnetic field distribution at the (x, y) plane, described by:

$$B_{xy} = B_0 + x \cdot G_x + y \cdot G_y. \tag{39}$$

If a cell in this array is regarded as rectangular, and it has values in the coordinates as (x_1, x_2) and (y_1, y_2), its enclosed flux will be:

$$F = \int_{y_1}^{y_2} \int_{x_1}^{x_2} B_{xy} dx dy. \tag{40}$$

Simplifying equation (40) with (39), and assuming the area of the cell $S = (x_2 - x_1)(y_2 - y_1)$ and the center of the cell (x_c, y_c) at $x_c = \frac{1}{2}(x_1 + x_2)$ and $y_c = \frac{1}{2}(y_1 + y_2)$, we obtain the enclosed magnetic flux as:

$$F = S(B_0 + x_c \cdot G_x + y_c \cdot G_y). \tag{41}$$

The area of each cell, S, can be seen as the same, if the variation introduced by the fabrication process is ignored. The magnetic flux in each cell is then distinguished by the variables indicating its position, x_c and y_c. The gradient parameters G_x and G_y can be chosen so that the magnetic flux enclosed in each cell is unique. The magnetic field gradient can be realized through a pair of gradient coils with currents of opposite directions.

The use of a magnetic field gradient provides a unique magnetic bias to each cell, so that, when single frequency microwave pulses are applied to the whole array or a chip, only one cell will respond due to the resonance in frequency. It is also possible to have a number of selected cells respond at one frequency by tuning the parameters G_x and G_y. If, for instance, only the gradient G_x or G_y is used (by setting $G_y = 0$ or $G_x = 0$), the cells in a column or a row will be addressed by a single frequency radiation.

The magnetic field gradient scheme presents a practical approach for the manipulation of an integrated circuit of Josephson junctions. However, the use of magnetic field gradient presents challenges. First, each cell has a different flux bias, which implies each cell operates with different energies. This will increase the complexity in setting circuit parameters and implementing algorithms. Second, to individually manipulate a cell, microwave pulses with different frequencies are injected in a sequential order. Other measures are required to have cells working in a synchronized pattern. Finally, the accuracy and stability of a flux bias that can be achieved by using a magnetic gradient need to be investigated.

7. Summary

A classical SIMD computer architecture and an array-based quantum computer structure have been presented as possible applications of superconducting circuits of Josephson junctions. The classical computer may serve as a pre- and post-processor for the quantum computing performed in the heart of the Josephson circuit array, establishing a heterogeneous quantum/classical computer for, e.g. an implementation of Shor's factoring algorithm.

Quantum computing represents an important application based upon the reversibility of computation [90], while reversible computing is also of interest in classical digital systems where little or no energy is dissipated [91]. The Josephson circuit, operating at a low temperature and consuming little power, might be favorable for the implementation of a reversible circuit. A reversible network could thus be obtained from the superconducting circuits and perform both quantum and classical computations. These issues on reversible computing are, however, not specifically discussed in our study, and await further investigations.

A quantum CNN architecture using the Josephson circuits, with the quantum dynamics formulated as the CNN state dynamics, has been proposed, presenting a novel computing paradigm for Josephson circuits. Since classical computing architectures (SIMD arrays), quantum computing architectures and semi-quantum computing architectures (quantum CNNs) can be simultaneously studied on the same device, the Josephson circuit is a good vehicle for investigating the architectural issues of quantum and nanoelectronic computer systems, independently from the question of which device will be the ultimate implementation vehicle.

References

[1] *International Technology Roadmap for Semiconductors*, 2003 ed. http://public.itrs.net/.

[2] R. Compañó (ed.), *Technology Roadmap for Nanoelectronics*, 2nd ed. European Commission IST programme Future and Emerging Technologies, 2000.

[3] A. Bachtold, P. Hadley, T. Nakanishi and C. Dekker, "Logic circuits with carbon nanotube transistors," *Science,* vol. 294, pp. 1317-1320, 2001.

[4] Y. Huang, X. Duan, Y. Cui, L. J. Lauhon, K. Kim and C. M. Lieber, "Logic gates and computation from assembled nanowire building blocks," *Science,* vol. 294, pp. 1313-1317, 2001.

[5] C. P. Collier, E. W. Wong, M. Belohradsky, F. M. Raymo, J. F. Stoddart, P. J. Kuekes, R. S. Williams and J. R. Heath, "Electronically configurable molecular-based logic gates," *Science,* vol. 285, pp. 391-394, 1999.

[6] C. P. Collier, G. Mattersteig, E. W. Wong, Y. Luo, K. Beverly, J. Sampaio, F. M. Raymo, J. F. Stoddart and J. R. Heath, "A [2]catenane-based solid state electronically reconfigurable switch," *Science,* vol. 280, pp. 1172-1175, 2000.

[7] N. A. Melosh, A. Boukai, F. Diana, B. Gerardot, A. Badolato, P. M. Petroff and J. R. Heath, "Ultrahigh-density nanowire lattices and circuits," *Science,* vol. 300, pp. 112-115, 2003.

[8] Z. Zhong, D. Wang, Y. Cui, M. W. Bockrath and C. M. Lieber, "Nanowire crossbar arrays as address decoders for integrated nanosystems," *Science,* vol. 302, pp. 1377-1379, 2003.

[9] M. R. Stan, P. D. Franzon, S. C. Goldstein, J. C. Lach and M. M. Ziegler, "Molecular electronics: from devices and interconnect to circuits and architecture," in *Proc. IEEE*, vol. 91, pp. 1940-1957, 2003.

[10] J. R. Heath, P. J. Kuekes, G. S. Snider and R. S. Williams, "A defect-tolerant computer architecture: opportunities for nanotechnology," *Science,* vol. 280, pp. 1716-1721, 1998.

[11] S. C. Goldstein and M. Budiu, "Nanofabrics: spatial computing using molecular nanoelectronics," in *Proc. 28th Int. Symp. Computer Architecture*, pp. 178-189, 2001.

[12] A. DeHon, "Array-based architecture for FET-based nanoscale electronics," *IEEE Trans. Nano*, vol. 2, pp. 23-32, 2003.

[13] J. M. Tour, W. L. Van Zandt, C. P. Husband, S. M. Husband, L. S. Wilson, P. D. Franzon and D. P. Nackashi, "Nanocell logic gates for molecular computing," *IEEE Trans. Nano*, vol. 1, pp. 100-109, 2002.

[14] P. J. Kuekes and R. S. Williams, "Demultiplexer for a molecular wire crossbar network (MWCN DEMUX)," *U. S. Patent 6256767*, July 2001.

[15] J. von Neumann, "Probabilistic logics and the synthesis of reliable organisms from unreliable components," *Automata Studies*, Shannon C.E. & McCarthy J., eds., Princeton University Press, Princeton N.J. pp. 43-98, 1956.

[16] N. Pippenger, "Reliable computation by formulas in the presence of noise," *IEEE Trans. Inform. Theory*, vol. 34, pp. 194-197, 1988.

[17] T. Feder, "Reliable computation by networks in the presence of noise," *IEEE Trans. Inform. Theory*, vol. 35, pp. 569-571, 1989.

[18] R. L. Dobrushin and S. I. Ortyukov, "Upper bound on the redundancy of self-correcting arrangements of unreliable functional elements," *Prob. Inf. Trans.*, vol. 13, pp. 203-218, 1977.

[19] R. L. Dobrushin and S. I. Ortyukov, "Lower bound for the redundancy of self-correcting arrangements of unreliable functional elements," *Prob. Inf. Trans.*, vol. 13, pp. 59-65, 1977.

[20] N. Pippenger, G. D. Stamoulis and J. N. Tsitsiklis, "On a lower bound for the redundancy of reliable networks with noisy gates," *IEEE Trans. Inform. Theory*, vol. 37, pp. 639-643, 1991.

[21] N. Pippenger, "On networks of noisy gates," in *Proc. 26th Ann. Symp. Foundations Comput. Sci.*, pp. 30-38, 1985.

[22] N. Pippenger, "Invariance of complexity measures for networks with unreliable gates," *J. ACM*, vol. 36, pp. 531-539, 1989.

[23] N. Pippenger, "Developments in "The Synthesis of Reliable Organisms from Unreliable Components"," in *Proc. Symposia in Mathematics*, vol. 50, pp. 311-324, 1990.

[24] D. P. Siewiorek and R. S. Swarz, *Reliable Computer Systems: Design and Evaluation,* 1998. A K Peters, Natick, Massachusetts, USA.

[25] J. G. Tryon, "Quadded logic," *Redundancy Techniques for Computing Systems*, pp. 205-228, 1962. Spartan Books, Washington D.C., USA.

[26] P. A. Jensen, "Quadded NOR logic," *IEEE Trans. Reliability*, vol. 12, pp. 22-31, 1963.

[27] W. H. Pierce, *Failure-Tolerant Computer Design,* Academic Press, 1965.

[28] J. A. Abraham, "A combinatorial solution to the reliability of interwoven redundant logic networks," *IEEE Trans. Computers*, vol. 24, pp. 578-584, 1975.

[29] J. A. Abraham and D. P. Siewiorek, "An algorithm for the accurate reliability evaluation of triple modular redundancy networks," *IEEE Trans. Computers*, vol. 23, pp. 682-692, 1974.

[30] A. E. Barbour and A. S. Wojcik, "A general, constructive approach to fault-tolerant design using redundancy," *IEEE Trans. Computers*, vol. 38, pp. 15-29, 1989.

[31] C. E. Stroud, "Reliability of majority voting based VLSI fault-tolerant circuits," *IEEE Trans. VLSI*, vol. 2, pp. 516-521, 1994.

[32] S. Spagocci and T. Fountain, "Fault rates in nanochip devices," in *Electrochemical Society Proc.*, vol. 98-19, pp. 582-593, 1999.

[33] M. Forshaw and K. Nikolić, "Algorithms and Architectures for Nanoelectronic Computers," in *Technical report MEL-ARL Project ANSWERS*, June 2000.

[34] K. Nikolić, A. Sadek, M. Forshaw, "Fault-tolerant techniques for nanocomputers," *Nanotechnology, 13*, pp. 357-362, 2002.

[35] J. Han and P. Jonker, "A system architecture solution for unreliable nanoelectronic devices," *IEEE Trans. Nanotechnology*, vol. 1, no. 4, pp. 201-208, 2002.

[36] A. S. Sadek, K. Nikolić and M. Forshaw, "Parallel information and computation with restitution for noise-tolerant nanoscale logic networks," *Nanotechnology, 15*, pp. 192-210, 2004.

[37] J. Han and P. Jonker, "A defect- and fault-tolerant architecture for nanocomputers," *Nanotechnology*, vol. 14, no. 2, pp. 224-230, 2003.

[38] D. Mange, M. Sipper, A. Stauffer and G. Tempesti, "Toward robust integrated circuits: the embryonics approach," in *Proc. IEEE*, vol. 88, pp. 516-541, 2000.

[39] I. Koren and Z. Koren, "Defect tolerance in VLSI circuits: techniques and yield analysis," in *Proc. IEEE*, vol. 86, pp. 1819-1836, 1998.

[40] C. H. Stapper, "A new statistical approach for fault-tolerant VLSI systems," in *Proc. 22nd Int. Symp. Fault-Tolerant Computing*, pp. 356-365, 1992.

[41] J. Lach, W. H. Mangione-Smith and M. Potkonjak, "Low overhead fault-tolerant FPGA systems," *IEEE Trans. VLSI*, vol. 6, pp. 212-221, 1998.

[42] F. Distante, M.G.Sami and R. Stefanelli, "Fault-tolerance and reconfigurability issues in massively parallel architectures," in *Proc. CAMP, Computer Architecture for Machine Perception 1995*, pp. 340-349, 1995.

[43] G. Norman, D. Parker, M. Kwiatkowska and S. K. Shukla, "Evaluating the reliability of defect-tolerant architectures for nanotechnology with probabilistic model checking," in *Proc. Int. Conf. on VLSI Design*, pp. 907-912, 2004.

[44] W. G. Brown, J. Tierney and R. Wasserman, "Improvement of electronic-computer reliability through the use of redundancy," *IRE Trans. Electronic Computers*, vol. 10, pp. 407-416, September 1961.

[45] M. J. B. Duff, CLIP4, *Special Computer Architectures for Pattern Processing*, CRC Press, Boca Raton, Florida, USA, pp.65-86, 1982.

[46] K. E. Batcher, Design of a massively parallel processor, *IEEE Trans. Comput.*, vol. 29, pp. 836-840, 1980.

[47] T. Oya, T. Asai, T. Fukui and Y. Amemiya, "A majority-logic device using an irreversible single-electron box," *IEEE Trans. Nanotechnology*, vol. 2, no. 1, pp. 15-22, 2003.

[48] T. J. Fountain, *Processor Arrays: Architecture and Applications*, 1987. Academic Press, London, UK.

[49] P. P. Jonker, *Morphological Image Processing: Architecture and VLSI Design,* 1992. Kluwer Publishers, Dordrecht, The Netherlands.

[50] J. Han and P. Jonker, "A Study on Fault-Tolerant Circuits using Redundancy," in *Proc. VLSI 2003 (Multionference in Computer Science and Engineering)*, pp. 65-69, 2003.

[51] J. Han and P. Jonker, "From Massively Parallel Image Processors to Fault-Tolerant Nanocomputers," in *Proc. ICPR 2004 (Int. Conf. on Pattern Recogniton)*, pp. unknown yet, 2004.

[52] J. Han, *Fault-Tolerant Architectures for Nanoelectronic and Quantum Devices*, Ph.D. dissertation, Delft University of Technology, 2004. To be published.

[53] M. Forshaw, D. Crawley, P. Jonker, J. Han, and C. Sotomayor Torres, *Nano_Arch_Review: A Review of the Status of Research and Training into Architectures for Nanoelectronic and Nanophotonic Systems in the European Research Area*, EU 6th Framework Programme Information Society Technologies FP6/2002/IST/1, Specific Support Action, Contract no. 507519, University College, London, UK, July 2004.

[54] C. S. Lent, P. D. Tougaw, W. Porod and G. H. Bernstein, Quantum cellular automata, *Nanotechnology*, vol. 4, pp. 49-57, 1993.

[55] L. O. Chua and L. Yang, Cellular Neural Networks: Theory, *IEEE Tran. Circuits Sys.*, vol. 35, pp. 1257-1272; and Cellular Neural Networks: Applications, *ibid.* pp. 1273-1290, 1988.

[56] M. J. B. Duff and T. J. Fountain, *Cellular logic Image Processing*, 1986. Academic Press, London, UK.

[57] S. Kyo, T. Koga and S. Okazaki, IMAP-CE: a 51.2 GOPS video rate image processor with 128 VLIW processing elements, in *Proc. Int. Conf. Image Processing*, pp. 294-297, 2001.

[58] R. Kleihorst, A. Abbo, A. van der Avoird, M. O. de Beeck, L. Sevat, P. Wielafe, R. van Veen, and H. van Herten, Xetal: a low-power high-performance smart camera processor, in *proc. IEEE ISCAS 2001*, pp. 215-218, 2001.

[59] T. J. Fountain, M. J. B. Duff, D. G. Crawley, C. D. Tomlinson and C. D. Moffat, The use of nanoelectronic devices in highly parallel computing systems, *IEEE Trans. VLSI*, vol. 6, pp. 31-38, 1998.

[60] P. Julián, R. Dogaru, M. Itoh, M. Hänggi and L. O. Chua, On the RTD implementation of simplicial cellular nonlinear networks, in *Proc. 7th IEEE Int. Workshop CNNs Appl.*, pp. 140-147, 2002.

[61] C. Gerousis, S. M. Goodnick and W. Porod, Toward nanoelectronic cellular neural networks, *Int. J. Circ. Theor. Appl.*, vol. 28, pp. 523-535, 2000.

[62] T. Yang, R. A. Kiehl and L. O. Chua, Tunneling phase logic cellular nonlinear networks, Int. J. of Bifurcation and Chaos, vol. 11 (12): 2895-2911, DEC 2001.

[63] G. Toth, C. S. Lent, P. D. Tougaw, Y. Brazhnik, W. Weng, W. Porod, R.-W. Liu and Y.-F. Huang, Quantum cellular neural networks, *Superlattices and Microstructures*, vol. 20, pp. 473-478, 1996.

[64] J. Han and P. Jonker, Quantum cellular nonlinear networks using Josephson circuits, in *Proc. IEEE-NANO 2003, 3rd IEEE Conference on Nanotechnology* (San Francisco, CA, USA, Aug.12-14), pp. 457-460, 2003.

[65] M. A. Nielsen and I. L. Chuang, *Quantum Computation and Quantum Information*, Cambridge University Press, 2000.

[66] D. P. DiVincenzo, Quantum Computation, *Science*, Vol. 285, pp. 255, 1995.

[67] J. E. Mooij, T. P. Orlando, L. Levitov, L. Tian, Caspar H. van der Wal and Seth Lloyd, Josephson persistent-current qubit, *Science*, vol. 285, pp. 1036-1039, 1999.

[68] T. P. Orlando, J. E. Mooij, L. Tian, Caspar H. van der Wal, L. S. Levitov, Seth Lloyd and J. J. Mazo, Superconducting persistent-current qubit, *Phys. Rev. B*, vol. 60, pp. 15398-15413, 1999.

[69] C. H. van der Wal, A. C. J. ter Haar, F. K. Wilhelm, R. N. Schouten, C. J. P. M. Harmans, T. P. Orlando, S. Lloyd and J. E. Mooij, Quantum superposition of macroscopic persistent-current states, *Science*, vol. 290, pp. 773-777, 2000.

[70] I. Chiorescu, Y. Nakamura, C. J. P. M. Harmans and J. E. Mooij, Coherent quantum dynamics of a superconducting flux qubit, *Science*, vol. 299, pp. 1869-1871; published online 13 Feb. 2003, 10.1126/science. 1081045

[71] P. Jonker and J. Han, On quantum and classical computing with arrays of superconducting persistent current qubits, in *Proc. CAMP2000, Fifth IEEE International Workshop on Computer Architectures for Machine Perception* (Padova, Italy, Sep.11-13, 2000), IEEE Computer Society, Los Alamitos, California, USA, pp. 69-78, 2000.

[72] J. Han and P. Jonker, On quantum computing with macroscopic Josephson qubits, in *Proc. IEEE-NANO 2002, 2nd IEEE Conference on Nanotechnology* (Washington D.C., USA, Aug.26-28), pp. 305-308, 2002.

[73] J. Han and P. Jonker, Novel computing architecture on arrays of Josephson persistent current bits, in *Proc. MSM 2002, Fifth International Conference on Modeling and Simulation of Microsystems* (San Juan, Puerto Rico, USA, April 22-25), pp. 636-639, 2002.

[74] Y. Shimazu, Two four-junction qubits coupled by a superconducting flux transporter , an internal report in the Quantum Transportation group at the Delft University of Technology (4/5/2000).

[75] FastHenry, a multipole-accelerated inductance analysis program developed by the RLE Computational Prototyping Group at Massachusetts Institute of Technology, U.S.A. http://rleweb.mit.edu/vlsi/codes.htm

[76] T. van Duzer and C. W. Turner, *Principles of Superconductive Devices and Circuits*, 2nd ed. Upper Saddle River, New Jersey: Prentice Hall PTR, 1998.

[77] A. Eket and R. Jozsa, Quantum Computation and Shor's Factoring Algorithm, *Reviews of Modern Physics*, Vol. 68, No. 3, pp. 733, 1996.

[78] P. Shor, Algorithms for quantum computation: discrete log and factoring, in *Proceedings of the 35th Annual Symposium on Foundations of Computer Science*, IEEE Computer Society Press, Los Alamitos, CA, USA, pp.124-134, 1994.

[79] F. G. Paauw, Spectroscopy experiments on two coupled Josephson persistent current qubits, a Master thesis in the Quantum Transportation group at the Delft University of Technology, November 2002.

[80] I. L. Chuang, L. M. K. Vandersypen, X. Zhou, D. W. Leung, S. Lloyd, Experimental Realization of a Quantum Algorithm, *Nature*, Vol. 393, 14 May 1998.

[81] D. Deutsch and R. Jozsa, Rapid solutioin of problems by quantum computation, *Proc. R. Soc. Lond. A439*, pp. 553-558, 1992..

[82] A. Barenco, C. Bennett, R. Cleve, D. DiVincenzo, N. Margolus, P. Shor, T. Sleator, J. Smolin, and H. Weinfurter, Elementary gates for quantum computation, *Physical Review A*, Vol. 52, 3457, 1995.

[83] V. Vedral, A. Barenco, and A. Ekert, Quantum Networks for Elementary Arithmetic Operations, *Physical Review A*, Vol. 54, No. 1, July 1996.

[84] K. R. Crounse and L. O. Chua, The CNN universal machine is as universal as a Turing machine, *IEEE Tran. Circuit Sys. I*, vol. 43, pp. 353-355, 1996.

[85] D. S. Crankshaw, E. Trías and T. P. Orlando, Magnetic Flux Controlled Josephson Array Oscillators, *IEEE Tran. Applied Superconductivity*, vol. 11, pp. 1223-1226, 2001.

[86] R. C. Rey-de-Castro, M. F. Bocko, A. M. Herr, C. A. Mancini and M. J. Feldman, Design of an RSFQ Control Circuit to Observe MQC on an rf-SQUID, *IEEE Tran. Applied Superconductivity*, vol. 11, pp. 1014-1017, 2001.

[87] D. S. Crankshaw, J. L. Habif, X. Zhou, T. P. Orlando, M. J. Feldman and M. F. Bocko, An RSFQ Variable Duty Cycle Oscillator for Driving a Superconductive Qubit, *IEEE Tran. Applied Superconductivity*, vol. 13, pp. 966-969, 2003.

[88] T. P. Orlando, S. Lloyd, L. S. Levitov, K. K. Berggren, M. J. Feldman, M. F. Bocko, J. E. Mooij, C. J. P. Harmans and C. H. van der Wal, Flux-based Superconductive Qubits for Quantum Computation, *Physica C*, 372-376, pp. 194-200, 2002.

[89] J. P. Hornak, *The Basics of MRI*, online at: http://www.cis.rit.edu/htbooks/mri/inside.htm.

[90] C. Bennett, Logical Reversibility of Computation, *I.B.M. J. Res. Dev.*, Vol. 17, pp. 525-535, 1973.

[91] A. De Vos, Reversible Computing, *Progress in Quantum Electronics*, Vol. 23, pp. 1-49, 1999.

SHORT COMMUNICATIONS

In: Computer-Aided Design...
Editors: C.M. De Smet et al, pp. 415-425
ISBN 978-1-60456-860-8

Short Communication A

INTERPOLATION OF A DATA POINT SET USING THE PROGRESSIVE ITERATION APPROXIMATION PROPERTY

***J. Delgado*[1]* *and J.M. Peña*[2]**
[1]Departamento de Matemticas, Universidad de Oviedo, Spain
[2]Departamento de Matemtica Aplicada, Universidad de Zaragoza, Spain

Abstract

In Computer Aided Geometric Design, several methods for approximating a data point set with a parametric curve or a parametric surface have been considered: approximation by least squares, approximation using radial basis functions and approximation using the progressive iteration approximation property. In this paper, we present with a unified notation a concise survey on the approximation method derived from the progressive iteration approximation property.

1. Introduction

In Computer Aided Geometric Design (CAGD) is usual the need of interpolating or approximating a data point set with a parametric curve or a parametric surface. In the literature several methods have been considered for this purpose: approximation by least squares (see [9]), approximation using radial basis functions (see [13]) and approximation using the progressive iteration approximation property of a curve and a surface (see [20], [2], [14] and [8]). This paper deals with this last approach.

Qi et al. as well as de Boor showed (see [20] and [2]) that the uniform cubic B-spline basis satisfied the progressive iteration approximation property and extended the property for surfaces, showing that the nonuniform cubic B-spline tensor product surface satisfies such property. In [14] it was extended the application of the progressive iteration approximation method to normalized totally positive representations. In [8] it was compared the convergence rates of the different normalized totally positive bases of a space of functions.

*E-mail address: delgadojorge@uniovi.es

Let us recall that a basis $(u_0, \ldots, u_n)$ defined on a set I formed by nonnegative functions and such that $\sum_{i=0}^{n} u_i(x) = 1$ for all $x \in I$ is called a *blending basis*.

Given a sequence of points $\{P_i\}_{i=0}^{m}$ whose i^{th} point is assigned to a parameter value t_i, for $i = 0, 1, \ldots, m$, and a blending basis $(u_0, \ldots, u_m)$, we generate a starting curve as $\gamma^0(t) = \sum_{i=0}^{m} P_i^0 \, u_i(t)$ where $P_i^0 = P_i$ for $i = 0, 1, \ldots, m$. Then, by calculating the adjusting vector for each control point $\Delta_i^0 = P_i - \gamma^0(t_i)$, and taking $P_i^1 = P_i^0 + \Delta_i^0$ for $i = 0, 1, \ldots, m$, we get the curve $\gamma^1(t) = \sum_{i=0}^{m} P_i^1 \, u_i(t)$. Iterating this process we can get a sequence of curves $\{\gamma^k\}_{k=0}^{\infty}$. Then, when $\lim_{k\to\infty} \gamma^k(t_i) = P_i$ for all $i \in \{0, 1, \ldots, n\}$ we say that the initial curve satisfies the *progressive iteration approximation* property.

Given a sequence of points $\{P_{ij}\}_{0\le i\le m}^{0\le j\le n}$, such that the point P_{ij} is assigned to a couple of parameter values (x_i, y_j), for $i = 0, 1, \ldots, m$ and $j = 0, 1, \ldots, n$, and a blending basis $(u_{ij})_{0\le i\le m}^{0\le j\le n}$, we generate a starting surface as $F^0(x, y) = \sum_{i=0}^{m} \sum_{j=0}^{n} P_{ij}^0 \, u_{ij}(x, y)$ where $P_{ij}^0 = P_{ij}$ for $i = 0, 1, \ldots, m$ and $j = 0, 1, \ldots, n$. Then, by calculating the adjusting vector for each control point $\Delta_{ij}^0 = P_{ij} - F^0(x_i, y_j)$, and taking $P_{ij}^1 = P_{ij}^0 + \Delta_{ij}^0$ for $i = 0, 1, \ldots, m$ and $j = 0, 1, \ldots, n$, we get the curve $F^1(x, y) = \sum_{i=0}^{m} \sum_{j=0}^{n} P_{ij}^1 \, u_{ij}(x, y)$. Iterating this process we can get a sequence of surfaces $\{F^k\}_{k=0}^{\infty}$. Then, when $\lim_{k\to\infty} F^k(x_i, y_j) = P_{ij}$ for all $i \in \{0, 1, \ldots, m\}$ and $j \in \{0, 1, \ldots, n\}$, we say that the initial surface satisfies the *progressive iteration approximation* property.

Section 2 provides explicitly an algorithm in pseudo-code of the progressive iteration approximation property of curves and it provides sufficient conditions on the representations for the convergence of the iterative method. In Section 3, analogously to Section 2, we present explicitly an algorithm in pseudo-code of the progressive iteration approximation property of tensor product surfaces and some conditions ensuring the convergence of the method. In Section 4 we compare the convergence rate of the progressive iteration approximation property through different representations. Finally, in Section 5 we present the conclusions of the paper and some open problems related to this technique.

2. Progressive Iteration Approximation of Curves

In [14] it was studied in general under what conditions the curves generated through a blending system $(u_0, \ldots, u_n)$ satisfies the progressive iteration approximation property.

Before of stating this general result we need to define some concepts. The *collocation matrix* of a system of functions $(u_0(t), \ldots, u_n(t))$ at a sequence of ordered points $t_0 < \cdots < t_n$ in $\mathbb{R}$ is given by

$$M \begin{pmatrix} u_0, \ldots, u_n \\ t_0, \ldots, t_m \end{pmatrix} := (u_j(t_i))_{i=0,\ldots,m; j=0,\ldots,n}. \qquad (1)$$

A matrix is *totally positive (TP)* if all its minors are nonnegative and a system of functions is TP when all its collocation matrices (1) are TP. In case of a normalized totally positive (NTP) basis one knows that the curve imitates the shape of its control polygon, due to the variation diminishing properties of TP matrices (see [19]). In fact, shape preserving representations are associated with NTP bases.

Let $(P_i)_{0 \le i \le n}$ be a sequence of control points, $t_0 < t_1 < \cdots < t_n$ a sequence of parameters and $(u_0, \ldots, u_n)$ a blending basis. As we have commented in the previous Section, first we parameterize the control points P_i with the parameters t_i, assigning the parameter t_i to the control point P_i for all $i \in \{0, 1, \ldots, n\}$. Thc progressive iteration approximation method for curves generates the first curve of the following way

$$\gamma^0(t) = \sum_{i=0}^{n} P_i^0 \, u_i(t) \tag{2}$$

with $P_i^0 = P_i$ for all $i \in \{0, 1, \ldots, n\}$. Then, at the step $k \ge 0$ the progressive iteration approximation method computes from the curve γ^{k-1} obtained at the previous step the curve γ^k of the following way

$$\gamma^k(t) = \sum_{i=0}^{n} P_i^k \, u_i(t)$$

with

$$P_i^k = P_i^{k-1} + \Delta_i^{k-1}$$

where

$$\Delta_i^{k-1} = P_i - \gamma^{k-1}(t_i).$$

This process must be repeated as many times as necessary to get a precise enough approximation. An algorithm in pseudo-code can be written in the following way:

Algorithm

Input: $(P_i)_{0 \le i \le n}$, $(u_0, \ldots, u_n)$, $nTol$, $xTol$

For $i = 0 : n$

  $P_i^0 = P_i$

End-For

$\gamma^0(t) = \sum_{i=0}^{n} P_i^0 \, u_i(t)$

$k = 1$

$\gamma^{-1}(t_i) = \infty \; i = 0, 1, \ldots, n$

While $k \le nTol$ and $\max_{0 \le i \le n} \|P_i - \gamma^{k-1}(t_i)\| \ge xTol$

  For $i = 0 : n$

    $\Delta_i^{k-1} = P_i - \gamma^{k-1}(t_i)$

    $P_i^k = P_i^{k-1} + \Delta_i^{k-1}$

  End-For

  $\gamma^k(t) = \sum_{i=0}^{n} P_i^k \, u_i(t)$

  $k = k + 1$

End-While

Output: $\gamma^{k-1}(t)$ and, if $nTol$ is exceeded, a warning message.

Taking into account that $\Delta_i^k = P_i - \gamma^k(t_i)$ for all $i \in \{0, 1, \ldots, n\}$ and that $\gamma^k(t) = \sum_{j=0}^{n} P_j^k u_j(t)$ we have that

$$\Delta_i^k = P_i - \sum_{j=0}^{n} P_j^k u_j(t).$$

Since $P_i^k = P_i^{k-1} + \Delta_i^{k-1}$ for all $i \in \{0, 1, \ldots, n\}$ the previous expression is equivalent to

$$\Delta_i^k = P_i - \sum_{j=0}^{n} (P_j^{k-1} + \Delta_j^{k-1}) u_j(t)$$

and operating in this expression we have that

$$\Delta_i^k = (P_i - \gamma^{k-1}(t_i)) - \sum_{j=0}^{n} \Delta_j^{k-1} u_j(t).$$

Then, from the previous formula, taking into account that $\Delta_i^{k-1} = P_i - \gamma^{k-1}(t_i)$ for $i \in \{0, 1, \ldots, n\}$, we can deduce that

$$\begin{aligned}\Delta_i^k &= \Delta_i^{k-1} - \sum_{j=0}^{n} \Delta_j^{k-1} u_j(t) \\ &= -\sum_{j=0}^{i-1} \Delta_j^{k-1} u_j(t) + (1 - u_i(t_i)) \Delta_i^{k-1} - \sum_{j=i+1}^{n} \Delta_j^{k-1} u_j(t).\end{aligned}$$

So we can express the iterative method in matrix form of the following way

$$(\Delta_0^{k+1}, \Delta_1^{k+1}, \ldots, \Delta_n^{k+1})^T = (I - M)(\Delta_0^k, \Delta_1^k, \ldots, \Delta_n^k) \tag{3}$$

where I is the identity matrix of $n+1$ order,

$$M := M \begin{pmatrix} u_0, \ldots, u_n \\ t_0, \ldots, t_n \end{pmatrix}$$

and the Δ_j^l's are row-vectors. Iterating formula (3) we get

$$(\Delta_0^{k+1}, \Delta_1^{k+1}, \ldots, \Delta_n^{k+1})^T = (I - M)^{k+1}(\Delta_0^0, \Delta_1^0, \ldots, \Delta_n^0).$$

The iterative method converges if and only if $\lim_{k \to \infty} \Delta_i^k = 0$ for all $i \in \{0, 1, \ldots, n\}$. Hence, from the last expression we deduce that the progressive iteration approximation converges if and only if $\rho(I - M) < 1$, where $\rho(B)$ denotes the spectral radius of B. Theorem 2.1 of [14], using that all the eigenvalues of a totally positive matrix are real and positive (see Corollary 6.6 of [1]), gives a sufficient condition in order that the curve (2) satisfies the progressive iteration approximation property.

Theorem 1 *Let $U = (u_0, \ldots, u_n)$ be a blending basis. Then, if the basis U is totally positive and its collocation matrix M at $t_0 < t_1 < \cdots < t_n$ is nonsingular, the curve (2) satisfies the progressive iteration approximation property.*

The following examples of normalized totally positive bases of the space of polynomials satisfy the progressive iteration approximation property.

Examples 2

Let Π_m be the space of polynomials of degree less than or equal to m defined on $[0,1]$. The following bases are normalized totally positive bases of Π_m:

1. *Bernstein basis of degree m, $(b_0^m, \ldots, b_m^m)$, given by $b_i^m(t) = \binom{m}{i} t^i (1-t)^{m-i}$ for all $i \in \{0, 1, \ldots, m\}$.*

2. *The Said-Ball basis of degree m, $(s_0^m(t), \ldots, s_m^m(t))$, $m \geq 1$, $t \in [0,1]$, is defined by:*

$$\begin{aligned} s_i^m(t) &= \binom{\lfloor \frac{m}{2} \rfloor + i}{i} t^i (1-t)^{\lfloor \frac{m}{2} \rfloor + 1}, \qquad 0 \leq i \leq \left\lfloor \frac{m-1}{2} \right\rfloor, \\ s_i^m(t) &= \binom{\lfloor \frac{m}{2} \rfloor + m - i}{m-i} t^{\lfloor \frac{m}{2} \rfloor + 1} (1-t)^{m-i}, \qquad \left\lfloor \frac{m}{2} \right\rfloor + 1 \leq i \leq m, \end{aligned}$$

and, if m is even

$$s_{\frac{m}{2}}^m(t) = \binom{m}{\frac{m}{2}} t^{\frac{m}{2}} (1-t)^{\frac{m}{2}},$$

where $\lfloor r \rfloor$ $(r > 0)$ is the greatest positive integer less than or equal to r. For more details in this basis see [7].

3. *The DP basis of degree m, $(c_0^m(t), \ldots, c_m^m(t))$, $m \geq 2$, is defined by:*

$$\begin{aligned} c_0^m(t) &= (1-t)^m, \\ c_i^m(t) &= t(1-t)^{m-i}, \ 1 \leq i \leq \left\lfloor \frac{m}{2} \right\rfloor - 1, \\ c_i^m(t) &= t^i(1-t), \ \left\lfloor \frac{m+1}{2} \right\rfloor + 1 \leq i \leq m-1, \\ c_m^m(t) &= t^m. \end{aligned}$$

In addition, if m is even,

$$c_{\frac{m}{2}}^m(t) = 1 - t^{\frac{m}{2}+1} - (1-t)^{\frac{m}{2}+1},$$

and, if m is odd,

$$\begin{aligned} c_{\frac{m-1}{2}}^m(t) &= t(1-t)^{\frac{m+1}{2}} + \frac{1}{2}\left[1 - t^{\frac{m+1}{2}} - (1-t)^{\frac{m+1}{2}}\right], \\ c_{\frac{m+1}{2}}^m(t) &= \frac{1}{2}\left[1 - t^{\frac{m+1}{2}} - (1-t)^{\frac{m+1}{2}}\right] + t^{\frac{m+1}{2}}(1-t). \end{aligned}$$

For more details in this basis see [6].

Hence, by Theorem 1 the parametric curves generated by Bernstein, Said-Ball and DP bases satisfy the progressive iteration approximation property.

3. Progressive Iteration Approximation of Surfaces

In this section we present the most important result on the progressive iteration approximation property of tensor product surfaces. Let us recall that, given two matrices $A = (a_{ij})_{1\le i\le m}^{0\le j\le n}$ and $B = (b_{ij})_{1\le i\le p}^{0\le j\le q}$, their Kronecker product is denoted by $A \otimes B$ and is defined to be the block matrix

$$A \otimes B = \begin{pmatrix} a_{11}\, B & \cdots & a_{1n}\, B \\ \vdots & \ddots & \vdots \\ a_{m1}\, B & \cdots & a_{mn}\, B \end{pmatrix},$$

and so $A \otimes B$ is an $(m\,p) \times (n\,q)$ matrix.

Let us consider the particular case of tensor product surfaces. Given a control net $(P_{ij})_{0\le i\le m}^{0\le j\le n}$, the real increasing sequences $x_0 < x_1 < \cdots < x_m$ and $y_0 < y_1 < \cdots < y_n$, two blending bases $(u_0, \ldots, u_m)$ and $(\overline{u}_0, \ldots, \overline{u}_n)$. First, as we have stated in Section 1, we parameterize the control points P_{ij}, assigning the parameter (x_i, y_j) to the control point P_{ij} for all $i \in \{0, 1, \ldots, m\}$ and $j \in \{0, 1, \ldots, n\}$. The progressive iteration approximation method generates the first tensor product surface of the following way

$$F^0(x, y) = \sum_{i=0}^{m} \sum_{j=0}^{n} P_{ij}^0\, u_i(x)\, \overline{u}_j(y) \tag{4}$$

with $P_{ij}^0 = P_{ij}$ for all $i \in \{0, 1, \ldots, m\}$ and $j \in \{0, 1, \ldots, n\}$. Then, at the step $k \ge 0$ the progressive iteration approximation method computes the tensor product surface F^k from the tensor product surface F^{k-1} obtained at the previous step as

$$F^k(x, y) = \sum_{i=0}^{m} \sum_{j=0}^{n} P_{ij}^k\, u_i(x)\, \overline{u}_j(y)$$

with

$$P_{ij}^k = P_{ij}^{k-1} + \Delta_{ij}^{k-1}$$

where

$$\Delta_{ij}^{k-1} = P_{ij} - F^{k-1}(x_i, y_j).$$

As in the curve case, this process must be repeated as many times as necessary to get a precise enough approximation. An algorithm in pseudo-code can be written in the following way:

Algorithm

Input: $(P_{ij})_{0\le i\le m}^{0\le j\le n}$, $(u_0, \ldots, u_m)$, $(\overline{u}_0, \ldots, \overline{u}_n)$, $nTol$, $xTol$

For $i = 0 : m$
    For $j = 0 : n$
        $P_{ij}^0 = P_{ij}$
    End-For
End-For

$F^0(x, y) = \sum_{i=0}^{m} \sum_{j=0}^{n} P_{ij}^0\, u_i(x)\, \overline{u}_j(y)$

$k = 1$

$F^{-1}(x_i, y_j) = \infty \; i = 0, 1, \ldots, m$ and $j = 0, 1, \ldots, n$

While $k \leq nTol$ and $\max_{0\leq i\leq m; 0\leq j\leq n} \|P_{ij} - F^{k-1}(x_i, y_j)\| \geq xTol$

For $i = 0 : m$

For $j = 0 : n$

$\Delta_{ij}^{k-1} = P_{ij} - F^{k-1}(x_i, y_j)$

$P_{ij}^{k} = P_{ij}^{k-1} + \Delta_{ij}^{k-1}$

End-For

End-For

$F^k(x, y) = \sum_{i=0}^{m} \sum_{j=0}^{n} P_{ij}^k \, u_i(x) \, \overline{u}_j(y)$

$k = k + 1$

End-While

Output: $F^{k-1}(x, y)$ and, if $nTol$ is exceeded, a warning message.

Taking into account that $\Delta_{hl}^k = P_{hl}^k - F^k(x_h, y_l)$ for all $h \in \{0, 1, \ldots, m\}$ and $l \in \{0, 1, \ldots, n\}$, and that $F^k(x, y) = \sum_{i=0}^{m} \sum_{j=0}^{n} P_{ij}^k \, u_i(x) \, \overline{u}_j(y)$ we have that

$$\Delta_{hl}^k = P_{hl} - \sum_{i=0}^{m} \sum_{j=0}^{n} P_{ij}^k \, u_i(x) \, \overline{u}_j(y).$$

Since $P_{ij}^k = P_{ij}^{k-1} + \Delta_{ij}^{k-1}$ for all $i \in \{0, 1, \ldots, m\}$ and $j \in \{0, 1, \ldots, n\}$ the previous expression can be written as

$$\Delta_{hl}^k = P_{hl} - \sum_{i=0}^{m} \sum_{j=0}^{n} (P_{ij}^{k-1} + \Delta_{ij}^{k-1}) \, u_i(x) \, \overline{u}_j(y),$$

an operating in this expression we have that

$$\Delta_{hl}^k = (P_{hl} - F^{k-1}(x_h, y_l)) - \sum_{i=0}^{m} \sum_{j=0}^{n} \Delta_{ij}^{k-1} \, u_i(x) \, \overline{u}_j(y).$$

Then, from the previous formula, taking into account that $\Delta_{hl}^{k-1} = P_{hl} - F^{k-1}(x_h, y_l)$ for $h \in \{0, 1, \ldots, m\}$ and $l \in \{0, 1, \ldots, n\}$, we can deduce that

$$\Delta_{hl}^k = \Delta_{hl}^{k-1} - \sum_{i=0}^{m} \sum_{j=0}^{n} \Delta_{ij}^{k-1} \, u_i(x) \, \overline{u}_j(y).$$

Then we can express this iterative method in matrix form of the following way

$$\begin{aligned}&(\Delta_{00}^{k+1}, \Delta_{01}^{k+1}, \ldots, \Delta_{0n}^{k+1}, \Delta_{10}^{k+1}, \ldots, \Delta_{1n}^{k+1}, \ldots, \Delta_{m1}^{k+1}, \ldots, \Delta_{mn}^{k+1})^T \\ &= (I - B) \, (\Delta_{00}^{k}, \Delta_{01}^{k}, \ldots, \Delta_{0n}^{k}, \Delta_{10}^{k}, \ldots, \Delta_{1n}^{k}, \ldots, \Delta_{m1}^{k}, \ldots, \Delta_{mn}^{k})^T\end{aligned}$$

where I is the identity matrix of $(m+1)(n+1)$ order and the matrix B is the Kronecker product of the collocation matrices

$$B_1 = M\begin{pmatrix} u_0, u_1, \ldots, u_m \\ x_0, x_1, \ldots, x_m \end{pmatrix} \quad \text{and} \quad B_2 = M\begin{pmatrix} \overline{u}_0, \overline{u}_1, \ldots, \overline{u}_n \\ y_0, y_1, \ldots, y_n \end{pmatrix}.$$

Taking into account that, if the eigenvalues of a matrix A of order m are $\lambda_1, \ldots, \lambda_m$, and the eigenvalues of a matrix B of order n are $\mu_1, \ldots, \mu_n$, every eigenvalue of the Kronecker product $A \otimes B$ can be expressed as the product of an eigenvalue of A and an eigenvalue of B, $\lambda_i\, \mu_j$, in Theorem 2.2 of [14] sufficient conditions for the convergence of the progressive iteration approximation property for tensor product surfaces have been provided.

Theorem 3 *Let $U = (u_0, \ldots, u_m)$ and $\overline{U} = (\overline{u}_0, \ldots, \overline{u}_n)$ be two blending bases. Then, if the bases U and $\overline{U}$ are totally positive and the collocation matrices of U at $x_0 < x_1 < \cdots < x_m$ and of $\overline{U}$ at $y_0 < y_1 < \cdots < y_n$ are nonsingular, the tensor product surface (4) satisfies the progressive iteration approximation property.*

Examples 4 *By Theorem 3 the parametric surfaces generated through the tensor product of Bernstein, Said-Ball and DP bases introduced in Examples 2 satisfy the progressive iteration approximation property.*

4. Comparison of the Convergence Rates

Let $(u_0, \ldots, u_n)$ be a totally positive basis of a vector space of functions $\mathcal{U}$. Then we say that $(u_0, \ldots, u_n)$ is a B-basis if for any other totally positive basis $(v_0, \ldots, v_n)$ of $\mathcal{U}$ the matrix K of change of basis

$$(v_0, \ldots, v_n) = (u_0, \ldots, u_n)\, K$$

is totally positive. Let us remind that, if a vector space of functions has a totally positive (resp., normalized totally positive) basis then it has a B-basis (resp., normalized B-basis). For a normalized B-basis, the control polygon "exaggerates" the form of the curve and the curve imitates the form of the control polygon. It has been proved that in a vector space of functions with normalized totally positive bases its normalized B-basis has optimal shape preserving properties among all the normalized totally positive bases of the space. In this section we state the optimality of the normalized B-basis with respect to the progressive iteration approximation property.

Let us start comparing the convergence rates of the progressive iteration approximation for curves through different representations. Using some strong results of Linear Algebra (see Section 3 of [8] for more details) Theorem 4 of [8] shows the basis with the fastest convergence rate among all NTP bases of a space of functions.

Theorem 5 *Given a space of functions $\mathcal{U}$ with an NTP basis, the normalized B-basis of $\mathcal{U}$ provides a progressive iteration approximation with the fastest convergence rates among all NTP bases of $\mathcal{U}$.*

The following examples of normalized B-bases satisfy the PIA with the fastest convergence rates.

Examples 6

1. *The Bernstein basis of degree m is the normalized B-basis of Π_m (see [3]). Hence, by Theorem 5 it provides a progressive iteration approximation with the fastest convergence rate among all normalized totally positive bases of Π_m.*

2. *The space of trigonometric polynomials span$\{1, \cos t, \ldots, \cos mt\}$ on $[0, \pi]$ has normalized B-basis (see [18]), which provides a progressive iteration approximation with the fastest convergence rate among all normalized totally positive bases of that space.*

3. *The space span$\{\sin kt, \cos kt\}_{k=0}^{p}$ on $[-\Delta, \Delta]$ where $\Delta \in (0, \pi/2)$ has normalized B-basis (see [21]), which provides a progressive iteration approximation with the fastest convergence rate among all normalized totally positive bases of that space.*

4. *The spaces span$\{1, t, \sin t, \cos t\}$ and span$\{1, t, t^2, \cos t, \sin t\}$ on $[0, \alpha]$ where $\alpha \in (0, 2\pi)$ have normalized B-bases (see [16]), which provide a progressive iteration approximation with the fastest convergence rate among all normalized totally positive bases of the corresponding spaces.*

For the case of surfaces in Corollary 6 of [8] it was used that the $m\,n$ eigenvalues of the Kronecker product of an $m \times m$ matrix and an $n \times n$ matrix are given by the $m\,n$ products of an eigenvalue of one matrix by an eigenvalue of the other matrix in order to prove the following result.

Theorem 7 *Given two spaces of functions $\mathcal{U}$ and $\mathcal{V}$ with NTP bases, the tensor product of the normalized B-bases of $\mathcal{U}$ and $\mathcal{V}$ provides a progressive iteration approximation with the fastest convergence rates among all bases which are tensor product of NTP bases of $\mathcal{U}$ and $\mathcal{V}$.*

Examples 8 *By Theorem 7 the bases formed by the tensor product of the normalized B-bases mentioned in Examples 6 provides a progressive iteration approximation with the fastest convergence rates among all bases which are tensor product of NTP bases of the corresponding spaces.*

5. Conclusions

This paper has analyzed the progressive iteration approximation property of curves and surfaces, showing its interest and applications. The bases associated to shape preserving representations of curves and tensor product surfaces always satisfy this property. Moreover, the bases with optimal shape preserving properties in CAGD are always the bases with the fastest convergence rates of the progressive iteration approximation property of the corresponding space of functions. Let us mention an open problem in this field: for a given dimension, which space of functions provides a basis with the fastest convergence rate?

References

[1] T. Ando (1987), Totally Positive Matrices, *Linear Algebra and its Applications* **90**, 165-219.

[2] C. de Boor (1979), How does Agee's method work?, Proceedings of the 1979 *Army Numerical Analysis and Computers Conference*, ARO Report 79-3, Army Research Office, 299-302.

[3] J. M. Carnicer and J. M. Peña (1993), Shape preserving representations and optimality of the Bernstein basis, *Advances in Computational Mathematics* **1**, 173-196.

[4] J. M. Carnicer and J. M. Peña (1994), Totally positive bases for shape preserving curve design and optimality of B-splines, *Computer Aided Geometric Design* **11**, 633-654.

[5] N. Dejdumrong and H. N. Phien (2000), Efficient algorithms for Bezier curves, *Comput. Aided Geom. Design* **17**, 247-250.

[6] J. Delgado and J. M. Peña (2003), A shape preserving representation with an evaluation algorithm of linear complexity, *Comput. Aided Geom. Design* **20**, 1-10.

[7] J. Delgado and J. M. Peña (2006), On the generalized Ball bases, *Advances in Computational Mathematics* **24**, 263-280.

[8] J. Delgado and J. M. Peña (2007), Progressive iterative approximation and bases with the fastest convergence rates, *Comput. Aided Geom. Design* **24**, 10-18.

[9] M. S. Floater (1998), *How to Approximate Scattered Data by Least Squares*, SINTEF Report No. STF42 A98013, Oslo.

[10] T. N. T. Goodman (1989), Shape preserving representations. In: *Mathematical methods in CAGD*, T. Lyche, L. L. Schumaker, eds., Academic Press, Boston, pp 333-351.

[11] T. N. T. Goodman and H. B. Said (1991), Shape preserving properties of the generalised Ball basis, *Comput. Aided Geom. Design* **8**, 115-121.

[12] R. A. Horn and C. R. Johnson (1994), *Topics in matrix analysis*, Cambridge University Press.

[13] A. Iske (2002), *Scattered Data Modelling Using Radial Basis Functions*, in **Tutorials on multiresolution in geometric modelling**, A. Iske, E. Quak, and M. S. Floater (eds.), Springer-Verlag, Heidelberg, 205-242.

[14] H. Lin, H. Bao and G. Wang (2005), Totally positive bases and progressive iteration approximation, *Computer & Mathematics with Applications* **50**, 575-586.

[15] H. Lin, G. Wang and C. Dong (2003), Constructing iterative non-uniform B-spline curve and surface to fit data points (in Chinese), *Science in China (Series E)* **33**, 912-923.

[16] E. Mainar, J. M. Peña and J. Sánchez-Reyes (2001), Shape preserving alternatives to the rational Bézier model. *Comput. Aided Geom. Design* **18**, 37-60.

[17] H. Minc (1988), *Nonnegative matrices*, Wiley Interscience, New York.

[18] J. M. Peña (1997) Shape preserving representations for trigonometric polynomial curves, *Comput. Aided Geom. Design* **14**, 5-11.

[19] J. M. Peña (1999), *Shape preserving representations in Computer Aided-Geometric Design*, Nova Science Publishers, Inc.

[20] D. Qi, Z. Tian, Y. Zhang and J. B. Zheng (1975), The method of numeric polish in curve fitting (in Chinese), *Acta Mathematica Sinica* **18**, 173-184.

[21] J. Sánchez-Reyes (1998), Harmonic rational Bézier curves, p-B-ezier curves and trigonometric polynomials, *Comput. Aided Geom. Design* **15**, 909-923.

[22] B. Stephen (1979), *Matrix methods for engineers and scientists*, McGraw-Hill, Berkshire, UK.

In: Computer-Aided Design...
Editors: C.M. De Smet et al, pp. 427-486
ISBN 978-1-60456-860-8

Short Communication B

EMERGENT COMPUTATIONAL PARADIGMS: HOW QUANTUM MECHANICS SHAPES THE FUTURE OF INFORMATION PROCESSING

*Marius Nagy**
School of Computing, Queen's University
Kingston, Ontario K7L 3N6, Canada

Abstract

The weird quantum mechanical effects governing the behavior of sub-atomic particles are about to revolutionize the way we perform computation and manipulate information. Genuine quantum mechanical features, like superposition of states, entanglement and interference, can be harnessed in order to speed up computation or enhance the security of data communications. But the fundamental ability of a quantum computer to process information at a deeper physical level than a conventional computer is able to, allows the former to tackle a much broader palette of information processing tasks, thus establishing its superiority in terms of computational power. Specifically, we uncover a class of information processing tasks (based on the problem of distinguishing among entangled quantum states) whose members are readily carried out by a quantum computer, yet are impossible to perform on any classical machine (whether deterministic or probabilistic).

We also demonstrate the importance of parallelism for the emerging field of quantum computation and quantum information by providing two examples of tasks for which a parallel approach can make the difference between success and failure. In the first case, we analyze the quantum distinguishability problem restricted to direct quantum measurements and show that the failure of a sequential approach accounts for the impossibility of constructing a Universal Computer. The second example deals with a practical instance of the rank-varying computational complexity paradigm, identified in the procedure for computing the quantum Fourier transform. We show that under the constraints imposed by quantum decoherence, only a parallel approach can guarantee a reliable solution or, alternatively, improve scalability.

The quantum Fourier transform is a very powerful tool, allowing for the design of fast quantum algorithms. We show herein that the quantum Fourier transform and its

*E-mail address: marius@cs.queensu.ca

inverse can also be successfully used to build quantum key distribution protocols that offer improved eavesdropping detection rates due to an innovative disruption amplification process.

1. Introduction

The computations carried out today are qualitatively different from those performed more than half a century ago, when the age of computers was only just beginning. The traditional concept of computation is best captured by the functioning of the Turing machine. A sequence of operations (or transformations) forming the *algorithm* is applied to a set of *input* data to produce an *output* (or result).

In time, this rather simplistic view on computation has been challenged by increasingly demanding applications and real-world problems. We need better solutions, faster, to problems whose input specifications may vary with time. Often, our results need to be obtained before certain deadlines, or else various penalties can be applied.

The quest to make computation more efficient and meet today's requirements has led to the development of entirely new computational paradigms. These are based on revolutionary principles like the laws of quantum mechanics, the Watson-Crick complementarity of the building blocks forming DNA strands, the dynamics of complex chemical reactions or the structure of a living cell.

Quantum computation and quantum information can be defined as the study of information processing tasks accomplished using quantum mechanical systems. It could rise to meet the expectations of enthusiasts of the field, causing computer science to be reconsidered (and effectively rewritten) in the new *quantum* light. In such a case, quantum computers and practical applications of quantum information theory will substantially impact our everyday life.

The theory of quantum computation is already well-developed and a great deal of effort is put nowadays into filling the gap between theory and practical implementations of quantum computing devices. Quantum computation harnesses the quantum mechanical principles of *superposition* and *interference* in order to achieve a potential exponential speed-up over classical algorithms. And if building a practical quantum computer still proves out of reach in the near future, quantum cryptography definitely looks as the most promising practical application of quantum information theory, at least in the short term. The *uncertainty principle*, the *no-cloning* theorem and the genuine quantum mechanical resource of *entanglement* can be exploited to exchange secret keys securely over public channels. The unbreakability of quantum key distribution schemes seems to be guaranteed by the very laws of physics, unlike the public-key systems in use today, whose security rests on unproven assumptions about the presumptive intractability of some problems on a classical computer.

Throughout this chapter we will investigate how the unique features of quantum mechanics are pushing the classical limits of function computability and data security, while highlighting the importance of parallelism for the emerging quantum technology. The context of our discussion is established in section 3, where we analyze the relation between the quantum and the classical models of computation with respect to their information processing power. The characteristics of the physical level at which a device registers and processes information are ultimately responsible for its computational power. We show that there are problems involving purely quantum mechanical features for which only a machine operating in accord with quantum mechanics is naturally suited. A new class of information processing tasks is thus uncovered whose members are readily carried out by a quantum computer, yet are impossible to perform on any classical machine (whether deterministic or probabilistic).

Sections 4 and 5 demonstrate that the concept of *parallelism* transcends the boundaries between computational paradigms, being also applicable to unconventional models of computation, like quantum computing. In section 4 we study the implications of parallelism for quantum measurements and show that a parallel approach can make the difference between success and failure when trying to distinguish among (entangled) quantum states. An interesting consequence of this fact is the impossibility of constructing a Universal Computer. Section 5 presents the benefits of using a parallel architecture when computing the quantum Fourier transform or its inverse in the critical context of avoiding the undesired effects caused by *quantum decoherence*.

The quantum Fourier transform is traditionally used to design quantum algorithms that are exponentially faster than their best classical counterparts, as in the case of Shor's quantum algorithms for factoring integers and computing discrete logarithms [65]. In section 6 we show that the quantum Fourier transform and its inverse can also be successfully used to build quantum key distribution protocols that offer improved eavesdropping detection rates while maximizing the eavesdropper's uncertainty over the binary sequence transmitted. Employing the quantum Fourier transform in a key distribution protocol allows the detection of a possible eavesdropper even when the qubit tested was not directly tampered with. This is a unique feature, not present in any of the previous quantum key distribution protocols. A summary of the topics addressed in this chapter together with some conclusions regarding the results obtained bring our exploration into quantum information and computation to an end in section 7.

But first, in order to familiarize the reader with the concepts manipulated throughout this chapter, we begin by introducing the basic elements of quantum computation and quantum information to the extent needed for a clear exposition of the main ideas presented hereafter. For a more detailed overview of the field we refer the unfamiliar reader to what we consider a few good introductions to quantum information and computation [57, 46, 61, 48, 18, 51, 41]. For those acquainted with the quantum paradigm, section 2 can be skipped altogether.

2. Fundamentals of Quantum Computation and Quantum Information

The field of quantum information and quantum computation is based on the postulates governing quantum mechanics. The aim of this section is to provide a basic description of these postulates and the mathematical formalisms required to work with them from a computational point of view.

Quantum mechanics takes place in the framework provided by linear algebra. We can associate to any isolated physical system a complex vector space with an inner product defined on it, known as the state space of the system. Mathematically, such a vector space with an inner product is called a Hilbert space. At any given point in time, the system is completely described by its state vector, which must be a unit vector in the system's state space.

Quantum state spaces and the transformations acting on them are traditionally described in terms of vectors and matrices using the compact *bra/ket* notation introduced by Dirac [32]. According to his conventional notation, *kets* like $|x\rangle$ are simply column vectors, typically used to describe quantum states. Similarly, the matching *bra* $\langle x|$ is a row vector denoting the conjugate transpose of $|x\rangle$.

2.1. The Qubit

At an abstract level, the simplest quantum mechanical system is the quantum bit, or *qubit*. A qubit is a unit vector in a two-dimensional state space, for which a particular orthonormal basis, denoted by $\{|0\rangle, |1\rangle\}$ has been fixed. The two basis vectors $|0\rangle$ and $|1\rangle$ correspond to the possible values a classical bit can take. However, unlike classical bits, a qubit can also take many other values. In general, an arbitrary qubit $|\Psi\rangle$ can be written as a linear combination of the computational basis states:

$$|\Psi\rangle = \alpha|0\rangle + \beta|1\rangle, \tag{1}$$

where α and β are complex numbers such that $|\alpha|^2 + |\beta|^2 = 1$. This is the fundamental difference distinguishing quantum bits from classical ones and is a direct application of the quantum principle of superposition of states. The qubit $|\Psi\rangle$ in equation (1) is in a superposition of $|0\rangle$ and $|1\rangle$, a state in which it is not possible to say that the qubit is definitely in the state $|0\rangle$, or definitely in the state $|1\rangle$. After all, what better intuition about the superposition principle than the idea (quite old and widely accepted now) that each particle is also a wave.

For a single qubit, there is a very intuitive graphical representation of its state as a point on the unit three-dimensional sphere (also called the *Bloch sphere*). Figure 1 depicts four possible states of a qubit using the Bloch sphere representation. Note that the states corresponding to the points on the equatorial circle have all equal contributions of 0-ness and 1-ness. What distinguishes them is the *phase*. For example, the two states displayed above, $1/\sqrt{2}(|0\rangle + |1\rangle)$ and $1/\sqrt{2}(|0\rangle - |1\rangle)$ are the same up to a relative phase shift of π, because the $|0\rangle$ amplitudes are identical and the $|1\rangle$ amplitudes differ only by a relative phase factor of $e^{i\pi} = -1$.

We have described qubits as mathematical objects, but there are real physical systems which may be described in terms of qubits. Possible physical realizations of a qubit include two different polarizations of a photon, the alignment of a nuclear spin in a uniform magnetic field or two electronic levels in an atom.

2.2. Measurements

We now turn our attention on the amount of information that can be stored in a qubit and, respectively, retrieved from a qubit. Since any point on the Bloch sphere can be characterized by a pair of real-valued parameters taking continuous values, it follows that, theoretically, a qubit could hold an infinite amount of information. However, we cannot extract more

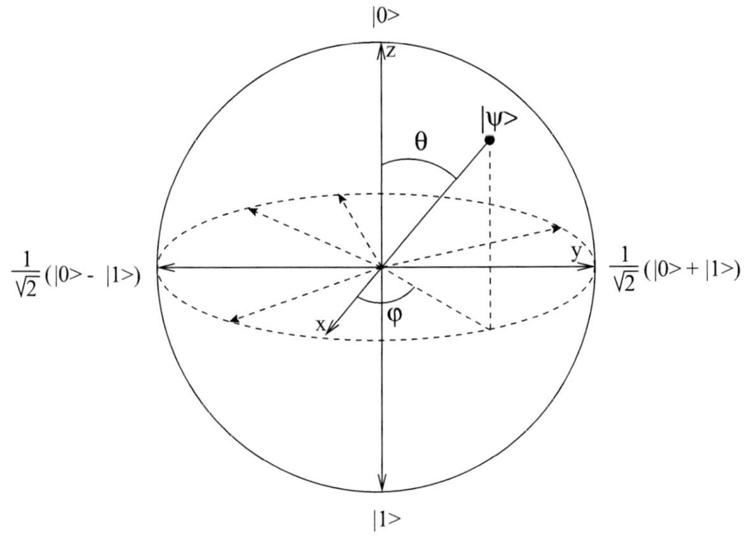

Figure 1. The Bloch sphere representation of a qubit.

information from such a qubit than we are able to do it from a classical bit. The reason is that we have to *measure* the qubit in order to determine which state it is in. And another of the fundamental postulates of quantum mechanics, the one regarding measurements, restricts us in the amount of information that can be gained about a quantum state through measurement. According to this postulate, when we measure a qubit $|\Psi\rangle = \alpha|0\rangle + \beta|1\rangle$ with respect to the standard basis for quantum computation $\{|0\rangle, |1\rangle\}$, we get either the result 0 with probability $|\alpha|^2$, or the result 1 with probability $|\beta|^2$. The condition that the probabilities must sum to one corresponds geometrically to the requirement that the qubit state be normalized to length 1, that is the inner product $\langle\Psi|\Psi\rangle$ equals 1.

Furthermore, measurement alters the state of a qubit, collapsing it from its superposition of $|0\rangle$ and $|1\rangle$ to the specific state consistent with the measurement result. For example, if we observe $|\Psi\rangle$ to be in state $|0\rangle$ through measurement, then the post-measurement state of the qubit will be $|0\rangle$, and any subsequent measurements (in the same basis) will yield 0 with probability 1. In general, measurement of a state transforms the state into one of the measuring device's associated basis vectors. The probability that the state is measured as basis vector $|u\rangle$ is the square of the norm of the amplitude of the component of the original state in the direction of the basis vector $|u\rangle$.

2.3. Uncertainty Principle

As noted by Julian Brown (in [21] page 120), Berthiaume and Brassard connect Heisenberg's uncertainty principle with the idea that any measurement yielding information in the classical form induces an irrevocable destruction of some remaining information, making further measurements less informative, if not completely useless [19]. Our objection to this point of view is that while it is perfectly true that, in general, measurement disturbs the quantum state of the observed system, this is not what Heisenberg's uncertainty principle is trying to quantify. Heisenberg showed that it is not possible, according to quantum mechanics, to simultaneously know both the position and momentum of a particle with arbitrary accuracy. Position and momentum form a pair of canonically conjugate quantum variables and the more we know about one of them, the more we are restricted in the precision with which the other one can be measured.

Later, Heisenberg's uncertainty principle was generalized to any two quantities corresponding to non-commuting operators [63]. An equivalent formulation of this general uncertainty relation is developed in [57] based on expressing projective measurement and standard deviations in terms of observables. Of course, there are many other pairs of conjugate variables (beside position and momentum), and we only mention here energy and time (who actually needs a special treatment, as given in [66]), horizontal and vertical polarizations or right-handed and left-handed circular polarizations. It is also important to stress that uncertainty relations of any kind do not express the incapacity of the measurement device to provide accurate observations of the variables, due to their imperfections. These relations are mathematical results derived from the principles governing quantum mechanics and therefore hold regardless of the performances of the measuring devices used.

2.4. No-clonability

Naturally, measurements in bases other than the computational basis are always possible, but this will not help us in determining α and β from a single measurement. One might think of solving this problem by making multiple copies of the initial qubit $|\Psi\rangle$ and then measuring each of the copies in order to obtain an estimation of α and β. In fact, it turns out to be impossible to make a copy of an unknown quantum state. The *no-cloning* theorem, one of the earliest results of quantum computation and quantum information [72], states that quantum mechanics prevents us from building a quantum cloning device capable of copying non-orthogonal quantum states. The ability to clone orthogonal quantum states translates into the ability to copy classical information, since the different states of classical information can be thought of merely as orthogonal quantum states. So it seems that quantum mechanics places severe limitations on the accessibility of quantum information, but sometimes this can be used to our advantage, as we will see in the case of quantum cryptography.

2.5. Quantum Registers

Let us examine now more complex quantum systems, composed of multiple qubits. In classical physics, individual two-dimensional state spaces of n particles combine through the Cartesian product to form a vector space of $2n$ dimensions, representing the state space of the ensemble of n particles. However, this is not how a quantum system can be described in terms of its components. Quantum states combine through the tensor product to give a resulting state space of 2^n dimensions, for a system of n qubits. It is this exponential growth of the state space with the number of particles that quantum computers try to exploit in their attempt to achieve exponential speed-up of computation over classical computers.

For a system of two qubits, each with basis $\{|0\rangle, |1\rangle\}$, the resulting state space is the set of normalized vectors in the four dimensional space spanned by basis vectors $\{|0\rangle \otimes |0\rangle, |0\rangle \otimes |1\rangle, |1\rangle \otimes |0\rangle, |1\rangle \otimes |1\rangle\}$, where $|x\rangle \otimes |y\rangle$ denotes the tensor product between column vectors $|x\rangle$ and $|y\rangle$. It is customary to write the basis in the more compact notation $\{|00\rangle, |01\rangle, |10\rangle, |11\rangle\}$. This generalizes in the obvious way to an n-qubit system with 2^n basis vectors.

2.6. Entanglement

Similar to single qubits, multiple-qubit systems can also be in a superposition state. The vector

$$|\Psi\rangle = \frac{1}{2}(|00\rangle + |01\rangle + |10\rangle + |11\rangle) \tag{2}$$

describes a superposition state of a two-qubit system in which all four components (corresponding to the four basis vectors) have equal amplitudes. What about the two qubits composing the system? Can we characterize their states individually? If we rewrite equation (2) in order to express $|\Psi\rangle$ as the tensor product

$$|\Psi\rangle = (\frac{1}{\sqrt{2}}|0\rangle + \frac{1}{\sqrt{2}}|1\rangle) \otimes (\frac{1}{\sqrt{2}}|0\rangle + \frac{1}{\sqrt{2}}|1\rangle) \tag{3}$$

then we can legitimately assert that each of the component qubits is also in a superposition state, perfectly balanced between $|0\rangle$ and $|1\rangle$. Now let us drop the two middle terms in equation (2) and consider the superposition state described by

$$|\Phi\rangle = \frac{1}{\sqrt{2}}|00\rangle + \frac{1}{\sqrt{2}}|11\rangle \tag{4}$$

In this case it is no longer possible to find complex numbers α, β, γ and δ such that

$$(\alpha|0\rangle + \beta|1\rangle) \otimes (\gamma|0\rangle + \delta|1\rangle) = \frac{1}{\sqrt{2}}|00\rangle + \frac{1}{\sqrt{2}}|11\rangle \tag{5}$$

The state of the system cannot be decomposed into a product of the states of the constituents. Even though the state of the system is well defined (through the state vector $|\Phi\rangle$), neither of the two component qubits is in a well-defined state. This is again in contrast to classical systems, whose states can always be broken down into the individual states of their components. Furthermore, if we try to measure the two qubits, the superposition will collapse into one of the two basis vectors contributing to the superposition and the outcomes of the two measurements will always coincide. In other words, if one of the qubits is found to be in state $|0\rangle$, then the second one will necessarily be in the same state, while a state $|1\rangle$ assumed after measurement will be shared by both qubits. Therefore, we say that the two qubits are entangled and $|\Phi\rangle$ describes an entangled state of the system.

Entanglement defines the strong correlations exhibited by two or more particles when they are measured and which cannot be explained by classical means. This does not imply that entangled particles will always be observed in the same state, as entangled states like

$$\frac{1}{\sqrt{2}}|01\rangle \pm \frac{1}{\sqrt{2}}|10\rangle \tag{6}$$

prove it. States like these or the one in equation (4) are known as Bell states or EPR pairs after some of the people who pointed out their strange properties [9, 34].

In some sense, we can say that superposition encompasses entanglement, since entanglement can be viewed as a special case of superposition. It is also interesting to make an analogy between entanglement and the concept of primality from number theory. Indeed, an entangled state of the system corresponds to a prime number, since it cannot be factored or decomposed as a product of subsystem states.

2.6.1. Entanglement as a Physical Resource

Today, entanglement is no longer regarded as merely a quantum curiosity. It has become the essential feature of quantum mechanics and people are seeing it as a *physical resource* that can be spent in order to solve information-processing tasks in new ways. Some researchers have even begun to quantify entanglement by introducing a standard unit of entanglement in the form of a maximally entangled pair, which is said to carry one *e-bit* of entanglement [56]. By contrast, incompletely entangled pairs carry less than one *e-bit*. They developed ways to weigh entanglement using entanglement distillation and dilution.

Therefore, the question whether this "resource" really exists in Nature and can be exploited in the ways we currently believe it can, is of crucial importance for the future of quantum computation and quantum information. Superdense coding, teleporting a quantum state or finding the prime factors of a composite integer in polynomial time on a quantum computer are only a few of the most important applications of entanglement. The current potential with which quantum computation and quantum information are credited will certainly be affected if some day entanglement is disproved.

2.7. Quantum Evolution

Let us assume for now that we can harness entanglement to increase the efficiency of computation and information-processing tasks in general. What are the "circuits" composing a hypothetical quantum computer? The answer to this question is in strong relation with the way an isolated quantum system evolves over time. We already saw what happens when we try to measure such a quantum system. If, for example, we are trying to read the content of a quantum memory register, the system will undergo a sudden, unpredictable jump into one of the classical bit string configurations composing the original superposition. In other words, there will be a discontinuity in the evolution of the quantum memory register. But, if we leave the register unobserved, the system will undergo a smooth, continuous evolution governed by Schrödinger's equation, a deterministic differential equation which enables us to predict the future or uncover the past evolution of the memory register. Consequently, any quantum computation is reversible and therefore quantum gates (the quantum analog of classical gates) must always have as many outputs as they have inputs, in order to avoid any loss of information that would prevent the computation from being undone.

2.8. Quantum Gates

A quantum NOT gate acting on a single qubit will evolve the initial state $\alpha|0\rangle + \beta|1\rangle$ into the final state $\alpha|1\rangle+\beta|0\rangle$, in which the roles of $|0\rangle$ and $|1\rangle$ have been interchanged. Because every quantum gate acts linearly, the transformation is fully specified by its effect on the

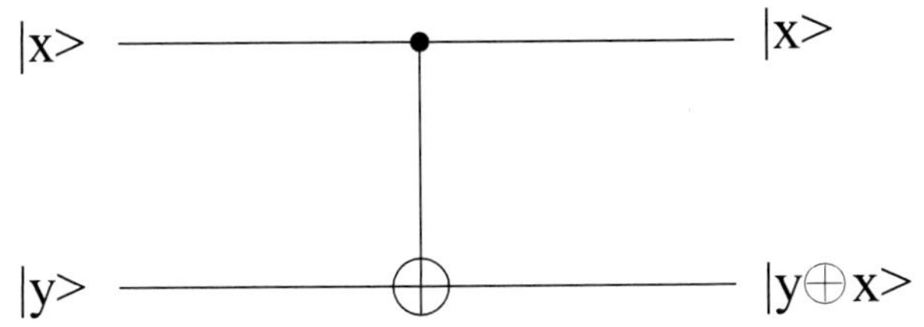

Figure 2. Controlled-NOT quantum gate.

basis vectors. Hence, there is a very convenient representation of a quantum gate in matrix form. The matrix X representing the quantum NOT gate is then defined as follows:

$$X = \begin{bmatrix} 0 & 1 \\ 1 & 0 \end{bmatrix}.$$

The first column represents the effect of applying the NOT gate to state $|0\rangle$, while the second column is the result of applying the NOT gate to state $|1\rangle$. We can now describe the operation of the quantum NOT gate, acting on an arbitrary qubit state, through the following equation:

$$X \cdot \begin{bmatrix} \alpha \\ \beta \end{bmatrix} = \begin{bmatrix} \beta \\ \alpha \end{bmatrix}.$$

Other examples of single qubit gates are the Z gate:

$$Z = \begin{bmatrix} 1 & 0 \\ 0 & -1 \end{bmatrix},$$

which leaves $|0\rangle$ unchanged, but introduces a phase shift by flipping the sign of $|1\rangle$, and the Hadamard gate:

$$H = \frac{1}{\sqrt{2}} \begin{bmatrix} 1 & 1 \\ 1 & -1 \end{bmatrix},$$

which is one of the most useful quantum gates, because it creates superpositions of $|0\rangle$ and $|1\rangle$.

Although there are an infinite number of single qubit gates, not any two by two matrix is a legitimate representation of a quantum gate. Schrödinger's equation states that the dynamics of a quantum system must take states to states in a way that preserves orthogonality. In other words, the normalization condition $|\alpha|^2 + |\beta|^2 = 1$ for the initial state $\alpha|0\rangle + \beta|1\rangle$ must also be true for the quantum state after the gate has acted. This translates into the requirement that the matrix U describing the single qubit gate be *unitary*, that is $U^* \cdot U = I$, where U^* is the conjugate transpose of U. Single qubit gates can be conveniently visualized as rotations of the arrow representing the qubit state on the surface of the Bloch sphere.

Quantum gates on multiple qubits can also be defined. Figure 2 depicts a controlled-NOT gate, an instance of the more abstract controlled-U gate, where $U = X$. The target bit $|y\rangle$ is flipped if and only if the control bit $|x\rangle$ is set to 1.

Multiple qubit gates must also satisfy the requirement that probability be conserved, so they too must be unitary transformations. Since any unitary matrix is invertible and the inverse is also a unitary matrix, it follows that a quantum gate can always be inverted by another quantum gate. The set of all 1-qubit rotations (gates) together with the controlled-NOT gate is universal for quantum computation. But finite universal sets of gates exist as well. Two researchers working independently have shown that any imaginable quantum computation can be performed by connecting together multiple copies of a certain 2-qubit gate [7, 33]. Such universal quantum gates are similar to the NAND gate in classical computation.

This radical departure from the classical ways of treating information and the potential of the quantum model to significantly increase computational efficiency have raised questions about the computational power of a quantum machine relative to a conventional one. Is a quantum computer strictly more powerful than a classical one? Are there information processing tasks for which only a machine based on quantum mechanical principles is naturally suited? What are the limitations when trying to simulate a quantum process on a classical computer?

These questions have concerned researchers in quantum computation and quantum information theory ever since the field originated. Despite the impressive advancements made in the quantum computation and quantum information areas, the fundamental question about the relative power of a quantum computer with respect to its classical counterpart is still not fully answered. Perhaps this is partly due to the multitude of contexts (or paradigms) in which such a question might be asked. Consequently, there may not be a single answer. In the next section, we analyze the relation between the quantum and the classical models of computation from the broad perspective offered by quantum mechanics.

3. Beyond the Limits of Conventional Computation

We begin by reviewing and making explicit some of the contexts in which the comparison between the classical and the quantum computer took place. This will help emphasize the variety of angles under which the problem can be attacked and also put our approach into perspective.

The first step towards an analytical investigation of the computational power specific to a quantum mechanical device was the elaboration of a model that should be abstracted away from any particular physical realization. The breakthrough came when David Deutsch described the operation of a universal quantum computer $\mathcal{Q}$, a model of computation inspired by the classical Turing machine, but whose functioning obeys the principles of quantum mechanics. Even in this early paper [29], several features are identified with respect to which the Quantum Turing Machine is superior to any classical device.

3.1. True Randomness

The first example given is the generation of *true* random numbers. In particular, valid programs are shown to exist for $\mathcal{Q}$ that deal with arbitrary irrational probabilities, a feature that the universal Turing machine $\mathcal{T}$ could not truly match. It could only simulate such discrete finite stochastic systems with arbitrary accuracy, provided it has access to a "random oracle", which really cannot be implemented by classical means.

3.2. Entanglement

But the property of $\mathcal{Q}$ that cannot be even approximately simulated by any classical system is the generation of *entangled* (or *non-separable*) states like

$$\frac{1}{\sqrt{2}}(|0\rangle|0\rangle + |1\rangle|1\rangle). \tag{7}$$

The strong correlations exhibited by the two qubits composing state (7) are only characteristic to the quantum resource known as *entanglement*, and they are simply beyond the scope of any classical Turing machine. Bell's theorem [9] is a mathematical formulation of the fact that no classical system can reproduce the statistical results obtained by measuring these two qubits.

3.3. Quantum Speed-up

As another argument intended to prove the superior computational power of the Quantum Turing Machine, Deutsch provides an example which demonstrates how *quantum parallelism* can be used to speed up computation. Quantum parallelism refers to the capability of a quantum computer to evaluate a function $f(x)$ for exponentially many different values of x in the time it takes a classical computer to evaluate the function for just one value. This is possible due to the quantum mechanical principle of the *superposition* of states. Deutsch exploited this feature and devised an example in which quantum parallelism augmented with *interference* can "beat" a classical computer. Thus, given a function $f : \{0, 1\} \rightarrow \{0, 1\}$, he presented a quantum algorithm able to compute $f(0) \oplus f(1)$ in a single evaluation of the function f.

Later, Deutsch's algorithm was generalized by Deutsch and Jozsa [31], who addressed the n-bit case by allowing the domain of f to be the set of all integers in the interval $[0, 2^n - 1]$. In just one evaluation of the function f, the Deutsch-Jozsa algorithm is able to determine whether f is constant or perfectly balanced (the latter property meaning that f maps exactly half of the input values in the domain to the image 0, and the other half to 1). Although the problem seems somewhat contrived, with no immediate practical applications, this was the first example in which the quantum computer achieved an exponential speed-up over the classical one (note that a classical Turing machine needs an exponential number of evaluations of f in order to make the decision between constant and perfectly balanced).

The same superiority of the quantum computer was proved by Shor's factorization algorithm [65], only this time for a problem of huge practical importance. Factoring large integers and computing discrete logarithms in quantum polynomial time threatens the security of a large class of public-key cryptographic systems in use today. For a classical computer these tasks remain intractable, despite remarkable advances that could only bring their running time to a sub-exponential level [43]. So, in the context of essentially speeding up the computation for some problems, we can affirm that a quantum computer is definitely more powerful than a classical one. However, we should keep in mind that these problems can also be solved by the universal Turing Machine, given enough time (even if this time is more than the age of the Universe).

3.4. Quantum Simulations

Another class of tasks at which quantum computers could naturally outperform any classical machine is simulating quantum mechanical systems occurring in Nature. As the size (number of constituents) of a quantum system increases, the number of variables required to describe the state of the system grows exponentially. So, in order to store the quantum state of a system with n distinct components, a classical computer would need some c^n bits of memory, with the constant c depending upon the system being simulated and the desired accuracy of the simulation. Furthermore, calculating its evolution over time would require the manipulation of a huge matrix, involving $c^n \times c^n$ bits. As Feynman noted in 1982 [36], this is prohibitively inefficient for a simulator observing the laws of classical physics. On the other hand, a machine that worked by quantum means would intrinsically make a much more efficient simulator, requiring only a linear number of qubits.

Following the same logic, it is not difficult to envisage a classical Turing machine that simulates an arbitrary quantum circuit, if one does not care about efficiency. The simulation in [10] requires space, and therefore time, exponential in the number of qubits in the quantum circuit. Bernstein and Vazirani [17] have given a simulation that takes polynomial space, but exponential time. The lack of an efficient classical simulation of a quantum computer induced the idea that a quantum computing machine may be inherently faster and therefore strictly more powerful. However, any computation a quantum computer can perform, by applying a series of unitary evolutions to its quantum register, can be replicated (even if highly inefficiently) by a Deterministic Turing Machine (DTM). Similarly, a Probabilistic Turing Machine (PTM) can simulate the inherent probabilistic nature of a quantum measurement operation.

3.5. QTM versus DTM and PTM

The contest between the quantum and the classical computer can also be judged from these two points of view: comparing the Quantum Turing Machine (QTM) with a DTM or a PTM. The Deutsch-Jozsa algorithm, for instance, achieves an impressive speed-up over a DTM, but the problem is also easy for a PTM, which can solve it very quickly with high probability.

The first hint that QTMs might be more powerful than PTMs was given by Bernstein and Vazirani, who showed how to sample from the Fourier spectrum of any Boolean function on n bits in polynomial time on a QTM [17]. No algorithm was known to replicate this result on a PTM. Then, Berthiaume and Brassard were able to construct an oracle, relative to which a decision problem exists that could be solved with certainty in polynomial time in the worst case on a quantum computer, but could not be solved classically in probabilistic expected polynomial time, if errors were not tolerated [19]. In the same paper, they also show that there is a decision problem solvable in exponential time on a QTM and in double exponential time on all but finitely many instances on any DTM. These two results, besides being a victory of quantum computers over classical machines (deterministic or probabilistic) also prove that the power of quantum computation cannot simply be ascribed to the indeterminism inherent in quantum theory.

3.6. Quantum vs. Classical Complexity

The great hope for quantum computers at the inception of the quantum paradigm of computation was that they would be able to make NP-complete problems tractable. Relative to this criterion, we still don't know whether a quantum machine is more powerful than a classical one, in spite of Shor's results concerning factorization and computing discrete logarithms. The trouble is that neither of these two problems is known to be *NP*-complete, despite the general belief that they are not in *P*. Furthermore, the current belief is that a quadratic improvement in the running time may be the best we can get out of a quantum computer in these kinds of tasks [64].

The relative power of quantum computers with respect to classical ones can also be couched in the relationships between classical and quantum complexity classes. In this sense, the complexity classes *BPP* (Bounded error Probability in Polynomial time) and its quantum analogue *BQP* have attracted a lot of interest. Proving that $BPP \subset BQP$ is regarded as proving that quantum computers are strictly more powerful than classical computers. This may be quite non-trivial to demonstrate, since $BPP \subset BQP$ implies that *P* is not equal to *PSPACE*, a result that many researchers have unsuccessfully attempted to prove. However, if we adopt a non-classical approach and allow the input to be described in non-classical terms (genuine quantum mechanical terms, in our case) then we can show that the set of problems solvable efficiently by a classical computer (deterministic or probabilistic) is strictly included in the set of problems having an efficient quantum solution.

3.7. Super-Turing Computations

We end this exposition of working hypotheses, when comparing quantum and classical computers, with the most "exotic" cases. Some researchers have shown that there are quantum processes which can be used to compute the solution to Turing uncomputable (or undecidable) problems. Calude and Pavlov [22] describe a mathematical quantum device that is able to determine with a pre-established precision whether an arbitrary program halts or not. Kieu [42] uses quantum adiabatic processes to provide a single, universal procedure, taking the form of a quantum algorithm that solves Hilbert's tenth problem (which has been shown to be equivalent to Turing's halting problem). The essence of these results is that there exist mathematical constructions, built within the framework provided by the physical theory of quantum mechanics, which are powerful enough to tackle with success problems that have been proved to be out of the capabilities of the Turing machine.

A few observations have to be made with respect to the features empowering these quantum "hypercomputers". They manage to compute the "uncomputable" by eluding in one way or another the *finiteness condition* [2]. The method employed by Calude and Pavlov (a quadratic form of an iterated map acting on randomly chosen vectors, the latter viewed as special trajectories of two Markov processes working in two different scales of time) encodes the whole data into an infinite superposition. Kieu too works with a dimensionally infinite Hilbert space in his quantum adiabatic algorithm. However, he argues that the number of dimensions is only required to be sufficiently large, but finite.

Furthermore, an important common characteristic of both algorithms is their probabilistic nature. The answer they give to a problem has only a certain probability to be the correct one. This probability can be made arbitrarily close to 1, but it can never reach 1 as long as the quantum procedure is only allowed to run for a finite amount of time. Finally, we note that the models of computation capable of such performances are mathematical objects with no constructive indications being offered to attempt the experimental realization of such a machine (assuming this thing is possible). From this point of view, they can rather be characterized as quantum "hypercomputers", as opposed to a "standard" quantum computer, capable of running Shor's algorithm, for example.

Although a bit more philosophical, Roger Penrose's claim that some quantum phenomena occurring in the neurons composing the human brain could be used to explain our conscious mentality is made along the same lines. He submits that no computational model is strong (or powerful) enough to fully explain the actions of the human brain [59, 60]. In particular, no classical Turing machine is capable of simulating the complex quantum processes that are supposed to take place inside our "quantum hypercomputer" (that is, our brain).

3.8. A Different Perspective

Information manipulation is still regarded today as the transformation and/or communication of *classical* information. This assumption is *implicit* and is well justified by the fact that virtually all computing devices in use today operate in accord with classical physics. The problems we can solve and the tasks we can accomplish with the aid of a computer are defined in terms of the classical input data provided to the computer. Quantum computation and quantum information, however, are challenging the current viewpoint, which may seem natural at this particular moment in time. But if a quantum computer will ever become a practical reality, this perception will necessarily have to change. By representing and manipulating information at a deeper physical level, the quantum computer can tackle problems that are impossible for a conventional computer.

The quantum model of computation not only offers entirely new ways to manipulate information, but also allows information processing tasks to be formulated in unconventional, genuine quantum mechanical terms. In the new framework established by the laws of quantum mechanics, the concept of information acquires new dimensions due to the principle of superposition of states. Quantum information is, consequently, qualitatively different from classical information, the latter becoming just a simple, particular case of the former.

Although classical information about quantum systems can be acquired through quantum measurements and, in general, it is possible to simulate a quantum process on a conventional machine (even if inefficiently), there are tasks that can only be successfully accomplished if one has the ability to operate directly at the physical (quantum) level used to encapsulate information. Therefore, in the same way quantum mechanics augments the understanding of physical reality, pointing out the limitations of previous physical theories, quantum computation enlarges the scope of information processing, exposing the limitations of conventional computation. Non-determinism and operating on quantum superpositions can each be successfully simulated on a machine whose functioning obeys the laws of classical physics. However, we show that there are problems merging non-determinism and entanglement[1] in such a way that a solution based on classical means is no longer possible [53].

[1] seen as a particular instance of superposition involving multiple qubits.

Let us now describe the terms under which we compare, in the following, the quantum computer with the classical computer. The quantum machine is assumed to have a set of quantum gates that is universal for quantum computation (although for our purposes the controlled-NOT and Hadamard gates will suffice), together with the ability to perform single-qubit measurements in the standard computational basis $\{|0\rangle, |1\rangle\}$. This description corresponds to a standard quantum computer that can have various physical realizations.

On the other hand, the classical computer in consideration is a conventional computing device whose capabilities match those of the Universal Turing Machine. Due to the nature of the problems addressed, the classical computing machine is augmented with the same measurement capabilities as the quantum computer. After all, quantum measurements in the standard computational basis are just a means of acquiring classical information (about quantum states).

In the context delimited by these specifications, we can identify a whole class of information processing tasks which clearly separate the quantum computer from its classical counterpart in terms of computability.

3.9. Quantum Distinguishability

At the heart of this class of problems is the task of distinguishing among entangled quantum states. We introduce the quantum distinguishability problem through a metaphor involving two prototypical characters, named Alice and Bob. Suppose we have a fixed set of quantum states described using the usual Dirac notation $|\Psi_i\rangle$ $(1 \leq i \leq n)$ known to both Alice and Bob. Alice randomly chooses a state from the set and prepares a qubit (or set of qubits) in that particular state. She then gives the qubit(s) to Bob who is free to investigate them in any way he likes. To be more specific, Bob can apply any kind of measurement on the qubit(s) and possibly process and/or interpret the information acquired through measurement. In the end, his task is to identify the index i of the state characterizing the qubit(s) Alice has given him.

The only case in which a set of quantum states can be reliably (that is, 100% of the time) distinguished from one another is if they are pairwise orthogonal. For example, the four states $|00\rangle$, $|01\rangle$, $|10\rangle$ and $|11\rangle$ form an orthonormal basis (each vector is a unit vector and distinct vectors have a zero inner product) for the state space spanned by two qubits. Consequently, they can be reliably distinguished by an appropriate measurement. In this case, we can simply measure each qubit (sequentially) in the computational basis (defined by the basis vectors $|0\rangle$ and $|1\rangle$).

On the other hand, it is impossible to reliably distinguish $|0\rangle$ from $\frac{1}{\sqrt{2}}|0\rangle+\frac{1}{\sqrt{2}}|1\rangle$. While the first state will consistently yield a 0 upon measurement, the second state also has a 50% chance to be observed as a 0. It is this component in the direction of the basis vector $|0\rangle$ which is present in both quantum states that prevents us from distinguishing them reliably. If the vectors describing the quantum states would be orthogonal, then a measurement basis would exist with respect to which the quantum states share no common components.

Consider now the case in which we try to distinguish among the four Bell states: $\frac{1}{\sqrt{2}}|00\rangle + \frac{1}{\sqrt{2}}|11\rangle$, $\frac{1}{\sqrt{2}}|00\rangle - \frac{1}{\sqrt{2}}|11\rangle$, $\frac{1}{\sqrt{2}}|01\rangle + \frac{1}{\sqrt{2}}|10\rangle$, $\frac{1}{\sqrt{2}}|01\rangle - \frac{1}{\sqrt{2}}|10\rangle$. No sequential approach (that is, measuring the qubits one after the other) will be of any help here, regardless of the basis in which the measurements are performed. By measuring the two qubits, in sequence, in the computational basis, Bob can distinguish the states $\frac{1}{\sqrt{2}}(|00\rangle \pm |11\rangle)$ from $\frac{1}{\sqrt{2}}(|01\rangle \pm |10\rangle)$. He does this by checking if the outcomes of the two measurements are the same or not. But this kind of measurement makes it impossible to differentiate between $\frac{1}{\sqrt{2}}(|00\rangle + |11\rangle)$ and $\frac{1}{\sqrt{2}}(|00\rangle - |11\rangle)$, or between $\frac{1}{\sqrt{2}}(|01\rangle + |10\rangle)$ and $\frac{1}{\sqrt{2}}(|01\rangle - |10\rangle)$.

Alternatively, Bob can decide to perform his measurements in a different basis, like $(|+\rangle, |-\rangle)$, where the basis vectors are

$$|+\rangle = \frac{1}{\sqrt{2}}|0\rangle + \frac{1}{\sqrt{2}}|1\rangle,$$

$$|-\rangle = \frac{1}{\sqrt{2}}|0\rangle - \frac{1}{\sqrt{2}}|1\rangle.$$

Due to the fact that

$$\frac{|00\rangle + |11\rangle}{\sqrt{2}} = \frac{|++\rangle + |--\rangle}{\sqrt{2}}$$

and

$$\frac{|00\rangle - |11\rangle}{\sqrt{2}} = \frac{|+-\rangle + |-+\rangle}{\sqrt{2}},$$

Bob can now reliably distinguish the quantum state $\frac{1}{\sqrt{2}}(|00\rangle + |11\rangle)$ from $\frac{1}{\sqrt{2}}(|00\rangle - |11\rangle)$. Indeed, if the two qubits yield identical outcomes when measured in this new basis, then we can assert with certainty that the state was not $\frac{1}{\sqrt{2}}(|00\rangle - |11\rangle)$. Similarly, if the measurement outcomes for the qubits are different, the original state could not have been $\frac{1}{\sqrt{2}}(|00\rangle + |11\rangle)$. Unfortunately, in this new setup, the quantum states $\frac{1}{\sqrt{2}}(|00\rangle + |11\rangle)$ and $\frac{1}{\sqrt{2}}(|01\rangle + |10\rangle)$ become indistinguishable and the same is true about $\frac{1}{\sqrt{2}}(|00\rangle - |11\rangle)$ and $\frac{1}{\sqrt{2}}(|01\rangle - |10\rangle)$.

The computational bases $(|0\rangle, |1\rangle)$ and $(|+\rangle, |-\rangle)$ are, respectively, the two extremities of an (theoretically) infinite number of choices for the basis relative to which the quantum measurements are to be performed. But even though the separation line between the four Bell states will drift with the choice of the basis vectors, the two extreme cases discussed above offer the best possible distinguishability.

Intuitively, this is due to the entanglement exhibited between the two qubits in all four states. As soon as the first qubit is measured (regardless of the basis), the superposition describing the entangled state collapses to the specific state consistent with the measurement result. In this process, some of the information originally encapsulated in the entangled state is irremediably lost. Consequently, measuring the second qubit cannot give a complete separation of the four EPR states. But the Bell states do form an orthonormal basis, which means that (at least theoretically) they can be distinguished by an appropriate quantum measurement. However, this measurement must be a *joint* measurement of both qubits simultaneously, in order to achieve the desired distinguishability. Not surprisingly, this is very difficult to accomplish in practice.

The distinguishability of the four Bell (or EPR) states is the key feature in achieving superdense coding [16]. However, in the experimental demonstration of this protocol [47] two of the possibilities cannot be distinguished from one another, precisely because of the difficulties associated with implementing a joint measurement.

3.10. Generalization

The general formulation of the problem is given in the following. Suppose we have a quantum system composed of n qubits whose state is not known exactly. What we know with certainty is that the system can be described by one of the following 2^n entangled[2] states:

$$\begin{aligned} &\frac{1}{\sqrt{2}}(|000\cdots 0\rangle \ \pm \ |111\cdots 1\rangle), \\ &\frac{1}{\sqrt{2}}(|000\cdots 1\rangle \ \pm \ |111\cdots 0\rangle), \\ &\qquad\qquad\vdots \\ &\frac{1}{\sqrt{2}}(|011\cdots 1\rangle \ \pm \ |100\cdots 0\rangle). \end{aligned} \tag{8}$$

The challenge for the two candidate computers is to correctly identify the state of the system resorting to all their measurement and computational abilities. Alternatively, the problem can also be formulated as a function computation (evaluation), with the unknown quantum state as the input and the corresponding index (between 0 and $2^n - 1$) as the output. We have to say from the very beginning that this function is computable. The 2^n states in (8) are perfectly distinguishable since they form an orthonormal basis for the state space corresponding to the n-qubit system.

The immediate, theoretical solution to this problem is to perform a single joint measurement of the whole system by defining each of the 2^n states that are to be distinguished to be a projector associated with the measurement operation. Although mathematically this is a perfectly valid solution, it is very difficult in practice to perform such a joint measurement, even for the simplest case involving only two qubits [47]. Furthermore, as we will detail in the next section, if a joint measurement of all qubits in the system is not feasible, then no solution is better than measuring each qubit individually, one after the other. Of course, in this way we will not be able to distinguish between quantum states that differ only through a relative phase factor, like $\frac{1}{\sqrt{2}}(|000\cdots 0\rangle + |111\cdots 1\rangle)$ and $\frac{1}{\sqrt{2}}(|000\cdots 0\rangle - |111\cdots 1\rangle)$, for example. But note that this is the best that can be achieved, given the measurement capabilities of both the classical and quantum computer.

However, if we resort to their processing capabilities, the situation changes. Unitary operators preserve inner products, so any unitary evolution of the system described by (8) will necessarily transform it into another orthonormal basis set. Therefore, a unitary transformation must exist that will allow a subsequent measurement in the standard computational basis without any loss of information. The following result shows that such a transformation not only exists, but that in fact it can be implemented efficiently.

---

[2]For the case $n = 1$ the term *entanglement* is inappropriate. A single qubit is just in a balanced *superposition* of 0 and 1. However, we still choose to use *entanglement* throughout our exposition because for any n greater than 1 the superposition is actually an entangled state.

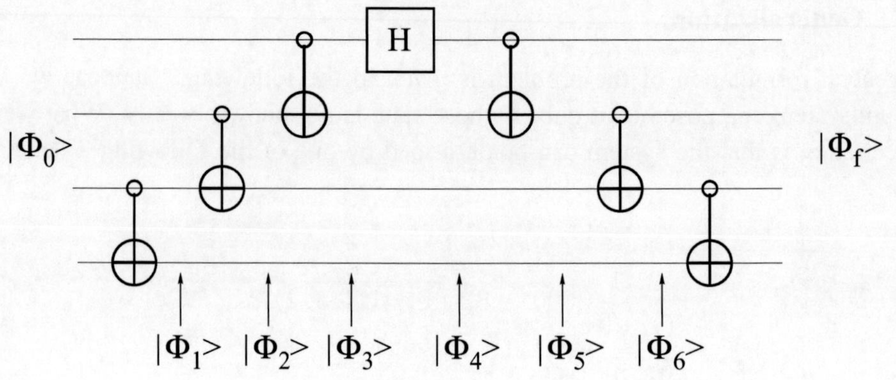

Figure 3. Quantum circuit for Proposition 1.

Proposition 1 *The transformation between the following two orthonormal basis sets for the state space spanned by n qubits:*

$$
\begin{aligned}
\frac{1}{\sqrt{2}}(|000\cdots 0\rangle + |111\cdots 1\rangle) &\longleftrightarrow |000\cdots 0\rangle, \\
\frac{1}{\sqrt{2}}(|000\cdots 0\rangle - |111\cdots 1\rangle) &\longleftrightarrow |111\cdots 1\rangle, \\
\frac{1}{\sqrt{2}}(|000\cdots 1\rangle + |111\cdots 0\rangle) &\longleftrightarrow |000\cdots 1\rangle, \\
\frac{1}{\sqrt{2}}(|000\cdots 1\rangle - |111\cdots 0\rangle) &\longleftrightarrow |111\cdots 0\rangle, \\
&\vdots \\
\frac{1}{\sqrt{2}}(|011\cdots 1\rangle + |100\cdots 0\rangle) &\longleftrightarrow |011\cdots 1\rangle, \\
\frac{1}{\sqrt{2}}(|011\cdots 1\rangle - |100\cdots 0\rangle) &\longleftrightarrow |100\cdots 0\rangle.
\end{aligned}
\tag{9}
$$

can be realized by a quantum circuit comprising only a linear number of controlled-NOT and Hadamard gates.

Proof

It is easy to check that the circuit depicted in Figure 3 performs the required quantum transformation for the case $n = 4$. To see this, we show the intermediate quantum states for the particular input

$$|\Phi_0\rangle = \tfrac{1}{\sqrt{2}}|0000\rangle + \tfrac{1}{\sqrt{2}}|1111\rangle.$$

These are:

$$|\Phi_1\rangle = \frac{1}{\sqrt{2}}|0000\rangle + \frac{1}{\sqrt{2}}|1110\rangle,$$

$$|\Phi_2\rangle = \frac{1}{\sqrt{2}}|0000\rangle + \frac{1}{\sqrt{2}}|1100\rangle,$$

$$|\Phi_3\rangle = \frac{1}{\sqrt{2}}|0000\rangle + \frac{1}{\sqrt{2}}|1000\rangle = (\frac{1}{\sqrt{2}}|0\rangle + \frac{1}{\sqrt{2}}|1\rangle) \otimes |000\rangle,$$

$$|\Phi_4\rangle = |\Phi_5\rangle = |\Phi_6\rangle = |\Phi_f\rangle = |0000\rangle.$$

The generalization to an arbitrary number of qubits is straightforward. In the general case the circuit consists of $2n - 2$ controlled-NOT gates and one Hadamard gate. Due to its symmetric nature, the same quantum circuit can also perform the inverse transformation, from the normal computational basis set to the entangled basis set. □

By applying the transformation realized by this circuit, the quantum computer can disentangle the qubits composing the system and thus make the act of measuring each qubit entirely independent of the other qubits. This is possible because the final states (after the transformation) are actually classical states which can be interpreted as the indices corresponding to the original entangled quantum states. Obtaining the correct answer to the distinguishability problem amounts to accurately compute the index associated with the given input state. The procedure detailed above gives us a reliable way to do this, 100% of the time. In other words, the function is efficiently computable (in quantum linear time) by a quantum computer.

Can the classical computer replicate the operations performed by the quantum machine? We know that a classical computer cam simulate (even if inefficiently) the continuous evolution of a closed quantum system (viewed as a quantum computation in the case of an ensemble of qubits). So, whatever unitary operation is invoked by the quantum computer, it can certainly be simulated mathematically on a Turing machine. The difference resides in the way the two machines handle the uncertainty inherent in the input. The quantum computer has the ability to transcend this uncertainty about the quantum state of the input system by acting directly on the input in a way that is specific to the physical support employed to encode or describe the input. The classical computer, on the other hand, lacks the ability to process the information at its original physical level, thus making any simulation at another level futile exactly because of the uncertainty in the input.

We have to emphasize that had the input state been perfectly determined, then any transformation applied to it, even though quantum mechanical in nature, could have been perfectly simulated using the classical means available to a Turing machine. However, in our case, the classical computer does not have a description of the input in classical terms and can only try to obtain one through direct measurement. This will in turn collapse the superposition characterizing the input state, leaving the classical computer with only a 50% probability of correctly identifying the original quantum state. This means that the problem cannot be solved classically, not even by a PTM. There is no way to improve the 50% error rate of the classical approach to distinguish among the 2^n states.

So this problem tells us that what draws the separation line between a quantum and a classical computer, in terms of computational power, is not the ability to extract information from a quantum system through measurements, but the ability to process information at the physical level used to represent it. For the distinguishability problem discussed, this is the only way to deal with the non-determinism introduced by superposition of states.

The fact that a function with an argument expressible only in quantum mechanical terms (as a superposition of states) is not computable by a conventional computing device capable to process information only at the classical level may appear as unfair to the classical computer. In fact, such functions are just revealing the natural, physical limitations of conventional computing devices. Thus, a quantum computer is intrinsically more powerful than a classical (conventional) one, as the set of problems solvable (functions computable) by the latter is a proper subset of those solvable (computable) by the former. It is only when we restrict the input to be classical for both machines, that the relative power of a quantum computer with respect to a classical one still remains debatable.

3.11. Some Consequences

Distinguishing among entangled quantum states forms the basic building block for a series of information processing tasks that can only be accomplished by a quantum computer. Here are two such examples.

3.11.1. Conveying Quantum Information through a Classical Channel

The first one addresses the problem of transmitting unknown quantum information through a classical channel. In the general case, when we have no knowledge whatsoever about the quantum state to be transmitted, the task is obviously impossible. It requires a classical description of the quantum state, which cannot be obtained since a quantum measurement would ruin the original state and cloning an unknown quantum state was proven to be impossible.

Quantum teleportation actually requires the existence of a classical channel between the source and the destination, so it could be interpreted as the transmission of an unknown quantum state through a classical channel. There is an important point to make, however. Quantum teleportation refers only to a single qubit and requires an EPR state to be shared by the sender and the receiver prior to the teleportation. This entangled pair of qubits is actually a resource that will be consumed in the process. The same argument can be formulated in the case of another task that is not possible through classical means, namely, superdense coding. Unlike these remarkable applications of entanglement as a physical resource, the information processing tasks investigated in this paper do not assume the creation and distribution of entanglement in order to be completed.

After this necessary clarification, we note that the problem investigated in our first example is unsolvable (in its most general formulation) by both our classical and quantum computers. However, if we restrict the unknown quantum state to be a member of the set (8), then the task is only out of the capabilities of the classical machine. The quantum computer can still use the circuit in Figure 3 to obtain a "label" of the original quantum state in classical terms, which can be subsequently transmitted via the classical channel. At the other end, the same quantum circuit can reconstruct the original quantum state, based on the classical information received.

3.11.2. Protecting Quantum Information from Classical Attacks

The second example is taken from the field of cryptography and gives a more plastic representation of the physical limitations of a classical computer to process information. A simple protocol may be devised to enable the transmission of information through a quantum channel, without any possibility of eavesdropping from a third party resorting only to the computational power of a classical computer. For this purpose, each pair of qubits transmitted through the channel encodes one bit of information in the following way: $\frac{1}{\sqrt{2}}(|00\rangle+|11\rangle)$ or $\frac{1}{\sqrt{2}}(|01\rangle+|10\rangle)$ represent a 0 bit, while $\frac{1}{\sqrt{2}}(|00\rangle-|11\rangle)$ or $\frac{1}{\sqrt{2}}(|01\rangle-|10\rangle)$ represent the bit 1. Since the information is encoded (hidden) in the relative phase between the two terms of the superposition, no single-qubit measurements[3] are better than just flipping a coin in order to guess the *bit* transmitted, so no information whatsoever can be gained by the classical machine.

The quantum computer would be in the same situation if it would resort only to its measurement abilities. However, the quantum computer can first "evolve" the Bell basis into the normal computational basis (using the quantum circuit from Figure 3 for the case $n = 2$) and then identify the bit transmitted by reading the measurement outcome for the first qubit. Note that this protocol can be generalized to "beat" any classical computer endowed with *finite* measuring capabilities. If the classical computer is able to perform a joint measurement of k qubits (where k is unbounded, but finite) then it suffices to encode a bit of information into the relative phase of an entangled quantum state comprising $k + 1$ qubits. In this way, the information conveyed through the quantum channel is safely kept out of reach for the classical computer, due to its limitations in processing information at the very physical level chosen to embody it.

3.12. Discussion

When he devised the Quantum Turing Machine as the first abstract model of quantum computation, David Deutsch already pointed to some features that set it apart from the classical Turing machine: intrinsic genuine non-determinism and entanglement. Naturally, these features have created a lot of speculations about the superiority of the quantum computer in terms of computability and complexity. Consequently, the computational powers of the quantum and classical machine have been evaluated and compared in a variety of contexts.

We have shown in this section that there is a whole class of information processing tasks relative to which a clear separation line exists between quantum computers and classical computers with respect to their computational powers. The set of problems solvable by classical means is therefore strictly smaller than the set of functions computable through quantum means. At the heart of this separation lies a problem (namely, distinguishing among entangled quantum states) that combines uncertainty and entanglement in a way that renders a classical simulation of the quantum solution impossible. Otherwise, taken separately, uncertainty can be dealt with (through measurements) in the absence of entanglement, while entanglement, as a particular case of superposition, can be simulated by a classical machine for the purpose of computation (due to the linearity of the unitary operators describing quantum transformations).

[3]including those performed in other bases than the standard computational basis.

While quantum measurements are certainly required to distinguish among different quantum states, this is most emphatically not what gives the Quantum Turing Machine the advantage over the classical Turing machine. Also, this superiority is not due to some theoretical property specific to "hypercomputers", which breaks in one way or another the finiteness condition by implicitly assuming some form of unlimited computational resources. It is also not a matter of complexity, the ability to solve problems much faster than it is possible classically. This section shows that quantum computers are better than classical ones (whether deterministic or probabilistic) in terms of computability (function evaluation) due to the power conferred to their computations by the way they represent information at the physical level.

At this point, it is important that we make clear the implications of our discussion on the Church-Turing thesis. The definition of the Turing machine was an extraordinary achievement in abstracting out computation as an information manipulating process. But although the model was thought to be free of any physical assumptions, it is clear today that the description of the Turing machine harbors an implicit assumption: the information it manipulates is classical. Computation is a physical process and the Turing machine computes in accord with the laws of classical physics (it was Rolf Landauer who first noted that "Information is physical." and Seth Lloyd extended this observation, stating that "Information processing is also physical." [45]).

However, the success of quantum mechanics in explaining the reality of the microcosmos is challenging our traditional views on information processing, forcing us to redefine what we mean by computation. In the context of quantum computation, the data in general, and the input in particular, are not restricted to classical, orthogonal values, but can be arbitrary superpositions of them. Therefore, computational problems like distinguishing among entangled quantum states are not an attack on the validity of the Church-Turing thesis, but rather they precisely define its scope. It is in these terms that the main result of this section has to be understood:

The set of functions computable by a classical Turing machine is a proper subset of those computable using a quantum Turing machine.

It is worth emphasizing that the gap between a quantum and a classical machine is qualitatively different from the relationship between an analog and a discrete (or digital) machine. The difference between an analog computer and a digital one is purely quantitative, in the sense that while the former can operate with real numbers (theoretically), the latter can only approximate them. But this approximation can be arbitrary accurate, given the digital model has enough time and memory. Consequently, when presented with an analog input, the digital computer can always obtain a representation of it, which is as close to the original as the computer's resources are permitting. Since both machines are working at the same physical level (manipulating voltage levels, for example), there is no task that one machine could do and the other would not be able to tackle it. In contrast, the operating principles of a quantum computer are qualitatively different from those governing the behavior of a conventional computer, thus allowing the former to address information processing tasks that are simply out of the scope of the latter.

Classical physics is just a particular, trivial case of quantum mechanics. Sometimes,

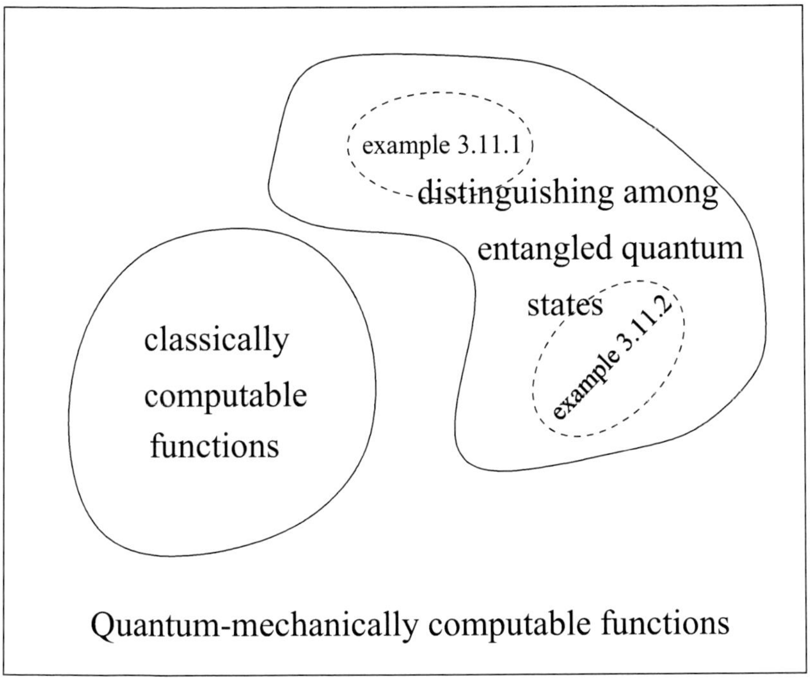

Figure 4. Relationship between quantum and classical computation.

information encoded in genuine quantum mechanical terms cannot be successfully manipulated unless the computing device has the power to process this information directly at the physical level used to represent it. The properties of the physical level chosen to embody information in a computational model ultimately determine its computational capabilities and power. The limitations of the classical Turing machine are therefore purely physical. So, is a machine that computes following the principles of quantum mechanics really more powerful than a computing device designed in accord with classical physics? We think that the answer is definitely affirmative. And the difference is made by those problems, defined in purely quantum mechanical terms, whose quantum solutions are impossible to simulate classically.

4. Parallelism and Universal Computation

Parallel computing was originally motivated by the need to speed up computation, especially for those tasks whose sequential running time is prohibitively long. This traditional view of the role played by parallelism in computation has since evolved dramatically, with implications almost impossible to foresee when the field originated.

We know today that there are tasks and computational paradigms for which a parallel approach offers much more than just a faster solution. A real-time environment, constraining the input data provided and the output produced at various moments in time, can have drastic effects on the quality of the solution obtained for a certain problem, unless parallelism is employed [49, 55]. A general framework is developed in [1] to show how a superlinear (with respect to the number of processors employed in the parallel approach) improvement in the quality of the solution computed to a real-time problem can be obtained.

In other cases, a sequential machine fails to tackle a certain task altogether, and parallelism is the only hope to see that task accomplished. Examples of this kind include measuring the parameters of a dynamical system [3] or setting them in such a way as to avoid pushing the system into a chaotic behavior [6]. Also, some geometric transformations can only be performed successfully if we act simultaneously on a certain number of objects [4].

Progress in science and technology influences the way computations are carried and the emergence of novel computational environments and paradigms continually broadens the applicability and importance of parallelism. In this section, we highlight the role of parallelism for quantum information theory through an example [52] that also reinforces the argument developed in [2] demonstrating the infeasibility of a Universal Computer obeying certain conditions.

4.1. Quantum Distinguishability through Joint Measurements

In the following we show that a parallel approach can make the difference between success and failure when trying to distinguish among (entangled) quantum states. The distinguishability problem, introduced in the previous section, assumes a set of 2^n entangled states, any one of which could characterize the quantum state of an ensemble composed of n qubits, at a given moment in time. Unlike the analysis performed in section 3, we now restrict the set of actions that can be undertaken to distinguish among these states to direct quantum measurements, without any pre-processing. There are no restrictions concerning the number of measurements allowed or the time when the task has to be completed.

The vectors composing the set (8) form an orthonormal basis for the state space corresponding to the n-qubit system. The only chance to differentiate among them using quantum measurement(s) is to observe the n qubits simultaneously, that is, perform a single joint measurement of the entire system. In the given context, *joint* is really just a synonym for *parallel*. Indeed, the device in charge of performing the joint measurement must posses the ability to "read" the information stored in each qubit, in parallel, in a perfectly synchronized manner. In this sense, at an abstract level, the measuring apparatus can be viewed as having n probes. With all probes operating in parallel, each probe can "peek" inside the state of one qubit, in a perfectly synchronous operation. The information gathered by the n probes is seen by the measuring device as a single, indivisible chunk of data, which is then interpreted to give one of the 2^n entangled states as the measurement outcome.

From a mathematical (theoretical) point of view, such a measurement operator can be easily constructed by defining each of the 2^n states that are to be distinguished to be a projector associated with the measurement operation. We are well aware though, that a physical realization of this mathematical construction is extremely difficult, if not impossible to achieve in practice, with today's technology. The experimental demonstration of the superdense coding protocol mentioned in the previous section clearly shows this difficulty (for just two qubits!). Yet, if there is any hope to see a joint measurement performed in the future, then only a device operating in a parallel synchronous fashion on all n qubits (as explained above) would succeed.

It is perhaps worth emphasizing that if such a measurement cannot be applied then the desired distinguishability can no longer be achieved regardless of how many other measuring operations we are allowed to perform. In other words, even an infinite sequence of measurements touching at most $n - 1$ qubits at the same time cannot equal a single joint measurement involving all n qubits.

Furthermore, with respect to the particular distinguishability problem that we have to solve, a single joint measurement capable of observing $n - 1$ qubits simultaneously offers no advantage whatsoever over a sequence of $n - 1$ consecutive *single* qubit measurements. This is due to the fact that an entangled state like

$$\frac{1}{\sqrt{2}}(|000\cdots 0\rangle + |111\cdots 1\rangle)$$

cannot be decomposed neither as a product of $n-1$ individual states nor as a product of two states (one describing a single qubit and the other describing the subsystem composed of the remaining $n-1$ qubits). Any other intermediate decomposition is also impossible. This is an important characteristic of the task, defining it as inherently parallel. Consequently, if the degree of parallelism necessary to successfully solve the problem is not available, then the solution is no better than a purely sequential approach.

Overall, our distinguishability problem can only be tackled successfully within a parallel approach, where we can measure all qubits simultaneously. In this sense, distinguishing among entangled quantum states can be viewed as a quantum variant of the measure-compute-set problem formulated in [3], which also admits only a parallel solution.

4.2. Universal Computation

Although it may seem surprising, there is a connection between the quantum distinguishability problem with its parallel solution and the hypothetical notion of a Universal Computer, introduced in [2]. Such a machine must be able to follow (execute) the steps of any program made up of basic input, output and internal processing operations. The Universal Computer is intended to be the most general possible model of computation, encompassing all existing or imagined computational paradigms. Specifically, its internal processing capabilities include (but are not limited to) basic arithmetic and logical operations, unitary quantum gates, operations specific to DNA and natural computing, etc. It must also have a means of communicating with the outside world at any time during a computation, either for receiving input or producing output (results). The machine is endowed with the ability to acquire input data through measurements on outside-world systems, performed by a set of probes (or sensors). The program, the input data (either received or acquired), the output and all intermediate results are stored in (and can be retrieved from) a memory which is generously allowed to be unlimited.

To make this Universal Computer a "realistic" model of computation, it is subjected to the *finiteness condition*: In one step, requiring one time unit, the Universal Computer can execute a finite and fixed number of basic operations (including measurements). Some physicists have tried to quantify this finiteness condition showing that special and general relativity, together with quantum mechanics, limit the number of operations that a computer can perform in a step. More precisely, general relativity limits the energy density of some volume of space, and then quantum mechanics limits the number of elementary logical operations that can be performed in that volume within a certain time [37, 44]. It is precisely this limitation (quite natural and reasonable) that makes the Universal Computer a utopian concept. Specifically, three classes of computable functions $\mathcal{F}$ are described in [2], which cannot be computed by any machine obeying the finiteness condition.

One of these classes of problems involves measuring a set of interacting variables. Formally, suppose there are n variables $x_0, x_1, \cdots, x_{n-1}$. Although these variables may represent the parameters of a physical or biological system, the following formalism is abstracted away from any particular realization and does not necessarily describe the dynamics of a quantum system. The dependence of each variable on all others induces the system to continually evolve until a state of equilibrium may eventually be reached. In the absence of any external perturbations, the system can remain in a stable state indefinitely. We can model the interdependence between the n variables through a set of functions, as follows:

$$\begin{aligned} x_0(t+1) &= f_0(x_0(t), x_1(t), \ldots, x_{n-1}(t)) \\ x_1(t+1) &= f_1(x_0(t), x_1(t), \ldots, x_{n-1}(t)) \\ &\vdots \\ x_{n-1}(t+1) &= f_{n-1}(x_0(t), x_1(t), \ldots, x_{n-1}(t)) \end{aligned} \tag{10}$$

This system of equations describes the evolution of the system from state

$$(x_0(t), x_1(t), \ldots, x_{n-1}(t))$$

to state

$$(x_0(t+1), x_1(t+1), \ldots, x_{n-1}(t+1)),$$

one time unit later. In the case where the system has reached equilibrium, its parameters will not change over time. It is important to emphasize that, in most cases, the dynamics of the system are very complex, so the mathematical description of functions $f_0, f_1, \ldots, f_{n-1}$ is either not known to us or we only have rough approximations for them.

Assuming the system is in an equilibrium state, our task is to measure its parameters in order to compute a function $\mathcal{F}$, possibly a global property of the system at equilibrium. In other words, we need the values of $x_0(\tau), x_1(\tau), \ldots, x_{n-1}(\tau)$ at moment τ, when the system is in a stable state, in order to compute

$$\mathcal{F}(x_0(\tau), x_1(\tau), \ldots, x_{n-1}(\tau)).$$

We can try to estimate the value of $x_0(\tau)$, for instance[4], by measuring the respective parameter at time τ. Although, for some systems, we can acquire the value of $x_0(\tau)$ easily

[4]The choice of x_0 here is arbitrary. The argument remains the same regardless of which of the n parameters we choose to measure first.

in this way, the consequences for the entire system can be dramatic. Unfortunately, any measurement is an external perturbation for the system, and in the process, the parameter subjected to measurement may be affected unpredictably.

Thus, the measurement operation will change the state of the system from $(x_0(\tau), x_1(\tau), \ldots, x_{n-1}(\tau))$ to $(x_0'(\tau), x_1(\tau), \ldots, x_{n-1}(\tau))$, where $x_0'(\tau)$ denotes the value of variable x_0 after measurement. In those cases where the measurement process has a non-deterministic effect upon the variable being measured, we cannot estimate $x_0'(\tau)$ in any way. But, regardless of the particular instance of the model, the transition from $(x_0(\tau), x_1(\tau), \ldots, x_{n-1}(\tau))$ (that is, the state before measurement) to $(x_0'(\tau), x_1(\tau), \ldots, x_{n-1}(\tau))$ (that is, the state after measurement) does not correspond to the normal evolution of the system according to its dynamics described by functions f_i, $0 \leq i < n$.

However, because the equilibrium state was perturbed by the measurement operation, the system will react with a series of state transformations, governed by equations (10). Thus, at each time step after τ, the parameters of the system will evolve either towards a new equilibrium state or maybe fall into a chaotic behavior. In any case, at time $\tau + 1$, all n variables have acquired new values, according to the expressions of functions f_i:

$$\begin{aligned}
x_0(\tau+1) &= f_0(x_0'(\tau), x_1(\tau), \ldots, x_{n-1}(\tau)) \\
x_1(\tau+1) &= f_1(x_0'(\tau), x_1(\tau), \ldots, x_{n-1}(\tau)) \\
&\vdots \\
x_{n-1}(\tau+1) &= f_{n-1}(x_0'(\tau), x_1(\tau), \ldots, x_{n-1}(\tau))
\end{aligned} \tag{11}$$

Consequently, unless we are able to measure all n variables, in parallel, at time τ, some of the values composing the equilibrium state

$$(x_0(\tau), x_1(\tau), \ldots, x_{n-1}(\tau))$$

will be lost without any possibility of recovery.

The finiteness condition restricts in this case the number of variables that can be measured in parallel. So, if the Universal Computer is able to measure n variables in parallel (that is, during one step), where n can be arbitrarily large, but finite, then the Universal Computer will fail to solve the same problem for a system involving $n + 1$ variables. In other words, the Universal Computer cannot simulate a computation that is perfectly possible for another machine. However, it is exactly the principle of *simulation* that lies at the heart of *universality*.

Choosing a machine endowed with $n + 1$ probes (and therefore capable of measuring $n + 1$ variables in parallel) as the Universal Computer is not a solution. By an adversary argument, we can construct an instance of the above problem, only this time involving $n+2$ parameters to be measured, and the Universal Computer will fail once again to compute the required function $\mathcal{F}$, although it can be trivially computed by a machine with $n+2$ probes. This argument is valid for *any* given Universal Computer, having a fixed (and finite) number of probes and therefore a limited degree of parallelism to tackle such inherently parallel tasks.

It is important to emphasize that the computational paradigm to which the above setting belongs is not a conventional one. The input data necessary to compute $\mathcal{F}$ is not available at the outset and have to be acquired through measurement operations. Perhaps some readers may object to labeling the process of obtaining the necessary information as *computation*. They may be accustomed to seeing computation from the conventional point of view (like, for example, performing a basic arithmetic operation on a pair of numbers). However, the qualitatively new ways of manipulating information nowadays is forcing us to challenge the limitations of the classical computational paradigm and adopt a broader perspective (often called *unconventional* or *non-classical*) on computation [67].

From this new perspective, a computing machine is seen as an open system whose output depends on the interaction with its environment, a system capable of taking on new information (either communicated to it by an external agent or acquired directly through measurements). The emergence of this new model of computation is motivated by applications as diverse as data acquisition in signal processing [58] and the control of nuclear power plants [8]. Furthermore, such a computational paradigm can be realized through various physical means including, of course, a quantum mechanical one.

Coming back to the quantum example presented in this section, it is easy to see that a device capable of measuring at most n qubits simultaneously (where n is a fixed, finite number) will fail to solve the distinguishability problem for $n+1$ qubits. Our example, taken from the quantum information area is similar in nature with the interacting variables example formalized above and supports the idea advanced in [2] about the impossibility of realizing the concept of a Universal Computer. In the case that we have described, interdependence between variables takes the form of entanglement between qubits, the phenomenon ultimately responsible for making a parallel approach imperative.

5. Coping with Decoherence: Parallelizing the Quantum Fourier Transform

The role played by parallelism in the theory of computation depends on the particular paradigm or computational environment considered, but the benefits of its use have been confirmed with the emergence of each novel computing technology. We have just demonstrated the importance of parallelism for quantum measurements. Now we turn our attention on quantum computation and present an instance of a rank-varying complexity algorithm which can only be reliably implemented in a parallel setting. The example we describe involves computing the quantum Fourier transform, under the constraints imposed by avoiding the undesired effects caused by coupling with the environment [50].

5.1. Quantum Fourier Transform

The Fourier transform is a very useful tool in computer science and it proved of crucial importance for quantum computation as well. Since it can be computed much faster on a quantum computer than on a classical one, the discrete Fourier transform allows for the construction of a whole class of fast quantum algorithms. Shor's quantum algorithms for factoring integers and computing discrete logarithms [65] are the most famous examples in this category.

The quantum Fourier transform is a linear operator whose action on any of the computational basis vectors $|0\rangle, |1\rangle, \cdots, |2^n - 1\rangle$ associated with an n-qubit register is described by the following transformation:

$$|j\rangle \longrightarrow \frac{1}{\sqrt{2^n}} \sum_{k=0}^{2^n-1} e^{2\pi ijk/2^n} |k\rangle, \; 0 \leq j \leq 2^n - 1. \tag{12}$$

However, the essential advantage of quantum computation over classical computation is that the quantum mechanical principle of superposition of states allows all possible inputs to be processed at the same time. Consequently, if the quantum register is in an arbitrary superposition of the basis vectors

$$\sum_{j=0}^{2^n-1} x_j|j\rangle,$$

then the quantum Fourier transform will rotate this state into another superposition of the basis vectors

$$\sum_{k=0}^{2^n-1} y_k|k\rangle,$$

in which the output amplitudes y_k are the classical discrete Fourier transform of the input amplitudes x_j. Classically, we can compute the numbers y_k from x_j using $\Theta(2^{2n})$ elementary arithmetic operations in a straightforward manner and in $\Theta(n2^n)$ operations by using the Fast Fourier Transform algorithm.

In contrast, a circuit implementing the quantum Fourier transform requires only $\Theta(n^2)$ elementary quantum gates. Such a circuit can be easily derived if equation (12) is rewritten as a tensor product of the n qubits involved:

$$|j_1 j_2 \cdots j_n\rangle \longrightarrow \frac{(|0\rangle + e^{2\pi i 0.j_n}|1\rangle) \otimes (|0\rangle + e^{2\pi i 0.j_{n-1}j_n}|1\rangle) \otimes \cdots \otimes (|0\rangle + e^{2\pi i 0.j_1 j_2 \cdots j_n}|1\rangle)}{2^{n/2}}. \tag{13}$$

using the binary representation $j_1 j_2 \cdots j_n$ of j and binary fractions in the exponents (for full details see [57]).

Note that each Fourier transformed qubit is in a balanced superposition of $|0\rangle$ and $|1\rangle$. These qubits differ from one another only in the relative phase between the $|0\rangle$ and the $|1\rangle$ components. For the first qubit in the tensor product, j_n will introduce a phase shift of 0 or π, depending on whether its value is 0 or 1, respectively. The phase of the second qubit is determined (controlled) by both j_n and j_{n-1}. It can amount to $\pi + \pi/2$, provided j_{n-1} and j_n are both 1. This dependency on the values of all the previous qubits continues up to (and including) the last term in the tensor product. When $|j_1\rangle$ gets Fourier transformed, the coefficient of $|1\rangle$ in the superposition involves all the digits in the binary expansion of j.

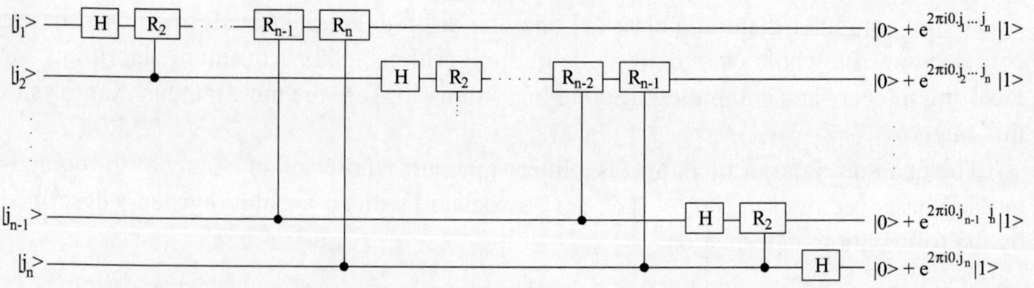

Figure 5. Quantum circuit performing the discrete Fourier transform.

In the case of each qubit, the Hadamard gate (see Figure 5) creates the superposition and induces a 0 or π relative phase between the two components, according to the binary value presented as input. The dependency on the previous qubits is reflected in the use of controlled phase shifts, as depicted in Figure 5. In the figure, a gate R_k implements a $\pi/2^{k-1}$ phase shift of the $|1\rangle$ component, according to the unitary transformation

$$R_k \equiv \begin{bmatrix} 1 & 0 \\ 0 & e^{2\pi i/2^k} \end{bmatrix}.$$

5.2. Rank-Varying Complexity

When analyzing the computational complexity of a given algorithm, we usually focus on how this quantity varies as a function of the problem size, without paying too much attention to how the complexity of each step in the algorithm varies throughout the computation. Though in many cases the complexity of each step is a constant, there are computations for which the cost of executing essentially similar steps is different from one step to another.

One factor determining such a variation could be *time*. Data may be affected by the passage of time, making the same computation increasingly harder as time goes by. A variety of instances demonstrating time-varying complexity are described in [5]. In other computational environments, it is rather the *rank* of a step, defined as the order of execution of that step, which dictates its complexity [5]. Examples of this kind are hardly new. Euclid's algorithm for computing the greatest common divisor of two numbers executes the same basic operation (a division) at each step, but the size of the operands (and implicitly the complexity of the operation) decreases continually. Algorithms for which an amortized analysis can be applied also make good examples of rank-varying computational complexity. Incrementing a binary counter [27] is a procedure in which the number of bit flips at each step is not constant, though it's neither strictly increasing nor strictly decreasing with the rank.

Computing the quantum Fourier transform and its inverse are also examples of algorithms with rank-varying complexity. According to the quantum circuit in Figure 5, we need n Hadamard gates and $n - 1 + n - 2 + \cdots + 1$ conditional rotations, for a total of $n(n+1)/2$ gates required to compute the Fourier transform on n qubits. But this total amount of work is not evenly distributed over the n qubits. The number of gates a qubit

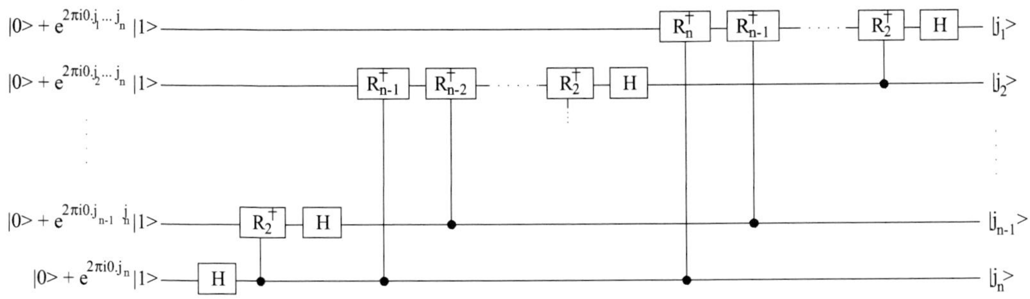

Figure 6. Quantum circuit performing the inverse Fourier transform.

needs to be passed through is in inverse relation with its *rank*. $|j_1\rangle$ is subjected to n elementary quantum gates, $n-1$ elementary unitary transformations are applied to $|j_2\rangle$, and so on, until $|j_n\rangle$, which needs only one basic operation.

If we break down the quantum Fourier transform algorithm into n steps (one for each qubit involved), then its complexity varies with each step. Starting with $|j_1\rangle$, the time needed to complete each step decreases over time. Since the rank of each step dictates its complexity, the circuit implementing the quantum Fourier transform is an example of a rank-varying complexity algorithm.

Naturally, the computation of the inverse quantum Fourier transform can also be decomposed into steps of varying complexity. Reversing each gate in Figure 5 gives us an efficient quantum circuit (depicted in Figure 6) for performing the inverse Fourier transform. Note that the Hadamard gate is its own inverse and $R_k^\dagger$ denotes the conjugate transpose of R_k:

$$R_k^\dagger \equiv \begin{bmatrix} 1 & 0 \\ 0 & e^{-2\pi i/2^k} \end{bmatrix}.$$

Getting back to the original $|j_1 j_2 \cdots j_n\rangle$ from its Fourier transformed expression has a certain particularity however. Because of the interdependencies introduced by the controlled rotations, the procedure must start by computing $|j_n\rangle$ and then work its way up to $|j_1\rangle$. The value of $|j_n\rangle$ is needed in the computation of $|j_{n-1}\rangle$. Both $|j_n\rangle$ and $|j_{n-1}\rangle$ are required in order to obtain $|j_{n-2}\rangle$. Finally, the value of all the higher rank bits are used to determine $|j_1\rangle$ precisely. Thus, computing the inverse Fourier transform by the quantum circuit illustrated in Figure 6 is a procedure the complexity of whose steps increases with their rank.

5.3. Semiclassical Solution

Although the circuits for computing the quantum Fourier transform and its inverse are efficient in terms of the total number of gates employed, the majority of these gates operate on two qubits. This makes a practical implementation difficult, since arranging for one qubit to influence another in a desired way is far greater a challenge than evolving a single-qubit closed quantum system in accordance with any unitary transformation.

A method to replace all the two-qubit gates in the circuit performing the quantum Fourier transform by a smaller number of one-qubit gates controlled by classical signals

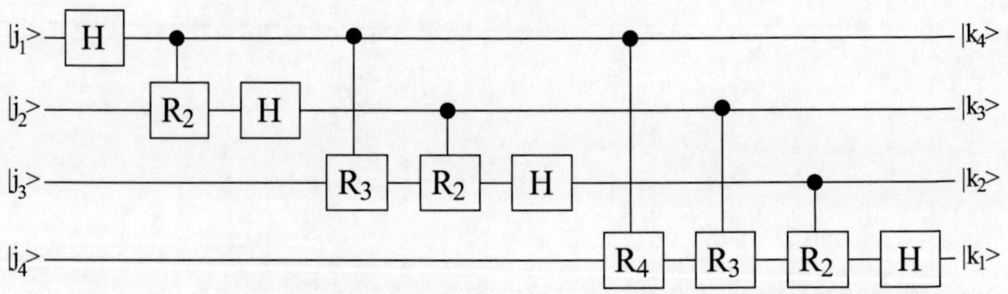

Figure 7. Alternative arrangement of gates in the circuit performing the quantum Fourier transform.

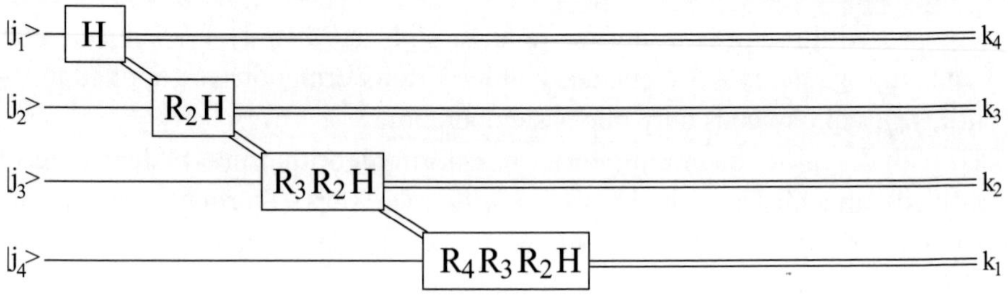

Figure 8. Semiclassical circuit for computing the quantum Fourier transform.

has been developed by Griffiths and Niu [38]. Their approach takes advantage of the fact that the roles of the control and target qubits in any of the two-qubit gates required to carry on the computation of the quantum Fourier transform are interchangeable. Consequently, the quantum circuit in Figure 5 is equivalent to the one depicted in Figure 7 (for inputs restricted to four qubits).

Note that, from this new perspective, the computation of the quantum Fourier transform appears to be a procedure whose steps are of increasing complexity. However, under the assumption that the Fourier transform is immediately followed by a quantum measurement, the complexity of each step in the computation can be made constant. Since a control qubit enters and leaves a two-qubit gate unchanged, it follows that the top qubit in Figure 7 yields the same result regardless of whether it is measured as it exits the circuit or immediately after undergoing the Hadamard transform. In the latter case, the result of the measurement can be used to determine the phase shift that needs to be applied on the second qubit, before it too is subjected to a Hadamard transform and then measured. The phase computed for the second qubit together with the result of the second measurement are passed down as classical inputs for the rotation applied to the third qubit.

The computation proceeds in this manner all the way down to the last qubit, with a phase rotation, a Hadamard gate and a measurement being performed at each step. The process is illustrated in Figure 8, where double lines have been used to denote a classical signal, according to the usual convention. Although the phase shift applied to each qubit is considered a single operation, conceptually, it is a combination of the gates depicted in the corresponding box, with each component being applied only if the controlling qubit was measured as 1.

Example: Here is an example of how the outcome of measurements determines the phase rotation that will be applied to subsequent qubits. If the top qubit in Figure 8 yields a 1 ($k_4 = 1$) when measured, then the second qubit undergoes a $\pi/2$ phase shift before the Hadamard gate and then it is measured. Supposc now that the outcome of this measurement is a 0 ($k_3 = 0$). Then the third qubit is phase shifted by

$$k_4\frac{\pi}{4} + k_3\frac{\pi}{2} = \frac{\pi}{4}$$

and then the Hadamard gate is applied. Again, without loss of generality, let the measurement yield a 1 ($k_2 = 1$). Then the phase shift applied to the bottom qubit is

$$k_4\frac{\pi}{8} + k_3\frac{\pi}{4} + k_2\frac{\pi}{2} = \frac{5\pi}{8}.$$

This semiclassical approach to computing the quantum Fourier transform achieves optimality in terms of the number of elementary unitary transformations that have to be applied. It also has the important advantage of employing only quantum transformations acting on a single qubit at a time. However, there is still room for improvement, as the total time needed to complete the computation can be further squeezed down if parallelism is brought into play. In what follows, we show how a quantum pipeline architecture is able to speed up the computation of the Fourier transform.

5.4. Parallel Approach

The solution developed in [38] to reduce the complexity of the quantum Fourier transform envisages a purely sequential approach, which is motivated by the same data dependency that causes the complexity of a step to vary with its rank. Nevertheless, there is a certain degree of parallelism that is worth exploiting in the computation of the quantum Fourier transform (or its inverse) in order to minimize the overall running time.

Our parallel approach is based on the observation that once a qubit has been measured, all phase shift gates classically controlled by the outcome of that measurement can be applied in parallel. The arrangement, again for just four qubits, is shown in Figure 9. The one-qubit gates are ordered into a linear array having a Hadamard transform at the top and followed by a $\pi/2$ phase shift gate. The phase shift induced by any other gate down the array is just half the rotation performed by the immediately preceding gate.

This architecture allows R_2, R_3 and R_4 to be performed in parallel during the first cycle. Since each phase shift gate acts on a different qubit, they can all be applied simultaneously, if the top qubit yielded a 1 upon measurement. In the second cycle, each qubit in the array travels up one position, except of course for the top one, which has already been measured. Now, depending on the outcome of the second measurement, R_2 and R_3 can be simultaneously effected on the corresponding qubits. In the third cycle, only R_2 is needed and only if the control is 1. The computation ends with the last qubit reaching the Hadamard gate and being measured afterwards. A formal description of the procedure, in the general case, is given below.

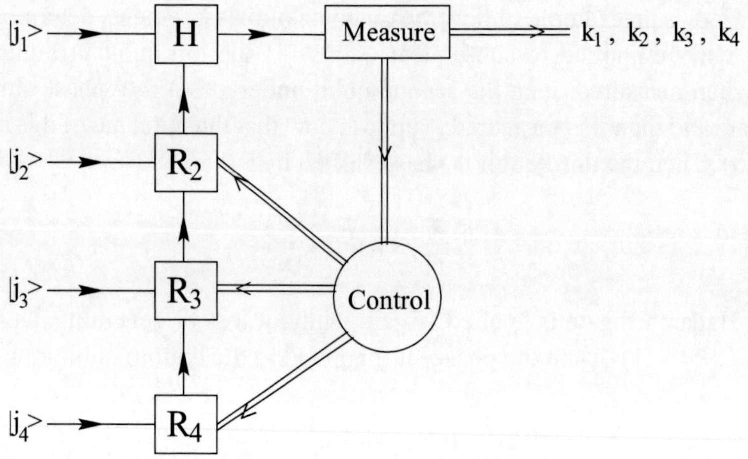

Figure 9. Quantum pipeline array for computing the Fourier transform.

Procedure *Parallel_Quantum_Fourier_Transform*

Input: $|j_1 j_2 \cdots j_n\rangle$
Output: $k_1 k_2 \cdots k_n$

for $i = 1$ **to** n **do**

$|j_i\rangle \longleftarrow H|j_i\rangle$;
Measure $|j_i\rangle$ as k_{n-i+1};
if $k_{n-i+1} = 1$ **then**
for $l = 2$ **to** $n - i + 1$ **do in parallel**
$|j_{i+l-1}\rangle \longleftarrow R_l|j_{i+l-1}\rangle$;
$|j_{i+l-1}\rangle$ moves one position up in the array
endfor
endif

endfor

In the worst case, when all qubits are measured as 1, there is no difference between the parallel algorithm outlined above and the sequential solution envisaged by Griffiths and Niu [38] with respect to the overall running time. Assuming, for analysis purposes, that measuring a qubit, applying a phase shift, and performing a Hadamard transformation, each takes one time unit, then the total time necessary to complete the Fourier transform on a quantum register with n qubits is $3n - 1$, as the top qubit in both the sequential circuit of Figure 8 and the parallel circuit of Figure 9 does not require a phase shift.

However, in the average case, some of the classical signals controlling the array of phase shift gates in Figure 9 will have been observed as 0, meaning that no phase shifts have to be performed during those respective cycles. In contrast, the sequential solution depicted in Figure 8 requires the application of a phase shift at every step following the first measurement with outcome 1. If the expected probability of a measurement yielding 0 equals the expected probability to observe a 1 following a measurement, then the running time of the parallel solution is shorter than the sequential running time by a difference proportional to the time it takes to effect a number of $O(n)$ phase shift gates, where n is the size of the input register.

The difference between the sequential running time and the parallel running time is maximum when $|j_1\rangle$ is measured as 1 and all the other qubits are observed in the state 0. In this case, the circuit in Figure 8 still performs $n - 1$ phase shifts, for a total running time of $3n - 1$ time units, while the circuit in Figure 9 executes all $n - 1$ phase shifts in parallel during the first cycle, thus completing the computation in $2n + 1$ time units.

The second advantage of the parallel approach is that the phase shift gates that need to be applied during the computation are known at the outset, making it easy to set them up beforehand in order to form the required linear array architecture. In other words, regardless of the initial quantum state of the register on which the QFT is to be performed, the first gate in the linear array (top gate in Figure 9) will always perform a Hadamard gate, the second gate always performs a $\pi/2$ phase shift, the third gate is "hardwired" to effect a $\pi/4$ phase shift and so on. The systolic mode of operation of the quantum array compensates for the fixed characteristics of each gate, the qubits traversing the array to undergo a specific quantum evolution at each node. In the current context, the attribute "systolic" describes the rhythmic mode in which data travel through the array of gates, much like blood does through the circulatory system.

In the sequential approach, on the other hand, the phase shift applied to each qubit is not known at the outset, as it is computed on the fly based on the information about the measurements performed so far and transmitted as classical signals. This means that the gates effecting the necessary phase shifts in the semiclassical approach of Griffiths and Niu [38] have to be "programmed" or adjusted during the computation, in order to accommodate a discrete set of possible values for the phase shift.

In the example given at the end of previous section, the phase shift applied to the bottom qubit is $5\pi/8$ because the previous measurements yielded $k_4 = 1$, $k_3 = 0$ and $k_2 = 1$. But the phase shift could have been $7\pi/8$ if all the measurements yielded a 1 or just $\pi/8$ if $k_4 = 1$ and $k_3 = k_2 = 0$. Therefore, we don't know at the outset how to "set" the quantum gates responsible with the phase shift performed on each qubit, as this information becomes available only during the computation, depending on the probabilistic results of the measurements. Technologically, this is more difficult to implement than a linear array of gates whose characteristics are fixed for any possible course of the computation.

The semiclassical Fourier transform and its parallelization are applicable to those quantum computations in which the Fourier transform immediately precedes a measurement of the qubits involved in the computation, like in Shor's algorithms for factoring integers and computing discrete logarithms [65]. Furthermore, the quantum systolic array architecture works equally fine if the input is already classical, in which case the restriction to measure the qubits after applying the Fourier transform can be lifted altogether.

When $j_1, j_2, \cdots, j_n$ are classical bits, the topology of the circuit in Figure 9 remains unchanged, except that no measurements are performed and the flow of data through the linear array is reversed, as shown in Figure 10. As more data are fed into the linear array through the Hadamard gate, after having "controlled" the parallel execution of a set of phase shifts, the computational complexity of each step increases with its rank. When j_1 enters

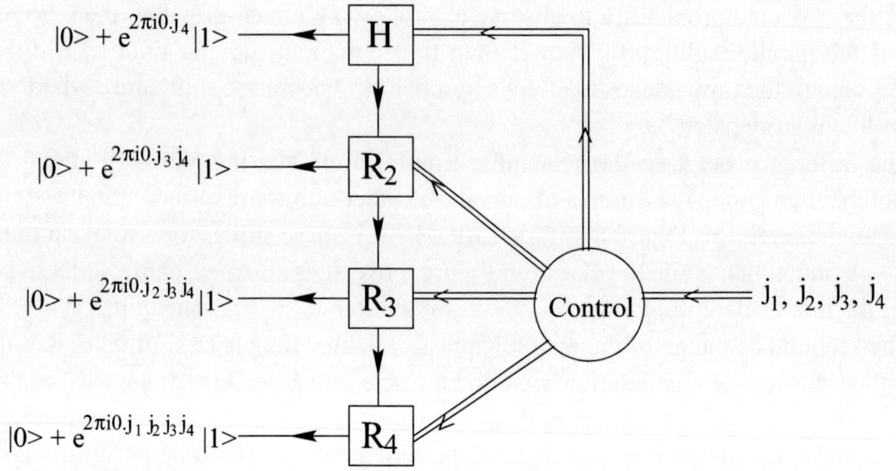

Figure 10. Quantum pipeline array for computing the Fourier transform on classical inputs.

the array, only the Hadamard gate is active, but with each consecutive step, a new gate down the array joins the ones above it to operate on the qubits traversing the array. Because these gates operate in parallel, the execution time of each step is maintained constant. Also note that, in this case, all outputs are simultaneously obtained during the last step of the computation.

The overall parallel running time, in the worst case, is therefore $2n - 1$ time units, as there are no measurements to perform. The worst case occurs when $j_2, j_3, \ldots, j_n$ have all value 1. For all other inputs (that is, when at least one of $j_2, j_3, \ldots, j_n$ is 0), the parallel running time is smaller than the time needed to complete the computation in a purely sequential manner, where each qubit is dealt with one after the other, in decreasing order of their ranks.

Quantum algorithms employ the Fourier transform in order to create an interference among the terms in a superposition. From this point of view, the quantum Fourier transform offers little advantage, if any, when applied to a classical input. However, the situation is different for quantum cryptography. Distributing classical keys through quantum means is a procedure that may use the quantum Fourier transform and its inverse as encoding and decoding algorithms to protect vital information while in transit [54]. We will explore this topic in section 6.

Naturally, the parallel approach detailed above for the computation of the direct Fourier transform is also applicable, with the same results, to the circuit in Figure 6, performing the inverse Fourier transform. The difference in time complexity between the sequential approach and the parallel one, although seemingly insignificant from a theoretical perspective, may prove essential under practical considerations, as we show next.

5.5. Quantum Decoherence

Qubits are fragile entities and one of the major challenges in building a practical quantum computer is to find a physical realization that would allow us to complete a computation before the quantum states we are working with become seriously affected by quantum errors. In an ideal setting, we evolve our qubits in perfect isolation from the outside world. But any practical implementation of a quantum computation will be affected by the interactions taking place between our system and the environment. These interactions cause quantum information to leak out into the environment, leading to errors in our qubits. Different types of errors may affect an ongoing computation in different ways, but *quantum decoherence*, as defined below, usually occurs extremely rapidly and can seriously interfere with computing the quantum Fourier transform and its inverse.

In the context of a quantum key distribution protocol [54], consider the task of recovering the original (classical) bit string $j = j_1 j_2 \cdots j_n$ from its quantum Fourier transformed form. The circuit performing this computation (see Figure 6) takes as input n qubits. The state of each qubit can be described by the following general equation:

$$|\psi_k\rangle = \frac{1}{\sqrt{2}}|0\rangle + \frac{e^{i\theta_k}}{\sqrt{2}}|1\rangle, \ 1 \leq k \leq n \tag{14}$$

where the relative phase θ_k, characterizing the qubit of rank k, depends on the values of bits $j_k, j_{k+1}, \cdots, j_n$. The corresponding density operator is given by

$$\rho_k = |\psi_k\rangle\langle\psi_k| = \frac{1}{2}|0\rangle\langle 0| + \frac{e^{-i\theta_k}}{2}|0\rangle\langle 1| + \frac{e^{i\theta_k}}{2}|1\rangle\langle 0| + \frac{1}{2}|1\rangle\langle 1|, \tag{15}$$

or in matrix form

$$\rho_k = \frac{1}{2}\begin{bmatrix} 1 & e^{-i\theta_k} \\ e^{i\theta_k} & 1 \end{bmatrix}. \tag{16}$$

The diagonal elements (or the *populations*) measure the probabilities that the qubit is in state $|0\rangle$ or $|1\rangle$, while the off-diagonal components (the *coherences*) measure the amount of interference between $|0\rangle$ and $|1\rangle$ [26]. Decoherence then, resulting from interactions with the environment, causes the off-diagonal elements to disappear. Since that is where the whole information carried by a qubit is stored, the input qubits for computing the inverse Fourier transform are very sensitive to decoherence. When they become entangled with the environment, the interference brought about by the Hadamard gate is no longer possible, as the system becomes effectively a statistical mixture. In other words, decoherence makes a quantum system behave like a classical one.

Naturally, this process is not instantaneous, but it usually occurs extremely rapidly, subject to how well a qubit can be isolated from its environment in a particular physical realization. Because of decoherence, we must obtain the values of $j_1, j_2, \cdots, j_n$ before time limit δ, after which the errors introduced by the coupling with the environment are too serious to still allow the recovery of the binary digits of j.

The precise value of δ will certainly depend on the particular way chosen to embody quantum information. If the qubits are implemented as trapped ions, then usually such a physical system is relatively well-isolated and decoherence is not a major concern. Nevertheless, other impediments make the design of a scalable quantum architecture a very challenging task. As a consequence, current experiments are only able to manipulate a handful of qubits. An illustrative example is a result from 2005 reporting the implementation of the semiclassical QFT on a "quantum register" composed of three beryllium ion qubits [23].

At the other end of the spectrum, we have attempts to implement the QFT, and quantum algorithms in general, using the well-established technology of nuclear magnetic resonance (NMR). In this case, decoherence plays a much more important role, directly affecting the accuracy of the results and placing a serious limitation on the scalability of this type of quantum computing architecture.

Experimental arrangements to compute the QFT on a 3-qubit NMR quantum information processor are reported by Weinstein et al. [70, 71]. Also, a 7-qubit experiment to implement the simplest meaningful instance of Shor's algorithm for factoring the number 15 uses the QFT as an important step of the computation [69]. Again we can see that scalability is the main obstacle towards building a practical quantum computer.

Of course, one of the possibilities to cope with the errors introduced by quantum decoherence is to use quantum codes to correct them. But here too, there are limitations. The more serious the errors are, the more ancillary qubits are required to correct them and consequently, the higher the probability of an error occurring in the correcting circuit itself. Therefore, we can only use that many auxiliary qubits to correct quantum errors before no advantage whatsoever in the accuracy of the solution is gained. From this point of view, parallelism offers a "clean" solution, avoiding the errors caused by quantum decoherence altogether and completing the computation before the entanglement with the surrounding environment seriously affects the ongoing quantum transformations.

The point we wish to make here is that when all other means have been used, a parallel approach like the one described in this paper may be the only way to further improve scalability by reducing the running time of the quantum algorithm and keep it below the decoherence threshold. Returning to our example, when δ lies between the parallel completion time and the sequential completion time, then the quantum pipeline array may be the only architecture capable to precisely recover all digits in the binary expansion of j. From a different perspective, the parallel solution allows for longer bit strings to be transmitted between the communicating parties, thus achieving better scalability over the purely sequential approach. With respect to scalability, it is also important to note that our parallel solution scales up linearly in the number of quantum gates employed, when the number of qubits on which the QFT is performed increases.

Griffiths and Niu [38] also point to decoherence as a possible problem when discussing their semiclassical solution to computing the quantum Fourier transform, and suggest to counter it by arranging the computation in such a way that the more significant bits of the input register are produced earlier than the less significant ones. This may or may not be possible, depending on the particular characteristics of a certain application. In the case of the inverse Fourier transform used as a decoding method in a quantum key distribution protocol [54], starting to work early on qubits of higher rank is not possible because the rank of each qubit is not disclosed until the second stage of the protocol, when all qubits are available to the receiving party. In such a situation, the parallel approach previously described can make the difference between success and failure when computing the quantum Fourier transform or its inverse in a practical setting. Alternatively, since the overall running time scales up with the number of input qubits, parallelism may be a way to improve scalability and still complete the computation before decoherence effects take hold.

5.6. Discussion

The difficulty of devising a parallel algorithm for computing the quantum Fourier transform comes from the data dependency between the different steps of the procedure. In most cases, it is exactly this precedence among the steps composing an algorithm that determines the variation in complexity. As a consequence, it is not easy, in general, to design a parallel solution to a problem whose steps are characterized by rank-varying complexity. The data dependency may impose a strict order of execution, making the resulting algorithm inherently sequential (think about Euclid's algorithm again). But, there is also a positive aspect of the data dependency characterizing the quantum Fourier transform. It may be exploited in cryptographic applications, for example to increase the security and intrusion detection rate in quantum key distribution protocols.

On the other hand, perhaps there exist computations made up of steps of various rank-dependent complexities, for which the order of execution is of no consequence to the correctness of the computation. Imagine, for instance, a task made up of n steps: $S_1, S_2, \ldots, S_n$, where the steps can be executed in any order, but the more steps we execute before a certain step S_j $(1 \leq j \leq n)$, the more time it will take to complete S_j. For example, S_j may require i elementary operations (time units) if executed i^{th}, for $i = 1, 2, \ldots, n$. This rank-driven increase in complexity may be due to how many pieces of data have to be taken into consideration at each consecutive step, how the data were affected by executing the previous steps, or it may be justified by the size of the partial solution that has to be constructed at each step.

In any case, the problem of coping with steps of ever increasing complexity is avoided altogether by a parallel machine endowed with n processing units. All steps would then be executed simultaneously, and since each step has the rank 1 in such a parallel approach, the computational complexity is kept constant (one time unit, in our example) for all steps. The difference between a sequential and a parallel approach is even more dramatic if the complexity of a step grows faster with its rank. In the case where step S_j $(1 \leq j \leq n)$ needs 2^i elementary operations (time units) to be completed, if executed i^{th}, $i = 1, 2, \ldots, n$, the benefits of using a parallel approach would be much higher.

6. Quantum Key Distribution

In this section we show that the quantum Fourier transform is a very versatile tool that can be employed not only to design fast quantum algorithms, but has applications in quantum cryptography as well. Two of the most important problems in cryptography are concerned with the *security* and *authenticity* of exchanged messages. There are perfectly good ways to achieve these two goals, provided the two parties (generically referred to as Alice and Bob) wishing to communicate over an insecure (public) channel share a secret key. Therefore, the *key distribution* step, allowing Alice and Bob to establish a secret key prior to exchanging any messages, is of capital importance for many areas of cryptography.

Various schemes have been proposed over time to ensure the security and authenticity of communications without resorting to a previously shared private key (Diffie-Hellman, Digital Signature Algorithm, RSA). Probably, the most successful example of such a public-key system is the RSA cryptographic system, based on the RSA algorithm [62]. The security of public-key cryptographic communication systems rests on unproved assumptions about the difficulty to compute the decryption key, even when the encryption key is known. The RSA algorithm, for example, so popular today, capitalizes on the presumed intractability of factoring large numbers in a reasonable amount of time, although nobody was able to prove that factoring is not in P.

With the advent of processing information at the quantum level, the security of cryptographic protocols was set on a firmer foundation. Quantum key distribution (QKD) schemes were proposed whose security is guaranteed by the very laws of physics (quantum mechanics, more precisely). What really distinguishes them from the classical cryptographic protocols is that they make the difference in terms of *intrusion detection*. In a classical scheme, one can only hope that the adversary simply does not have enough computational resources to gain knowledge of the information in transit. There is no protocol that allows for the detection of an eavesdropper. The ability to copy classical information without restriction is responsible for this situation. In contrast, since arbitrary quantum bits cannot be cloned [72], it is much more difficult for an eavesdropper to spy on a quantum communication without being detected.

Several techniques exist that exploit quantum effects for key distribution [12, 11, 35]. Their aim is to maximize the intrusion detection rate, upon which the security of the protocols rests. In these protocols, Alice conveys the secret information to Bob by encoding it into some quantum properties of photons. At the other end, Bob has to subject each photon to a quantum measurement, as soon as it is received, in order to agree with Alice on a common key. In the following, we review the main existing techniques for QKD in order to provide a context for the discussion of the new protocols proposed in this section. Thus, when analyzing their features and performance, we will use the work reviewed below for reference and comparison.

6.1. An Overview of Previous QKD Protocols

Generally, QKD protocols involve two stages. The first one is usually a one-way communication (from Alice to Bob) over a quantum channel. In this stage, a random sequence of bits generated by Alice is transmitted over to Bob, each 0 or 1 encoded in some quantum observable (photon polarization is the natural choice). Having measured each incoming qubit in one of the pre-defined bases, Bob must now communicate with Alice over a public channel to exchange information about the encoding of each qubit and eventually agree upon a common secret key. This two-way communication between Alice and Bob over a classical channel represents the second stage of QKD protocols. The above two-stage scenario forms the backbone of all schemes developed so far in order to distribute classical keys through quantum means. They differ only in the particular quantum mechanical features or principles chosen to achieve their goal.

The first quantum protocol for key distribution was developed in 1984 by Charles Bennett and Gilles Brassard and is hence known as BB84 [12]. It is characterized by the use of

Alice	0	1	1	0	0	1	0	0	0	1	0	0	1	1	0
	$\times$	+	$\times$	+	+	+	$\times$	$\times$	+	+	$\times$	+	$\times$	$\times$	$\times$
	$\nearrow$	$\uparrow$	$\nwarrow$	$\rightarrow$	$\rightarrow$	$\uparrow$	$\nearrow$	$\nearrow$	$\rightarrow$	$\uparrow$	$\nearrow$	$\rightarrow$	$\nwarrow$	$\nwarrow$	$\nearrow$
Bob	+	+	$\times$	+	$\times$	$\times$	+	$\times$	$\times$	+	+	+	$\times$	+	$\times$
	1	1	1	0	0	1	1	0	1	1	0	0	1	1	0
key		1	1	0				0		1		0	1		0

Figure 11. Quantum key distribution in the absence of eavesdropping.

two quantum alphabets (orthonormal bases) for encoding and decoding the bits transmitted. One consists of the vertical and horizontal polarization states of photons, while the other orthonormal basis corresponds to polarization directions formed respectively by 45° clockwise and counter-clockwise rotations off from the vertical. The convention used for the two quantum alphabets could be

$$\begin{cases} \text{“0”} & = \; |\rightarrow\rangle \\ \text{“1”} & = \; |\uparrow\rangle \end{cases}$$

in the case of the vertical/horizontal basis, and

$$\begin{cases} \text{“0”} & = \; |\nearrow\rangle \\ \text{“1”} & = \; |\nwarrow\rangle \end{cases}$$

for the oblique basis. In the first stage of BB84, Alice randomly chooses one of these two agreed-upon quantum alphabets for each bit transmitted. At the receiving end, Bob also selects one basis, at random, to measure each incoming photon and decode the bit carried. By comparing the alphabet used for encoding with that used for decoding, in the second stage of the protocol, Alice and Bob can reach an agreement for a common binary substring called the *raw key*, by keeping only those bits for which the encoding and decoding basis was the same and discarding all the others (roughly half of the total number of bits transmitted). Figure 11 illustrates this process.

Using a pair of conjugate (incompatible) observables, the BB84 protocol relies on Heisenberg's uncertainty principle coupled with the inevitable disturbance caused by quantum measurements to detect potential eavesdroppers. On average, 25% of the photons that Eve (the prototypical eavesdropper) chooses to tamper with will give rise to disagreements between Alice's raw key and Bob's raw key. Things get more complicated when such disagreements can also be the result of imperfections or noise in the quantum channel. Consequently, Eve could adopt the strategy of gaining only partial knowledge about the key by trying to hide behind the noise level. To cope with such low levels of eavesdropping, Bennett et al. [15] have proposed the method of *privacy amplification*, a mathematical technique based on the principle of hashing functions that magnifies Eve's uncertainty over the final form of the key.

Using pairs of orthogonal polarization states as quantum alphabets for the transmitted bits is not a necessary condition. Bennett showed [11] that any two non-orthogonal quantum states can be used to achieve key distribution in a practical interferometric realization using low-intensity coherent light pulses. The protocol (known as B92) needs only one quantum alphabet, but with non-orthogonal polarization states. Therefore, Bob must be equipped with a POVM (positive operator value measure) receiver in order to interpret the incoming photons properly. As in the case of BB84, eavesdropping attempts are made apparent by an unusual error rate in Bob's raw key. Specific to B92 is the possibility of detecting eavesdroppers by an unusual erasure rate (inconclusive receptions) for Bob.

The protocols that offer the best security, at least from a theoretical viewpoint, are based on entanglement (EPR pairs). Inspired by EPR experiments designed to test Bell's inequality, Artur Ekert thought of a way of using entangled pairs for distributing cryptographic keys by quantum means [35]. In the first stage of his scheme, Alice and Bob receive entangled particles from a central source and perform independent measurements upon them. The shared secret key is established in the second stage, when Alice and Bob publicly confront the orientations they adopted for each measurement.

Similarly to BB84, the key will consist of only those bits that were measured in the same basis by both participants. Unlike the BB84 protocol, however, the remaining bits are not discarded, but the strength of their correlations is used to test for eavesdroppers. These correlations must exceed anything that is possible classically, according to Bell's theorem, if the original EPR pairs were untampered with. A related, but simpler EPR cryptographic scheme was described by Bennett, Brassard and Mermin [14] that is proved secure without the need to invoke Bell's theorem. They also show the equivalence between their scheme and the original BB84 key distribution protocol.

Protocols resorting to EPR pairs offer a qualitatively new level of security, that becomes apparent by considering the scenario in which someone attempts to make measurements on the particles before they arrive at the legitimate receiver. For an entanglement-free protocol, such an eavesdropping strategy aims at gaining knowledge of the information encoded in the qubits transmitted. But in the case of schemes based on EPR pairs, Eve cannot elicit any information from the transiting particles simply because there is no information encoded there. The information about the secret key has yet to come into being once Alice and Bob perform their measurements.

Another advantage of entanglement-based schemes refers to the issue of privacy amplification. The limitations of the classical privacy amplification based on hashing algorithms are overcome in the quantum privacy amplification technique developed in 1996 [30]. The quantum procedure, which is applicable only to entanglement-based quantum cryptography, is in fact an entanglement purification process that can be repeatedly applied to impurely entangled particles to cleanse them of any signs of tampering by Eve.

However, these advantages of entanglement-based cryptography are rather theoretical at the moment because storing entangled particles is only possible for a fraction of a second as yet, and entanglement purification depends on quantum computational hardware that, although simple, has yet to be built. In contrast, implementations of the original BB84 protocol are well within the capabilities of current technology, reaching the point where they have become commercially viable.

6.2. Motivation for Our Approach

At an abstract level, a QKD protocol could be described in terms of qubits transmitted over a quantum channel. For practical implementations, the physical realization usually chosen to embody a qubit is the photon. Since it travels at the speed of light and its polarization can be easily manipulated, the photon is naturally suited for transmitting information. Still, in some cases, other realizations are equally possible, like manipulating the spin of an electron, for instance. Regardless of their possible implementations, all QKD protocols share one basic constraint: qubits are measured individually as soon as they are received. Storing the incoming qubits for later processing and/or measurement is not taken into consideration. This is quite intuitive, especially if we think about photons, which, by their nature, are made to travel and not to store information locally, in a static fashion.

This section investigates the opportunities created by the relaxation of the aforementioned constraint. More explicitly, we are interested in what benefits can be gained and at what cost, if we allow the qubits transmitted over the quantum channel to be stored for a determined amount of time by the receiving party. In the following, we motivate the feasibility of this assumption, even if the qubits are realized as photons.

Two of the main proposals for building a practical quantum computer are based on "ion traps" and cavity QED (quantum electrodynamics), respectively. In the ion trap scheme imagined by Cirac and Zoller [24], a quantum memory register would be physically realized by using "fences" of electromagnetic fields to trap a number of ions within the central region of an evacuated chamber. Each imprisoned ion embodies a qubit, with the ground state representing $|0\rangle$ and a metastable state representing $|1\rangle$. The operation of a quantum gate is effected by shining a pulse of light from a laser beam of the appropriate frequency onto the target ion. Although very simple quantum algorithms have been implemented on an ion trap quantum computer [40], the technology's main drawback remains scalability.

In the other proposal, which goes by the name of "flying qubit"-based quantum computer, quantum information is encoded in the polarization states of photons. The interaction necessary to emulate the functionality of a controlled-NOT quantum gate can be mediated by a drifting cesium atom, when the photons are placed inside a small cavity with highly reflecting walls. Quantum-phase gates based on cavity QED have been successfully realized experimentally [28, 68], yet again, it is a very challenging endeavor to extend this technology to complicated quantum circuits.

One of the ideas that emerged in order to overcome the scalability problem is a hybrid approach that combines the advantages of both ion trap and cavity QED technologies. In this approach, ion traps of limited size each would be interconnected through fiber optics, forming a quantum network. Thus, photons could be used to transfer quantum information between distant trapped atoms, while each of the multibit ion traps is responsible for storing information and local processing. The cavity QED interactions can provide the necessary methods for exchanging quantum information between the two different carriers [25]. Alternatively, the same goal can be achieved by using entanglement between a trapped atom and a photon [20].

The techniques proposed to implement a quantum network can also be applied in a cryptographic context. The qubits "flying" through the quantum channel will still be realized as photons, but whenever the receiving party wishes to store them (until it has better

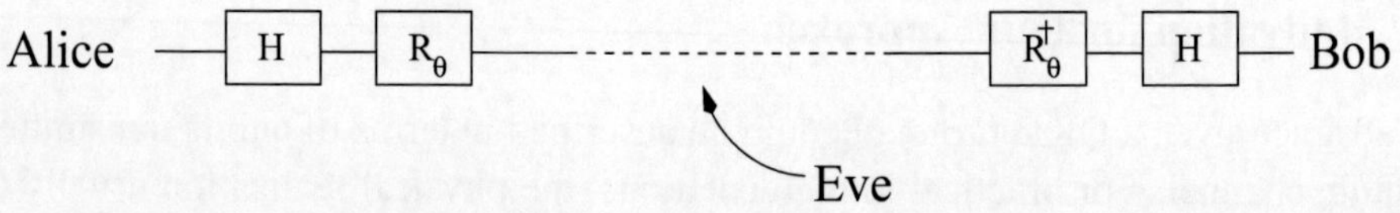

Figure 12. Schematics of random phase shift protocol for QKD.

knowledge about their encoding, for example), the information they carry is transferred to a local ion trap quantum register, which is much more suited for storing information over an extended length of time. Hence, our working assumption is motivated practically by the advancements made on the way toward building a quantum computer.

The immediate benefit of storing qubits during a quantum protocol for a more "intelligent" processing/measurement is an important reduction in the communication volume required, both quantum and classical. In the case of BB84, for instance, if Bob can safely store the qubits received from Alice until the second stage of the protocol, when he is informed of the exact encoding for each of them, then an appropriate measurement can be performed for each qubit. In this way, no qubit has to be discarded due to a mismatch between the encoding and decoding alphabet. For a shared secret key of a specified length, this leads to a 50% reduction in the total number of qubits that have to be transmitted. With fewer qubits transmitted, the volume of the classical communication in stage 2 of the protocol is reduced too. The fact that an eavesdropper may gain knowledge about the correct measurement basis for each qubit is of no advantage to her, since the qubits are no longer in her possession.

But reducing the amount of communication between Alice and Bob is not the only advantage offered by temporarily storing qubits. This possibility opens the door for designing new QKD schemes that have higher rates of intrusion detection and are therefore more secure. In the remainder of this section we show explicitly how storing qubits for a limited time can be exploited to enhance security.

6.3. Random $\frac{\pi}{2}$ Phase Shift Protocol

We first describe a BB84 equivalent protocol that we will use as a building block in designing a QKD scheme based on the Quantum Fourier Transform. The main idea of the protocol described herein is to encode each transmitted bit (0 or 1) into the relative phase between the $|0\rangle$ and $|1\rangle$ components of a balanced superposition and then encrypt the resulting qubit by applying a random phase shift gate, as depicted in Figure 12. The Hadamard gate provides the encoding alphabet

$$\begin{cases} \text{"0"} & \mapsto \frac{1}{\sqrt{2}}(|0\rangle + |1\rangle) \\ \text{"1"} & \mapsto \frac{1}{\sqrt{2}}(|0\rangle - |1\rangle) \end{cases}$$

and the R_θ gate rotates the relative phase with an angle θ

$$R_\theta = \begin{bmatrix} 1 & 0 \\ 0 & e^{i\theta} \end{bmatrix}, \ \theta \in \{0, \frac{\pi}{2}\}.$$

Note that R_0 does not affect the state of the qubit onto which the gate is applied, while $R_{\pi/2}$ rotates the qubit halfway between the two symbols of the encoding alphabet. The gate $R_\theta^\dagger$ denotes the inverse of R_θ. The protocol conforms to the generic two-stage structure, sketched in section 2.

Random $\frac{\pi}{2}$ phase shift protocol for QKD

Stage 1: Communication over a quantum channel

Step 1. Alice flips a fair coin to generate a random binary sequence that she intends to share with Bob.

Step 2. For each bit j in the sequence, Alice chooses , again at random, an angle $\theta = 0$ or $\theta = \pi/2$. She then prepares, accordingly, a qubit in the state $|\psi\rangle = R_\theta H|j\rangle$ that she sends over to Bob.

Step 3. Bob applies the necessary procedures for safely storing the qubits received from Alice until the second stage of the protocol, when he gains knowledge of which qubits have been phase shifted.

Stage 2: Communication over a public channel

Phase 1. Raw key extraction

Step 1. Alice informs Bob about her choice of θ for each transmitted bit.

Step 2. Knowing the relative phase shift θ for each stored qubit $|\psi\rangle$, Bob recovers the original bit transmitted, by computing $|j\rangle = HR_\theta^\dagger|\psi\rangle$ and then measuring $|j\rangle$ in the normal computational basis $\{|0\rangle, |1\rangle\}$. Following this procedure, Bob obtains a binary sequence that should be identical to the one randomly generated by Alice, provided no eavesdropping or errors interfered with the quantum transmission.

Phase 2. Error estimation

Step 1. Over the public channel, Alice and Bob compare portions of their raw keys to estimate the error rate Err. The bits tested are deleted from their raw keys. If $Err = 0$ the remaining bits form their final secret key.

Step 2. If $Err > 0$, but still sufficiently small, Alice and Bob may decide to apply privacy amplification techniques to minimize Eve's knowledge about their final secret key. Otherwise, if Err exceeds a certain threshold, they discard the whole sequence and start all over again.

The analogy with BB84 becomes apparent if we assimilate the encoding alphabet with the horizontal/vertical basis and the $\pi/2$ relative phase shift with the oblique basis. What are Eve's chances to break the above protocol and find a loophole that may allow her to elicit information about the secret key? In what follows, we analyze two main eavesdropping strategies that Eve may adopt.

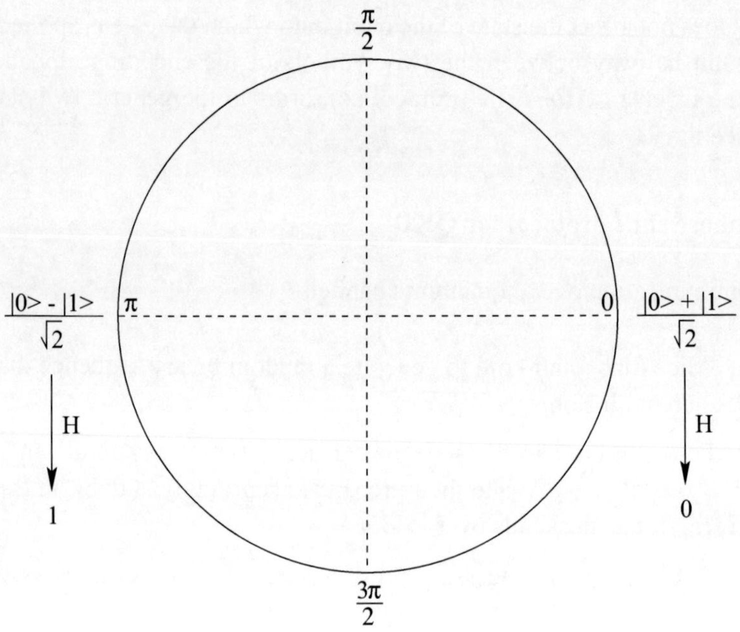

Figure 13. Bit encoding in the random $\frac{\pi}{2}$ phase shift protocol.

6.3.1. Opaque Eavesdropping

The most straightforward way in which Eve could spy on the quantum communication between Alice and Bob would be to intercept Alice's information carriers and measure them in some appropriate basis. If she could undo the rotation (with angle θ) applied by Alice, then she could measure the intercepted qubit using the basis $\{\frac{1}{\sqrt{2}}(|0\rangle+|1\rangle), \frac{1}{\sqrt{2}}(|0\rangle-|1\rangle)\}$. Such a measurement is carried out by first passing the qubit through a Hadamard gate and then measuring it in the normal computational basis $\{|0\rangle, |1\rangle\}$.

Since Eve has no information about θ, trying to rotate the qubit back with $\pi/2$ (see Figure 13) is in no way a better strategy than applying the Hadamard gate directly. Without loss of generality, consider what happens if the qubit intercepted by Eve encodes the bit 0 (the other case proceeds in an analogous way yielding a symmetric result). Before is acted upon, its state is given by

$$|\psi^0\rangle = R_\theta H|0\rangle = \frac{1}{\sqrt{2}}|0\rangle + \frac{1}{\sqrt{2}}e^{i\theta}|1\rangle. \tag{17}$$

Eve is assumed to have knowledge of the encoding alphabet, so she reverses the effect of the Hadamard gate by also applying a Hadamard gate (which is its own inverse):

$$H|\psi^0\rangle = \frac{1}{2}(|0\rangle + |1\rangle) + \frac{e^{i\theta}}{2}(|0\rangle - |1\rangle) = \frac{1+e^{i\theta}}{2}|0\rangle + \frac{1-e^{i\theta}}{2}|1\rangle. \tag{18}$$

Upon observing the above state, Eve will see a 0 with probability

$$p^0_{Eve} = |\frac{1+e^{i\theta}}{2}|^2 = \frac{1+\cos\theta}{2}. \tag{19}$$

and a 1 with probability

$$p_{Eve}^1 = |\frac{1 - e^{i\theta}}{2}|^2 = \frac{1 - \cos\theta}{2}. \tag{20}$$

where θ is either 0 or $\pi/2$ (see Figure 13). Next, Eve uses the Hadamard transform again to prepare a qubit in an encoded state compatible with the measurement's outcome and sends it to Bob. Bob keeps the qubit untouched until Alice informs him of the correct rotation angle θ. Then, he applies the $R_\theta^\dagger$ gate, thus inducing a relative phase of $-\theta$, since he received the qubit from Eve and not from Alice. Finally, Bob measures the qubit in the Hadamard basis, obtaining a 0 with the following probability:

$$p_{Bob}^0 = p_{Eve}^0 \cdot |\frac{1 + e^{-i\theta}}{2}|^2 + p_{Eve}^1 \cdot |\frac{1 - e^{-i\theta}}{2}|^2 = \frac{1 + \cos^2\theta}{2}. \tag{21}$$

For $\theta = 0$, $p_{Bob}^0 = 1$ and Eve gets undetected, but if $\theta = \pi/2$, p_{Bob}^0 is only $1/2$, so, on average, there is a 25% probability of detecting Eve for each qubit she chooses to eavesdrop on (same as BB84). Of course, this probability can be made arbitrarily close to 1 by testing a sufficiently large number of qubits. In turn, this requires a large number of qubits to be transmitted through the quantum channel. If Bob can store these qubits until the second stage of the protocol, the cost of the total communication (both quantum and classical) is effectively halved. Parity checking techniques, to avoid discarding bits when testing for eavesdropping, are also applicable.

6.3.2. Translucent Eavesdropping

In order to avoid the inevitable disturbance caused by a measurement, Eve could decide for a more subtle eavesdropping technique. She could choose, for instance, to entangle Alice's information carrier with her own probe, sending half of the entangled pair to Bob while keeping the other half for herself. Then, upon finding about the correct θ angle, by listening in on the conversation between Alice and Bob on the classical channel, Eve can apply the $R_\theta^\dagger$ and Hadamard gates to the qubit in her possession, hoping to unlock the information hidden within it. We focus again on the case when Alice encodes a 0, with the observation that the analysis for the other case would proceed in a similar way. The entanglement operation, performed by Eve, is described by the following equation:

$$CNOT((\frac{1}{\sqrt{2}}|0\rangle + \frac{e^{i\theta}}{\sqrt{2}}|1\rangle) \otimes |0\rangle) = \frac{1}{\sqrt{2}}|00\rangle + \frac{e^{i\theta}}{\sqrt{2}}|11\rangle. \tag{22}$$

where *CNOT* denotes the application of a controlled-*NOT* operation, with the qubit intercepted from Alice acting as the control qubit. When Alice discloses to Bob whether she applied the $\pi/2$ relative phase shift or not, Eve can proceed to effect the $R_\theta^\dagger$ and Hadamard transformations on the qubit remained in her possession. This will change the state of the ensemble Eve-Bob as follows:

$$\begin{aligned} H \otimes I(R_\theta^\dagger \otimes I(\tfrac{1}{\sqrt{2}}|00\rangle + \tfrac{e^{i\theta}}{\sqrt{2}}|11\rangle)) &= H \otimes I(\tfrac{1}{\sqrt{2}}|00\rangle + \tfrac{1}{\sqrt{2}}|11\rangle) \\ &= \frac{1}{2}(|00\rangle + |01\rangle + |10\rangle - |11\rangle). \end{aligned} \tag{23}$$

Similarly, if a bit with the value 1 would have been transmitted by Alice, the state of the entangled ensemble would have been

$$\frac{1}{2}(|00\rangle - |01\rangle + |10\rangle + |11\rangle). \tag{24}$$

Although distinguishing among states (23) and (24) is possible by applying a two-qubit gate on the whole ensemble, no information can be elicited by acting only on one qubit. In particular, a quantum measurement in the normal computational basis will yield a 0 or a 1 with equal probability.

The description and analysis of the protocol assumed an error-free quantum channel. The issue of noise can be addressed by introducing an additional phase to the second stage of the protocol. During this phase, Alice and Bob remove all errors from their tentative final key, producing a common error-free key, called *reconciled key* (see [46], chapter III, for details).

We conclude the analysis of the random $\pi/2$ phase shift protocol with a few observations that, although formulated for the protocol presented in this section, can be generalized, in a suitable form, to probably any existing QKD scheme. For each qubit Eve decides to tamper with, there is a certain chance (25% in our case, as well as for BB84) that she will be caught. It is important to emphasize that this probability is independent of the actions performed on the other qubits transmitted through the quantum channel. The only way Eve can be detected is to test one of the qubits she decided to spy on. In half of the cases, when she is lucky, the quantum state retransmitted to Bob is identical to the one intercepted from Alice, so she gains knowledge of the bit transmitted without any possibility of being detected. On the other hand, if she gets unlucky, then her uncertainty about the bit transmitted is total and, in addition, she disturbs the state of the qubit, introducing an error rate in Bob's raw key.

Consequently, Eve could settle for a low level of eavesdropping, trying to gain only partial knowledge of the secret key, while minimizing the chances of being detected. She could even take advantage of the imperfections in the quantum channel, trying to hide behind the "noise". In order to also address attack strategies based on low level of eavesdropping, we propose a conceptually new kind of QKD scheme that aims to maximize Eve's uncertainty about the bits she eavesdropped on, even after the public discussion between Alice and Bob, while giving Bob higher chances of detecting Eve, even for a smaller number of bits tested. The main idea of the protocol is to propagate the disruption caused by Eve when measuring a qubit to other qubits in the sequence as well. To this end we take advantage of the data dependencies introduced by the application of the Quantum Fourier Transform.

6.4. QKD Scheme Based on the Fourier Transform

In the discussion concluding the previous section, we pointed out to data dependency as the main challenge in designing a parallel solution to the computation of the quantum Fourier transform (QFT) and its inverse. However, the fixed order of execution characterizing the steps of the procedure for inverting the quantum Fourier transform can also be exploited to design secure QKD schemes.

The protocol that we describe in the following can be seen as a generalization of the random $\pi/2$ phase shift protocol, both relying on encapsulating information in the relative phase between the two components in a superposition. However, the Fourier transform brings into play the *rank* of a qubit in the sequence, thus giving a *context* to each qubit transmitted.

Employing the Fourier transform instead of the random $\pi/2$ phase shift as the encryption method does not alter the main structure of the protocol, so we will just point out the differences relative to the description we provided in the previous section. Figure 14 gives a pictorial representation of the entire protocol, with time flowing downwards.

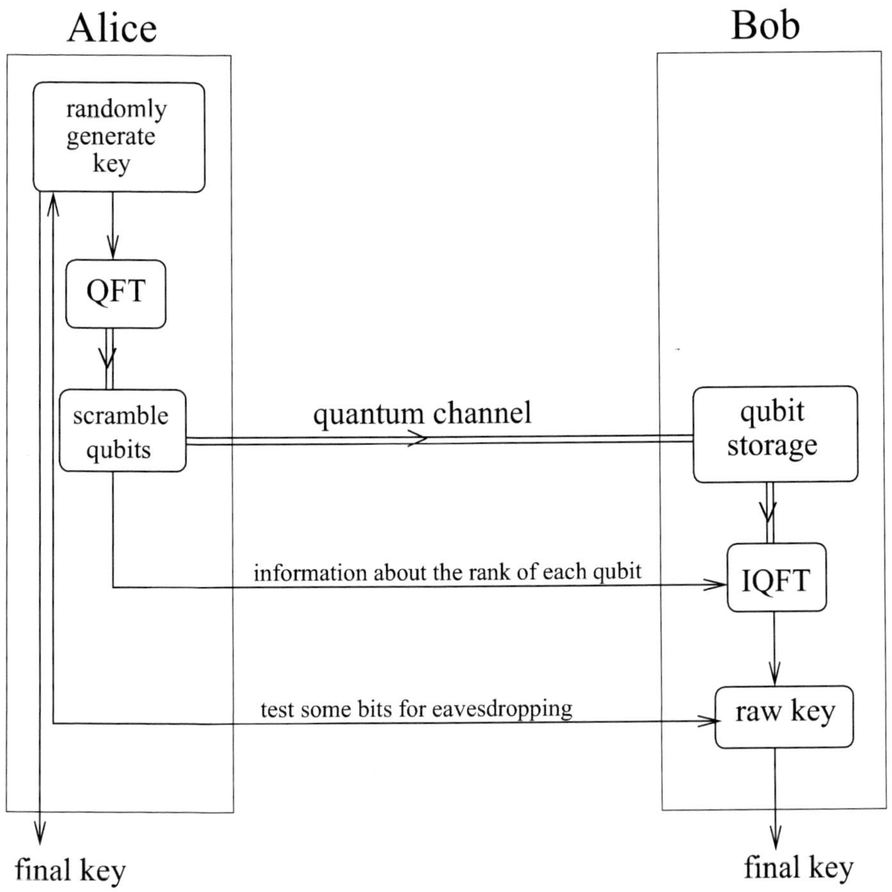

Figure 14. Schematics of a quantum key distribution protocol using the quantum Fourier transform (QFT) and its inverse (IQFT) as encoding and decoding algorithms. This is the first protocol that allows the detection of an eavesdropper even if the qubit tested was not "disturbed" while in transit.

In step 2 of the quantum communication stage, Alice applies the QFT to the binary sequence generated in the previous step, by passing it through the quantum circuit depicted in Figure 5. Then, she scrambles the resulting qubit sequence by choosing an arbitrary permutation of the qubits and sends them to Bob.

In the second stage of the protocol (involving classical communication), Alice informs Bob of the correct order in which he must place the received qubits (in other words, the *rank* of each qubit is disclosed). Consequently, the raw key extraction step can proceed with Bob applying the inverse Fourier transform to the properly re-arranged qubit sequence. In the absence of any eavesdropping or transmission errors, Bob must end up with the same bit sequence that Alice randomly produced at the outset of the protocol.

When Eve decides to spy on an arbitrary qubit in the sequence, she doesn't know its rank and is therefore ignorant of the influence exerted on it by the previous qubits in the ordered sequence. Without access to this additional information (the qubit's context), Eve can have no confidence in the outcome of an eventual measurement in the Hadamard basis pointing to a 0 or a 1.

6.4.1. An Example

Suppose that the bit string that Alice wants to convey to Bob is 10011010, so that $j_1 = 1$ and $j_8 = 0$. Consider what happens if Eve intercepts the qubit of rank 6 and measures it in the Hadamard basis. Since its state is

$$|0\rangle + e^{2\pi i 0.010}|1\rangle = |0\rangle + e^{\frac{\pi}{2}i}|1\rangle, \tag{25}$$

exactly halfway between $|0\rangle$ and $|1\rangle$ (relative phase $\pi/2$), there is an equal probability for either outcome to be realized. Consequently, even after learning it's context, Eve's uncertainty over this bit is total. Following her measurement, Eve can either send $H|0\rangle$ or $H|1\rangle$ to Bob. In any case, Bob will undo the $\pi/2$ rotation supposedly caused by $j_7 = 1$, therefore having a 50% chance of detecting Eve, provided he and Alice choose to test bit j_6. But if Bob measures bit j_6 as 1, then the error introduced by Eve's action is still detectable, even if the qubit whose state she disturbed is not checked by Alice and Bob. Thus, when applying the inverse Fourier transform on the qubit of rank 5, its quantum state becomes

$$|0\rangle + e^{(\pi+\frac{\pi}{4}-\frac{\pi}{4}-\frac{\pi}{2})i}|1\rangle \tag{26}$$

and in 50% of the cases Alice and Bob will discover a mismatch in their values for this bit. An erroneous bit j_6 will continue to influence the outcome of the following bits, up to j_1. The strength of this influence decreases with the rank and probably becomes negligible in a few steps. Nevertheless, if the error in j_6 propagates to one of its neighbors, then this bit acts as a new source of error, creating the mechanism for the initial disturbance to propagate indefinitely. So, unlike other QKD schemes, in this case, eavesdropping on one qubit has the potential to introduce a large number of errors. In general, for an arbitrary qubit of rank k ($0 < k \leq n$), the relative phase shift caused by errors in the previous bits (from n to $k+1$) varies between 0 and $\sum_{i=1}^{n-k} \pi/2^i$, as the errors induced may interfere with each other, adding up or canceling out.

Since Eve's uncertainty over an observed value is based on her ignorance about the context involved, it appears that the weak spot of the protocol lies in the high rank qubits. The highest rank qubit, for instance, is context-free (having no predecessors), so Eve can be certain of its value, provided she has performed a measurement on it. But because she doesn't know the ranks of the qubits transmitted during the quantum communication stage, she must eavesdrop on many qubits to increase her chances of learning the value of j_n. This, in turn, will cause more disturbance and therefore increase the risk of being detected.

In our example, by learning that the value of j_8 equals 0, Eve also becomes aware that j_8 has no influence on j_7, so her measurement on j_7 (if performed) must have yielded its true value. However, since $j_7 = 1$, there is an equal probability that a hypothetical measurement on j_6 has revealed the correct or incorrect value. For an arbitrary bit string $j_1 \cdots j_n$, Eve can end up knowing the values of the last k bits, where $j_{n-k+1} = 1$ and $j_{n-k+2}, \cdots, j_{n-1}, j_n$ are all zeroes, assuming that she performed all the necessary measurements on the qubits in transit. In practice, since the binary sequence transmitted is chosen at random, the probability of it ending in more than two or three consecutive zeroes is very low.

One immediate solution is for Alice and Bob to discard those bits from their raw keys. Alternatively, the protocol described above, and based on the Fourier transform, could be combined with the random $\pi/2$ phase shift protocol presented in the previous section. In this way, each qubit may get an additional $\pi/2$ relative phase shift, increasing Eve's uncertainty about the trailing bits in the sequence while maintaining the uncertainty level for the others.

6.5. Simulations

In order to better assess the improvement in performance brought by the QFT-based protocol with respect to the traditional BB84 protocol, a series of simulations for various input parameters were performed. To ensure a fair comparison between the two protocols, we assumed that Bob has knowledge of the encoding bases chosen by Alice, such that no qubits are discarded in the BB84 protocol because of a mismatch between the encoding and decoding bases. A series of 1000 simulations were performed for each possible configuration allowed by varying the following input parameters:

- total number of qubits transmitted (128, 256, 512),
- percentage of qubits eavesdropped on by Eve (10, 25, 50),
- percentage of qubits checked for eavesdropping by Alice and Bob (10, 25, 50).

Figure 15 shows the results in terms of the number of times Eve managed to remain undetected during each batch of 1000 simulations of the two protocols. For the same number of qubits eavesdropped on and the same number of qubits checked, the QFT-based protocol consistently outperforms BB84 because the errors introduced by eavesdropping propagate to other qubits as well and thus Eve may get caught even if the bit checked was not eavesdropped on. We can see that the improvement is bigger for lower levels of eavesdropping and/or fewer bits checked.

Figure 16, on the other hand, shows the average number of qubits (out of 256) that were detected as corrupted by Eve in each 1000-trial batch. The improvement in performance in favor of the QFT-based protocol is evident for each combination of input variables.

6.6. Discussion

When compared with existing QKD schemes, the protocol using the QFT offer better eavesdropping detection rates by propagating the disruption caused to one qubit to the following qubits in the sequence. This makes the protocol more efficient in terms of the number of bits that have to be tested in order to achieve a certain level of security. Also, the lack of

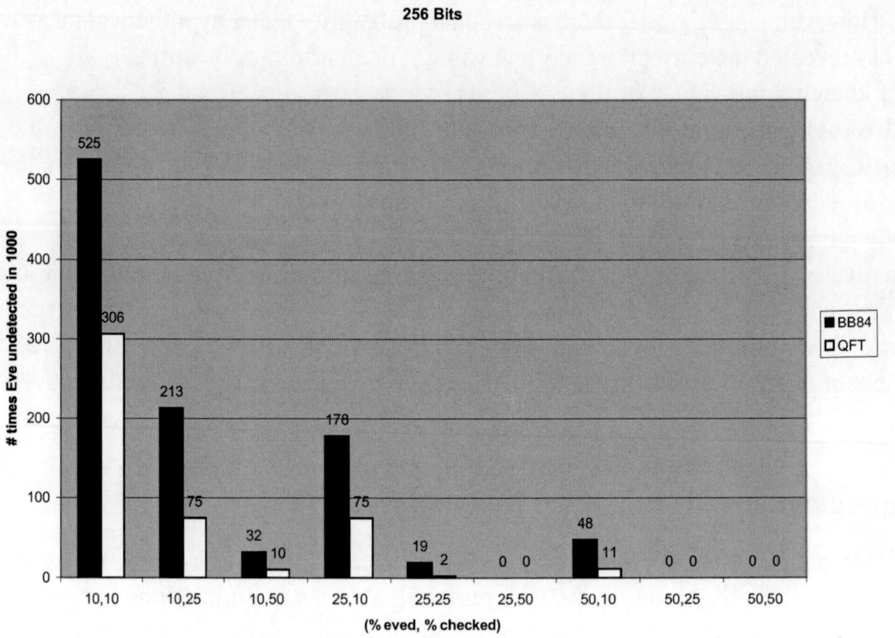

Figure 15. A comparison between the QFT-based and the BB84 protocol, in terms of the number of times Eve escapes detection in 1000 trials, for various percentages of bits eavesdropped on and checked.

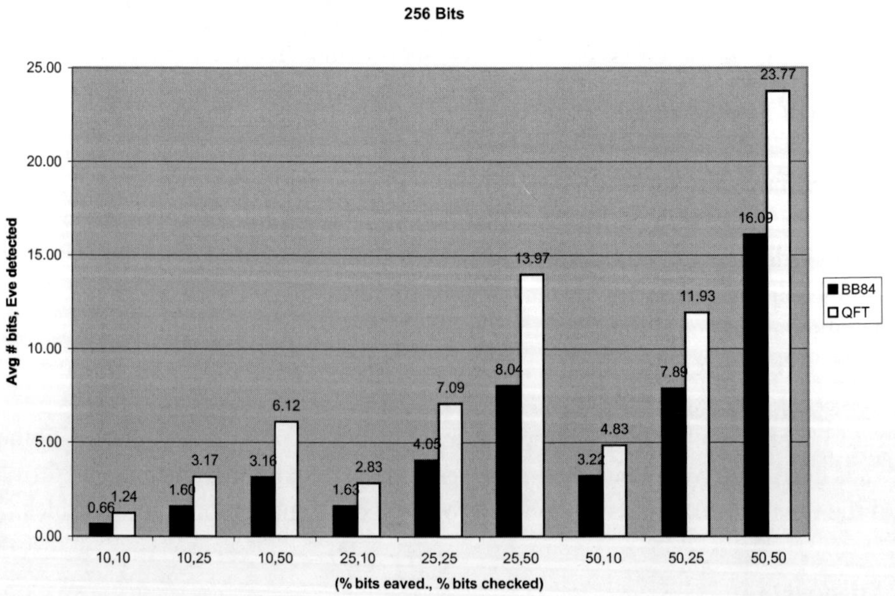

Figure 16. A comparison between the QFT-based and the BB84 protocol, in terms of the average number of corrupt bits detected in 1000 trials, for various percentages of bits eavesdropped on and checked.

knowledge over a qubit's context, at the time of eavesdropping, maximizes Eve's uncertainty about the information encoded within its quantum state, thus making the protocol more secure.

These benefits come at the cost of a more complex processing required at both ends of the link. However, the computational power assumed to be available for Alice and Bob is not that of a quantum computer. Computing the QFT and its inverse in the special case of a sequence made up of classical bits requires only the application of single-qubit gates. Although all the phase shift gates in Figures 5 and 6 are controlled-rotations, the control qubit is in fact always classical. Consequently, the net effect of such a controlled-gate is the application of the phase shift rotation onto the target qubit, if the control is 1, or no transformation at all, if the control is 0. Therefore, Alice and Bob need only to be able to perform Hadamard and phase shift rotations of single-qubit quantum states. As we have seen in section 5, parallel processing can also be applied in order to avoid decoherence.

The protocol for QKD developed in this section demonstrates that the QFT is a versatile tool, with important applications not only in quantum algorithms, but also in quantum cryptography. It allows for the design of new QKD schemes with clear advantages over the existing ones, especially for low levels of eavesdropping. Furthermore, the results obtained herein suggest that the role of QFT in the general area of data security is much more important than previously believed. Finally, another possible direction for future research is to discover other ways in which to exploit the assumption of storing the transmitted qubits for a pre-determined amount of time.

7. Conclusion

The progress made by physicists towards a better understanding of the principles behind the strange effects witnessed at the quantum level have had a remarkable impact on the evolution of computer science. The quantum mechanical principle of superposition of states found an unexpected, but fundamental application to the theory of computation, giving rise to the concept of *quantum parallelism*. This syntagm is used to denote the ability to perform a certain computation simultaneously on all terms of a quantum superposition, regardless of the number of qubits composing the quantum register whose state is described by that superposition.

From a mathematical point of view, quantum parallelism allows us to compute the values of an arbitrary function $f(x)$, simultaneously, for all possible inputs x. It is this massive parallelism coupled with the *interference* between various computational paths (brought about by the quantum Fourier transform, for example) that quantum computation tries to harness in order to obtain an important advantage in speed over conventional algorithms. However, this is not an easy task due to the difficulties associated with extracting the desired result from a superposition, through measurement.

Nevertheless, two notable results have contributed decisively to the interest shown today towards this novel and unconventional way of registering and processing information. One is the possibility to factorize integers and compute discrete logarithms in quantum polynomial time [65], a result that achieves an exponential speed-up over the best corresponding classical methods and, at the same time, delivers a serious blow to the security of many public-key cryptographic schemes in use today. The second is Grover's unstructured search algorithm [39], whose optimal quadratic speed-up over the classical solution may seem low, but it is certainly compensated by the broad spectrum of possible applications for the algorithm.

Yet the quantum paradigm is not merely a way to speed up computations. The unique features of quantum mechanics have revolutionized the way we represent and process information, allowing for achievements that cannot be replicated within a conventional setup. Harnessing entanglement as a physical resource makes possible quantum teleportation [13] and superdense coding [16]. The classical limits on data security in cryptographic protocols are improved with the aid of quantum mechanical principles, like the impossibility of copying unknown quantum states or the Heisenberg uncertainty principle. The classical computability limits have also been revised as a natural consequence of enlarging the framework within which information processing tasks can be defined and the availability of conceptually novel ways to address them.

Distinguishing among entangled quantum states turns out to be of pivotal importance in defining a whole class of information processing tasks that clearly separates a quantum computer from a classical one, in terms of computational power (function evaluation). The superiority of the quantum machine is not given by its ability to perform quantum measurements, but by the ability to process information (compute) at the quantum level.

There are cases in which this ability is mandatory in order to successfully tackle problems involving non-determinism and entanglement, features that are specific to quantum mechanics but not to classical physics. Therefore, much in the same way the physical theory of quantum mechanics subsumes classical physics as a particular case, the computational power of a quantum computer is strictly greater than that of a classical computer. The way information is physically represented in a certain model of computation directly determines its computational power, because information is intrinsically physical and cannot be abstracted away from its physical support.

We have also shown that if a machine lacks the ability to process information at the physical level used to represent it, then only a parallel approach can be successful in distinguishing among the elements of a set of quantum states. Furthermore, parallel processing may be the only way to see a quantum computation completed before decoherence effects take hold, as we have demonstrated in the case of the Fourier transform and its inverse. This last example is important from yet another point of view, underlining the importance of parallel processing for those computational environments in which the complexity of each step evolves with its rank. This also extends to the cases where the variation in complexity is time-driven [5]. The use of a parallel approach becomes critical when the solution to such a problem must accommodate a deadline. In the particular case we have investigated, quantum decoherence places an upper bound on the scalability of computing the quantum Fourier transform or its inverse, and the only chance to reach beyond that limit is through a parallel solution.

These examples prove that parallelism is equally important for quantum computation and quantum information as it is for the classical theory of computation. Note that we refer here to the common understanding of the term *parallelism* and not to *quantum parallelism*. Unlike the interpretation given to quantum parallelism, we want to express the ability to act simultaneously on a certain number of qubits. Thus, we can rightfully assert that parallelism transcends the laws of physics and represents a fundamental aspect of computation, regardless of the particular physical way chosen to embody information.

There is also a remarkable connection between parallelism and the concept of *universality* in computation [2]. In this respect, the problem of distinguishing among entangled quantum states, as an instance of measuring interdependent variables, strengthens the conclusion that there is no *finite*[5] computing device (conventional or unconventional) upon which the attribute *universal* can be bestowed. This result holds as long as the candidate Universal Computer cannot apply its (internal) set of basic processing operations ("gates") onto systems from the outside world. In other words, its processing capabilities can only be exercised on data already stored in its (internal) memory. For the problem we have analyzed in this chapter, all the input data on which the machine can work must be acquired through measurement(s).

Since the early 1980's, when the field began to materialize, quantum computation and quantum information has come a long way to impose itself as a stand-alone multidisciplinary science. A great deal of effort is put nowadays into closing the gap between a well developed theory and practical realizations. And if a large scale quantum computer is still out of reach, practical implementations of quantum cryptographic protocols have already become a reality. In this context, we have also shown how progress in quantum networks research together with the data dependency given by the rank of each qubit in the quantum Fourier transform can improve efficiency, security and eavesdropping detection in quantum key distribution schemes.

This chapter is a testimony to the indelible mark that quantum mechanics has already left on computer science. Indeed, today we can rightfully acknowledge the existence of a *quantum computer science* with deep ramifications into information theory, algorithms and complexity, cryptography, networking and communications, fault tolerance and error correction.

References

[1] Selim G. Akl. Discrete steepest descent in real time. *Parallel and Distributed Computing Practices*, **4**(3):301–317, 2001.

[2] Selim G. Akl. The myth of universal computation. In R. Trobec, P. Zinterhof, M. Vajteršic, and A. Uhl, editors, *Parallel Numerics, Part 2, Systems and Simulation*, pages 211–236. University of Salzburg, Austria and Jožef Stefan Institute, Ljubljana, Slovenia, 2005.

[3] Selim G. Akl. Coping with uncertainty and stress: A parallel computation approach. *International Journal of High Performance Computing and Networking*, **4**(1/2):85–90, 2006.

[4] Selim G. Akl. Inherently parallel geometric computations. *Parallel Processing Letters*, **16**(1):19–37, March 2006.

[5] Selim G. Akl. Evolving computational systems. In Sanguthevar Rajasekaran and John H. Reif, editors, *Parallel Computing: Models, Algorithms, and Applications*.

[5] in the sense introduced in [2] and briefly described in section 4.

CRC Press, 2007. A modified version is available as Technical Report No. 2006-526, School of Computing, Queen's University, Kingston, Ontario, Canada.

[6] Selim G. Akl, Brendan Cordy, and Weiguang Yao. An analysis of the effect of parallelism in the control of dynamical systems. *International Journal of Parallel, Emergent and Distributed Systems*, **20**(2):147–168, June 2005.

[7] Adriano Barenco. A universal two-bit gate for quantum computation. *Proceedings of the Royal Society of London A*, **449**:679–683, 1995.

[8] B. Barutçu, S. Şeka, E. Ayaz, and E. Türkcan. Real-time reactor noise diagnostics for the Borsele (PWR) nuclear power plant. *Progress in Nuclear Energy*, **43**(1–4):137–143, 2003.

[9] John Bell. On the Einstein-Podolsky-Rosen paradox. *Physics*, **1**:195–200, 1964.

[10] Eric Benjamin, Kenny Huang, Amir Kamil, and Jimmy Kittiyachavalit. Quantum computability and complexity and the limits of quantum computation. `http://www.cs.berkeley.edu/~kamil/quantum/qc4.pdf`, December 2003.

[11] Charles H. Bennett. Quantum cryptography using any two nonorthogonal states. *Physical Review Letters*, **68**(21):3121–3124, May 1992.

[12] Charles H. Bennett and Gilles Brassard. Quantum cryptography: Public key distribution and coin tossing. In *Proceedings of IEEE International Conference on Computers, Systems and Signal Processing*, pages 175–179, IEEE, New York, 1984. Bangalore, India, December 1984.

[13] Charles H. Bennett, Gilles Brassard, Claude Crépeau, Richard Jozsa, A. Peres, and W. Wootters. Teleporting an unknown quantum state via dual classical and EPR channels. *Physical Review Letters*, **70**:1895–1899, 1993.

[14] Charles H. Bennett, Gilles Brassard, and N. David Mermin. Quantum cryptography without Bell's theorem. *Physical Review Letters*, **68**(5):557–559, Feb 1992.

[15] Charles H. Bennett, Gilles Brassard, and Jean-Marc Robert. Privacy amplification by public discussion. *SIAM Journal on Computing*, **17**(2):210–229, April 1988.

[16] Charles H. Bennett and Stephen J. Wiesner. Communication via one- and two-particle operators on Einstein-Podolsky-Rosen states. *Physical Review Letters*, **69**(20):2881–2884, 1992.

[17] Ethan Bernstein and Umesh Vazirani. Quantum complexity theory. *Special issue on Quantum Computation of the SIAM Journal on Computing*, **26**(5):1411–1473, October 1997. `http://arxiv.org/abs/quant-ph/9701001`.

[18] André Berthiaume. Quantum computation. In Lane A. Hemaspaandra and Alan L. Selman, editors, *Complexity Theory Retrospective II*, pages 23–51. Springer-Verlag, New York, 1997.

[19] André Berthiaume and Gilles Brassard. Oracle quantum computing. *Journal of Modern Optics*, **41**(12):2521–2535, December 1994.

[20] B. B. Blinov, D. L. Moehring, L.-M. Duan, and Chris Monroe. Observation of entanglement between a single trapped atom and a single photon. *Nature*, **428**:153–157, March 11, 2004.

[21] Julian Brown. *The quest for the quantum computer*. Simon & Schuster, Touchstone edition, 2001.

[22] Cristian S. Calude and Boris Pavlov. Coins, quantum measurements, and Turing's barrier. *Quantum Information Processing*, **1**(1–2):107–127, April 2002.

[23] John Chiaverini et al. Implementation of the semiclassical quantum fourier transform in a scalable system. *Science*, **308**(5724):997–1000, May 2005.

[24] Ignazio Cirac and Peter Zoller. Quantum computations with cold trapped ions. *Physical Review Letters*, **74**:4091–4094, 1995.

[25] Ignazio Cirac, Peter Zoller, H. J. Kimble, and H. Mabuchi. Quantum state transfer and entanglement distribution among distant nodes in a quantum network. *Physical Review Letters*, **78**(16):3221–3224, April 21, 1997. `http://arxiv.org/abs/quant-ph/9611017`.

[26] C. Cohen-Tannoudji, B. Diu, and F. Laloe. *Quantum Mechanics*, volume 1 and 2. Wiley, New York, 1977.

[27] Thomas H. Cormen, Charles E. Leiserson, Ronald L. Rivest, and Clifford Stein. *Introduction to Algorithms*. MIT Press, Cambridge, Massachusetts, 2001.

[28] L. Davidovich et al. Quantum switches and nonlocal microwave fields. *Physical Review Letters*, **71**(15):2360–2363, October 11, 1993.

[29] David Deutsch. Quantum theory, the Church-Turing principle, and the Universal Quantum Computer. *Proceedings of the Royal Society of London A*, **400**:97–117, 1985.

[30] David Deutsch, Artur Ekert, Richard Jozsa, Chiara Macchiavello, Sandu Popescu, and Anna Sanpera. Quantum privacy amplification and the security of quantum cryptography over noisy channels. *Physical Review Letters*, **77**:2818–2821, 1996. `http://arxiv.org/abs/quant-ph/9604039`.

[31] David Deutsch and Richard Jozsa. Rapid solution of problems by quantum computation. *Proceedings of the Royal Society of London A*, **439**:553–558, 1992.

[32] P. Dirac. *The Principles of Quantum Mechanics*. Oxford University Press, 4th edition, 1958.

[33] David DiVincenzo. Two-bit gates are universal for quantum computation. *Physical Review A*, **51**:1015–1022, 1995.

[34] Albert Einstein, Boris Podolsky, and Nathan Rosen. Can quantum-mechanical description of physical reality be considered complete? *Physical Review*, **47**:777–780, May 1935.

[35] Artur Ekert. Quantum cryptography based on Bell's theorem. *Physical Review Letters*, **67**:661–663, 1991.

[36] Richard Feynman. Simulating physics with computers. *International Journal of Theoretical Physics*, **21**(6 & 7):467–488, 1982.

[37] Vittorio Giovannetti, Seth Lloyd, and Lorenzo Maccone. Quantum-enhanced measurements: Beating the standard quantum limit. *Science*, **306**:1330–1336, November 2004.

[38] Robert Griffiths and Chi-Sheng Niu. Semiclassical Fourier transform for quantum computation. *Physical Review Letters*, **76**:3228–3231, 1996.

[39] Lov K. Grover. A fast quantum mechanical algorithm for database search. In *Proceedings of the 28th Annual ACM Symposium on the Theory of Computing*, pages 212–219, Philadelphia, Pennsylvania, 22–24 May 1996, 1996.

[40] Stephan Gulde et al. Implementation of the Deutsch-Jozsa algorithm on an ion-trap quantum computer. *Nature*, **421**:48–50, January 2, 2003.

[41] Mika Hirvensalo. *Quantum Computing*. Springer-Verlag, 2001.

[42] Tien D. Kieu. Quantum adiabatic algorithm for Hilbert's tenth problem: I. The algorithm. `http://arxiv.org/abs/quant-ph/0310052`, October 2003.

[43] Arjen K. Lenstra and H. W. Lenstra, Jr., editors. *The Development of the Number Field Sieve*. Springer-Verlag, New York, 1993.

[44] Seth Lloyd. Quantum limits to the measurement of spacetime geometry. `http://arxiv.org/abs/quant-ph/0505064`, May 2005.

[45] Seth Lloyd. *Programming the Universe: A Quantum Computer Scientist Takes On the Cosmos*. Knopf, 2006.

[46] Samuel J. Lomonaco Jr., editor. *Quantum Computation: A Grand Mathematical Challenge for the Twenty-First Century and the Millennium*, volume 58 of *Proceedings of Symposia in Applied Mathematics*. American Mathematical Society, Short Course, Washington, DC, January 17-18 2000.

[47] Klaus Mattle, Harald Weinfurter, Paul G. Kwiat, and Anton Zeilinger. Dense coding in experimental quantum communication. *Physical Review Letters*, **76**(25):4656–4659, 1996.

[48] N. David Mermin. From Cbits to Qbits: Teaching computer scientists quantum mechanics. `http://arxiv.org/abs/quant-ph/0207118`, July 2002.

[49] Marius Nagy and Selim G. Akl. Computing nearest neighbors in real time. *Journal of Parallel and Distributed Computing*, **66**(3):359–366, March 2006.

[50] Marius Nagy and Selim G. Akl. Coping with Decoherence: Parallelizing the Quantum Fourier Transform. In *19th International Conference on Parallel and Distributed Computing Systems*, pages 108–113, San Francisco, California, September 2006.

[51] Marius Nagy and Selim G. Akl. Quantum computation and quantum information. *International Journal of Parallel, Emergent and Distributed Systems*, **21**(1):1–59, February 2006.

[52] Marius Nagy and Selim G. Akl. Quantum measurements and universal computation. *International Journal of Unconventional Computing*, **2**(1):73–88, 2006.

[53] Marius Nagy and Selim G. Akl. Quantum computing: Beyond the limits of conventional computation. *International Journal of Parallel, Emergent and Distributed Systems, Special Issue: Emergent Computation*, **22**(2):123–135, April 2007.

[54] Marius Nagy, Selim G. Akl, and Sean Kershaw. Key distribution based on the quantum Fourier transform. In *Proceedings of the International Conference on Security and Cryptography (SECRYPT 2008)*, pages 263–269, Porto, Portugal, July 2008.

[55] Naya Nagy and Selim G. Akl. The maximum flow problem: A real-time approach. *Parallel Computing*, **29**:767–794, 2003.

[56] Michael A. Nielsen. Simple rules for a complex quantum world. *Scientific American*, **13**(1):24–33, 2003. Special edition: The edge of physics.

[57] Michael A. Nielsen and Isaac L. Chuang. *Quantum Computation and Quantum Information.* Cambridge University Press, 2000.

[58] G. Okša, M. Bečka, and M. Vajteršic. Parallel computation with structured matrices in linear modeling of multidimensional signals. *Parallel and Distributed Computing Practices*, **5**(3):289–299, 2004.

[59] Roger Penrose. *The Emperor's New Mind.* Oxford University Press, New York, 1989.

[60] Roger Penrose. *Shadows of the Mind.* Oxford University Press, New York, 1994.

[61] Eleanor Rieffel and Wolfgang Polak. An introduction to quantum computing for non-physicists. *ACM Computing Surveys*, **32**(3):300–335, September 2000.

[62] Ronald L. Rivest, Adi Shamir, and Len M. Adleman. A method of obtaining digital signatures and public-key cryptosystems. *Communications of the ACM*, **21**(2):120–126, 1978.

[63] H. P. Robertson. The uncertainty principle. *Physical Review*, **34**:163–164, 1929.

[64] Sara Robinson. Emerging insights on limitations of quantum computing shape quest for fast algorithms. *SIAM News*, **36**(1), January/February 2003.

[65] Peter W. Shor. Polynomial-time algorithms for prime factorization and discrete logarithms on a quantum computer. *Special issue on Quantum Computation of the SIAM Journal on Computing*, **26**(5):1484–1509, October 1997.

[66] Warren D. Smith. The energy-time uncertainty principle. `http://citeseer.ist.psu.edu/238921.html`, typeset 811 September 21 1999.

[67] Susan Stepney, Samuel L. Braunstein, John A. Clark, Andy Tyrrell, Andrew Adamatzky, Robert E. Smith, Tom Addis, Colin Johnson, Jonathan Timmis, Peter Welch, Robin Milner, and Derek Partridge. Journeys in non-classical computation I: A grand challenge for computing research. *International Journal of Parallel, Emergent and Distributed Systems*, **20**(1):5–19, March 2005.

[68] Q. Turchette et al. Measurement of conditional phase shifts for quantum logic. *Physical Review Letters*, **75**(25):4710–4713, 1995.

[69] Lieven M. K. Vandersypen, Matthias Steffen, Gregory Breyta, Constantino S. Yannoni, Mark H. Sherwood, and Isaac L. Chuang. Experimental realization of Shor's quantum factoring algorithm using nuclear magnetic resonance. *Nature*, **414**:829–938, December 2001.

[70] Yaakov S. Weinstein et al. Implementation of the quantum fourier transform. *Physical Review Letters*, **86**(9):1889–1891, February 2001.

[71] Yaakov S. Weinstein et al. Quantum process tomography of the quantum fourier transform. *Journal of Chemical Physics*, **121**(13):6117–6133, 2004. `http://arxiv.org/abs/quant-ph/0406239v1`.

[72] William K. Wootters and Wojciech H. Zurek. A single quantum cannot be cloned. *Nature*, 299:802–803, 1982.

INDEX

A

B

C

D

E

F

G

J

K

L

M

N

O

P

Q

R

S

T

U

V

W

Y